PRACTICAL SOFTWARE ENGINEERING

LESZEK A. MACIASZEK, BRUC LEE LIONG

With contributions from STEPHEN BILLS

PRACTICAL SOFTWARE ENGINEERING

A Case Study Approach

PEARSON

Addison
Wesley

Harlow, England • London • New York • Boston • San Francisco • Toronto • Sydney • Singapore • Hong Kong
Tokyo • Seoul • Taipei • New Delhi • Cape Town • Madrid • Mexico City • Amsterdam • Munich • Paris • Milan

Pearson Education Limited
Edinburgh Gate
Harlow
Essex CM20 2JE
England

and Associated Companies throughout the world

Visit us on the World Wide Web at:
www.pearsoned.co.uk

First published 2005

ISBN 0 321 20465 4

British Library Cataloguing-in-Publication Data
A catalogue record for this book is available from the British Library

Library of Congress Cataloging-in-Publication Data
Maciaszek, Leszek.
    Practical software engineering : a case study approach / Leszek A. Maciaszek,
  Bruc Lee Liong; with contributions from Stephen Bills.
        p.   cm.
    Includes bibliographical references and index.
    ISBN 0-321-20465-4
        1. Software engineering.   I. Liong, Bruc Lee.   II. Bills, Stephen.   III. Title.

QA76.758.M248 2004
005.1–dc22   2004046604

10 9 8 7 6 5 4 3 2 1
09 08 07 06 05

Typeset in 10/12 pt Time by 35
Printed and bound in the United States of America

The publisher's policy is to use paper manufactured from sustainable forests.

MOTTO

Make everything as simple as possible,
but not simpler

– Albert Einstein

DEDICATIONS

For Diana, Dominika, and Tomasz
– Leszek A. Maciaszek

To my parents, Edison and Tina

– Bruc Lee Liong

Brief Contents

Guided tour   *xxvi*
Preface   *xxix*
Acknowledgements   *xxxv*

Part 1   Software Projects   **1**

Chapter 1   Software Development Lifecycle   5

Chapter 2   Software Modeling Language   37

Chapter 3   Software Engineering Tools   63

Chapter 4   Software Project Planning and Tracking   112

Chapter 5   Software Process Management   153

**Part 2   From Requirements via Architectural Design
to Software Release**   **195**

Chapter 6   Business Object Model   199

Chapter 7   Domain Object Model   215

Chapter 8   Iteration 1 Requirements and Object Model   234

Chapter 9   Architectural Design   248

Chapter 10   Database Design and Programming   301

Chapter 11   Class and Interaction Design   331

Chapter 12   Programming and Testing   365

Chapter 13   Iteration 1 Annotated Code   414

Part 3   **Software Refactoring and User Interface Development**   **461**

Chapter 14   Iteration 2 Requirements and Object Model   463

Chapter 15   Architectural Refactoring   478

Chapter 16   User Interface Design and Programming   509

Chapter 17   Web-Based User Interface Design and Programming   541

Chapter 18   Iteration 2 Annotated Code   584

Part 4   **Data Engineering and Business Components**   **637**

Chapter 19   Iteration 3 Requirements and Object Model   639

Chapter 20   Security and Integrity   660

Chapter 21   Transactions and Concurrency   700

Chapter 22   Business Components   729

Chapter 23   Iteration 3 Annotated Code   750

Bibliography   **811**

Index   **816**

Contents

Guided tour		*xxvi*
Preface		*xxix*
Acknowledgements		*xxxv*

Part 1   Software Projects   **1**

Chapter 1   Software Development Lifecycle   5

1.1   Software Engineering Quintessence   7

1.1.1 Software System is less than Enterprise Information System   7
1.1.2 Software Process is part of Business Process   8
1.1.3 Software Engineering is different from Traditional Engineering   10
1.1.4 Software Engineering is more than Programming   11
1.1.5 Software Engineering is about Modeling   12
1.1.6 Software System is Complex   13

1.2   Lifecycle Phases   15

1.2.1 Requirements Analysis   16
1.2.2 System Design   17
1.2.3 Implementation   18
1.2.4 Integration and Deployment   19
1.2.5 Operation and Maintenance   21

1.3   Lifecycle Models   21

1.3.1 Waterfall Lifecycle with Feedback   22
1.3.2 Iterative Lifecycle with Increments   25
        Spiral model   25
        Rational Unified Process (RUP)   27
        Model Driven Architecture (MDA)   29
        Agile lifecycle with short cycles   29

Summary   32
Key Terms   34
Review Questions   35

Chapter 2		Software Modeling Language	37
	2.1	Structured Modeling Language	38
		2.1.1 Data Flow Modeling	39
		2.1.2 Entity–Relationship Modeling	42
	2.2	Object-Oriented Modeling Language	43
		2.2.1 Class Diagrams	43
		2.2.2 Use Case Diagrams	46
		2.2.3 Interaction Diagrams	50
		Sequence diagrams	50
		Collaboration (communication) diagrams	51
		2.2.4 Statechart Diagrams	53
		2.2.5 Activity Diagrams	55
		2.2.6 Implementation Diagrams	56
		Component diagrams	56
		Deployment diagrams	59
		Summary	*59*
		Key Terms	*60*
		Review Questions	*61*
		Problem-Solving Exercises	*62*
Chapter 3		Software Engineering Tools	63
	3.1	Project Management Tools	64
		3.1.1 Project Scheduling and Controlling	65
		3.1.2 Aligning Project and Performance Management with Strategic Objectives	66
		3.1.3 Unifying Project Management with Web-Based Collaboration and Content Management	67
		3.1.4 Unifying Project Management with Web-Based Portfolio Management	68
		3.1.5 Integrating Project Management with Metrics	69
		3.1.6 Integrating Project Management with Risk Management	72
	3.2	System Modeling Tools	73
		3.2.1 Managing Requirements	74
		3.2.2 Visual UML Modeling	79
		3.2.3 Report Generation	82
		3.2.4 Database Modeling	82
	3.3	Integrated Development Environments	83
		3.3.1 Routine Programming Tasks	85
		Writing the program	86
		Executing the program	89
		Debugging the program	90
		3.3.2 Integration with Software Modeling	93

3.3.3 Enterprise Application Development 93
3.3.4 Integration with Business Components 95
3.3.5 Integration with Change and Configuration Management 97

3.4 Change and Configuration Management Tools 99

3.4.1 Support for Changes 99
3.4.2 Support for Versions 102
3.4.3 Support for System Building 102
3.4.4 Support for Reengineering 104

Summary 107
Key Terms 108
Review Questions 109
Problem-Solving Exercises 109

Chapter 4 Software Project Planning and Tracking 112

4.1 Project Plan Development 113

4.2 Project Scheduling 116

4.2.1 Tasks, Milestones, and Deliverables 117
4.2.2 Task Scheduling in a Bar Chart 118
4.2.3 Resources and Resource Calendars 121
4.2.4 Effort-Driven Scheduling in a Bar Chart 122
4.2.5 Resource Underallocation and Overallocation 123

4.3 Project Budget Estimation 126

4.3.1 Schedule-Driven Budget Estimation 127
4.3.2 Algorithmic Budget Estimation 130
Principles of algorithmic models 131
COCOMO 81 133
COCOMO II 135

4.4 Tracking Project Progress 138

4.4.1 Tracking the Schedule 139
4.4.2 Tracking the Budget 141
Actual costs from schedule 142
Actual costs from accounting 143
Earned value 146

Summary 149
Key Terms 150
Review Questions 150
Problem-Solving Exercises 151

Chapter 5 Software Process Management 153

5.1 People Management 155

5.1.1 Acquiring and Motivating People 155

Team creation 156
Motivational theories 157
5.1.2 Project Communications 158
Forms of communication 158
Lines of communication 159
Factors in communication 160
Communication in conflict resolution 161
5.1.3 Team Development 162

5.2 Risk Management 163
5.2.1 Risk Identification 163
5.2.2 Risk Assessment 164
5.2.3 Risk Handling 167

5.3 Quality Management 168
5.3.1 Software Qualities 169
5.3.2 Quality Control 171
Software testing 171
Testing techniques 173
Test planning 176
5.3.3 Quality Assurance 177
Checklists 178
Reviews 178
Audits 179

5.4 Change and Configuration Management 180
5.4.1 Requirements Changes 181
5.4.2 Artifact Versions 182
5.4.3 Defects and Enhancements 185
5.4.4 Metrics 187

Summary 190
Key Terms 191
Review Questions 193

Part 2 From Requirements via Architectural Design to Software Release 195

Chapter 6 Business Object Model 199

6.1 Advertising Expenditure Measurement – The Business 200

6.2 Business Context Diagram 201

6.3 Business Use Case Model 202
6.3.1 Business Use Cases and Business Actors 202
6.3.2 Business Use Case Model for AEM 203
6.3.3 Alternative Business Use Case Model for AEM 204

6.4 Business Glossary   207
      6.4.1 Business Glossary for AEM   207

6.5 Business Class Model   207
      6.5.1 Business Entities   207
      6.5.2 Business Class Model for AEM   208
      6.5.3 Alternative Business Class Model for AEM   209

      Summary   *210*
      Key Terms   *211*
      Review Questions   *211*
        Discussion Questions   *211*
        Case Study Questions   *211*
      Problem-Solving Exercises   *212*
        Case Study Exercises   *212*
        Minicase – Advertising Expenditure Measurement   *212*

Chapter 7   Domain Object Model   215

7.1 Contact Management – The Domain   216

7.2 Domain Use Case Model   217
      7.2.1 Use Cases and Actors   217
      7.2.2 Use Case Relationships   217
      7.2.3 Use Case Model for Contact Management   219
      7.2.4 Alternative Use Case Model for Contact Management   220

7.3 Domain Glossary   222
      7.3.1 Domain Glossary for Contact Management   222
7.4 Domain Class Model   224
      7.4.1 Classes and Attributes   224
      7.4.2 Class Relationships   226
      7.4.3 Class Model for Contact Management   227
      7.4.4 Alternative Class Model for Contact Management   228

      Summary   *229*
      Key Terms   *230*
      Review Questions   *231*
        Discussion Questions   *231*
        Case Study Questions   *231*
      Problem-Solving Exercises   *231*
        Case Study Exercises   *231*
        Minicase – Time Logging   *232*

Chapter 8   Iteration 1 Requirements and Object Model   234

8.1 Use Case Model   235

8.2 Use Case Document   236

8.2.1 Brief Description, Preconditions, and Postconditions 236

8.2.2 Basic Flow 237

8.2.3 Subflows 239

8.2.4 Exception Flows 241

8.3 Conceptual Classes 241

8.4 Supplementary Specification 243

Summary 245

Key Terms 245

Review Questions 246

Discussion Questions 246

Case Study Questions 246

Problem-Solving Exercises 246

Case Study Exercises 246

Minicase – Time Logging 247

Chapter 9 Architectural Design 248

9.1 Architectural Layers and Dependency Management 249

9.1.1 Architectural Modules 249

Design classes 250

Packages 250

9.1.2 Package Dependencies 251

9.1.3 Layer Dependencies 253

9.1.4 Class Dependencies 254

9.1.5 Inheritance Dependencies 255

Inheritance without polymorphism 258

Extension and restriction inheritance 258

Down-calls 259

Up-calls 260

9.1.6 Method Dependencies 260

Method dependencies in the presence of delegation 262

Method dependencies in the presence of
implementation inheritance 262

9.1.7 Interfaces 264

Implementation dependency 266

Usage dependency 266

Breaking circular dependencies with interfaces 267

9.1.8 Event Processing 268

Event processing and layer dependencies 270

Event processing and interfaces 270

9.1.9 Acquaintance 273

Acquaintance dependencies and interfaces 273

Acquaintance package 275

9.2 Architectural Frameworks 277

9.2.1 Model–View–Controller 277

9.2.2 Presentation–Control–Mediator–Entity–Foundation 279
PCMEF layers 280
PCMEF principles 282
Acquaintance in PCMEF+ 283
Deployment of PCMEF layers 285

9.3 Architectural Patterns 285

9.3.1 Façade 286
9.3.2 Abstract Factory 286
9.3.3 Chain of Responsibility 287
9.3.4 Observer 288
9.3.5 Mediator 290

Summary 292
Key Terms 293
Review Questions 294
Problem-Solving Exercises 295
Case Study Exercises 295
Minicase – Contact Information Management 295

Chapter 10 Database Design and Programming 301

10.1 Quick Tutorial in Relational Databases from a Software
Engineering Viewpoint 302

10.1.1 Table 303
10.1.2 Referential Integrity 305
10.1.3 Conceptual versus Logical Database Models 306
10.1.4 Implementing Business Rules 307
10.1.5 Programming Database Application Logic 310
10.1.6 Indexes 311

10.2 Mapping Transient Objects to Persistent Records 315

10.2.1 Object Databases, SQL:1999, and Impedance Mismatch 316
10.2.2 Object-Relational Mapping 317
Mapping a one-to-many association and aggregation 317
Mapping a many-to-many association 319
Mapping a one-to-one association 320
Mapping a one-to-many recursive association 320
Mapping a many-to-many recursive association 321
Mapping generalization 321

10.3 Database Design and Creation for Email Management 322

10.3.1 Database Model 323
10.3.2 Creating the Database Schema 325
10.3.3 Sample Database Content 326

Summary 328
Key Terms 328

Review Questions		*329*
Discussion Questions		*329*
Case Study Questions		*329*
Problem-Solving Exercises		*330*
Case Study Exercises		*330*
Minicase – Contact Information Management		*330*

Chapter 11	Class and Interaction Design	331
11.1	Finding Classes from Use Case Requirements	332
	11.1.1 Finding Classes from Use Case Requirements for Email Management	333
	11.1.2 Initial Class Design for Email Management	337
	Constants in interface	339
11.2	Architectural Elaboration of Class Design	339
	11.2.1 Architectural Elaboration of Class Design for Email Management	342
	11.2.2 Class Design for Email Management after Architectural Elaboration	343
	11.2.3 Class Instantiation	344
	Who instantiates the first object?	345
	Instantiation diagram for Email Management	345
11.3	Interactions	346
	11.3.1 Sequence Diagrams	347
	11.3.2 Communication Diagrams	349
	11.3.3 Interaction Overview Diagrams	351
11.4	Interactions for Email Management	351
	11.4.1 The 'Login' Interaction	352
	11.4.2 The 'Exit' Interaction	353
	11.4.3 The 'View Unsent Messages' Interaction	354
	11.4.4 The 'Display Message Text' Interaction	356
	11.4.5 The 'Email Message' Interaction	357
	11.4.6 The 'Incorrect User Name or Password' Interaction	358
	11.4.7 The 'Incorrect Option' Interaction	358
	11.4.8 The 'Too Many Messages' Interaction	359
	11.4.9 The 'Email Could Not Be Sent' Interaction	361

Summary		*361*
Key Terms		*362*
Review Questions		*362*
Discussion Questions		*362*
Case Study Questions		*362*
Problem-Solving Exercises		*363*
Case Study Exercises		*363*
Minicase – Time Logging System		*363*
Minicase – Contact Information Management		*364*

Chapter 12   Programming and Testing   365

   12.1   Quick Tutorial in Java from a Software Engineering Viewpoint   366

        12.1.1 Class   366
        12.1.2 Class Associations and Collections   369
              From conceptual to design class model   369
              Java collections   371
              Associations on entity objects   373
              C++ parameterized types   375
        12.1.3 Database Access in Java   377
              Comparison of JDBC and SQLJ   378
              Establishing a database connection   379
              Executing SQL statements   379
              Calling stored procedures and functions   383

   12.2   Test-Driven Development   385

        12.2.1 JUnit Framework   386
        12.2.2 Test-Driven Development in Email Management   389

   12.3   Acceptance and Regression Testing   395

        12.3.1 Test Scripts in Email Management   396
        12.3.2 Test Input, Output, and Regression Testing in Email Management 398
        12.3.3 Implementation of Test Script in Email Management   401

   12.4   Iteration 1 Runtime Screenshots   404

        Summary   409
        Key Terms   410
        Review Questions   411
        Problem-Solving Exercises   411
            Tutorial and Case Study Exercises   411
            Minicase – Time Logging System   412
            Minicase – Contact Information Management   413

Chapter 13   Iteration 1 Annotated Code   414

   13.1   Code Overview   415

   13.2   Package Acquaintance   417

        13.2.1 Interface IAConstants   417
        13.2.2 Interface IAEmployee   419
        13.2.3 Interface IAContact   419
        13.2.4 Interface IAOutMessage   420

   13.3   Package Presentation   422

        13.3.1 Class PMain   422
        13.3.2 Class PConsole   423
              Constructing a PConsole object   424
              Displaying login and menu   426

Viewing outmessages 426
Requesting to email an outmessage 429

13.4 Package Control 430

13.4.1 Class CActioner 430
Constructing a CActioner object 432
Initiating login 433
Routing retrieval of outmessages 433
Emailing an outmessage 434
Using JavaMail™ API 435

13.5 Package Entity 435

13.5.1 Interface IEDataSupplier 435
Object identifiers and identity field pattern 438
13.5.2 Class EEmployee 439
Constructing an EEmployee object 439
Getting unsent outmessages 440
Removing sent outmessages 440
13.5.3 Class EContact 441
Constructing an EContact object 442
Getting unsent outmessages 442
Removing sent outmessages 442
13.5.4 Class EOutMessage 443
Constructing an EOutMessage object 444
Getting and setting a contact for Outmessage 444
Getting and setting a creator employee for outmessage 445
Getting and setting a sender employee for outmessage 445

13.6 Package Mediator 446

13.6.1 Class MBroker 447
Constructing an MBroker object 448
Requesting login connection 448
Creating Employees Cache 450
Retrieving unsent outmessages 450
Creating an outmessages cache 452
Creating a contacts cache 453
Updating outmessages after emailing and restoring the cache 454

13.7 Package Foundation 455

13.7.1 Class FConnection 455
Constructing an FConnection object 456
Obtaining database connection 456
13.7.2 Class FReader 458
13.7.3 Class FWriter 458

Summary 459
Key Terms 459
Iteration 1 Questions and Exercises 459

Part 3   Software Refactoring and User Interface Development   461

Chapter 14   Iteration 2 Requirements and Object Model   463

14.1   Use Case Model   464

14.2   Use Case Document   465

14.2.1 Brief Description, Preconditions, and Postconditions   466
14.2.2 Basic Flow   466
14.2.3 Subflows   468
14.2.4 Exception Flows   472

14.3   Conceptual Classes and Relational Tables   474

14.4   Supplementary Specification   476

Summary   477
Key Terms   477
Review Questions   477

Chapter 15   Architectural Refactoring   478

15.1   Refactoring Targets   479

15.2   Refactoring Methods   479

15.2.1 Extract Class   480
15.2.2 Subsume Method   481
15.2.3 Extract Interface   483

15.3   Refactoring Patterns   484

15.3.1 Identity Map   485
15.3.2 Data Mapper   487
    Load – check-out   487
    Unload – check-in   488
15.3.3 Alternative Data Mapper Strategies   490
    Many data mappers   490
    Metadata mapping   492
15.3.4 Lazy Load   493
    Lazy Initialization   494
    Virtual Proxy   495
    OID Proxy   495
    Navigation in Identity Map   498
    Navigation in Entity Classes   500
15.3.5 Unit of Work   501

15.4   Refactored Class Model   502

Summary   505
Key Terms   506

	Review Questions	*507*
	Discussion Questions	*507*
	Case Study Questions	*507*
	Problem-Solving Exercises	*507*
Chapter 16	**User Interface Design and Programming**	**509**
16.1	User Interface Design Guidelines	510
	16.1.1 User in Control	511
	16.1.2 Interface Consistency	512
	16.1.3 Interface Forgiveness	512
	16.1.4 Interface Adaptability	513
16.2	User Interface Components	514
	16.2.1 Containers	515
	Layout management	518
	Layering management	519
	16.2.2 Menus	520
	16.2.3 Controls	521
16.3	User Interface Event Handling	523
16.4	Patterns and the User Interface	527
	16.4.1 Observer	528
	16.4.2 Decorator	530
	16.4.3 Chain of Responsibility	530
	16.4.4 Command	531
16.5	User Interface for Email Management	532
	Summary	*537*
	Key Terms	*538*
	Review Questions	*539*
	Problem-Solving Exercises	*540*
Chapter 17	**Web-Based User Interface Design and Programming**	**541**
17.1	Enabling Technologies for the Web Client Tier	543
	17.1.1 Basic HTML	543
	17.1.2 Scripting Language	545
	17.1.3 Applet: Thin and Thick	547
17.2	Enabling Technologies for the Web Server Tier	551
	17.2.1 Servlet	551
	17.2.2 JSP	555
17.3	Transactions on Stateless Internet Systems	559
17.4	Patterns and the Web	561
	17.4.1 Observer	563

17.4.2 Composite   563
17.4.3 Factory Method   564
17.4.4 Strategy   565
17.4.5 Decorator   565
17.4.6 Model–View–Controller   566
17.4.7 Front Controller   567
17.4.8 Reuse of Tags in JSP   567
17.4.9 Decoupled Control: Struts   572

17.5   Servlet Implementation of Email Management   573

       Summary   *581*
       Key Terms   *582*
       Review Questions   *582*
       Problem-Solving Exercises   *583*

Chapter 18   Iteration 2 Annotated Code   584

18.1   Code Overview   585

18.2   Package Acquaintance   586
       18.2.1 Interface IAEmployee   587

18.3   Package Presentation   588
       18.3.1 Class PWindow   588
              Constructing and launching PWindow   588
              Data retrieval in PWindow   590
              Filter activation   593
       18.3.2 Class PMessageDetailWindow   595
       18.3.3 Class PMessageTableModel   598
       18.3.4 Class PDisplayList   601
       18.3.5 Class PDisplayList.Filter   604

18.4   Package Control   607
       18.4.1 Class CAdmin   607
       18.4.2 Class CMsgSeeker   607

18.5   Package Entity   608
       18.5.1 Class EIdentityMap   609

18.6   Package Mediator   612
       18.6.1 Class MModerator   613
       18.6.2 Class MDataMapper   613
              Outmessage retrievals and loading   615
              Outmessage saving and unloading   618

18.7   Presentation Layer: Applet Version   620

18.8   Presentation Layer: Servlet Version   622

18.8.1 Class PEMS   623
        Login in servlet   624
        Showing outmessages in servlet   626
18.8.2 Class PEMSEdit   630

Summary   632
Key Terms   633
Iteration 2 Questions and Exercises   633

Part 4   Data Engineering and Business Components   **637**

Chapter 19   Iteration 3 Requirements and Object Model   639

19.1   Use Case Model   640

19.2   Use Case Document   641

       19.2.1 Brief Description, Preconditions, and Postconditions   641
       19.2.2 Basic Flow   642
       19.2.3 Subflows   644
       19.2.4 Exception Flows   651

19.3   Conceptual Classes and Relational Tables   653

19.4   Supplementary Specification   655

19.5   Database Specification   657

       Summary   659
       Key Terms   659
       Review Questions   659

Chapter 20   Security and Integrity   660

20.1   Designing Security   661

       20.1.1 Discretionary Authorization   662
               System and object privileges   663
               Programmatic discretionary authorization   664
       20.1.2 Mandatory Authorization   671
       20.1.3 Enterprise Authorization   672

20.2   Designing Integrity   675

       20.2.1 Null and Default Constraints   676
       20.2.2 Domain and Check Constraints   677
       20.2.3 Unique and Primary Keys   677
       20.2.4 Foreign Keys   678
       20.2.5 Triggers   680

20.3   Security and Integrity in Email Management   685

       20.3.1 Security in Email Management   685
               Explicit Authorization table   688

Using individual schemas, global schema, and stored procedures 689
Using individual schemas, global schema, views, and
stored procedures 689
Authorization administration 692
20.3.2 Integrity in Email Management 693

Summary 697
Key Terms 698
Review Questions 699
Problem-Solving Exercises 699

Chapter 21 Transactions and Concurrency 700

21.1 Concurrency in System Transactions 701

21.1.1 ACID Properties 702
21.1.2 Isolation Levels 703
21.1.3 Lock Modes and Levels 705
21.1.4 Transactional Models 706
21.1.5 Concurrency Control Schemes 707

21.2 Concurrency in Business Transactions 711

21.2.1 Business Transaction Execution Contexts 711
21.2.2 Business Transactions and Component Technology 712
21.2.3 Transaction Services across Tiers 712
Web tier 713
Application tier 714
Database tier 716
21.2.4 Offline Concurrency Patterns 717
Unit of Work 718
Optimistic Offline Lock 719
Pessimistic Offline Lock 721

21.3 Transactions and Concurrency in Email Management 722

21.3.1 Flat Transaction Model 722
21.3.2 Unit of Work and Transactional Support 723

Summary 725
Key Terms 726
Review Questions 727
Problem-Solving Exercises 727

Chapter 22 Business Components 729

22.1 Enterprise JavaBeans 730

22.1.1 EJB Fundamentals 732
22.1.2 Entity Beans 735
22.1.3 Session Beans 739

22.2	Business Components for Java	741
	22.2.1 Creating Entity Components	741
	XML for entity components	742
	Java for entity components	744
	22.2.2 Creating View Components	744
	XML for view components	745
	Java for view components	746
	22.2.3 Creating the Application Module	747
	Summary	*748*
	Key Terms	*749*
	Review Questions	*749*
Chapter 23	**Iteration 3 Annotated Code**	**750**
23.1	Code Overview	751
23.2	Package Acquaintance	751
	23.2.1 Interface IAReportEntry	751
23.3	Package Presentation	753
	23.3.1 Class PWindow	754
	Populating the report contact list	754
	Report window	755
	Activity report	757
	Printing the report	757
	Populating the report table	758
	Showing the authorization window	759
	Conversion from rule matrix to authorization table	762
	Saving modified authorization rules	762
	Conversion from authorization table to rule matrix	764
	Deleting an outmessage	764
	Modifying an outmessage	766
	Creating an outmessage	766
	23.3.2 Class PTableWindow	767
	Dynamic registration of buttons	767
	Adding listeners to dynamically generated buttons	769
	Button return status	770
	Printing in PTableWindow	770
23.4	Package Control	771
23.5	Package Entity	771
	23.5.1 Class EIdentityMap	773
	Report registration and removal	773
	Report retrieval	774

23.6   Package Mediator   776

    23.6.1 Class MModerator   777
            Authorization rules   777
            Report retrieval   779
            Creating an outmessage   781
            Updating an outmessage   781
    23.6.2 Class MDataMapper   782
            Changes to previous methods   782
            Report retrieval in MDataMapper   784
            Authorization rules loading in MDataMapper   786
            Saving authorization rules in MDataMapper   786
    23.6.3 Class MUnitOfWork   789
            Acquiring MUnitOfWork   790
            New entity registration in MUnitOfWork   791
            Dirty entity registration in MUnitOfWork   791
            Entity removal in MUnitOfWork   792
            Committing MUnitOfWork   792
            Execution of a transaction   793
            Starting a transaction   795

23.7   Package Foundation   795

    23.7.1 Transactions on FConnection   796
    23.7.2 Execute Statements in FWriter   796
    23.7.3 Querying the Database in FReader   798

23.8   Database Code   799

    23.8.1 Ref Cursor for ResultSet   800
    23.8.2 Retrieval of Outmessages   801
    23.8.3 Retrieval of Departmental Outmessages   801
    23.8.4 Deleting an Outmessage   802
    23.8.5 Creating an Outmessage   803
    23.8.6 Report Generation   805
    23.8.7 Trigger on OutMessage Table   807

    Summary   809
    Key Terms   810
    Iteration 3 Questions and Exercises   810

Bibliography   811

Index   816

The accompanying CD   826

Guided Tour

Chapter

17

Web-Based User Interface
Design and Programming

An obvious trend in enterprise application development is to make applications web-enabled. A web-based application is ubiquitous – it can be used at any time from anywhere. Clearly, there are very few situations where availability of a web application is not an attractive proposition. Unfortunately, the challenges in building such applications are considerable. Most serious challenges are with the server software, not addressed in this chapter. This chapter concentrates on the client software.

A web-based application means that an Internet browser manages the rendering of UI content, but the business logic and database state exists on a server. This means, to begin with, that the HyperText Markup Language (HTML) is used. An HTML-formatted web page is a mix of the presentation content (e.g. some text) and rendering instructions (e.g. font size). HTML can be used to apply rendering instructions on a text in standard UI components, including Swing components. This can improve the presentation in applications that are not necessarily web-enabled.

A *Japplet* component in Swing provides a UI container that can be placed in a web page. Java applets and JavaScript are but two technologies that make the UI dynamic within a browser. This means that a web-based UI can be changed dynamically in both layout and content. HTML uses the <object> tag to download an object that lives in the URL space to the client. An applet can be such an object within an HTML page and retrieved from a web server.

For security reasons, an applet can be digitally signed. Applet lives in a *sandbox* environment. It is termed *sandbox* as it has limited and restricted access to system resources. An applet cannot access system resources unless an explicit permission is given to it. In technical terms, a Java applet consists of one or more *JavaBeans*, reusable components that are stored in a compressed form in a *Java Archive* file (JAR). This improves the download time.

The server technologies for web-based applications include servlets and Java Server Pages. A servlet is a Java code which creates HTML pages on the fly and which is managed by a web server. The code may be supported by Java Server Pages (JSPs). A web server provides a channel of communication between HTML client browsers and

---

Chapter openings
set the scene for more
detailed discussion

**Numerous annotated
screenshots** to draw
out key points

---

104 | Chapter 3 ■ Software Engineering Tools

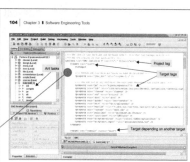

Project tag

Target tags

Target depending on another target

Figure 3.33 Sun ONE Studio and Apache Ant: system building

Each Ant task starts with a tag called 'target', such as "init" or "compile". The "init" target is used as the base for other targets by setting the initial properties of the project. A target may rely on other targets to achieve its job. In Figure 3.33, the target "compile" depends on "init". This dependence forces Ant to execute the "init" target before the "compile" target.

3.4.4 Support for Reengineering

The greatest battle of software engineering, yet to be won, is the automatic recovery of the designs present in existing legacy systems in order to reimplement them in a new form. A legacy system is a programming solution still in use, typically a large business information system, which was implemented a long time ago in traditional technology and has acquired extensive additional functionality through evolutionary maintenance.

A legacy system is the organization's history which stays from an earlier time but cannot be abandoned or replaced. The organization depends on the system in day-to-day business activities. Evolutionary maintenance done on the system over years has broken

---

**Extensive use of UML
diagrams**

Real code shows
readers how to put
concepts into practice

---

374 | Chapter 12 ■ Programming and Testing

Listing 12.3 ListedAs.java

```
ListedAs.java

5:    public class ListedAs {
6:       private double position;
7:
8:       private Movie movie;
9:
10:      private Actor actor;
11:
12:      public ListedAs(Movie m, Actor s, double position){
13:         this.movie = m;
14:         this.actor = s;
15:         this.position = position;
16:
17:         //register this ListedAs to the Movie and Actor
18:         movie.addListedAs(this);
19:         actor.addListedAs(this);
20:      }
69:   }
70: }
```

Figure 12.4 C++ parameterized types

---

608 | Chapter 18 ■ Iteration 2 Annotated Code

Listing 18.28 Message retrieval methods in CMsgSeeker

```
Method retrieveMessagesForCurrentEmployee(),retrieveMessagesFor-
Department(), and retrieveAllMessages() in CMsgSeeker

48:    public int retrieveMessagesForCurrentEmployee(
49:       Collection msgs,
50:       int numMsgs,
51:       Collection msgIDs) {
52:       int remainder = moderator.retrieveUnsentMessages(
           smp, msgs, numMsgs)
56:       if (msgIDs == null ) ) msgIDs.isEmpty())
57:          return remainder;
60:       Iterator it = msgs.iterator();
61:       while (it.hasNext()) {
62:          IAOutMessage msg = (IAOutMessage) it.next();
63:          Integer id = new Integer(msg.getMessageID());
64:          if (!msgIDs.contains(id)) {
65:             it.remove();
66:             remainder++;
67:          }
68:       }
69:       }
70:       return remainder;
71:    }
91:    public int retrieveMessagesForDepartment(String departmentCode,
92:       Collection msgs,
93:       int numMsgs,
94:       Collection msgIDs) {
96:       int remainder = moderator.retrieveUnsentMessages(
           departmentCode, msgs, numMsgs)
           ...[same as Line 56-77]
134:   public int retrieveAllMessages(
135:      Collection msgs,
136:      int numMsgs,
137:      Collection msgIDs) {
139:      int remainder = moderator.retrieveUnsentMessages(msgs,
           numMsgs)
           ...[same as Line 56-77]
```

18.5   Package Entity

The most visible changes in the entity package are the introduction of the IRObjectID interface and the EIdentityMap class (Figure 18.12). Changes to other entity objects are minimal. The changes relate to the inclusion of necessary code to help EIdentityMap

Key terms highlighted within text
Summary at the end of each chapter
reinforces readers' learning

To aid revision, **key terms** and their **in-text definitions** are noted at the end of every chapter

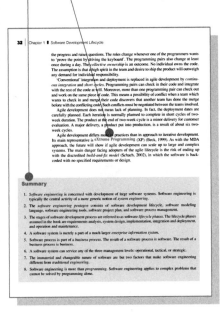

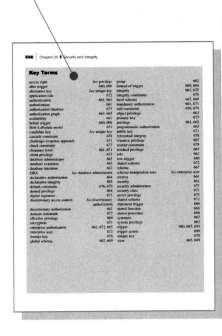

General end-of-chapter **review questions**
End-of-chapter review questions specific to
the **running case study**

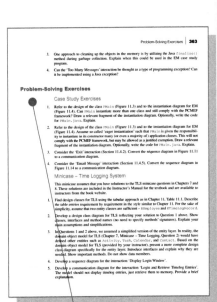

End-of-chapter **problem-solving exercises**
take readers deeper into the case study to ensure
understanding
Additional end-of-chapter **minicase exercises**
to test understanding further

The Book's Story

This book has a history of iterative and incremental development. It has certainly undergone all four major phases of one popular lifecycle model: project inception, elaboration, construction, and transition. The book has been an agile development by a pair of authors, with user stories as requirements, with continuous integration and lots of refactoring, but unfortunately not with short cycles to delivery.

The *inception* of the book dates back to the publication in 1990 of Maciaszek's *Database Design and Implementation* (Prentice Hall). Many readers of that book requested a follow-up text with more complete case studies, short and long examples, and with a stepwise (i.e. iterative and incremental) increase of technical difficulty and content sophistication. The business case for the book was made and the project entered the *elaboration* phase – the vision was refined, the risks resolved, the requirements and scope identified, but the target platform ended up to be . . . lots of industry training and consulting instead of a book.

Ten years later, and after countless industrial projects, the amount of practical material collected was screaming for publishing to a wider audience. But the audience has changed – the industry entered the Internet age. A new textbook was needed to define the prerequisite knowledge demanded by modern software engineering. That textbook was Maciaszek's *Requirements Analysis and System Design: Developing Information Systems with UML* (Addison-Wesley, 2001), going into its 2nd edition concurrently with this book. Soon after, the book you are holding entered the construction phase.

The *construction* phase was bumpy. Originally the book was perceived as a companion to Maciaszek's 2001 textbook or any similar book. Later the emphasis shifted to a stand-alone textbook that uses an iterative case study approach to teaching practical software engineering. The book concentrates on software design, programming and management. It emphasizes modern development practices, methods, techniques, and tools.

The *transition* phase of this book is in your – the reader's – hands. The beta-tests of this book were conducted in classrooms and on software projects. The deployment is at the reader's mercy. Please submit change requests, defects and enhancements to the development team.

Book Outline and Organization

The distinctive character of this book stems from two endeavors. Firstly, this book is about the way software engineering is done *in practice*. Secondly, it is about software engineering for *enterprise applications*. The following description of what enterprise applications include and exclude applies fully to this book: 'Enterprise applications include payroll, patient records, shipping tracking, cost analysis, credit scoring, insurance, supply chain, accounting, customer service, and foreign exchange trading. Enterprise applications don't include automobile fuel injection, word processors, elevator controllers, chemical plant controllers, telephone switches, operating systems, compilers, and games' (Fowler, 2003, p.3).

The book is pivoted on one main **case study**, two **minicases** with related exercises, a large number of supporting **examples**, **tutorials** to review basic modeling and programming concepts, and end-of-chapter **problem-solving exercises** which contain mostly **case study exercises**. The organization that is a reference for the case study, and for some minicases and examples, is a company specializing in *advertising expenditure measurement*. The book names this organization after its core business activity – AEM (in reality the organization is ACNielsen's Nielsen Media Research in Sydney, Australia). The case study is *Email Management* (EM) – a subsystem of AEM's *Contact Management* (CM) system.

As shown in the Venn diagram, AEM is the business, CM is one of the business domains, and EM is the case study. Examples and minicases are drawn from a cross-section of domains of the AEM business, including CM. Some examples are not related to AEM. The case study is enriched by examples and by case study exercises. Tutorials are used to quickly teach introductory topics with relation to UML modeling, Java programming, relational databases, GUI (graphical user interface) construction, and working with business components.

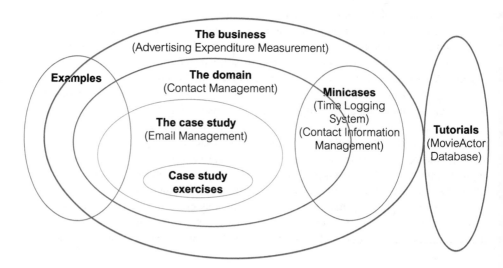

The book endeavors to give broad software engineering knowledge and to provide background information prior to presenting case study solutions. However, a distinguishing emphasis of the book is to show how to apply this knowledge on software projects. For given requirements, the book iteratively develops design and implementation models. Case study, minicases, examples and problem-solving exercises are carefully selected to emphasize various aspects of software development as necessitated by the unique characteristics of different applications and target software solutions.

The book consists of four parts. Part 1 (**Software Projects**) discusses software lifecycle, modeling languages, engineering tools, project planning, and process management. The next three parts (2, 3, and 4) introduce the case study, minicases and examples. The discussion in these three parts concentrates on the methods, techniques, processes, and development environments of software engineering.

Parts 2, 3 and 4 correspond to three project (case study) iterations. Each iteration starts with use case specifications enriched by an initial object model. The generic theory and practical knowledge underpinning each iteration are explained prior to demonstrating the case study design and programming solutions. Any knowledge specific to the case study solutions, and without significant generic appeal, is presented within or as a subsection of the case study discussion. Each iteration results in a complete solution and concludes with a chapter that contains the source code with necessary annotations and references to explanations in prior chapters.

Part 2 (**From Requirements via Architectural Design to Software Release**) starts by giving the business context for the EM case study. The first two chapters in this part present the business object model for AEM and the domain object model for CM. Next, the EM requirements are defined and the EM Iteration 1 is successively developed. The cornerstone of the first iteration is a sound architectural design amenable to successive stepwise enhancements. The 'deliverable' of the first iteration is the software release to the users (i.e. the readers of this book).

Part 3 (**Software Refactoring and User Interface Development**) concentrates on determining the front end of the system and on the presentation and domain layers of the application. It discusses the graphical user interface (GUI) design, including a web-enabled front end. The transformation from Iteration 1 to Iteration 2 is achieved through architectural refactoring and the development of an attractive user interface.

Part 4 (**Data Engineering and Business Components**) moves the focus point from the system front end to its backbone and to the middle tier. This part discusses the storage and manipulation of data, implementation of business rules, transaction processing, and security control. It explains also how the application logic can be moved to an application server in the middle tier.

Although Iteration 3 of the case study is developed from Iteration 2, Parts 3 and 4 of the book can be studied relatively independently. A reader can elect to concentrate on one of these parts and only skim through the other part. For example, a database designer/programmer may have a marginal interest in Part 3, whereas a GUI designer or Java programmer may have a marginal interest in Part 4. An expectation is that some readers will concentrate on Parts 1 and 2 of the book and will fully identify with Parts 3 and 4 after a period of experimentation and gaining better appreciation of the knowledge contained in earlier parts. It is also possible, in more advanced project-oriented courses, to begin using the book from Part 2.

From the total number of 23 chapters in the book, 6 are dedicated to the EM case study (these are Chapters 8, 13, 14, 18, 19, and 23). The educational value of these six chapters is through understanding and analyzing the case study. This is truly learning by example. By contrast, the first five chapters (Part 1) explain the foundations of software engineering and they do not refer to the case study. The remaining 12 chapters have both theoretical parts and the parts that link the theory to the case study, minicases, or other examples.

Distinguishing Features

The main distinguishing feature of the book is in its subtitle: **A Case Study Approach**. If you believe – as many educators do – that the best teaching formula is to *teach by example*, then this book is for you. If you want to be challenged and invited to *learn from mistakes*, then this book gives you plenty of opportunity to experiment with your solutions and compare them with the authors' answers and explanations. If on top of that, you would like to *customize learning to your current needs and level of knowledge* then each iteration has different emphasis, different modeling difficulty and may demand a different subset of development techniques and models.

An overriding objective of this book is to relate theories to reality by giving special attention to software design and implementation (while not neglecting analysis) and by addressing non-trivial practical problems. In its objective of 'exemplifying to explain', the book is unique in a number of ways:

1. *Education in mind.* The book was written with education in mind. The case study, examples and problem-solving exercises are not just plainly taken from real-world solutions; they are molded to suit educational needs. Real-world solutions are part of a complex business and software implementation context. That context is likely to be overwhelming and uninteresting to the reader, so it is simplified as much as possible. Presentation of GUI and database designs as well as programming examples eliminates unnecessary dependencies, 'information noise', and repetitive tasks.

2. *Annotated solutions.* There are no black-or-white, true–false, zero–one solutions in information systems. Frequently, a solution serves a particular purpose and may look plainly wrong when analyzed from a different perspective. Therefore, answers and solutions are carefully annotated.

3. *Alternative solutions.* Sometimes a single solution, no matter how annotated and explained, is not distinctly better than other potential solutions. To this end, alternative solutions are frequently provided and explained.

4. *Lists of key terms* at the end of each chapter compiled as indexes with references to page numbers. The lists can be used for self-study reviews of the understanding of the basic terminology introduced in each chapter. They can also be used by instructors to query the students' knowledge of each chapter.

5. *Review questions* to reinforce the reader's knowledge by insightful questions to each chapter. The questions are divided, when appropriate, into discussion questions and case study questions. Answers to all review questions are available to instructors from the book's website.

6. *Problem-solving exercises* to challenge the reader to research the issues before attempting a solution and to attempt extended or alternative solutions to the case study, minicases or other examples. Sample solutions to all review questions are available to instructors from the book's website.

7. *Website* with complete set of supporting material, including models and programming code (mostly UML, Java and database (Oracle) code). All programming code, including code not presented in the text, is available on the book's website.

8. *Emphasis on principles.* There are some well-defined principles (patterns, frameworks, standards, libraries, etc.) of good software engineering and system development. The book identifies and explains these principles and makes linkages to sources of information.

9. *Balanced mixture of professional depth and educational benefit.* In general, writing software and writing educational books are somewhat disjoint activities. Hopefully, this book contradicts this observation.

10. *Substituting for professional education and training courses.* Busy professionals tend to perform routine tasks and they can quickly fall behind the state-of-art and frequently the state-of-practice in the discipline. Finding time and funds to attend expensive professional education and training courses with case studies similar to those in this book may be difficult. Perhaps this book can give professionals an opportunity to catch up on latest developments at the time of their choice or between normal work duties.

Intended Readership

This book is aimed at a wide readership of students and IT professionals. An ideal reader is a student of a software engineering course or a software developer (or project leader/manager). The book is written so that it can be fully understood by students and professionals who possess basic knowledge of information systems and basic programming skills (hopefully in an object-oriented language and with some database use). For most readers, this corresponds to the first year of a university degree in computer science or informatics (information systems, information technology).

For *students*, the primary use of this textbook is in software engineering courses with a software development component. The book can also be used as a textbook in courses in information systems development, software projects, or systems analysis and design when taught in higher years or to more mature students. Moreover, the book can be used as a recommended reading in courses on object technology, object programming, web-based systems, database design and programming, and similar.

Practitioners most likely to benefit from the book include system designers, programmers, software architects, business and system analysts, project leaders and managers, web and content developers, reviewers, testers, quality assurance managers and industry trainers. The book can be used for professional education and training courses and workshops. It can also be adopted as a source of information for project teams. For practitioners already using UML, Java and relational databases on software projects, this book can serve as a validation of their software development practices and as a source of development ideas and directions.

Supplementary Materials

A comprehensive package of supplementary material is provided for the companion website. Most of the website content is freely available to all readers, but some material is password-protected for the benefit of instructors who have adopted the book in their teaching. The home page for this book is maintained at:

http://www.comp.mq.edu.au/books/pse
http://www.booksites.net/maciaszek

The web package for this book contains two sets of resources: for all readers and for instructors who adopted the textbook for teaching. The instructor resources are password-protected.

Instructor resources on the web include (but are not limited to):

1. *Instructor's Manual* with:
    (a) *questions and answers* to all end-of-chapter review questions and problem-solving exercises
    (b) extra *projects and solutions* – not contained in the textbook and available from the website to assist instructors in setting up student assignments and projects
2. *Lecture slides* – in PowerPoint and in modifiable Acrobat pdf formats
3. *UML models and Java/Database source code* for solutions to:
    (a) exercises and minicases
    (b) projects provided on the book's website
    (c) alternative design/programming approaches to the book's case study

Resources for all readers include (but are not limited to):

1. *Lecture slides* – in printable-only Acrobat pdf format
2. *Errata and addendum* document
3. *UML models and Java/Database source code* for the book's case study and examples, complete with instructions on how to compile and run the code.

Your comments, corrections, suggestions for improvements, contributions, etc. are very much appreciated. Please, direct any correspondence to:

Leszek A. Maciaszek
Department of Computing
Macquarie University
Sydney
NSW 2109, Australia
email: leszek@ics.mq.edu.au
web: http://www.comp.mq.edu.au/~leszek
phone: +61 2 9850-9519
facsimile: +61 2 9850-9551
courier: North Ryde, Herring Road, Bld. E6A, Room 319

Acknowledgements

Author's Acknowledgements

This book took a considerable time to write but that time shrinks to insignificance in comparison with the time taken to gain the knowledge and skills necessary for its writing. Our special gratitude goes to our friends and colleagues at ACNielsen, Sydney, Australia, who provided the initial 'testbed' for much of the knowledge transferred to the readers in this book. Our thanks go in particular to Stephen Bills (who is also this book's named contributor) and his team of developers, including Paul Antoun, Bruno Beira, Sue Dayes, Steven Grotte, Jeff Hong, Yijun Li, Kevin Mathie, Denise McCrae, Chantal O'Connell, James Rees, Jovan Spoa, Eric Zurcher.

Writing a book is a considerable project. As explained in Chapter 4 and elsewhere in the book, a successful project requires that sufficient work and material resources be allocated to project tasks. Work resources consist of people and equipment, including hardware and software. Material resources are consumables and supplies. The authors of this book allocated themselves to the tasks, but the project would dismally fail without all accompanying work and material resources. The resources were provided by Macquarie University, Sydney, Australia, and University of Economics, Wrocław, Poland. We are indebted to our friends, colleagues and students at these two universities for their advice, support, and assistance, for all the resources that they have provided to this project.

Talking about resources, this book could not have been written without intensive and wide-ranging use of software tools and environments. The software necessary for the book was obtained by various means, from purchase via downloads of demonstration copies to using open software sources. People behind software obtained through such means are anonymous to us, so acknowledgements are not possible. Our acknowledgements are, however, in place to these software vendors who responded to our requests to provide software free of charge for educational use by us and our students. We are particularly indebted to Oracle Corporation (Oracle and JDeveloper), Rational Software Corporation, currently IBM (Rational Suite), Sybase (PowerDesigner), and yWorks (yDoc).

Most significantly, we are grateful to Keith Mansfield of Pearson Education, the editor of this book as well as the editor of Maciaszek's *Requirements Analysis and Systems Design*. Thank you, Keith, for having the vision for both books and for your hard work from inception to production and deliverables. Book production is a real team effort. Risking the omission of quite a few names, we would like to thank especially: Anita Atkinson (senior desk editor), Helen MacFadyen (proofreader), Ruth Freestone King (copyeditor) and Owen Knight (editorial assistant). Thank you all for your corrections, improvements, insights, advice and great cooperation.

Publisher's Acknowledgements

We are grateful to the following for permission to reproduce copyright material:

Table 1.1 based on information from *Fundamentals of Software Engineering*, Prentice Hall (Pearson Education, Inc.), (Ghezzi, C., Jazayeri, M. and Mandrioli, D., 2003); Figure 1.10 adapted from figure of *Rational Unified Process*, reprinted by permission from http://www.rational.com/products/rup/, © Copyright 2003 by International Business Machines Corporation. All Rights Reserved; Figures 3.1, 4.3, 4.4, 4.5, 4.7, 4.8, 4.9, 4.10, 4.11, 4.13, 4.14, 4.16, 4.17, 4.19, 4.20, 4.21, 4.22, 4.23, 4.25, 4.26, 4.28 and 4.29 from screen shots of Microsoft® Office Project (2003), reprinted by permission from Microsoft Corporation, Copyright © 1998–2003 Microsoft Corporation; Figure 3.2 from screen shot of Manage-Pro™ 6.1 from www.managepro.net, March 2004, Performance Solutions Technology, LLC, reproduced by kind permission of Performance Solutions Technology, LLC; Figure 3.3 from screen shot of eRoom from www.eroom.net/eRoomNet/, July 2003, Documentum, Inc., reproduced by kind permission of Documentum, Inc.; Figure 3.4 from a screen shot of eProject Enterprise, July 2003, reproduced by kind permission of eProject, Inc.; Figures 3.5 and 3.6 from screen shots of *Small Worlds*, reprinted by permission from www.thesmallworlds.com/, © Copyright 2003 by International Business Machines Corporation. All Rights Reserved; Figure 3.8 from screen shot of @Risk from www.palisade-europe.com, reproduced by kind permission of the Palisade Corporation; Figures 3.9, 3.10, 3.12, 3.14, 3.16, 3.30, 3.31, 5.14, 5.15 from screen shots of *IBM Rational Suite*, reprinted by permission from *Rational Suite Tutorial, Version 2002.05.00*, © Copyright 2002 by International Business Machines Corporation. All Rights Reserved; Figure 3.9 from screen shot of Microsoft® Word, reprinted by permission from Microsoft Corporation, Copyright © 1998–2003 Microsoft Corporation; Figure 3.11 from screen shot of DOORS® from www.telelogic.com, reprinted by kind permission of Telelogic UK Ltd., Copyright © 2004 Telelogic AB; Figure 3.13 from screen shot of Enterprise Architect from www.sparxsystems.com.au, August 2003, Sparx Systems Pty Ltd., reproduced by kind permission of Sparx Systems Pty Ltd.; Figure 3.15 from a screen shot of Gentleware's Poseidon Sales Application model, August 2003, reproduced by kind permission of Gentleware AG; Figures 3.16, 3.34 and 3.35 from screen shots of No Magic's MagicDraw™ from www.magicdraw.com, July 2003, © Copyright No Magic, Inc. 1998–2004, reproduced with permission. All Rights Reserved; Figure 3.17 from screen shot of Sybase® PowerDesigner® version 9.5, from www.sybase.com, July 2003, © Copyright 2002, Sybase, Inc., All Rights Reserved; Figure 3.25 from screen shot of *Borland® Together® ControlCenter® example* (2003), www.borland.com, reprinted by permission of Borland Software Corporation; Figure 3.27 from screen shot of Oracle JDeveloper from www.otn.oracle.com, reproduced by permission of Oracle Corporation; Figure 3.29 from screen shot of Perforce, from www.perforce.com, reproduced by kind permission of Perforce Software, Inc.; Figure 3.32 from screen shot of Microsoft® Visual SourceSafe from http://msdn.microsoft.com/ssafe/default.asp, (2003), reprinted by permission from Microsoft Corporation, Copyright ©

1998–2003 Microsoft Corporation; Tables 4.2 and 4.3 based on information from *Software Cost Estimation with COCOMO II*, Prentice Hall (Pearson Education, Inc.), (Boehm, B.W., Abts, C., Brown, A.W., Chulani, S., Clark, B.K., Horowitz, E., Madachy, R., Reifer, D. and Steece, B., 2000); Figures 5.11 and 20.4 from *Requirements Analysis and Systems Design with UML*, Addison Wesley, (Pearson Education), (Maciaszek, L.A., 2001); Figure 12.11 from screen shot of Microsoft® DOS, reprinted by permission from Microsoft Corporation, Copyright © 1990–2003 Microsoft Corporation; Figure 17.18 adapted from *Mastering Jakarta Struts* by James Goodwill. Copyright © 20002 by Ryan Publishing Group. Reproduced here by permission of Wiley Publishing, Inc. All rights reserved; Figures 22.3 and 22.4 from screen shots of Oracle Business Component Browser from www.otn.oracle.com, reproduced by permission of Oracle Corporation.

In some instances we have been unable to trace the owners of copyright material, and we would appreciate any information that would enable us to do so.

Part

1

Software Projects

Chapter 1   Software Development Lifecycle   5

Chapter 2   Software Modeling Language   37

Chapter 3   Software Engineering Tools   63

Chapter 4   Software Project Planning and Tracking   112

Chapter 5   Software Process Management   153

I t is good practice in knowledge transfer domains, such as in book writing or in software production, to start by defining the main terminology. Terms need just to be defined and clarified, not invented. Surely, most terms we are working with have been invented before.

This book is about software and systems. It is about software engineering and software system development. It is about large software projects and about enterprise information systems. The book subscribes to the following definitions, provided by the prominent experts in the field.

'*Software engineering* is the field of computer science that deals with the building of software systems that are so large or so complex that they are built by a team or teams of engineers' (Ghezzi *et al.*, 2003, p.1). In this definition, there are few important observations.

'The building of software systems' is another way of saying *system development*. In reality, software engineering goes beyond software development. It applies also to *software maintenance*. Like any engineering product, such as a bridge or house, the software must be maintained. Unlike in the case of a typical engineering product, the maintenance of software includes software evolution (addition of new modules) and extensive changes to the very foundations of the product. In this sense, software development subsumes software maintenance.

'A *system* is a purposeful collection of interrelated components that work together to achieve some objective" (Sommerville, 2001, p.21). System development (and maintenance) is concerned with processes, methods and tools to support software production. Because software is a model of reality, software development is about *modeling* of software artifacts.

System is more than software. '*System engineering* is concerned with all aspects of the development and evolution of complex systems where software plays a major role' (Sommerville, 2001, p.7). 'System engineering focuses on a variety of elements, analyzing, designing, and organizing those elements into a system that can be a product, a service, or a technology for the transformation of information or control' (Pressman, 2001, p.245). And because software plays a major role in most contemporary systems, this book is also about system engineering.

Most software projects are undertaken in response to organizational needs to tackle an identified problem in a business process or to improve a business process to hold up to competitive pressures. A *software project* is a planned undertaking which is intended to deliver a software product or service and is completed over a period of time. Software projects of special interest in this book are those aimed at delivery of *enterprise information systems*. These are large and complex systems. As noted by Fowler (2003, p.2): 'Enterprise applications often have complex data – and lots of it – to work on, together with business rules that fail all tests of logical reasoning.'

The Standish Group (Standish, 2003) researches into the reasons for *software failures*. The seminal *Chaos Report* produced by the Standish Group in 1994, reported that only 16.2 percent of software projects were completed on time and on budget. As far as large and complex systems go, the news was even worse: only 9 percent of such projects were completed on time and on budget. The *Chaos Report* for 2003 showed an improvement – 34 percent of projects completed on time and on budget. Although the improvement is significant, it is dismal when compared with traditional engineering disciplines, such as architecture or electrical engineering.

Success of a software project is conditioned on five interrelated facets – the *software engineering pentagon*, depicted graphically below. The facets are:

■ software development lifecycle – Chapter 1
■ software modeling language – Chapter 2
■ software engineering tools – Chapter 3
■ software project planning – Chapter 4
■ software process management – Chapter 5.

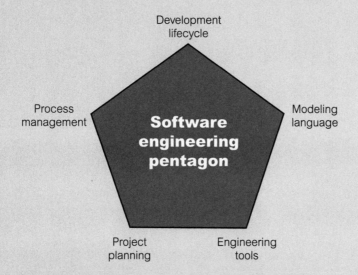

The main learning objectives of Part 1 are to gain knowledge of:

■ the quintessence of software engineering
■ lifecycle phases and models, in particular iterative and incremental development
■ software modeling languages, in particular the UML object-oriented modeling language
■ software engineering tools for project management, system modeling, integrated teamwork programming, and change and configuration management
■ project scheduling and budget estimation
■ techniques to track project progress
■ management of human resources allocated to the project
■ project risk management
■ software quality management
■ change and configuration management.

Chapter

1

Software Development Lifecycle

In normal usage, the term 'life cycle' means 'the changes that happen in the life of an animal or plant' (Cambridge, 2003). In software engineering, the term lifecycle (normally written as a single word) is applied to artificial software systems to mean the changes that happen in the 'life' of a software product. Various identifiable phases between the product's 'birth' and its eventual 'death' are known as lifecycle phases.

The changes, and therefore the phases, are gradual. The product is *phased in* – introduced in stages. Hence, iterative and incremental development. Eventually, the product is *phased out* – its usage is gradually stopped. Hence, stepwise retirement. A reasonable way of thinking is that software is, at any time except deployment stage, either in phase-in or phase-out period. Software maintenance, despite its evolutionary character, begins the phasing-out process.

Figure 1.1 shows typical software lifecycle phases (explained in more detail in Section 1.2). The phases are:

1. requirements analysis
2. system design
3. implementation
4. integration and deployment
5. operation and maintenance.

Figure 1.1 demonstrates that once a software product is introduced into an organization, it stays there forever, although under different 'reincarnations'. There is no possibility for an organization to return to a manual way of conducting business. Once in operation, the software product is maintained 'to death'.

Maintenance, even if it evolves the system, leads eventually to deterioration of its original architectural design. The system becomes a legacy system – it cannot be 'perfected' any more, and even housekeeping and corrective maintenance become a major challenge. The entire system, or major components of it, must be phased out. The realization that the system is a legacy results in a decision to develop a new

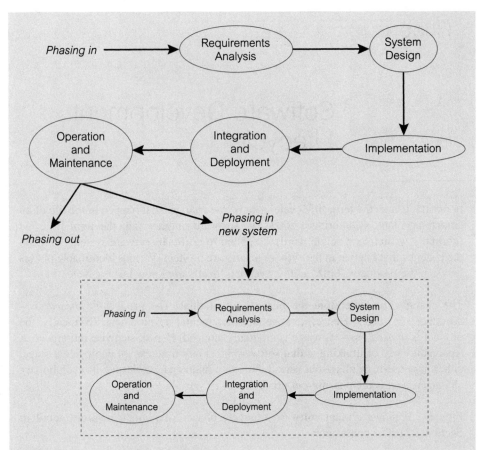

Figure 1.1 Software lifecycle phases

system. This starts a new lifecycle shown at the bottom of Figure 1.1. The phasing out of the old system and the phasing in of a new system are conducted in parallel until the new system is deployed to the users. Even after deployment, the old system may stay operational for some time until the new system can demonstrate its production usefulness.

Characteristic to Figure 1.1 is the absence of *testing* as a lifecycle phase. Testing – like project management activities, including the collection of project *metrics* – is an all-encompassing activity that applies to all phases of the lifecycle.

Software Engineering Quintessence

Understanding of the software lifecycle is conditional on the understanding of the quintessence of software engineering – its fundamental nature, the context of software production. The quintessence of software engineering is captured in the following key observations:

- the software system is less than the enterprise information system
- the software process is part of the business process
- software engineering is different from traditional engineering
- software engineering is more than programming
- software engineering is about modeling
- the software system is complex.

Software System is less than Enterprise Information System

A software system is merely a part of a much larger enterprise information system. An implication is that the development of a software system is just an activity (albeit a fundamental one) in the development of an enterprise information system. A Venn diagram in Figure 1.2 demonstrates the inclusion of a software system in an enterprise information system. It shows also that an enterprise information system is a component of the enterprise as the whole and that the enterprise is a part of the business environment.

An information system is concerned with generating and managing information for people. Some of this information is generated automatically by computer systems. Other information is generated manually by people. The point is that information systems are *social systems* that encompass and use software and other components for the benefit of the enterprise. Benson and Standing (2002) list the following components of an information system:

Figure 1.2

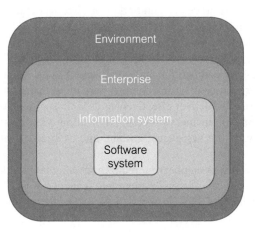

- people
- data/information
- procedures
- software
- hardware
- communications.

For example, a bank account management system consists of bank tellers, data/information about customers and their accounts, procedures governing the withdrawal and depositing of money, software able to process data/information, hardware on which the software can run (including automatic teller machines), and personal and automated communication channels that shackle all these components together.

1.1.2 Software Process is part of Business Process

A *process* refers to the manner in which work activities are scheduled, organized, coordinated, and performed at a certain period of time in a given place in order to produce product or service. The difference between software process and business process stems from and relates to a product or service expected from these processes. The result of a software process is software. The result of a business process is business.

There is a clear relationship between software and business. Software is potentially a major contributor to business success. Software is part of business, but not vice versa. In fact, this subset/superset relationship has been depicted in Figure 1.2. Enterprise in Figure 1.2 is another term for business. The purpose of enterprise is to realize a value creation chain, which serves the realization of business mission, objectives, and goals.

The difference between software process and business process is akin to the difference between process efficiency and effectiveness. Efficiency means doing something right. Effectiveness means doing the right thing. In organizational terms, effectiveness implies attainment of business mission, objectives, and goals. These are all deliverables of *strategic planning* processes conducted by the enterprise. Part of strategic planning is *business modeling*. Hence, business processes aim to deliver effectiveness.

By contrast, software processes aim to deliver efficiency. It is, therefore, possible for a software process to deliver a very *efficient* product or service, which will be *ineffective* to the business. At best, ineffective can mean neutral to the business. At worst, it can make the business vulnerable to competition and even bring it to bankruptcy.

Clearly, a software process is an inherent part of a business process, vital to the success of an enterprise. To deliver effectiveness as well as efficiency, a software process must be a contributor to a business process. After all, a decision to develop a software product or service is, in the first place, an outcome of strategic planning and business modeling.

The discipline of software engineering realizes the alignment of software and business processes. On the one hand, software development is increasingly placed in the context of business modeling. Chapters 6 and 7 of this book are a clear manifestation of this trend. On the other hand, software development strives to deliver products and services of

Knowledge systems

Knowledge bases

OLAP (online analytical
processing) systems

Data warehouses

OLTP (online transaction
processing) systems

Databases

Figure 1.3
Software for
different
management
levels

increasing business value to an enterprise. This has to do with three **management levels** that business processes service: operational, tactical, and strategic.

Placing software development in the context of business modeling means that a software process is derived from a wider business model and it tries to support and implement a particular business process in that model. This means that a software product/ service cannot be just an information service. It should also implement and assist in business actions. The design of an information system should either explicitly identify a business process it serves or, better, it should be a part of a (business) *knowledge management system*. One aspect of such design is a coordination between automated informational actions, manual supportive actions, and creative decision-making actions.

Usually, a software system services a single management level – operational, tactical, or strategic (Figure 1.3). The *operational level* processes business operational data and documents, such as orders and invoices. This is the realm of **online transaction processing** (OLTP) systems assisted by conventional *database* technology. The *tactical level* processes information obtained from the analysis of data, such as monthly trends in product orders. This is the realm of **online analytical processing** (OLAP) systems assisted by *data warehouse* technology. The *strategic level* processes the organizational knowledge, such as rules and facts behind a highly profitable product selling. This is a realm of knowledge systems assisted by *knowledge base* technology.

Software products/services at operational management level are indispensable to the enterprise. Without them, a modern enterprise cannot function. However, operational software does not provide to the enterprise any competitive edge. Competitors work with similar software systems. The business value of software increases with higher management levels that the software applies to.

Interestingly, software products/services that are potentially of highest business value to the enterprise are the most difficult to automate. Understandably so. Strategic management is about organizational *knowledge* and *wisdom*. As noted by Benson and Standing: 'Wisdom and knowledge exist only in the minds of people. When people talk about knowing something such as a telephone number, they are really talking about data. Understanding how to use that piece of data is knowledge. Deciding not to call someone at 3.00 a.m. is an example of wisdom' (Benson and Standing, 2002, p.77). Processing and transfer of knowledge (not to mention wisdom) is and will remain mostly a social phenomenon, motivational and intuitive, not technical and predictable.

1.1.3 Software Engineering is different from Traditional Engineering

The fact that a software system is a component of an information system implies that software engineering is an aspect of a broader discipline of systems engineering. Consequently, a software engineer must understand the requirements of the whole system and must be competent in the system's application domain to engineer the interfaces that the software must supply to its environment. A software engineer must also understand that some data/information processing can be better done in hardware than in software and that some processing may not need to (or cannot) be automated at all.

System engineering is concerned with studying principles that govern the internal workings of complex systems. There is a long history of using system engineering in **traditional engineering** disciplines, such as mechanical or electrical engineering. The discovered principles of system engineering are formalized in mathematical models. The models are validated and applied in engineering products. These products are material in nature – bridges, buildings, power stations.

Not so with software products. As observed in the seminal work of Brooks (1987), software is immaterial in nature. Classical mathematical models apply to some but not to all aspects of software. Software is defined in fuzzy terms – 'good', 'bad', 'acceptable', 'satisfying user requirements', etc. Similar qualities are used in the service sector where quality is associated with fuzzy terms such as 'good service', 'customer convenience', 'competence', 'job knowledge', etc. Software engineering may be tackling 'fuzzy' problems but this does not mean that it must be less rigorous or not provable. It is just that software engineering should use different branches of mathematics, such as fuzzy logic or rough sets, to provide rigor and proof.

In this context it is worth observing that *rigor* is not the same as *formality*. A software process may be rigorous even though not formally proven by mathematical laws. Indeed, this is the case even in classical mathematics. As pointed out by Ghezzi *et al.* (2003, p.43): 'Textbooks on functional calculus are rigorous, but seldom formal: proofs of theorems are done in a very careful way, as sequences of intermediate deductions that lead to the final statement; each deductive step relies on an intuitive justification that should convince the reader of its validity. Almost never, however, is the derivation of a proof stated in a formal way, in terms of mathematical logic.' Interested readers are advised to reach for a seminal paper on social processes and proofs of theorems and programs by De Millo *et al.* (1979).

Software engineering does not need to be a poor cousin of traditional engineering. It is just different. Nobody in traditional engineering expects that a bridge built to mathematical models will collapse. Similarly, a 'good' software 'satisfying user requirements' should not fail. But, there is a but – provided that the user requirements and expectations or external circumstances have not changed drastically in the meantime.

Nobody expects a bridge to be moved by ten meters after it has been built. Similarly, nobody should expect a software product to happily perform different tasks after it has been built. If this is what is expected then the software has not failed. The software has only become unusable or unacceptable because the business conditions or external environment changed. If a river corridor moved by ten meters because of the recent flooding, a civil engineer cannot be blamed and must not be expected to effortlessly move the existing bridge to span the new corridor.

This said, a software engineer must be prepared to build software that can accommodate change. That is the demanded nature of software. Software must be **supportable** – understandable, maintainable, and scalable. This is what makes software different from a bridge and makes software engineering different from traditional engineering.

Each software system is unique and its production process is unique. Unlike in traditional engineering disciplines, an application software product is not *manufactured* – it is *implemented*. It is not a car or refrigerator. It must be implemented to fit its environment. Each instance of a software system is unique – whether built from scratch or customized from a commercial off-the-shelf (COTS) software package. Only system software and software tools, such as operating systems and word processors, are massively manufactured once engineered. *Application software*, which is the subject of this book, is implemented not manufactured.

Software Engineering is more than Programming   1.1.4

In introductory pages to Part 1 of this book, software engineering has been defined as 'the field of computer science that deals with the building of software systems that are so large or so complex that they are built by a team or teams of engineers' (Ghezzi *et al.*, 2003, p.1). The definition emphasizes teams of people and complex systems.

Programming refers to 'code cutting' – writing a series of instructions to make a computer perform a particular task. If the task is large, programming may involve a team of programmers but each act of programming is primarily a personal activity. Programming is a skill. Given a definition and specification for the problem, a programmer applies the skills to express the problem in a programming language.

Software engineering is more than programming. Software engineering applies to complex problems that cannot be solved by programming alone. Complex systems must be designed before they can be programmed. Like in the building industry, a complex system must be *architected* before it can be built. It must be *modularized* using abstraction and 'divide-and-conquer' methods. Each module must be then carefully specified and its interfaces to other modules defined, before it can be given to programmers for coding.

A programmer has a limited understanding of the entire system. S/he codes one programming module at a time – a **software component** that needs to be integrated (by a software engineer) with other components to configure a working system. (Of course, this distinction between programmer and software engineer is only to illustrate the issue. In practice, the distinction may or may not apply.)

Frequently, multiple **versions** of the same component are available to a software engineer. A software **configuration** is built by assembling specific versions of different components. It is, therefore, possible to have multiple configurations of the same system.

Before a system can be designed, a software engineer must understand its requirements. This means that the requirements analysis must be done and specified in some modeling language. A standard modeling language in contemporary practice is **Unified Modeling Language** (UML). Both analysis and design models are expressed in UML.

A software engineer is responsible for bringing UML models for a system to the point where the initial programming code can be generated from these models. Programmers can take over from that point but the software engineer remains in charge of roundtrip engineering between the design and the code. **Roundtrip engineering** is an iterative cycle of forward (from design to code) and reverse (from code to design) engineering activities.

Finally, software engineering is a team activity. Teams must be managed. Consequently, software engineering is affected by and contributes to **project management**. This includes planning, budgeting and scheduling, quality control and risk management, and change and configuration management.

To recap, software engineering is concerned with providing an architectural solution for the system, with designing architectural components, with integrating components into an operational system, with roundtrip engineering, with project management, etc. Software engineering is an elaborate knowledge within which programming is a useful skill.

1.1.5 Software Engineering is about Modeling

Software engineering is about modeling (Lee and Tepfenhart, 2002). **Models** are abstractions from reality. They are abstract representations of reality. Is a computer program a model or reality? Well, one can argue that a program stored in computer memory or printed on paper is a reality. But the purpose of programming is not the program code per se; it is rather the functionality it provides. Is a football game played on a computer a reality? Is it really for real? These are clearly rhetorical questions.

Abstraction is a powerful technique in software engineering. By allowing concentration on important aspects of a problem and by ignoring aspects that are currently not relevant, abstraction allows to systematically conquer the problem's complexity (Section 1.1.6). Abstraction applies to both software products and software processes. A **software process model** is an abstract representation of the software process. In practical terms, a software process model defines the lifecycle phases and how they interact (Section 1.2). A **software product model** is an abstract representation of a software product. A software product model identifies a discrete product in a discrete stage of the lifecycle.

A software process model determines what software products, at various levels of abstraction, need to be produced by lifecycle phases. The following is a list of generic software product models:

■ **Requirements model** – a relatively informal model that captures user requirements and describes the system in terms of its business value.

■ **Specifications model** – a model that specifies requirements in more formal terms using a modeling language such as UML.

■ **Architectural model** – a model that defines the desired architecture of the system.

■ **Detailed design model** – a model that defines the software/hardware details of the demanded programming solution.

■ **Program model** – an implementation model that constitutes an ultimate executable software model.

Each of these product models can be further divided to identify more specific models. For example, a detailed design model can include user interface model, database model, program logic model, etc.

Finally, the software engineering paradigm used in system development influences the modeling abstractions. The two main paradigms are the old-style functional (procedural, imperative, structured) development and the modern object-oriented development.

The **functional paradigm** breaks a complex system down to manageable units using the approach known as functional decomposition. The technique called data flow modeling is used for this purpose. The software model is successively divided into processes (at decreasing levels of abstraction) linked by data flows.

The **object-oriented paradigm** breaks a system down into packages/components of classes linked by various relationships. Abstraction can be applied by allowing nested structures, i.e. a package/component can contain multiple levels of other packages/components. This book concentrates on object-oriented software engineering.

Software System is Complex 1.1.6

Software systems are *complex*. In the past, software was monolithic and procedural in nature. A typical Cobol program of the past was a single entity with subroutines called as required. The logic of the program was sequential and predictable. The complexity of such software was a consequence of its mere size.

Modern object-oriented software is distributed (it can reside on many computer nodes) and its execution is random and unpredictable. The size of modern software is the sum of the sizes of its components. Each component is designed to be of limited manageable size. As a result, the size is not the main factor in the complexity of modern software.

The complexity of modern software is in the 'wires' – in the linkages and communication paths between components. The inter-component linkages create dependencies between distributed components that may be difficult to understand and manage. The difficulty is inflated by the fact that components are frequently developed and managed by people and teams not even known to each other.

Figure 1.4 shows a possible object-oriented system in which objects in various packages communicate indiscriminately. This creates a network of intercommunicating objects. In the diagram, the complexity within packages (components) is still manageable due to the limited size of the packages. However, the dependencies created by inter-package communication links will grow exponentially with the introduction of more packages. The responsibilities of managing such dependencies are not always clear, as the responsibilities for packages remain with different teams. More importantly, the fact that any object in one package can communicate with any object in another package creates *potential dependencies* between all objects in the system. This means that a change in an object can potentially impact (can have a '*ripple effect*') on any other object in the system.

More formally, the cumulative measure of object dependencies with unrestricted inter-package (inter-component) communication links is the number of different combinations of pairs of objects. Such a measure can be computed using a probability theory method known as the *combinations counting rule*. The formula below calculates cumulative class

Figure 1.4
Complexity in the
'wires'

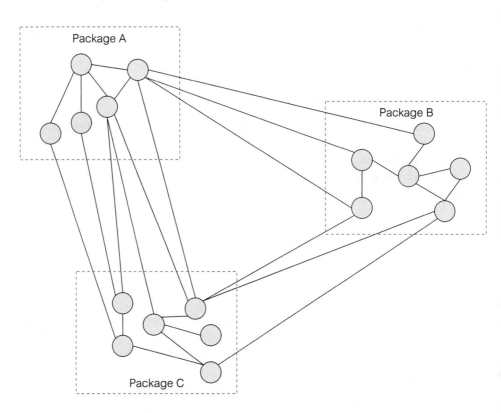

dependency (CCD) in a system with n classes of objects. For 5 classes, CCD equals 10. For 57 classes (for example), CCD equals 1,596. Such growth in complexity quickly becomes *unsupportable*.

$$_nCCD_2 = \frac{n!}{2!(n-2)!}$$

The formula computes the worst complexity, where each object communicates with all other objects. Although the worst scenario is unlikely in practice, it must be assumed in any dependency impact analysis conducted on the system (simply because real dependencies are not known beforehand). If a change in a class can potentially impact on any other class, then this fact must be checked to ensure that the change has been conquered. Systems permitting an indiscriminate network of intercommunicating objects, like in Figure 1.4, are considered unsupportable from a software engineering perspective. They are not understandable, not maintainable, and not scalable.

The solution to the dilemma lies in replacing networks of objects with hierarchies of objects. All complex systems that are supportable take the form of a *hierarchy*. This topic is so important that a separate chapter is dedicated to it (Chapter 9). Figure 1.5 shows merely how the complexity of a system can be reduced by allowing only single channels of communication between packages. Each package defines an interface object (this could be a Java-style interface or so called dominant class) through which all communication with the package is channeled. Despite the introduction of three extra objects, the

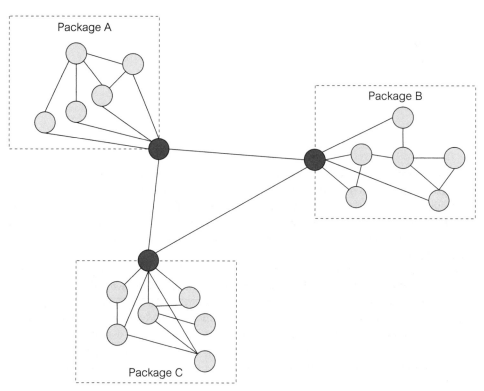

Figure 1.5
Reduction in
complexity due
to introduction
of interfaces
between
packages

complexity of the system in Figure 1.5 is visibly reduced in comparison with the same system in Figure 1.4.

Note also that the design in Figure 1.4 makes a mockery of a principal tool in the hands of the software engineer – the **abstraction** mechanism. Abstraction allows us to reason about selected parts of the system in a way that suppresses (abstracts from) irrelevant details. Although objects in Figure 1.4 are grouped in three packages, the complexity of the system (measured as a cumulative class dependency) is the same as for the similar system with no packages at all. The packages in Figure 1.4 do not introduce any useful layer of abstraction. They may as well not exist.

Lifecycle Phases

1.2

The **software lifecycle** is an abstract representation of a software process. It defines the phases, steps, activities, methods, tools, as well as expected deliverables, of a software development project. It defines a software development strategy.

There exist a number of useful lifecycle models (Section 1.3), which are in general agreement on lifecycle phases but differ on the importance of particular phases and on interactions between them. Lifecycle phases assumed in this book were identified at the beginning of this chapter. They are:

1. requirements analysis
2. system design
3. implementation
4. integration and deployment
5. operation and maintenance.

1.2.1 Requirements Analysis

'**User requirements** are statements, in a natural language plus diagrams, of what services the system is expected to provide and the constraints under which it must operate' (Sommerville, 2001, p.98). **Requirements analysis** is the activities of determining and specifying requirements. In contemporary practice, requirements analysis is assisted by a good degree of engineering rigor, and it is therefore sometimes identified with **requirements engineering**.

Requirements determination proves to be one of the greatest challenges of any software development lifecycle. Users are frequently unclear about what they require from the system. Frequently, they do not know real requirements, exaggerate them, provide requirements that conflict with requirements of fellow users, etc. There is also a risk, as in any communication between people, that the true meaning of a requirement is misunderstood. Developers are faced with the following anonymous observation: 'I know you believe you understood what you think I said, but I'm not sure you realize that what you heard is not what I meant.'

There are many methods and techniques of eliciting requirements. They include (Maciaszek, 2001):

- interviewing users and domain experts
- questionnaires to users
- observation of users performing their tasks
- study of existing system documents
- study of similar software systems to learn about the domain knowledge
- prototyping of working models of the solution to discover and confirm requirements
- joint application development sessions between developers and customers.

Requirements specification follows requirements determination. In current practice, UML is the standard modeling language for requirements specification (as well as for system design). Requirements are specified in graphical models as well as in textual descriptions. Because a complex system cannot be understood from a single viewpoint, the models provide complementing and by necessity overlapping viewpoints on the system.

Both graphics and text are stored in a repository of a **computer assisted software engineering** (CASE) tool. The tool facilitates making changes to the models as needed. It enables the integration of various models with overlapping concepts. It also enables transformations between analysis models (where this is possible) and assists in transformations to design models.

Requirements analysis results in a **requirements document** (Maciaszek, 2001). Most organizations adopt some templates for requirements documents. A template defines the structure of the document and provides guidelines on how to write it. The main body of a requirements document contains models and descriptions for system services and for system constraints. *System services* (what the system does) are frequently classified into functional requirements and data requirements. *System constraints* (how the system is constrained) include considerations related to the user interface, performance, security, operational conditions, political and legal restrictions, etc.

As mentioned in passing, the outcome of each lifecycle phase should be validated and tested. A professional approach to testing demands the creation of a **software quality assurance** (SQA) group within the organization. The SQA team consists of professional system testers. The team is relatively independent from developers. To make the whole process work, the SQA team, not the developers, is made responsible for the quality of the software product (i.e. the SQA is blamed for any undetected inadequacies and defects in the software).

Testing of abstract models is difficult because, most of the time, it cannot be automated. *Walkthroughs* and *inspections* are two popular and effective techniques. The techniques are similar. These are pre-organized meetings of developers and users during which the requirements models and documents are 'walked through'. The discussion that follows in the meetings is likely to uncover some problems. The essence of these techniques is that, during the meetings, the problems are identified but their resolution is not attempted, and there is no finger-pointing at people potentially responsible for the problems.

System Design   1.2.2

'A **software design** is a description of the structure of the software to be implemented, the data which is part of the system, the interfaces between system components and, sometimes, the algorithms used' (Sommerville, 2001, p.56). This definition is consistent with the definition of a software system as a union of data structures and algorithms. In enterprise information systems, data structures imply databases. Algorithms are not always fully described during design in order to leave some level of implementation freedom to the programmers (and, to put it bluntly, designers are not programmers and they may not be in a position to take knowledgeable algorithmic decisions).

Design begins where the analysis ends. As true and trivial as this statement is, the line separating analysis and design is not that clear in many projects. Theoretically the issue is simple. Analysis is the modeling unconstrained by any implementational (hardware/software) considerations. Design is the modeling that takes into consideration the platform on which the system is to be implemented.

In practice the distinction between analysis and design is blurred. There are two main reasons for this. Firstly, modern lifecycle models are *iterative with increments* (Section 1.3.2). In most such models, at any point in time, there are multiple incremental versions of the software under development. Some of the versions are in analysis, others in design; some in development, others in production, etc. Secondly, and more significantly, the same modeling language (UML) is used for analysis and design. The movement from analysis to design is 'by elaboration', rather than by translation between different representations.

The analysis model is elaborated into the design model by smooth addition of specification details. Drawing the line between analysis and design is very difficult in these circumstances.

The design discussed above is called, more precisely, the **detailed design**, i.e. the design that adds details to the analysis models. But there is another aspect of system design, namely the architectural design. The **architectural design** is concerned with setting up an architectural framework for the system, the component structure that the detailed design must adhere to, and the principles and patterns of internal communications between components.

The architectural design decides the 'beauty' of the system. A major objective of architectural design is to lead to a system that is *supportable* – understandable, maintainable, and scalable. The detailed design must conform to architectural design. Because of the blurry separation line between analysis and detailed design, some early architectural decisions may need to be taken within or even prior to requirements specifications (but after requirements determination).

Testing of architectural design is two-faceted. Firstly, the superiority of an architectural framework offered to the designers must be demonstrated. It must be shown that the framework addresses software complexity, ensures supportability, streamlines development, etc. Secondly, testing of architectural design has to do with verifying that the design of components conforms to the principles and patterns of the adopted architectural framework.

Testing of detailed design also has two aspects. Firstly, to be testable, the detailed design must be traceable. **Traceability management** is the whole branch of software engineering concerned with maintaining links between software artifacts at various stages of development. In the case of detailed design, each design artifact must be linked to requirements in the requirements document that motivated the production of that artifact. The existence of an artifact does not mean that it is acceptable. Hence, the second aspect of design testing employs walkthroughs and inspections to assess the quality of the design product so far.

1.2.3 Implementation

Implementation is mostly programming. But programming does not just imply a bunch of people sitting in a common area and coding in some programming language from design specifications. Programming is much more intellectually demanding than that. As indicated in the previous sections, the designs will be 'underspecified' in some areas when they reach programmers, in particular in the area of algorithm design. Completing the specifications requires extra designing before coding can take place. In this sense, a programmer is also a designer.

A programmer is a *component engineer.* Today's programming is rarely done from scratch. Much of programming is based on reusing pre-existing components. This means that the programmer must have the knowledge of component software and must know how to find this software in order to plug to it the newly coded application components. This is a tough ask.

A programmer is a *roundtrip engineer.* Programming begins as a transformation of design into code. Initial code does not have to be manually programmed. Using CASE tools and **integrated development environments** (IDEs), the code can be generated (forward engineered) from design models. Once generated, the code must be programmed manually to fill in the missing bits (these 'bits' are substantial and are the most difficult bits to program). Once modified by the programmer, the code can be reverse engineered back to update the design models. These forward and reverse engineering cycles are called **roundtrip engineering**.

If all this sounds simple, it is not. Roundtrip engineering is not perfect. The existing tools are powerful and clever, but they still fail in properly doing some aspects of the job. To keep the design and implementation in sync, both the designers and programmers must know the limitations and make manual corrections and additions as needed. Much of the responsibility in this task rests on project managers. They must schedule and monitor the work of designers and programmers so that they do not step on each other's toes. The practical requirement is that forward-engineering and reverse-engineering cannot overlap in time (Maciaszek, 2002).

In many projects, implementation is the longest of the development phases. In some lifecycle models, such as in the agile software development (Section 1.3.2), implementation is a dominant development phase. Implementation is an error-prone activity. The time spent in the creative writing of programs may be less than the time spent on program debugging and testing.

Debugging is an act of removing software 'bugs' – errors in programs. Errors in program syntax and some logic errors can be spotted and rectified by commercial debugging tools. Other errors and defects need to be discovered during program tests. **Testing** can take the form of code reviews (walkthroughs and inspection) or it can be execution-based (observing the program behavior during its execution). Traceability management supports testing in establishing if the programs satisfy user requirements.

There are two kinds of *execution-based testing*: **testing to specs** (black box testing) and **testing to code** (white box testing). Both kinds use the same strategy of feeding the program with input data and observing if the output is as expected. The difference lies in that testing to specs feeds the program with data without any consideration given to the program logic. The assumption is that the program should be behaving reasonably for any input data. In testing to code, the input data is provided to test specific execution paths in the program; as many of them and as diverse as possible. Because testing to specs and testing to code tend to uncover different kinds or errors and defects, both of them should be used.

Integration and Deployment 1.2.4

'The whole is more than the sum of its parts.' This seminal truth by Aristotle (384–322 BC) captures the essence of system integration and deployment. **Integration** assembles the application from the set of components previously implemented and tested. **Deployment** is the handing over of the system to customers for production use.

Software integration signifies the movement from the 'programming in the small' to the 'programming in the large' (Ghezzi *et al.*, 2003). Enterprise information systems are all sufficiently large and complex systems (Section 1.1.6) to make integration a very significant phase in the lifecycle. As another saying goes: 'For every complex problem there is a simple solution – that won't work' (H.L. Mencken). Integration cannot be swept under the carpet. Integration is a stage in its own right, even if it is sometimes difficult to disassociate it from implementation, such as in the *continuous integration* of the agile development (Section 1.3.2).

Integration is also difficult to disassociate from testing. In fact, the integration phase of the lifecycle is frequently referred to and discussed under the term of **integration testing**. With the omnipresent acceptance of iterative lifecycle models (Section 1.3.2), software is produced as a sequence of frequent incremental releases. Each increment is an integration of components, individually tested before, but in need of integration testing prior to deployment.

To a large degree, integration is driven by the architectural design of the system. The architecture of the system identifies its components and dependencies between them. It is of paramount importance that the architectural solution is in the form of a *hierarchy* (Section 1.1.6). A hierarchy means elimination of any circular dependencies between components. With circular dependencies, integration testing of some software increments (builds) may be impossible.

Consider a component dependency structure where component c_i uses (depends on) c_j and c_j uses c_k. Suppose that c_i and c_j have been implemented and individually tested but c_k is yet to be developed. The task is to integrate c_i and c_j. This task requires the programming of a **test stub** for c_k, i.e. a piece of code that simulates the behavior of the missing component c_k. The stub provides an integration context for the execution of c_j. A usual way to imple- ment the stub is by allowing it to take the same input/output parameters as in the ultimate c_k and to produce the results expected by c_j by hard-coding them or reading from a file.

All this works provided there are no circular dependencies between c_j and c_k. In the presence of circular dependencies both components must be fully implemented and individually tested prior to integration. Even then, the circular dependencies will create a testing nightmare. With extensive cycles in architectural design, integration testing would have to be done as a single activity called a *big-bang testing*. Big-bang testing can only be successfully performed for small programming solutions. It is not a reasonable proposition in modern software development.

Coming back to the example, suppose now that c_j and c_k have been implemented and individually tested but c_i is yet to be developed. How do we integrate c_j and c_k so that the integrated increment (build) gets the data and other context that would be normally given to it by c_i and so that we can assert that the increment does the job expected by c_i? To do this, a **test driver** for c_i must be programmed to 'drive' the integration.

All in all, integration requires writing of extra software, stubs and drivers, which are useful only during integration. This supporting test software is called **test harness** or *test scaffolding*, to refer to temporary scaffolding used in the building industry.

Integration can be conducted *top-down* (from the root of the dependency hierarchy) or *bottom-up* (from the components at the leaves of the hierarchy). The top-down approach requires the implementation of stubs. The bottom-up approach demands drivers. In reality, the integration rarely follows one of these approaches exclusively. A mixed approach, sometimes called *middle-out*, prevails.

Like integration, deployment is not a one-off activity. Software is deployed in releases. Each *release* combines a number of increments (builds) that offer coherent and usable functionality to the users. Prior to deployment, software is *system tested* by developers under realistic conditions. This is sometimes called *alpha-testing*. Alpha-testing is followed by **acceptance testing** by user-testers. This is sometimes called *beta-testing* (alpha- and beta-testing are terms accepted more in tests conducted on system software on behalf of software vendors, as opposed to the application software development).

Apart from system and acceptance testing, deployment includes a range of other activities. The most important of these activities is *user training*. In practice, user training may start well before the system is ready for release. The training coincides with the production of *user documentation*.

Operation and Maintenance 1.2.5

Operation signifies the lifecycle phase when the software product is used in day-to-day operations and the previous system (manual or automated) is phased out. *Phasing out* is usually a staged process. In situations where this is possible and feasible, the organization runs the new and old systems in parallel for some time. This provides a fallback if the new product fails the business demands.

Operation coincides with the start of product **maintenance**. In software engineering, maintenance has a slightly different meaning to the normal use of this word. Firstly, maintenance is not just an unplanned fixing of problems arising. Maintenance is planned and costed in the early stages of the lifecycle. Secondly, maintenance includes product evolution. In some iterative lifecycle models (Section 1.3.2), it may even be difficult to distinguish between development and maintenance.

In literature (Maciaszek, 1990; Ghezzi *et al.*, 2003), maintenance is usually divided into:

- *corrective* (housekeeping) – fixing defects and errors discovered in operation
- *adaptive* – modifying the software in response to changes in the computing or business environment
- *perfective* – evolving the product by adding new features or improving its quality.

Maintenance cost is considerable in the life of software. It is considerable because the product remains in operation for a long time. Large enterprise systems are so fundamental to organizations that they are kept alive using any available 'life support' technologies. Such systems are called **legacy systems**. They should be retired but there is no replacement for them. Indeed, when the decision of system *retirement* is eventually made, it is made not because the legacy system is not useful to the organization any more, but because it is not technically possible to keep it alive much longer. It should not come as a surprise that maintenance is the main reason why this is not technically possible – over time maintenance destroys the architectural clarity of software to the point that it cannot be supported any more.

Lifecycle Models 1.3

Software lifecycle determines the 'what', but not the 'how', of software engineering. Software engineering is to a considerable degree a social phenomenon constrained by a particular organizational culture of an enterprise. An enterprise may elect a generic

lifecycle model but the specifics of the lifecycle, how the work is done, is unique for each organization and may even differ considerably from project to project. This is consistent with the observations, made in Section 1.1.3, that a software product is not manufactured – it is implemented. Software process is not an experiment that can be repeated over and over again with the same degree of success.

The following is a short list of reasons why lifecycle specifics must be tailored to organizational cultures and why they differ from project to project:

- Software engineering experience, skills and knowledge of the development team (if not sufficient, the time for the 'learning curve' must be included in the development process).

- Business experience and knowledge (this is much more troublesome than the previous point because business experience and knowledge are not acquired easily).

- Kind of application domain (different processes are needed to develop an accounting system and a power station monitoring system).

- Business environment changes (changes in external political, economic, social, technological, and competitive factors).

- Internal business changes (changes to management, working conditions, enterprise financial health, etc.).

- Project size (a large project demands different processes from a small one; a very small project may even not need any processes as the developers can cooperate and exchange information informally).

Under the proviso of the above discussion, the approaches to software lifecycle can be broadly divided into two main groups:

- waterfall with feedback
- iterative with increments.

1.3.1 Waterfall Lifecycle with Feedback

The **waterfall model** is a traditional lifecycle introduced and popularized in the 1970s. The model has been reported as used with great success on many large projects of the past. Most of these projects were for batch (i.e. not interactive) systems implemented in Cobol language. Today, the waterfall lifecycle is used less frequently.

Using the lifecycle phases assumed in this chapter, the waterfall lifecycle with feedback can be visualized as in Figure 1.6. It is a linear sequence of phases, in which the previous phase must be completed before the next one can begin. The completion of each phase is marked with *signing off* of a project document for that phase. Feedbacks (back-arrows in Figure 1.6) between phases are possible, and indeed likely. A feedback signifies an undocumented but necessary change in a later phase, which should result in a corresponding change in the previous phase. Such backtracking should, but rarely does, continue to the initial phase of Requirements Analysis.

There are many variants of the waterfall lifecycle model. One such variant, depicted in Figure 1.7, allows for overlaps between phases, i.e. the next phase can begin before the

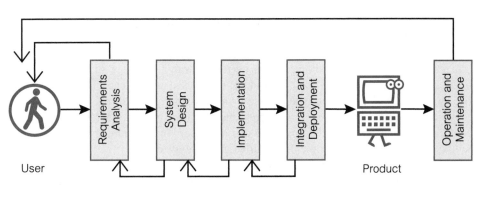

Figure 1.6
Waterfall lifecycle with feedback

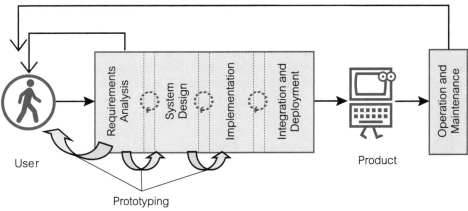

Figure 1.7
Waterfall lifecycle with feedback, overlaps, and prototypes

previous one is fully finished, documented and signed off. This is indicated in Figure 1.7 by arrowed circles between phases. Another popular variant, sometimes called the **prototyping model**, allows for construction of software prototypes in phases preceding the implementation phase. This is also indicated in Figure 1.7.

A crucial point about the waterfall approaches is that they are *monolithic* – they are applied 'in one go' to the whole system under development and they aim at a single delivery date for the system. The user is involved only in early stages of requirements analysis and signs off the requirements specification document. Later in the lifecycle, the user is in the dark until the product can be user-tested prior to deployment. Because the *time lag* between project commencement and software delivery can be significant (in months or even years), the trust between users and developers is put to the test and the developers find it increasingly difficult to defend the project to the management and justify expended resources.

The introduction of *overlaps* between phases can address another drawback of the lifecycle, namely stoppages in some parts of the project because developers from various teams wait for other teams to complete dependent tasks. The overlaps also allow for greater feedback between neighboring phases.

Prototyping in any lifecycle has a useful purpose, but it does offer special advantages to the waterfall model by introducing some flexibility to its monolithic structure and by cushioning against the risk of delivering product not meeting user requirements. A **software prototype** is a partial 'quick and dirty' example solution to the problem. From that example solution, successive forms of the software product can be developed.

In software engineering, prototyping has been used with a great deal of success to elicit and clarify user requirements for the product. Once used in this capacity, the question arises what to do with the prototype software. One possibility is to throw it away once its requirements validation purpose has been achieved. The justification for 'throw-away' prototyping is that retaining the prototype can introduce 'quick and dirty' solutions into the final product. After all, people do not drive in prototype cars.

However, software implementation is not car manufacturing. With component-based dynamic software development environments, the conversion of a prototype to a good final product without any traces of 'quick and dirty' solutions is achievable. This is depicted with forward-arrows in Figure 1.7. A prototype created in requirements analysis can serve to refine system design and an improved design prototype can be refined into an implemented final product.

Table 1.1 classifies the main characteristics of waterfall lifecycles into advantages and disadvantages (Schach, 2002; Ghezzi *et al.*, 2003). Sometimes, a characteristic is both advantage and disadvantage. This is shown by comments placed in both cells of a table row.

Table 1.1 Waterfall lifecycle with feedback

Advantages	Disadvantages
∎ Enforces disciplined approach to software development. Defines clear milestones in lifecycle phases, thus facilitating project management	∎ Completion criteria for requirements analysis and for system design are frequently undefined or vague. Difficult to know when to stop. Danger to deadlines
	∎ A monolithic approach, applying to the whole system, that may take a very long time to final product. This may be outright unacceptable for a modern enterprise demanding short 'return on investment' cycles
	∎ No scope for abstraction. No possibility to 'divide and conquer' the problem domain to handle the system complexity
∎ Produces complete documentation for the system	∎ Documentation can give a false sense of confidence about the project progress. Its dry, inanimate statements can be easily misinterpreted. Also, there is a risk of bureaucratizing the work
∎ Signing off the project documents before moving to successive phases clarifies the legal position of development teams	∎ Freezing the results of each phase goes against software engineering as a social process, in which requirements change whether we like it or not
∎ Requires careful project planning	∎ Project planning is conducted in early stages of the lifecycle when only limited insight into the project is available. Risk of misestimating of required resources

Source: Based on information from Ghezzi *et al.* (2003)

Iterative Lifecycle with Increments 1.3.2

Iteration in software development (as contrasted with iteration in a program) is a repetition of some process with an objective to enrich the software product. Every lifecycle has some elements of an iterative approach. For example, feedbacks and overlaps in the waterfall model introduce a kind of iteration between phases, stages or activities. However, the waterfall model cannot be considered iterative because an iteration means movement from one version of the product to the next version of it. The waterfall approach is monolithic with only one final version of the product.

An **iterative lifecycle** assumes **increments** – an improved or extended version of the product at the end of each iteration. Hence, the iterative lifecycle model is sometimes called evolutionary or incremental.

An iterative lifecycle assumes **builds** – executable code that is a deliverable of an iteration. A build is a vertical slice of the system. It is not a subsystem. The scope of a build is the whole system, but with some functionality suppressed, with simplified user interfaces, with limited multi-user support, inferior performance, and similar restrictions. A build is something that can be demonstrated to the user as a version of the system, on its way to the final product. Each build is in fact an increment over the previous build. In this sense the notions of build and increment are not different.

An iterative lifecycle assumes *short iterations* between increments, in weeks or days, not months. This permits continual planning and reliable management. The work done on previous iterations can be measured and can provide valuable metrics for project planning. Having a binary deliverable at the end of each iteration, that actually works, contributes to reliable management practices.

Figure 1.8 demonstrates that each iteration is a small waterfall of typical lifecycle phases. The differences are in the 'small print', as discussed above. The uppermost loop from Operation and Maintenance to the user is now fully and frequently employed. Lessons of the previous iteration are taken immediate advantage of in the next iteration. The user, equipped with the new experience of using the previous build, can be very helpful in refining requirements for the next iteration. The current design of the build is a starting point for System Design in the next iteration. Deployment of Iteration 2 Product is a start to Iteration 3, etc.

A classic iterative lifecycle model is the spiral model (Boehm, 1988). A modern representative of the iterative lifecycle is the IBM Rational Unified Process® (RUP®) (RUP, 2003), which originated from Rational Unified Process (RUP) (Kruchten, 1999). More recent representatives of the iterative lifecycle model are Model Driven Architecture (MDA®) (Kleppe *et al.*, 2003; MDA, 2003) and the agile development (Agile, 2003; Martin, 2003).

Spiral model

As rightly noticed by Ghezzi *et al.* (2003), the **spiral model** (Boehm, 1988) is really a *metamodel* in which all other lifecycle models can be contained. The model consists of four quadrants of the Cartesian diagram (Figure 1.9). The quadrants are: planning, risk analysis, engineering, and customer evaluation. The first loop around the spiral starts in the *planning* quadrant and is concerned with initial requirements gathering and project

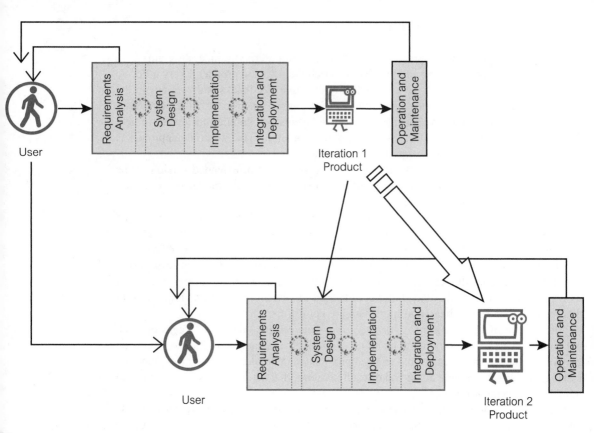

Figure 1.8 Iterative lifecycle with increments

planning. The project then enters the *risk analysis* quadrant, which conducts cost/benefit and threats/opportunities analyses in order to take a 'go, no-go' decision of whether to enter the *engineering* quadrant (or kill the project as too risky). The engineering quadrant is where the software development happens. The result of this development (a build, prototype or even a final product) is subjected to *customer evaluation* and the second loop around the spiral begins.

The spiral model treats the software development per se as just one of the four quadrants – the engineering quadrant. The emphasis on repetitive project planning and customer evaluation gives it a highly iterative character. Risk analysis is unique to the spiral model. Frequent risk analyses allow an early identification of any emerging risks to the project. The risks can be internal (under the organization's control) or external (risks that the organization cannot control). Either way, the task of risk analysis is to look in the future and if it is clear that the risks are not sustainable, the project must be killed without regard to the costs expended so far.

Each loop fragment within the engineering quadrant can be an iteration resulting in a build. Any successive loop fragment in the outward direction is then an increment. This said, other interpretations of engineering loop fragments are possible. For example, the

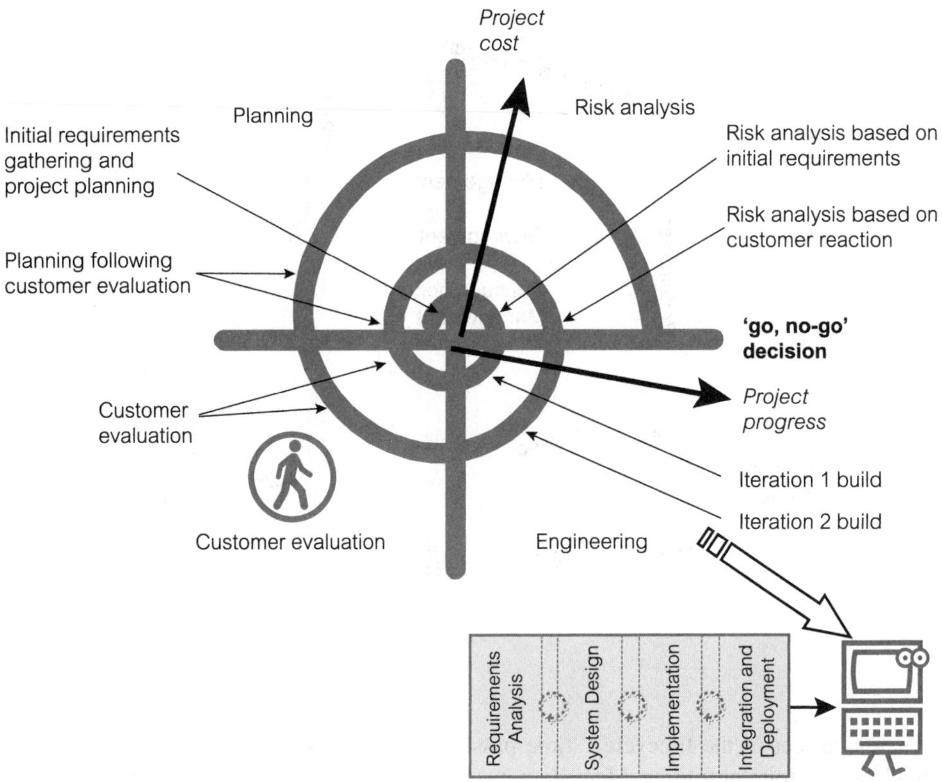

Figure 1.9
Spiral model
lifecycle

whole loop around the spiral may be concerned with requirements analysis. In such case, the engineering loop fragment may be concerned with requirements modeling and building an early prototype to solicit requirements. Alternatively, the spiral model can contain the monolithic waterfall model. In such case, there will be only one loop around the spiral.

The spiral model is rather a reference model or a metamodel for other models. Attractive and realistic as it may be, it does not translate to a specific documented lifecycle that organizations use in software development. The spiral model is a 'way of thinking' about software development principles.

Rational Unified Process (RUP)

The IBM **Rational Unified Process**® (RUP®) (RUP, 2003) is more than a lifecycle model. It is also a support environment (called the RUP platform) to assist developers in using and conforming to the RUP lifecycle. This support comes in the form of HTML and other documentation providing online help, templates and guidance. The RUP support environment constitutes an integral part of IBM (previously Rational) suite of software engineering tools, but it can be used as a lifecycle model for any software development.

The level of RUP acceptance has suffered from an obscure RUP process structure, which has been presented as two-dimensional. The *horizontal dimension* represents the

Figure 1.10
Rational Unified
Process
Source: adapted
from figure of
*Rational Unified
Process* reprinted
by permission
from http://
www.rational.com/
products/rup/,
© Copyright 2003
by International
Business Machines
Corporation. All
Rights Reserved

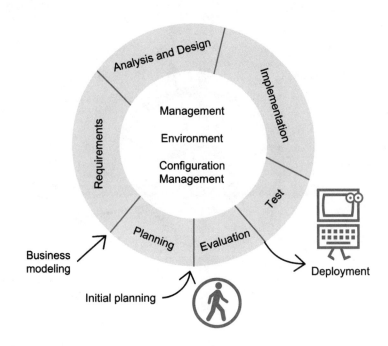

dynamic aspect of the lifecycle – time passing in the process. This dimension has been divided into four unfolding lifecycle aspects: inception, elaboration, construction, and transition. The *vertical dimension* represents the static aspect of the lifecycle – software development disciplines. This dimension has been divided into lifecycle activities: business modeling, requirements, analysis and design, implementation, test, deployment, as well as supporting activities of configuration and change management, project management, and environment.

Although appealing at first, the process explained as the combination of the two RUP dimensions lacks clarity. What is the difference between construction and implementation or between inception and business modeling or between transition and deployment? These questions are difficult to answer. To rectify these problems (it seems), a simplified visualization of the RUP® process has been offered. Figure 1.10 is this simplified representation (RUP, 2003).

Apart from some small variations in lifecycle phases, the RUP process aligns very well with the generic iterative lifecycle in Figure 1.8. The main difference is an explicit Test phase after Implementation. As mentioned a few times in passing, the lifecycle phases adopted in this book consider testing as an all-encompassing activity to be applied to each lifecycle phase, not just to implementation. In RUP, testing results in the Deployment of an iteration (increment).

Following the spiral model, RUP tries to be explicit about risk management. One aspect of risk management in RUP is the explicit Evaluation phase. More importantly though, and consistently with the spiral model, RUP advocates that a 'go, no-go' decision should be taken at the end of each lifecycle phase.

Model Driven Architecture (MDA)

The **Model Driven Architecture**® (MDA®) (Kleppe *et al*., 2003; MDA, 2003) is a lifecycle framework from Object Management Group (OMG). MDA attempts to take the UML to its next natural stage – executable specifications. The idea of **executable specifications**, i.e. turning specifications models into executable code, is not new, but MDA takes advantage of existing standards and modern technology to make the idea happen.

The MDA is a modern representative of the *transformation model* (Ghezzi *et al*., 2003), which in turn has its origins in **formal systems development** (Sommerville, 2001). The transformation model treats systems development as a sequence of transformations from the formal specifications for the problem, via more detailed (less abstract) design stages, to an executable program. Each transformation step is carefully verified to guarantee that each output is a true representation of the input.

The transformation model assumes extensive automatization of transformations, but recognizes that some transformations can only be performed manually. Accordingly, the machine-readable representations of models, created and stored within computer assisted software engineering (CASE) environments, are assumed. Machine-readability supports the iterative nature of the transformation model. Unlike in the waterfall lifecycle, the transformation model supports evolution of models through multiple iterations.

The MDA lifecycle is depicted in Figure 1.11. MDA distinguishes between informal Requirements and more formal Analysis specifications. This separation allows us to exclude Requirements from the transformations of the MDA process. The remaining artifacts (models) of the process are in the machine-readable form susceptible to transformations.

The result of Analysis is a Platform Independent Model (PIM), highly abstract and detached from any software/hardware constraints. The result of Design is a Platform Specific Model (PSM), less abstract and constrained by the implementation software/hardware platform. For each platform, a separate PSM is generated. If the system under development spans multiple platforms, then additional PSMs are provided and linked by MDA interoperability *bridges*. Multiple PSMs transform to multiple codes, also linked by bridges.

The MDA promise extends into the **component technology** and the whole area of constructing systems from reusable building blocks – models and programs (this is sometimes called the *component-based lifecycle* (Pressman, 2001)). The architecture goes beyond executable UML models and encompasses a range of OMG-specified services, such as repository services, persistence, transactions, event handling, and security. The aim is to create reusable and transformable models for specific vertical industries, such as telecommunications or hospitals. Time will tell if MDA will prove itself in practice. For this to happen, MDA must be able to demonstrate that it scales up to large and complex systems.

Agile lifecycle with short cycles

The **agile software development** process, proposed in 2001 by Agile Alliance, a non-profit organization of enthusiasts, is a daring new approach to software production. In the Manifesto of Agile Alliance (Agile, 2003), the spirit of the agile development is captured in four recommendations:

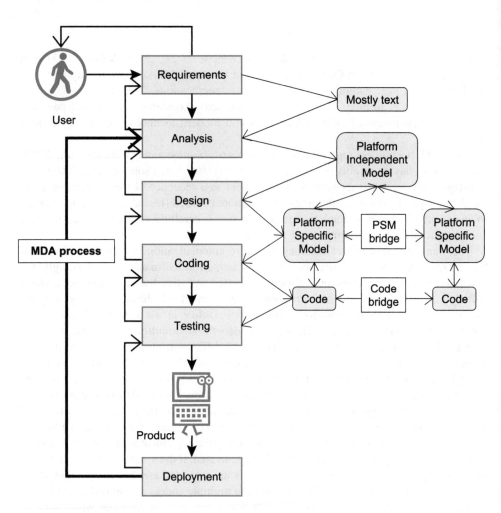

Figure 1.11
Model Driven
Architecture
lifecycle

1. Individuals and interactions over processes and tools.
2. Working software over comprehensive documentation.
3. Customer collaboration over contract negotiation.
4. Responding to change over following a plan.

The agile development stresses that software production is a creative activity that depends on people and team collaboration far more than on processes, tools, documentation, planning, and other formalities. Agile development subscribes to the maxim that 'great software comes from great people', everything else is secondary. 'People' includes all project stakeholders – developers and customers. Unlike in other software processes, in agile development, customers (users and system owners) work closely with the development team throughout the lifecycle, not just at the beginning of it. Constant customer feedback alleviates the need for signing a formal contract for the entire product. Intense collaboration alleviates the need for these parts of documentation that serve the purpose of knowledge transfer.

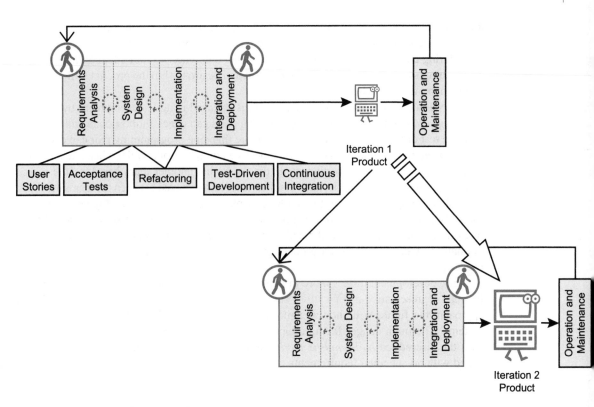

Figure 1.12 Agile software development

Despite all these 'revolutionary' propositions, agile development sits well among other iterative lifecycles. As shown in Figure 1.12, an agile lifecycle may not be using the terminology of typical lifecycle phases, but it does in effect follow the normal cycle of analysis, design, implementation, and deployment.

'Conventional' requirements analysis is replaced in agile development by *user stories* – features that the customer would like the system to support. The development team estimates how long it will take to implement each story, and how much each story will cost. The customer can then select stories to be implemented in the first and successive iterations.

'Conventional' system design and implementation are replaced in agile development by a combination of acceptance tests, refactoring, and test-driven development. *Acceptance tests* are programs that an application program must pass to be accepted by customers. This process is called **test-driven development** or *intentional programming* – the developer programs his/her intent in an acceptance test before s/he implements it. The whole approach is facilitated by frequent **refactorings** – improvements to the structure of the system without changing its behavior.

Agile development encourages other practices, such as **pair programming** and *collective ownership*. All programming is done by pairs of programmers – two programmers working together at a single workstation. One programmer writes the code and the other observes the progress and raises questions. The roles change whenever one of the programmers wants to 'prove the point by driving the keyboard'. The programming pairs also change at least once during a day. The *collective ownership* is an outcome. No individual owns the code. The assumption is that a high spirit in the team and desire to ship the product will outweigh any demand for individual responsibility.

'Conventional' integration and deployment is replaced in agile development by *continuous integration* and *short cycles*. Programming pairs can check in their code and integrate with the rest of the code at will. Moreover, more than one programming pair can check out and work on the same piece of code. This means a possibility of conflict when a team which wants to check in and merge their code discovers that another team has done the merge before with the conflicting code. Such conflicts must be negotiated between the teams involved.

Agile development does not mean lack of planning. In fact, the deployment dates are carefully planned. Each iteration is normally planned to complete in short cycles of two-week duration. The product at the end of two-week cycle is a minor delivery for customer evaluation. A major delivery, a product put into production, is a result of about six two-week cycles.

Agile development differs more in practices than in approach to iterative development. Its main representative is **eXtreme Programming** (XP) (Beck, 1999). As with the MDA approach, the future will show if agile development can scale up to large and complex systems. The main danger facing adopters of the agile lifecycle is the risk of ending up with the discredited *build-and-fix model* (Schach, 2002), in which the software is hack-coded with no specified requirements or design.

Summary

1. *Software engineering* is concerned with development of large software systems. Software engineering is typically the central activity of a more generic notion of *system engineering*.

2. The *software engineering pentagon* consists of software development lifecycle, software modeling language, software engineering tools, software project plan, and software process management.

3. The stages of software development process are referred to as software *lifecycle phases*. The lifecycle phases assumed in the book are requirements analysis, system design, implementation, integration and deployment, and operation and maintenance.

4. A software system is merely a part of a much larger *enterprise information system*.

5. Software process is part of a *business process*. The result of a software process is software. The result of a business process is business.

6. A software system can service any of the three management levels: operational, tactical, or strategic.

7. The immaterial and changeable nature of software are but two factors that make software engineering different from *traditional engineering*.

8. Software engineering is more than *programming*. Software engineering applies to complex problems that cannot be solved by programming alone.

9. Software engineering is about *modeling*. All products of software engineering, including programs, are models of reality. Modeling uses *abstraction* to represent concepts with various levels of detail.

10. Software systems are *complex*. The complexity of modern software is in the 'wires' – in the linkages and communication paths between components.

11. *Requirements analysis* is the activity of determining and specifying user requirements. Accordingly, requirements analysis is divided into *requirements determination* and *requirements specification*. *Requirements engineering* comprises all more rigorous and formal tasks in support of requirements analysis.

12. *System design* follows requirements analysis and it is the modeling that takes into consideration the platform on which the system is to be implemented. There are two different aspects of system design: *architectural design* and *detailed design*. A major objective of architectural design is to lead to a system that is *supportable* – understandable, maintainable, and scalable. The detailed design must conform to architectural design.

13. *Implementation* is mostly programming, but it includes other engineering activities such as component engineering and roundtrip engineering. Debugging and testing are an integral part of implementation.

14. *Integration* assembles the application from the set of components previously implemented and tested. *Deployment* is the handing over of the system to customers for production use. *Integration testing* is an important contributor to successful integration and *acceptance testing* must be done prior to deployment.

15. *Operation* signifies the lifecycle phase when the software product is used in day-to-day operations and the previous system (manual or automated) is phased out. *Phasing out* is usually a staged process. Operation coincides with the start of product *maintenance*. The maintenance can be corrective, adaptive, or perfective.

16. There are various *lifecycle models* that can be adopted for software development. They are broadly divided into the waterfall models with feedback and the iterative models with increments.

17. The *waterfall models* are characterized by a linear sequence of phases, in which the previous phase must be completed before the next one can begin. Waterfall models are not suitable for modern software production.

18. There are four main representatives of *iterative models*: spiral, Rational Unified Process (RUP), Model Driven Architecture (MDA), and the agile model.

19. The *spiral model* is really a generic metamodel that encompasses all iterative models. The model consists of four lifecycle quadrants: planning, risk analysis, engineering, and customer evaluation. Risk analysis is the most characteristic feature of the spiral model.

20. *RUP* is more than a lifecycle model. It is also a support environment (called the RUP platform) to assist developers in using and conforming to the RUP lifecycle. Like the spiral model, RUP is explicit about risk management.

21. The *MDA* model is based on the idea of executable specifications. It is a modern representative of the transformation model, which in turn has its origins in formal systems development. The component technology is at the heart of the MDA model.

22. *Agile development* stresses that software production is a creative activity that depends on people and team collaboration far more than on processes, tools, documentation, planning, and other formalities.

Key Terms

abstraction	12, 15
acceptance testing	21
agile software development	29
architectural design	18
architectural model	12
build	25
business process	8
CASE *See* computer assisted software engineering	
component technology	29
computer assisted software engineering	16
configuration	11
debugging	19
deployment	19
detailed design	18
detailed design model	12
effectiveness	8
efficiency	8
enterprise information system	7
executable specifications	29
eXtreme Programming	32
formal systems development	29
functional paradigm	13
IDE *See* integrated development environment	
implementation	18
increment	25
information system	7
integrated development environment	19
integration	19
integration testing	20
iteration	25
iterative lifecycle	25
legacy system	5, 21
lifecycle	5
lifecycle model	22
lifecycle phases	5
maintenance	21
management levels	9
MDA *See* Model Driven Architecture	
model	12
Model Driven Architecture	29
object-oriented paradigm	13
OLAP *See* online analytical processing	
OLTP *See* online transaction processing	
online analytical processing	9
online transaction processing	9
operation	21

pair programming	31
program model	12
programming	11
project management	12
prototyping model	23
Rational Unified Process®	27
refactoring	31
requirements analysis	16
requirements determination	16
requirements document	17
requirements engineering	16
requirements model	12
requirements specification	16
roundtrip engineering	12, 19
RUP® *See* Rational Unified Process®	
software component	11
software design	17
software engineering	7
software lifecycle	15
software process	8
software process model	12
software product model	12
software prototype	24
software quality assurance	17
specifications model	12
spiral model	25
supportability	11
system	7
system design	17
system engineering	10
test driver	20
test harness	20
test stub	20
test-driven development	31
testing	19
testing to code	19
testing to specs	19
traceability management	18
traditional engineering	10
UML *See* Unified Modeling Language	
Unified Modeling Language	12
user requirements	16
version	11
waterfall model	22
XP *See* eXtreme Programming	

Review Questions

1. Explain how software engineering and system engineering relate to each other. Is this a containment or intersection relationship? Is it possible that the two concepts may not relate at all?

2. What are the five main facets of software engineering? Can you think of any software engineering concerns not obviously covered by these facets?

3. What factors decide that a system is labeled as legacy system? Can a legacy system be turned into a modern system? How can this be done, if at all?

4. What do we mean by saying that information systems are social systems? Can a system be social? Consider the following explanation of the term 'social' – 'relating to activities in which you meet and spend time with other people and which happen during the time when you are not working' (Cambridge, 2003).

5. In the management science there is a strong distinction made between efficiency and effectiveness of systems and people. In normal usage, the term 'efficiency' means 'when someone or something uses time and energy well, without wasting any' (Cambridge, 2003). The term 'effectiveness' means 'how successful it is . . . in achieving the results you want' (Cambridge, 2003). How do these two terms apply to software engineering? Is software engineering about efficiency or effectiveness, or both? Explain. Give examples.

6. What are the principal differences between a database and a data warehouse? How do these two concepts relate to management levels in an organization?

7. What is a supportable system? Can a supportable system become a legacy system? Explain.

8. What do we mean by roundtrip engineering? How does it relate to programming?

9. Software engineering is concerned with system modeling. What is modeling in software engineering? How does it relate to the notion of abstraction? Does it make sense to talk about program modeling?

10. How do you understand the distinction between the functional and object-oriented paradigms in system development?

11. Which factor is most important in deciding about the complexity of a modern object-oriented system? What is the main technique of controlling and minimizing the complexity? Explain.

12. Explain the relationship between requirements analysis and requirements engineering.

13. What is the distinction between requirements determination and requirements specification? Explain.

14. Draw a line between requirements analysis and system design. When does analysis become designing?

15. How do detailed design and architectural design relate to each other?

16. What are the main approaches and techniques of testing?

17. Explain the use of stubs and drivers in integration testing.

18. In modern software engineering, the waterfall lifecycle model is replaced by iterative models. Are there any aspects of the waterfall model, missing or not feasible in iterative models, that would benefit iterative approaches? Discuss.

19. What is risk management? Which lifecycle models are most explicit about risk management? Explain.

20. What are executable specifications? Which lifecycle model uses executable specifications as its focal point? Explain.

21. What are the most uncommon aspects of the agile development? (uncommon in comparison with other iterative approaches). Explain.

Chapter

2

Software Modeling Language

Language is a means of communication between people. Software is produced by people for people. Software models need to be communicated. Software modeling requires a language as a means of expressing software development processes and artifacts. The language must be universal (must be a standard) and understood by a large community of people. The language must be rich semantically to convey the required meaning with minimal amount of syntactic constructs. The language must contain powerful abstract concepts to express ideas at multiple levels of abstraction without a need to use another language suiting that level of abstraction better.

As argued in Section 1.1.5, software engineering is about modeling. The outcome of software engineering – a program – is simply an executable model. A programming language is therefore a modeling language, albeit at a very low level of abstraction, representing bits and bytes of a computer system. Ideally one software modeling language should serve the combined purpose of analysis, design, and implementation. This is in fact the premise of the standard modeling language of today – the **Unified Modeling Language** (UML) (UML, 2003b).

In reality, neither UML or any other modeling language has reached the status of the language for the entire development lifecycle. In particular, the intricacies of programming have resisted the temptation of a one-language-fits-all proposition. Programmers work with different languages, which suit them better for whatever reason. This means that when it comes to programming, UML models have to be translated to a programming language. Moreover, when it comes to the detailed design for various application domains and for various technologies, UML has insufficient power and diversity to serve all design purposes. The **UML profiles**, such as UML for web modeling or UML for business modeling (UML, 2003a), address this issue but there is still a long way to go.

'A picture is worth thousand words.' This old truth has been embraced by software modeling languages. Modeling languages are *visual* but supplemented with *text*. Sometimes, a graphical model needs to be further clarified to avoid misinterpretation. At other times, a graphical model does not give the whole story and additional information is provided in text. In some cases, text dominates over visual representation. Interestingly, requirements determination at the beginning of the software lifecycle and programming towards the end of it are predominantly specified in text. The middle stages of analysis and design are mostly visual.

Software specifications consist, therefore, of a large number of *visual models*, supplemented with text, defining various stages of product development and providing various (frequently overlapping) viewpoints on software artifacts. A broad division of models distinguishes between analysis, design, and implementation models. Each model consists of one or more diagrams and any additional information stored in the project repository.

A diagram is a graphical view of a model that displays software symbols. Each diagram represents different aspects of the model or represents the model at a different (less or more detailed) level of abstraction. A general division of diagrams distinguishes among diagrams capturing a system's state, behavior, and state changes.

Diagrams and textual descriptions of models are stored in a project repository. Repository is a major component of any *visual modeling tool*. It is a database of project artifacts. The word 'database' implies a persistent and integrated storage allowing concurrent access to it by many users (developers). Software development is a collaborative effort of many developers and all of them have to have concurrent access to development models. Most visual modeling tools employ the full power of database technology, or even use commercial database management systems (DBMSs), to implement their repositories. Traditionally, visual modeling tools are called computer assisted software engineering (CASE) tools.

This chapter concentrates on UML. UML is a lingua franca of the software development community – developers as well as (increasingly) users. For completeness and for contrast, the chapter starts by explaining the modeling language of the past – the structured modeling language. Understandably, the chapter is not the complete specification of modeling languages; the UML specification at the time of writing consists of 736 pages (UML, 2003b). The chapter presents just the main 'vocabulary' and provides examples of modeling using a small application domain – a MovieActor application, also used elsewhere in the book. Parts 2 through 4 of the book explain and use the UML with detail and rigor.

2.1 Structured Modeling Language

Structured modeling was popularized at the end of the 1970s as a result of the popularity of structured programming. Structured programming epitomized programming without using the `goto` statements, with the loops and `if` statements as the main control constructs, and with the top-down approach to program design. The top-down approach of structured programming was embraced by the design and analysis phases resulting in a number of structured analysis and design methods. Particular methods were known by the names of the authors of books that defined them – De Marco, Yourdon and Constantine, Gane and Sarson, Jackson.

Structured modeling is a top-down function-oriented approach to software development that decomposes the system into sets of interacting functions in the process known as functional decomposition. Functional decomposition is a stepwise process, which relies on a good use of abstraction. The system models are presented at multiple levels of abstraction, starting with a top 'bird's eye' overview of it and ending on primitive functional modules defined in details sufficient for implementation. Structured modeling expresses the monolithic and procedural character of Cobol-style systems of the past.

Structured modeling offers a range of visualization techniques, most popular of which have been data flow diagrams (DFDs), entity–relationship diagrams (ERDs), and structure charts. The first two are discussed next.

Data Flow Modeling 2.1.1

Undoubtedly, data flow diagrams (DFDs) are one of the most popular modeling techniques in the history of software engineering. Today they are used infrequently because of the mismatch with the object-oriented approach. Nevertheless, DFDs remain an applicable technique in some circumstances. Suffice to say that early versions of UML attempted to include a variation of DFDs for modeling of systems behavior. This attempt was discarded after criticisms from the object-oriented 'purists'.

The cornerstone of DFDs is functional decomposition. Figure 2.1 depicts the idea. Functional decomposition is a method of gradually defining functional processes of the system. This is a top-down activity that starts with a context diagram and finishes with module specifications.

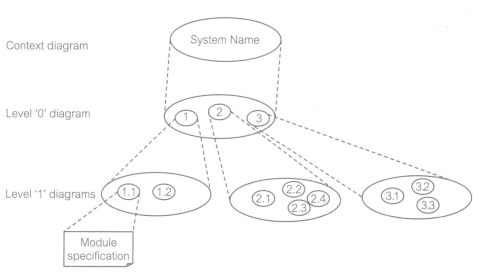

Figure 2.1
Functional decomposition in DFDs

Figure 2.2
Context diagram

A **context diagram** consists of one **process** only – the process that corresponds to the system under development. The purpose of the context diagram is to determine the place of the system with regard to its environment. A context diagram determines the boundaries of the system by defining its inputs and outputs with external entities. **External entities** are organizations, departments, people, other systems, etc., which are outside of the system under development, and which supply input data to it or expect output data from it, or do both. The flow of data is shown by arrows that are called **data flows**.

Figure 2.2 is an example of a context diagram for the system (context process) named `Movies on the Web`. The system is used by a cinema chain to advertise movies on the Internet, provide information about the movies and details about screenings, so that movie goers can get information and order tickets online. There are two external entities identified in Figure 2.2: `Customers` and `Distributors`. `Distributors` provide `MovieDetails` to the system. The system displays `ScreeningDetails` to `Customers` and `Customers` may place `TicketOrder` with the system. These are data flows outside the context process. All other processing is done inside the 'bubble', i.e. inside the context process.

The specification of what is done inside the context 'bubble' is provided by the *Level '0' diagram*, also called the **overview diagram**. The decomposition of the context diagram into Level '0' diagram is shown in Figure 2.3. The system consists of three processes: `CRUD MovieActor`, `CRUD Screenings`, and `Manage Ticketing` (`CRUD` stands for Create, Read, Update, and Delete – the four main activities done on data in database-driven applications). The external data flows are assigned to the processes, but without duplicating external entities from the context diagram. The internal data flows are now more specific. Process 1 supplies `movie_title` and `duration` of the movies to Process 2. Process 2 determines screening times and locations, and supplies this information to Process 3. Processes are numbered but the sequence of numbering is not important, other than for linking a process to its further decomposition.

Figure 2.3
Level '0' DFD
diagram

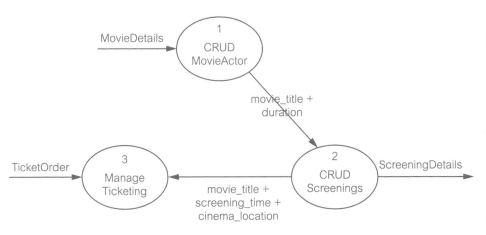

Figure 2.4
Level '1' DFD
diagram

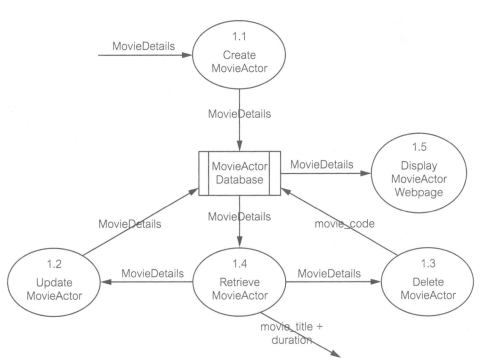

Figure 2.4 is a decomposition of **Process 1** (CRUD MovieActor) from Figure 2.3. Figure 2.4 is one of three possible *Level '1' diagrams*. The data flows coming in and out of Process 1 are accounted for in Figure 2.4 (this is one aspect of so-called *flow balancing*). The Level '1' diagram in Figure 2.4 introduces the last modeling element in DFDs – the data store, represented here by MovieActor Database. A **data store** is a data storage for data flows. A data flow put by one process into a data store can be accessed by another process at another time.

Theoretically, functional decomposition can be conducted many levels down the hierarchy tree. In practice, three or four levels of decomposition are sufficient for even quite large systems. The depth of decomposition can vary for processes identified in the Level '0' diagram.

The processes at the bottom-level of the hierarchy (the leave nodes of the tree) are further defined in text. This is called **module specification** (Figure 2.1). The text is really a pseudo-code known as **Structured English**. A Structured English definition uses typical programming language concepts, such as assignment statement, conditional statement, and a loop construct.

From Structured English specifications is only one step into coding. DFDs, with their multiple levels of abstract models, cover quite a space between analysis and design. They concentrate on processes, but they also identify data structures (data flows). Although not discussed here, data flows are carefully defined in DFDs.

DFDs constitute quite a complete description of the system, but they still need to be complemented by other techniques in at least two areas. One area is on the intersection of design and implementation. This is the area filled by *structure charts*, not discussed here.

The second area is in data modeling. This is the area filled by entity–relationship modeling, discussed next.

2.1.2 Entity–Relationship Modeling

Entity–relationship (ER) modeling is a data modeling technique which has been popularized by structured analysis and design and which remains a popular technique for modeling database structures at higher (conceptual) levels of abstraction. The technique has many variants of which the most popular is known as the *crow's foot notation*.

ER models are presented visually as **entity–relationship diagrams** (ERDs). The diagrams define just three modeling elements – entities, relationships, and attributes.

An **entity** is a conceptual data structure, which represents a business fact or rule and which can be distinctly identified (usually). The identification allows distinguishing an entity as a concept (*entity set* or *entity type*) from *entity instances* (*entity occurrences*). ERDs visualize entity sets but the proper interpretation of the models requires reasoning that takes into consideration entity instances.

A **relationship** represents an association between entity instances from different entity sets and, in some important cases, from a single entity set. Relationships are visualized as lines connecting entity sets. The lines are adorned and annotated in various ways to define various properties of relationships.

Entities are data containers. Data in these containers is structured by attributes. An **attribute** is a data–value pair. In contemporary practice, influenced by relational database technology, attributes are *single-valued*. *Multi-valued* attributes and *composite* attributes (i.e. attributes containing other attributes) are not normally supported in ER visual modeling tools.

Figure 2.5 uses the ER crow's foot notation to represent a (highly simplified) conceptual model for MovieActor database. The diagram consists of three named entities and two unnamed relationships. The *multiplicity* properties of relationships are shown graphically and with two-digit notation. The notation 0,n on the relationship between movie and listed_as means that an entity instance of movie may be linked to minimum zero (shown graphically by a small circle) and maximum many (shown graphically by three small lines known as the crow's foot) entity instances of listed_as.

Figure 2.5
Entity–relationship diagram in crow's foot notation

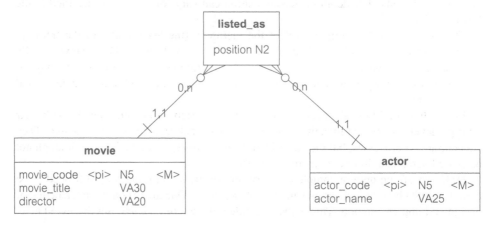

The notation 1,1 means minimum one and maximum one, i.e. exactly one. This also means that listed_as has the *mandatory participation* in the relationship with movie (each instance of listed_as must be linked to one instance of movie). A small bar on the relationship line shows the mandatory participation graphically.

Attributes are listed in entity boxes. Attributes are given names (e.g. movie_code), types (e.g. N5 – numeric integer of maximum five digits), if an attribute is an identifier (<pi> – primary identifier), and if it always has to have a value (<M> – mandatory).

An ERD must be consistent with the data structures (data flows and data stores) defined in the corresponding DFD. To ensure the consistency, the initial ERD can be derived from the DFD. Unfortunately this possibility, of an automatic generation of ERD from DFD, has never been sufficiently supported in commercial CASE tools.

Object-Oriented Modeling Language   2.2

Modeling of contemporary (object-oriented) systems is done in the Unified Modeling Language (UML). The UML 'is a language for specifying, visualizing, constructing, and documenting the artifacts of software systems, as well as for business modeling and other non-software systems. The UML represents a collection of the best engineering practices that have proven successful in the modeling of large and complex systems' (UML, 2003b, p.1-1).

In the UML, visual modeling is an arrangement of so-called classifiers. A classifier is a model element that describes the system's behavior or structure and that normally has a visual representation. Examples of classifiers include class, actor, use case, relationship.

An object, as per object-oriented paradigm, is defined as a piece of software that has state, behavior, and identity (Maciaszek, 2001). The object state is defined by its attribute values. The object behavior is defined by services (operations) that an object can perform when requested by other objects. The object identity is a unique property of an object by means of which any two objects in the system are considered different even if they share the same attribute values and operations. This means that two objects can be equal, but they are never identical. By the same principle, an object can change its state and behavior considerably, but it remains the same object with the same identity.

Associated with the above characteristics of objects, there exists a classification of object-oriented models into *state models*, *behavior models*, and *state change models*. Each of these models is represented by one or more diagrams.

The UML specification defines six kinds of diagrams: state structure, use case, interaction, statechart, collaboration, activity, and implementation diagrams. These diagrams are discussed next.

Class Diagrams   2.2.1

Static structures of models, called also *state models*, are expressed in the UML in class diagrams. A class diagram visualizes classes (and interfaces), their internal structure, and their relationships to other classes.

UML defines a **class** as a description for 'a set of objects that share the same specifications of features, constraints, and semantics' (UML, 2002, p.45). An alternative definition is that 'a *class* is the descriptor for a set of objects with similar structure, behavior, and relationships' (UML, 2003b, p.3-35).

Features are attributes and operations. An **attribute** is a structural (typed) feature of a class. An **operation** is a behavioral feature of a class that declares a service that can be performed by instances (objects) of that class.

In programming languages, such as Java, features are referred to as class members. An attribute is a **data member**, frequently called a **member variable**, **instance variable** or **field** (note that a local variable defined within an operation is not a data member). An operation is a **member function**, typically called a **method**. An act of calling a service provided by a method is referred to as sending a **message** to an object or a **message passing** between objects.

A **relationship** is a meaningful connection between classifiers (i.e. classes in the case of a class diagram). Association, aggregation, and generalization relationships can be used in class modeling.

Figure 2.6 shows main modeling elements of a class diagram. Classes are represented as rectangular boxes with three compartments. The top compartment contains class name, the middle compartment lists attributes of the class, and the bottom compartment lists operations of the class. Relationships are shown by lines connecting classes.

Although an **association** is specified on classes (types), a true meaning of it is that it is a relationship between instances of those classes (types). Hence, multiplicity of *association ends* is so significant. Figure 2.6 demonstrates possible use of multiplicities. **Multiplicity** specifies how many instances of one class relate to one instance of another class. Multiplicity ought to be defined on both ends of an association. The presence of zero in the multiplicity (0..n or 0..1) indicates that the **participation** of a class instance in the association is optional.

Aggregation is in the UML a special kind of association where an instance of one class (a whole; **superset class**) contains instances of another class (a part; **subset class**). In most situations, a domain class model can be sufficiently expressive without using aggregations.

Figure 2.6
Modeling elements of a class diagram

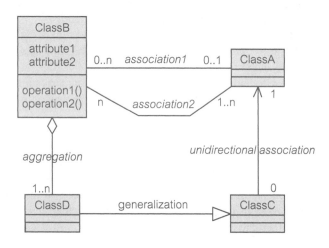

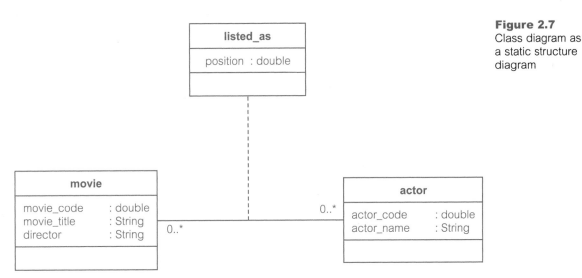

Figure 2.7
Class diagram as
a static structure
diagram

Deciding on aggregations in domain modeling may be an over-commitment to what really is (in the UML) a specialized form of association.

Generalization is a relationship on classifiers (i.e. classes (types) in the domain class model). Each instance of the more specific class (subclass) is also an instance of the more generic class (superclass). Hence, this is not a relationship on instances of those classes. As per the definition of generalization, multiplicity does not apply to it.

The above definitions should make it clear that a class diagram expresses more than the static structure of a system. A class diagram represents also the dynamic behavior of a system. In many ways, the role of class diagrams in object-oriented modeling resembles the dominant role of DFDs in structured modeling. Both define processes (operations) and data structures. The difference is that the driving force of DFDs are processes and the driving force of class diagrams are data structures. It is also possible to construct class diagrams without visualizing operations. A class diagram is then a pure static structure diagram.

A class diagram in Figure 2.7 corresponds to the ER diagram in Figure 2.5. An interesting aspect of this example is that it leads to the UML concept of association class. An association class is a class that represents an association relationship between other classes. Modeling with an association class is needed when an association itself has attributes and a class is required to store these attributes. listed_as is an association class. An association class is illustrated by a dashed line from it to a relationship between two other classes.

Figure 2.8 shows a UML design of the Movie class with both state and behavior features. The class consists of three data members, a *constructor* method to instantiate objects of the class, and a number of instance methods with their *signatures* – lists of arguments and their types. Note that *return types* of methods are not displayable in the UML class notation.

Figures 2.7 and 2.8 differ also in the applied level of abstraction. Figure 2.7 is an analysis-level diagram and Figure 2.8 is a design-level model of a Java class. The next

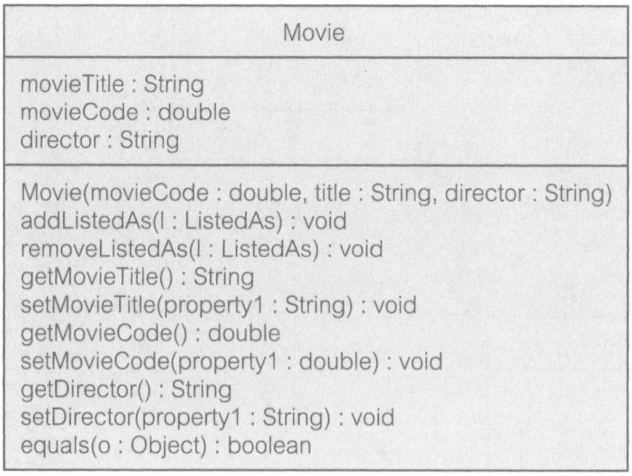

Figure 2.8
Class design with
state and behavior
features

Movie
movieTitle : String movieCode : double director : String
Movie(movieCode : double, title : String, director : String) addListedAs(l : ListedAs) : void removeListedAs(l : ListedAs) : void getMovieTitle() : String setMovieTitle(property1 : String) : void getMovieCode() : double setMovieCode(property1 : double) : void getDirector() : String setDirector(property1 : String) : void equals(o : Object) : boolean

figure, Figure 2.9, is a design-level model for the MovieActor application. The model consists of five classes and an interface from the `java.util` library (`Collection`).

Out of the three main kinds of the UML relationships – **association**, **aggregation**, and **generalization** – the first two are represented in Figure 2.9. All relationships are unidirectional (indicated by arrows on the lines). This means, for example, that `Movie-Searcher` contains the attribute named `conn`, type of which is `Connection` and which value in any `MovieSearcher` object is an *object identifier* (OID) of a `Connection` object. However, `Connection` does not contain an attribute linking it to `MovieSearcher`.

`Connection` does not have any attributes (member variables). This is possible in classes dedicated to doing computations or other processing not involving *entity objects* (business data objects). Attributes in `MovieSearcher` are *constants* (static values). In practice, `MovieSearcher` has two variable attributes, `conn` and `listedAs`, acquired from its relationships to two other classes. More detailed explanation of Figure 2.9 is not essential here; but it is given in Chapter 12.

2.2.2 Use Case Diagrams

Use case diagrams are the main analysis-level behavior modeling technique in UML. It is possible to develop many use case diagrams to represent various aspects of a system at various levels of abstraction. In general, use case diagrams do not create hierarchical structures reminiscent of DFDs.

The principal point about use case diagrams is that the power of them does not rest in graphical diagrams. The real power of use case diagrams is in textual specifications of use cases stored in the repository. Textual *use case specifications*, such as given for the EM case-study in Chapters 8, 13 and 19, are detailed descriptions of user requirements. Use case specifications guide the developers in all lifecycle phases and in most modeling tasks. They are guiding the analysis, design and implementation tasks. They are used to develop test cases, record defects, and identify future enhancements. They are essential for establishing maintenance and evolution tasks.

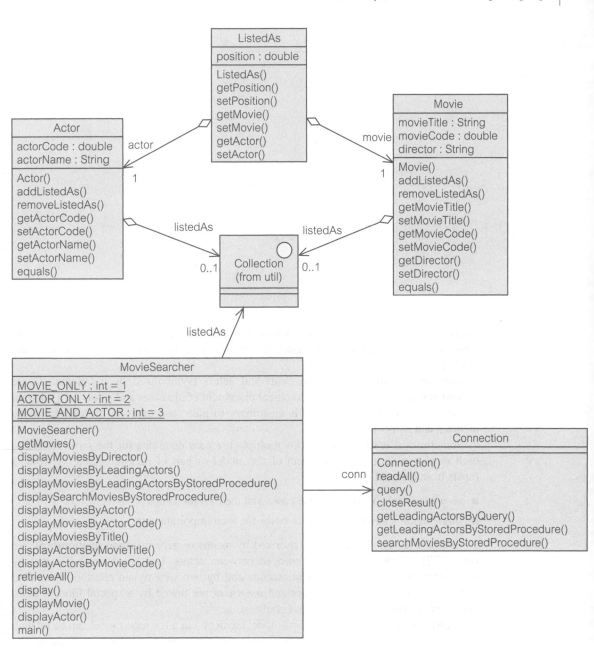

Figure 2.9 Design class diagram with state and behavior

Use case represents a major piece of system functionality. An actor is a role that somebody or something plays with regard to a use case. An actor communicates with a use case (via the «communicate» relationship) and expects from it some feedback – a value or observable result. (In the UML, the name surrounded by French guillemet symbols

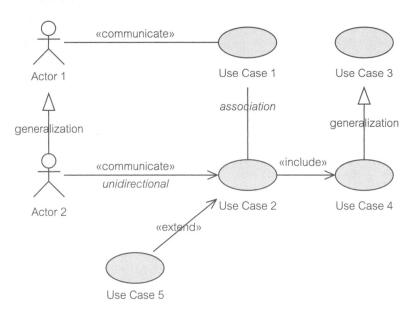

Figure 2.10
Modeling
elements of a use
case diagram

(such as «communicate») is known as a stereotype. A UML **stereotype** is used to introduce a new concept into a model, if that concept is not inherently supported by the UML.)

Use cases (symbolized by an oval) and actors (symbolized by a 'stickman') are presented in a use case diagram. Graphical placement of use cases and actors on a diagram has only a visual connotation. It is customary to place use cases in the middle of the diagram and actors on its borders.

Sometimes it is desirable to draw multiple use case diagrams for the same domain – each emphasizing a different aspect of the model or part of it. Two typical viewpoints (apart from a global model) are:

■ *no actors* – this means only use cases and their relationships

■ *single actor's viewpoint* – all use cases for each important actor.

Actors in the model can be categorized by means of generalization relationships. No other UML relationships are encouraged between actors. Use cases can be related by association and generalization relationships and by two stereotyped relationships called «include» and «extend». Actors and use cases are linked by a special kind of association called the «communicate» **relationship.**

Figure 2.10 shows how classifiers (model elements) in a use case model can be related. Use cases are interlinked because they need to collaborate to perform the tasks of the system. However, a recommended practice is to limit relationships between use cases. Showing all relationships obscures the intent of the model. Showing only selected relationships raises a question why these relationships are more important than others. It must be remembered that ultimately use case diagrams take secondary stage to text documents defining each use case.

The principle of a prudent use of relationships applies also to two relationships specifically stereotyped in the UML for use case modeling – the «include» relationship and the «extend» **relationship**. The «include» relationship means that the execution of one use case enfolds (always) the functionality of the included use case. For example, Withdraw Money includes Check Account Balance. Withdraw Money is called a **base use case** and Check Account Balance is called an **addition use case**. The «include» relationships allow the common functionality to be factored out so that the same addition use case is accessed from many base use cases. The «include» relationships can also be used to reduce the size of a complex use case by extracting from it addition use cases.

The «extend» relationship means that the execution of one use case may need to be extended (sometimes) by the functionality of the extending use case. For example, Print Transaction Record extends Withdraw Money. Print Transaction Record is called an **extension use case** and Withdraw Money is called a base use case. The «extend» relationships may be used to model exceptional or optional behavior, but the primary imperative is that the base does not depend on the extension for its own functionality (hence, the direction of the arrowhead – from extension to base).

The «include» and «extend» relationships are always **unidirectional** to denote the direction of inclusion or extension. The «communicate» and association **relationships** may or may not have an arrowhead to denote if the navigation is in one direction. A lack of arrowhead implies either that the **navigation** is in both directions or that the navigation direction is not defined (i.e. perhaps it will be defined in the future but we do not bother for now).

Figure 2.11 is a use case diagram for the MovieActor application. The diagram corresponds to two processes (Processes 1 and 2) of the DFD in Figure 2.3. It consists of

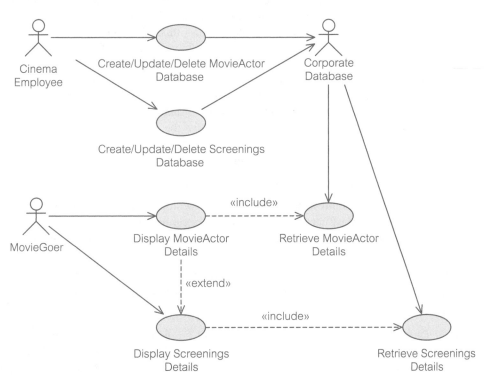

Figure 2.11
Use case diagram

three actors and six use cases. `Corporate Database` is shown as an actor to emphasize that it is separate from the modeled application. Displaying information to `MovieGoer` requires including the functionality of two database retrieval use cases. Displaying screening information is extended by showing MovieActor details whenever `MovieGoer` wants to find out more about movies and actors played in current screenings.

2.2.3 Interaction Diagrams

Interaction diagrams are the main design-level behavior modeling technique in UML. Interaction diagrams are developed for uses cases, groups of use cases, or parts thereof. They can be presented at various levels of abstraction and with various details.

Successive UML standards have been introducing significant changes to interaction diagrams and to interpretation of modeling elements used in these diagrams. The approach taken in this chapter is to distinguish two kinds of interaction diagrams: *sequence diagrams* and *collaboration diagrams* (called *communication diagrams* in Section 11.3.2). These two diagrams are interchangeable and many CASE tools provide for automatic conversion between them.

Sequence diagrams

A **sequence diagram** (Section 11.3.1) is a graphical visualization of sequences of messages between objects, i.e. sequences of method invocations on objects, which result in accomplishing some tasks. The emphasis in a sequence diagram is on the sequence of messages. Placing messages one under another shows this. The optional numbering of messages also indicates the sequence. An object receiving a message activates the relevant method. The time when the flow of control is focused in an object is called **activation**. Activations are shown as narrow rectangles on object *lifelines* (vertical dotted lines).

Hierarchical numbering of messages shows activation dependencies between messages. In particular, a message to self (i.e. a method call on the same object) within one activation results in a new activation. This is shown both by the hierarchical numbering and graphically by the attachment of a new narrow rectangle.

As shown in Figure 2.12, sequence diagrams differentiate among:

- **synchronous messages** – represented by a filled arrow head
- **callback messages** – represented by a dashed line with an open arrow; this is called *a* **method reply** and must not be confused with a **method return** from a message call, which is implicit at the end of the activation and normally not shown on interaction diagrams
- **asynchronous messages** – represented by an open arrow head
- **object creation messages** – represented by a dashed line with an open arrow to an object rectangle.

Interactions focus on sequences of messages, not on the data that the messages pass around. Therefore, the signatures of messages do not need to be shown and the return types are normally not visualized. The return types are frequently understood from the context.

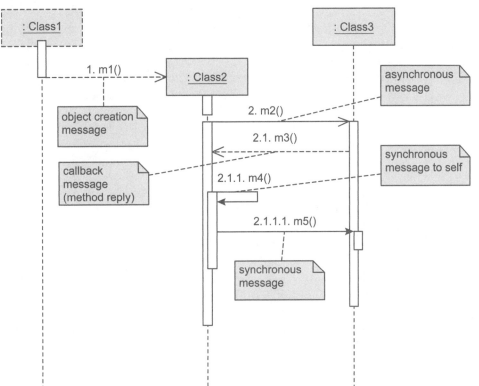

Figure 2.12
Messages in a
sequence diagram

To load entity objects to memory, the MovieActor application needs to query the database and to create entity objects from result sets returned by queries. For simplicity, the MovieActor application consists of only five classes: three entity classes, the MovieSearcher class, and the Connection class. The MovieSearcher class initiates processing and displays the results of database access to the screen. The Connection class interacts with the database.

Figure 2.13 presents a sequence diagram for the use case Retrieve MovieActor Details. This use case requires loading entity objects to memory (i.e. populating the entity cache upon retrieving the data from the database).

The searcher:MovieSearcher object instantiates the conn:Connection object and then sends to it the readAll() message. The readAll() method constructs a SQL query string and passes it to the query() method. The query() method sends the createStatement() message on the conn object. This is shown in Figure 2.13 as a message to the JDBC Connection interface. The createStatement() returns a Statement object. The executeQuery() message on the Statement object produces a ResultSet object that is returned to the readAll() method.

Collaboration (communication) diagrams

A **collaboration (communication) diagram** (Section 11.3.2) is a variation of a sequence diagram. Figure 2.14 is a collaboration diagram that corresponds to Figure 2.13. Messages

Figure 2.13
Sequence
diagram

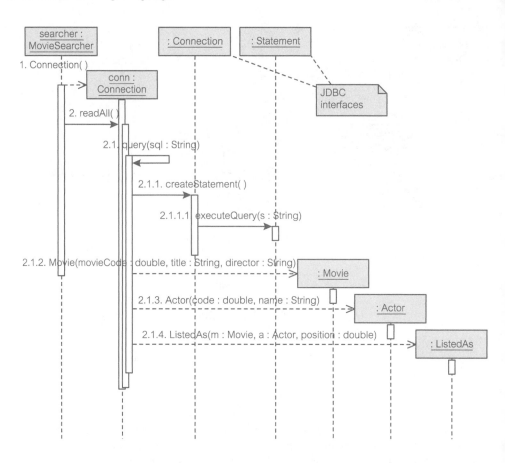

in the collaboration diagram are shown with a solid line and an arrow with the message name. The solid line is also an indication of how an object sending the message acquired the 'handle' on the receiving object (this could be, for example, by an association link or by acquaintance).

A collaboration diagram does not illustrate lifelines (but the objects represent the lifelines). Activations are implicit in the hierarchical numbering of messages. An object creation message is also implicit (to some degree) in the numbering – the newly created object continues the numbering from the next sequential value. Apart from that there is no visual distinction between an object creation and callback messages.

In practice, the developers tend to use sequence diagrams much more than collaboration diagrams. From the visual perspective, sequence diagrams have an advantage for presenting more complex models in which the explicit visualization of message sequences is essential – even though they may require printing on large paper formats using printers (plotters) capable of taking large formats.

Collaboration diagrams may be more useful for the analysis of messages from/to a given object. They may be more convenient when drawing initial draft interactions and when doing 'iterative' trial-and-error modeling. Because of this, they are quite handy for brainstorming sessions.

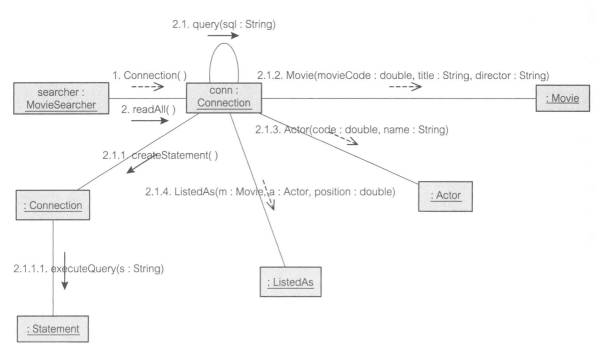

Figure 2.14 Collaboration (communication) diagram

Statechart Diagrams   2.2.4

Unlike most other UML diagrams, statechart diagrams are not specific to object-oriented modeling. Statechart diagrams apply the notation and ideas of traditional state machine models (Sommerville, 2001), used for decades in modeling engineering real-time applications. These kinds of applications have to model possible states of devices and systems such as chemical containers, elevators, electrical switches, power plants, etc.

A **statechart diagram** captures states of an object and actions that lead to state transitions on that object. A statechart diagram is drawn for each class, which has interesting state changes worthy of modeling. A **state** of an object (class instance) changes when the values of some of its attributes change. For example, the object Student, whose attribute enrollmentStatus is set to the value 'part-time', is in a PartTime state. The same Student object may have another attribute paymentStatus set to 'paid'. The Student is then in states PartTime and Paid.

Attaching a statechart diagram to a class is not the only use of statecharts. Statechart diagrams can be constructed for other modeling elements, which have interesting dynamic behavior, such as use cases, actors, operations, interactions.

An example of statechart diagram for a Movie class is depicted in Figure 2.15. The example is conceived so as to illustrate a variety of modeling constructs and options. States, represented by rectangles with rounded corners, specify the responses of an object to input events. **Transitions**, shown as arrowed lines, originate from a *source state* and terminate on a *target state*. The *initial state* is indicated by a black circle. The *final state* is

Figure 2.15
Statechart
diagram

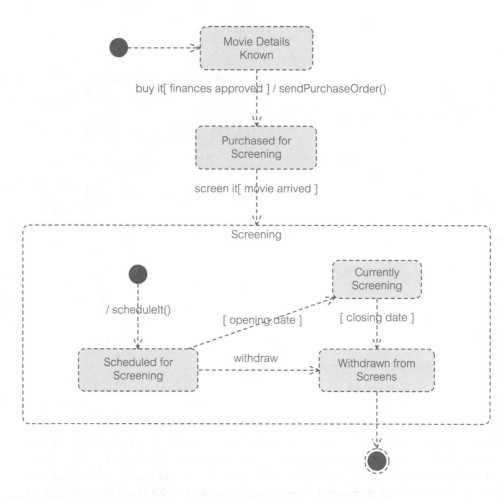

represented by an encircled black circle, known in the jargon as the bull's eye. A diagram can have more than one initial state and more than one final state.

'A state is a condition during the life of an object or an interaction during which it satisfies some condition, performs some action, or waits for some event. A *composite* state is a state that, in contrast to a *simple* state, has a graphical decomposition' (UML, 2003b, p.3-137). Screening in Figure 2.15 is a composite state. The initial simple state within Screening is Scheduled for Screening.

States have durations. They correspond to intervals of time between two transitions. Duration is a relative concept. Normally, states take more time on our relative timescale than transitions. States can also represent computations.

A transition may be annotated according to the following format. The use of any of the three elements in the format is optional.

event-signature [guard-condition] /*action-expression*

Events can be of different types. In particular they can be call events, i.e. messages. As such, events can take parameters. **Guard conditions** are boolean expressions specifying under what conditions the transition will 'fire' (will succeed). **Actions** are executed once the transition fires. They usually signify methods of the owning object.

Activity Diagrams

An activity diagram is a state machine that represents a computation, i.e. the performance of actions, and such that the transitions are triggered by the completion of the actions. Typically, an activity diagram is attached to the implementation of an operation or a use case. In the current version of UML (UML, 2002, 2003b), activity diagrams are used exclusively for depicting behavior using the control and data flow model reminiscent of *Petri nets* (Ghezzi *et al.*, 2003). In previous versions of UML, activity diagrams served a combined purpose of behavior specification and state machine (Maciaszek, 2001).

Figure 2.16 is a UML **activity diagram** annotated with UML notes explaining the meanings of graphical symbols. The diagram depicts activities (action states) triggered by the class CAdmin when it requests a get EMovie service from the class MDataMapper. The first decision box is used to indicate that EMovie may be found in the program's memory cache, but if it is not there then the class FReader retrieves it from the database.

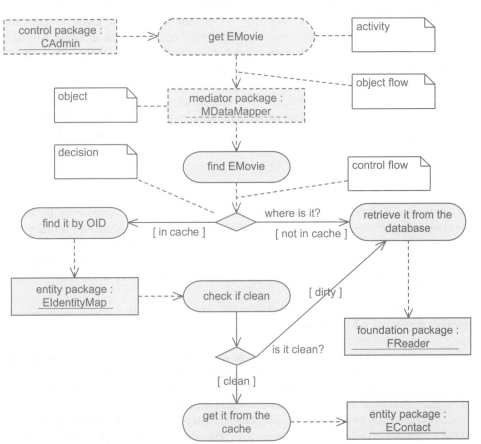

Figure 2.16
Activity diagram

Even if `EMovie` is in the cache, but it is dirty (i.e. it has been modified since it was retrieved from the database), the computation is redirected to `FReader`.

An **action state** of an activity diagram differs in several ways from a *normal state* of a statechart diagram. Unlike normal states, which can have recursive (internal) transitions to themselves, action states are computations that should not be interrupted by external events or have any outgoing transitions based on explicit events. Outgoing transitions from an action state are the result of completing the activity of that state.

An *object* of an activity diagram is similar to an object (lifeline) of an interaction diagram. **Object flows** (dashed arrows) between objects and action states specify which object sends a message and which object has a method to service that message. An object which is the output of an action is usually the input to one or more successive actions. **Control flows** (solid arrows) are used when an action state produces an output (usually a decision output) that is the input to a successive action state.

2.2.6 Implementation Diagrams

Implementation diagrams are models for physical implementation of the system. They show system components, their structure and dependencies and how they are deployed on computer nodes. 'Implementation diagrams' is a generic term for two kinds of diagrams: component diagrams and deployment diagrams. Component diagrams show the structure of components, including their interface and implementation dependencies. Deployment diagrams show the runtime deployment of the system on computer nodes.

The UML documentation (UML, 2003b) points out that implementation diagrams can be used in an extended way for business and organizational modeling. In such modeling, components can represent business entities, procedures and other artifacts. Deployment nodes can represent organizational units and resources (people, machines, money, etc.) of a business project.

Component diagrams

'A **component diagram** shows the dependencies among software components, including the classifiers that specify them (for example, implementation classes) and the artifacts that implement them; such as, source code files, binary code files, executable files, scripts' (UML, 2003b, p.3-169). 'A **component** represents a modular, deployable, and replaceable part of a system that encapsulates implementation and exposes a set of interfaces' (UML, 2003b, p.3-174).

A component is denoted by a rectangular box equipped with two smaller rectangles. It does not have its own features such as attributes or operations. It acts as container for other *specifiers* that have the features. A component *implicitly* exposes a set of interfaces, which represent services provided by elements residing on the component. *Explicitly*, such interfaces can be denoted by a circle annotated with the name of the interface. A link, represented by a straight line, connects a component to an interface to indicate that a particular component exposes services defined in the interface.

Components may be connected to other components by physical containment (direct nesting of a component in its enclosing component). Physical containment represents a compositional relationship called the «`reside`» relationship (hence, a relationship line can be used

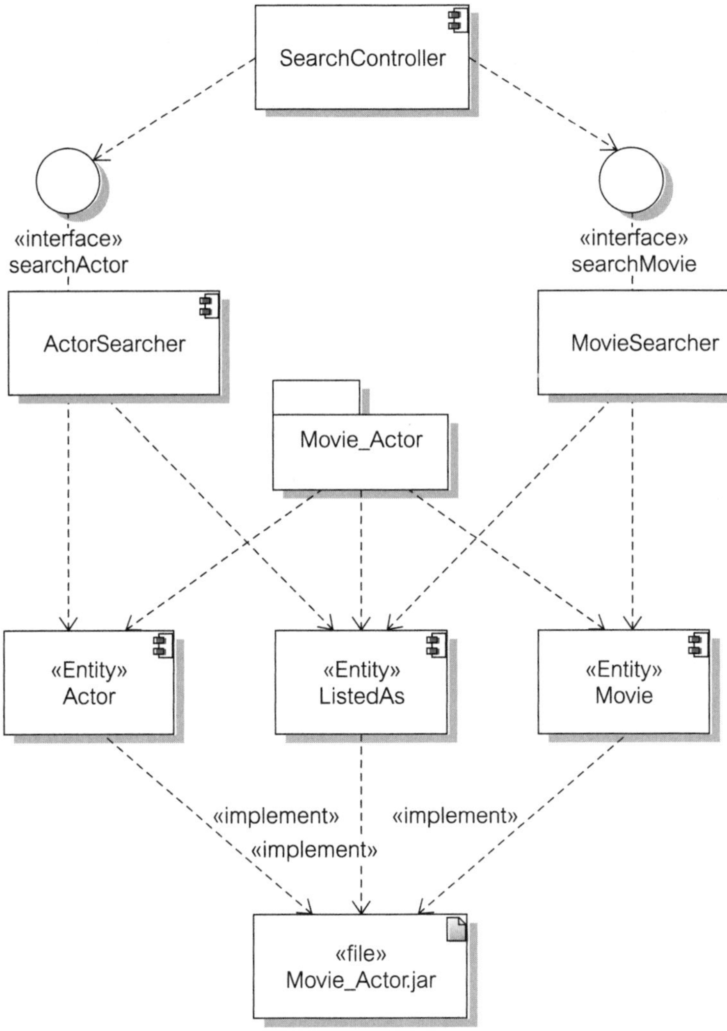

Figure 2.17
Component
diagram

in the diagram as an alternative notation for containment). Equivalently, a physical contain-ment between component and artifact can be illustrated by the «implement» relationship.

Dashed arrows are used to depict dependencies between components. The same arrows are used to show dependencies between a component and an interface. The meaning then is that a particular component depends on the services defined in the interface, rather than on services defined in another component.

Packages can be used in a component diagram to illustrate the grouping of the components. Stereotypes can be used to indicate implementation-specific dependencies or characteristics of components.

Figure 2.17 shows a component diagram for the MovieActor minicase application. The stereotype «Entity» is used to indicate that the component houses entity objects. The package Movie_Actor contains three entity components, namely Actor, Movie, and ListedAs. These entity components are physically stored in the file called Movie_Actor.jar. The containment is illustrated by the «implement» relationship.

The `SearchController` component is responsible for performing searches on the MovieActor database based on search criteria specified by users. To do this job, `Search-Controller` takes advantage of two interfaces, called `searchMovie` and `searchActor`. These interfaces are implemented by `MovieSearcher` and `ActorSearcher`, respectively. Whenever `SearchController` needs certain information regarding movie information, it queries `searchMovie`. Similarly, `searchActor` is used to find information regarding actors.

Component diagrams can easily accommodate changes resulting from using different implementation platforms. For example, if Enterprise Java Beans (EJB) were used as an implementation platform, Figure 2.17 can be modified with appropriate stereotypes on the components. In the EJB case, `SearchController`, `ActorSearcher`, and `MovieSearcher` would be stereotyped as «EJB Session» to indicate that they are *EJB*

Figure 2.18
Deployment
diagram

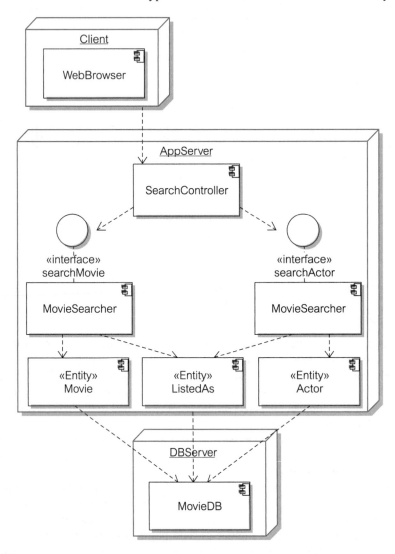

Session beans. `Movie`, `ListedAs`, and `Actor` would be stereotyped as «`EJB Entity`» to represent *EJB Entity beans*.

Deployment diagrams

'**Deployment diagrams** show the configuration of run-time processing elements and the software components, processes, and objects that execute on them. Software component instances represent run-time manifestations of software code units' (UML, 2003b, p.3-171). Component instances are contained in nodes, which indicates that the components run or execute on these nodes.

'A **node** is a physical object that represents a processing resource, generally, having at least a memory and often processing capability as well. Nodes include computing devices but also human resources or mechanical processing resources' (UML, 2003b, p.3-173).

The deployment of components, shown in Figure 2.17, is shown in Figure 2.18. In this diagram, the focus is on the placement of components and the interaction between resources. Nodes are denoted by three-dimensional rectangle boxes. Figure 2.18 identifies a `Client` machine that houses the `WebBrowser` component. Most components defined in Figure 2.17 are placed on an application server `AppServer`. The `Movie`, `ListedAs`, and `Actor` components access the database, provided by the `MovieDB` component, and located on the `DBServer` node.

Summary

1. The *Unified Modeling Language* (UML) is the standard modeling language for modern *object-oriented* software systems. Various extensions of UML, known as *UML profiles*, exist to tailor UML to specific application domains and technologies.

2. The language for *structured modeling*, in support of developments conforming to the old-style *functional paradigm* (Chapter 1), includes a range of visualization techniques, most popular of which have been data flow diagrams (DFDs), entity–relationship diagrams (ERDs), and structure charts.

3. Structured modeling is normally centered on functional decomposition represented in DFDs. ERDs and structure charts are used as supporting techniques. DFDs have three main modeling elements: processes, data flows, and data stores.

4. ERDs are a data modeling technique which is widely used outside of structured modeling for representing database structures. ERDs are constructed using two graphical elements: entities and relationships. Both entities and relationships can contain attributes.

5. The UML offers a wide range of modeling techniques to represent various viewpoints on the modeled system. The range of diagrams includes class diagrams, use case diagrams, interaction diagrams, statechart diagrams, activity diagrams, and implementation diagrams.

6. *Object-oriented UML modeling* is centered on class diagrams but driven by use case diagrams. The use case model is a reference point for all other models. Other models refer to the use case model to find out user requirements and/or to verify if they conform to user requirements. Class diagrams represent both the state and behavior of the system. Eventually, class models constitute the main input to programming.

7. *Class diagrams* visualize object classes, their attribute and operation content, and relationships between classes. There are three kinds of relationships: associations, aggregations, and generalizations.

8. *Use case diagrams* provide a simple visualization of use cases, their relationships, and actors communicating with the use cases. However, the real strength of use cases is not in visual models but in text definitions of user requirements that use cases must satisfy.

9. *Interaction diagrams* are the main design-level behavior modeling technique in UML. They represent message passing in the system. There are two kinds of interaction diagrams: sequence diagrams and collaboration (communication) diagrams.

10. *Statechart diagrams* capture states of objects and actions that lead to state transitions on the objects. Statechart diagrams are drawn for individual classes, although they can also be used to model state changes in larger modeling elements, such as packages or the entire system.

11. An *activity diagram* is a state machine that represents a computation. Typically, an activity diagram is attached to the implementation of an operation or a use case.

12. *Implementation diagrams* are models for physical implementation of the system. They show system components, their structure and dependencies and how they are deployed on computer nodes. There are two kinds of implementation diagrams: component diagrams and deployment diagrams.

Key Terms

«communicate» relationship	48	control flow	56
«extend» relationship	48, 49	data flow	40
«include» relationship	48	data flow diagrams	39
action	55	data member	44
action state	56	data store	41
activation	50	deployment diagram	59
activity diagram	55	DFD	*See* data flow diagrams
addition use case	49	diagram	38
aggregation	44, 46	entity	42
association	44, 46	entity–relationship diagram	42
association class	45	ERD	*See* entity–relationship diagram
asynchronous message	50	event	54
attribute	42, 44	extend relationship	49
base use case	49	extension use case	49
callback message	50	external entity	40
class	44	feature	44
class diagram	43	field	*See* data member
classifier	43	functional decomposition	39
collaboration diagram	51	generalization	45, 46
communication diagram	*See* collaboration diagram	guard condition	54
component	56	implementation diagram	56
component diagram	56	instance variable	*See* data member
context diagram	40	interaction diagram	50

member function	*See* method	repository	38
member variable	*See* data member	sequence diagram	50
message	44	state machine	53
message passing	44	state	53
method	44	statechart diagram	53
method reply	*See* callback message	stereotype	48
method return	50	structured analysis and design	39
model	38	Structured English	41
module specification	41	structured modeling	39
multiplicity	44	structured programming	38
navigation	49	subclass	45
node	59	subset class	44
object behavior	43	superclass	45
object creation message	50	superset class	44
object flow	56	synchronous message	50
object identity	43	transition	53
object state	43, 53	UML	*See* Unified Modeling Language
operation	44	UML profile	37
overview diagram	40	unidirectional relationship	49
participation	44	Unified Modeling Language	37, 43
process	40	use case	47
relationship	42, 44, 49	use case diagram	46

Review Questions

1. Explain the place and role of a repository in software modeling. What is it? What does it contain?

2. Why is structured analysis and design called 'structured'? What could be alternative terms? Discuss.

3. In DFDs, is it possible to have a data flow between two data stores or between an external entity and a data store? Explain.

4. Explain the requirement of data flow balancing in DFDs. Give an example demonstrating possible cases where the balancing requirement is broken.

5. Explain how the ERD notions of multiplicity and participation are related.

6. Explain similarities and differences between aggregation relationships and associations in class modeling.

7. Refer to Figure 2.8. Explain how the Java `Collection` interface is used to represent relationships between the classes in the model.

8. The «extend» relationship in the use case models is drawn as an arrow from the extension to the base use case (for example, 'check luggage' extends the 'check-in for flight' use case). Would it not be better to draw the arrow in the opposite direction and change the stereotype name of the relationship to «is extended by» (i.e., 'check-in for flight' is extended by 'check luggage')? Explain.

9. Discuss the situations in which modeling with a sequence diagram is advantageous compared with using a collaboration diagram, and vice versa.

10. Explain and exemplify differences between events, guard conditions, and actions in statechart models.

11. What is an object flow and a control flow in an activity diagram?

12. What is the meaning of an interface in a component diagram?

Problem-Solving Exercises

1. Refer to the context diagram in Figure 2.2. Is this diagram complete for the problem described? If not, how would you improve the model.

2. Consider an entity called `Student` with attributes such as `student_id`, `student_name`, etc. Consider also that the system needs to store details of student addresses so that it is possible to group students by their postcodes or even the street names they live on. Additionally, any multiple telephone numbers of students need to be kept. How would such information be modeled in an ERD? Draw various models and explain their pros and cons.

3. Refer to the class diagram in Figure 2.7. Draw an alternative diagram to represent the same modeling situation. Explain the semantics of both diagrams and point to any semantic differences.

4. Using an online reservation system to buy theater tickets involves actions such as selecting a seat, making the payment with a credit card, optionally getting a price discount based on the client's history of buying tickets, and taking a decision about whether the ticket should be posted to the client's address or collected at the venue. Draw a use case diagram for the above scenario, complete with any «include» and «extend» relationships.

5. Why does the component `ListedAs` in Figure 2.17 not show the fact that it is a map between an `Actor` and a `Movie`, i.e. `ListedAs` is a relationship object that maps actors to movies, and vice versa? Should the diagram show something similar to Figure 2.19 instead? Note that Figure 2.19 shows only the three components involved and assumes that other components are the same as in Figure 2.17.

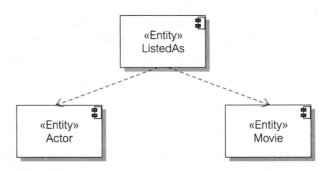

Figure 2.19 Dependencies of ListedAs to Actor and Movie

Chapter

3

Software Engineering Tools

There are two important dimensions to software engineering tools: personal and organizational. A tool can be used for personal productivity and/or for teamwork (workgroup, collaborative) productivity. In both cases, a tool demands certain level of knowledge, skill, and management. The term 'maturity' (Chapter 5) is used to define these demands. Without an adequate level of maturity, the use of a tool can hurt more than help.

There is an important difference between personal maturity and organizational teamwork maturity. The former is under the control of a single person. The latter is not. The lesson is obvious. Unless the maturity of the whole development team is sufficient, the use of tools can impede organizational productivity. A tool introduces a level of rigor into doing things. If an organization is in a mess, the introduction of tools to the development process will only generate more mess.

Understandably, software engineering tools for **teamwork** productivity is a big investment in people and technology. Tools in this category belong to the category of software products known as **computer-supported collaborative work** (CSCW) or **workgroup computing**. CSCW tools are complex products; in fact they belong to some of the most sophisticated software products that money can buy. There are quite a few reasons for that.

Firstly, the collaboration aspect requires the database technology to support storing, retrieving, and sharing of development artifacts. Secondly, many development artifacts are graphical models. Storing, retrieving and sharing of such multimedia objects creates a real challenge for conventional (relational) database technology. Thirdly, a creative development work takes a long time, may produce results that conflict with other solutions, must allow for mistakes and experiments, etc.

In a nutshell, the collaborative aspect requires the database technology that can manage historical versions of various artifacts and combine them in various development configurations. And again, conventional database technology has not been targeting these kinds of issues. Vendors of software engineering tools have frequently no choice but to develop by themselves a 'bleeding-edge' technology and build it into their products.

A generic term for software engineering tools is computer assisted software engineering (CASE). In practice, however, the meaning of CASE is commonly restricted to visual modeling tools for system analysis and design. Although most such tools have a capability of forward engineering (generating the code) and reverse engineering from existing code to visual models, they do not normally provide a more complete programming environment. Tools that comprehensively assist programmers are termed integrated development environments (IDEs).

CASE and IDEs do not encompass all tools used in software processes. A software lifecycle requires *project management* tools to schedule and manage project resources. It also requires *change management* tools to manage defects, enhancements, and to take care of the overall maintenance of the software. Being a teamwork activity, software engineering requires the technology of software *configuration management*. Accordingly, the following discussion classifies software engineering tools into the following groups:

- project management tools
- system modeling tools (CASE)
- software programming environments (IDEs)
- change and configuration management tools.

Software engineering tools is a big and fiercely competitive business. The tools referred to in this chapter, while representative to the industry, may or may not exist in the presented form by the time this book reaches the readers. The reader should refer to the book's website for updates or to attempt to make relevant Internet searches for latest information (as requested in 'Problem-Solving Exercises' at the end of this chapter).

3.1 Project Management Tools

Project management brings together a set of tools, methods, and techniques related to planning the project and managing the associated process. Methods and techniques of project and process management are discussed in the next two chapters. The tools, their major properties and capabilities, are discussed in this chapter. Discussion about change and configuration management tools, sometimes considered a part of project management, is delayed to Section 3.4.

Project management is about distribution and control of budgets, time, and people. The main questions asked are: How much will it cost to develop a system?, How long will it take to develop a system?, and What people do we need to develop a system?

An old maxim says that if you can't plan it, you can't do it. But planning cannot be done 'out of the blue'. It requires some prior knowledge about what it takes to develop a system in this organization, with these people, with these resources, in this organizational culture, etc. To have this kind of knowledge, the organization must know its past. The organization must measure what has been happening on past projects. The organization must be collecting various *metrics* from previous projects. This leads to another maxim: 'unless you know your past, you cannot properly plan your future'.

Project management requires tools for effective scheduling and controlling project activities, for estimating project costs, for collecting metrics, etc. Contemporary tools are frequently included in integrated management support environments that tie together typical project management with strategic planning, business modeling, portfolio management, document management, workflows, etc. Such integrated environments provide a single collaborative tool for the management of projects in the wider context of setting strategic initiatives, conducting tactical management, performing daily tasks, and managing individuals. Integrated management environments can reach outside of an enterprise to suppliers, customers, and other business partners.

Management of large projects is best done using web-based tools, which enable dynamic, interactive, and just-in-time managing of large teams and processes. Many traditional project management tools are available in web-based versions (PMC, 2003).

Project Scheduling and Controlling 3.1.1

Tools for **scheduling and controlling** project activities assist in preparing activity graphs. Activity **network graphs** identify events that must occur before an activity can begin, specify the duration of each activity and its due date, assign human and other resources to all activities, etc. Two traditional activity graphs are the **critical path method** (CPM) networks and **Gantt charts**. A well-known extension of CPM is a **Program Evaluation and Review Technique** (PERT) chart.

Project management tools are capable of generating activity graphs once necessary project information is provided. Required project information includes identification of activities (tasks), their durations and resources, precursor events and events that result from activities, etc. Project information can be provided in text or entered by direct manipulation of a graph.

Project management tools are also capable of automatically converting graphs (e.g. PERT to Gantt charts or vice versa) and of presenting graphs to emphasize various viewpoints and with different details. For example, separate graphs can be produced for the whole project and for various individuals working on the project. Graphs can be visualized using different timescales, showing (or not) specific human and other resources, showing durations for activities, and/or showing their starting and finishing dates, etc.

Project management tools adjust and rebuild schedules whenever changes occur to an activity or to a resource. Schedules are adjusted and new start and finish dates are recalculated with new information about the latest progress. Schedules can be recalculated to account for the impact of adding resources to a project. This allows managers to understand if additional resource can bring better results (sometimes managerial overheads associated with adding a new resource can increase the time to delivery).

Figure 3.1
MS Project®:
CPM chart
Source: Screenshot
of Microsoft® Office
Project (2003),
reprinted by
permission
from Microsoft
Corporation,
Copyright © 1998–
2003 Microsoft
Corporation

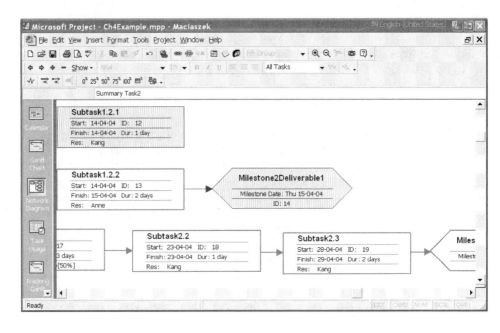

Figure 3.1 is a simple example of a CPM network presented by MS Project® from Microsoft (Microsoft, 2003c) – one of the best-known project management tools. The diagram shows a few project tasks (activities) and milestones. Each task specifies start and finish dates, duration, and the assigned human resource. The example in Figure 3.1 is discussed in more detail in Chapter 4.

3.1.2 Aligning Project and Performance Management with Strategic Objectives

Organizations function in competitive and dynamic surroundings. To survive and to compete successfully, organizations must constantly adapt their objectives, goals, plans as well as development projects to changes in customer needs, new technologies, changing external factors, etc. Under these conditions, project management becomes subservient to demands of effectiveness, efficiency, and performance improvement.

Not surprisingly, some project management tools are included in larger environments to support a wide variety of managerial activities. In particular, they support project management in the context of providing reinforcement to **performance management** and strategic planning. They help in managing people and teams to plan, track, and achieve business goals. The emphasis is shifted from projects to people. People are not treated as mere 'resources' allocated to activities or tasks. People are managed by assigning to them business goals and tracking the results.

Figure 3.2 presents an overview of ManagePro™ from Performance Solutions Technology (ManagePro, 2003). This is a tool for goal-driven team-based management of projects. ManagePro™ is designed to be a general management tool, which provides facilities to manage goals, projects, development plans, meetings, email, documents, and performance reviews including annual reviews.

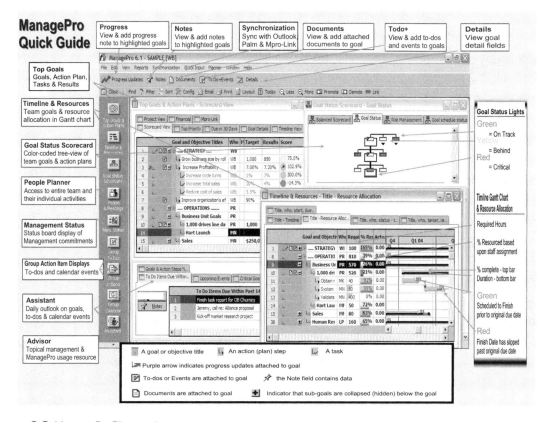

Figure 3.2 ManagePro™: overview

Source: Screenshot of ManagePro™ 6.1 from www.managepro.net, March 2004, reproduced by kind permission of Performance Solutions Technology, LLC

Unifying Project Management with Web-Based Collaboration and Content Management

3.1.3

Many software projects are distributed – they span multiple people and cross organizational boundaries. Communication between stakeholders of such projects must be web-enabled. Project management becomes a 'component' in a web-based collaboration of *knowledge workers*. The workers belong to various distributed teams. To deliver the project they need to plan, communicate, collaborate, take decisions, and assign responsibilities, etc. over the Internet.

Collaboration management includes support for project stakeholders to lodge issues, define and assign actions, document outcomes. Collaboration rules can be set up to remind about events and activities by means of email notifications. Timesheets of stakeholders become an integral part of project management and stakeholders are automatically informed about project progress.

Along with collaboration, web-based project management relies on easy access and sharing of documents and other informational content, such as web pages and emails. Tools in this category maintain public libraries of documents and other content – they

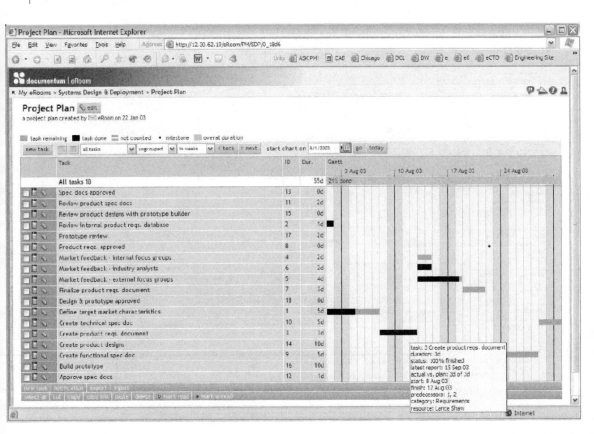

Figure 3.3 eRoom: Gantt chart

Source: Screenshot of eRoom from www.eroom.net/eRoomNet/, July 2003, reproduced by kind permission of Documentum, Inc

support what is known today as **content management**. Subscription mechanisms are used to inform project stakeholders of content changes.

eRoom from Documentum (eRoom, 2003) is an example of a web-centric software tool that unifies project management with collaboration and content management. Figure 3.3 illustrates a Gantt chart in eRoom's web-enabled collaborative environment.

3.1.4 Unifying Project Management with Web-Based Portfolio Management

Unifying project management with collaboration and content management, all over the Internet, is an important step towards planning and scheduling that is *multi-project* and *resource-constrained*. Tools supporting such planning and scheduling concentrate on collaborative resource profiling and resource allocation, and on integrated time reporting. This process of enabling the enterprise to align resources and investments with strategic objectives is called enterprise **portfolio management**.

Tools that unify project management with enterprise portfolio management tend to combine the whole set of related management tools, such as team and resource management, communication and collaboration management, document and content management. Tools in this category, such as eProject Enterprise from eProject (eProject, 2003) or Primavera Enterprise® Product Suite from Primavera Enterprise (Primavera, 2003), foster a web-based work environment for

- project discussions, tracking and work assignment
- team calendars and timesheets
- electronic meetings to reach consensus and take consultative decisions
- sharing project documents and maintaining versioning of them
- workflow automation and tracking of decisions
- conventional planning and scheduling with Gantt, CPM and PERT charts
- document templates and patterns to encourage best practices
- aligning projects with strategic plans and business models
- managing individual and shared resources
- allocating skills to human resources and allocating resources to projects
- generation of cross-project summaries and status indicators.

Figure 3.4 illustrates a project summary report produced by eProject Enterprise (eProject, 2003). It shows a pie chart for budget spent versus budget remaining, a graph depicting task planned costs versus actual cost, and a hierarchy of tasks informing how they contribute to overall project health. The toolbar at the top of the window reveals how the tool can be used for personal management and for enterprise-wide collaboration.

Integrating Project Management with Metrics 3.1.5

Metrics in software engineering have nothing to do with the European metric system. Metrics is the discipline of measuring software development processes and products so that collected information can aid future project planning.

Despite their significance, metrics are neglected on most projects. They tend to be sacrificed in the name of day-to-day pressures to deliver the current project. Metrics require resources, and shifting resources from the development work to the collection of metrics is a tough call. It is also a call that can send up red flags in selected areas although the project may be on a right track.

Because collection of metrics is an expensive proposition, sometimes resisted by developers and managers, the availability of easy to use and informative metrics tools is even more important. The metrics tools must allow easy entry of information. Whenever possible, information should be obtained automatically from development models and program codes.

Analysis of the architectural design of the code is an important example of how project management can be enhanced by critically important metrics. Architectural design

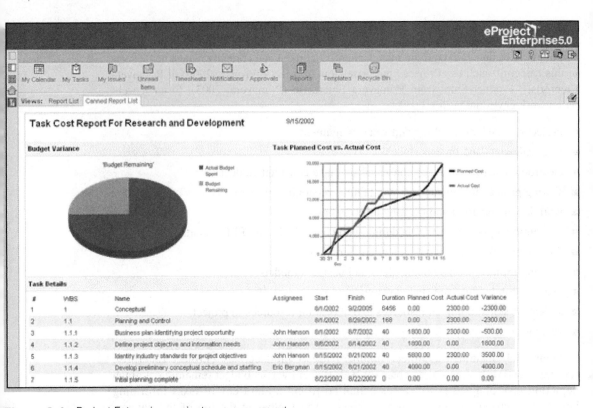

Figure 3.4 eProject Enterprise: project summary report
Source: Screenshot of eProject Enterprise, July 2003, reproduced by kind permission of eProject, Inc

(Chapter 9) bears responsibility for system *supportability*, i.e. its understandability, maintainability and scalability. It is, therefore, important to measure system supportability early in the software lifecycle as well as later when the impact of changes on existing code must be evaluated. Metrics aim at setting targets for minimizing component dependencies so that overall stability and quality of the system can be improved.

Figure 3.5 shows an example of *what-if* analysis performed on the code with 7 packages (6 of them visible) and 62 classes with 201 relationships. The analysis has been conducted on the class FWriter (the left-most circle). The lines show potential dependencies from FWriter so that the impact of changing FWriter on other classes can be understood. The list on the right of potentially affected objects includes Java inner classes. Java inner classes account also for a large number of circles in the top-right package. Figure 3.5 was created with Small Worlds (SmallWorlds, 2003). This tool was acquired in July 2003 by IBM (the functionality of this tool is to be incorporated in the IBM product portfolio known as IBM Rational Quality by Design).

Figure 3.6 is another screenshot from Small Worlds. The graph presents internal dependencies to classes and interfaces that exist in the class called CAdmin. The dotted arrows capture *uses* dependencies. The solid arrows show *contains* dependencies.

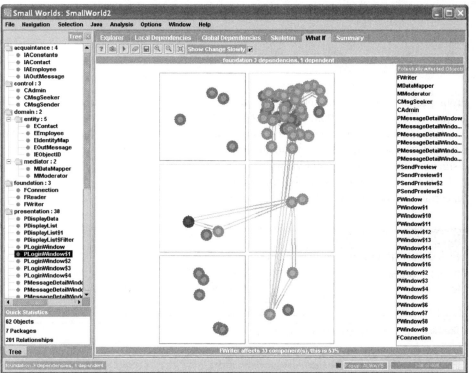

Figure 3.5
Small Worlds:
what-if analysis
Source: Screenshot
of *Small Worlds*
reprinted by
permission from
www.thesmallworlds.
com/, © Copyright
2003 by International
Business Machines
Corporation. All
Rights Reserved

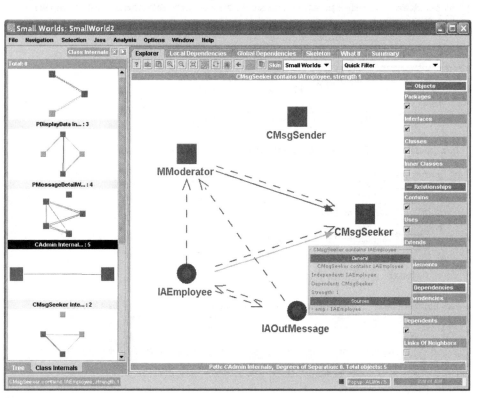

Figure 3.6
Small Worlds:
class internals
analysis
Source: Screenshot
of *Small Worlds*
reprinted by
permission from
www.thesmallworlds.
com/, © Copyright
2003 by International
Business Machines
Corporation. All
Rights Reserved

3.1.6 Integrating Project Management with Risk Management

From project management and metrics, there is only a small step to risk analysis of projects. Ghezzi *et al.* (2003, p.416) define **risks** as 'potentially adverse circumstances that may impair the development process and the quality of products'. Risks are everyday occurrences that accompany any human activity. Not surprisingly, risk management is a distinct branch of management theory.

Risk management is a decision-making activity that assesses the impact of risks (uncertainties) on decisions. It weighs distributions of possible project outcomes versus the

Figure 3.7
Risk Radar™:
risk data input
Source: Integrated
Computer
Engineering (ICE,
2003)

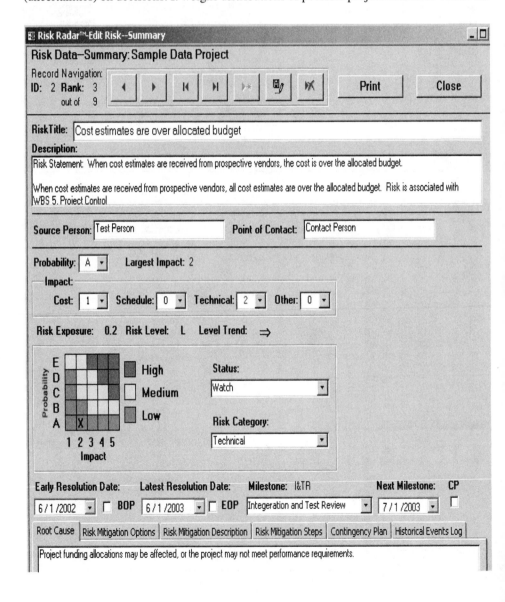

probabilities of arriving at these outcomes. Given the acceptable level of tolerance on risk, it estimates the likelihood with which a desired outcome will happen.

Project risk management uses the same way of thinking as that employed in risk analyses of financial portfolios. A simple method of financial planning is to take the initial portfolio and estimate future earnings by applying average interest rates on return on the assets. Using average returns can at best bring average results. Better outcomes may be achieved by employing probability theory and considering various odds. The odds are defined with various probability distribution functions and the range of possible outcomes is computed using simulation. Project risk management uses similar approaches.

Assuming that the desired project outcomes are defined, typical steps of risk analysis are:

1. Identify risks and represent them using ranges of possible values. This is done by replacing a risk value with a selected probability distribution function, such as Poisson, uniform, chi-square, triangular, etc.

2. Use simulation, such as Monte Carlo or Latin Hypercube method, to generate possible outcomes and likelihood of these outcomes.

3. Take a decision based on graphical outputs (histograms, cumulative graphs, etc.) and using personal judgment and acceptable tolerance for risk.

Tools that integrate project management with risk management are frequently implemented as add-ins to conventional project management tools (such as Microsoft Project), add-ins to spreadsheets (such as Microsoft Excel), or as database applications (e.g. on top of Microsoft Access). For example, the range of products called @Risk from Palisade (Palisade, 2003) consists of add-ins to Microsoft Project and Excel. On the other hand, the Risk Radar™ products from ICE (Integrated Computer Engineering) (ICE, 2003) are Access applications.

Figure 3.7 illustrates a Risk Radar™ data entry window to specify a risk (ICE, 2003). Each risk is defined this way and stored in Microsoft Access database before a simulation is used to perform risk analysis.

Figure 3.8 shows outcomes of a Monte Carlo simulation using @Risk (Palisade, 2003). The simulation was conducted by replacing uncertain values, in a spreadsheet of risk variables, with probability distribution functions representing ranges of possible values. The resulting graphs show distributions of possible outcomes and the probabilities of getting these outcomes. Graphs are supplemented with summary statistics. For further dynamic analysis, probability bars and sliding delimiters are provided to answer specific questions, such as 'What are the chances that the number of defects in the code will exceed a certain value?'

System Modeling Tools

3.2

As discussed in Section 1.1.5, software engineering is about modeling. Hence, the range of *system modeling tools* embraces all tools that support software engineers in development tasks – from analysis via design to implementation. These are largely **visual modeling**

Figure 3.8
@Risk: simulation outcomes
Source: Screenshot of @Risk from www.palisade-europe.com, reproduced by kind permission of the Palisade Corporation

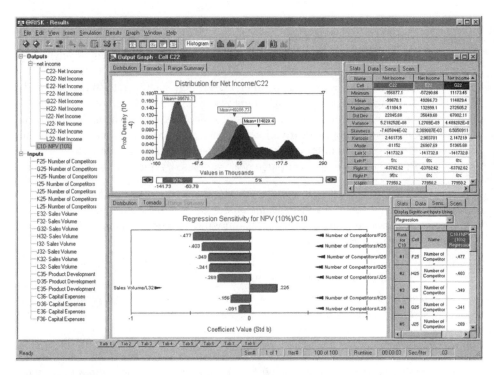

tasks in the UML language. Visual modeling tools are commonly known as CASE tools. Although formally the notion of software modeling includes programming, integrated programming environments are discussed separately in Section 3.3.

Modern system modeling tools are workgroup tools and support multiple developers in accessing a shared repository of development artifacts, checking out the artifacts to local workstations, working on these artifacts, and checking them back into the repository. The teamwork aspects of system modeling tools are covered in Section 3.4.

System modeling tools concentrate on the requirements analysis and system design phases. They typically include capabilities of generating (forward engineering) initial code from the models as well as reverse engineering the models from the code. One of the main features of modeling tools is managing dependencies between user requirements (expressed as text statements) and visual modeling concepts representing these requirements.

Visual modeling uses the Unified Modeling Language (UML) (Chapter 2). UML is sufficient for all modeling tasks related to business requirements, system state and behavior, and dynamic state changes. Other modeling issues, such as database modeling or web content design, are likely to need a specialized modeling language or a specially developed UML variation (UML profile).

3.2.1 Managing Requirements

Requirements are text statements within a requirements document. Normally, there is one requirements document per use case (Section 2.2.2). Requirements are defined at multiple

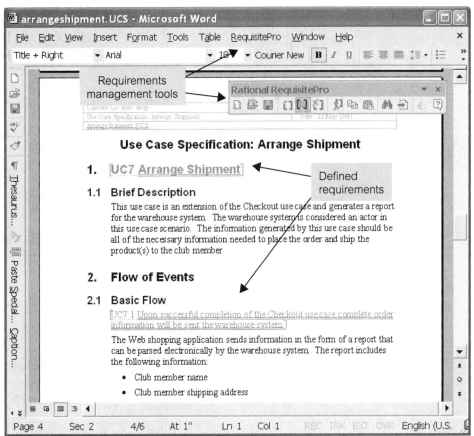

Figure 3.9
IBM Rational
RequisitePro:
requirements
document
Source: Screenshot
of *IBM Rational
Requisite Pro*
reprinted by
permission from
*Rational Suite
Tutorial, Version
2002.05.00*,
© Copyright 2002
by International
Business Machines
Corporation. All
Rights Reserved;
Screenshot of
Microsoft® Word,
reprinted by
permission from
Microsoft
Corporation,
Copyright © 1998–
2003 Microsoft
Corporation

levels of abstraction and there is a hierarchical arrangement between requirements. A use case descriptive name is also a requirement.

A system modeling tool must facilitate team collaboration by providing ways of writing requirements documents, identifying various categories of requirements in the documents, managing changes to requirements, and making requirements accessible to all developers. The universal accessibility of requirements to developers underscores the importance of requirements in the development lifecycle. Requirements are used by analysts to produce analysis models, by designers to define system architecture and detailed design specifications, by testers to develop test cases, and by project managers to create schedules and budgets.

Figure 3.9 contains a fragment of a requirements document created with IBM RequisitePro (Rational, 2003). This tool extends Microsoft Word with operations necessary to create and manage multiple levels of requirements within a text document. Specific RequisitePro operations are available on a menu and in a toolbar. The document in the figure defines two requirements UC7 and UC7.1.

Requirements defined in a requirements document are stored in the modeling tool's *repository*. They can be displayed and modified by developers. Changes to requirements

Figure 3.10
IBM Rational
RequisitePro:
Requirements
properties
Source: Screenshot
of *IBM Rational Suite*
reprinted by
permission from
Rational Suite
Tutorial, Version
2002.05.00,
© Copyright 2002
by International
Business Machines
Corporation. All
Rights Reserved

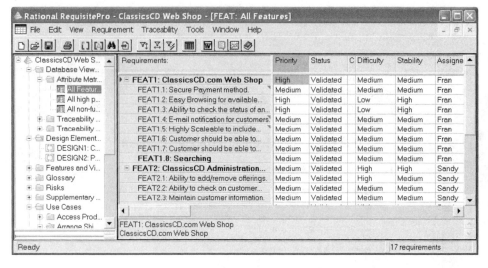

names are automatically reflected in the requirements document, and vice versa. The tool must support navigation between related requirements and between requirements and other modeling artifacts.

A typical way of displaying requirements for manipulation is a spreadsheet-like format. This familiar format makes it easy to assign various property (attribute) values to requirements. Requirement properties define issues such as the status of the requirement, its difficulty, stability (i.e. if it is likely to change), who owns it, whom it is assigned to, when it was created and/or updated. Figure 3.10 shows a list of high-level requirements, called features, and their properties.

It is desirable to represent various characteristics of requirements using color. Figure 3.11 shows a spreadsheet-style view of requirements in Telelogic's DOORS (Telelogic, 2003). The open dropdown menu shows how a risk level (high, medium, or low) can be assigned to a requirement. Each risk level is color-coded and the names/definitions of the requirements are displayed in their risk colors.

An integration of requirements management with the UML visual modeling necessitates maintaining bidirectional associations between requirements (at various levels) and visual model elements (artifacts). In early development stages, associations between requirements and use cases are established. Figure 3.12 is an IBM Rational Rose dialog box that links a use case to a requirements document and a requirement UC7 representing the use case. A similar dialog box would be displayed in the opposite direction, i.e. if a developer working within RequisitePro wanted to link a requirements document to a use case specification in Rational Rose.

Requirements management intersperses with the rest of lifecycle processes. Requirements management includes the ability to link requirements (from different levels of the requirements hierarchy) to the model elements that implement these requirements. Integration of requirements into the model and its various elements (use cases, classes, components, methods, etc.) strengthens the value of the design. This type of *all-in-one* tool tries to incorporate requirements management into all major processes of software lifecycle, from requirements modeling to software generation (forward engineering).

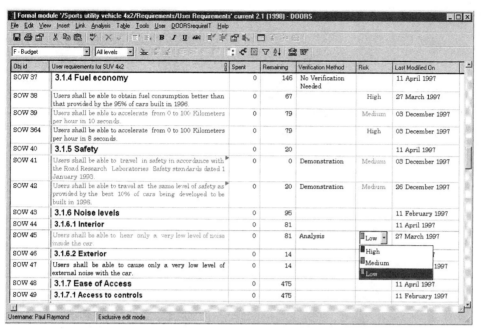

Figure 3.11
DOORS:
spreadsheet-style
requirements
management
Source: Screenshot
of DOORS® from
www.telelogic.com,
reprinted by kind
permission of
Telelogic UK Ltd.,
Copyright © 2004
Telelogic AB

Figure 3.12
IBM Rational
Rose: managing
associations
between
requirements
and use cases
Source: Screenshot
of *IBM Rational Suite*
reprinted by
permission from
*Rational Suite
Tutorial, Version
2002.05.00*,
© Copyright 2002
by International
Business Machines
Corporation. All
Rights Reserved

Integration of requirements and other modeling elements requires clever representation of models at various levels of detail and strong navigability between the elements. With a possibility of large number of diagrams and model elements created in a project, it is easy to get lost in the 'project space'. Those who observed the changes in Windows Explorer, for example, would notice a *thumbnails view* feature that allows the user to put pictures on folders as a reminder of the content of the folder. Thumbnails view is also generated automatically for folders that contain images by displaying the thumbnails of the images on the folder image. Users do not need to browse the folder to see its content as viewing

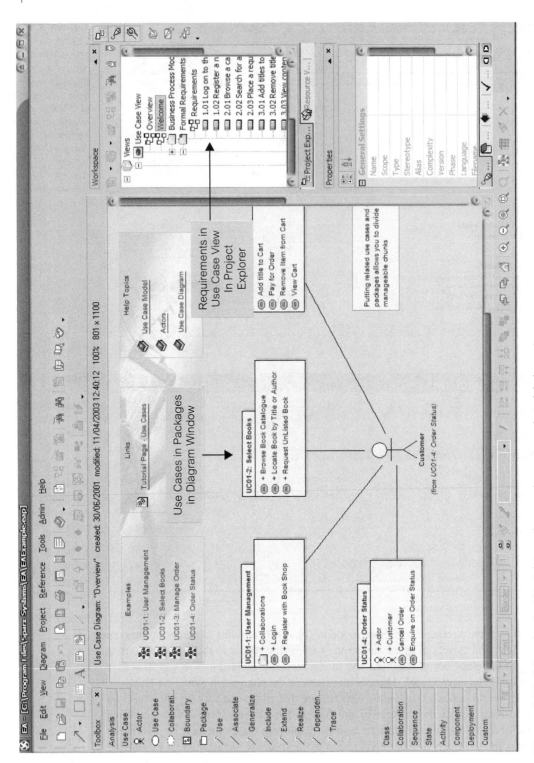

Figure 3.13 Enterprise Architect: integrating requirements and model elements

Source: Screenshot of Enterprise Architect from www.sparxsystems.com.au, August 2003, reproduced by kind permission of Sparx Systems Pty Ltd

the thumbnails already gives a good idea of its content. A similar approach can be incorporated into modeling tools to avoid unnecessary traversal of diagrams and simply to remind the designer about the content of the diagram.

Short of implementing thumbnails or similar techniques, grouping the related requirements and model elements into UML packages (possibly into various levels of packages) can greatly enhance the manageability of the system. Figure 3.13 shows how use cases can be grouped into packages and shown graphically while at the same time linking to requirements in a tree browser window. The example is from Sparx Systems' Enterprise Architect (Sparx, 2003).

Visual UML Modeling   3.2.2

Tools for visual **UML modeling** range from simple graphics-only tools to repository-based tools supporting teamwork and allowing customization of graphical representations. The most sophisticated tools have a repository set up on a commercial database, provide complete integration of models, interface to other software engineering tools, support multiple versions of design artifacts and models, generate code for a variety of programming languages and databases, etc. All these issues are addressed in detail in relevant chapters of this book.

Visual UML modeling tools are quite similar in the GUI presentation aspect. They consist of the graphical modeling area and the corresponding toolbox of modeling elements. A navigational (Explorer-style) browser window assists in navigation between different diagrams and modeling concepts within the project. There is some sort of a documentation window to allow text descriptions for modeling elements. Context-sensitive specification windows can be launched to enter detailed specifications (including text descriptions) for modeling elements. All diagrams and specifications are stored in a single repository for multi-user access by developers.

Figure 3.14 is an example of UML modeling workspace provided by IBM Rational Rose (Rational, 2003). The window displays design elements of one of this book's minicases – the Time Logging System (TLS). Although this may not be obvious from the figure, the presented class diagram was obtained by reverse engineering the Java program into the Rose model. The Class Specification window is for the `IFReader` interface visible in the upper right part of the diagram. The Operation Specification window is for the `readEmployee()` operation of `IFReader`.

Figure 3.15 confirms that GUI aspect of the UML modeling tools are quite similar. All tools provide a navigational browser, the model drawing area, and repository specification windows. The example in Figure 3.15 presents the visual modeling workspace of Gentleware's Poseidon (Gentleware, 2003). Poseidon is based on ArgoUML (ArgoUML, 2003). An interesting feature of Poseidon is that it maintains the design documentation with the model in tabbed-paged windows (in the lower part of the workspace). This technique allows entering repository information simultaneously with creation of graphical elements, without a need to launch separate repository windows like in Rational Rose.

In Poseidon, the visibility, understandability and manipulation of diagrams is facilitated by a meaningful use of color and by providing an overview window to assess the size of the entire diagram. The graph overview window is visible in the left bottom corner in

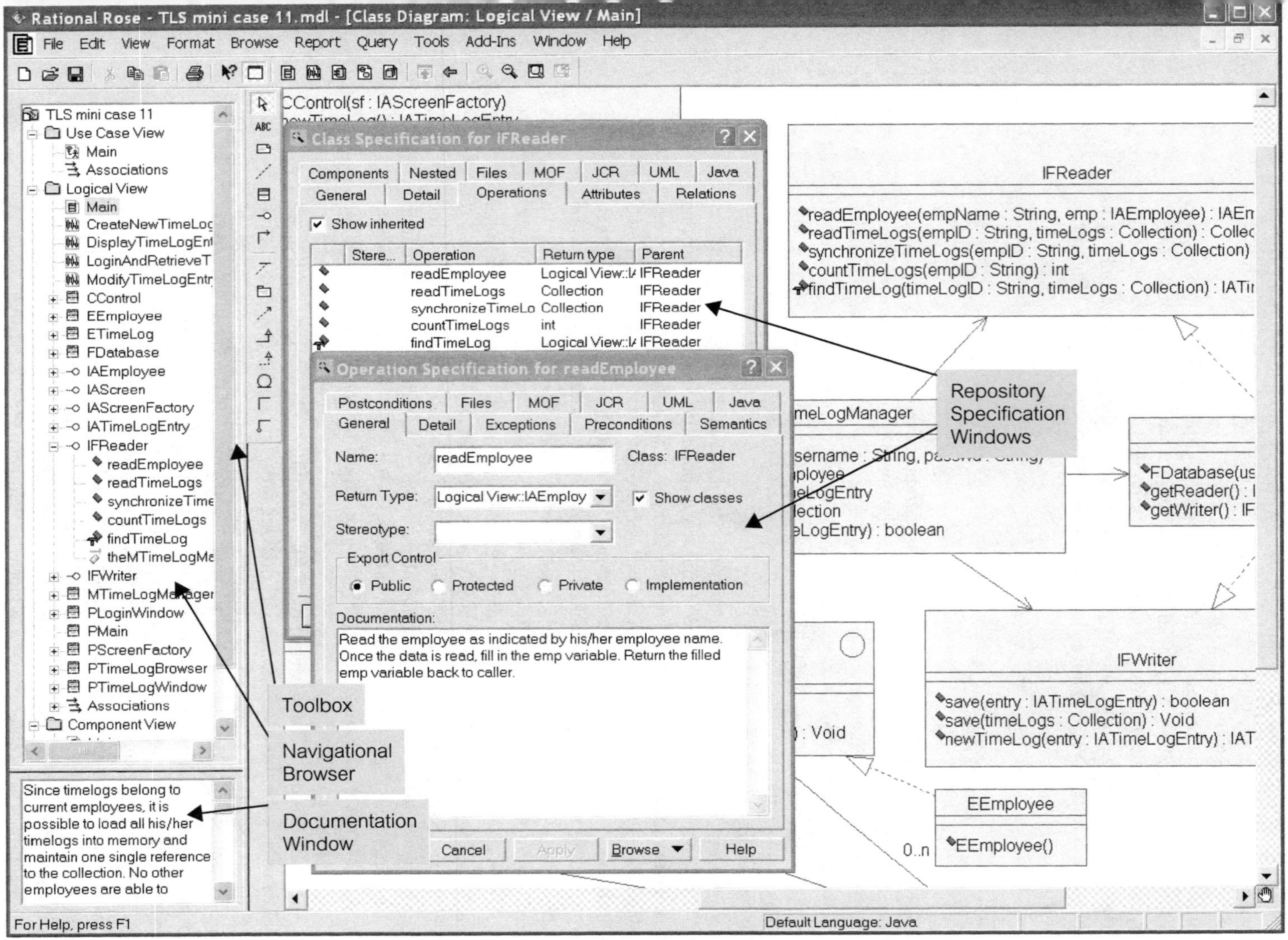

Figure 3.14 IBM Rational Rose: visual modeling workspace

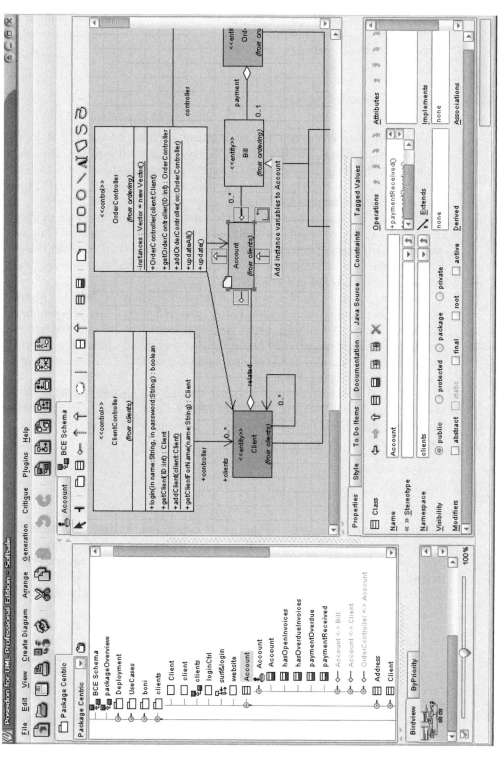

Figure 3.15 Gentleware's Poseidon visual modeling workspace

Source: Screenshot of Gentleware's Poseidon Sales Application model, August 2003, reproduced by kind permission of Gentleware AG

Figure 3.15. The overview window has two tabs – for a 'bird's-eye view' of the model and by priority of modeling elements. The overview window is a distinctive help when working with large models.

3.2.3 Report Generation

Visual modeling dominates software development activities, on par only with programming and testing. These are also the most teamwork-oriented activities. It is, therefore, essential that visual models and related documentation are easily viewable and shareable among all project stakeholders, not just developers. This is where the **report generation** capabilities come in handy.

Reports can be generated according to various templates and various file formats. Good tools support a range of predefined document templates and allow creation of user-defined templates. The templates determine the structure of documents. The content can also be defined by the users who can specify which models and modeling elements should be included or excluded from generation.

File formats usually supported by modeling tools include HTML, Microsoft Word, and/or Acrobat's pdf. Because external tools exist to convert easily between these three formats, the support for all formats in a tool is not essential. The issue that matters more is if the report should be generated for viewing/browsing on the Internet or for printing. A tool generating HTML files should give an option to generate HTML reports to one screen, thus allowing for convenient printing.

Figure 3.16 demonstrates two reports generated by separate modeling tools: No Magic's MagicDraw (Nomagic, 2003) and IBM Rational SODA (Rational, 2003). The former is in the HTML file format aimed for browsing by the user. The latter is in the Microsoft Word format aimed at printing.

3.2.4 Database Modeling

Database modeling requires a unique set of capabilities. Although high-level database models can be developed using UML class diagrams, specific logical/physical models require referencing tables, not classes. Database-specific concepts, not known to UML, include also referential integrity, indexes, stored procedures, triggers. Moreover, there are differences between different database management systems that must be considered when the designs are used for code generation.

Figure 3.17 shows a visual modeling workspace of a database modeling tool PowerDesigner from Sybase (Sybase, 2003). Like in UML modeling tools, the workspace contains a navigational browser window and a drawing window with a floatable palette of applicable modeling elements. The diagram shows relational database tables and referential integrity relationships between them. Database modeling tools integrate with various database management systems. It is possible to generate schema code as well as code for triggers and stored procedures. Some tools also support generation of test data. Reverse engineering from a database to graphical models is also supported.

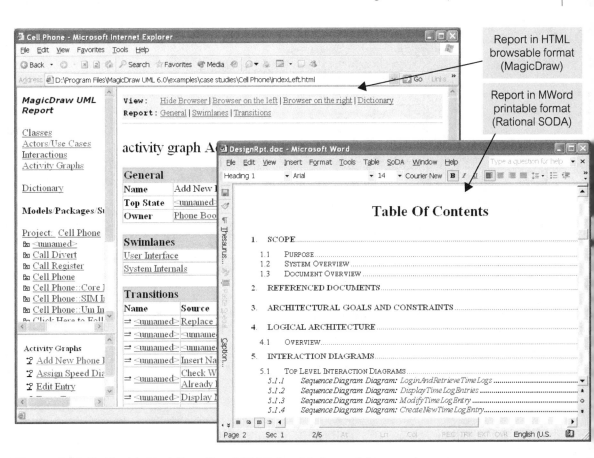

Figure 3.16 No Magic's MagicDraw™ and IBM Rational Suite: modeling reports
Source: MagicDraw case study (Nomagic, 2003), Screenshot of No Magic's MagicDraw, © Copyright No Magic, Inc., reproduced with Permission. All Rights Reserved; Screenshot of *IBM Rational Suite* reprinted by permission from *Rational Suite Tutorial, Version 2002.05.00*, © Copyright 2002 by International Business Machines Corporation. All Rights Reserved

The example in Figure 3.17 refers to the book's Email Management (EM) case-study. The presented diagram is part of the model used in Iteration 3 of EM case study (Part 4 of the book). Although not shown here, PowerDesigner has also UML modeling capability which allows the generation of a UML class diagram from a logical/physical database model. The reverse mapping is possible as well. It is possible to generate a database model from a UML class diagram (although the model would have to be further elaborated to define database-specific properties).

Integrated Development Environments

Software programming environments are commonly called **integrated development environments** (IDEs). IDEs automate many tedious programming processes and allow developers to focus on more important issues. Standard capabilities of IDEs include code

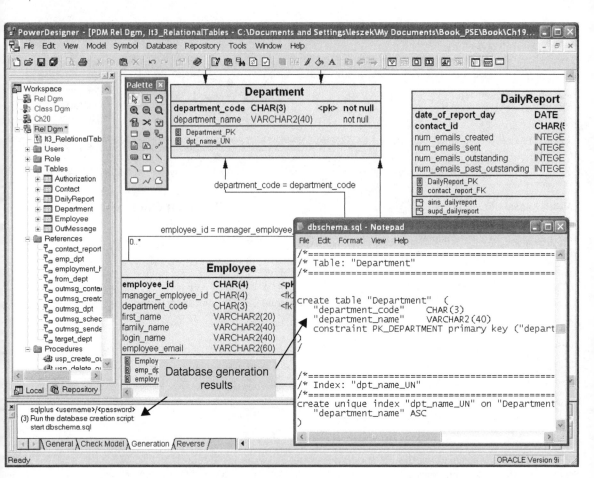

Figure 3.17 Sybase PowerDesigner: visual modeling workspace

Source: Screenshot of Sybase® PowerDesigner® version 9.5, from www.sybase.com, July 2003, © Copyright 2002, Sybase, Inc

completion, support for programming standard features (code auditing), integration with the build tools such as Ant or make, etc. This section, like the rest of the book, discusses Java-related programming environments. Nevertheless, much of the discussion applies to other environments as well.

Although IDEs converge in standard features, there are still differences between the tools. Some differences relate to the integration of IDEs with other software engineering tools, in particular with the modeling tools (Section 3.2) and with the tools supporting teamwork (change and configuration management tools) (Section 3.4). Also, different IDE vendors target different developer markets. IDEs can be distinguished with regard to the following features:

- integration with software modeling
- support for the scope and nature of application development
- integration with distributed development environments and with change and configuration management tools.

As UML becomes the standard modeling language, its support and availability in IDEs become important. UML designs provide programmers with abstractions necessary to view software under development in different and more understandable perspectives. This is important as it is not uncommon for the programmers to get trapped in details of a particular functionality and lose the overall perspective.

Java technologies are released by platforms. The notion of platform is used to signify the support given for the scope and nature of application development domain. The main kinds of **Java technologies** are (Java, 2003):

- Java 2 Platform, Standard Edition (J2SE)
- Java 2 Platform, Enterprise Edition (J2EE)
- Java 2 Platform, Micro Edition (J2ME).

The J2SE types of IDE address rapid application development and integration in the cycle design–develop–deploy. IDEs in this category provide an essential set of tools for program editing and compiling and APIs for writing, deploying, and running Java applets and applications.

The J2EE types of IDE provide a wide range of tools to ease the development of enterprise-level software. IDEs in this category usually integrate with existing application servers and are capable of generating the configurations needed to deploy the application into an application server. This is the foundation technology for web services. It aims at implementation of interoperable business applications.

Many IDEs to support development of embedded applications are becoming available on the market with the more recent introduction of J2ME. Development of a J2ME application requires a unique set of tools to support resource-constrained and highly optimized runtime environments in devices and consumer products, such as mobile phones, personal digital assistants, or in-car navigation systems.

Open-source and component software requires a distributed programming environment. Developers are frequently in dispersed locations. Teamwork activities between developers need to be centrally controlled by tools to allow synchronization of work and speedy software development. To assist in this kind of development, IDEs need to be integrated with change and configuration management tools.

The boundaries between market segments are fading as IDEs support richer combinations of features. It is not uncommon to see an enterprise programming environment that has UML support as well as capability to develop embedded software or a database-driven IDE that integrates with roundtrip engineering with Java.

Routine Programming Tasks 3.3.1

A universal purpose of every IDE is to help developers to write programs fast and avoid errors. To this end, an IDE provides a friendly graphical workspace for all typical programming tasks. This section and its subsections demonstrate how routine programming tasks are performed in Sun ONE Studio environment (Sun ONE, 2003), previously known as Forte for Java IDE. Sun ONE Studio is developed on top of open-source software called NetBeans. Other IDEs have similar capabilities.

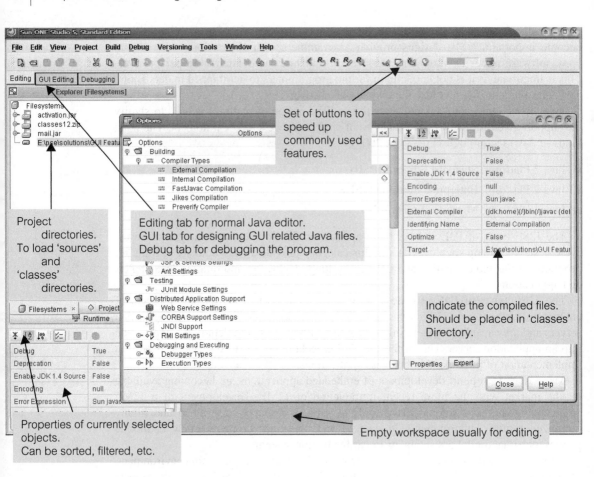

Figure 3.18 Sun ONE Studio: development workspace
Source: Sun Microsystems, Inc

Figure 3.18 shows a typical IDE development workspace – Sun ONE Studio in this case. To start programming, a set of project files need to be loaded to a 'source' directory (where all the source files will be placed), and to a 'target' directory (where the compiled files will go). Prior to loading, some settings have to be configured to inform IDE how to locate/place the files.

Writing the program

Modern IDEs are equipped with wizards to guide the developer through various tasks, including creation of Java files. Figure 3.19 shows a wizard window for creating a new Java source file. The class name is `HelloWorld`. The class will be placed in the package `pkg`. The class declaration, which is based on the option chosen in 'Access Level', indicates that it is a `public` class.

Figure 3.20 presents a resulting Java file with blank methods ready for the programmer to edit. The standard text editor has the following capabilities:

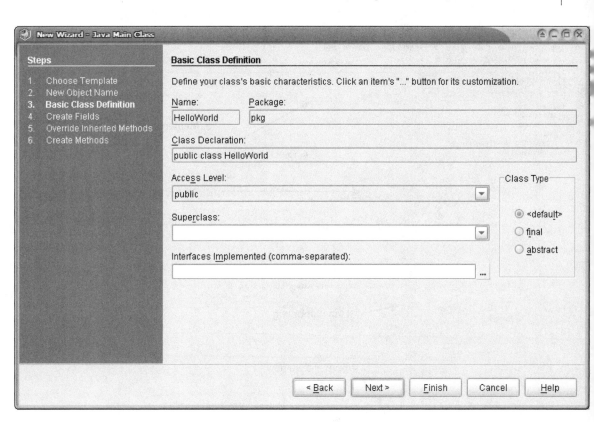

Figure 3.19 Sun ONE Studio: file creation wizard
Source: Sun Microsystems, Inc

- Line numbering, which helps programmers to figure out where they are and, in case of error, get to the line number quickly.

- Syntax highlighting that helps a programmer to identify which word is a keyword, variable, comment, string, space, etc. (usually the use of color is customizable).

- Indication if a particular file has been modified or not. This eliminates a need to click through multiple files to find out whether something has been changed in them.

- A quick navigation toolbar to help jump between methods and variables.

- Indication of current cursor (line number and column number) and other indications, such as 'ins' mode (insert mode) as compared to 'ovr' (override) mode.

Editing of a Java source file is easy by having popup tool tips to help programmers in a variety of ways (Figure 3.21). A tool tip can tell what methods are available in the current object invoked (1). Figure 3.21 shows that a programmer is in `System.out` and a set of `println()`s is available (there are many overloaded versions of `println()`, each has different parameters). A tooltip can display the description of current method (2). During editing, it is sometimes useful to bring to the programmer's attention that something is missing, such as the fact that the above method does not have a 'javadoc' tag and

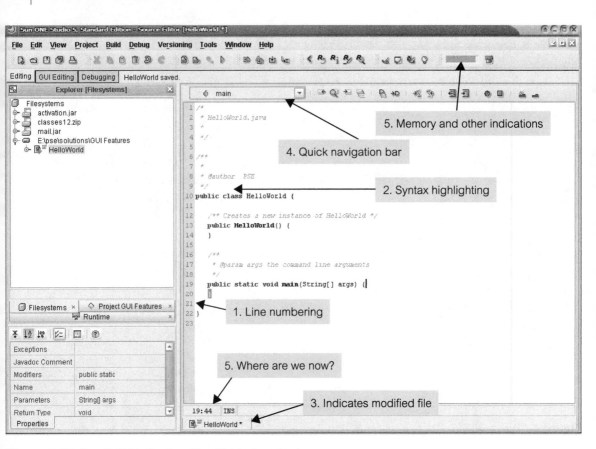

Figure 3.20 Sun ONE Studio: Java file with blank methods
Source: Sun Microsystems, Inc

therefore it will not have a proper documentation when the `javadoc` is executed (to generate the documentation for the project).

A variety of other editing gadgets is also expected to be available. A tool should be able to do all of the following:

■ Automatically fill appropriate arguments for the method once the programmer decides which method to choose. For example, if the programmer chooses `println(boolean)` from the list, then the tool tries to find if there is a readily available `boolean` variable that can be used as the parameter.

■ Fill out the method name once the programmer has chosen the method. This frees the programmer from typing the name of the method.

■ Automatically eliminate unmatched method names from the popup. For example, if the programmer types `System.out.pri` then there is no need to show `flush()`, `clone()`, `toString()`, and other methods as they do not start with the 'pri' string.

■ Automatically move the cursor to the nearest empty spot that requires programmer's attention. For example, the cursor should be moved inside the position of an empty parameter that requires to be typed in by the programmer. That is, if the programmer

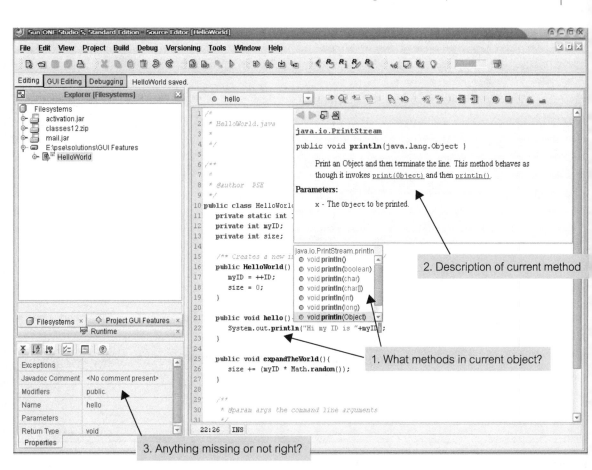

Figure 3.21 Sun ONE Studio: editing made easy. Source: Sun Microsystems, Inc

chooses `println(Object)` from the popup, then the cursor should be moved to `System.out.println(|)` (the | indicates the new position of the cursor).

■ Provide popup tool tip to offer list of methods or variables available on the current workspace (current files or any files under development). This is quite important as there are times when the programmer needs to refer to methods developed in other classes and it is inconvenient to switch back and forth to find the method names or signatures, etc.

■ Provide brace highlighting to indicate to the programmer whether the braces are matched. Brace highlighting should work for function braces (i.e. '`functionName()`') and any other braces, such as '`[]`'.

■ Indicate syntax errors as the programmer types.

Executing the program

Once the program is successfully compiled and linked to libraries, it can execute within an IDE (Figure 3.22). An IDE should support the program's execution by presenting the

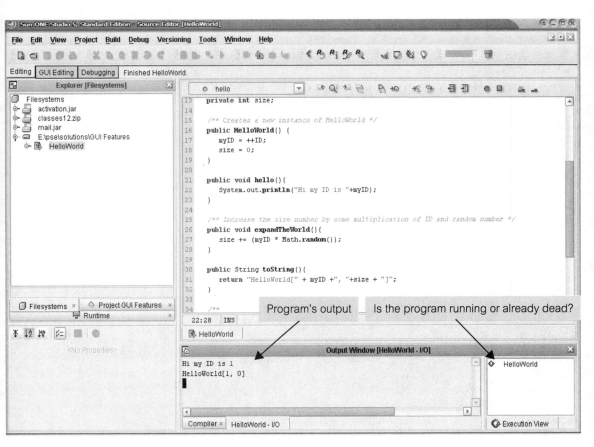

Figure 3.22 Sun ONE Studio: executing the program. Source: Sun Microsystems, Inc

output of the program, by providing (if necessary) a way for the user to give input to the program, and by indicating if the program is running or already dead. Nothing is more annoying than waiting for a long time for a dead program to finish because there is no indication whether it is running in the first place.

Debugging the program

Debugging should be made available in an IDE. Lack of the debugging feature means a nightmare for developers since they will have to rely on a bunch of `println()` statements to achieve an approximate result (not to mention the time wasted to type in the `println()` statements and deleting them when not needed any longer).

An IDE editor usually allows integration with the debugger by setting breakpoints (the debugger will momentarily pause on the breakpoint during program execution) and variable expressions (the value of a variable or expression is displayed during program execution) (Figure 3.23). A simple double-click on the line number usually sets a breakpoint for the current line. Clicking the menu item or toolbar button is another approach to set breakpoints or watch variables.

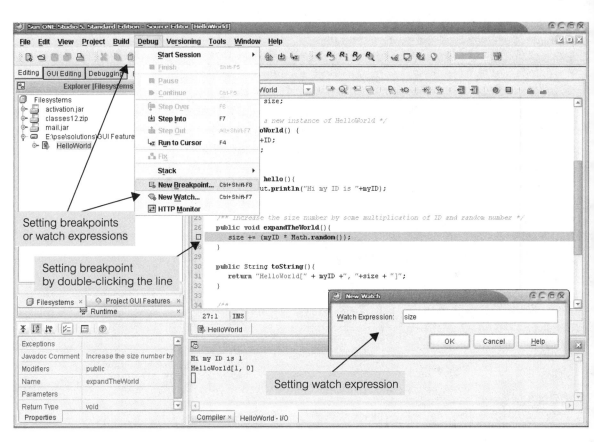

Figure 3.23 Sun ONE Studio: setting the program for debugging
Source: Sun Microsystems, Inc

Figure 3.23 includes a dialog box with the 'size' variable set for watching during program execution. A complex expression can be used in place of the variable, if required. For example, getSizeMult2() is a valid expression in the watch to indicate to the debugger that the programmer wants to be informed regarding the result of the method getSizeMult2() at any time when the debugger is running.

Other features of debugging include:

■ Watching the HTTP 'post' and 'get' requests from a client (if the debugger is running on a web server).

■ Checking the stack trace window of a hierarchy object calling graph.

■ 'Run to cursor' to execute program in the debugger and stop when the execution reaches current cursor position.

■ 'Step Into' to start program execution and get into the current method's body.

■ 'Step Out' to fast-forward the execution till the end of the currently executed method and go to the next invocation call.

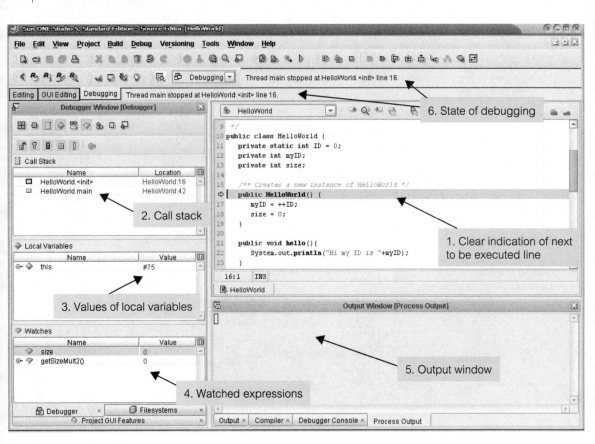

Figure 3.24 Sun ONE Studio: Step Into debugging
Source: Sun Microsystems, Inc

- 'Step Over' to start program execution and 'jump over' the currently executed method. This speeds up the execution if the developer is sure regarding the correctness of the current method and does not feel a need to check it.

- 'Pause' to pause the current debugging session and 'Continue' to continue the paused session. This could be useful, for example, if the program is thread-based and there are currently many threads running concurrently and there is a need to 'freeze' for a while.

- 'Finish' or 'Stop' to bail out of the debugging session altogether.

- Line coloring is important to indicate various breakpoints, current line of invocation, etc.

Figure 3.24 shows a result of 'Step Into' debugging. The debugger stepped into the active method (which is HelloWorld()). It then stopped on the method definition line waiting for the user's next instruction. Figure 3.24 points to the following issues:

- Clear indication of the next-to-be-executed line. The debugger stepped into this line from a statement new HelloWorld(), not visible on the current display.

- Clear indication of the call stack (i.e. the hierarchical nature of objects called) and other information (line number, etc).
- Some information regarding the currently executing method, what's the value of its parameters, etc.
- What are the values for all 'watches'? Show whether they have values or are not applicable in current context.
- As usual, the output window to see what is going on in terms of the program's results.
- Some other information to inform the developer about the state of the debugger.

Integration with Software Modeling 3.3.2

The coming together of software engineering tools is particularly evident in the inclusion of **UML modeling** capabilities in IDEs. This trend is also visible in the other direction, but it is less strong. An outcome of the integration is a teamwork environment facilitating communication and collaboration using synchronized graphical models and code. The developer can work on a model or watch automatic changes in the code, or vice versa.

A popular tool that integrates modeling and coding is Borland's Together ControlCenter (Borland, 2003) (Figure 3.25). This is a fully fledged UML diagramming tool that supports automatic forward and reverse engineering (roundtrip engineering) between code and model. The developed model can be analyzed for its pattern conformance, for example with the Gang of Four (GoF) patterns (Gamma *et al.*, 1995). Figure 3.25 shows a UML model with a code editor where actions performed on the model are immediately reflected in the code.

Enterprise Application Development 3.3.3

A software programming environment is qualified to be considered an enterprise IDE when it specifically allows the design, development, and deployment of J2EE applications. J2EE applications range from development of simple Enterprise JavaBeans (EJB) with Bean-Managed Entity Persistent beans (BMP) or Container-Managed Entity Persistent beans (CMP) to the development of JSP, Servlet and web services.

Integration with an application server (where the beans will be placed) is a core feature of this type of IDE. The knowledge required by the developers to successfully develop and deploy a J2EE application is considerable. Typically a development of J2EE application will have the following sequence:

1. Design components required for the application (does the application need JSP, HTML, Servlet, BMP/CMP, etc.?).
2. Develop the 'skeletons' of components via wizards' point-and-click facilities.
3. Fill the logic of the component.
4. Test the component.
5. Generate a deployment configuration for the application.

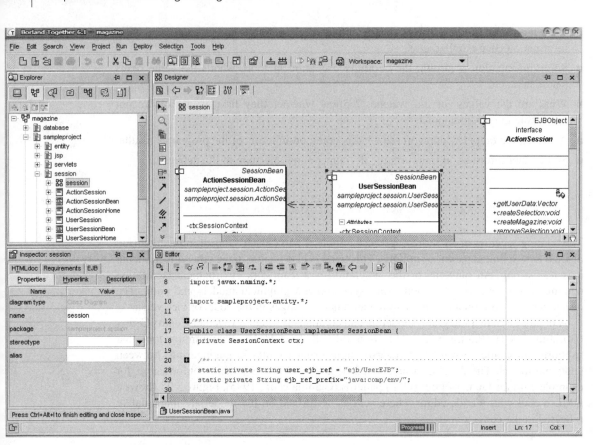

Figure 3.25 Borland Together ControlCenter: integration of UML modeling and programming

Source: Screenshot of *Borland* ® *Together* ® *ControlCenter* ® example (2003), www.borland.com, reprinted by permission of Borland Software Corporation

Component testing requires the IDE to provide either internal or external support for testing. Internally, the IDE could have a test application server optimized for standard testing features, such as variable monitoring, thread tracing, etc. Externally, the IDE could have a remote debugger and tester to allow execution of the application in a pre-existing application server.

The Email Management (EM) case-study discussed in this book was developed as an enterprise J2EE application. One of the main tools used in the programming phase was Sun ONE Studio. Figure 3.26 shows the Sun One Studio workspace as used during a GUI editing of the EM class PWindow (Part 4 of the book).

An enterprise-strength IDE is expected to support various templates to get a job done quickly, including templates for JSP, EJB, Java files, web services, etc. Multiple GUI types should be supported. Changes in the GUI should be reflected immediately in the code allowing rapid application development (RAD) of visual applications. Database connectivity should be JDBC-compliant and allow reverse engineering of pre-existing database tables into entity beans ready to be deployed on an application server.

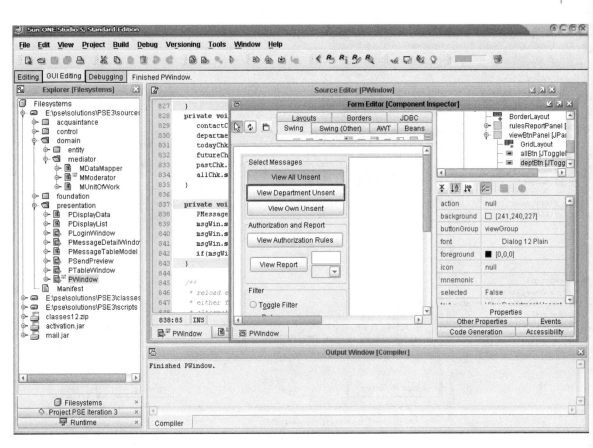

Figure 3.26 Sun ONE Studio for J2EE development
Source: Sun Microsystems, Inc

Integration with Business Components   3.3.4

Development of a J2EE application can be further enhanced with the appropriate support for a business components framework. **Business components** constitute the middle tier of a multi-tier system architecture. This is a tier between the application GUI and the application data in a database. Business components are best deployed on a separate server – an application server.

One such J2EE development tool targeting business components is Oracle JDeveloper (Oracle, 2003). It supports standard Java development as well as development of enterprise applications to be deployed on a not-necessarily Oracle-based infrastructure. It is tightly integrated with Oracle's Business Components for Java (BC4J) that allows development of database back-end applications (Chapter 22).

BC4J provides business-tier building blocks to integrate with any JDBC-compliant database. Reverse engineering of database tables is a matter of point-and-click. Linking between application (so-called Views) and database tables is done in XML-based configuration files. Both JDBC and SQLJ technologies can be used to communicate with

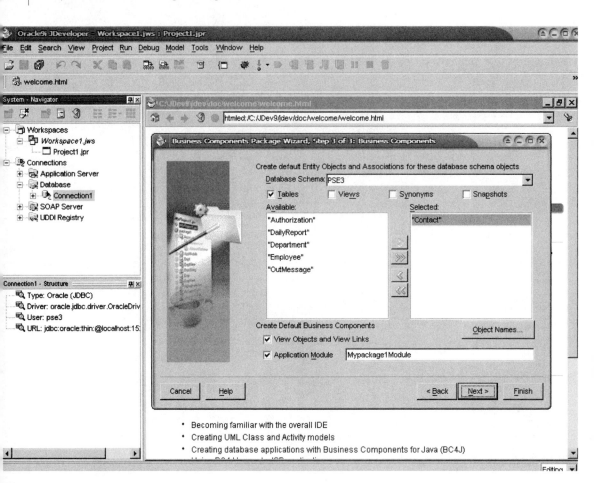

Figure 3.27 JDeveloper in developing a BC4J application
Source: Screenshot of Oracle JDeveloper from www.otn.oracle.com, reproduced by permission of Oracle Corporation

databases. During the development of BC4J components, JDeveloper uses its internal Oracle Container for Java (OC4J) – a subset of Oracle Application Server that handles EJB and database related issues.

Development of a database back-end application is usually performed in the following sequence:

1. Reverse engineer pre-existing database schema/tables (this is included in the wizard for BC4J).

2. Generate a set of views that reflect the database tables.

3. Customize the views to apply business logic.

A simple application browser with BC4J implementation is shown in Chapter 22 (Figure 22.2). Figure 3.27 shows a step to generate BC4J from existing database schema (PSE3 in this case). After a successful connection to the database, the wizard will use the database definitions of tables, views, synonyms, and snapshots to generate GUI views (application windows).

Integration with Change and Configuration Management 3.3.5

The next section, Section 3.4, discusses change and configuration management tools indispensable for collaborative development and necessary for system maintenance. Industry-strength IDEs must support multi-developer work and they have built-in team-work features. **Teamwork** capabilities are frequently achieved by linking to independent change and configuration management tools. Typically, the integration is so transparent that the IDE looks and feels like it is also a change and configuration management tool. In some cases, change and configuration management capabilities are an inherent part of an IDE.

In programming circles, a configuration management tool is frequently considered synonymous with a version control system (VCS). Undoubtedly, **version control** is the dominant component of configuration management, but a full-blown configuration management tool embraces artifacts modeled in all lifecycle phases. Many VCSs are concerned only with the programming code.

One of the most comprehensive IDEs based on Eclipse open-source software (Eclipse, 2003), IBM's WebSphere Studio Application Developer (WSAD) (IBM, 2003) integrates team programming, configuration management, and version control. It integrates with Concurrent Versions Systems (CVS) and comes packaged with IBM Rational ClearCase LT (CCLT).

As seen in Figure 3.28, Sun ONE Studio provides integration to a range of VCSs, one of which is Perforce (Perforce, 2003). Perforce and any other VCS works on a project basis. A depot (or repository) specifies the location of documents managed by Perforce. Users can connect to Perforce to add, edit or delete a document (program). The system

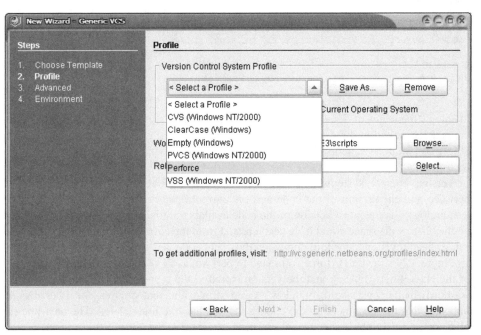

Figure 3.28
Sun ONE Studio: version control integration
Source: Sun Microsystems, Inc

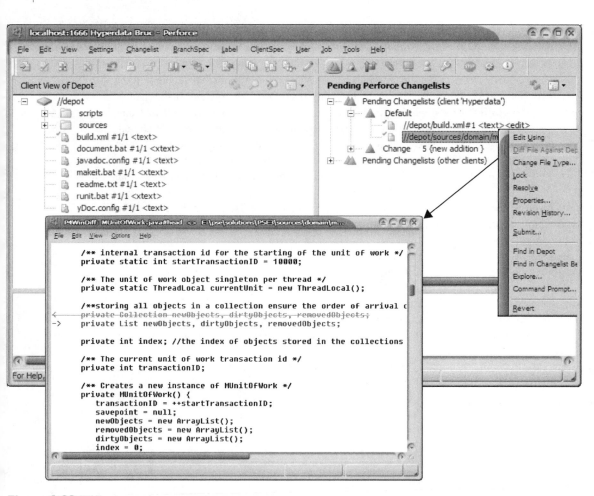

Figure 3.29 Perforce: version comparison
Source: Screenshot of Perforce, from www.perforce.com, reproduced by kind permission of Perforce Software, Inc

maintains the states of documents checked out to the user's work space. Such documents are usually locked in the depot. When the user has finished working with the document, s/he may want to synchronize (or check in) the document and therefore update the repository.

Version control systems provide graphical 'diff' tools to perform comparisons between a client version of the code and the current *head revision*, which – in Perforce terminology – is the latest version of the code available on the server (depot). The version on the client workspace could have been created from the current head revision or from an earlier head revision, depending on when the client code was checked out from the depot.

Figure 3.29 shows a Perforce command to perform a 'diff' between a client's revision of the class MUnitOfWork and the version stored in the repository. The result of 'diff' is shown in the overlapping window. A red stroke line that crosses one line of code indicates that the document on the client's version has one line deleted. The next line (in blue and pointed to by a side arrow) is a new statement in the code.

Change and Configuration Management Tools

Although, technically, change and configuration management are distinct, in practice both are always integrated. A **change management tool** records changes that have occurred during the software lifecycle. Change management is particularly prominent in the implementation–testing cycle when defects encountered necessitate changes in the code. However, recording just changes without maintaining the history of changes is not sustainable in practice. There is a need to keep track of various versions of development artifacts, including versions of the same artifact developed by different developers, so that old versions can be brought alive again when needed. **Version control** is the domain of **configuration management tools**.

Unified activities of change and configuration management can be explained in the following typical sequence of steps (Rational, 2002):

1. A developer joins the project by logging in to the tools and the project repository. This creates a **private workspace** on the developer's workstation from which the developer gains access to the **public workspace** (database) of artifacts available to the team.

2. A private workspace of a developer consists of a development view and a development stream. A *view* consists of one version of each artifact in the developer's workspace. A *stream* (or configuration) is a current set of versions for which the development activities are tracked by the configuration management tool.

3. *Activities* to be performed by a developer are entered into the repository via the change management tool. They can be retrieved by the developer to create a to-do list.

4. The developer *checks out* the artifacts to the private workspace. While performing activities on checked-out objects, the configuration management tool maintains a *change set* (the list of modified artifacts).

5. The developer *checks in* the (modified) artifacts to the public workspace. The changes to artifacts become visible to the team upon declaring them as *delivered*. The delivery of changes relates to the whole change set. A more sophisticated tool would allow collaboration between developers for proposed changes to be discussed so that any conflicts between versions delivered by different developers can be resolved.

6. Subject to a managerial decision, change sets delivered by the development team can be made into a new *baseline* (or *build*) – a consistent set of product and process artifacts that creates a new common continuation point for the project team. New baselines can be established frequently, even daily.

7. Baselines undergo the scrutiny of quality control and assurance and can be *promoted* to *recommended baselines*. A recommended baseline is used to *rebase* the development streams of developers so that they can work from the current recommended baseline.

Support for Changes

One of the most important truths of software engineering is that changes to or within a project must be managed, for otherwise the changes will 'manage' the project. Change is omnipresent. The whole project management is a form of **change management**. Changes to a project can be due to external or internal project conditions (budget, resources, competition, etc.). They can be due to changes in user requirements. They are also due to defects in software and to necessary software enhancements (future features). The reasons abound.

Change management tools provide facilities to support the change process. The change process itself should be defined in a workflow that the change management tool implements. Technically, a **workflow** can be modeled as a statechart diagram (Section 2.2.4). A workflow defines sequences of activities and *transition* states for all well-defined *initial* states in order to arrive at one or more *final* states. There can be many workflows created for various initial states.

Workflow management is a discipline in its own right. A change management tool can integrate with a workflow management tool or it can have intrinsic ways of specifying possible workflows. These intrinsic ways may or may not allow generating and printing of workflow documents. The workflows may be just implemented by allowing/disallowing state transitions that the developer can perform depending on the current state of the artifact undergoing change. The transitions are allowed or disallowed subject to the current

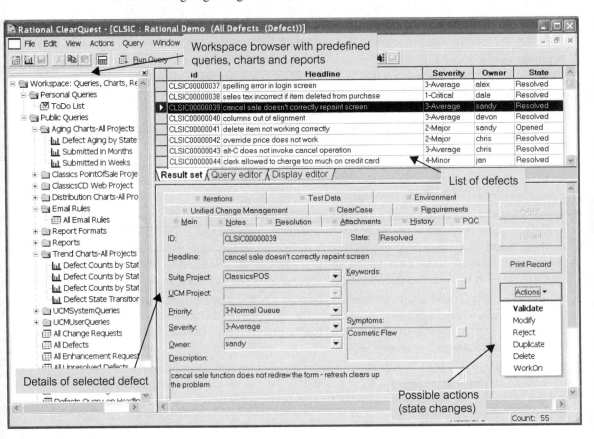

Figure 3.30 IBM Rational ClearQuest: managing defects

Source: Screenshot of *IBM Rational Suite* reprinted by permission from *Rational Suite Tutorial*, Version 2002.05.00, © Copyright 2002 by International Business Machines Corporation. All Rights Reserved

status of the artifact (unconfirmed, assigned, reopened, etc.) and possible status of resolution, if any (fixed, invalid, duplicate) (Bugzilla, 2003).

Figure 3.30 shows a screenshot from a change management tool IBM Rational ClearQuest (Rational, 2003). The screenshot relates to management of **defects**. It lists all the defects submitted to the system and allows viewing and manipulating the details of a selected defect. The defect shown in the figure is in a `Resolved` state. When in this state, the change workflow definition permits actions (state transitions) as shown in the dropdown list in the lower right corner of the display.

Apart from the state, each defect is characterized by additional properties, such as priority, severity, owner, etc. The tool gives a possibility of searching for defects with certain properties and generating various reports and charts. The workspace browser contains system and user-predefined queries, charts, and reports. The developer can specify personal queries, such as the `ToDo List` in Figure 3.30.

Figure 3.31 demonstrates a predefined trend chart for current project defects. The chart shows defect counts by their states: submitted, resolved, opened, assigned, and closed. The counts are obtained for each day in a two-week period.

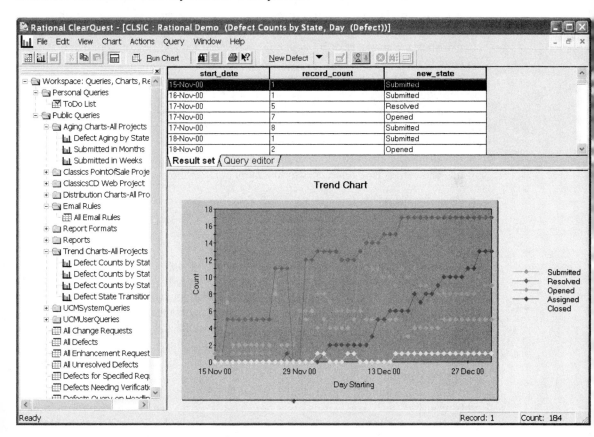

Figure 3.31 IBM Rational ClearQuest: defect trend chart

3.4.2 Support for Versions

Configuration management is tightly related to change management. The main task of configuration management is to maintain the history of changes. The history consists of *versions* of product and process artifacts. A configuration management system has an internal facility to maintain various **version derivation graphs**. The graphs allow tracking of changes applied to an artifact as well as composing versions of various objects to create a higher-level *configuration* of versions.

Developers need to know what changes have been made to an artifact they currently work on. As an example, an interesting question that always arises throughout development lifecycle is 'When did we inadvertently introduce this bug?' Answering such a question requires tracing through the set of changes made to the software to pinpoint the version where the bug was introduced. Finding the cause of the problem gives a hope for unraveling the situation.

Another situation when 'knowing the changes' is important occurs when the developer is ready to check in the work to the public workspace (database repository). At some point – prior, during, or after the check-in – there is a need to compare the differences between the current version of the artifact and a version registered for the public. Such comparisons are made easy by *compare-and-merge* capabilities of configuration management tools.

In some situations, the compare-and-merge action is performed in the background, but configuration management tools provide also GUI facilities for graphical comparisons, complete with highlighting of differences. Figure 3.32 shows a merge facility of Visual SourceSafe from Microsoft (Microsoft, 2003b). The facility uses color to highlight differences in lines of code between two versions being compared. Additional lines of code are represented in green, while modified lines are in red. Comparison is usually done side by side and can include references to line numbers (not shown in the figure).

3.4.3 Support for System Building

'**System building** is the process of compiling and linking software components into a program which executes on a particular target configuration' (Sommerville, 2001, p.655). The ultimate aim of system building is to create a **distributable** – an executable version of software that can be distributed to its users. The main challenge in system building is to adhere to all dependencies between software components and their various versions and to resolve all references to data files. The process of building specifies also the tools to be used in successive build (make) tasks.

System building facilities are always integrated into configuration management tools and, therefore, naturally extend IDEs (Section 3.3.5, Figure 3.29). There are many build tools available, such as `make` or `gnumake`, but a favorite among Java-based build tools must be considered to be Apache Ant (Another Neat Tool) (Apache, 2003). Apache Ant is particularly useful for building systems that work across multiple platforms.

Ant **configuration files** (also called **build files**) are written in XML and can be extended using Java classes. Build files call out a target tree containing build tasks. Targets

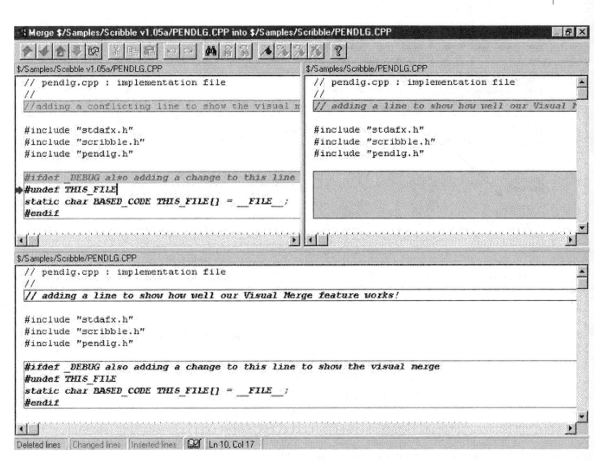

Figure 3.32 Microsoft SourceSafe: merging differences between versions

Source: Screenshot of Microsoft® Visual SourceSafe from http://msdn.microsoft.com/ssafe/default.asp (2003), reprinted by permission from Microsoft Corporation, Copyright © 1998–2003 Microsoft Corporation

can depend on each other, such that a target to make a distributable depends on a target to compile the code.

Figure 3.33 is an example of using Apache Ant within Sun ONE Studio. The left panel shows a `build.xml` as the current Ant file visible in the main window. Inside `build.xml`, there are a number of Ant tasks registered (init, compile, jar, all, clean, javadoc, etc.). Each of these tasks can be executed directly from the IDE. The example demonstrates that an Ant file is an XML-style document. The document consists of XML tags identifiable to the Ant processor.

The 'project' tag signifies the highest element in Ant. In Figure 3.33, this is `"EMS Iteration 3"` with the base directory of `"."` (current directory). When this project is processed by the Ant processor, and the task name is not specified prior to the processing, the processor will execute the task labeled on the default property (currently it is `"all"`).

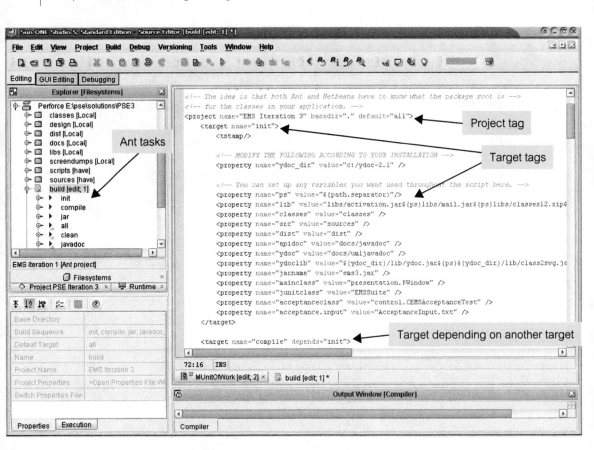

Figure 3.33 Sun ONE Studio and Apache Ant: system building
Source: Sun Microsystems, Inc

Each Ant task starts with a tag called 'target', such as `"init"` or `"compile"`. The `"init"` target is used as the base for other targets by setting the initial properties of the project. A target may rely on other targets to achieve its job. In Figure 3.33, the target `"compile"` depends on `"init"`. This dependence forces Ant to execute the `"init"` target before the `"compile"` target.

3.4.4 Support for Reengineering

The greatest battle of software engineering, yet to be won, is the automatic recovery of the designs present in existing legacy systems in order to reimplement them in a new form. A legacy system is a programming solution still in use, typically a large business information system, which was implemented a long time ago in traditional technology and has acquired extensive additional functionality through evolutionary maintenance.

A legacy system is the organization's history which stays from an earlier time but cannot be abandoned or replaced. The organization depends on the system in day-to-day business activities. Evolutionary maintenance done on the system over years has broken its core architectural design. Introduction of new changes is still needed because of growing users' demands and competitive pressures. So, evolutionary maintenance must continue even though changes to the system can bring entirely unpredictable results. There is no one in the organization who understands in detail how the system produces its results.

The organization finds itself in a vicious circle. There is a realization that a brand new system is needed to replace the legacy system. However, the task is overwhelming. The legacy system is not just some information system in the organization – it is the very business of the organization. It cannot be put on a side track while a new system is developed from scratch. Even more importantly, to replace a system means that the functionality of the system must be understood in the first place. In most cases, no documentation exists for the system or the documentation does not match what the system really does. The complexity of the system precludes manual means of discovering (recovering) the system's current design. Automated tools are necessary.

Software reengineering is a branch of knowledge concerned with methods, techniques, and tools for examining and altering legacy systems to recover their designs and re-implement them in a new form. Reengineering consists of a range of technologies:

- reverse engineering
- re-documentation from source code
- restructuring of program logic
- re-targeting the system to a modern platform
- source code translation to another language
- data reengineering (as opposed to process reengineering)
- forward engineering.

The current reality is that legacy systems are predominantly systems programmed in Cobol and accessing pre-relational databases (i.e. network and hierarchical databases). However, the history has a tendency to repeat itself. There is lots of evidence that the systems developed and deployed 'as we speak' become legacy 'the day' they are deployed in organizations. This is true for systems developed in Java and C#, and especially true for developments in C++ where diversions to low-level C programming and procedural (non-object-oriented) coding style are a frequent practice.

The first activity of reengineering is reverse engineering. In the object-oriented world, **reverse engineering** means obtaining UML models from an object-oriented program. There are two main reverse engineering *sources*: the program source code or the program compiled code. The main *target* is a class model.

Most modeling tools provide some kind of reverse engineering. In fact, as discussed in Section 3.3.2, many IDEs allow synchronized development of graphical models and code. This means that these tools have built-in forward and reverse engineering capabilities. More complete reverse engineering allows working with multiple sources and generating more complete UML designs.

Figure 3.34 shows a number of windows that start the process of reverse engineering in MagicDraw (Nomagic, 2003). The *source* is a Java source code (one of this book's case-study programs). The target is a new class diagram.

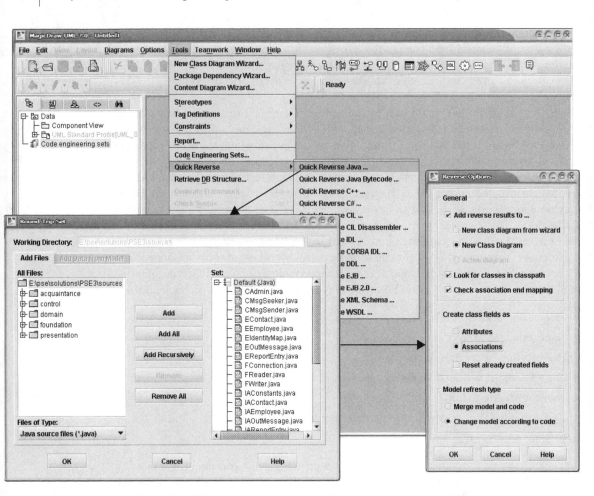

Figure 3.34 No Magic's MagicDraw™ prior to reverse engineering
Source: Screenshot of No Magic's MagicDraw (Prior to Reverse Engineering). © Copyright No Magic, Inc., reproduced with Permission. All Rights Reserved

The result of reverse engineering defined in Figure 3.34 is shown in Figure 3.35. Reversed Java packages and classes are generated into the project browser window. The class model is shown in the 'bird's-eye view' window, which has the zooming capability to present parts of the diagram in a readable form in the main window. As seen, the layout of the diagram requires human intervention to eliminate lines crossing over multiple classes, etc. (this is a universal problem as no 'perfect' automatic layout algorithm exists).

The current state of the art in reverse engineering is such that layout limitations are the least of the worries. On the face of it, the tools seem to be doing a good job, but they still leave much to be desired when reengineering legacy systems. Legacy systems, developed over years by many programmers using various compiler versions, have code fragments that use unusual programming features and unique compiler options. These issues add to the problems in the state of the art, which is incapable of properly reverse engineering certain code features. For example, very few tools can do a satisfactory job in reverse engineering inner classes or relationships based on collections.

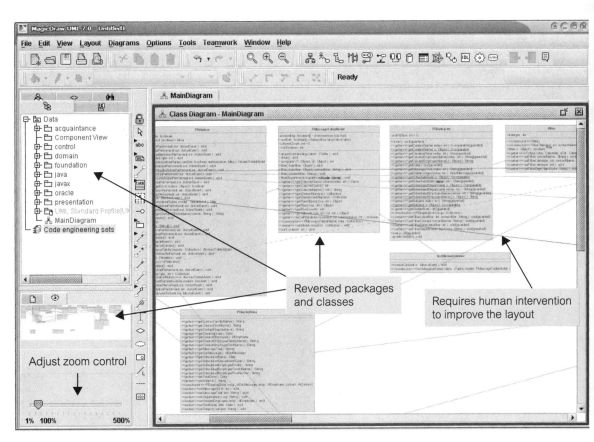

Figure 3.35 No Magic's MagicDraw™ after reverse engineering

Summary

1. Software engineering tools belong to the category of software products known as *computer-supported collaborative work* (CSCW) or *workgroup computing*.

2. Software engineering tools can be classified into four groups: (1) project management tools, (2) system modeling tools (traditionally known as CASE tools), (3) integrated development environments (IDEs), and (4) change and configuration management tools.

3. *Project management tools* are concerned with project scheduling and controlling. However, modern project management tools implement a range of related functions or provide seamless integration to related tools. These related functions are in the areas of performance management, web-based collaboration, content management, portfolio management, metrics, and risk management.

4. *System modeling tools* embrace all tools that assist software engineers in development tasks – from analysis via design to implementation. All modern tools support the UML language. Although they are able to generate code from the models, they normally do not constitute a complete programming environment. System

modeling tools concentrate on requirements management and specification, system design (including database modeling), and generation of reports and design documents.

5. *IDEs* are sophisticated programming workbenches that provide a friendly programming environment to assist teams of programmers in all typical programming tasks. They can greatly improve productivity of programmers in the cycle of writing, executing and debugging programs. Modern IDEs provide integration and connectivity to visual modeling, databases, and sources of business components in an attempt to assist in the development of enterprise applications. They also integrate to change and configuration management tools to ensure smooth collaboration of the entire programming team.

6. *Change and configuration management tools* are really two sides of the same coin. A change management tool records changes that have occurred during the software lifecycle. Change management is prominent in the implementation–testing cycle to allow management of defects revealed by tests. Programming, being a creative activity, results in production of various versions of software components. There is a need to keep track of versions produced by different developers as well as to store past versions in case they need to be revisited. *Version control* is the domain of *configuration management tools*. Change and configuration management tools have facilities to *build* systems that can work on specified target platforms. They can also integrate with reengineering tools to assist in reverse engineering of legacy systems.

Key Terms

build file	*See* configuration file	network graph	65
business components	95	performance management	66
CASE	*See* computer assisted software engineering	PERT	*See* Program Evaluation and Review Technique
change management	100		
change management tools	99	portfolio management	68
collaboration management	67	private workspace	99
computer assisted software engineering	64	Program Evaluation and Review Technique	65
computer-supported collaborative work	63	project management tools	64
configuration file	102	public workspace	99
configuration management	102	report generation	82
configuration management tools	99	requirements	74
content management	68	reverse engineering	105
CPM	*See* critical path method	risk	72
critical path method	65	risk management	72
CSCW	*See* computer-supported collaborative work	scheduling and controlling	65
database modeling	82	software reengineering	105
debugging	90	system building	102
defect	101	teamwork	63, 97
distributable	102	UML modeling	79, 93
evolutionary maintenance	104	version control	97, 99
Gantt chart	65	version derivation graph	102
IDE	*See* integrated development environment	visual modeling	79
integrated development environment	64, 83	visual modeling tools	73
Java technologies	85	workflow	100
legacy system	104	workgroup computing	*See* computer-supported collaborative work
metrics	69		

Review Questions

1. How important is it for project management tools to be web-based? Discuss pros and cons.

2. How do project management tools support the drawing of activity network graphs?

3. How does the inclusion of performance management in a project management tool change the tool's emphasis? Explain.

4. What is content management? How is it used in the context of project management?

5. What is portfolio management? How does it relate to project management?

6. Explain the relationship of metrics to project management?

7. Explain the relationship between risk management and project management?

8. What are the main capabilities expected from a requirements management tool?

9. What is the role of a repository in visual modeling?

10. Is UML sufficient for database modeling? Could it be extended to allow database modeling sufficient for database code generation?

11. Explain the difference in debugging between 'Step Into' and 'Step Out'.

12. Explain the notions of change, version and configuration and how these concepts are related.

13. What is a workflow in change management? How is it defined and expressed?

14. What are the technologies of software reengineering? Explain them briefly.

Problem-Solving Exercises

1. The website addresses of project management tools referred to in this chapter are listed in Table 3.1 below. Visit the websites to learn about the latest developments regarding these tools. If the website link is not valid any more, try to establish what happened to it (to the tool and/or to the vendor). Search the Internet for the latest trends in project management tools and for tools making the headlines. Prepare a list of important tools, with current website addresses and a short list of main features.

Table 3.1 Project management tools referred to in Chapter 3

Tool name	Website address
MS Project (Microsoft, 2003c)	http://www.microsoft.com/office/project/default.asp
Manage Pro (ManagePro, 2003)	http://www.managepro.net/
eRoom (eRoom, 2003)	http://www.eroom.net/eRoomNet/
eProject (eProject, 2003)	http://www.eproject.com/
Primavera Enterprise (Primavera, 2003)	http://www.primavera.com
Small Worlds (SmallWorlds, 2003)	http://www.thesmallworlds.com/
@Risk (Palisade, 2003)	http://www.palisade-europe.com/
Risk Radar (ICE, 2003)	http://www.iceincusa.com/products_tools.htm

2. The website addresses of system modeling tools referred to in this chapter are listed in Table 3.2 below. Visit the websites to learn about the latest developments regarding these tools. If the website link is not valid any more, try to establish what happened to it (to the tool and/or to the vendor). Search the Internet for latest trends in system modeling tools and for tools making the headlines. Prepare a list of important tools, with current website addresses and a short list of main features.

Table 3.2 System modeling tools referred to in Chapter 3

Tool name	Website address
RequisitePro (Rational, 2003)	http://www.rational.com
DOORS (Telelogic, 2003)	http://www.telelogic.com/
Enterprise Architect (Sparx, 2003)	http://www.sparxsystems.com.au/
Rational Rose (Rational, 2003)	http://www.rational.com
Poseidon (Gentleware, 2003)	http://www.gentleware.com/
ArgoUML (ArgoUML, 2003)	http://argouml.tigris.org/
MagicDraw (Nomagic, 2003)	http://www.magicdraw.com/
Rational SODA (Rational, 2003)	http://www.rational.com
PowerDesigner (Sybase, 2003)	http://www.sybase.com/products/enterprisemodeling

3. The website addresses of integrated development environments (IDEs) referred to in this chapter are listed in Table 3.3 below. Visit the websites to learn about the latest developments regarding these tools. If the website link is not valid any more, try to establish what happened to it (to the tool and/or to the vendor). Search the Internet for latest trends in IDEs and for tools making the headlines. Prepare a list of important tools, with current website addresses and a short list of main features.

Table 3.3 IDEs referred to in Chapter 3

Tool name	Website address
Sun ONE Studio (Sun ONE, 2003)	http://wwws.sun.com/software/sundev/jde/
Together ControlCenter (Borland, 2003)	http://www.borland.com/together/
Oracle JDeveloper (Oracle, 2003)	http://otn.oracle.com/products/jdev/content.html
WSAD (IBM, 2003)	http://www-3.ibm.com/software/awdtools/studioappdev/

4. The website addresses of change and configuration management tools referred to in this chapter are listed in Table 3.4 below. Visit the websites to learn about the latest developments regarding these tools. If the website link is not valid any more, try to establish what happened to it (to the tool and/or to the vendor). Search the Internet for latest trends in change and configuration management tools and for tools making the headlines. Prepare a list of important tools, with current website addresses and a short list of main features.

Table 3.4 Change and configuration management tools referred to in Chapter 3

Tool name	Website address
Perforce (Perforce, 2003)	http://www.perforce.com/
Rational Clear Quest (Rational, 2003)	http://www.rational.com
Visual SourceSafe (Microsoft, 2003b)	http://msdn.microsoft.com/ssafe/default.asp
Ant (Apache, 2003)	http://www.apache.org/

5. Search the Internet to learn about Java technologies. What are the main Java technologies? Are they the same as discussed in the book? Are there any new significant technologies not defined in the book?

6. Refer to Figure 3.23. Why did the programmer set the breakpoint on Line 27? What bug does s/he try to fix? Assume that the initial value of `myID` is 1 and `size` is initially 0.

Chapter 4

Software Project Planning and Tracking

Software project planning and tracking, discussed in this chapter, and software process management, discussed in the next chapter, constitute the management aspect of the software engineering pentagon. The distinction between project planning and process management is rather vague. *Software project planning and tracking* is an *ongoing* activity of estimating how much time, money, effort, and resources need to be expended on the project.

Being not just once-off but an ongoing activity, software project planning can be treated as an all-encompassing activity of managing software engineering product and process. In particular, software project planning includes not just scheduling, budgeting and tracking, but also risk analysis, quality assurance, people management, and configuration management. However, for the purpose of this chapter, planning is equivalent to project scheduling and tracking. Related issues are introduced here only if necessary, and elaborated in their own right in Chapter 5.

Interestingly, related issues of risk analysis, quality assurance, configuration management, etc. have a rather multi-project connotation. They apply across multiple projects. This is another reason to separate planning for a single project from the multi-project aspects. These multi-project aspects are discussed in more detail in Chapter 5.

Software project planning starts where strategic planning and business modeling stop. Strategic planning and business modeling decide about an organization's mission, objectives, and goals. These objectives and goals determine the need for software projects.

Project Plan Development

4.1

As argued in Chapter 1, **project planning** is not a separate phase of the development lifecycle. It is an umbrella activity spanning the lifecycle phases. Although some lifecycle models, e.g. RUP (Section 1.3.2), consider planning as the very first activity at the start of the project, they make it clear that this is only initial planning. No reasonable estimates of cost (budget) and time (schedule) are possible until at least user requirements for the project are determined.

Research by Boehm *et al.* (2000) indicates that early planning estimates, after project feasibility studies, can vary up or down by a factor of four compared with real cost/time spent on the project completion. If the real cost/time expended is equal to some value x, then initial estimates could have ranged from $0.25x$ to $4x$. As illustrated in Figure 4.1, successive corrections to plan estimates approximate ever closer to the real value of x. The approximations in Figure 4.1 are just that – approximations. They differ for different projects and they vary from Boehm's original work because of the different lifecycle phases used in Figure 4.1.

Estimating cost/time (budget/schedule) is only one aspect of a software project plan. In practice, a budget/schedule plan can be one of several planning documents. Other documents may include a quality plan, test plan, people development plan, configuration management plan, etc. These may be separate documents or parts of a comprehensive project plan document. Sommerville (2001) recommends the following sections in a typical project plan:

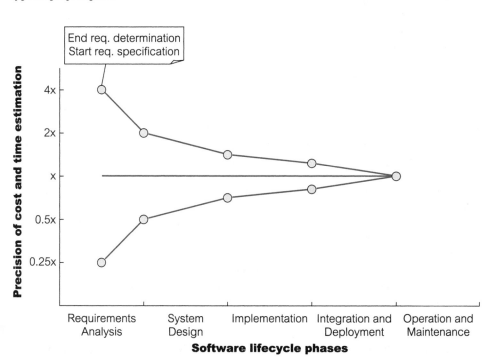

Figure 4.1
Project plan
approximation

1. *Introduction* – to define project objectives and main cost and time constraints.

2. *Project organization* – to describe organization of the development team.

3. *Risk analysis* – to identify risks and the ways of managing them.

4. *Hardware and software resource requirements* – to specify hardware/software needs for the development work.

5. *Work breakdown* – to define project activities, milestones and deliverables.

6. *Project schedule* – to define allocation of time and resources to activities.

7. *Monitoring and reporting mechanisms* – to determine the needs for monitoring mechanisms and management reports.

The steps in developing a software project plan are similar to those needed in other kinds of innovative project (Lientz and Rea, 2002). Figure 4.2 is a UML activity diagram that illustrates the typical sequence of steps.

Project planning starts with the definition of *objectives*, *scope*, and *constraints* for the project. In reality, the project objectives and scope will have been identified prior to project planning (as these are the responsibilities of strategic planning and business modeling). Two typical project constraints are time and money – projects have due dates and limited budgets. Other constraints may relate to the availability of resources, in particular human resources.

Project **deliverables** are software products or services that meet project objectives. Deliverables are delivered to project stakeholders (project owners and users). They need to satisfy user requirements, conform to design specifications, and meet the set quality standards. In contemporary practices of iterative and incremental developments, a project is likely to have multiple deliverables.

Once deliverables are known, the work can be organized in milestones, phases and tasks. This is sometimes called **work breakdown structure**. A **milestone** is a significant event in the project. It marks the end of some process activity and is used to monitor project progress. A milestone is normally used to represent the completion of a deliverable, but a milestone can signify other kinds of project outputs, such as the completion of an important design step. A milestone can also signify the completion of a project **phase** (and a deliverable is typically a result of some closing phase). Projects (and phases) are made up of **tasks**, which are **activities** with a clear beginning and end.

The early steps of project planning concentrate on *the what* of the project. Estimating resource needs is about *the how* of the project – how to carry out the project tasks. **Resources** are people, equipment, materials, supplies, software, hardware, etc. required by project tasks. Estimation of resource needs can be just an initial step in the whole range of planning activities, such as related to staff acquisition and procurement planning.

Establishing the *project team* is an activity driven by human resource needs. It is one thing to know what human resources are needed, but building up a team is quite a different matter. Some team members may come from inside the organization, others need to be hired as full-time employees or as contract people. Building up a good team with complementary skills, the right team spirit, with no personal tensions, and dedicated to the project is one of the most critical challenges for a project manager.

Project planning includes determination of quality standards. **Quality** is a relative term. Quality is in the eye of the beholder. Ultimately, the quality product is a product that satisfies the user. This means a software product that has been delivered on time and within

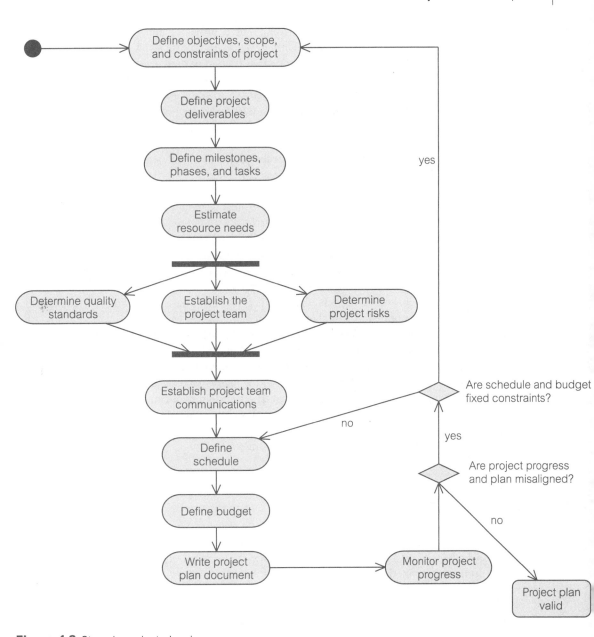

Figure 4.2 Steps in project planning

budget, implements user requirements, is friendly in use, does not fail, etc. Higher quality may mean higher cost. Determination of quality standards must consider the impact of quality policies on project duration and budget, and even on the project scope.

Project planning includes also determination of project risks. **Risks** are adverse events that are frequently difficult to anticipate and, even when identified and known, they may or may not happen. It is a responsibility of a project planner to determine the *risk avoidance* strategies and to define *contingency plans* in case a risk occurs.

Establishing project *team communications* is an important task in all but small projects. In small projects, team members may communicate sufficiently through informal meetings, exchanges of emails, etc. In large projects, team communications must be planned and supported by the technology. The technology solutions include workgroup, time management, configuration management and related software systems capable of exchanging multimedia documents.

The step of defining the **schedule** for the project is about estimation of time needed not only for the development but also for project management, product quality assurance, and risk management. Scheduling includes also allocation of resources to tasks.

The step of defining the **budget** for the project is about estimation of costs required by resources needed for tasks. There are various estimation techniques. None of them is perfect and at least a couple of them should be used on a project for verification purposes. In some cases, costs may be calculated based on the schedule and using base rates, set fees for the use of a resource, set costs for a task, etc. In other cases, costs may be obtained based on known cost metrics from similar projects. It is also possible to estimate budget based on algorithmic models that predict the cost based on project characteristics (parameters) supplied to a mathematical model.

Writing the project **plan document** is the culmination of the earlier planning steps. The plan document needs to be distributed to management and to project team members. The distribution may be in electronic form by email and by placing it on the Intranet website.

The project plan is regularly revised by the processes of **tracking project** progress and identifying misalignments with the plan. If a misalignment can be addressed by updating the project schedule and budget, then the revision is relatively straightforward. Otherwise, the revision may need to start from the very first step of project planning, i.e. from redefinition of objectives, scope, and constraints.

4.2 Project Scheduling

Project scheduling and tracking is a daily activity of project managers. Building time schedules assumes that the *work breakdown structure* and the task list are known. Simple as it may sound, the determination of tasks in a large project is a very difficult undertaking. *Tasks* are activities with clear start and end days, ideally of between one day and two weeks' duration. Different lifecycle models (Section 1.3) result in different work breakdown structures and different task lists. Many tasks just happen as a reaction to unexpected developments on the project and cannot be easily predicted.

Project scheduling is a moving target. There are complex interdependencies between tasks, various constraints on when the tasks can be performed, and the variety of possible interruptions. Missing a deadline on a single task has a ripple effect on the rest of the schedule. *Resources* allocated to the project, in particular human resources, are heavily constrained and frequently impossible to reschedule conveniently.

Fortunately, project management tools, such as Microsoft Project used for examples in this chapter, are capable of automatically creating and re-creating schedules to reflect changes in tasks and resources. They are also able to identify critical paths in the schedules. A **critical path** is any sequence of linked tasks in the project that must be done on time for the project to finish by the deadline. A **slippage** (delay) in any task on a critical path will result in the project missing the deadline. On the other hand, tasks that are not on a critical path can afford delays (they have so-called **slack time**). CPM **network charts** (Figure 3.1) are a good technique to visualize critical paths and slippages.

Tasks, Milestones, and Deliverables   4.2.1

Schedule creation begins with defining a **task** list for each phase of the project. Tasks can be hierarchically organized in multiple levels of subtasks. Each task is assigned a *duration* – an estimate of how long it will take to complete the task. Durations can be provided using different timescales, such as hours, days, and weeks. A good practice is not to have tasks of more than two weeks' duration.

Once task durations are available, the schedule can be constructed *forward* (from the project's start date) or *backward* (from the project's end date). The backward construction may be preferred if the project must be finished by a certain date. Durations are used to calculate the amount of work. If the task list and the end date are firm constraints, the schedule can only be adjusted by varying allocation of resources to tasks.

The schedule reflects the **project calendar**. The calendar specifies working times and nonworking times. Working times are work hours on weekdays, such as Monday to Friday 9.00 a.m. to 5.00 p.m. Nonworking times are all other times with no work done on the project. This includes weekends, holidays, lunch breaks, etc.

A **milestone** is a task that results in a significant event or outcome. Although a task with some duration can be marked as resulting in a milestone, it is customary to create milestones as separate tasks with zero duration. A milestone can be a sign of the end of a project's phase or the end of the whole project.

A milestone can represent a **deliverable**. The fact that a milestone denotes a deliverable can be reflected in the name of the milestone task. It is also possible to create a separate task for a deliverable with zero duration. Both milestones and deliverables represent a particular state in the project. As such, they should be named starting with a noun (e.g. 'database is loaded and ready for testing'). By contrast, other tasks start with a verb (e.g. 'implement database triggers').

Figure 4.3 is an example of Microsoft Project's interface for creating a task list for a project. Tasks are successively entered in rows. They are named and duration estimates are provided. The figure uses notional names reflecting the task types. Tasks that are milestones or deliverables are given zero duration. The horizontal bars symbolize tasks. Milestones and deliverables are pictured with small diamonds and specific dates.

Apart from regular tasks, Figure 4.3 demonstrates a recurring task and a summary task with two levels of subtasks. A **recurring task** is a task that repeats at regular time intervals, such as every day, once per week, etc. (e.g. 'conduct the code review meeting every Friday'). The recurring task in Figure 4.3 occurs every Friday and it has four instances of two-hour duration (four successive Fridays).

Tasks can be organized in a hierarchy of subtasks. The task at the top of a hierarchy is known as a **summary task**. The duration and other characteristics of the summary task are

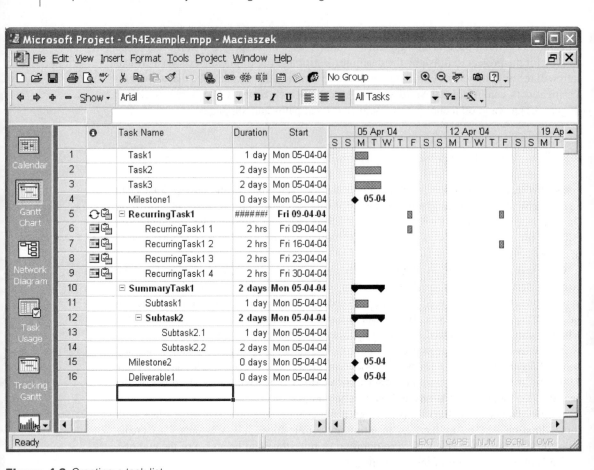

Figure 4.3 Creating a task list
Source: Screenshot of Microsoft® Office Project (2003), reprinted by permission from Microsoft Corporation, Copyright © 1998–2003 Microsoft Corporation

computed from its constituent subtasks. A subtask is any task that is a part of the summary task or a part of any higher-level subtask.

4.2.2 Task Scheduling in a Bar Chart

Tasks are related to each other and may depend on specific dates. **Task dependencies** need to be defined before the project schedule can be computed. Task dependencies occur between two or more *linked tasks*. Unlinked tasks are considered to have no dependencies so that they can be conducted in parallel. There are two main kinds of task dependencies (Lientz and Rea, 2002):

■ task dependencies based on the work organization
■ task dependencies due to competing for the same resources (Section 4.2.3).

Task dependencies based on the work distinguish between predecessor and successor tasks. Microsoft Project recognizes four basic categories of predecessor-to-successor dependencies:

- *finish-to-start (FS)* – successor task cannot start until predecessor task is finished
- *start-to-start (SS)* – successor task cannot start until predecessor task is started
- *finish-to-finish (FF)* – successor task cannot finish until predecessor task is finished
- *start-to-finish (SF)* – successor task cannot finish until predecessor task is started.

Once dependencies between linked tasks are established, changes to a predecessor's dates and duration affect the successor's dates. It is also possible to specify more complex predecessor-to-successor dependencies, in particular:

- *delay dependencies* in which a *lag time* is introduced between the predecessor and successor tasks
- *overlap dependencies* in which a *lead time* exists between the predecessor and successor tasks.

Delay dependencies introduce a delay (lag time) between linked tasks. For example, a lag time of three days is specified if the successor task can start only after three days of completion of the predecessor task. By contrast, **overlap dependencies** introduce an overlap (lead time) between linked tasks. This allows the successor task to start before the predecessor task is finished. Lag and lead times can be specified in absolute values (e.g. +3 days for lag time or −2 days for lead time). They can also be specified as percentages of the predecessor task duration.

With task dependencies in place, a bar chart can be automatically constructed. A **Gantt bar chart** displays tasks on the vertical axis and the start and end dates of tasks on the horizontal axis. The bar chart in Figure 4.4 is known as a Gantt chart, after the name of its inventor. A Gantt chart can be applied for time scheduling for the entire project, for individual project phases, or for individual human resources. A project management tool can synchronize between the master Gantt chart for the project and the individual charts.

The arrows represent the time dependencies in Figure 4.4. At first, all dependencies in the chart were created as finish-to-start (FS). Later, a delay dependency was specified between `Subtask2.2` and `Subtask2.3` and an overlap dependency was allowed between `SummaryTask1` and `Task4`. Few tasks have no dependencies and can be done in parallel (e.g. `Task1` and `Task2`).

Normally the tasks are scheduled on an *As Soon As Possible* (ASAP) basis. This means that the task will be scheduled as soon as possible subject to dependencies on predecessor tasks and subject to availability of resources. All tasks in Figure 4.4 are scheduled on ASAP principle.

As an alternative, tasks can be scheduled on an *As Late As Possible* (ALAP) basis. This is useful in two situations. Firstly, the ALAP principle allows the task to obtain maximum input from earlier tasks before it starts. Having more information may allow costly mistakes to be avoided in the task's execution. Secondly, the ALAP principle allows the calculation of how much a task can be delayed without delaying the project finish date (i.e. without extending the project's critical path).

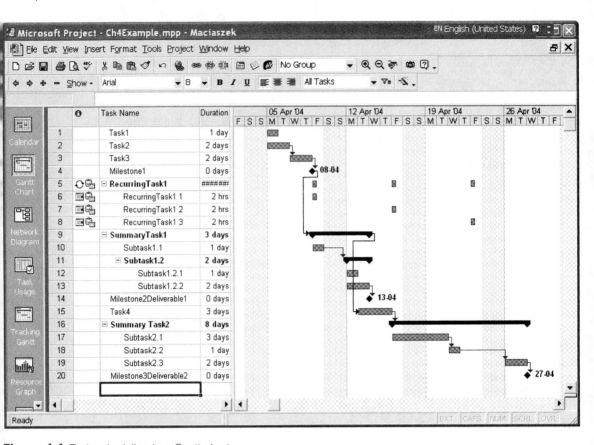

Figure 4.4 Task scheduling in a Gantt chart

Source: Screenshot of Microsoft® Office Project (2003), reprinted by permission from Microsoft Corporation, Copyright © 1998–2003 Microsoft Corporation

In some cases additional constraints may need to be imposed on selected tasks, which determine specific dates for tasks' start or finish. These are called **inflexible constraints**. Microsoft Project allows six inflexible constraints:

- Must Finish On (MFO)

- Must Start On (MSO)

- Finish No Earlier Than (FNET) – inflexible for projects scheduled from the finish date

- Finish No Later Than (FNLT) – inflexible for projects scheduled from the start date

- Start No Earlier Than (SNET) – inflexible for projects scheduled from the finish date

- Start No Later Than (SNLT) – inflexible for projects scheduled from the start date.

Inflexible constraints should be used only if necessary as they remove flexibility from the project scheduling. There are no inflexible constraints in the schedule in Figure 4.4.

Resources and Resource Calendars   4.2.3

Each task must be assigned resources. **Resources** can be broadly classified into work resources and material resources. **Work resources** consist of people and equipment, including hardware and software. **Material resources** are consumables and supplies, such as the printing paper. A task may require multiple resources. In the case of human resources, many people can work on a task. Depending on the complexity of the project and on the level of detail demanded in the plan, it may be advisable to allocate only the *accountable* human resource to the task (i.e. only the person responsible for the task).

Resource assignment introduces both flexibility and constraints to scheduling. On the one hand, it is possible to 'move resources around' to minimize unwanted dependencies between tasks. On the other hand, tasks may be delayed because they have to wait for availability of demanded resource.

Resource assignment has an important *tracking function* (Section 4.4). With a resource assigned it is possible to track the amount of work performed by people and equipment and to monitor the use of materials. Underutilized resources may be allocated to tasks in need or trouble. Costs of resources can also be tracked.

Prior to assigning resources to tasks, resources have to be defined. As shown in Figure 4.5, the resource definition includes giving the name to a resource, specifying its type, and indicating the number of *resource units* available for the resource. The last feature applies only to work resources. In the case of people resources, treated as individuals rather than as groups of people, the maximum applicable number of resource units is 100 percent. The 100 percent signifies a resource employed on a full-time basis. For half-time employees, the maximum number of resource units is 50 percent.

A full-time employee, with 100 percent of units, may still not be available 100 percent of the time (say, 8 hours per day) to work on a task. This depends on the **resource calendar**

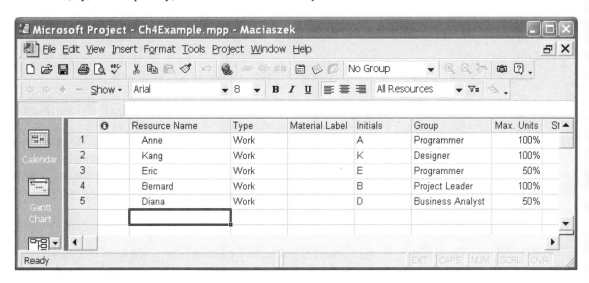

Figure 4.5 Resource list
Source: Screenshot of Microsoft® Office Project (2003), reprinted by permission from Microsoft Corporation, Copyright © 1998–2003 Microsoft Corporation

Figure 4.6
Resource calendar

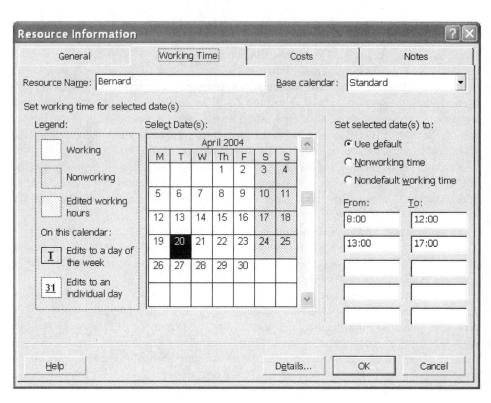

(as opposed to the project calendar). The resource calendar permits entering any days and times when the resource is not available as well as specifying work patterns different from defined in the project calendar (such as working on weekends) (Figure 4.6).

4.2.4 Effort-Driven Scheduling in a Bar Chart

Assignment of resources to tasks is based on the maximum amount of working time that a resource can offer. The maximum working time is determined from maximum available number of resource units and any constraints in the resource calendar. If the resource is a part-time employee (50 percent resource units) with no constraints in the resource calendar, then (in the example) the resource is available for 4 hours per day. If the work assigned to the resource exceeds the resource daily availability, then such a resource is over allocated.

Assignment of additional resources on a task may shorten the task duration and it can, therefore, affect the project schedule. The approach to scheduling where the duration of tasks can change (up or down) as resources are added or removed from tasks is known as **effort-driven scheduling**. In this approach, the effort required to complete a task remains unchanged, but the duration of the task can change.

For example, duration of `Task3` in Figure 4.4 is 2 days. This implies 16 hours of effort. In Figure 4.7, `Task3` is allocated 50 percent of the Kang resource, which means 4 hours

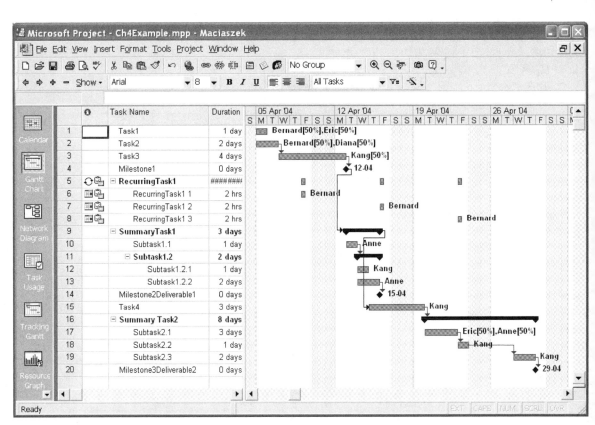

Figure 4.7 Effort-driven scheduling in a Gantt chart
Source: Screenshot of Microsoft® Office Project (2003), reprinted by permission from Microsoft Corporation, Copyright © 1998–2003 Microsoft Corporation

per day. This in turn means that Kang needs 4 days to complete Task3. In the effort-driven scheduling used in the Gantt chart in Figure 4.7, the project schedule is adjusted based on the effort required and resources provided.

If it is required that task durations should not change in the presence of event-driven scheduling, then the planner should assign the amount of resource that can deliver the effort within the prescribed duration. For example, Task 1 and Task 2 are given double resources, each able to perform 50 percent of prescribed effort. As a result, the durations of these two tasks have not changed. The same principle is applied elsewhere in the Gantt chart in Figure 4.7.

Resource Underallocation and Overallocation 4.2.5

Project management tools are capable of providing multiple views on project scheduling information. **Resource usage** is one such view (Figure 4.8). The resource usage view shows scheduled work hours of each resource and the hours divided across tasks. The analysis of resource usage (allocation) allows identification of *underallocated and*

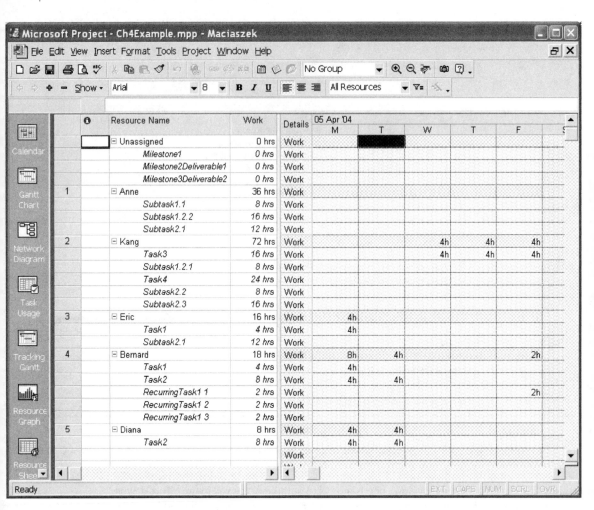

Figure 4.8 Resource usage
Source: Screenshot of Microsoft® Office Project (2003), reprinted by permission from Microsoft Corporation, Copyright © 1998–2003 Microsoft Corporation

overallocated resources. There are no overallocated resources in Figure 4.8, but clearly all of them are underallocated in the sense that there is no work defined for them on some days.

The resource underallocation is frequently not factual. Resources are often used on many projects and a single project schedule is not evidence of resource underutilization. It is also likely that some aspects of the resource's work are not captured in any management schedules.

By contrast, the resource overutilization creates immediate scheduling problems and must be addressed. Consider a change to resource allocation for Task1 in Figure 4.9. Diana has replaced the Eric resource. At first glance, everything looks fine as Diana provides 50 percent of the effort in Task1 and in Task2, which means 4 hours in each task. However, Diana is a part-time resource in Figure 4.5, which means that Diana cannot work 8 hours on Monday 05 Apr 04.

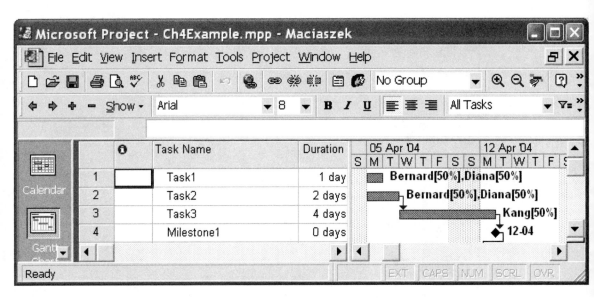

Figure 4.9 Change in resource allocation causing overallocation
Source: Screenshot of Microsoft® Office Project (2003), reprinted by permission from Microsoft Corporation, Copyright © 1998–2003 Microsoft Corporation

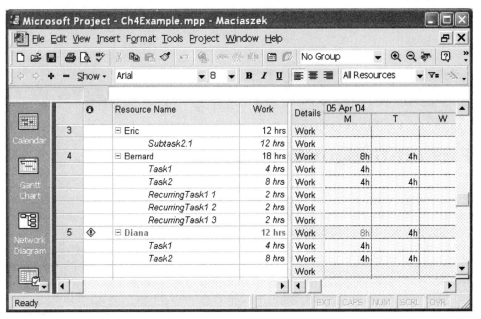

Figure 4.10
Resource usage showing overallocated resources
Source: Screenshot of Microsoft® Office Project (2003), reprinted by permission from Microsoft Corporation, Copyright © 1998–2003 Microsoft Corporation

The project management tool immediately notices Diana's overallocation. Figure 4.10 is the resource usage view showing Diana as an overallocated resource (shown in red and by a warning sign in the 'information' column). The allocation of 8 hours on Monday 05 Apr 04 is twice as much as Diana can deliver as a half-time employee.

Figure 4.11
Resource graph
for overallocated
resource
Source: Screenshot
of Microsoft® Office
Project (2003),
reprinted by
permission
from Microsoft
Corporation,
Copyright © 1998–
2003 Microsoft
Corporation

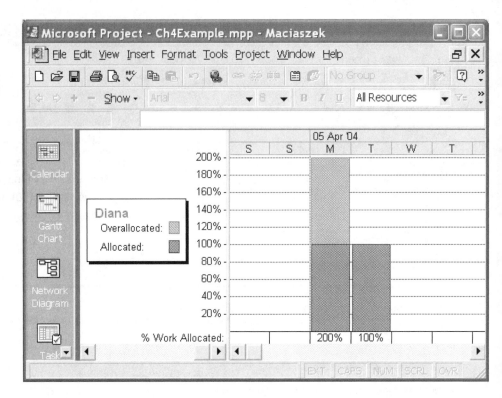

The fact that a resource is overallocated can be visualized in a resource graph, as shown in Figure 4.11. The graph shows clearly that the work allocated to Diana on 05 Apr 04 amounts to 200 percent of what she can do (again, the coloring of the bars indicates this).

4.3 Project Budget Estimation

Project **budget estimation** is a thorny issue. There are many suggested approaches to cost estimation but only a couple of them have a scientific merit. Moreover, approaches that resemble science are costly. There is a tradeoff between the effort needed to arrive at a more accurate and maintainable budget and the value provided by the budget.

As noticed by Lientz and Rea (2002) and shown in Figure 4.12, the effort to produce the budget increases rapidly with the level of detail considered in determining the factors that influence calculations. The budget accuracy is likely to be steadily improving with more detail. The budget maintainability, however, is high for simplistic evaluation methods, but starts to decrease rapidly at some point when the amount of detail gets in the way of quick and correct adjustments. The real budget value is itself a tradeoff between accuracy and maintainability. Up to a certain point, the cumulative effect of these three factors improves the budget value. However, at some level of detail, the budget value starts decreasing.

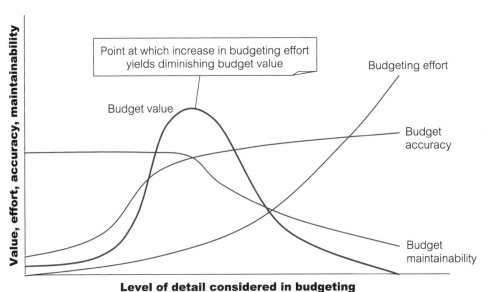

Figure 4.12
Budget value
versus budgeting
effort

Graphs such as that in Figure 4.12 provide some justification for such cost evaluation methods as expert judgment or estimation by analogy (Sommerville, 2001). **Expert judgment** is a method in which estimates are solicited from multiple experts, and then discussed and reconciled to arrive at an agreed estimate. **Estimation by analogy** can be used when similar projects in the same application domain have been completed and the actual costs of them are known. The budget of the project is then estimated by analogy with what happened in the past.

More sophisticated methods of budget estimation can be divided into two broad groups. The first group consists of bottom-up methods, which consider tasks and resources allocated in the project schedule prepared earlier, and obtain the budget by summing the costs of resources plus other fixed costs. These methods are discussed next under 'schedule-driven budget estimation'.

The second robust approach to budget estimation is known as 'algorithmic budget estimation'. In this approach, some estimated software size metric, such as the number of lines of code or the number of function points in the code, is used to derive the cost. The cost is obtained by feeding the metric values and a large number of adjusting parameters to a mathematical model. The model itself is an outcome of extensive studies on past projects.

Schedule-Driven Budget Estimation 4.3.1

Schedule-driven budget estimation assumes that there exists a prior schedule with resources allocated to tasks. This is called the **baseline** schedule or plan. Because schedules are subject to changes, a project management tool can maintain multiple baselines and separate budget estimations can be done for each baseline.

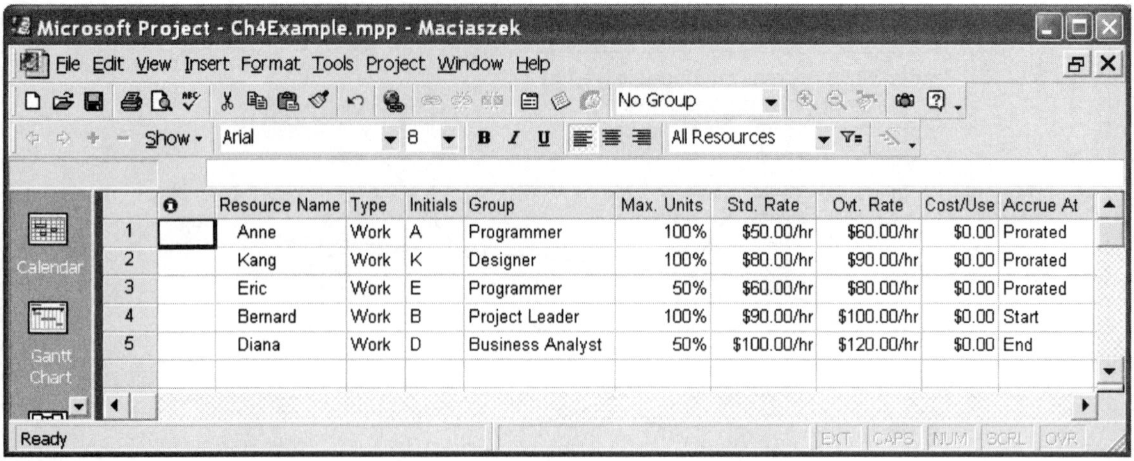

	Resource Name	Type	Initials	Group	Max. Units	Std. Rate	Ovt. Rate	Cost/Use	Accrue At
1	Anne	Work	A	Programmer	100%	$50.00/hr	$60.00/hr	$0.00	Prorated
2	Kang	Work	K	Designer	100%	$80.00/hr	$90.00/hr	$0.00	Prorated
3	Eric	Work	E	Programmer	50%	$60.00/hr	$80.00/hr	$0.00	Prorated
4	Bernard	Work	B	Project Leader	100%	$90.00/hr	$100.00/hr	$0.00	Start
5	Diana	Work	D	Business Analyst	50%	$100.00/hr	$120.00/hr	$0.00	End

Figure 4.13 Assigning rates and other costs to resources
Source: Screenshot of Microsoft® Office Project (2003), reprinted by permission from Microsoft Corporation, Copyright © 1998–2003 Microsoft Corporation

Theoretically, the schedule-driven budget estimation seems easy to do. Since resources are assigned to tasks in the baseline, everything that is left to be done is to assign costs to resources, add overhead and other fixed costs, and make the project management tool to compute the budget for the project. The devil is in the detail. For example, resources can accrue costs at various times during the task duration. Rates and fixed costs can differ in different time periods. There may be some legal rules affecting pay rates and costs. Accounting principles can affect calculation, etc. Still, initial budget calculation is trivial when compared with budget tracking in response to schedule changes, varying baselines, and other project conditions (Section 4.4).

As stated, the budget estimation requires **rates** and other costs for work and material resources to be entered. As shown in Figure 4.13, apart from **standard rates**, there may be overtime rates and per-use rates. An **overtime rate** is paid to a work resource if the resource is used outside regular working hours. Overtime work is not additional work on the task but it can be used to shorten the duration of the task. **Per-use rate** is in fact not a rate but a set cost for the use of a resource. It can be used as a replacement for other rates or in addition to them.

Cost **accrual methods** must be defined for resources, alongside rates and other costs. Accrual can be at the start of a task, at the end of a task, or prorated (as worked). The prorated method is the most frequently used and accrues the cost based on the completion percentage of the task. Accrual methods apply to flexible costs and to fixed costs. In Figure 4.13, the prorated method is used for the first three resources. Bernard's accrual method is at the start, and Diana's at the end.

Figure 4.14 demonstrates how different accrual methods affect cost calculations. Eric's costs are accrued on a day-by-day basis. Bernard's costs are accrued on the first day when the task starts. By contrast, Diana's costs are accrued only when the task completes.

Rates and other costs can change depending on the time when the resource is consumed (e.g. as a result of pay raises). Figure 4.15 demonstrates a dialog box that can be used to specify the changes that take effect from some particular date.

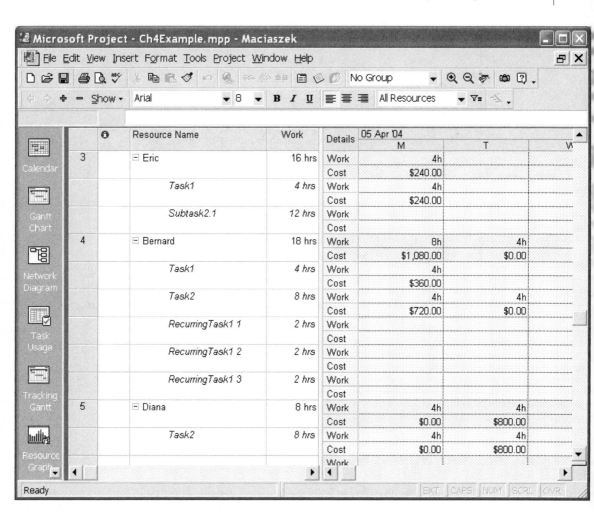

Figure 4.14 Resource costs with different accrual methods
Source: Screenshot of Microsoft® Office Project (2003), reprinted by permission from Microsoft Corporation, Copyright © 1998–2003 Microsoft Corporation

Once resource costs are known, it is possible to compute total costs of tasks, as shown in Figure 4.16. Note that task costs can include fixed costs assigned to the task per se, rather than to a resource consumed by the task. For example, a fixed cost may be with regard to consumables and similar expenses. In Figure 4.16, fixed costs are added to all milestones (which have no resources allocated). A fixed cost is also added to RecurringTask1. Note that the current budget has been saved as a baseline and that the project has not committed any money yet, as seen in the Actual column.

A project management tool can also maintain the distribution of costs across resources (Figure 4.17). As before, the resource costs have not been committed yet.

The planner is now in position to calculate the cost of the entire project. Figure 4.18 shows such a calculation. Because the project has not started yet, the current, actual, and remaining costs are the same. The actual cost is zero. According to the plan, the project should complete within 19 days, have a workload of 150 hours, and a cost of $13,596.

Figure 4.15
Rate changes
over time

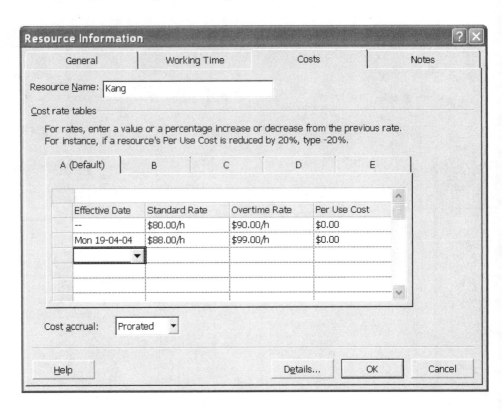

4.3.2 Algorithmic Budget Estimation

Done well, schedule-driven budget estimation delivers good value with reasonable effort (Figure 4.12). However, in practice, budget estimation should not rely exclusively on one estimation technique. The accuracy of budget estimation should be verified by applying a second technique. The issue is reminiscent of obtaining multiple quotes for the services provided by tradespeople: a single quote may not reflect the real value provided.

The **algorithmic budget estimation** is the second best estimation technique after the schedule-driven estimation. The algorithmic estimation takes some measure (metric) of the size of the problem and applies to it an empirically obtained algorithm to arrive at the budget for solving the problem. In manufacturing disciplines, such as car manufacturing, the issue is simple. Given the time and cost of producing one car, it is possible to obtain the time and cost for the whole manufacturing 'project'.

In engineering disciplines, and in particular in software engineering, the issue is much more tricky. To begin with, an engineering project produces a single unique product, not a large quantity of the same product. Even if a metric can be obtained that decomposes the product to multiple components, the components are not the same. Software does not scale up easily (Section 1.1.6). Each component demands different effort, even if the component is as primitive as a line of code or a function point. Most costs are attributed to work

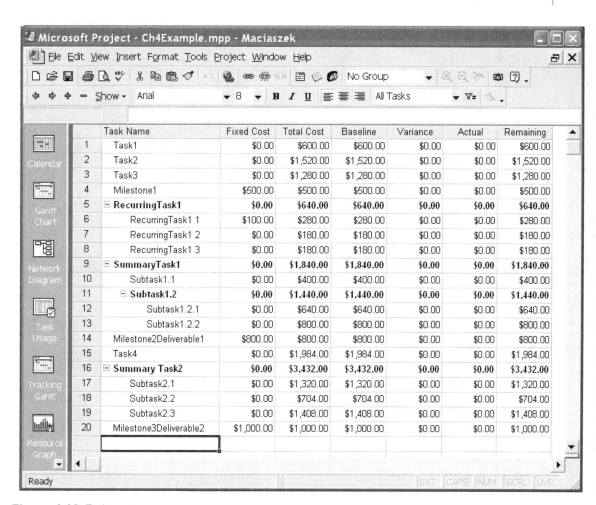

Figure 4.16 Task costs
Source: Screenshot of Microsoft® Office Project (2003), reprinted by permission from Microsoft Corporation, Copyright © 1998–2003 Microsoft Corporation

resources, and human resources in particular, not to material resources. Finally, because each product is unique, it is difficult to know in advance the size of the problem.

Principles of algorithmic models

Algorithmic models use empirically derived formulas to estimate cost of human resources (**effort**) as a function of the project size. The **size** is typically expressed in the lines of code (LOCs), in function points (FPs), or in object points (OPs). The software size is also estimated (Pressman, 2001).

The **lines of code** value relates to the number of thousands (K) of non-comment source statements in the program. Hence, the LOC variable is shown in formulas as KLOC. KLOCs are one of the most detailed sizing metrics possible and can potentially lead to the most valuable budget estimates (Figure 4.12). On the negative side, in modern software

	Resource Name	Cost	Baseline Cost	Variance	Actual Cost	Remaining
1	Anne	$1,800.00	$1,800.00	$0.00	$0.00	$1,800.00
2	Kang	$6,016.00	$6,016.00	$0.00	$0.00	$6,016.00
3	Eric	$960.00	$960.00	$0.00	$0.00	$960.00
4	Bernard	$1,620.00	$1,620.00	$0.00	$0.00	$1,620.00
5	Diana	$800.00	$800.00	$0.00	$0.00	$800.00

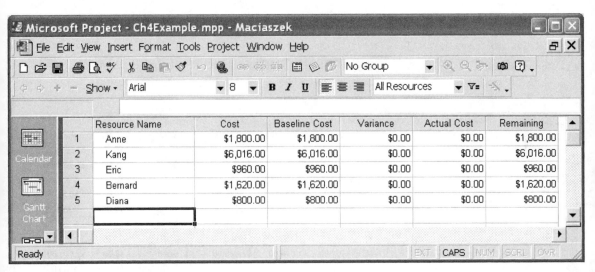

Figure 4.17 Resource costs
Source: Screenshot of Microsoft® Office Project (2003), reprinted by permission from Microsoft Corporation, Copyright © 1998–2003 Microsoft Corporation

Figure 4.18
Project cost

	Start	Finish
Current	Mon 05-04-04	Thu 29-04-04
Baseline	Mon 05-04-04	Thu 29-04-04
Actual	NA	NA
Variance	0d	0d

	Duration	Work	Cost
Current	19d	150h	$13,596.00
Baseline	19d	150h	$13,596.00
Actual	0d	0h	$0.00
Remaining	19d	150h	$13,596.00

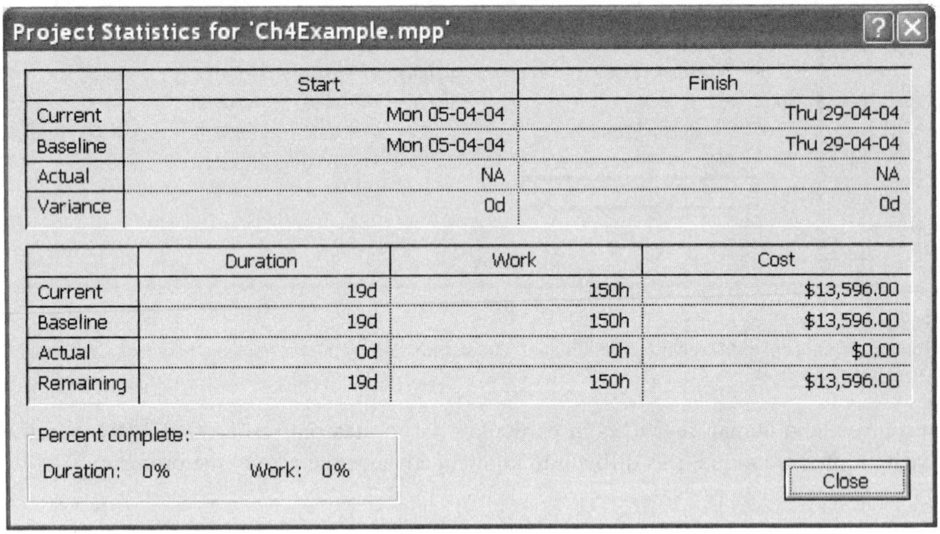

production, which favors code generation and code reuse, it is very hard to estimate lines of code and distinguish them from reused or generated code.

Function points are at a higher level of code decomposition than lines of code (i.e. they provide less detailed sizing information). Function points are not software modules or components, as the name may suggest. In their most frequent guise, function points are computed by decomposing software across five features (inputs, outputs, data files, inquiries, and external interfaces) and calculating the number of these features while adjusting the calculation depending on the features' perceived complexity.

Object points are at an even higher level of code decomposition than function points. Like function points, they are obtained by using counts of different software features. The features are user interface screens, software reports, and software components. As with function points, the calculation is adjusted using weighting factors to reflect features' complexity. The calculation is also adjusted to remove reused object points. This leads to the measure called new object points (NOPs).

With sizing information in place, an algorithmic model of cost estimation takes the nominal form:

$$effort = c * size^k$$

The constants c and k are established empirically and given by the model. The exponent k reflects the complexity of the problem and the non-proportional increase of effort in larger projects. This exponent is typically in the range from 1 to 1.5. The multiplier c is another scaling factor of project difficulty based on assessments of attributes such as required product reliability, skills of the team, available software tools, etc.

The best-known algorithmic models are so-called COCOMO models. The acronym COCOMO stands for COnstructive COst MOdel (Boehm, 1981; Boehm *et al.*, 2000; Pressman, 2001; Sommerville, 2001; Schach, 2002; Ghezzi *et al.*, 2003). There are two COCOMO models, both developed under the guidance of Barry Boehm. The original model, developed in the 1980s, is now known as COCOMO 81. An improved version published in 2000 is known as COCOMO II.

COCOMO 81

COCOMO II has effectively subsumed COCOMO 81 for all but traditional software projects based on the third generation languages such as Cobol or C. However, there is an educational merit in explaining the principles of COCOMO 81 before addressing COCOMO II.

COCOMO 81 is really a set of three approaches to cost estimation. The three approaches distinguish among small, medium size, and complex systems. Each approach is given a generic estimation formula based on the predicted size of the code. In reality, there are multiple formulas to choose from for each approach based on project characteristics. The three modes and associated generic formulas are (Boehm, 1984):

- Basic (or organic) COCOMO:

$$effort = 3.2 * size^{1.05}$$

- Intermediate (or semidetached) COCOMO – this mode includes a set of *cost drivers* in the estimation to scale the nominal development effort based on assessments of product, hardware, personnel, and project attributes:

$$effort = 3.0 * size^{1.12}$$

- Advanced (or embedded) COCOMO – this mode builds up on the intermediate version but uses cost drivers to assess their impact on each phase of the development lifecycle:

$$effort = 2.8 * size^{1.20}$$

For example, using the basic COCOMO and assuming that the system will consist of 10,000 lines of code (10 KLOCs), the estimated effort expressed in person-months is:

$$\text{effort} = 3.2 * 100^{1.05}$$
$$= 3.2 * 125.9$$
$$\approx 403 \text{ person-months}$$

One of the most interesting indirect contributions of COCOMO 81 was the definition of relative importance of various **cost drivers** in the project cost and effort (Boehm, 1981). For example, the range of values for the cost driver known as 'product complexity' states that the difference between a simple and a complex product is a factor of $2.36 \ (1.65/0.70)$ in the cost estimate. If this factor value was the only differentiating factor between two products, then the effort to develop a complex product would be 2.36 times higher than for a simple product.

By comparison, some other cost drivers (in descending order of significance) are (Boehm, 1984):

- 'analyst capability' is a factor of $2.06 \ (1.46/0.71)$
- 'programmer capability' is a factor of $2.03 \ (1.42/0.70)$
- 'required software reliability' is a factor of $1.87 \ (1.40/0.75)$
- 'execution time constraints' is a factor of $1.66 \ (1.66/1.00)$
- 'application experience' is a factor of $1.57 \ (1.29/0.82)$
- 'use of modern programming practices' is a factor of $1.51 \ (1.24/0.82)$
- 'programming language experience' is a factor of $1.20 \ (1.14/0.95)$

There are interesting lessons from studying the above numbers. Despite being based on empirical research about a quarter of a century old, the reported significance of the cost drivers strikes a chord with modern software production. For example, one cannot agree more with the observation that the application experience gives more value to the project than the programming language experience. After all, one can learn programming by working in isolation with a computer as one's only company. Gaining application experience can only be done 'in the field' by interacting with others and observing the working environment. Even then, the experience obtained in one environment may not fully apply to another environment.

In the schedule-driven budget estimation (Section 4.3.1), the schedule is used to obtain the budget for the project as well as the detailed budget for individual tasks and resources. Algorithmic methods do not link to the schedule except for the possibility of estimating development time corresponding to estimated effort. The empirical formulas for estimating total development time, for the three COCOMO approaches, are, respectively (Boehm, 1984):

- simple COCOMO: $\text{time} = 2.5 * \text{effort}^{0.38}$
- intermediate COCOMO: $\text{time} = 2.5 * \text{effort}^{0.35}$
- advanced COCOMO: $\text{time} = 2.5 * \text{effort}^{0.32}$

Clearly, COCOMO is not as simple as taking the software size and using it in the formula to estimate the effort. The accuracy of the estimation is paramount to the accuracy of provided cost drivers and other scaling factors. This in turn depends on the availability of metrics from the past projects. A software development organization must know its history (and have it in numbers) in order to plan its future.

COCOMO 81 has provided a wealth of historical measurement information from a large number of organizations in the hope that the experience of other organizations can be used where local metrics are not available. This was helpful in times when Cobol was used as a universal language for business system programming and the applications were not as diverse as today. No such historical information exists for modern projects. Each organization must collect metrics from previous projects to have any hope of planning reliably for the future.

COCOMO II

COCOMO II (Boehm *et al.*, 2000) is based on the same principles as COCOMO 81, but it addresses a couple of important COCOMO 81 deficiencies. The model has been calibrated from the analysis of experience data collected (originally) from 83 software projects. Like all algorithmic models, COCOMO II requires sizing information. Apart from the LOCs and the FPs, COCOMO II introduces the object points (OPs) as a sizing option. Like COCOMO 81, COCOMO II uses a variety of cost drivers, scale factors, and other adjustment procedures.

COCOMO II is significantly more complex than COCOMO 81, which reflects:

- the increased complexity of software and application domains
- a wider variety of lifecycle models and software engineering techniques
- the proportional growth of software generation and reuse compared with manual programming
- the continuing nature of planning and cost estimation.

Unlike COCOMO 81, which provided estimations for the waterfall lifecycle and procedural programming, COCOMO II is responsive to iterative lifecycles and object-oriented programming. It recognizes the prototyping, increments, short cycles, use of program generators, development by component composition, etc.

COCOMO II is sensitive to a lifecycle phase in which estimates are being obtained. It gives merit to the growing precision of cost and time estimation with the project progress (Figure 4.1). Accordingly, COCOMO II consists of three different models corresponding to three successive phases of the project. The models are called the:

- *application composition model* – to be used in early analysis phase or during early prototyping
- *early design model* – to be used after requirements analysis is completed
- *post-architecture model* – to be used after the software architecture design is known.

The **application composition model** uses weighted object points (OPs) for sizing information. The OPs are counts of anticipated user interface screens, software reports, and software components. The OP count is reduced by the percentage of object points obtained by reuse, so that only new object points (NOPs) are considered for effort estimation. The formula for NOPs is:

$$NOP = OP * [(100 - \%reuse)/100]$$

Table 4.1 Productivity metrics in COCOMO II application composition mode

Combined developers' experience/ capability and organization's maturity/capability	Productivity in NOP/month
Very low	4
Low	7
Nominal	13
High	25
Very high	50

The application composition model uses only two weighting factors to determine the development productivity level (capability). The two factors are the developers' experience/capability and the organization's maturity/capability. The two factors are combined to determine five productivity levels. Associated with the five levels are productivity 'cost drivers' expressed in terms of NOPs that the project team is capable of producing per month. The five levels and corresponding productivity metrics are shown in Table 4.1.

Once the productivity metric is chosen, the formula to calculate the effort in COCOMO II application composition model is:

```
effort = NOP/productivity
```

For example, if the count of new object points is 500 and the productivity is 4, then the effort (in person-months) will be estimated at 125. By contrast, if the productivity is 50, then the effort will be only 10 person-months.

The **early design model** uses function points (FPs) for sizing information in cost prediction. In practice, however, COCOMO II (like COCOMO 81) provides standard tables for converting FPs to KLOCs, and the size is ultimately expressed in KLOCs. The estimation formula is:

```
effort = c * size^k * m + autoeffort
```

Based on COCOMO II research, the value of the constant coefficient `c` is set to 2.5 in the early design model. The value of the exponent `k` varies between 1.01 and 1.26.

The multiplier `m` expresses the influence of cost drivers on the estimated effort. COCOMO II defines seven sets of cost drivers: (1) product reliability and complexity, (2) reuse required, (3) platform difficulty, (4) personnel capability, (5) personnel experience, (6) schedule, and (7) support facilities. Each of the seven cost drivers is assigned a value. The value of 1 means that the cost driver is inconsequential – it does not affect the estimation. The value of `m` is then the result of the multiplication of the seven numbers.

The last term in the formula, `autoeffort`, is computed separately according to its own algorithm. The meaning of `autoeffort` is the effort put by developers in the automatic code generation and the integration of this code with the manually created programs. Because the rest of the formula refers only to the code created manually, `autoeffort` is added to the result of the other computation.

The following is a hypothetical computation of the effort assuming that all terms of the formula have been decided before.

Table 4.2 Cost drivers in COCOMO II post-architecture model

Cost driver category	Cost driver code	Cost driver name
Product attributes	RELY	Required system reliability
	CPLX	Complexity of system modules
	DOCU	Extent of documentation required
	DATA	Size of database used
	RUSE	Required percentage of reusable components
Computer attributes	TIME	Execution time constraints
	PVOL	Volatility of development platform
	STOR	Memory constraints
Personnel attributes	ACAP	Capability of project analysis
	PCON	Personnel continuity
	PEXP	Programmer experience in project domain
	PCAP	Programmer capability
	AEXP	Analyst experience in project domain
	LTEX	Language and tool experience
Project attributes	TOOL	Use of software tools
	SCED	Development schedule compression
	SITE	Extent of multi-site working and quality of site communications

$$
\begin{aligned}
\text{effort} &= 2.5 * 100^{1.15} * 1.3 + 35 \\
&= 2.5 * 199.5 * 1.3 \\
&\approx 678 \text{ person-months}
\end{aligned}
$$

The **post-architecture model** uses adjusted lines of code (LOCs) for sizing information in cost prediction. The lines of code are adjusted from the early design model by considering two factors: (1) the requirements volatility and (2) the extent of reuse. The first factor considers the LOCs necessary in any rework due to changing requirements. The second factor accounts for initial high investment in searching for and understanding reusable components. The estimation formula is the same as in the early design model. The changes relate to the details of how the coefficients and terms are established.

The post-architecture model uses 17 cost drivers and 5 scale factors. The cost drivers are grouped in 4 categories. It is not necessary to consider all cost drivers. Cost drivers with a nominal value of 1 do not affect the computation. Other ratings are multiplied to obtain the value of the multiplier m. Table 4.2 lists the cost drivers (Boehm *et al.*, 2000; Sommerville, 2001).

The scale factors are used in the post-architecture model to derive the value of the exponent k applied to the `size` value. Each factor is rated with integer values from 5 to 0. The values are added, divided by 100, and the result is added to the nominal value of the exponent 1.01 to give the value to be used in the formula. The scale factors and their explanations are listed in Table 4.3 (Boehm *et al.*, 2000; Sommerville, 2001).

The algorithmic budget estimation is an important alternative and addition to the schedule-based estimation. Each approach can constitute a good 'sanity check' for the other approach. Using these two approaches turns software cost estimation within project planning and tracking into an engineering discipline.

Table 4.3 Scale factors in COCOMO II post-architecture model

Scale factor	Explanation
Precedentedness	To capture the prior experience of the organization with similar projects
Development flexibility	To capture the extent to which the project client intervenes in the development. A high flexibility means that the client is not involved or sets only generic goals
Architecture/risk resolution	To capture the extent to which risk management is done on the project
Team cohesion	To capture the extent to which the development team is integrated and effective
Process maturity	To capture the software engineering maturity of the organization in conducting projects

4.4 Tracking Project Progress

Tracking project progress involves two main sets of comparisons:

- the *baseline schedule* versus the *actual schedule* (this includes work tracking – the baseline work allocated to resources versus the actual work performed), and
- the *baseline budget* versus the *actual budget*.

Apart from the original *baseline* plan, *interim* plans may be created as checkpoints of project progress. An interim plan can be compared with the baseline to assess the project progress or slippage. An interim plan can also serve as an additional (or new) baseline for assessing the current plan.

Tracking project progress is therefore conditional on prior creation and saving of the baseline schedule and the baseline budget. After the project has started, costs begin to accumulate in a way that may not be exactly as planned. New information is coming not just from the modifications to the schedule, but also from the accounting system that charges costs to the project (Lientz and Rea, 2002). The information coming from these two sources may conflict.

The complications due to *changes to the planned schedule* may be significant. Tasks may be interrupted and therefore they need to be split into parts. Task splitting introduces difficulties in cost calculation because costs can be accrued at start, at end, or can be prorated. Resources may become unavailable causing slippages. Tasks may be set with absolute start and end dates causing havoc in rescheduling.

The complications due to the *accounting system* may be even trickier. The accounting system uses time sheets and invoices to assign costs to projects. Human resources can work on multiple projects and on multiple tasks within the same project. Unless the time recording system is synchronized with the project management system and unless it forces clear splits of costs, the accounting system has no way of knowing how much time was spent on various tasks. Invoices reach the accounting systems days after the work was done and are usually paid as late as possible.

The picture is clear. Comparing the baseline and the actual is a real challenge. Additionally, the time tracking and cost tracking can bring up conflicting information. The project can be behind schedule but on or under budget. It can also be on or ahead of schedule but over budget. All other combinations apply as well, such as ahead of schedule and under budget or behind schedule and over budget.

Tracking the Schedule 4.4.1

Changes to the planned schedule must be tracked as the project progresses (this is called schedule tracking). The completion state of each task needs to be recorded and shown on the bar chart. The same applies to splitting of tasks due to interruptions and to reallocation of resources. A task's progress can be updated in absolute terms by changing its duration or start/end dates or in relative terms by specifying percentage of completion.

Assuming that the current project date is 12 Apr 04, Figure 4.19 shows actual execution of Task1, Task2, and Task3 as compared with the baseline schedule in Figure 4.7. A narrow black bar inside a task bar indicates the completion status of the task.

Task1 has been completed as scheduled. However, Task2 started one day later and lasted one day longer. As a result, Task3 could only start on Friday instead of Wednesday. This introduced the risk of two days' slippage in the project. To address this problem, the

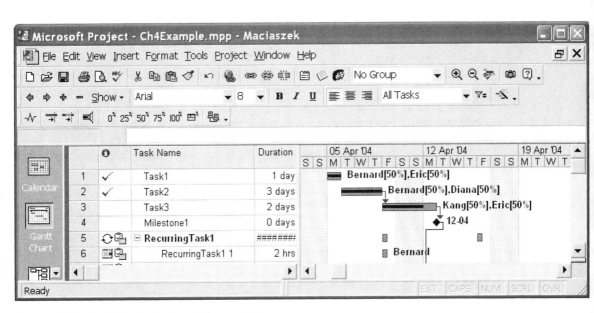

Figure 4.19 Gantt chart showing task completion
Source: Screenshot of Microsoft® Office Project (2003), reprinted by permission from Microsoft Corporation, Copyright © 1998–2003 Microsoft Corporation

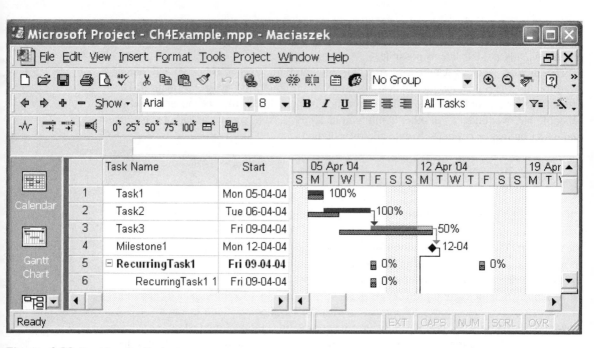

Figure 4.20 Tracking Gantt chart
Source: Screenshot of Microsoft® Office Project (2003), reprinted by permission from Microsoft Corporation, Copyright © 1998–2003 Microsoft Corporation

planner added the Eric resource to the task, thus making it possible to complete `Task3` according to the baseline schedule. After one day (Friday), `Task3` has been marked as 50 percent complete.

These explanations about the actual schedule status as compared with the baseline can be illustrated by means of a **tracking Gantt chart** (Figure 4.20). A tracking Gantt chart shows pairs of bars for each task, one above the other. The lower bar represents the baseline task. The upper bar represents the actual task. The upper bars are colored to indicate if they are completed, not started yet, or partially completed.

Apart from the graphical representation, the tracking Gantt chart provides textual information about each task's Baseline Start, Baseline Finish, Start Variance and Finish Variance. A **variance** is the difference between the baseline and the actual.

Since resources are assigned to tasks, tracking the completion of tasks also provides information about how much work was done by each resource. This information can be presented on a task-by-task basis, as in Figure 4.21. The view presented in Figure 4.21 can also be used to update the value of actual work performed by the resource. When compared with the planned amount of work, the information provided about actual work can be used to calculate the work remaining on a task.

From the people management perspective, it is essential to track actual work done by each resource. Figure 4.22 illustrates a relevant view. The variance between the actual work and the baseline work is an indication of how a resource is used compared with the schedule.

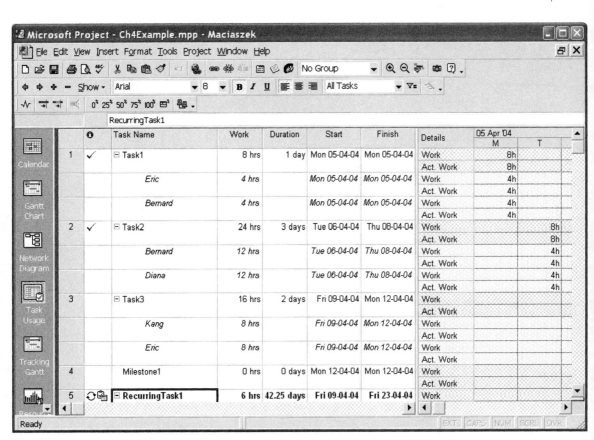

Figure 4.21 Tracking the work on task-by-task basis
Source: Screenshot of Microsoft® Office Project (2003), reprinted by permission from Microsoft Corporation, Copyright © 1998–2003 Microsoft Corporation

Tracking the Budget   4.4.2

One way of looking at **budget tracking** is to treat it as a direct continuation of schedule tracking. It is possible to automatically track actual costs on tasks completed, or in progress, by applying resource rates, accrual methods, and any fixed costs. This approach can reflect any changes in the schedule, such as changes to task durations or reallocation of resources.

However, as mentioned earlier, the actual costs reported by the *accounting system* may be different from the costs calculated from actual work performed. In some cases, the accounting system may be the only source of information of actual cost. This will happen, for example, when the tradeoff between the budget value and the budget effort (Figure 4.12) has not warranted the level of detail in the schedule that would support accurate budget calculation.

Budget tracking is essential for operational and tactical decision making. Accordingly, the findings from budget tracking must be summarized and presented in a form suitable for managers. One of the most useful methods that succinctly informs if the project is on budget is called the *earned value analysis*.

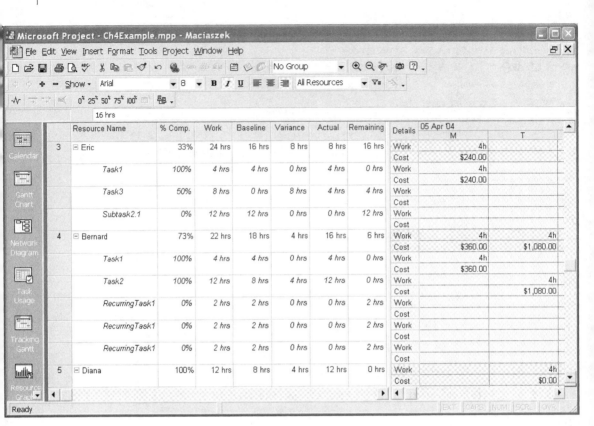

Figure 4.22 Tracking work on a resource-by-resource basis
Source: Screenshot of Microsoft® Office Project (2003), reprinted by permission from Microsoft Corporation, Copyright © 1998–2003 Microsoft Corporation

Actual costs from schedule

A project management tool can calculate total **actual costs** of tasks that have consumed resources. Figure 4.23 shows such calculation for tasks undertaken prior to Monday 12 Apr 04. The calculations are done by multiplying hourly resource rates (Figure 4.13) by hours worked. The actual execution of Task2 and Task3, shown in Figure 4.23, differs from the baseline schedule for these tasks (Figure 4.7). Figure 4.23 demonstrates the calculations. Note that Task3 is (prior to 12 Apr 04) only 50 percent completed (Figure 4.22), but the calculation is done assuming its 100 percent completion in both the baseline and actual schedules.

Knowing the baseline, actual, and remaining costs for individual tasks allows calculation of the project's current cost. The **current cost** is currently scheduled cost, or the total project cost after considering the project's progress and any related cost adjustments. The current cost is the actual cost up to the current project date plus baseline cost of all remaining tasks. The **remaining cost** is the difference between the current and actual costs.

Task2	Baseline 2 days	Actual 3 days
Bernard 50%	8h * $90 = $720	12h * $90 = $1,080
Diana 50%	8h * $100 = $800	12h * $100 = $1,200
Total	$1,520	$2,280

Task3	Baseline 4 days	Actual 2 days
Kang 50%	16h * $80 = $1,280	8h * $80 = $640
Eric 50%		8h * $60 = $480
Total	$1,280	$1,120

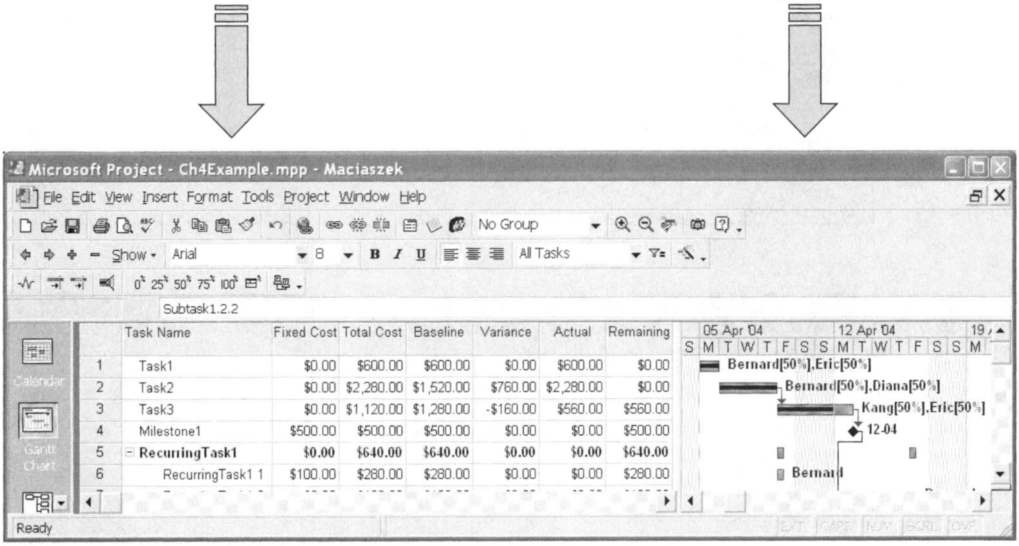

	Task Name	Fixed Cost	Total Cost	Baseline	Variance	Actual	Remaining	05 Apr 04	12 Apr 04	19
1	Task1	$0.00	$600.00	$600.00	$0.00	$600.00	$0.00	Bernard[50%],Eric[50%]		
2	Task2	$0.00	$2,280.00	$1,520.00	$760.00	$2,280.00	$0.00	Bernard[50%],Diana[50%]		
3	Task3	$0.00	$1,120.00	$1,280.00	-$160.00	$560.00	$560.00	Kang[50%],Eric[50%]		
4	Milestone1	$500.00	$500.00	$500.00	$0.00	$0.00	$500.00	12-04		
5	RecurringTask1	$0.00	$640.00	$640.00	$0.00	$0.00	$640.00			
6	RecurringTask1 1	$100.00	$280.00	$280.00	$0.00	$0.00	$280.00	Bernard		

Figure 4.23 Calculating baseline and actual costs
Source: Screenshot of Microsoft® Office Project (2003), reprinted by permission from Microsoft Corporation, Copyright © 1998–2003 Microsoft Corporation

Figure 4.24 represents the costs for the entire project. The figures show current, baseline, actual, and remaining costs of the project. The values reflect the earlier discussion.

Actual costs from accounting

Calculating actual costs from the schedule rarely gives a true and final account of costs committed. Firstly, the schedules are unlikely to include all resources consumed by tasks or even to include all tasks. Secondly, the sluggishness of the accounting system can distort the real story. In all cases when the reality is found not to match the figures in the budget, the budget needs to be modified manually. From the technical point of view, this requires turning off the automatic updating of actual costs in the project management tool and overriding the actual costs for the tasks or resources.

In some cases, the actual cost obtained from the accounting system may be attributed to the *fixed cost* for the task that failed to be entered during scheduling (refer, for example, to the Fixed Cost column in Figure 4.23). In other cases, the actual cost may be attributed to the *per-use cost* charged for a work resource in addition to normal *rate-based fees* (the Cost/Use column in Figure 4.13). In cases like that the modifications to the baseline plan can remove the mismatch.

Figure 4.24
Project costs and other statistics

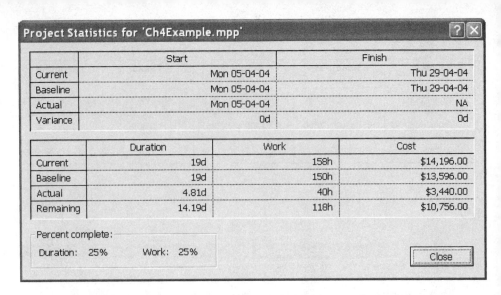

Figure 4.25 Budget changes reported by the accounting system

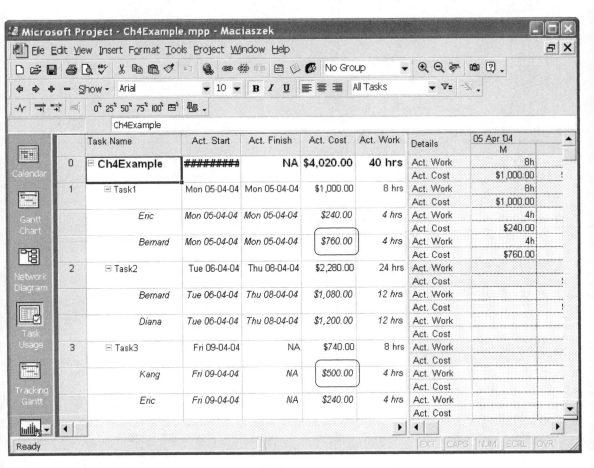

Source: Screenshot of Microsoft® Office Project (2003), reprinted by permission from Microsoft Corporation, Copyright © 1998–2003 Microsoft Corporation

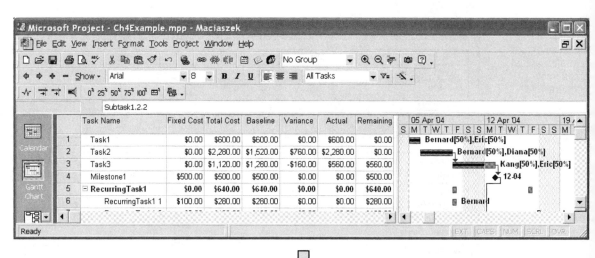

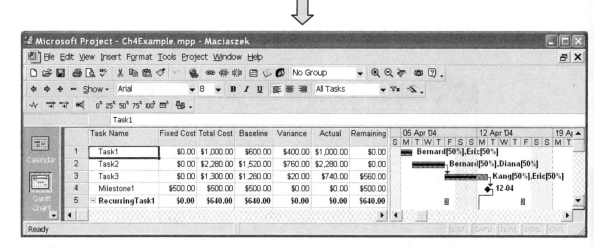

Figure 4.26 Budget before and after actual costs from accounting
Source: Screenshot of Microsoft® Office Project (2003), reprinted by permission from Microsoft Corporation, Copyright © 1998–2003 Microsoft Corporation

Discussion in this chapter concentrates on human resources. Frequently, discrepancies between budgeted costs and actual costs reported by the accounting system are due to non-human resources. All discrepancies between budgeted and actual, whether due to human or non-human resources, must be corrected in the budget (in order to match the actual costs). In the case of human resources, the discrepancies can be corrected by making changes in the schedule. To exemplify the consequences of manual modification of actual costs, Figure 4.25 shows modifications to the actual costs of two resources (encircled), after the costs were provided by the accounting system.

Changes in Figure 4.25 constitute an increase of $400 to Bernard in `Task1` and an increase of $180 to Kang in `Task3`. These increases are automatically reflected in the new budget (Figure 4.26) and in the project cost statistics (Figure 4.27).

Figure 4.27
Project cost
statistics before
and after actual
costs from
accounting

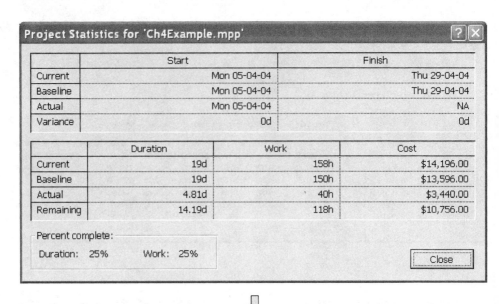

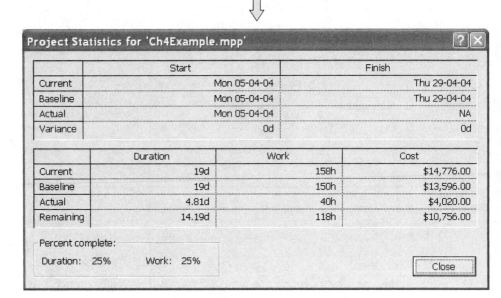

Earned value

Earned value analysis is a quantitative technique to determine if the project is on budget (Pressman, 2001; Lientz and Rea, 2002). The technique uses the baseline estimate of the schedule and the actual progress to date to determine the completeness status ('completeness health') of the project. The analysis is conducted for individual tasks and for the

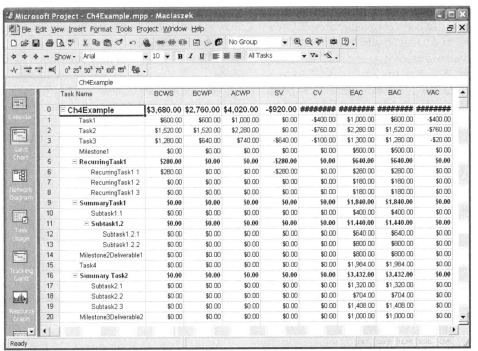

Figure 4.28
Earned value
analysis
Source: Screenshot
of Microsoft® Office
Project (2003),
reprinted by
permission
from Microsoft
Corporation,
Copyright © 1998–
2003 Microsoft
Corporation

BCWS – Budgeted Cost of Work Scheduled
BCWP – Budgeted Cost of Work Performed
ACWP – Actual Cost of Work Performed
SV – Scheduled Variance (SV = BCWP – BCWS)
CV – Cost Variance (CV = BCWP – ACWP)

EAC – Estimate at Completion
BAC – Budget at Completion
VAC – Variance at Completion (VAC = BAC – EAC)

whole project. It can also be taken down to the level of resources within each task.
Earned value analysis is also known as *performance management* and *management by
objectives*.

Earned value analysis can only be conducted if resources and their rates/costs have been
assigned to tasks. From the quantitative point of view, a task without resources cannot have
any work done and cannot have costs or *earned value*.

As Figure 4.28 shows, the earned value analysis provides a variety of complementary
performance measures. The measures are:

■ BCWS – Budgeted Cost of Work Scheduled

■ BCWP – Budgeted Cost of Work Performed

■ ACWP – Actual Cost of Work Performed

■ SV – Scheduled Variance (SV = BCWP – BCWS)

■ CV – Cost Variance (CV = BCWP – ACWP)

■ EAC – Estimate at Completion

■ BAC – Budget at Completion

■ VAC – Variance at Completion (VAC = BAC – EAC)

BCWS is the earned value of the task (or project, or resource) based on the scheduled work. In daily communication, BCWS is known as **scheduled work**. BCWS is calculated for tasks that should have consumed resources and be completed by the date for which the progress is assessed (i.e. `12 Apr 04` in the example). Tasks that have not started have BCWS equal to zero.

BCWP is the earned value of the task (or project, or resource) based on the percentage of scheduled work that has actually been completed by the date for which the progress is assessed. It is also known as **performed work**. For example, in Figure 4.28, BCWS for `Task3` is $1,280. This task is 50 percent complete on `12 Apr 04`. Hence, its BCWP is $640.

ACWP is the sum of all actual costs incurred to date. This includes rate-calculated and fixed costs obtained from the schedule and any manually entered costs obtained from the accounting system. For example, ACWP is $1,000 for `Task1` and $740 for `Task2`, consistent with the changes introduced from accounting (Figure 4.25). ACWP for `Task3` is $2,280 because of changes due to allocation of an extra resource to this task (Figure 4.23).

SV is the difference between BCWP and BCWS. The scheduled variance equal to zero indicates that a task has been completed (except, of course, when both BCWP and BCWS are equal to zero, which means that the tasks have not started). In most other cases, SV is negative and reflects (in absolute money terms) the fact that the work has not been completed.

CV is the difference between BCWP and ACWP. It is an indication of actual cost savings or overruns compared with the baseline budget. In the example, `Task1`, `Task2`, and `Task3` record overruns. More money was spent on the work done on these tasks than scheduled.

EAC is the estimated cost of the task at completion based on the current progress. For completed tasks, EAC is equal to ACWP. For tasks that have not started yet, EAC is equal to the scheduled costs in the baseline (Figure 4.16). For tasks that started but have not completed, EAC is the estimated total cost, including changes from accounting. EAC for `Task3` is $1,300, as explained in Figure 4.26.

BAC is the budgeted cost of the task at completion based on the current progress. For completed tasks, BAC is equal to BCWP. For tasks that have not started yet, BAC is equal to the scheduled costs in the baseline (Figure 4.16). For tasks that started but have not completed, BAC is the actual cost from the schedule. BAC for `Task3` is $1,280, as shown in Figure 4.23.

VC is simply the difference between BAC and EAC. For completed tasks, VC is equal to CV. It is zero for tasks that have not started. For tasks partially completed, VC indicates budget overruns (negative value) or underruns (positive value) when actual costs from accounting are considered.

Earned value analysis is an indispensable tool in the hands of project leaders and managers. It allows for *in-time management* of project progress, early discovery of cost trends, and taking corrective actions to avoid major budget overruns.

Summary

1. *Software project planning and tracking* is an *ongoing* activity of estimating how much time, money, effort, and resources needs to be expended on the project. It is not a separate phase of the development lifecycle – it is an umbrella activity spanning the lifecycle phases.

2. Project *deliverables* are software products or services that meet project objectives. Once deliverables are known, the work can be organized in *milestones*, *phases*, and *tasks*. The work needs *resources*, i.e. people, equipment, materials, supplies, software, hardware, etc. required by project tasks.

3. *Scheduling* for the project is about estimation of time needed for the development and about allocation of resources to tasks. *Budgeting* for the project is about estimation of costs required by resources needed for tasks.

4. Project *scheduling* is a moving target. There are complex dependencies between tasks, various constraints on when the tasks can be performed, and variety of possible interruptions. *Task dependencies* are due to the way the work is organized and due to competition for the same resources. *Inflexible constraints* set specific dates for tasks' start or finish.

5. *Resources* are broadly classified into work resources and material resources. *Work resources* consist of people and equipment, including hardware and software. *Material resources* are consumables and supplies. Resource assignment introduces both flexibility and constraints to scheduling.

6. The approach to scheduling where the duration of tasks can change (up or down) as resources are added or removed from tasks is known as *effort-driven scheduling*. The *resource usage* view shows scheduled work hours of each resource and the hours divided across tasks. The analysis of resource usage allows identification of underallocated and overallocated resources.

7. *Budget estimation* methods range from simplistic methods, such as expert judgment and estimation by analogy, to more rigorous methods, such as schedule-driven estimations and algorithmic estimations.

8. *Schedule-driven budget estimation* assumes that there exists a *baseline* schedule with resources allocated to tasks. The estimation requires entering *rates* and other costs for work and material resources. It requires also defining *accrual methods* for resources.

9. *Algorithmic budget estimation* takes some measure (*metric*) of the size of the problem and applies it to an empirically obtained algorithm to arrive at the budget for solving the problem. The budget estimates cost of human resources (*effort*) as a function of the project size. The *size* is typically expressed in the lines of code (LOC), in function points (FPs), or in object points (OPs).

10. COCOMO 81 and COCOMO II are the best-known algorithmic models. Both models recognize the relative importance of various *cost drivers* in the project cost and effort. There are three COCOMO 81 models: basic, intermediate, and advanced. There are also three COCOMO II models: application composition, early design, and post-architecture.

11. *Tracking project progress* involves two main sets of comparisons: (1) the baseline schedule versus the actual schedule, and (2) the baseline budget versus the actual budget. The tracking considers changes to the planned schedule and the actual costs coming from the accounting system.

12. A tracking Gantt chart can be used in *schedule tracking* to represent the actual schedule status compared with the baseline.

13. *Budget tracking* is a direct continuation of schedule tracking. It tracks actual costs on tasks completed, or in progress, by applying resource rates, accrual methods, and any fixed costs.

14. *Earned value analysis* is a quantitative technique of determining if the project is on budget. The technique uses the baseline estimate of the schedule and the actual progress to date to determine the completeness status of the project.

Key Terms

accrual method	128	overtime rate	128
activity	114	performed work	148
actual	139	per-use rate	128
actual cost	142, 143	phase	114
algorithmic budget estimation	130	plan document	116
application composition model	135	post-architecture model	137
bar chart	*See* Gantt bar chart	project calendar	117
baseline	127, 139	project planning	113
budget	116	quality	114
budget estimation	126	rate	128
budget tracking	141	recurring task	117
COCOMO 81	133	remaining cost	142
COCOMO II	135	resource	114, 121
cost driver	134	resource calendar	121
critical path	117	resource usage	123
current cost	142	risk	115
delay dependencies	119	schedule	116
deliverable	114, 117	schedule tracking	139
early design model	136	scheduled work	148
earned value analysis	146	schedule-driven budget estimation	127
effort	131	size	131
effort-driven scheduling	122	slack time	117
estimation by analogy	127	slippage	117
expert judgment	127	standard rate	128
function points	132	summary task	117
Gantt bar chart	119	task	114, 117
inflexible constraints	120	task dependencies	118
lines of code	131	tracking Gantt chart	140
material resource	121	tracking project	116, 138
milestone	114, 117	variance	140
network chart	117	work breakdown structure	114
object points	133	work resource	121
overlap dependencies	119		

Review Questions

1. What is a typical sequence of steps in project planning?

2. What is a critical path? Draw a simple example of a CPM network graph to show the significance of a critical path for project planning and tracking.

3. Explain the differences between slack time, lag time, and lead time.

4. Explain the principles behind As Soon As Possible (ASAP) and As Late As Possible (ALAP) scheduling.

5. Explain the observation that there is a point at which the increase in budgeting effort yields diminishing budget value.

6. What are accrual methods? How do they affect cost calculations? Give a simple example.

7. Explain the three 'sizing' options in budget estimation: lines of code, function points, and object points. How are they used? How do they compare?

8. How do various cost drivers influence budget estimation? How do they differ? Are there any interesting lessons about software development in general from studying cost drivers?

9. What is the difference between cost drivers and scale factors in COCOMO II?

10. Explain the differences between baseline, actual, variance, and remaining costs.

11. What is the earned value? Explain the concepts of the scheduled work and the performed work.

Problem-Solving Exercises

1. Refer to the Gantt chart in Figure 4.29. Consider the following two changes to the project calendar. The days 8, 9, and 12 April 2004 are nonworking because of Easter holidays. Also,

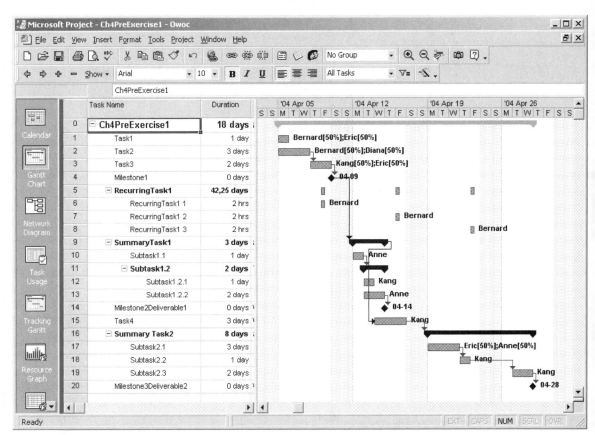

Figure 4.29

Source: Screenshot of Microsoft® Office Project (2003), reprinted by permission from Microsoft Corporation, Copyright © 1998–2003 Microsoft Corporation

Bernard works only half a day (4 hours) each Monday. Make necessary changes to the Gantt chart in Figure 4.29. What is the new delivery date? Is there a change to overall project duration?

2. Refer to the Gantt chart in Figure 4.29 again (Question 1 above). Consider the following three changes: (1) `Task1` is linked to `Subtask1.2.1`, (2) `Task1` is scheduled for As Late As Possible (ALAP), and (3) `Subtask1.2.1` is set to the Must Finish (MFO) constraint for `20 Apr 04`. Make necessary changes to the Gantt chart in Figure 4.29. What is the new delivery date?

3. Consider the post-architecture model of COCOMO II and the effort estimation formula as below:

$$\text{effort} = c \; * \; \text{size}^k \; * \; m \; + \; \text{autoeffort}$$

Assume that the value of the constant coefficient `c` is 2.5, the predicted code `size` is 100 KLOCs, and that `autoeffort` is 35 person-months. Next consider the following values of cost drivers and scale factors in two software projects – Project A and Project B (Tables 4.4 and 4.5). Calculate the values of exponent `k` and multiplier `m` for the two projects. Use these values to estimate the effort required on these two projects.

Table 4.4 Cost drivers for Projects A and B

Driver code	Cost driver name	Project A	Project B
RELY	Required system reliability	1.23 (high)	0.73
CPLX	Complexity of system modules	1.31 (very high)	0.80
DOCU	Extent of documentation required	N/A	0.76
DATA	Size of database used	1.15 (moderate)	0.87
RUSE	Required % of reusable components	1.00 (neutral)	0.94
TIME	Execution time constraints	1.30 (high)	N/A
PVOL	Volatility of development platform	N/A	0.84
STOR	Memory constraints	N/A	N/A
ACAP	Capability of project analysis	N/A	N/A
PCON	Personnel continuity	1.18 (rather low)	N/A
PEXP	Programmer domain experience	1.25 (low)	0.77
PCAP	Programmer capability	1.24 (low)	0.79
AEXP	Analyst experience in project domain	1.33 (very low)	N/A
LTEX	Language and tool experience	1.15 (rather low)	0.90
TOOL	Use of software tools	1.21 (low)	N/A
SCED	Development schedule compression	N/A	N/A
SITE	Extent of multi-site working and quality of site communications	1.05 (not bad)	N/A

Table 4.5 Scale factors for Projects A and B

Scale factor	Project A	Project B
Precedentedness	5 (very low)	1
Development flexibility	4 (low)	2
Architecture/risk resolution	3 (relatively low)	1
Team cohesion	2 (not bad)	0
Process maturity	5 (very low)	1

Chapter

5

Software Process
Management

Software planning and tracking, discussed in the previous chapter, constitutes an important and compelling part of software process management. Project planning and tracking imposes process discipline on software engineers. However, to talk about process management in its own right, a range of other activities must be managed. Project managers need to also manage people, risk, quality, change, etc. Process management applies to multiple projects and aims at overall process improvement in the organization.

Software organizations strive to continuously improve their development procedures and practices. This continuous process improvement requires prior determination of the current **process maturity** level. It also requires that the organization has the knowledge of *key factors* that would result in process improvement, if introduced to the organization's procedures and practices. The concepts of process maturity and of key factors in process improvement underpin the **Capability Maturity Model** (CMM) defined by the Software Engineering Institute (SEI) at Carnegie Mellon University in Pittsburgh, USA (CMM, 2003).

As seen in Figure 5.1, the CMM model defines five increasing levels of process maturity: (1) initial, (2) repeatable, (3) defined, (4) managed, and (5) optimizing (Paulk *et al.*, 1995; Pfleeger, 1998). CMM has become an effective process quality standard. The model has an associated accreditation mechanism, which allows organizations to subject themselves to auditing procedures that attest their process maturity. Many software development contracts demand proof of a particular minimal level of process maturity from software suppliers and contractors.

At the *initial level* of maturity, the organization does not really have any predictable process. Any successful project is a matter of luck, not the result of a managed process. It is just an outcome of good work by some key individuals. If these individuals leave the organization or when some other crisis situation arises, there are no established procedures to follow to put the project back on track.

Moving to the *repeatable level* of maturity requires an improvement in the process discipline. The discipline is the result of planning and tracking activities facilitated by a degree of quality assurance and configuration control. The process at this level is still

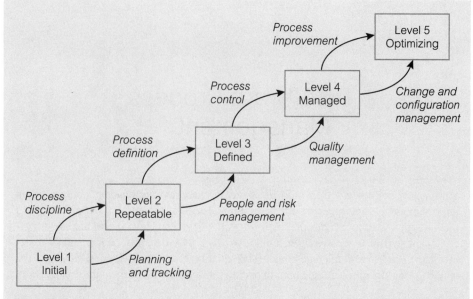

Figure 5.1 CMM levels

quite intuitive, rather than codified, but the experience from the planning and tracking of previous projects can be leveraged (repeated) on the current project.

Moving to the *defined level* of maturity requires improvement in the process definition. The key factors in reaching the defined level are people and risk management. Risk and crisis situations can be addressed with a defined process. Processes are facilitated by an extensive use of software engineering tools.

Moving to the *managed level* of maturity requires improvement in the process control. At this level, process and product metrics are meticulously collected to measure the software quality and people productivity. The metrics allow early detection of problems and the taking of evasive or corrective actions.

Moving to the *optimizing level* of maturity requires improvement in the very area of process improvement. A key factor in process improvement is change and configuration management, including defect and enhancement management as well as changes in the technology and the process itself. The whole area of process improvement is scheduled and budgeted.

The organization of this chapter is consistent with the CMM model and the key factors for moving between levels. The key factor of moving from Level 1 to Level 2 (planning and tracking) was addressed in Chapter 4. The remaining key factors constitute the main sections in this chapter.

People Management

People management is not what it used to be. This is so for several reasons:

- Technology is changing all aspects of business.
- The changing business environment impacts organizational structures resulting in network organizations of loosely connected cooperating units.
- New organizational structures imply new management styles.
- New management styles must be risk tolerant and innovative.
- Risk tolerance and innovation do not square well with bureaucratic people management based on accountability and procedures.
- Modern work teams draw strength from opportunistic collaboration of people, where individuals do not automatically owe any loyalty to the organization but are motivated by the working environment and more abstract work-unrelated needs.

Modern organizations tend to resemble *network structures* of loosely coupled units related by alliances rather than ownership. People in a **network organization** have unique notions of motivation, loyalty, organizational power, leadership, achievement, satisfaction, gratification, etc. (Benson and Standing, 2002). The old style of hierarchical management does not apply for teams in a network organization. Software engineering teams are at the forefront of this wave of change.

Acquiring and Motivating People

Acquiring and motivating people is the essence of the team-building process. The team is formed based on the project plan (Chapter 4) and an associated **staffing management plan**. The team building exercise includes selection of project managers, project leaders and all other team members. Depending on the situation, team members can be the current employees assigned to the project or the team may need to be formed by hiring new employees or acquiring external contractors and consultants.

Modern network organizations may favor **self-directed teams**, but good management and leadership are necessary conditions for the success of any project. The larger the project, the more true this is. Selecting a good project manager, who knows how and when to manage and how and when to lead, is a critical decision of the project owner.

Heldman (2002) assigns the following diverse set of characteristics to **project leaders** and **managers**.

Leaders have a knack for getting others to do what needs done and rallying them around a vision. Good leaders have committed team members who believe in the vision of the leader. Leaders set direction and time frames, and have the ability to attract good talent to work for them. . . . Managers are generally task oriented, concerned with things like plans, controls, budgets, policies, and procedures. They're generalists with a broad base of planning and organizational skills, and their primary goal is satisfying stakeholder needs. They also possess motivational skills and the ability to recognize and reward behavior.

(Heldman, 2002, p.304)

An important point is that a project manager must also be a leader, while the converse is not necessarily true. A good manager must control as well as inspire. The leadership is particularly instrumental on large projects. In such projects, the distance between managers and executors of decisions may include multiple levels of management. To get things done, managers must trust team members and team members must be inspired as well as motivated.

Team creation

The team members are acquired by assigning employees to the project and/or by hiring new employees. *Reassignment of employees* between projects is the responsibility of top management. A project manager should try to find the names of suitable, potentially available and interested employees, and request their reassignment. Suitable does not necessarily mean the best employees (Lientz and Rea, 2002). Best people are in high demand. Reassigning them means that other projects lose out. Having best people raises management expectations about the project. Finally, the best people may not fit into the team and may introduce undesirable tensions.

Hiring new employees provides a better possibility of finding people who can fill in specific needs of the project and the team, but it is always at a greater risk of misjudging the applicants. The decision whom to employ is taken by considering three kinds of input (Sommerville, 2001):

- information provided by the applicants in their employment portfolio
- references obtained on the applicants from their past employers and other external referees
- outcomes from interviews and any employment tests performed by applicants.

Thorough execution of all three inputs is mandatory unless there is another 'trusted' input from people who know the applicant. Although such input is frequently 'off protocol', it certainly plays a role in the hiring practices.

The *tests* to assess applicants fall in two groups: (1) aptitude tests, and (2) psychometric tests (Sommerville, 2001). **Aptitude tests** are designed to uncover a person's skills to perform certain tasks, such as to program in a particular language. **Psychometric tests** are designed to uncover a person's attitude and suitability for certain types of tasks, such as ability to be decisive. Tests are typically conducted under time restrictions and other examination pressures. They may not be a true reflection of the person's problem-solving ability in normal working environment.

People are acquired to fill up specific needs of the project and the team. These needs are diverse and complementary. Typical factors that govern staff selection are (Sommerville, 2001; Lientz and Rea, 2002):

- application domain and business process experience
- technical knowledge, experience and expertise with the methods and tools

- educational background
- problem-solving ability
- communication skills
- adaptability, willingness, and availability
- attitude, ambition, and initiative
- personality.

As stated in passing, modern work teams draw strength from opportunistic collaboration of people, where individuals do not automatically owe any loyalty to the organization but are motivated by the working environment and more abstract work-unrelated needs. Acquiring employees is likely to be a lesser management worry than motivating and retaining them. As noted by Benson and Standing (2002), software engineers tend to be cash-rich and time-poor. Motivating and retaining such employees demands unorthodox approaches, such as allowing work from home or more leisure time.

Motivational theories

Motivation can be **extrinsic** or **intrinsic**.

Extrinsic motivators are material things and might include bonuses, the use of a company car, stock options, gift certificates, training opportunities, and so on. Intrinsic motivators are specific to the individual. Some people are just naturally driven to achieve – it's part of their nature. Cultural and religious influences are forms of intrinsic motivators as well. Reward and recognition . . . are examples of extrinsic motivators.

(Heldman, 2002, p.300)

There are many motivational theories, which try to identify what prompts people in their actions and what factors influence people professional behavior. Explicitly or implicitly, all popular theories acknowledge that people are motivated best when given the opportunity to fulfill high-level abstract 'soul' needs and aims. Low-level fundamental 'body' needs and aims, of obtaining tangible items such as food, clothing, or even money, are weak motivators over and above the 'continued existence level'. The continued existence level means here that these motivators are provided to a person in just sufficient quantity. Increasing this quantity to motivate people better brings only short-term effects.

Heldman (2002) summarizes four well-publicized motivational theories:

- Maslow's Hierarchy of Needs
- Hygiene Theory
- Expectancy Theory
- Achievement Theory.

Maslow's Hierarchy of Needs classifies motivational needs into five groups: (1) physiological needs for food, shelter, etc., (2) safety needs for physical welfare and the security of possessions, (3) social needs for interaction with other people, sense of belonging, love, friendship, etc., (4) esteem needs for recognition, respect, accomplishment, etc., and (5) self-realization needs for personal expression and development. Maslow's theory argues that once a lower-level need has been met and is continuously maintained, it does not serve as a motivator any more. The next higher level becomes the new motivator.

The **Hygiene Theory** of Frederick Herzberg (known also as the Motivation–Hygiene Theory) identifies two motivational factors: (1) hygiene factors, and (2) motivators. Hygiene factors relate to work conditions, personal relationships, pay, benefits, and similar work provisions. Hygiene factors prevent dissatisfaction but are not motivators in the true sense of the word. Motivators are the aspects of work that bring satisfaction from a job well done. Motivators are opportunities for personal advancement, training programmes, challenging but feasible tasks, etc.

The **Expectancy Theory** states that people act and behave according to expectations expressed by their environment, provided these expectations bring rewards. The desire to deliver an outcome that satisfies expectations drives motivation. To be true motivators, any rewards promised must always be fulfilled. Managers setting high expectations regarding performance and openly rewarding high performance are likely to create teams that will live up to the expectations, and vice versa.

The **Achievement Theory** identifies three motivational factors: (1) achievement (desire to succeed), (2) power (desire to influence others), and (3) affiliation (desire of belonging and companionship). The theory does not differentiate among these three motivators. It simply states that the strength of each of these desires determines the blend responsible for the performance of the team.

5.1.2 Project Communications

Communication is the activity of exchanging information and knowledge. It is the process of sending messages from senders to recipients. For many job tasks and roles, communication skills may be more important than technical skills. Arguably, this is true for management jobs. Every aspect of innovative undertakings, such as software engineering projects, is beset with communications.

Software process management addresses project communications from at least four viewpoints (Pfleeger, 1998; Sommerville, 2001; Heldman, 2002; Lientz and Rea, 2002):

- forms of communication
- lines of communication
- facilitating/inhibiting factors in communication
- communication in conflict resolution.

Forms of communication

Messages are exchanged in some encoded form. The code can be verbal, in text, in pictures, in symbols, conveyed by facial expression or intonation, etc. The recipient must understand the sender's code to communicate. The message can be confidential, public, formal, informal, internal, external, horizontal (between peers), vertical (between supervisors and subordinates), etc. Typical **communication forms** are:

- person-to-person casual communications
- person-to-person in-room meetings
- person-to-person telephone conversations
- person-to-person Internet conferencing (in text, voice and/or video)
- telephone voicemail
- facsimiles
- post mail
- courier mail
- electronic mail
- web pages.

Different communication forms have their own unique advantages and disadvantages (Lientz and Rea, 2002). *Person-to-person* forms can convey considerably more information by conversation tone, facial expressions, 'body talk', etc. If not recorded, person-to-person communications can convey even more information by allowing more freedom of expression without fearing the consequences of wider distribution of the text/voice/video record.

Email is a powerful but risky communication medium. Not only can email messages be distributed further, but they can also be forwarded or copied by mistake. Email gives a deceptive feeling of confidentiality of person-to-person communication, but it can end up being a formal and very public disseminator of information. Moreover, when disseminated, it is much more credible than other forms of person-to-person communication because it has been provided with confidentiality and it then becomes public. Unlike *post mail*, the sender of email can usually know if the recipient received it or even read it. In general, email should not be used with sensitive matters.

Web pages are a powerful medium of communication. Web pages allow for quick dissemination of information to large groups of people. They are not disruptive in the sense that intended recipients can access web pages at their will. However, communication through web pages has to ensure timely updating of web information, otherwise web pages will be perceived as unreliable and recipients will stop trying to access the information.

From all the *mail* forms, the text form dominates in formal communication. Voice and video forms are relatively infrequent. They take too much effort and time to 'decode' in order to play a significant role in formal exchanges of information.

Lines of communication

Communication must be managed, and the number of **communication lines** between people and teams must be minimized, while still sufficient to disseminate information and knowledge efficiently. The problem of communication lines brings a parallel with the issue of complexity in the 'wires' raised in Section 1.1.6. Complexity management requires communication via hierarchical structures, grouping people in teams and providing an optimal mix of vertical and horizontal communication lines.

In flat organizational structures, the number of communication lines grows exponentially with the increase of communication participants (Pfleeger, 1998). Figure 5.2 demonstrates the increase in communication lines when the number of participants grows from three to

n people = $n(n-1)/2$ lines of communication
n people = $2^n - 1$ possible teams

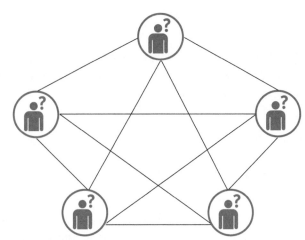

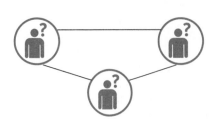

3 people = 3 communication lines, 7 possible teams

5 people = 10 communication lines, 31 possible teams

Figure 5.2 Communication lines and possible teams

five. Each communication line permits exchange of information in both directions, from sender to recipient and vice versa. The associated formula explains the calculation. A reduction in communication lines can be achieved by creating teams and channeling the communication between teams via team leaders/managers. The outcome is similar to that shown in Section 1.1.6 in Figure 1.5.

Figure 5.2 shows a formula for the calculation of a number of possible teams that can be created from a given number of participants. The formula computes the number of possible combinations from a given number of elements. For example, with three participants A, B, and C, the combinations are A, B, C, AB, BC, AC, and ABC. Naturally, at any particular point in time, the maximum number of teams is much smaller and is equal to the maximum number of participants (i.e. the number of one-person teams).

Factors in communication

In reality, it is never necessary for every single piece of information to be communicated to all people on the project. Both too much and too little communication can harm the project. Team members must be informed about everything that affects or relates to the tasks they perform. Project participants must also be informed about global issues, project directions, selected political decisions, etc. to feel that they are an integral part of the project and the organization.

A danger with hierarchical structures and vertical messages is that people at the same level do not communicate sufficiently (Sommerville, 2001). There are various ways of improving communication within such teams. One is the selection of team members to ensure a proper mix of extroverts and introverts (Pfleeger, 1998). An **extrovert** is a person who happily engages other people in communication. An **introvert** is the opposite – a shy, quiet person, frequently a very good listener. (Incidentally, effective listening skills are as important in communication as speaking capabilities.)

The previous point stipulates that a significant amount of communication is incidental. This is both true and desirable. The organization of the workplace can considerably facilitate or inhibit prearranged and/or **incidental communication** (Sommerville, 2001). For example, working within open-plan areas, with or without cubicles, both encourages communication and discourages it at the same time. The discouragement comes from the interruptions to others that open-plan offices facilitate and from the lack of privacy.

No amount of private communication can substitute the need for organized forms of **group communication**. The group communication requires group meeting rooms, properly equipped and sized, in easily accessible areas, and available for formal as well as informal meetings.

Communication in conflict resolution

Conflicts in teams are unavoidable and communication is the primary means of resolving them. Heldman (2002) discusses five techniques for **conflict resolution**. The first three have a lasting effect; the remaining two tend to bring only temporary outcomes. They are:

- forcing
- compromise
- confrontation
- smoothing
- withdrawal.

Forcing in conflict resolution does what it suggests. It forces a solution on team members who are in conflict. Forcing is possible under a supervisor–subordinate dependency. The forced party must accept the resolution but s/he is likely not to agree with it. A supervisor is a project manager or a project leader. Decisions that are forced onto people tend to increase the authority of a project manager (if not used too frequently), but to weaken the charisma and influence of a project leader. The passing of such a decision to interested parties may be done in a form of communication that is not face to face.

By contrast, **compromise** requires face-to-face communication. It requires that parties in conflict speak their minds and reach a middle ground solution with no winners or losers. Because compromise involves reconciliation, the resolution may be a lasting one.

Confrontation is the most effective and most desirable solution, provided one right answer to the conflict exists and that the conflict can be attributed to a specific issue (and not, for example, to personality clashes). Confrontation is known also as problem solving. Once facts are established and the solution to the problem is specified, the decision can be taken and the conflict goes away.

Smoothing is a rather temporary way of resolving conflict in which the problem underpinning the conflict is shown as less significant than it is. Therefore, the scale of the conflict diminishes. Smoothing is frequently just a 'brainwashing' exercise. The conflict is likely to re-emerge later, possibly with increased force. Only in some lucky cases, when the problem goes away by other seemingly unrelated decisions, does smoothing provide a permanent resolution to the conflict.

Withdrawal is another temporary way to resolve conflict in which one party sees no point in discussing the conflict any further. This is undoubtedly the worst conflict resolution outcome, at least as long as both parties remain on the team: not only does communication fail to solve the problem, but the withdrawal results in a diminished communication between team members on all other project issues too.

5.1.3 Team Development

Acquiring and motivating people (Section 5.1.1) and project communications (Section 5.1.2) are two dominating issues in **team development** (called also **team building**). Other issues include team organization, collocation, training, appraisals, performance reports, external feedback, etc.

Teams undergo four stages of development (Heldman, 2002):

- forming
- storming
- norming
- performing.

Team **forming** begins with the initial meeting of employees on the project (Lientz and Rea, 2002). This should be a 'strictly business' meeting in which team members are introduced, their roles are explained, the project schedule is introduced, initial issues are raised, methods and tools are described, etc. Some informal meetings may follow at a later time to 'break the ice'.

Inevitably, once difficult problems surface, the team enters the **storming** stage. Some project issues result in confrontation and conflicts. The backgrounds for problems can be diverse – schedules, priorities, control, money, procedures, personalities, etc. At this stage leaders are born and losers are identified.

The **norming** stage follows. Pushing and pulling gives way to collaboration. Team members know their places in the project. They confront the problems, not each other. Joint decisions are reached without frictions. Friendships are born.

The **performing** stage is reached only by great teams. At this stage the efficiency and effectiveness of the team is better than normal. There is a great understanding in the team and very strong motivation for success. All team members have a sense of belonging and purpose as well as high job satisfaction.

Team development includes **team organization**. There are numerous models suggested for team organization, but in practice it is rare to see teams built exactly according to theoretical models. This probably reflects the uniqueness of software projects, differences in software lifecycles, specificities of organizational cultures, and similar issues. Schach (2002) discusses and compares seven different approaches to team organization.

Team development is a continuing process. It requires constant reinforcement. Even small changes to team structure, work principles, project directions may force the four-stage cycle to start again. A great team can turn into a dysfunctional group of employees. To counteract this, team development should be an important part and contributor to software process improvement. Team development should define performance improvement activities, including work environments, collocation of employees in work areas, training plans, etc. Essential aspects of team development are performance appraisals. Good work should be publicly recognized after it happens, but not by setting up bonuses and rewards, which are likely to cause personal tensions in the team.

Risk Management 5.2

The notions of risk and **risk management** have been introduced in Section 3.1.6 and referred to throughout Chapter 4. References to risks in Chapter 4 signify that risk management is an important consideration in software planning and tracking.

As noted by Lientz and Rea (2002), a project may be much more advanced in terms of schedule and budget than in terms of risk issues because most of the issues may remain to be resolved. Hence, for example, a project may be 80 percent complete but its risk of failing may be as high as 50 percent. Even worse, the project may be completed and deployed to users while some issues remain unresolved. For example, it may be quite probable that the performance of the system will unacceptably deteriorate with occasional peak workloads or with the database growth.

Strategies to manage risks range from reactive to proactive. **Reactive risk strategies** delay handling of risks until they become critical factors in the project. **Proactive risk strategies** encourage acting on risks as soon as they arise or even in anticipation of them happening. Between these two approaches, there are strategies that encourage proactively addressing only the most pressing risk issues in terms of potential loss (impact) and in terms of necessary resolution time.

While, in general, proactive approaches are favored, Lientz and Rea (2002) note the undesirable consequences of 'plunging in too soon':

- Not every symptom ends up in a problem (hence resources may be expended on the issue which would never happen).
- Functional managers may not treat the issue seriously and may develop a wrong opinion of project managers/leaders reporting the issue as crying wolf and panicking.
- Overreacting or taking action with no complete information may worsen the problem.
- Time and patience could bring up a better solution.

This section concentrates on the process of risk management. A typical process involves at least three stages:

1. risk identification
2. risk assessment
3. risk handling.

Risk Identification 5.2.1

Risk identification is a tedious process of listing possible risk issues in brainstorming sessions and using experts' advice and managers' experience. The list must be deliberately restricted in size, e.g. up to 30 risks. Risks with a low potential harm and with a low probability of happening can be excluded from the list.

To help with identifications, risk types are first determined. Typical risk types are:

- project product (i.e. risks due to project size, uniqueness, complexity, etc.)
- project process (due to disregarding or not following the process)
- people (due to personality clashes, poor management, human resource allocations, etc.)
- business (due to changes in business conditions, policies, etc.)
- organizational (due to restructuring, financial difficulties, etc.)
- technology (due to technology inadequacies or technology changes)
- tools (due to incapability of software engineering tools, takeovers of tool vendors, etc.)
- customers (due to communication difficulties, lack of interest in the project, etc.)
- requirements (due to changing, incomplete, ill-defined requirements, etc.)
- other projects (due to dependence on and impact of other projects)
- external factors (due to government regulations, legal implications, etc.).

Specific risks vary greatly between projects. Risk types help in discovering them. In practice, organizations use comprehensive risk checklists, going through them and pinpointing those risks which apply to the project in hand. Sommerville (2001) provides a short list of frequent risks:

- staff turnover (loss of experienced staff during the project)
- management change (new management sets different priorities)
- hardware unavailability (hardware not available when needed)
- requirements change (greater volatility of requirements than built into the plan)
- specifications delays (delays with specifications of required components and interfaces)
- size underestimate (the system turns out to be larger and more complex than expected)
- CASE tool underperformance (incapabilities of CASE tools to sufficiently assist developers)
- technology change (change to the project's technology assumptions)
- product competition (competing products threaten the project's viability).

5.2.2 Risk Assessment

Risk assessment (called also risk analysis, risk estimation, or risk projection) ranks the identified risks in two ways:

1. by the likelihood or probability of the risk happening
2. by the negative impact on the project

Likelihood can use a five-point scale, such as very likely, quite possible, probable, improbable, unlikely. Alternatively, the **probability** can be measured on a nine-point scale,

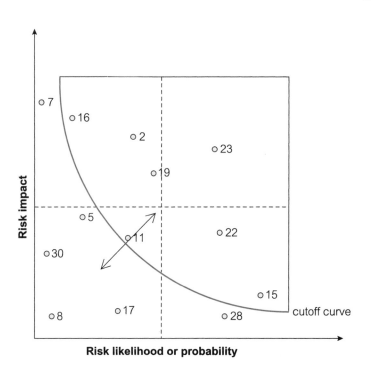

Figure 5.3
Risk exposure and
risk management
cutoff

i.e. 10 percent, 20 percent, etc. up to 90 percent. Risk with a 100 percent probability is not a risk, it is a certainty – a project constraint or requirement.

The negative **impact** can use a five-point scale, such as catastrophic, critical, serious, tolerable, marginal. A decision must be taken on risk reference issues against which the negative impact can be estimated. A usual set of such reference issues, or **risk components**, is as follows (Pressman, 2001):

- schedule risk (that the schedule will not be adhered to)
- budget risk (that budget overruns will happen)
- performance risk (that the product will not meet performance demands)
- supportability risk (that the product will be not maintainable or scalable).

To be able to rank the risks, the negative impact should be normalized and expressed in money terms. It is then possible to calculate the **risk exposure** of each risk by multiplying the likelihood/probability by the impact.

Risk exposure can also be addressed using a graphical layout as in Figure 5.3, where one of the axes indicates the scale of the risk likelihood/probability and the other the scale of the risk impact. Risks are shown as points on intersections between impact and likelihood/probability values. Risks under the cutoff curve are disregarded in further risk management. Risks above the cutoff curve need to be further managed. To change the number of risks to be managed, the cutoff curve can be moved in the direction of arrows.

Figure 5.3 assumes that risk impact and risk likelihood/probability are weighted equally in estimating the significance of risks. Out of thirteen risks depicted in Figure 5.3, seven

Figure 5.4
Changing risk
management
cutoff

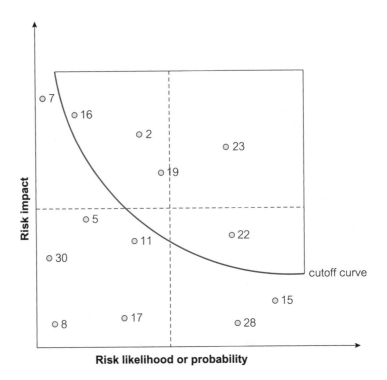

meet the cutoff curve and will be further managed. Six risks are under the cutoff curve and will be disregarded in further risk management.

Moving the cutoff curve in the direction of the arrows shown in Figure 5.3 changes the number of risks to be considered for further management. Figure 5.4 demonstrates the outcome of a double action of moving the cutoff slightly up and rotating it to give less weight to likelihood/probability. As a result, only five risks are included for further management.

It must be noted that, over time, some risks diminish or disappear and other risks strengthen or emerge. This means that risk positions on the graphs change. Like scheduling and budgeting, risk management is a moving target. If necessary, the decision to terminate the project due to unsustainable risks may need to be taken.

Research by Charette (1989) recommends **risk referent levels** as the basis for computing **project termination points**. A risk referent level is a combination of risk components (schedule, budget, performance, supportability). It defines the level of project tolerance for risks – a breakpoint at which the project should be terminated. Figure 5.5 is a graphical visualization of a possible referent termination curve for two of the four components (schedule and budget) (Sommerville, 2001). The project should be terminated if the current project *referent point* is in the project termination area above the reference curve.

In practice, the reference level cannot be graphically represented as merely a reference curve. Firstly, graphical visualization is not easily possible for more than two risk components. Secondly, reference points do not form a smooth curve. They create a ragged line, or rather a region with areas of possible termination.

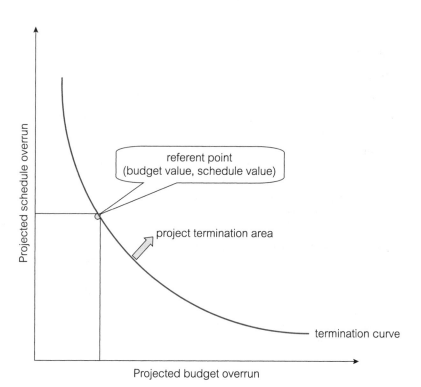

Figure 5.5
Risk referent
levels and project
termination points

Understandably, project termination is a difficult decision, normally with important personal consequences. The politics related to project termination frequently stand in the way of using solely the estimations of risk management for such decisions. Barring politics, assessing whether or not the project should be terminated is always full of subjective judgments. Subjectivity is not so much with regard to the computation of referent levels as with the inputs to such computation: risk impact and likelihood/probability values.

Risk Handling   5.2.3

As mentioned, risks change over time and need to be constantly monitored. Results of risk monitoring are used to modify risk plans and the planning–monitoring cycle continues. Risk planning and monitoring strategy can form a distinct **risk management plan** or can be included in the overall project management plan.

Apart from a document that defines risk management activities, a risk management plan is unlikely to be a hard-copy document. It is rather a **risk database** – a database tool/application allowing storing, searching, prioritizing, sorting, updating, and production of reports at will. The risk database is used for all three stages of risk management: identification, assessment, and handling.

Assuming a proactive approach to risk management, **risk handling** employs a combination of three strategies:

- risk avoidance
- risk minimization
- contingency planning.

The risk avoidance strategy attempts to eliminate the likelihood/probability of the risk occurring. For example, if there is a risk of losing a key team member due to his/her unhappiness about flexible working hours, an offer to work from home on some days can be made to that person.

The risk minimization strategy attempts to diminish the impact of the risk when it occurs. With relation to the previous example, to minimize the impact of the staff loss, another team member may be trained to match the knowledge and skills of the team member who may quit the job.

The contingency planning strategy accepts that risk may become a reality and there is a need to know how to react when this happens. A contingency plan defines the sequence of actions to be taken when other strategies have failed and the risk has become a fact. For example, the key team member is leaving with two weeks' notice and there is no immediate replacement available. The contingency plan may then specify that a replacement employee/contractor should be hired, the budget and schedule should be adjusted accordingly, and the departing employee should spend the remaining two weeks documenting the status of his/her work.

5.3 Quality Management

Software quality management is an umbrella activity that intertwines with most other management undertakings and cuts across the entire development lifecycle and process. It intertwines and cuts across, but it is an independent activity. A quality management team should be separate from the development team and have its own reporting channels. Quality management should be independent from project management. The quality management plan should have its own budget and schedule, at least as far as the quality assurance is concerned (Section 5.3.3).

Quality management has been the subject of intense standardization efforts. The Capability Maturity Model (CMM), discussed at the beginning of this chapter, is a de facto standard for a quality process. The International Organization for Standardization adopted the ISO 9000 series of quality standards. The standards apply to any industry and all types of activity domains, including software engineering. An ancillary document, known as ISO 9000-3, elucidates ISO 9000 for software engineering.

More recently, the key standards within the ISO 9000 series of standards have been merged into a single standard, known as ISO 9001:2000 (ISO, 2003). The emphasis of the standard is on managing key processes to continually improve them (this is analogous to CMM Level 5). As in the case of CMM certification, ISO provides an opportunity for organizations to register their conformance to ISO-defined processes.

Quality management standards are predominantly concerned with defining quality processes which would ensure quality in the products. This is different to quality mechanisms concerned with controlling quality in the products. Accordingly, *quality assurance* (Section 5.3.3) is distinguished from *quality control* (Section 5.3.2).

Software Qualities   5.3.1

Different users (and different developers) may have different opinions about what constitutes **software quality**. There are many desired qualities and, depending on a software project, some of them may be more important than others. Software qualities need to be identified, defined, and classified.

The main classification divides software qualities into **product** and **process qualities**. Usually it is not possible to produce a quality product without having a quality process that defines production activities. The purpose of the process is a product. Consequently, although qualities can be attributed to the process per se, all process qualities can be directly linked to product quality. The reverse is also true.

From the viewpoint of quality management, product quality must be assured and controlled not only on the **end product** delivered to the customer, but also (first of all) on all intermediate **work products** (known collectively as **artifacts**). Managing quality in work products demands support of *configuration management tools* able to store and manipulate multiple artifacts, their versions and relationships between them.

Ghezzi *et al.* (2003) provide an excellent account of representative qualities of software products and processes. The representative qualities are:

- correctness
- reliability
- robustness
- performance
- usability
- understandability
- maintainability (repair ability)
- scalability (evolvability)
- reusability
- portability
- interoperability
- productivity
- timeliness
- visibility.

Correctness is a set of formal properties of software that institutes one-to-one correspondence between the software product and its functional specifications. There are two problems with the correctness quality. Firstly, there is a strong argument in favor of the well-known observation that it is not possible to prove a program correct because it is not possible to guarantee the absence of errors in such complex products as software. Secondly, functional specifications are rarely defined with enough precision and stability to serve as an exhaustive reference point in deciding the correctness properties. It would be, therefore, possible to have correct software for incorrect requirements.

Reliability (also called **dependability**) is a property of software that makes the software trusted and believed in by the users because it behaves well and in the way users expect. Ideally, the notion of software reliability should include the notion of correctness. While this is true in traditional engineering disciplines, in software engineering a reliable software is allowed to contain 'known bugs'. Even if new errors are encountered, the software may be still considered reliable (enough).

Robustness implies that the software is unlikely to fail or break, or at least fail or break in an irrecoverable way. Robustness complements the notions of correctness and reliability. Jointly, these three qualities define whether the software performs its designated functions as expected. Moreover, all three properties can refer to product as well as process qualities.

Performance means to operate satisfactorily, according to predefined targets. The usual target is response time of the software system, which specifies how long the user is prepared to wait for the system to respond to the user's request. Unlike many other qualities, performance is a black-and-white quality: either the system meets the performance indicator or it does not.

Usability relates to the user friendliness of the software; how easy it is for the users to make the software work for them. This is a very subjective property. What is friendly and easy for one person may be unfriendly and difficult for another. The usability quality is predominantly a feature of the design of the user interface for the system. As in traditional engineering disciplines, the more standard and typical the user interface, the more usable it is. Innovative designs of user interfaces may look nice but they are not terribly usable, especially for novice but computer-literate users.

Understandability refers to the ease with which the meaning of the internal structure and behavior of the software can be analyzed and comprehended by a software maintainer. Understandability is a condition for maintainability.

Maintainability of software is unlike maintainability of other engineering products. Software parts do not break due to prolonged use, power surges, or similar causes. In software engineering, maintainability is an all-encompassing concept meaning any of the three tasks: (1) correcting software errors and deficiencies, (2) adapting the software to new requirements, and (3) perfecting the software to give it new qualities. In the narrow meaning of the word, accepted here, maintainability is restricted to the first point. This is called **repairability** by Ghezzi *et al.* (2003).

Scalability, or **evolvability**, is the ease with which the software can be scaled up or evolved in response to the growth in demand for its functionality. Scalability can only be achieved in systems with clear, understandable architectural design. Once the architecture of the system deteriorates due to maintenance (repairs), the scalability diminishes. Understandability, maintainability, and scalability are known under the combined name of **supportability**.

Reusability of software defines the level to which the software components can be used for construction of other products. Software can be reused in two ways. It can be used as a **component** of another product, or it can be used as a generic **framework** that needs to be customized to create another product. Reusability applies also to software processes.

Portability means that the software can run on various hardware/software platforms without any modifications or after undergoing minor customization or parameterization. Portability has an economic significance. This quality is essential in system software, less so in application software.

Interoperability defines the ability of software to coexist or work together with other software, possibly even with the future software that does not yet exist. Like portability, interoperability is crucial in system software. The interoperability quality underpins software known as **open systems**.

Productivity is a process quality factor. Productivity defines the rate at which the process allows software to be produced, given a certain amount of resources. Productivity is the measure of the process efficiency and performance.

Timeliness is another process quality factor, which defines the ability of the process to produce software on time. On time, usually means according to the baseline schedule (a revised schedule, according to which the product has been delivered, is unlikely to be timely). In case of commercial products, timeliness may mean on-time-to-market.

Finally, **visibility** is also a process quality factor. A visible process is a transparent process – the process with clearly defined and documented stages and activities. A visible process is a condition for good project and risk management. A visible process is also a condition for an organization to obtain a CMM certification or ISO registration.

Quality Control   5.3.2

Quality control is mostly about testing the quality of a product, as opposed to **quality assurance** that is about building quality into the product. Quality control has a reactive flavor. Quality assurance is very much a proactive undertaking. Quality control is mainly an operational and tactical effort. Quality assurance has a strong strategic aspect. Sometimes, quality control is considered a part of quality assurance.

Pressman (2001) equates quality control with **variation control**. Variation control is the concept used in manufacturing where multiple copies of the same product are produced and they should be identical. A copy, which shows variations compared with a model (template) copy, fails the quality test.

In software engineering, multiple copies of software product are not a concern. The majority of application software products exist in a single copy. When multiple copies are produced, such as with commercial system software, the duplication is a simple matter of producing compact disks or other storage media. Frequently, commercial software distribution does not even produce multiple copies – the software can be downloaded from the website of the software vendor.

Software testing

However, there is a parallel between software quality control and variation control. Quality control is about finding variations in a work or end product compared with a given specification. The specification can demand a fulfillment of a functional requirement and/or a satisfaction of the qualities listed in Section 5.3.1. The aim of software quality

Figure 5.6
Relative cost of
correcting an error

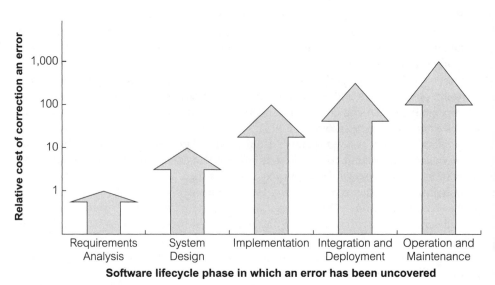

Software lifecycle phase in which an error has been uncovered

control is to subject the software to frequent tests in order to eliminate problems as early as possible. In many ways, software quality control is synonymous with **software testing**.

As explained in Section 1.2 and elsewhere in the book, testing is not a separate phase of the development lifecycle. Like quality management, testing is an umbrella activity that applies to all lifecycle phases. Naturally, testing is most intense when the code is available. Paradoxically, however, testing of code is not necessarily the most valuable kind of testing in terms of the project schedule and budget.

As reported in old studies by IBM, the relative cost of correcting an error grows almost exponentially depending on the lifecycle phase in which the error has been detected. The IBM research has established a belief that the cost of correcting an error may grow by a factor as high as 10s between lifecycle phases (Figure 5.6). Hence, assuming that correcting an error found during requirements analysis costs $1 to correct, correcting the same error would cost as much as $10 to correct if it was uncovered during system design, $100 if uncovered during implementation, and as much as $1,000 if detected after the system has been deployed to the users.

This universally accepted truth about the relative cost of correcting errors gives additional motivation and importance to quality control and testing activities. Testing takes different forms depending on the development phase. During requirements analysis, testing attempts to establish the completeness of requirements, to eliminate inconsistencies and contradictions, to validate any software prototypes with the users, etc. During system design, testing cross-checks various design models, traces design artifacts to specifications, ensures that all requirements are addressed, etc. During implementation and later, testing of the code takes a leading position.

There is an interesting dependency between software development artifacts and testing of code. The dependency is that later stages of testing concentrate on validating earlier development artifacts. This observation is pictured in Figure 5.7 (Pfleeger, 1998). Hence,

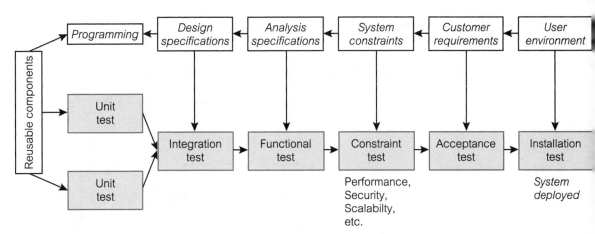

Figure 5.7 Dependencies between testing types and development phases

for example, integration tests are conducted against architectural and detailed design specifications. However, acceptance tests emphasize current customer requirements, which hopefully have not changed since they were documented for the analysis and design purpose. If they did change, acceptance tests may bring negative customer feedback and the issues raised need to be resolved between customers and project managers.

Testing techniques

There are many possible **testing techniques**, which can be intermixed to provide the best possible testing coverage and outcomes. No matter how extensive the testing is, it cannot be exhaustive and guarantee program/system correctness. It is never possible to test for all possible data inputs or code execution paths.

Testing techniques (strategies) can be classified according to various criteria (Unhelkar, 2003). The following discussion is based on five criteria: (1) visibility, (2) automation, (3) partitioning, (4) coverage, and (5) scripting (Figure 5.8). The criteria are not independent. For example, the two partitioning techniques apply mostly to black box testing, but not really to white box. The scripting techniques (regression tests and exercising tests) are automatic tests.

Black box testing (or **testing to specs**) assumes that the tester does not know or chooses to ignore the internal workings of the program unit under test. The test unit is considered a black box, which takes some input and produces some output. The testing is done by feeding the test unit with data inputs and verifying that the expected output is produced. Because no implementation knowledge is required, black box testing can be conducted by the users. Accordingly, this is the main technique of acceptance testing.

The black box technique tests system functionality, or the system functional outputs, to be precise. It is also applicable for constraint testing, such as system performance or security. A special target of black box testing is **missing functionality**, i.e. when an expected functional requirement has not been implemented in the software. In such a case,

Figure 5.8
Testing techniques

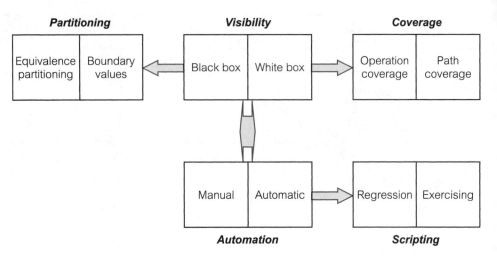

the test unit gets data to trigger such functionality and fails because the code to do the job is not there.

White box testing (or **testing to code**) is the opposite of black box testing. The test unit is considered a white box or, better, a transparent **glass box** that reveals its content. In this approach, the tester studies the code and decides on data inputs that are able to 'exercise' selected execution paths in the code. Black box testing must normally be followed by white box testing to pinpoint the errors discovered when testing to specs.

Unlike black box testing, white box testing is not restricted to code testing. It is equally suitable for other development artifacts, such as design models and specification documents. Testing of this kind uses review techniques, such as walkthroughs and inspections (Section 5.3.3). An interesting discovery possible with white box testing, but not with black box, is the existence of 'dead code'. The **dead code** are statements in the program that cannot be exercised, i.e. they will never be used no matter what input is given to the code.

The equivalence partitioning and boundary value techniques apply mostly to black box testing, although white box testing can also benefit from them. They are specific approaches to the black box technique to counteract the impossibility of conducting exhaustive tests.

Equivalence partitioning groups data inputs (and, implicitly, data outputs) into partitions constituting homogeneous test targets. The assumption is that testing with any one member of the partition is as good as testing with other members. Therefore, testing with the other members can be forfeited. Choosing the homogeneous partitions is the main difficulty. Partitions must be chosen with a good knowledge of data and the application demands for data. In this sense, partitioning per se is not really black box (it is not even a testing technique as such). Black box is the testing technique that equivalence partitioning supports.

Boundary value is merely an additional data analysis technique to assist in equivalence partitioning and, consequently, to assist in black box testing. Boundary values are extreme cases within equivalence partitions. For example, if the partition is a set of integer values from 1 to 100, the boundary value analysis will recommend tests to be done on the values on the edges of the partition, i.e. for −1, 0, +1 as well as for 99, 100, and 101. Naturally, the expected outcome for testing on −1 and 101 would be an error condition.

Coverage techniques determine how much code is going to be exercised by a white box test. **Operation coverage**, called also **method coverage**, ensures that each operation in the code is exercised at least once by the white box test. Operation coverage is a modern object-oriented substitute for statement and branch coverage, which apply in procedural programming languages.

Path coverage aims at numbering possible execution paths in the program and exercising them one by one. Clearly, the number of such paths is indefinite in large programs. The tester is only able to define the most critical and most frequently used paths, and only these paths will be exercised.

Testing can be manual or automatic (Unhelkar, 2003). A human tester who interacts with the application under test conducts manual testing. The tester launches the application, systematically executes its functions and observes the results. The execution steps are conducted according to a predefined *test script*. The test script defines step-by-step testing actions and expected outcomes. Use cases and other requirements specification documents are used to write test scripts.

The main problem with manual tests is that, in most practical situations, they are performed on 'live data'. There is no fixed baseline data predefined to guarantee the same output for repeating execution of manual tests. For this reason, expected output is not always defined precisely in the test scripts. Frequently, the output is not even presented to the screen, but it is manifested in database changes. This forces the tester to write and execute SQL scripts or other *test harnesses* to check the results of test actions.

Manual tests are expensive to prepare, execute, and manage. They are unable to satisfy the 'volume' demands of testing. **Automated testing** employs software testing tools to execute large volumes of tests without human participation. The tools are also able to produce necessary post-test reports to facilitate management of test outcomes. Naturally the preparatory tasks, such as deciding what to test, programming some test scripts, and setting up the testing environment, must still be done by human experts.

As indicated in Figure 5.8, automated testing can be divided into regression testing and exercising testing. **Regression testing** is a popular term to mean repetitive execution of the same test scripts on the same baseline data to verify that previously accepted functionality of the system has not been broken by successive changes to the code, i.e. changes seemingly unrelated to the tested functionality.

Regression testing is performed by automatic execution of pre-recorded test scripts at scheduled test times. Original test scripts are recorded by a **capture/playback tool** in the process of capturing the human tester's actions on the application under test. Regression testing is a playback activity of playing back the scripts. In many cases, the tool-captured scripts are modified (improved) by a test programmer to allow regression testing of features, which the tool could not record automatically.

Exercising, for the lack of a better term, is really an automated coverage testing. A tool that implements exercising testing generates automatically and randomly various possible actions that otherwise could be performed by the user on the application under test. This could be compared to a mad user hitting any possible key on the keyboard, selecting any possible menu item, pressing any available command button, etc.

Generated actions are recorded (captured) in a script, sometimes called the **best script**, which is deemed to be able to exercise the application. Any errors or application failures are recorded as well and a separate script is generated for actions that led to the problem. This is called a **defect script**. The defect script can be played back at any time to reproduce the error and try to determine the reason behind it.

Because both regression and exercising tests use capture/playback tools, which result in programs in some scripting language, they can feed off each other, thus creating a powerful automated testing environment. In practice, the difficulty with automated testing is not in conducting it, but in running consecutive tests on a stable testing environment, with an identical testbed database, with the same state of open and active applications on the test workstation, with predictable network speed, with network broadcasting to the workstation disabled, with the same desktop appearance (including video resolution, desktop colors, fonts), etc. Finally, all automatic tests should clean up after themselves and re-create the database and application testbed as it was before the tests started.

Test planning

A **test plan** is a part of the quality management plan. The test plan defines the testing schedule, budget, tasks (test cases) and resources. The plan must not be restricted to code testing. It should include testing of other project artifacts. It should also link to change management tasks responsible for handling defects.

Part of test planning is the identification of the **test environment**, as separate from the development environment. The plan should specify which test tasks should be conducted in a test environment and which in a development or production environment. A test environment requires allocation of human and material resources. Test workstations must be specified, the test database created, and the test software tools installed.

Figure 5.9 is a class model of testing concepts relevant to test planning. The test plan is developed around **test cases** (or tasks in a traditional planning sense). Requirements constitute test input to test cases. A requirement can be a use case requirement or test requirement. Ideally, test requirements are derived from and correspond to use case requirements. Therefore, test cases should contain statements about test requirements.

Each test case defines the hardware/software configurations for conducting the test as well as iterations recommending when the tests should be executed. A configured test case can be instantiated for execution as an automated test.

Test cases are realized in **test scripts**. Each test script consists of detailed listing of test steps and **verifications points** (which are the questions checking any significant outcomes of test steps). Test scripts can be combined in **test suites**. Test suites can contain other test suites. Automated testing is capable of performing test suites as single entities.

A test script can be destined for an automated or manual test. A human tester performs a manual test. A virtual tester, which is a workstation that can launch the application under test and execute a test program on that application, performs an automated test. Automated tests can be run on a local computer (within the development environment) or on an agent computer (within the test environment). Running the test on an agent computer does not preclude viewing and recording the test results on the local computer.

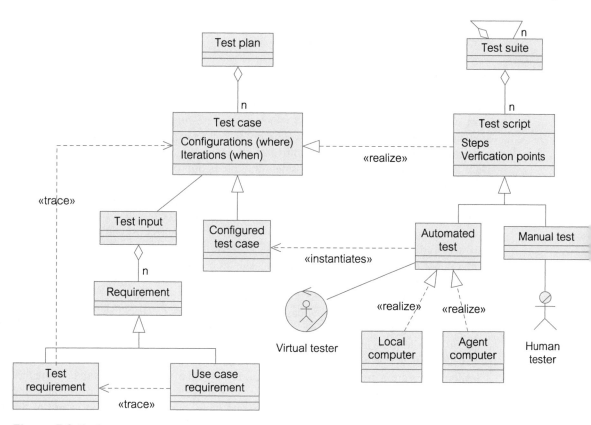

Figure 5.9 Testing concepts

Quality Assurance 5.3.3

Quality control and quality assurance are two sides of the same coin – quality management. Both include a feedback loop to the development process. Apart from the already mentioned differences between quality control and quality assurance, perhaps the most distinguishing difference is that **quality assurance** is a management-level function (even though some quality assurance activities are conducted by the developers alone).

The management-designated **software quality assurance** (SQA) group conducts quality assurance. The group is independent from developers and reports to functional management (this could be at operational, tactical or even strategic level, depending on the significance of the project). Being a management function, quality assurance monitors not just development product and processes, but also project plans – schedule, budget, allocation and utilization of resources.

Quality assurance verifies the compliance of software products and processes with the adopted standards. As the name suggests, quality assurance is a reassuring activity – to reassure all project stakeholders (owners, customers and developers) that the system quality is high.

From a range of quality assurance undertakings, three deserve closer look. These are: (1) checklists, (2) reviews, and (3) audits.

Checklists

In everyday life, a checklist is a list of things to do. In quality assurance, a **checklist** is a list of issues and questions against which a software product or process is verified for quality properties. It is a baseline of quality measures expected in software. Although a checklist is probably the most primitive of all quality assurance techniques, it is easy to use and can provide an early assessment and prediction of the quality of the product or process.

A checklist may be a simple list of relatively independent checkpoints or it can be a logical sequence of steps such that each step feeds off the previous step. In the former case, a checklist resembles a questionnaire. In the latter case, a checklist can contain branches to steer further checks to specific paths. Checklist items can be prioritized according to importance or to the time when the checks should be conducted.

Checklists can be used independently or as part of another quality assurance task, such as a review or audit. Indeed, a checklist guides the very conduct of a formal review (walkthrough or inspection). Standards organizations produce checklists, which software organizations use to check if their processes conform to standard requirements. Checklist questions need to be addressed to obtain a CMM certification or ISO registration.

Checklists are an important element of shaping the *quality culture* within an organization. They are a great educational device, in particular when used to validate whether software models, including programs, have been constructed according to the modeling principles and patterns. Making a mistake, and then being told about the nature of the mistake, is arguably the most effective learning technique. Checklists are about locating mistakes and informing about their nature.

The last point makes it clear that the quality of a checklist itself is a prerequisite for the successful use of the technique. The best people in the organization and people who have experience in software development must create checklists. Bad checklists will have a negative and long-lasting impact on the quality culture.

Reviews

A **review** in quality assurance refers to a formal meeting of developers, and possibly managers, to review a work product or process. The notion encompasses a range of pre-organized technical meetings, of which the best known are **walkthroughs** and **inspections**.

Reviews are document driven. A document is prepared in advance and made available to review participants prior to the meeting. Participants are expected to study the available material in preparation for the meeting. The review is restricted to a small number of people: a *review leader* (and meeting moderator), the developer whose work is reviewed (a *producer*), and a couple of fellow developers.

During the meeting, the producer explains ('walks through') the piece of work under review and allows the reviewers to raise issues. The meeting pinpoints and documents the problems, but does not attempt to solve them. Acknowledged problems are recorded in a review issues list (Pressman, 2001), which is handed to the producer after the meeting. The list guides the producer in making corrections to the work product or process. Once the corrections are made, the review leader is informed about it and evaluates the work and corrections made. If necessary, a follow-up meeting is called.

Special features of a formal technical review are as follows:

- It can be used for any work product and process that is contained in any kind of document (this can be a UML model, a test plan, user manual, a piece of code, a process definition, etc.).

- Complete materials for the meeting are distributed and studied in advance (the preparation should not demand more than a couple of hours of work by each reviewer).

- The membership of the meeting is clearly defined and normally restricted to up to five people.

- The duration of the meeting is short (two hours or less).

- The tasks allocated to the participants are clearly specified:
  - a review leader evaluates the material for readiness for the meeting, distributes documents to participants, organizes and moderates the meeting
  - a producer 'walks through' the document and answers questions
  - all reviewers, including the review leader, raise issues based on their advance studies (one of the reviewers takes notes and produces a review issues list; this person is called a recorder or secretary).

- The meeting pinpoints and documents the problems in a review issues list, but does not attempt to solve them (the review issues list is then filed as part of the formal project documentation).

- All care must be taken to ensure that the meeting reviews the work product or process, not the producer (and no personal appraisal consequences result from the meeting).

- The number of meetings is not restricted but any meeting is set at the discretion of a review leader or project leader.

Walkthroughs and inspections are similar. The main difference is that inspections are carried out under close management supervision, are less frequent, and address larger and less technical problems. There is lots of evidence that formal reviews work well provided they are done well. They contribute to overall quality culture, increased productivity, meeting deadlines, project awareness, development of professionalism, etc.

Audits

Audits have a much more comprehensive charter than checklists or reviews. An **audit** is an IS/IT quality assurance process similar in scope, required resources, and level of assumed expertise to traditional accounting audits. It is the most formal of all quality assurance techniques. An audit starts with extensive preparations and studies of the audited system and continues with interviews and inspections. Obtained information is validated as much as possible, and conclusions are reached. The conclusions about the status of the process or product are documented in a formal report, which also includes a risk assessment for the continuation of the project.

Unhelkar (2003) points out the following differences between an audit and other quality assurance techniques:

- The producer of the audited product or process is usually a team, not a person.
- An audit can be performed without the presence of the producer.
- Audits make extensive use of checklists and interview and less of reviews.
- Audits can be external, i.e. conducted by auditors external to the organization.
- An audit can last from a day to a week or more (but is always restricted to strictly defined scope and objectives).

The scope of an audit is normally much wider than that of other quality assurance undertakings. Auditing recognizes the strategic importance of IT to the business and focuses on IT governance and business reengineering issues. The audited project is analyzed from the viewpoint of overall IT investments and its alignment with the business mission.

Auditing involves the whole range of organizational plans and finances, not just the project plan. It considers legal implications and project management issues. Typical objectives are the detection and prevention of frauds and security breaches as well as planning for contingencies and disaster recovery. A particular emphasis is on evaluating the efficiency and effectiveness of the use of all project resources.

There is a close dependency between the audited product and process and wider business policies and procedures. An audit of the project provides inputs to ensure consistency with business policies and procedures. It also recommends complementary policies and procedures applicable to the project.

5.4 Change and Configuration Management

The topic of change and configuration management has been introduced in Section 3.4 in the context of capabilities of tools supporting these activities. In many ways, the sophistication of change and configuration management is evidence of the maturity of the whole development process. As noted at the beginning of this chapter, an improvement in change and configuration management is a key factor in reaching the optimal level of maturity on the CMM scale (Figure 5.1).

Change and configuration management is the process of managing product and process artifacts and managing the teamwork activities in an evolving software system. The process relates to the entire lifecycle of software, from its inception to retirement. Organizations must plan for change. Change and configuration management heralds and strengthens all other management processes, including quality management.

Figure 5.10 shows the main concepts and dependencies in change and configuration management. Change requests can result in changes to use cases and use case requirements. Some changes become enhancements (future features) and are not considered in the current development. There is a mapping between use case requirements and test requirements. Test requirements can be thought of as verification points in test scripts.

System modeling draws on use case requirements to create model artifacts, including the code. Artifacts are versioned, i.e. there may be multiple versions of the same artifact.

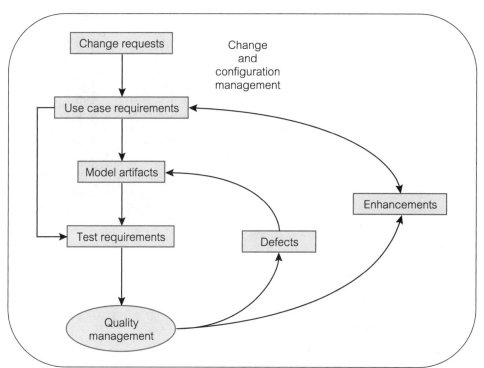

Figure 5.10
Concepts and
dependencies
in change and
configuration
management

Model artifacts have verification points in test requirements. Some test requirements fail quality management tasks. These are mostly defects, but some may be classified as enhancements. Making software failures into enhancements restricts, in effect, the system scope. Some use case requirements need to be taken out of the scope of the current project.

Requirements Changes   5.4.1

The reality of software projects is that user requirements change during the software development lifecycle. Some requirements cease to apply, other requirements get modified, and new requirements are introduced. Changes to requirements must not be taken lightly. They need to be approved in a formal change request process.

Change management involves both manual and automated processes. Any desire to make a change in requirements should be formally submitted as a change request. A **change request form** (CRF) contains recommendations about proposed change, name of the change submitter, date, projected costs, and other implications. The CRF can be manually filled or it can be generated from the change management system (this will happen if the change is the result of a proposed enhancement (Figure 5.10)). A manually filled form needs to be keyed in and registered in the change database.

Each change request undergoes careful assessment of technical and other merits. It is then passed to project managers for approval. In some organizations, a person or a group of people is charged with the responsibility for taking decisions on change requests. Such

Figure 5.11
Traceability
between use case
requirements and
test requirements
Source: Maciaszek,
2001. Reprinted
by permission of
Pearson Education

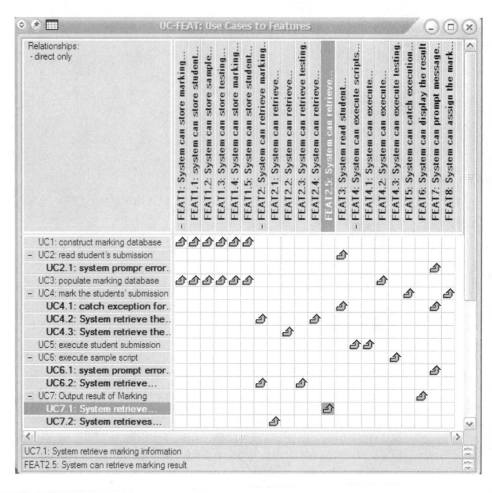

a group has the grandiose name of **change control authority** (CCA) or **change control board** (CCB). The decision considers strategic and organizational as well as technical impacts. Approved changes result in *engineering change orders* (ECO) (Pressman, 2001). An ECO specifies exact changes to be made, any constraints, and criteria for quality assurance.

Each use case requirement is analyzed for how it can be tested and one or more test requirements are associated with it (Figure 5.11). Any changes to requirements necessitate corresponding changes in test requirements. All CRFs and ECOs are archived for any future references, but typically there is no version control performed on them (Sections 3.4 and 5.4.2).

5.4.2 Artifact Versions

Development work results in production of model artifacts, including code. Various members of the development team produce the artifacts. There may be many useful

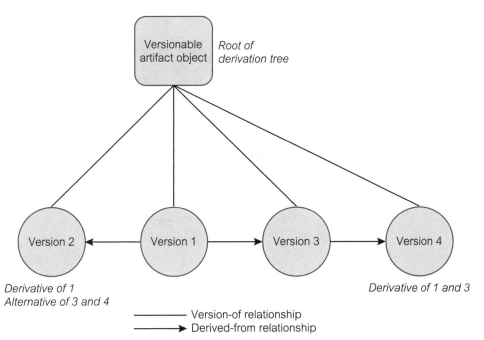

Figure 5.12
Versions

versions of the same artifact. Storing and manipulating versions is the domain of **configuration management** systems. Traditionally, object-oriented database management systems (Kim, 1990; Cattell, 1994) have excelled in managing versionable objects and many configuration management systems are based on object database technology.

Figure 5.12 explains the principles governing **version management** (Kim, 1990). Most development artifacts are stored as **versionable objects** in the **public workspace** (Section 3.4). Each time a developer checks in such an object to the **private workspace**, a new version is created. There can be multiple versions derived from each version. A version derived from another version is called its **derivative**. Versions that are not on the same path to the root are sometimes called **alternatives** (or parallel versions).

Versions can apply to objects of various granularity. Artifacts are frequently compositions of other artifacts. For example, a class contains methods. A new version of a method implies therefore a new version of a class. This process of creating a new version of an object as a result of modifying (also adding or deleting) a subset object is called **percolation**.

A selection of some set of mutually consistent versions, which results in a semantically distinct higher-level artifact, is called a **configuration**. Technically, a configuration is also a version that happens to consist of the whole range of object versions. Frequently, a configuration defines an entire software product.

A prerequisite condition for proper management of versions is an unambiguous *identification* of versionable objects. This means, in an object-oriented database world, that each versioned artifact is identified by the quadruple: {database id, class id, object id, version id}. Assuming a single database of artifacts, the notation c5o3v7 can mean version 7 of the 3rd object (instance) of class 5.

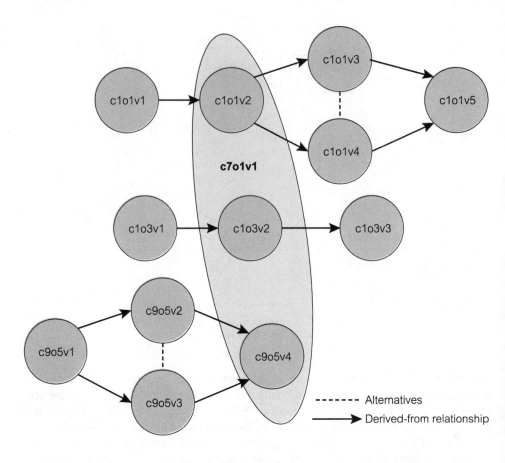

Figure 5.13
Configuration

Figure 5.13 is an example of configuration defined on versions of three objects (Cattell, 1994). The configuration `c7o1v1` is itself a version of a versionable artifact. Note that alternatives are not normally considered as good candidates for a configuration. They should be **merged** by developers (with the tool's help) into a reconciled version before they can be considered for a configuration. It is possible that versions of different objects of the same class can be included in a configuration. The configuration in Figure 5.13 has two versions of class `c1` (`c1o1v2` and `c1o3v2`).

A configuration in the public workspace can be registered as a current (latest) **baseline**. The baseline determines artifact versions that developers can check out to a private workspace and work on. The baseline configuration is frozen for changes in the public workspace, but a new configuration can be *promoted* to a baseline. Earlier configurations are retained in the configuration database so that older versions of objects can be used in new configurations, including new baselines.

From the developer's perspective, a baseline distributed to customers is called a system **release** (or **deliverable**). However, from the management perspective, a release is more than baseline software. A system release is a complex logistical and public relations exercise that must take into account a variety of customers and current installations. For example, new releases must be installable on any previous releases or from scratch.

Distribution media must be decided for software and documentation (this is likely to be the Internet). Various payment options must be worked out. Evaluation versions of software may need to be made available for downloads.

All things considered, a system release involves a significant number of products and processes (Sommerville, 2001):

- executable client code
- database server code (schema, trigger, stored procedures)
- database load data (if any) and any other data files
- configuration files and installation instructions
- system documentation and online help features
- distribution options and associated informational and accounting documentation.

Defects and Enhancements   5.4.3

A software **defect** is an error in the software discovered during formal reviews or tests or discovered by users in an operational system. An **enhancement** is a recommended feature of the system that can be implemented in the future. Enhancements come from two main sources. They can be formally submitted by stakeholders as a formal change request and have no relation to any defect. Alternatively, they can be some defects, which relate to an incomplete or missing implementation of a user requirement. Such defects can sometimes be postponed for later resolution as an enhancement to the system.

Defects and enhancements undergo state changes as a result of acting on them. The history of state changes is maintained by the change management system. The history of state changes replaces a need for version and configuration management on defects and enhancements. Defects and enhancements are independent objects; they are not compositions of other defects or enhancements. Apart from permitting access to the history of defects and enhancements, a change management tool allows them to be grouped according to different criteria, such as by owner, priority, and symptoms (Section 3.4.1).

Figure 5.14 shows an example of a *defect definition*. Each defect is numbered, it is in a particular state (Submitted), it is given a headline definition and a detailed description, it belongs to a project, it has priority, severity, owner, keywords, and symptoms. For each defect state, there is a set of possible actions specified. The action set is customizable according to a change management policy for defects employed on the project.

Figure 5.15 shows an example of an *enhancement definition*. Similarly to defects, each enhancement is numbered, it is in a particular state (Opened), it is given a headline definition and a detailed description, it belongs to a project, it has customer priority. For each enhancement state, there is a set of possible actions specified. The action sets are customizable according to a change management policy for enhancement employed on the project.

An open-source software website for the GCC bug tracking system Bugzilla (Bugzilla, 2003) recommends the following *states for defects*:

- new – when the defect is a new entry and has not been reported previously.
- resolved – the defect has been resolved but it can still be reopened later, if the resolution is found unsatisfactory.

Figure 5.14
Defect
Source: Screenshot
of *IBM Rational Suite*
reprinted by
permission from
Rational Suite Tutorial

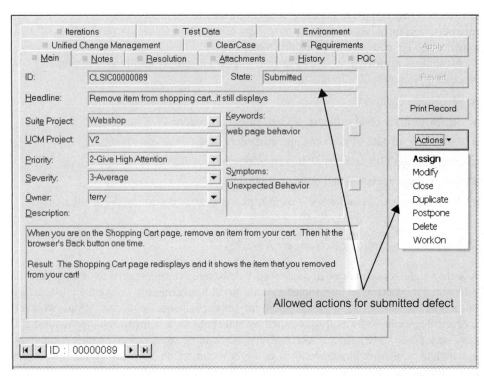

Figure 5.15
Enhancement
Source: Screenshot
of *IBM Rational Suite*
reprinted by
permission from
Rational Suite Tutorial

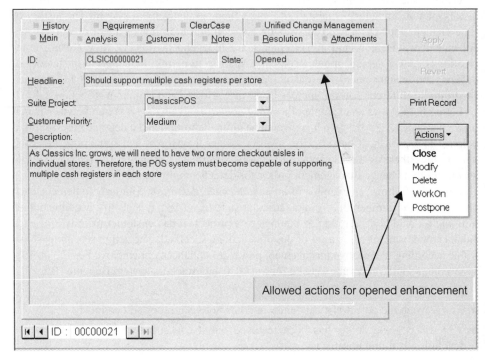

- `unconfirmed` – the defect has been noted but it is yet to be checked if it is a defect at all.
- `reopened` – the defect has been reopened because the previous fix did not really work.
- `assigned` – the defect is not yet resolved but has been assigned to an appropriate party.
- `suspended` – the work on the defect has been suspended as it takes longer than planned or is deemed not cost effective.
- `waiting` – more information is required for the defect to be properly identified.
- `closed` – the matter is closed as a result of its resolution or by other managerial decision.

In Bugzilla, an *enhancement* is merely a defect with a very low *severity* and therefore considered 'a nice to have feature'. In general, typical *severity levels for defects* are:

- `trivial` – the defect can trivially be fixed.
- `minor` – it will be nice to fix, otherwise life goes on with slight annoyance.
- `normal` – fix it in due time, some loss of functionality exists.
- `major` – the defect affects the main functionality, but it does not cause the software to die yet.
- `critical` – wow, how did this thing get here? Nobody says anything about crashing.
- `blocker` – the software will not even start up or it is not possible to use it.

When the defect is analyzed, its resolution can take on many different forms. Again the following list is just a recommendation; it may differ between vendors and it can be customized by project managers (Bugzilla, 2003):

- `invalid` – this defect cannot be reproduced or is no longer valid for the current version of the software or it is not even a defect at all.
- `duplicate` – some other defects have been reported that are similar to this one.
- `workaround` – the defect is acknowledged and will be fixed sometime later, but a workaround is known to resolve it for now.
- `fixed` – the defect has been resolved, this will result in a *resolved* state for the defect.
- `worksforme` – the defect is not reproducible on the current installation, this will result in an *unconfirmed* state.
- `wontfix` – the defect is not going to be fixed because of technical or other reasons.

Metrics

The topic of **metrics** was introduced in Chapter 4 in the context of project management. Project scheduling and budgeting is based on prior project experiences and on various product and process measurements (metrics) collected in the past. For example, metrics that estimate software size, such as the number of lines of code or the number of function points in the code, are indispensable in estimating the cost of the project. Metrics collection, like testing, is an activity pertaining to all phases of the lifecycle.

Software metrics is a large independent area of knowledge and one that generates much controversy. The main controversy relates to the very nature of metrics – the collection of quantitative numbers to assess such subjective issues as maintainability, scalability, complexity, or even the size of code or the size of effort. Nevertheless, even approximate, ambiguous and ballpark numbers are better than no numbers. Moreover, the evidence is that they serve management and planning decisions well.

The other important controversy relates to the fact that metrics have a side effect of evaluating people, not just products and processes. As observed by Ghezzi *et al.* (2003, p.366): 'It is clear, in fact, that, whichever quantity we adopt to evaluate whichever quality, if a designer feels that he or she is being evaluated through that quantity, that designer will try to maximize (or minimize) the measured quantity rather than the real quality.'

Rather than giving a generic introduction to metrics, this section presents a set of most referred to metrics for object-oriented software engineering. Known as the **CK metrics**, in connection with the names of their creators (Chidamber and Kemerer, 1994), they have not escaped their own degree of controversy (Henderson-Sellers *et al.*, 1996). Nevertheless, they are consistent with approaches adopted later in the book and are, therefore, explained next.

There are six CK metrics (Chidamber and Kemerer, 1994):

- weighted methods per class (WMC)
- depth of inheritance tree (DIT)
- number of children (NOC)
- coupling between object classes (CBO)
- response for a class (RFC)
- lack of cohesion in methods (LCOM).

Weighted methods per class (WMC) is computed as the sum of complexities of all methods in a class. The complexities are normalized values in the range from 0 to 1. The precise meaning of the notion of method complexity is not defined. It is at the discretion of those who use the metric, but it is suggested that some structural properties of methods may be used.

Chidamber and Kemerer (1994) offer the following viewpoints on the WMC metric:

- WMC is a *predictor metric* (as opposed to a *control metric*). The metric can serve as a predictor of time and effort needed to develop and maintain a class.
- A large value of WMC creates an increased potential inheritance dependency if the class is reused as a superclass.
- A large value of WMC is a likely indicator that the class is application specific, thus limiting the possibility for its reuse across many applications.

The inheritance hierarchy has a root (superclass) and leaves (subclasses). **Depth of inheritance tree** (DIT) is the maximum length (number of classes) from the node to the root of the tree. DIT applies per class, not per inheritance tree or per system. The definition applies trivially to single inheritance, but it applies also to multiple inheritance.

The viewpoints on DIT are (Chidamber and Kemerer, 1994):

- A class with larger DIT inherits a larger number of methods and it is, therefore, more difficult to understand its behavior.
- A significant number of classes with large DIT imply greater design complexity in terms of overall number of classes and methods in the system.
- A class with larger DIT is likely to be taking better advantage of reuse of inherited methods.

Like DIT, **number of children** (NOC) is an inheritance-related metric. NOC counts the number of immediate subclasses of a class. A large value of NOC is a rather negative property, as per the following list of viewpoints (Chidamber and Kemerer, 1994):

- Larger NOC means more reuse via inheritance (which may be good or bad depending on the perspective taken).
- Large NOC usually implies an improper or diluted abstraction of the superclass and the misuse of subclassing.
- A class with large NOC is likely to be doing too much (taking too much responsibility in the system). This creates an unbalanced design and makes testing more difficult.

Two classes are *coupled* if they depend on each other (but dependency, and therefore coupling, may sometimes be in one direction only). The dependency can be structural (via instance variables) or behavioral (due to method dependencies). **Coupling between object classes** (CBO) is a count of the number of classes coupled to a given class. Coupling is necessary for classes to collaborate; however, excessive coupling has significant undesirable effects.

Chidamber and Kemerer's (1994) viewpoints on CBO are:

- Excessive CBO is detrimental to architectural design quality.
- Large CBO for a class prevents its reuse because the class depends on other classes. (This is true for inheritance reuse, but it can be argued that coupling itself *is* a reuse.)
- Large CBO hinders class encapsulation and makes maintenance of the class more troublesome.
- Design with excessive CBO creates extra challenges for testing.

Response for a class (RFC) is the number of methods whose services are potentially needed in order to satisfy a message request received by an object of the class. In other words, RFC is a number of method invocations to perform a service. The methods can be internal to the class and/or external. The word 'potentially' implies the worst-case possibility, i.e. the maximum number of methods involved in doing the job (in practice, for any particular request, some methods in the chain of calls may be unnecessary and will not be used). Chidamber and Kemerer (1994) offer the following viewpoints on the WMC metric:

- The testing and debugging of the class is more complex with a larger value of RFC.
- A large RFC implies a complex class.
- Being the worst-case value, RFC can be a good indicator of the time needed to perform testing.

Lack of cohesion in methods (LCOM) is the final CK metric. A high value of cohesion in methods says that the methods of the class are not related to each other (are not similar) and, therefore, they possibly do not belong to a single abstraction (to a single class). The similarity may be measured by a number of methods accessing the same instance variables. The larger the number of similar methods, the more cohesive the class is. Total lack of cohesion means that the methods are fully independent.

Chidamber and Kemerer (1994) viewpoints on LCOM are:

- The existence of cohesion in methods promotes encapsulation and is, therefore, desirable.
- Lack of cohesion means that the methods are independent and the class should be split into two or more smaller classes.
- Low LCOM increases the complexity of the design and the potential for errors.

Software metrics are proposed as quantitative measures of assessing the quality of software products and processes. Despite their importance, the reality is that metrics are frequently neglected in software projects. Such projects are automatically at a low level of maturity, but this is not a consolation.

Summary

1. The *Capability Maturity Model* (CMM) model defines five levels of process maturity: (1) initial, (2) repeatable, (3) defined, (4) managed, and (5) optimizing. This chapter has concentrated on key factors defining higher levels of process maturity, namely: (1) people management, (2) risk management, (3) quality management, and (4) change and configuration management.

2. People in a *network organization* have unique notions of motivation, loyalty, organizational power, leadership, achievement, satisfaction, gratification, etc. Network organizations necessitate new approaches to people management, in particular in the area of acquiring and motivating people.

3. Acquiring and motivating people is the essence of the *team-building* process. There are many *motivational theories*, which try to identify what prompts people in their actions and what factors influence people's professional behavior.

4. Proper *forms and lines of communication* must be established in a project for its successful conduct. Both too much and too little communication can hurt the project. Apart from informational and managerial aspects, communication is the primary means of resolving conflicts in teams.

5. *Teams* undergo four stages of *development*: (1) forming, (2) storming, (3) norming, and (4) performing.

6. *Risk management* involves three stages: (1) risk identification, (2) risk assessment, and (3) risk handling. Strategies to manage risks range from reactive to proactive. *Reactive risk strategies* delay handling of risks until they become critical factors in the project. *Proactive risk strategies* encourage acting on risks as soon as they arise or even in anticipation of their happening.

7. Software *quality management* is an umbrella activity that intertwines with most other management undertakings and cuts across the entire development lifecycle and process. There are many desired *software qualities*, and depending on a software project some of them may be more important than others. Software qualities need to be identified, defined, and classified.

8. Quality management consists of quality control and quality assurance. *Quality control* is mostly about testing quality of a product, as opposed to *quality assurance* which is about building quality into the product. Quality control has a reactive flavor. Quality assurance is very much a proactive undertaking.

9. *Software testing* is a dominant activity of quality control. There are many possible *testing techniques*, which can be intermixed to provide the best possible testing coverage and outcomes. No matter how extensive the testing is, it cannot be exhaustive and guarantee the program/system correctness. The *test plan* defines the testing schedule, budget, tasks (test cases) and resources. The plan must not be restricted to code testing. It should include testing of other project artifacts.

10. The management-designated *software quality assurance* (SQA) group conducts quality assurance. Quality assurance endeavors include: (1) checklists, (2) reviews, and (3) audits.

11. *Change and configuration management* is the process of managing product and process artifacts and managing the teamwork activities in an evolving software system. The process relates to the entire lifecycle of software, from its inception to retirement.

12. *Change management* involves manual and automated processes. Proposed changes are formally submitted as *change requests*. Change requests can result in changes to use cases and use case requirements. Some changes become enhancements and are not considered in current development. There is a mapping between use case requirements and test requirements.

13. Development work results in production of model artifacts, including code. There may be many useful versions of the same artifact. Storing and manipulating versions is the domain of *configuration management* systems. A selection of some set of mutually consistent versions, which results in a semantically distinct higher-level artifact, is called a *configuration*.

14. A software *defect* is an error in software discovered during formal reviews or tests or discovered by users in an operational system. An *enhancement* is a recommended feature of the system that can be implemented in the future. Defects and enhancements undergo state changes as a result of acting on them.

15. *Metrics* collection, like testing, is an activity pertaining to all phases of the lifecycle. The *CK metrics* are the best-known metrics for object-oriented software engineering.

Key Terms

Achievement Theory	158	CCA	*See* change control authotity
alternative	183	CCB	*See* change control board
aptitude test	156	change control authority	182
artifact	169	change control board	182
audit	179	change management	180, 181
automated testing	175	change request form	181
baseline	184	checklist	178
best script	176	CK metrics	188
black box testing	173	CMM	*See* Capability Maturity Model
boundary value	174	communication	158
Capability Maturity Model	153	communication forms	158
capture/playback tool	175	communication lines	159

component	170
compromise	161
configuration	183
configuration management	180, 183
conflict resolution	161
confrontation	161
contingency planning	168
correctness	169
coupling between object classes	189
CRF	*See* change request form
dead code	174
defect	185
defect script	176
deliverable	184
dependability	*See* reliability
depth of inheritance tree	188
derivative	183
end product	169
enhancement	185
equivalence partitioning	174
evolvability	*See* scalability
exercising	175
Expectancy Theory	158
extrinsic motivator	157
extrovert	160
forcing	161
forming	162
framework	170
glass box testing	*See* white box testing
group communication	161
Hygiene Theory	158
incidental communication	161
inspections	178
interoperability	171
intrinsic motivator	157
introvert	160
lack of cohesion in methods	189
maintainability	170
Maslow's Hierarchy of Needs	157
merge	184
method coverage	*See* operation coverage
metrics	187
missing functionality	173
motivation	157
network organization	155
norming	162
number of children	189
open system	171
operation coverage	175
path coverage	175
percolation	183
performance	170
performing	162
portability	171
private workspace	183
proactive risk strategies	163
process maturity	153
process qualities	169
product qualities	169
productivity	171
project communication	158
project leader	155
project manager	155
project termination points	166
psychometric test	156
public workspace	183
quality assurance	171, 177
quality control	171
quality management	168
reactive risk strategies	163
regression testing	175
release	184
reliability	170
repairability	*See* maintainability
response for a class	189
reusability	170
review	178
review issues list	179
risk assessment	164
risk avoidance	168
risk components	165
risk database	167
risk exposure	165
risk handling	167
risk identification	163
risk impact	165
risk likelihood	164
risk management	163
risk management plan	167
risk minimization	168
risk probability	164
risk referent level	166
robustness	170
scalability	170

self-directed team	155	testing techniques		173
smoothing	161	testing to code	*See* white box testing	
software qualities	169	testing to specs	*See* black box testing	
software quality assurance	177	timeliness		171
software testing	172	understandability		170
SQA	*See* software quality assurance	usability		170
staffing management plan	155	variation control		171
storming	162	verifications point		176
supportability	170	version management		183
team building	*See* team development	versionable object		183
team development	162	visibility		171
team organization	162	walkthrough		178
test case	176	weighted methods per class		188
test environment	176	white box testing		174
test plan	176	withdrawal		162
test script	176	work products		169
test suites	176			

Review Questions

1. Explain CMM process maturity levels. What are the key factors for improving maturity levels?

2. What is a network organization? What are the main people management issues within a network organization? Relate your explanations to the team creation processes and to relevant motivational theories.

3. Discuss the interplay between communication forms and communication lines.

4. Discuss the interplay between communication forms and conflict resolution.

5. How useful are reactive risk strategies in risk management? Explain.

6. How is risk exposure calculated? What is a risk referent point?

7. What are risk handling strategies in proactive risk management? How are they applied? Give an example.

8. Explain the differences between quality control and quality assurance. What are the main quality management techniques used in quality control and in quality assurance?

9. Explain the quality of supportability.

10. Black box and white box testing are said to complement each other. Explain.

11. What is the relationship between regression tests and exercising tests? Can they be used collaboratively? Explain.

12. Explain the concepts of test case, test script, and test suite. How are these concepts related?

13. How do you understand the quality culture? Compare how the activities of quality control and quality assurance contribute to the quality culture.

14. Refer to Figure 5.10. They say that a picture is worth a thousand words. Explain the picture in your words (no need for a thousand words though).

15. Versions of modeling artifacts need to be merged? What does this mean? How is this done? At what points in the project do, the merges need to be conducted? Are the merges conducted automatically or is manual intervention necessary?

16. Refer to Figure 5.14. Assume that the defect is not in Submitted state but in Resolved state. What actions would you allow in the dropdown list for a defect in Resolved state? Explain.

17. Refer to Figure 5.15. Assume that the enhancement is not in Opened state but in Postponed state. What actions would you allow in the dropdown list for an enhancement in Postponed state? Explain.

18. Refer to the CK metrics. Which of these metrics have special significance for determining the supportability quality of a system. Explain.

Part

2

From Requirements via Architectural Design to Software Release

Chapter 6   Business Object Model   199

Chapter 7   Domain Object Model   215

Chapter 8   Iteration 1 Requirements and Object Model   234

Chapter 9   Architectural Design   248

Chapter 10 Database Design and Programming   301

Chapter 11 Class and Interaction Design   331

Chapter 12 Programming and Testing   365

Chapter 13 Iteration 1 Annotated Code   414

Modern software processes are *iterative*. Software production is done iteration by iteration. *Iteration* is a software development cycle with its own requirements analysis, system design, implementation, testing, and delivery to the users. Iterations are *incremental* – successive iterations deliver a larger product by extending and refining the previous iteration. Each iteration produces an executable, tested, and integrated software *release*. Iterations are of short durations (a few weeks), so that stakeholders' confidence in software development is maintained and the user feedback for successive iterations is obtained early.

This book teaches principles of information systems development by presenting iterations delivering incremental releases for the case-study. There are three iterations – addressed in Parts 2, 3, and 4 of the book. Each iteration has its own emphasis and requires a particular knowledge and set of skills. The background knowledge is provided in a way that is intertwined with the presentation of iteration tasks and solutions.

The teaching approach of the book is to relate the explanation to a case-study and to minicases. If, however, the required background knowledge is relatively complex, shorter examples (not necessarily derived from the case-study) are introduced in an attempt to explain the underlying concepts. The case-study, problem-solving exercises, minicases and most examples apply to a company nicknamed AEM, which specializes in *Advertising Expenditure Measurement*.

Part 2 of the book specifies a business object model for AEM (Chapter 6). The model identifies the main domains of AEM. A domain of interest to the book is *Contact Management* (CM). A domain object model for CM is given in Chapter 7. The remaining chapters of Part 2 address a CM subsystem called *Email Management* (EM), which is the subject of the book's case-study.

The EM system helps to manage email documents. The case-study focuses on composing and sending email messages (called outmessages) stored earlier in a database and scheduled to be sent to contacts (customers, suppliers, employees within organizations, etc.). The outmessages – queries to contacts, requests for meetings, etc. – are entered in the database in the process of conducting daily business transactions. An ultimate EM product may include capture, indexing, classification, and retrieval of all email business correspondence. Both outgoing and incoming emails may be stored and managed in the EM database.

To manage email content, a structure has to be imposed on what is in essence an unstructured email document. In initial iterations of the case-study, the structure is quite simple – it distinguishes among outmessage subject, outmessage text, email date, sender, and recipient. An outmessage text is an undifferentiated byte stream – nothing is known about its internal structure (this reflects the limitations of relational databases with regard to processing multimedia data types).

The case-study concentrates on the system's capability to send emails and update the database to indicate which outmessages and attached documents have been sent. The principal actors (to use the UML parlance) of EM are the organization's employees. The case-study addresses only formal business emails that have an AEM contact in mind. Informal (private) emails may be using the same mail servers but are of no interest to the case-study.

Iteration 1 (discussed in this part) aims at a simple console-based Java application that accesses the database via JDBC. Upon a user's login to the email database, the application can retrieve from the database and display the list of outmessages to be emailed to contacts. The user (employee) can then request automatic emailing of chosen outmessages. After a successful mailing, the database is updated accordingly.

Successive iterations of the case-study address more sophisticated means of managing email text content and storing unstructured (multimedia) documents attached to the email being sent. *Iteration 2* (discussed in Part 3) allows new outmessages to be entered into the database via a GUI or web-enabled interface. It supports also viewing outmessages based on different filters and search criteria. *Iteration 3* (discussed in Part 4) moves much of the application logic to the database and enforces additional business rules in the database that the application must obey. Problem-solving exercises at the ends of chapters extend the case-study further. Emailing is a work-related activity aimed at AEM contacts (customers, suppliers, etc.). This leads directly to the possibility of tracking contact-related events and managing employees' time logs.

The main learning objectives of Part 2 and Iteration 1 of the case-study are to gain knowledge of:

- the placement of an IS project within the business object model and within the domain object model
- software development that originates from a use case document, conceptual class model and supplementary specifications
- the significance of an architectural framework in iterative and incremental development
- the design and programming of database to support informational needs of application programs
- the design of classes and the design of interactions between objects
- accessing databases and caching entity objects in Java
- interdependence between programming and testing, test-driven development and acceptance testing
- the development of understandable, maintainable, and scalable software that is rigorous and documented and yet low-key on ritual and red tape.

Chapter

6

Business Object Model

Following the **Unified Process** (UP) (Kruchten, 1999; Rational, 2002), we make a distinction between the **business object model** (BOM) and the **Domain object model** (DOM) – called the domain model in RUP. Both are high-level (i.e. highly abstracted) object-oriented system models, but BOM applies to the entire business whereas DOM applies to an application domain under consideration. BOM is an enterprise-wide model. DOM is a conceptual model of a domain of interest. For this textbook, BOM describes the background and the context for the case-studies and is discussed only in this chapter. The remaining case-study chapters in Parts 2 through 4 define DOM or apply to it.

BOM consists of a business use case model and a business class model. The **business use case model** represents *business actors'* interactions with business use cases and shows basic relationships between business use cases. Business use cases are large granularity business processes – the main business functions of an enterprise. The **business class model** represents *business entities* and relationships between them. Business entities are the most fundamental classes ('business objects') necessary for the realization of business use cases (a *class* is used here in a typical object-oriented meaning as an abstraction that describes a set of objects with common attributes, operations, relationships, and semantic constraints).

A simplified variation of a business use case model, called a **business context diagram**, is used to depict the scope of an enterprise's core business. A context diagram is an old technique used in structured modeling to delineate the system scope. In structured modeling, context diagrams were an integrated part of once very popular and successful modeling practice called data flow diagrams (DFD) (Section 2.1.1). Although DFDs are not advocated by the UML, context diagrams remain a popular modeling choice in object-oriented analysis (e.g. Larman, 2002).

Models and diagrams are examples of software development artifacts. An **artifact** is any documented information produced by a system developer and used in a development lifecycle. One of the most important information system (IS) development artifacts, work on which should start as early as possible, is a *glossary* of terms and definitions. The main purpose of a glossary is to introduce clarity to communication between developers and other project stakeholders. Without a glossary, the following anonymous observation will haunt the project: 'I know you believe you understand what you think I said, but I'm not sure you realize that what you heard is not what I meant.'

Like all system modeling activities, BOM uses diagrams to visualize the main concepts. Although visual presentation is indispensable for reasoning about models, specifications of software systems consist predominantly of text documents. Diagrams serve rather a unifying purpose – they are particularly useful when categorizing and classifying modeling concepts and to express relationships and dependencies between modeling concepts. BOM establishes a framework for information system development strategy in an organization and introduces initial terminology for developer–customer communication.

6.1 Advertising Expenditure Measurement – The Business

AEM (**Advertising Expenditure Measurement**) is a *market research company*. AEM does not produce merchandise in the conventional meaning of the word. Its core business is obtaining, processing, and selling information about advertisements which appeared in various media. The AEM customer base consists of organizations and individuals who buy market research information about advertising expenditures.

The process of identifying advertisements and recording advertising content is partly automatic and partly manual. *Automatic data capture* involves modern scanning and multimedia recognition hardware and software. *Manual data capture* is a laborious process of watching TV advertisements, reading newspapers and magazines, etc. Advertisements are entered into the AEM database as new (not advertised before) or they get matched to an advertisement already stored in the database. The *matching* of incoming advertisements to those already in the database is performed during the data capture.

The advertising content of all advertisements is stored in a database (this includes advertised products, duration (for TV and radio), size (for press), monetary value, etc.). The process of identifying the advertising content is error-prone and requires frequent external and internal verification. *External verification* requires contacting advertising media outlets, advertising agencies, individual advertisers, etc. *Internal verification* is a quality control mechanism to ensure that the data capture by AEM system and employees is correct. AEM has contractual arrangements with many media outlets to regularly receive from them *electronic log files* with information pertaining to the advertising content of these outlets – this greatly facilitates the data collection and verification processes.

The advertising data provides two areas of reporting to the AEM customers. A customer may request a report that the advertisements they paid for appeared as they were supposed to (this is called *campaign monitoring*). A client can also request a report outlining their competitive advertising position in their specific industry (this is called *expenditure reporting*). The expenditure reports capture the expenditures achieved by an advertiser or an advertised product by various criteria (time, geographical regions, media, etc.).

Any AEM client (not just an advertising client) can purchase *expenditure reports* – in the form of custom-designed reporting software or as hard copies. AEM's customer base comprises individual advertisers, advertising agencies, media companies, media buying consultancies, as well as sales and marketing executives, media planners, buyers, etc.

Business Context Diagram

6.2

The description of the AEM core business in Section 1.1 is sufficient to develop a business context diagram for AEM. A **business context diagram** is a version of business use case model customized for the task. **Business actors** represent **external entities**, i.e. people, organizations, information systems, etc. that are external to AEM. External entities act as providers of information to AEM or recipients of information from AEM, or both. External entities are grouped to identify the main categories of providers/recipients of information rather than individual participants in the system.

There is only one **business use case** in a business context diagram. It depicts the overall 'system behavior', represents the core business activity, and expresses the system scope. The business use case receives information from external entities, processes it in some way, and sends the output information to external entities. The scope of the business use case is to process input information into output information. Anything else is outside its scope. The business use case will not process unsolicited input information and it will not produce uncalled-for output information.

Interactions between external entities and the business use case have a different meaning than in a conventional use case diagram. They represent the flow of input/output information (**data flows**) between external entities and the business use case.

Figure 6.1 is a business context diagram that depicts the AEM scope. There are two external entities: `Media Outlet` and `AEM Client`. Media outlets supply advertising

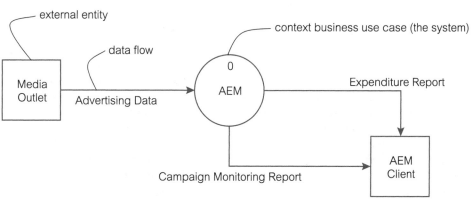

Figure 6.1
Business context diagram

data to AEM. AEM clients receive campaign monitoring reports and expenditure reports from AEM.

The transformation of advertising data to reports is the internal function of AEM. The advertisement verification, manual entry, and other AEM functions will acquire and supply data but these are considered internal data flows within the AEM business use case. For example, the supply of newspapers, magazines, video reels, etc. for manual entry is treated as an internal function within the scope of the system.

6.3 Business Use Case Model

A **business use case model** is a *decomposition* (to borrow the term from data flow diagrams) of the business context diagram. The business use case of the business context diagram is decomposed into a small number of component business use cases. When taken together, the business use cases of a business use case model define exactly the same functionality as the context business use case of the business context diagram.

6.3.1 Business Use Cases and Business Actors

A **business use case** is a high-level usage case (case of business use) within the system under consideration. It is a high-level piece of business functionality with well-defined boundaries. Business use cases are the first attempt at identifying major functional modules (major business activities) in the enterprise.

Business actors in a business use case model are a specialized version of actors of a conventional use case diagram (Chapter 2). An **actor** is a role played by a person, system, device, etc. when using or otherwise communicating with the services of a use case.

A business actor can be an external entity (i.e. outside the scope of the system) or it can be a role, which is internal to the system (such as an employee at a computer terminal). An internal business actor is typically a **primary actor** (it interacts directly with the system). An external entity is typically a **secondary actor** (a role that communicates with the system via an intermediary – normally a primary actor). Consider a banking application where a customer approaches a teller (a person or an ATM machine) and requests a money withdrawal from a bank account. The customer is a secondary actor (and an external entity). The primary actor is a teller. The use case can be called Withdraw Money or something similar.

Classifiers (model elements) in a business use case diagram can be linked by various kinds of relationships (Maciaszek, 2001), but the relationships should be used judiciously. Business use cases can be linked by an **association** relationship (other kinds of the UML use case relationships (Chapter 2) are not normally encouraged for business use cases).

Communication between an actor and a use case is expressed in the UML as a relationship stereotyped as «communicate». An important relationship, with a wide-spread application to modeling and programming, is **generalization**. This is a relationship between a more general classifier and a more specific classifier. The more specific classifier 'is a kind of' the more generic classifier. Generalizable classifiers include business use cases and business actors in business use case models and business entities in business class models.

Business Use Case Model for AEM 6.3.2

Figure 6.2 presents a business use case diagram for AEM. The model takes advantage of a small visual variation in the UML notation that distinguishes between a business use case and a regular (system) use case (Section 2.2.2). A business use case has a slash inside the use case oval. Similarly, a business actor has a slash in a circle representing the head of a 'stick-man' icon.

The business use case model divides the AEM system into four main business use cases: `Data Collection`, `Data Verification`, `Valorization` and `Reporting`. Business use cases are connected by **unidirectional associations** (i.e. associations with an arrow-head) to signify the main AEM business workflow – from data collection to verification, valorization, and reporting.

`Data Collection` communicates with `Media Outlet` to obtain advertising log information (this is normally done automatically via computer–computer communication). The log is used for data capture and matching it to advertisements already stored in the AEM database – partly automatic and partly manual. This is signified in Figure 6.2 by *generalization relationships*. `Auto Matching` 'is a kind of' `Data Collection`, and `Manual Matching` also 'is a kind of' `Data Collection`.

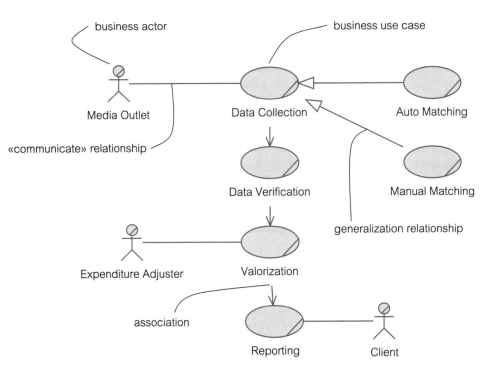

Figure 6.2
Business use case diagram for AEM

The advertisement data is entered into the database and it is then subjected to careful `Data Verification`. The task of verification is to confirm that all captured advertisement details are valid and logical in the context of surrounding information. This includes various reasonability checks, such as a TV ad of unreasonable duration or with times overlapping with a TV program (as opposed to a scheduled break for advertisement screening).

Once entered and verified, the advertisements undergo `Data Valorization` – the process of assigning expenditure estimates to advertisements. `Expenditure Adjuster` is a business actor – normally an external consultant with an inside knowledge about market prices of advertising in different media and under various additional conditions (such as the buying power of advertising agencies, the competitive position of various advertising media, the time when advertisements are shown (in the case of TV), etc.).

AEM is in the business of selling advertising information to its clients. `Client` is a business actor (external entity) prepared to pay for information from the last business use case in the diagram – `Reporting`. Reports are customized to individual clients. They can be delivered to clients on a periodic (subscribed) basis (by email, on compact disks, in paper form, etc.). Ad hoc reports to sporadic clients are also supplied.

6.3.3 Alternative Business Use Case Model for AEM

The business use case model in Figure 6.2 emphasizes a workflow of AEM activities (from data collection to reporting). The business actors in that model are all secondary actors – external contributors and beneficiaries of AEM. However, this is just one of many possible high-level views on the functional BOM architecture. Figure 6.3 represents an alternative view.

The model in Figure 6.3 uses the name `Quality Control` for a business use case previously called `Data Verification`. This is consistent with the name of the department responsible for the quality of collected advertisement data. The business use case called `Valorization` in Figure 6.2 is now included in `Reporting` and not shown as a separate business use case. This fact is indicated by a communication line between a business actor `Rates Consultant` and `Reporting`.

Figure 6.3 identifies two additional business use cases: `Contact Management` and `Data Maintenance`. `Contact Management` has a classic responsibility to bring new customers to the business and to keep existing customers happy. It is called `Contact Management` (rather than Customer Management) to indicate this business use case responsibility to also stay in contact with AEM suppliers (such as media outlets), consultants (such as `Rates Consultant`) and to maintain communication with other external entities (such as government media research bodies).

`Data Maintenance` is a surprisingly elaborate business use case. Its main responsibility is to ensure the correctness of a relatively 'stable data' in the AEM database. By 'stable data' we mean descriptive meta-information about advertisements (such advertisements types), media (such as media categories), outlet data logs (such as possible statuses of the log). Other 'stable data' is anything, which is not subject to constant changes in the main AEM workflow between data collection and reporting (things like outlet address or agency name).

Figure 6.3 presents the most important business actors and the most important communication lines to business use cases. By most important we mean most relevant to

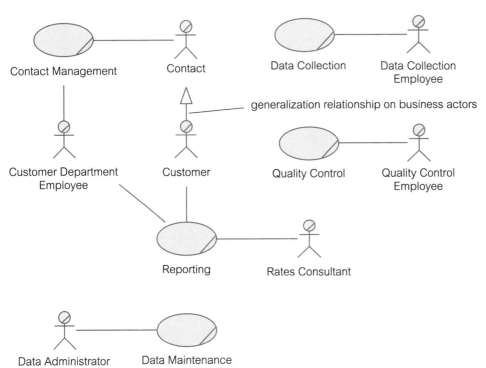

Figure 6.3
Alternative
business use case
diagram for AEM

what we want to emphasize in the model. This sounds pretty arbitrary but that's the nature of modeling. For a model of any reasonable complexity, no two modelers will come up with exactly the same models. This would not necessarily mean that one model is better than the other – both of them can be equally good or equally bad.

One could argue, for example, that Contact communicates with all five business use cases. However, we have to draw a line between what is important and what is not that important for a particular view represented by the model. In this case, we assumed that the main business use case that Contact communicates with is Contact Management. Less important «communicate» relationships for Contact are not shown, with the exception that a *subclass* of Contact, called Customer, communicates with Reporting.

Note that a generalization relationship can be set on business actors, not just on business use cases as in Figure 6.2. Customer 'is a kind of' Contact. This means that a Contact who is a Customer communicates with Reporting. Note the expressive power of generalization. Generalizations on business use cases and on business actors can simplify the graphical representation and still convey the same semantic information.

When comparing the models in Figures 6.2 and 6.3, we note that the same model elements are sometimes called differently. Data Verification in Figure 6.2 is called Quality Control in Figure 6.3, Expenditure Adjuster is called Rate Consultant, and Client is called Contact. This creates a potential for ambiguity in communication between various project stakeholders. Although, in practice, one of the two business use case models will end up as a project *artifact*, it is important that all terminological ambiguities are addressed and resolved in the system *glossary* (next section).

Table 6.1 Business glossary for AEM

Term	Definition and explanations
ad (advertisement)	A unique piece of creative work that may be broadcast, screened, published or otherwise exposed any number of times. Each ad exposure by a media outlet is known in the AEM system as an ad instance
ad instance	A particular occurrence of an ad, i.e. each incidence of an ad broadcast, screening, or publication
product	An item of merchandise or a service that may be advertised. Products may be categorized (i.e. a product can belong to a category of products). Categories are classifications of products as envisaged by AEM. The AEM system supports a hierarchical grouping of categories with an unlimited number of levels in the hierarchy. Products may only be categorized at the lowest level of the category hierarchy
category	A classification of products as envisaged by AEM for reporting purpose. Categories can be organized into hierarchical structures of categories and subcategories. Products are 'categorized' with categories at the bottom level of hierarchical structure
organization	A business entity that AEM deals with. There are different types of organizations, including advertisers, agencies, outlets, advertiser groups, agency groups, and data providers. An organization can be one, many, or none of these types
agency	An organization that handles the advertising planning and media buying for an advertiser. The goal of an agency is to optimize the advertising expenditure
outlet	An organization that exposes an advertisement. In the television and radio media, an outlet is defined as the station that airs ads. In the cinema and outdoor media, an outlet is defined as the company that organizes exposure of the ads. In the print medium, an outlet is defined as the publication in which ads are printed
advertiser	An organization that uses the media to expose its creative output (advertisement) in order to promote a product (merchandise or service). A large number of advertisers are known in the AEM system as 'Direct Advertiser'. These are advertisers that bypass an agency and book advertising space directly with a media outlet
advertiser group	An organization that directly or indirectly controls one or more other companies and is interested in viewing the accumulated advertising activity and expenditure of the associated companies. Advertiser groups do not pay for any advertising; the advertisers within the group handle this. Advertiser groups are also known as Holding Companies
agency group	A company that directly or indirectly controls one or more other agencies and is interested in viewing the accumulated planning and media buying for an agency or group of agencies. Agency groups do not do any planning or media buying; the agencies within the group handle this
provider (auxiliary supplier)	An organization that provides auxiliary data to the AEM system. This information includes demographics (divisions of groups of people based on specified attributes such as age, sex, and socio-economic factors), surveys (measured and projected viewing/listening/readership figures per different demographic categories and for different outlets), rates (advertising prices for different outlets to determine the cost of an ad), discounts (estimated reductions in advertising prices due to the purchasing power of an agency when booking ads through a specified medium)
adlink	An association between an ad, the product it advertises, the advertiser who pays for the exposure of the ad, and the agency responsible for the booking of that exposure. Outlets that have exposed the ad can be derived from the descriptions of ad instances of that ad

Business Glossary

The work on a glossary (Larman, 2002) should start very early in IS development and it should be an ongoing activity. The **glossary** defines the communication platform between all project stakeholders. It records all terms and definitions that have any – even remote – possibility of being unclear or ambiguous.

The glossary can be written as a simple text document in a table format. As a minimum, the table should consist of two columns: the term and the definition. Once the glossary grows to a substantial size, the terms should be listed in alphabetical order.

Business Glossary for AEM

Table 6.1 presents the initial AEM glossary. It contains terms necessary in the initial stages of the project, including those to consider when developing the business class model, which is our next task (Section 6.5). The terms are not alphabetically sorted – they are explained in the order that facilitates educational continuity.

Business Class Model

The **business class model** shows the most fundamental business entities ('business objects') and the principal relationships between them. The model is developed concurrently with the business use case model. A *business entity* is a classifier that characterizes and participates in the conduct of an organization's main business activities. Frequently, a business entity is an IS modeling representation of a term defined in the glossary (Table 6.1).

Business Entities

Business entity is a class but it ought to be contrasted with other UML classes necessary in an IS system, such as the classes responsible for handling the graphical user interface (GUI), program logic, or access to a database. UML provides a graphical variation to distinguish business entities from normal system classes. A business entity is presented as a circle with a slash and a horizontal line under it.

Being a class, business entity can have attributes and operations. However, being a highly abstract representation of a business object, attributes and operations are not expected to be specified.

Three forms of UML relationships can be used on business entities: **association**, **generalization** and **aggregation**. The basic meaning of association and generalization is as explained for business use case models. Aggregation is a stronger form of association with a containment or ownership property.

Multiplicities can be shown on suitable relationships, i.e. on associations and aggregations. Multiplicities can be listed in a basic form as one-to-one, many-to-many, or one-to-many, or they can also contain the definition of **participation** (or **optionality**). An entity instance may not participate in a relationship. This is shown by a 0 ahead of the indicator of multiplicity (e.g. 0..1 means optional (possibly 0) participation for multiplicity of one; 1..n means mandatory (at least 1) participation for multiplicity of many).

6.5.2 Business Class Model for AEM

Figure 6.4 shows a business class diagram for AEM. The model contains six business entities and the primary relationships between them. Two kinds of the UML relationship are used: *associations* and an *aggregation*. Basic *multiplicities* of relationships are also shown (all of them are either many-to-many or one-to-many).

`AdvertisementInstance` embodies individual occurrences of an advertisement. `Advertisement` is a unique piece of creative material that may be broadcast, screened, or published any number of times. `AdvertisedProduct` captures the product that is the aim of the advertisement.

There are also three organizational classes. `Outlet` stores information about media companies. `Advertiser` is an organization that uses the media to advertise a product.

Figure 6.4
Business class
diagram for AEM

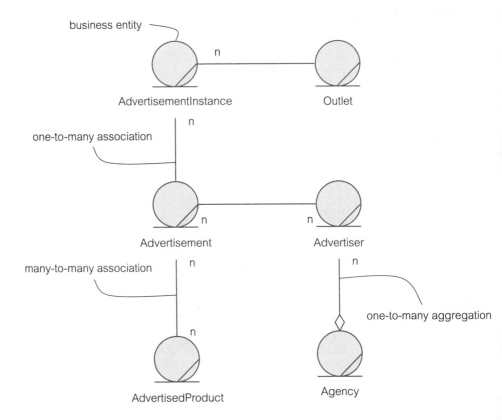

Agency is an organization that handles the advertising planning and media buying on behalf of an advertiser.

The diagram also shows the principal relationships between business classes. The relationship between Agency and Advertiser is an aggregation. Other relationships are associations. Each AdvertisementInstance is linked to a single Outlet and a single Advertisement. The same Advertisement may be used by more than one Advertiser and it may advertise more than one AdvertisedProduct. Agency represents many Advertisers, but – according to the model – an Advertiser can only be represented by a single Agency (if this is not the case, aggregation ought not to be used).

Alternative Business Class Model for AEM   6.5.3

The business class model in Figure 6.5 is an 'incremental' improvement over the model in Figure 6.4. The new model adds two business classes: Organization and Category. Organization is just a generic class for Outlet and Customer. The introduction of Category means that it is now possible to show that a Product can be categorized (i.e. linked to a Category).

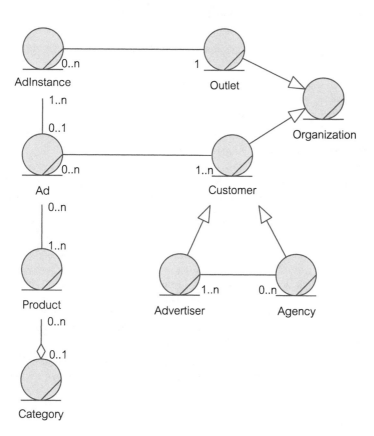

Figure 6.5
Alternative business class diagram for AEM

The model enhances the precision of association definitions by adding *participation* (*optionality*) properties to multiplicity definitions of relationships. Participation definitions add a remarkable amount of meaning to the model.

We know now that information about an `Outlet` can be stored in the AEM database even if there are no `AdInstances` for it. Similarly, `AdInstance` and `Product` can be stored even if we do not know (as yet) their `Ad` description. An `Advertiser` does not need to advertise using an `Agency` or it can advertise via multiple `Agencies` (if this is the case then the use of aggregation in Figure 6.4 is in error).

On the other hand, an `AdInstance` cannot exist in the database unless it is connected to an `Outlet`. An `Ad` cannot exist unless it is linked to at least one `AdInstance`, one `Product`, and one `Customer`. `Product` can be categorized with at most one `Category`. The same `Category` can apply to many `Products` but a `Category` can also exist on its own.

Summary

1. A *business object model* (BOM) is an object-oriented model that describes the core business of an enterprise. The description defines the enterprise boundary (business context diagram), its business responsibilities (business use case model), and its information entities (business class model).

2. Business object modeling is a software development and as such produces *artifacts* – documents, models, descriptions, software, etc.

3. A model artifact contains *classifiers* – model elements that describe behavioral and structural features of an enterprise or system.

4. The enterprise considered in the book is a market research company nicknamed AEM (Advertising Expenditure Measurement). Its core business is recording, processing, and selling value-added information about advertisements in all major audiovisual and printed media.

5. A *business context diagram* consists of one business use case representing the enterprise and input/output data flows from/to external entities (other organizations or systems).

6. A *business use case model* defines business use cases, business actors, and relationships between them. A *business use case* is a major functional module for the purpose of completing a business task of significance to the enterprise. A *business actor* represents anything that interacts with a business use case (via the «*communicate*» relationship). Business use cases can be related by *associations* and can be classified using *generalization* relationships.

7. A business *glossary* is a list of business terms and definitions. It is important to start building a glossary early in the development process.

8. The existence of a glossary facilitates development of the business class model, which defines business entities and relationships between them. A *business entity* is a classifier for business objects – something that can contain data and can exhibit behavior. Relationships include associations, aggregations, and generalizations. The multiplicity and optionality of a relationship (association or aggregation) specifies the business constraints and rules governing the relationship.

9. Although it is desirable that ultimately a single BOM is defined for an enterprise (and all key stakeholders agree on it), alternative models are possible. Alternative models serve a useful purpose by providing different modeling viewpoints on an enterprise.

Key Terms

«communicate» relationship	202	classifier	202
actor	202	data flow	201
Advertising Expenditure Measurement	200	domain object model	199
AEM *See* Advertising Expenditure Measurement		DOM	*See* domain object model
aggregation	207	external entity	201
artifact	199	generalization	202, 207
association	202, 207	glossary	207
BOM	*See* business object model	primary actor	202
business actor	201, 202	relationship multiplicity	208
business class model	199, 207	relationship optionality	*See* relationship participation
business context diagram	199, 201	relationship participation	208
business entity	207	secondary actor	202
business object model	199	unidirectional association	203
business use case	201, 202	Unified Process	199
business use case model	199, 202	UP	*See* Unified Process

Review Questions

Discussion Questions

1. What is the system scope? How can it be defined?

2. What is the difference between business actor and external entity?

3. What is the difference between business actor and actor?

4. What is the difference between primary actor and secondary actor?

5. What is the difference between data flow and the «communicate» relationship?

6. What is the difference between association and relationship?

7. How are generalization relationships useful in business use case diagrams and in business class diagrams.

8. How is a glossary useful in a business class model?

9. Discuss the significance of defining multiplicities on relationships in a business class diagram. Is it vitally important to define participation (optionality) properties of relationships in a business class diagram?

10. Discuss the usefulness of aggregation relationships in business class modeling.

11. What are the main artifacts of BOM?

Case Study Questions

1. What is data capture and matching? What is the difference between manual matching and auto matching? How do these activities relate to data collection and data verification? Can manual matching be considered to be a kind of or a part of data verification?

2. What is an adlink? How is it or can it be related to data matching? Is establishing adlinks the function of data collection or data verification? Discuss your position.

3. What is valorization? What are audience participation or readership figures? How do you think valorization and audience/readership figures are related? Should valorization be a stand-alone business use case or a part of the `Reporting` business use case?

4. There are two main categories of AEM report. What are they? Reflect on the importance of both report categories for AEM business.

5. What is data maintenance? Do you think it is a legitimate business use case?

Problem-Solving Exercises

Case Study Exercises

1. Read again Section 6.1 and consider business use case models in Section 6.3. Construct a business use case diagram that combines the diagrams in Figures 6.2 and 6.3 and takes into consideration possible extensions based on information in Section 6.1.

   By 'combining' we do not mean a straight union of Figures 6.2 and 6.3 (in any case, the union will not be possible because of discrepancies in terminology). A good use of the generalization relationship provides a nice mechanism to combine and extend the models.

2. Extend the glossary in Table 6.1 in Section 6.4 to reflect the terms discussed in the business use case models in Section 6.3 and not already included in the glossary.

3. Develop a business class model which uses glossary terms in Table 6.1 in Section 6.4 as business classes. For relationships, show multiplicities with participation properties.

Minicase – Advertising Expenditure Measurement

Consider the following 'problem statement' about AEM. The statement complements the description of the AEM core business in Section 6.1 but it is treated here as an idiosyncratic portrayal.

The AEM system needs to satisfy two sets of users: internal users (AEM employees) and external users (AEM customers and other contacts). We want to enable our external users to access our data with the shortest possible delay between the collection of advertising activity data and the availability of that information. This relates both to printed (hard-copy) and soft-copy reports and to data files that are delivered to some customers who purchased our reporting software AEM*Reporter*.

Our Customer Department has the task of searching for new customers by researching those areas where our data has a potential market. The sales staff will then use this information to establish contact with these prospective customers with the aim of negotiating a business contract for delivery of AEM reports. Once we win a customer, our primary focus is to ensure that they are completely satisfied with the service and data that they receive.

Contact management does not just relate to our customers. It embraces also our auxiliary suppliers. These are organizations that provide AEM with data (mostly advertising media outlets, but also organizations who supply us with auxiliary data – advertising rate cards, audience and readership figures, and similar supporting information). Contracts exist with some suppliers for the supply of auxiliary data.

The majority of AEM's customers are on annual contracts. The contract specifies its timeframe, limitations in terms of access to our information, frequency of information delivery, target advertising markets (including media outlets and geographical areas), and any other conditions for data provision. This information is linked to our Accounts Receivable for the purposes of billing and tracking of payments. A regular requirement is the production of sales analysis reports. This assists greatly in renegotiating the contracts.

AEM collects information from a variety of sources. The major form of data collection is the electronic transfer of advertising activity from the media outlets to activity logs (i.e. computer files). This takes place primarily in the middle of the night by establishing computer-to-computer communication with media outlets and capturing the previous twenty-four hours of activity. Advertising data that cannot be collected electronically is entered manually from the advertising source. In the case of the press, this is from the newspapers and magazines. For cinema and outdoor advertising we expect the corresponding media outlets to send us advertising reports for input.

AEM collects about half a million advertisement instances each week. In order to cope with this volume of data in the most efficient manner, we attempt – during data entry – to automatically link collected data to advertisements already stored in our database. The principle applied is that if we have seen the details of an advertisement before, we can apply the same decisions as last time to that record. Material not recognized is flagged for the attention of a member of our quality control staff.

The quality control staff perform verification of all automatically collected and flagged data as well as of all data collected manually (i.e. entered by data collection staff from an advertisement source when automatic recognition of an advertisement is not possible). The process of data collection and data verification aims to determine so-called adlinks. An adlink is an assignment of an advertisement to the advertised product, advertiser, and agency used by the advertiser.

Once collected and verified, the data undergoes a consolidation process for the purpose of producing aggregated reports to customers. Consolidation demands that the collected and verified data is first copied from our transactional database to the data warehouse (i.e. the database which contains all historical advertising activity data and which is designed specifically for data analysis).

To start with, the data collected in units of media outlet (e.g. a TV channel) and day is aggregated into units of media types (e.g. metropolitan television) and week. Both aggregated and more specialized reports require the updating of the advertisement information with advertising rates (charges) and audience/readership data. The rates must reflect as closely as possible the real prices being paid for that medium under the number of parameters (such as day and time advertised, buying power of an agency, our own intelligence and surveys, etc.). The audience/readership data is necessary to measure the effectiveness of our advertising on our customers' target audience/readership.

AEM sells advertising activity information to its customers. We can distribute this information in a number of ways. Printed reports are just one of them. As we progress in time, the provision of information on paper will reduce in importance until it is no longer a requirement. Soft-copy reports, sent electronically to our customers, will be demanded for the foreseeable future. Instead of reports, we can provide our customers with data files that a customer can use to produce their reports using our reporting software AEM*Reporter*. Finally, it is also feasible to allow our bigger customers to connect to our data warehouse and permit them to access data they have contracted for.

Exercises

1. Build a business use case model reflecting the problem statement for the minicase. Try not to be influenced by the business use case models for AEM presented in the book. A practical start

point is to read the problem statement and highlight the candidate business use cases and candidate business actors (using different color highlighters).

2. Build a business class model reflecting the problem statement for the minicase. Try not to be influenced by the business class models for AEM presented in the book. Ignore for now business entities required to support data warehouse (data consolidation and distribution of advertising activity information to customers). For relationships, show multiplicities with participation properties. A practical start point is to read the problem statement and highlight the candidate business classes. Note also that business actors from the business use case model are candidate business classes in a business class model.

Chapter

7

Domain Object Model

The business object model (BOM), discussed in Chapter 6, is a model of the enterprise. The **domain object model** (DOM) is a model for a subset of BOM. An enterprise has one BOM and many DOMs. In this book, the BOM is AEM – the Advertising Expenditure Measurement enterprise. Any major business use case of BOM can be treated as a DOM.

The scope of an IS project can be a domain as addressed in this chapter. A **domain** is an application area (a subsystem) of an enterprise information system. A domain defines the scope of an **application under development**. However, in an iterative and incremental approach to software production, a domain may be too large to constitute the scope for a development iteration. It is more likely that one or a couple of use cases defined within the DOM will define the scope of an iteration.

The DOM discussed in this chapter is Contact Management (CM) (see also Maciaszek, 2001). Contact Management contains the book's main case-study – Email Management (EM). EM is an *application under development*. Figure 7.1 is a Venn diagram showing dependencies between BOM, DOM, and the EM case-study. Note in this context that some minicases introduced at the ends of chapters belong to other DOMs, i.e. different from CM. However, all minicases are within the book's BOM.

DOM is more than the Unified Process (UP) definition of a domain model. In the UP, the domain model is an artifact of business modeling and a representation of real-world conceptual classes in the domain of interest. Risking oversimplification, the UP domain model is a class model reminiscent of semantic entity–relationship models popularized by structured analysis methods. In particular, the UP domain model visualizes classes, their attributes and relationships, but no operations.

DOM is a relatively complete UML analysis model, which can employ a wide range of the UML methods and techniques. However, a complete DOM will not be developed if the scope of the *application under development* is a subset of DOM. In this book, DOM is only a 'linkage' between BOM and the EM (Email Management) case-study. BOM and DOM together provide the background knowledge and the context for the application under development.

Figure 7.1
Dependencies
among BOM,
DOM, and the
case study

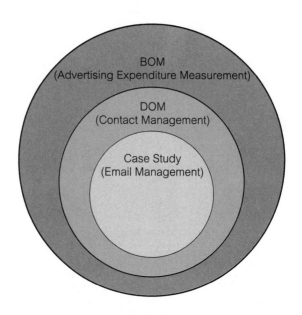

7.1 Contact Management – The Domain

CM (**Contact Management**) is a business function of AEM. CM is on a 'side road' of the main AEM *workflow chain* consisting of data collection, valorization (quality control), and reporting (Section 6.3). However, it is a major contributor to the AEM *value chain*, to use the concept popularized by Michael Porter (Porter, 1985; see also Maciaszek, 2001).

CM is responsible for communication with AEM contacts – predominantly customers and suppliers. This involves scheduling, initiating, recording outcomes of communication as well as handling informational details of contacts. CM can also be seen as a support function for the workflow chain, whenever a need for communication arises within the workflow chain but is passed to CM for handling. Examples include inquiries to media outlets regarding inaccuracies in electronic data logs (Section 6.1), inquiries to resolve unknown adlinks (Section 6.4), inquiries to agencies and advertisers to verify the accuracy of rates applied to advertisements, etc.

CM is about person-to-person communication, which is a critically important contributor to organizational knowledge that must be 'documented'. Documenting person-to-person communication is an attempt to manage **unstructured information** – letter correspondence, facsimile exchanges, emails, voice recordings, business presentations, web pages, etc. From a database perspective, these are all examples of **multimedia data**.

In contemporary practice, multimedia data is unstructured – it is stored as an undifferentiated byte stream with no structured knowledge about its informational content. **Descriptive attributes** (such as who created the data, subject area, keywords, etc.) are stored alongside the multimedia object to 'recover' its informational content. Descriptive attributes (which are themselves **structured information**) are stored in a database and used to access multimedia objects (in the same or another database or in a file system).

CM is a system of recording descriptive information about person-to-person communication and, if required and accessible, reaching to an unstructured source of this descriptive information. CM stores descriptions of new customer negotiations, contact details, follow-up actions, customer requirements, report deliveries, production queries from the 'workflow chain', etc.

Domain Use Case Model

7.2

In terms of modeling concepts, a **domain use case model** resembles a business use case model. Both are representations of business functions, relationships between them, and relationships with the environment. The difference is that a business use case model is enterprise-oriented and normally not aiming at immediate implementation, whereas a domain use case model is more 'down-to-earth', possibly project-oriented and can serve as a contract between developers and project stakeholders.

A domain use case model is created from a number of sources. The starting point is BOM – business use case model in particular, but also the glossary and business class model. Other sources of 'modeling inspiration' include business models, organizational structures and processes, stakeholder demands, any supplemental specifications for the system, etc.

Use Cases and Actors

7.2.1

Use case represents a major piece of system functionality. An **actor** is a role that somebody or something plays with regard to a use case. An actor communicates with a use case (via the «communicate» relationship) and expects from it some feedback – a value or observable result.

Sometimes it is desirable to draw multiple use case diagrams for the same domain – each emphasizing a different aspect of the model or part of it. Two typical viewpoints (apart from a global model) are:

- no actors – use cases and their relationships
- single actor's viewpoint – all use cases for each important actor.

Use case diagrams (Section 2.2.2 in Chapter 2) are the UML technique to visualize use cases, actors, and their relationships. Visualization is quite basic and frequently not very helpful. *Use case specifications*, which are text documents stored in a CASE tool repository, are the main power and attraction of use case modeling.

Use Case Relationships

7.2.2

Actors in the model can be categorized by means of generalization relationships. No other UML relationships are encouraged between actors. Use cases can be related by association

Figure 7.2
Relationships
between use case
model classifiers

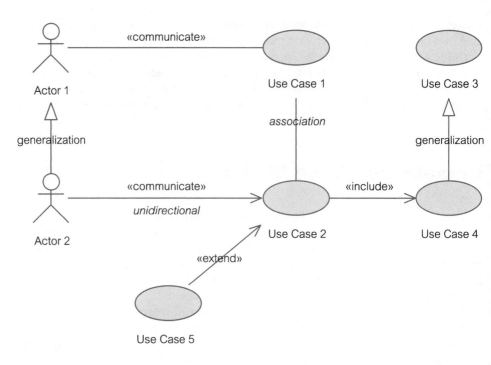

and generalization relationships and by two stereotyped relationships called «include» and «extend». Actors and use cases are linked by a special kind of association called the «communicate» relationship.

Figure 7.2 (duplicated here from Figure 2.10) shows how classifiers (model elements) in a use case model can be related. Use cases are interlinked because they need to collaborate to perform the tasks of the system. However, a recommended practice is to limit relationships between use cases. Showing all relationships obscures the intent of the model. Showing only selected relationships raises a question why these relationships are more important than others. It must be remembered that, ultimately, use case diagrams take a secondary role to text documents defining each use case.

The principle of a prudent use of relationships applies also to two relationships specifically stereotyped in the UML for use case modeling: the «include» relationship and the «extend» relationship (Section 2.2.2). The «include» relationship means that the execution of one use case enfolds (always) the functionality of the included use case. The «extend» relationship means that the execution of one use case may need to be extended (sometimes) by the functionality of the extending use case.

The «include» and «extend» relationships are always **unidirectional** to denote the direction of inclusion or extension. The «communicate» and association relationships may or may not have an arrowhead to denote if the navigation is in one direction. Lack of an arrowhead implies either that the **navigation** is in both directions or that the navigation direction is not defined (i.e. perhaps it will be defined in the future but we don't bother for now). Note that navigation in both directions is represented by a straight line rather than by a line with two arrowheads.

Use Case Model for Contact Management 7.2.3

Contact Management (CM) is a complex domain. The business of most organizations evolves around customers' satisfaction and suppliers' reliability. AEM is no exception. However, in this book, CM is merely a path towards the book's case-study – Email Management. For this reason, the view taken on CM is rather simplistic.

Figure 7.3 is a plausible use case model for CM. It consists of five use cases: Negotiate New Customer, Record Customer Requirements, Maintain Contact Information, Track Contact Events, Handle Production Queries. Consistently with our recommendation in Section 7.2.1, no relationships between use cases are modeled.

Generalization relationships on actors simplify the model. For example, we know that Customer Department Manager is the only actor that communicates with Negotiate New Customer. But Customer Department Manager can also communicate with Handle Production Queries. This is because Customer Department Manager 'is a kind of' Customer Department Employee and Customer Department Employee 'is a kind of' Employee.

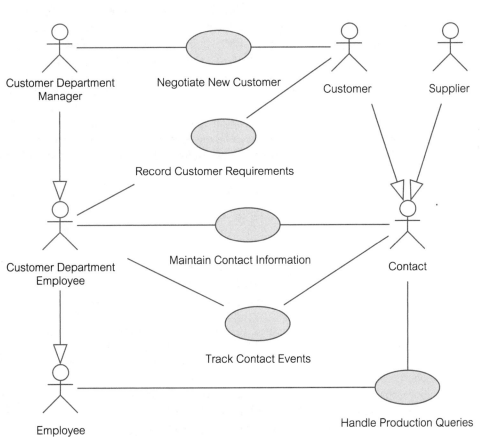

Figure 7.3
Use case diagram for CM

A vital CM activity is the search for new customers. This is done by researching those target contacts for which AEM advertising activity information is of potential interest. These contacts become prospective customers and are targeted by `Negotiate New Customer`. `Customer Department Manager` is responsible for engaging these prospects and conveying details of AEM services. The objective is to win a contract with the prospect. If no interest is generated, the exchange of communication is recorded in the system with a date to re-establish contact with this prospect.

`Record Customer Requirements` is responsible for managing specifications of AEM customers' needs for advertising activity information. The specifications capture the category and frequency of advertising activity information that the customer is interested in (including the range of advertised products or categories, the media outlets of interest, the spread of geographical markets, the time span for which reports are sought, the advertisers and agencies of interest to the customer).

`Maintain Contact Information` is a routine function of maintaining details of customers and suppliers, such as addresses, telephone and fax details, the type of advertising data supplied, contact persons. This use case is enriched by an internal know-how, such as the relative importance of a customer to AEM business, the reliability of a supplier, a change of the nature of the contract (e.g. when an agency with a current AEM contract loses an advertiser as its client).

All contact events and communication exchanges between Customer Department employees and AEM contacts are recorded within the system. These exclude ad hoc events that do not result in a noticeable value to AEM. `Track Contact Events` keeps track of events that lead to or have a potential to lead to an outcome of business value to AEM. `Track Contact Events` is able to link events, undertaken by one or more employees over a period of time, so that they can be viewed as a unit. A unit with a well-defined purpose is called a task.

`Handle Production Queries` manages all queries to contacts raised within the production 'workflow chain'. The queries can be raised in any step of the chain – in data collection, during data verification, during valorization of advertisements, and when generating and delivering advertising activity reports.

7.2.4 Alternative Use Case Model for Contact Management

Contact Management can be seen as a function in managing documents to/from contacts, scheduling employees' contact-related activities, recording activities already attended to, and of course in managing contact information.

Managing documents includes unstructured documents (Section 7.1). Scheduling of activities can be a part of a broader task of managing employees' electronic calendars (such as exemplified by Microsoft Outlook's Calendar). All entries with regard to a contact can be linked and tracked from the calendars. Calendar entries that have been dealt with can be recorded in employees' electronic time logs.

The above observations can lead to an alternative use case model, which emphasizes generic (less customized) functions of a typical CM application and hides specific CM responsibilities in more generic use cases. Figure 7.4 is an alternative model.

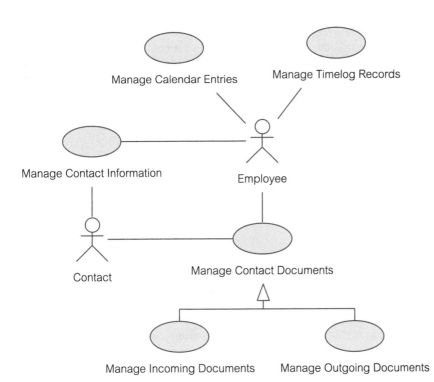

Figure 7.4
Alternative use
case diagram for
CM

The model in Figure 7.4 divides CM into four main use cases: Manage Calendar
Entries, Manage Timelog Records, Manage Contact Information and Manage
Contact Documents. There are just two generic actors identified in the model:
Employee and Contact. Contact does not communicate with Manage Calendar
Entries and Manage Timelog Records because these use cases are considered internal
to AEM employees.

Manage Calendar Entries is in charge of scheduling and tracking appointments,
meetings and other intercommunication between AEM employees and contacts. Each
employee has his/her own electronic calendar. The entries in the calendar can be entered
manually by an employee, can be scheduled for an employee by other employees
(supervisors), or can be automatically entered from other functions of the AEM system
(such as to handle any queries to contacts generated during data collection or data
verification).

Although not explicitly modeled in Figure 7.4, there are two main kinds of calendar
entry: timed and untimed. Timed entries designate the date and time of the activity:
appointment, meeting, telephone call, etc. Untimed entries are activities and events which
either do not have a specific due date/time or last for one or more days (such as 'being on'
a business trip).

It is assumed that Manage Calendar Entries includes the functionality of tracking
contact events and the scheduling of production queries (modeled explicitly in Figure 7.3).
Note, however, that tracking the outcomes of contact events and the outcomes of
production queries will involve two other use cases: Manage Timelog Records and

`Manage Contact Documents`. The latter will be engaged for retrieving documents related to contact events and production queries (including the content of email messages).

`Manage Contact Information` has the combined functionality of `Maintain Contact Information` and `Record Customer Requirements` in Figure 7.3. It handles details and requirements of persons and organizations, which are CM targets.

`Manage Contact Documents` enables the storage and retrieval of any documents, both structured and unstructured, and including emails associated with a contact. The documents are classified into incoming from contacts and outgoing to contacts.

7.3 Domain Glossary

The business glossary in Table 6.1, Section 6.4, defined basic terms related to advertising expenditure measurement. It was called a *business glossary* to signify that it contained vocabulary related to BOM. Since BOM defines DOMs, a business glossary needs to be expanded to include domain terms.

In practice, IS development relates to one *domain* at a time (and handles only one *application* at a time, i.e. the application under development). It is sensible, therefore, to talk about a **domain glossary** as the list of terms within the domain scope.

7.3.1 Domain Glossary for Contact Management

The CM domain defines the scope of the domain glossary in Table 7.1. The glossary contains all terms from the business glossary (Table 6.1) and adds terms related to contact management. Because glossaries grow in size quickly, the glossary in Table 7.1 is sorted. In the 'Definition and explanations' column, references to terms already defined in the glossary are typed in italics.

Table 7.1 Domain glossary for CM

Term	Definition and explanations
ad (advertisement)	A unique piece of creative work that may be broadcast, screened, published or otherwise exposed any number of times. Each ad exposure by a media outlet is known in the AEM system as an *ad instance*
ad instance	A particular occurrence of an *ad*, i.e. each incidence of an *ad* broadcast, screening, or publication
adlink	An association between an *ad*, the *product* it advertises, the *advertiser* who pays for the exposure of the *ad* and the *agency* responsible for the booking of that exposure. Outlets that have exposed the *ad* can be derived from the descriptions of *ad instances* of that *ad*
advertiser	An *organization* that uses the media to expose its creative output (*advertisement*) in order to promote a *product* (merchandise or service). A large number of advertisers are known in the AEM system as 'Direct Advertiser'. These are advertisers that bypass an *agency* and book advertising space directly with a media *outlet*

Table 7.1 (cont'd)

Term	Definition and explanations
advertiser group	A company that directly or indirectly controls one or more other companies and is interested in viewing the accumulated advertising activity and expenditure of the associated companies. Advertiser groups do not pay for any advertising; the advertisers within the group handle this. Advertiser groups are also known as Holding Companies
agency	An *organization* that handles the advertising planning and media buying for an *advertiser*. The goal of an agency is to optimize the advertising expenditure
agency group	An *organization* that directly or indirectly controls one or more other *agencies* and is interested in viewing the accumulated planning and media buying for an *agency* or group of agencies. Agency groups do not do any planning or media buying; the agencies within the group handle this
calendar entry	An appointment, meeting, event or other activity scheduled in an employee's electronic calendar to act upon. A calendar entry may be timed (when it has due date/time allocated) or it may be untimed (it appears as a 'things to do' entry without a specific date/time by which to act upon it)
category	A classification of *products* as envisaged by AEM for reporting purpose. Categories can be organized into hierarchical structures of categories and subcategories. *Products* are 'categorized' with categories at the bottom level of hierarchical structure
contact	A person or *organization* that AEM communicates or does business with
customer	A *contact* who receives data or services from AEM and typically pays for it
employee	A person who is employed by AEM or has other work arrangement with AEM with or without pay
organization	A business entity that AEM communicates or deals with. There are different types of organizations, including *advertisers*, *agencies*, *outlets*, *advertiser groups*, *agency groups*, and data *providers*. An organization can be one, many, or none of these types
outlet	An *organization* that exposes an *advertisement*. In the television and radio media, an outlet is defined as the station that airs *ads*. In the cinema and outdoor media, an outlet is defined as the company that organizes exposure of the *ads*. In the print medium, an outlet is defined as the publication in which *ads* are printed
product	An item of merchandise or a service that may be advertised. Products may be categorized (i.e. a product can belong to a category of products). *Categories* are classifications of products as envisaged by AEM. The AEM system supports a hierarchical grouping of *categories* with an unlimited number of levels in the hierarchy. Products may only be categorized at the lowest level of the *category* hierarchy
production query	A request for information, or just information, raised by the production staff with regard to an AEM *contact*. Production staff includes all *employees* involved in collecting and processing advertising activity data
prospect (prospective customer)	A *contact* that is targeted by AEM's sales staff as a potential *customer*
provider (auxiliary supplier)	A *contact* that provides auxiliary data or services to AEM. This information includes demographics (divisions of groups of people based on specified attributes such as age, sex, and socio-economic factors), surveys (measured and projected viewing/listening/ readership figures per different demographic categories and for different outlets), rates (advertising prices for different outlets to determine the cost of an *ad*), discounts (estimated reductions in advertising prices due to the purchasing power of an *agency* when booking *ads* through a specified medium)
query (to contact) (outmessage)	A request for information, or just information, raised by an AEM *employee* with regard to an AEM *contact*. Includes *production queries*

Figure 7.5
Classes and
relationships in
a domain class
model

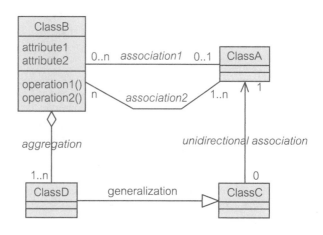

7.4 Domain Class Model

A **domain class model** defines classes and relationships between them. The definition is visual and descriptive. A class diagram provides the visual representation. The descriptive representation consists of specifications of various properties as they may apply to classes and relationships. Some of these properties cannot be effectively visualized in a class diagram.

Figure 7.5 (the same as Figure 2.6) is an abstract example of a class diagram. The three kinds of **relationship** (associations, aggregations, and generalizations) applicable to a business class model (Section 6.5) can also be used for a domain class model.

Model properties that cannot be shown visually in a class diagram and are supported by the UML can be recorded in a repository of an UML-compliant visual modeling tool. A **repository** is a database of a visual modeling tool that stores all model specifications, including diagrams.

Non-visual model properties can be entered via a dialog box for a classifier (see Section 6.3.1). Figure 7.6 shows a dialog box for a class. The dialog box has many tabs. The active tab – called `General` – allows the class in the `Documentation` field to be described. The content of the `Documentation` field will be stored in the repository as a text that will not be visible on the class diagram.

7.4.1 Classes and Attributes

A **class** represents a set of objects. Classes in a domain class model signify *business concepts*. A domain class model does not designate *software concepts*, such as classes for a graphical user interface or classes needed in the application program to communicate with a database. In this sense, **domain classes** resemble business entities of a business class model (Section 6.5).

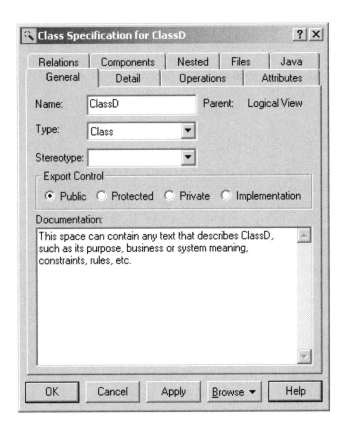

Figure 7.6
Repository
dialog box

Most domain classes are definitions for multiple **object instances**. An application program will need to *instantiate* many objects of a domain class. For example, a class called `Product` is a definitional template from which many products will be created. This is typical of classes representing business objects. By contrast, many classes representing software concepts are singleton classes. A **singleton class** means that only one instance of it can exist within the program. For example, a class called `DatabaseReader` is likely to be a singleton class.

An expectation is that a domain class model is more detailed (i.e. it is a lower level of abstraction) than a business class model. For example, important attributes of a domain class may be specified (but it would be too early to specify operations at this stage). Note, in this context, that the graphical representation for a business entity (Section 6.5.1) does not even provide for attribute and operation compartments.

An **attribute** represents a data value. For example, `product_name` is an attribute in `Product` class. An attribute has a name (such as `product_name`) and a **data type** (such as *string* of characters). An object-oriented way of thinking implies that data types of attributes are primitive types. A **primitive data type** means that no internal structure can be identified in the type. For example, `product_name` is a primitive type but `person_name` is not, if we want to distinguish between family name, first name, and middle name.

An object-oriented and the UML position is that a **non-primitive data type** is a class (notwithstanding the fact that a class can contain operations apart from attributes). This creates a certain level of difficulty when modeling domain classes. Without a skillful use of abstraction, a modeler can end up with a large number of insignificant classes such as `PersonName`.

7.4.2 Class Relationships

A **relationship** is a meaningful connection between classifiers (i.e. classes in the case of a domain class model). Association, aggregation, and generalization relationships can be used in domain class modeling (Figure 7.5). However, a recommended approach is to use associations freely, think twice before using aggregations, and resist using generalizations.

Although an **association** is specified on classes (types), a true meaning of it is that it is a relationship between instances of those classes (types). Hence, multiplicity of association ends is so significant. Figure 7.5 demonstrates a possible use of multiplicities. **Multiplicity** specifies how many instances of one class relate to one instance of another class. Multiplicity ought to be defined on both ends of an association. The presence of zero in the multiplicity ($0..n$ or $0..1$) indicates that the **participation** of a class instance in the association is optional.

Aggregation is, in the UML, a special kind of association where an instance of one class (a whole; **superset class**) contains instances of another class (a part; **subset class**). In most situations, a domain class model will be sufficiently expressive without using aggregations. Deciding on aggregations in domain modeling may be an overcommitment to what really is, in the UML, a specialized form of association.

Generalization is a relationship on classifiers, i.e. classes (types) in a domain class model. Each instance of the more specific class (**subclass**) is also an instance of the more general class (**superclass**). Hence, this is not a relationship on instances of those classes. As per the definition of generalization, multiplicity does not apply to it.

Using generalization in domain class modeling introduces a risk of misinterpretation of the real nature of relationships in the model (i.e. that object instances are related somehow). Generalization should be used only when the resulting visual simplification of a graphical model outweighs the risks of confusion when interpreting the model. (Clever use of generalization can radically reduce the number of other relationships in the model.)

Figure 7.5 shows a possibility (quite exceptional) where multiplicity for `ClassC` in association with `ClassA` is 0 (this corresponds to $0..0$, i.e. minimum zero and maximum zero). This is possible because association is unidirectional. The navigation is only allowed from `ClassC` to `ClassA`, but not vice versa. Hence, `ClassA` is not associated with `ClassC`.

Multiplicity on aggregation is usually defined only on one end of aggregation. A whole (superset class) contains a part (subset class). This means that an instance of the whole can contain zero, one or many instances of the part. By implication, an instance of the part is normally contained in one instance of the whole (if anything, it may not be contained at all and in that case the multiplicity would be $0..1$).

Class Model for Contact Management   7.4.3

A recommended practice is to develop the use case model and class model in parallel. Unfortunately, a textbook cannot show the process of going about doing things – it can only describe the products of the process. Two main products of DOM are the domain use case model and the domain class model. Since the domain use case model was described first (Section 7.2), we can use it to derive a corresponding domain class model.

To get a symbolic feel for the process the reader is encouraged to read again Section 7.2.3 and attempt to sketch a class diagram that would satisfy the informational needs of use cases described in that section. Without doubt, an experiment like that will open a Pandora's box of questions demanding clarification on both ends of the modeling spectrum – in the use case model and in the class model. This is precisely why the two models need to be built up iteratively and in sync.

Figure 7.7 is a domain class diagram matching the informational needs of the domain use case model in Section 7.2.3. The diagram shows the main relationships and basic attributes of classes. All relationships are associations. The data types of attributes are not specified but some attributes are clearly non-primitive data types. These attributes will become classes in their own right (Section 7.4.1), but this possibility is ignored for the sake of simplicity.

`Contact` is a person who represents an `Organization` or acts as an individual with business links to AEM (hence, the multiplicity `0..1`). The attribute `status` reflects the customer negotiation status, such as that the contact is a prospect (Section 7.3.1). The

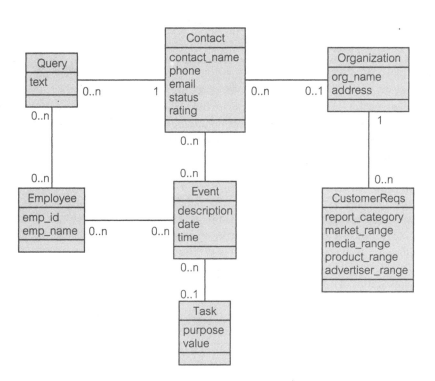

Figure 7.7
Class diagram for CM

attribute `rating` is a comparative ranking value that AEM currently attaches to a contact (this is managed by the use case `Maintain Contact Information`).

The model does not specialize `Contact` into subclasses but there is an understanding that `Contact` represents any AEM contact – customer, outlet, supplier, prospect, etc. (Section 7.3.1). Showing subclasses (generalization relationships) for `Contact` will not improve much (if at all) the intended semantics of the model but it will make the model more difficult to explore.

`Contact` is linked to multiple `Events` (ref. the use case `Track Contact Events`) and multiple `Queries` (ref. the use case `Handle Production Queries`), and so is `Employee`. In this way, contacts and employees are indirectly linked via events and queries.

`Events` may be combined into `Task`, but they do not have to be. `Event` can be a stand-alone, perhaps once-off, interaction between `Employee` and `Contact`. The association between `Event` and `Task` supports the use case `Track Contact Events`.

`CustomerReqs` supports the use case `Record Customer Requirements` and it feeds eventually into the function of managing customer contracts – the function that is outside the Contact Management DOM. Although negotiation of customer requirements is done with contacts, `CustomerReqs` is associated with `Organization`, which is represented by `Contact`.

Attributes of `CustomerReqs` are non-primitive data types. They will become classes in a refined class model. Creating separate classes now would change the overall 'balance' of the model too much in favor of one use case, `Record Customer Requirements` (one of five use cases in Figure 7.3).

7.4.4 Alternative Class Model for Contact Management

Figure 7.8 is a class model that corresponds to the alternative use case model given in Section 7.2.4. As compared with the model in Figure 7.7, the alternative model is less specific as far as managing contacts in AEM is concerned. The model can almost serve as a framework for any CM system, not just for AEM. This framework will need to be specialized and extended, in future project iterations, to handle AEM specifics.

The model separates personal information about employees (in `Employee` class) from schedules and records of employees' work activities (in `Calendar` and `TimeLog` classes). `Employee` contains many `Calendars` and `Timelogs` (modeled by aggregation relationships). The reason it contains 'many' is evident from the attributes of `Calendar` and `TimeLog`. `Calendar` stores descriptions and details of calendar entries (`entry_desc`). `Timelog` stores descriptions and details of time log records (`record_desc`).

A `Timelog` record may be an outcome of an employee's action on a `Calendar` entry. Hence the `0..1` multiplicity on one end of the relationship between `Timelog` and `Calendar`. A `Timelog` record and a `Calendar` entry may be linked to `0..n` `Contacts` (some work duties of employees, such as a meeting, may involve a group of contacts).

Storing and handling of documents takes a central stage in the model. `Document` can be from or to one or more `Contacts`, it can be addressed by one or more `Calendar` entries, and it can be referred to in one or more `Timelog` records.

`Contact` may or may not be associated with an `Organization`. `Organization` may exist even if its `Contacts` are not known to the system. An important implication (and

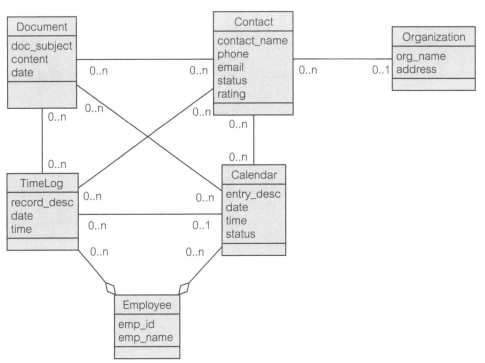

Figure 7.8
Alternative class
diagram for CM

assumption) is that documents, time log records, and calendar entries can be associated (indirectly) to an `Organization` as long as it is identified with at least one `Contact`.

Summary

1. A *domain object model* (DOM) is a model of one application area (domain) of an enterprise. It is one of possibly many models within a *business object model* (BOM). Usually, the DOM is a UML analysis model for one business use case of the BOM.

2. A *domain* defines the scope of an *application under development*. Typically, a development *iteration* addresses one or a couple of use cases identified within the DOM.

3. The domain taken up by the case-study of the book is CM (Contact Management). The application under development is EM (Email Management) – a use case with the DOM for CM.

4. CM is a system of recording descriptive *structured information* about exchanges of communication between an enterprise and its contacts (customers, suppliers, etc.) as well storing and managing *unstructured documents* related to these exchanges of communication.

5. A *domain use case model* is a UML use case diagram and associated use case documents defined for a domain.

6. A *use case diagram* is a graphical depiction of actors, use cases, and relationships between them.

7. *Actor* is a role that somebody or something plays with regard to a use case. *Use case* represents a piece of functionality.

8. An actor communicates with a use case via the «communicate» relationship. Use cases can be related by association and generalization relationships and by two stereotyped relationships called «include» and «extend».

9. A *domain glossary* expands a business glossary by adding to it terms and definitions specific to the domain.

10. A *domain class model* defines classes within a domain and relationships between these classes. The definition is both visual (domain class diagram) and descriptive (textual specifications for classes).

11. Domain classes define *business objects* (as opposed to *software objects*). Typically, a domain class represents many object instances. *Singleton classes*, which can instantiate only one object, are rare for domain classes (but quite frequent for other software classes).

12. An *attribute* represents a data value. An *attribute type* can be primitive or non-primitive. Non-primitive type designates a class.

13. There are three main kinds of *relationships*: associations, aggregations, and generalizations. *Multiplicity* and *participation* are important properties of associations. These properties apply also to aggregation, but not to generalization.

Key Terms

«communicate» relationship	218	generalization	226
«extend» relationship	218	multimedia data	216
«include» relationship	218	multiplicity	226
actor	217	navigation	218
aggregation	226	non-primitive data type	226
application under development	215	object instance	225
association	226	participation	226
attribute	225	primitive data type	225
class	224	relationship	224, 226
CM	*See* Contact Management	repository	224
Contact Management	216, 219	singleton class	225
data type	225	structured information	216
descriptive attributes	216	subclass	226
DOM	*See* domain object model	subset class	226
domain	215	superclass	226
domain class	224	superset class	226
domain glossary	222	unidirectional relationship	218
domain class model	224	unstructured information	216
domain object model	215	use case	217
domain use case model	217		

Review Questions

Discussion Questions

1. Explain how a BOM and a DOM relate to each other?

2. What is a typical scope of application under development with regard to DOM?

3. What is structured and unstructured information?

4. What is the meaning of the «communicate» relationship?

5. Explain the differences between an addition use case and an extension use case?

6. What is a repository?

7. What is meant by business objects and by software objects? How do these two concepts relate to domain object modeling?

8. What is a domain class?

9. What is a singleton class? Can you think of a domain class that is a singleton class?

10. Explain the role of non-primitive types in domain object modeling.

11. How does UML express multiplicity and participation? Would you consider these two concepts to be semantically dependent or independent? Is the UML way of expressing multiplicity and participation aligned with the semantics of these two concepts?

12. Compare the usefulness of association and aggregation in domain object modeling.

13. What is generalization? How should it be used in domain object modeling?

Case Study Questions

1. Consider the use case diagram in Figure 7.3. Suppose you would like to make the model more explicit by showing relationships between use cases. Try it. What is your conclusion? Does it make modeling sense to include relationships in this diagram?

2. What is a prospect in the CM terminology?

3. Analyze the class model in Section 7.4.3 and the diagram in Figure 7.7. Is it possible for AEM, according to the model, to get into a contractual arrangement with a private person (as opposed to an organization)?

Problem-Solving Exercises

Case Study Exercises

1. Consider the use case model for CM discussed in Section 7.2.3 and the corresponding use case diagram in Figure 7.3. Assume that current development iteration emphasizes the following CM aspects:

   (a) There is a need to separately track events that relate to contractual arrangements that AEM has with existing customers. Many contract-related events result from customers communicating to AEM their new requirements for advertising information or from AEM marketing of new services to customers under existing contracts. They also may be an outcome of routine or ad hoc communication with a contact.

(b) The glossary in Table 7.1 states that a contact is a person or organization that AEM communicates or does business with. There is a need to clarify the correlation between `PersonContact` and `OrganizationContact`. Assume that the requirements analysis of the nature of this correlation revealed that:

(i) There are frequently many individuals (`PersonContacts`) that AEM uses to commun-icate with a single organization (`OrganizationContact`).

(ii) Some communication with OrganizationContact is via an individual who is anony-mous to AEM. This can be, for example, one of many secretaries, and information about them is not recorded in the AEM database. However, a likely outcome of a communication with an anonymous individual may be linked to a `PersonContact` within that organization (e.g. when a secretary makes an appointment for AEM with a financial officer).

Produce a variant of the use case diagram in Figure 7.3 that emphasizes the above two aspects of CM. Retain existing use cases. Do not show any actors. Just add new use cases to the model and establish necessary relationships.

2. Consider the class model for CM in Section 7.4.3 and the corresponding class diagram in Figure 7.7. Take into account additional and specific requirements raised in Exercise 1 above. Whether or not you have attempted to solve Exercise 1, produce a variant of the class diagram in Figure 7.7 that models the new requirements.

Minicase – Time Logging

Contact Management is not just about managing contacts. It is also about managing employees engaged in contact management. The use case diagram in Figure 7.4 makes this point by including two use cases associated only with the `Employee` actor. The use cases are: `Manage Calendar Entries` and `Manage Timelog Records`. This minicase elaborates on the latter. (Maciaszek (2001) contains a case study that explores typical functionality of managing employees' electronic calendars.)

Time logging (TL) is a facility that allows employees to record time worked on various tasks during a specified period of time. In case of CM, time logging captures time spent on doing contact management. This includes exchanges of communications by telephone, fax, email, courier, and regular post. It includes meetings and conferences. It includes also the time spent preparing outgoing documents, letters, memos, contracts, etc., and the time spent reading and analyzing any incoming materials. Finally, it includes time related to maintaining contact details, such as address changes, tracing returned correspondence, etc.

The fundamental usability requirement of the time logging function is that it must be done with a minimum of overhead. In other words, the function must be transparent, coincidental, and concurrent to performing the contact management tasks. Without this ease-of-use, time logging will not work – either employees will not bother entering time information or they will not do it with sufficient precision and detail.

Time logging in CM is not about 'big brother' watching what employees are doing or about employees' performance evaluation. Time logging is about determining time and effort spent on dealing with various contacts, about the value of these contacts to the AEM business, about rating the contacts, about customer relations, about tracking events leading to successful contracts, about timely response to complaints, etc. In a nutshell, time logging is about business analysis, tactical decisions, and strategic planning with regard to the contact management function.

Time logging is not unique to AEM. Any organization can benefit from an application supporting this function. Indeed, there are commercial software tools for time logging. One such tool comes from Responsive Software (Responsive, 2002). The tool can be customized to allow easy entry of time information for specific projects and activities. Alternatively, this and similar tools can serve as a source of ideas for user interface design on a project aimed at in-house development of the time logging function.

For the purpose of this minicase, the time logging function is a use case of the CM application domain (Figure 7.4). The use case allows an employee to enter time records about *tasks* and *activities* (called also *events*) performed with regard to *contacts*. The use case determines from the CM database the lists of contacts and predefined tasks. All employees entering time records can refer to these lists. Individually, each employee can create in the CM database his/her own list of predefined *activities*. Each time record can contain a longer text description about the nature of the task/activity.

A time record relates always to one employee and one contact. Under this condition a time record can be entered for:

- a predefined task and a predefined activity within that task
- a predefined task with no activity recorded
- an employee-defined activity with no task recorded (the application allows a new employee-defined activity to be created, if the activity has not been defined before and is, therefore, not available from a dropdown list).

An entry of a time record includes the start date/time and the end date/time of the task/activity. The use case automatically calculates the duration of the task/activity. The duration may be less than the difference between the end and start time, if the employee took some breaks (pauses) between the start and end time. An employee can explicitly enter the duration of breaks within a time record.

Previous time log entries can be viewed and printed. They can also be sorted by different criteria, in particular by date/time, by contact, and by task. A customized display, such as one where certain entries are filtered out, is possible. The filter criteria are the same as the sort criteria. Existing entries can be modified or deleted, subject to some business rules, such as no changes are allowed on entries entered in the previous billing, accounting, or reporting period.

Exercises

1. Based on the minicase specifications, develop a use case model that identifies sub-use-cases of the `Manage Timelog Records` use case from Figure 7.4. As `Employee` is the only actor, there is no need to show it in the diagram.

2. Based on the minicase specifications, extend the domain class diagram in Figure 7.8. Add new domain classes and associate them with existing classes.

Chapter

8

Iteration 1 Requirements and Object Model

This book takes an iterative case-study approach to information systems development. The main case-study is **Email Management** (EM). EM is part of Contact Management (CM), which in turn is part of Advertising Expenditure Measurement (AEM) (Figure 7.1). Accordingly, EM can be seen as a use case of CM.

Figure 8.1 is an extension of the use case model in Figure 7.4. `Manage Email` is an *extension use case* (Section 7.2.2) for three *base use cases*: `Manage Calendar Entries`, `Manage Timelog Records`, and `Manage Contact Documents`.

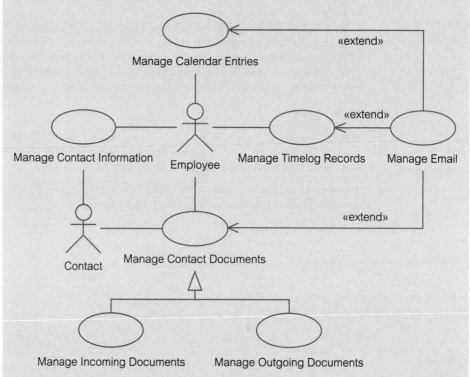

Figure 8.1 Manage Email as CM extension use case

Email itself is a document to a contact or from a contact. Additionally, an email may have document attachments. Hence, `Manage Email` extends `Manage Contact Documents`. Sending an email may be scheduled as an employee's work activity, and therefore inserted as a calendar entry under the control of `Manage Calendar Entries`. The act of sending and responding to emails entails a work record that may need to be stored in the time log of an employee. Therefore, `Manage Email` extends `Manage Timelog Records`.

Although not within the scope of the book's case-study, Email Management can have a wider appeal as a system for **Email Marketing**. Email Marketing is about targeted emailing to contacts (potential customers) of marketing information about products or services. As in the EM case study, Email Marketing stores information about contacts and their email addresses in the database, formats outgoing messages based on the information also kept in the database, automatically emails these messages, and updates the database accordingly.

Use Case Model

For educational reasons, this and successive iterations of the case-study introduce assumptions and simplifications. Iteration 1 assumes that messages to contacts are already stored in the EM database. The Iteration 1 system is responsible for composing and emailing of these messages and for updating the database after successful emails.

Figure 8.2 is a dedicated use case model aimed at presenting the scope, intended functionality, assumptions and simplifications of Iteration 1. The use case `Store Messages to Contacts` is outside the scope of Iteration 1.

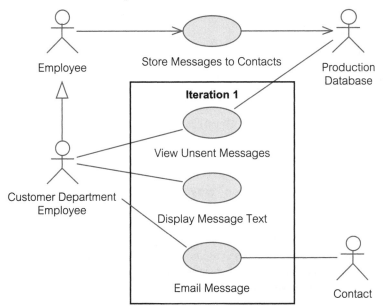

Figure 8.2
Use case diagram for Iteration 1

The purpose of `Store Messages to Contacts` is to store in `Production Database` the subject and text of email messages to contacts and to assign sending of these messages to appropriate `Customer Department Employees`. Normally this use case is activated during collecting and verifying advertising activity data and when preparing activity reports for customers. Iteration 1 assumes that such messages exist already in `Production Database`.

`View Unsent Messages` is responsible for displaying a list containing basic information about messages kept in `Production Database` and scheduled for emailing by `Customer Department Employee`. `Customer Department Employee` may wish to display the complete text of the message (`Display Message Text`) before deciding to email it (`Email Message`).

Once the message is successfully sent, `Email Message` flags it as dealt with. This action is not obvious in the use case diagram because the model does not commit itself to how and where the 'sent flag' will be set. It is possible, for example, that `Production Database` is used only by `View Unsent Messages`, which reads the messages and downloads them to a database internal to EM. An internal database cannot be an actor in the EM model.

8.2 Use Case Document

A graphical representation of a use case model (i.e. a use case diagram) serves an important visualization purpose ('a picture is worth thousand words'), but a real benefit of use case modeling is in text descriptions of use cases. A text description of a use case is sometimes called simply a **use case document**.

A use case document is written according to a format predefined by developers for the project. There exist various format templates (Larman, 2002). Templates divide the document into sections and introduce other writing conventions. Use case documents are user requirements. Since user requirements are linked and depend on each other, the writing convention for the use case document must offer a technique of linking various parts of the document.

The format template used in this book is presented Table 8.1. In practice the template will also contain the 'header' information – the author, creation date, version, development status, associated test case document, etc.

8.2.1 Brief Description, Preconditions, and Postconditions

In the following, the use case document is assumed to apply to Iteration 1 of the EM case-study; that is, Iteration 1 of the `Manage Email` use case (Figure 8.1) is the scope of the document.

Brief description

Iteration 1 of the `Manage Email` use case allows an employee to display and send email messages to contacts. It handles only messages already stored in the database. Only one message at a time can be emailed.

Table 8.1 Use case document

Brief description	Expanded description
Actors	Identified from a use case diagram and defined in the diagram repository. If actors are few and obvious, there is no necessity to repeat the diagram and repository information in the document
Preconditions	State the conditions that must be met before the use case can fulfill its contract (its tasks). The use case may fail when the preconditions are not met but this does not mean that the use case has the obligation of checking the preconditions before it 'fires'
Postconditions	State the conditions that the use case guarantees to fulfill on its completion. The postconditions define the state of the system when the use case completes satisfactorily and when the use case is forced to perform an alternative path of execution
Basic flow	Lists and briefly defines the main flow of use case logic – the main steps of it. The detailed definition of each step is deferred to a *subflow* description. Basic flow defines the 'happy path' scenario (Larman, 2002), i.e. it ignores any exceptional situations or error possibilities
Subflows	Define the steps of the basic flow in detail. They also assume the 'happy path' scenario. Sometimes called *extensions* or *alternative flows* in the literature (e.g. Larman, 2002)
Exception flows	Define the exception flow of logic caused by exceptions and errors. Unless the exception is an expected outcome of the use case, exception flows define the 'unhappy path' scenarios. Called also *alternative flows* in the literature (e.g. Maciaszek, 2001; Quatrani, 2000)

Preconditions

1. An Employee works for the Customer Department or is otherwise authorized by the System Administrator to access the EM application.

2. The EM database contains messages to be emailed to contacts.

3. An Employee is connected to an email server and is an authorized database user.

Postconditions

1. The program updated the EM database to reflect any successful emailing of messages.

2. The EM database is left in an intact state if any exception or error occurred.

3. Upon the Employee quitting the application, the console window is closed.

Basic Flow   8.2.2

The steps of the use case execution path are known as the **flow of events**. The flow of events divides into the **basic flow**, subflows, and exception flows. Below is the basic flow of Iteration 1 of the `Manage Email` use case. The flow of events may include sketches of

Figure 8.3
Sketch 1 of user–
computer interface

```
                    EMAIL MANAGEMENT SYSTEM - ITERATION 1


  Please enter your username: lburton
  Please enter your password: psswd
```

the user–computer interface. In Iteration 1, the interface is a text-based console window (i.e. not a GUI).

Providing sketches of user–computer communication in use case documents is a controversial topic. Some experts argue that use case documents must shy away from design/implementation decisions such as the look and feel of user–computer interfaces. However, the other school of thought is that the user–computer interface is a fundamental user requirement that must be considered very early in the development process. The user–computer interface not only sells the product but also serves as an important communication medium in gathering and clarifying user requirements.

Basic flow

The use case starts when an Employee wishes to view and email messages to contacts.

The system displays an informational message and requests that the Employee provides a username and password (Figure 8.3).

- The system attempts to connect the Employee to the EM database.

- Upon successful connection, the application displays a menu list of possible options that the Employee can request. There are four menu options numbered sequentially (Figure 8.4):
  1. to view unsent messages to contacts (see 'S1 – View Unsent Messages', below)
  2. to display the text of a message after the `message_id` is provided (see 'S2 – Display Message Text', below)
  3. to email a message identified by a `message_id` (see 'S3 – Email Message', below)
  4. to quit the application.

If the Employee chooses to exit the EM application by typing 4, the use case ends.

Figure 8.4
Sketch 2 of user–
computer interface

```
                    EMAIL MANAGEMENT SYSTEM - ITERATION 1

  Please enter your username: lburton
  Please enter your password: psswd

     1. View Unsent Messages
     2. Display Text of a Message
     3. Email a Message
     4. Quit this Program

  Please write an option number [1, 2, 3 or 4]:
```

```
              EMAIL MANAGEMENT SYSTEM - ITERATION 1

Please enter your username: lburton
Please enter your password: psswd

   1. View Unsent Messages
   2. Display Text of a Message
   3. Email a Message
   4. Quit this Program

Please choose an option [1, 2, 3 or 4]: 1

There are 2 unsent query message(s), as below:

Message ID: 14
Date Created: 2002-06-21
Message Subject: Product missing
Contact Name: Pablo Romero
Organization: SBS Sydney

Message ID: 19
Date Created: 2002-06-21
Message Subject: Log incomplete
Contact Name: Dorothy Norris
Organization: ABC Radio

   1. View Unsent Messages
   2. Display Text of a Message
   3. Email a Message
   4. Quit this Program

Please choose an option [1, 2, 3 or 4]:
```

Figure 8.5
Sketch 3 of user–computer interface

Subflows

8.2.3

The following defines the **subflows** referred to in the basic flow. Subflows are numbered for ease of reference from other places of the use case document. The convention used in this book identifies a subflow with a letter S followed by a consecutive number (i.e. S1, S2, etc.). The convention adheres to a well-known practice (e.g. Quatrani, 2000).

S1 – View Unsent Messages

The information displayed in the console window is as per the example in Figure 8.5.
   The menu list is presented after the last unsent message is displayed.

S2 – Display Message Text

The Employee is prompted for a `message_id` before the text of that message is displayed. A message text is displayed as shown in Figure 8.6.
   The menu list is re-displayed below the message text.

Figure 8.6
Sketch 4 of user–
computer interface

```
1. View Unsent Messages
2. Display Text of a Message
3. Email a Message
4. Quit this Program

Please choose an option [1, 2, 3 or 4]: 2

Please enter the message id: 14

Message ID: 14
Date Created: 2002-06-21
Contact Name: Pablo Romero
Organization: SBS Sydney
Message Subject: Product missing
Message text:
The Product name for your ad CI223375XY is missing. Can you please
supply it?

1. View Unsent Messages
2. Display Text of a Message
3. Email a Message
4. Quit this Program

Please choose an option [1, 2, 3 or 4]:
```

S3 – Email Message

The Employee is prompted to specify which `message_id` should be emailed. The Employee types in the `message_id`, the email is sent, and the database is updated. An informational message is displayed in the console window after successful emailing, as shown in Figure 8.7. The menu list is re-displayed after the message has been emailed.

Figure 8.7
Sketch 5 of user–
computer interface

```
1. View Unsent Messages
2. Display Text of a Message
3. Email a Message
4. Quit this Program

Please choose an option [1, 2, 3 or 4]: 3

Please enter the message id you want to email: 14

The message Id = 14 has been emailed.
Date Sent: 2002-06-22

1. View Unsent Messages
2. Display Text of a Message
3. Email a Message
4. Quit this Program

Please choose an option [1, 2, 3 or 4]:
```

Exception Flows 8.2.4

Exception flows describe flows of actions to be taken when an exception is raised. An exception can be an error condition but it does not have to be.

Like subflows, exception flows are numbered for ease of reference from other places of the use case document. The convention used in this book identifies an exception flow with a letter E followed by a consecutive number (i.e. E1, E2, etc.).

E1 – Incorrect username or password

If, in the basic flow, the actor provides an incorrect username or incorrect password (Figure 8.3), the system displays an error message. The system permits the actor to reenter the username and password or to quit the application. The actor is given three chances to provide the correct username and password. If three times unsuccessful, the system cancels the login and the use case terminates.

E2 – Incorrect option

If, in the basic flow, the actor provides an incorrect option number (Figure 8.4), the system ignores the entered value and re-displays the list of menu options. If three times unsuccessful, the system logs the actor out and restarts the use case (by displaying the login prompt – Figure 8.3).

E3 – Too many messages

If, in the S1 subflow, the number of unsent messages scheduled for the actor exceeds a parameter-predefined number of how many messages can be viewed at a time, the system displays an informational message stating that there are more messages in the database. The informational message is displayed after the predefined number of unsent messages is shown to the actor and before the menu list is re-displayed.

E4 – Email could not be sent

If, in the S3 subflow, the mail server returns an error that the email could not be sent, the system informs the actor that the email was not sent and the use case continues by displaying the menu list.

Conceptual Classes 8.3

The object model for BOM (Chapter 6) and for DOM (Chapter 7) defined classes for corresponding use case specifications. The classes were called business entities in BOM (Section 6.5.1) and domain classes in DOM (Section 7.4.1). Such classes are frequently referred to as conceptual classes (Larman, 2002).

Figure 8.8
Conceptual
classes in
Iteration 1

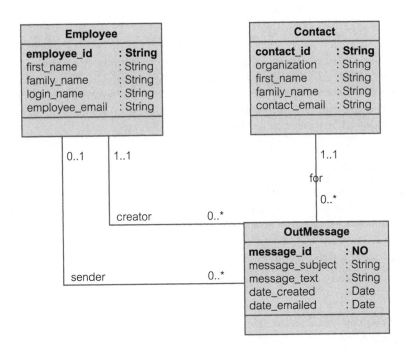

A **conceptual class** is a definition for a set of business objects, i.e. objects that have a business meaning to the organization. In an implemented system, instances (objects) of a conceptual class are stored in a database (such as the `Production Database` modeled as an actor in Figure 8.2). In this sense, conceptual classes represent the *database objects*.

An application program accesses the database objects as needed and creates copies of them in the program's memory. So, the notion of a conceptual class has both the database and the application program representation. Once implemented in the program, conceptual classes are but one category of **application classes**. All application classes for Iteration 1 are defined in Chapter 11. The initial object model discussed in this chapter defines conceptual classes only.

Figure 8.8 is a class diagram for conceptual classes needed in Iteration 1. The diagram establishes associations between classes. Associations are named and multiplicities are defined. Classes contain attribute names and types (string, number, date, etc.). Operations are not defined yet.

The class diagram contains three classes: `Employee`, `Contact`, and `OutMessage`. Associations are named `sender`, `creator`, and `for`. Naming associations makes referencing them easier, in particular in cases where multiple associations exist between the same two classes (as is the case for associations between `Employee` and `OutMessage`).

There is precisely one `Contact` for each `OutMessage`. `Contact` may be linked to zero or many `OutMessages`. The association named `creator` links `OutMessage` to `Employee` who created that `OutMessage` in the database. The association named `sender` identifies `Employee` who is scheduled to email the `OutMessage`. This association links to zero `Employees` if the sender for `OutMessage` is not scheduled yet.

Classes include all attributes except those representing associations. This is consistent with UML analysis modeling. In the UML design/implementation models, associations become attributes. An **association attribute** is typed with a class to which it links.

In the analysis model in Figure 8.8, most attributes are typed as `strings`. The type of `message_id` is `number` (signified by NO). The two date attributes are typed as `dates`.

Supplementary Specification

8.4

A **supplementary specification** is a document that defines requirements and constraints not captured in models and documents of use cases and conceptual classes. The document captures predominantly non-functional requirements and constraints, i.e. requirements and constraints that are not behavioral in nature, but rather restrictions and conditions on the implementation.

Table 8.2 lists the requirements and constraints addressed in a typical supplementary specification. The structure of the supplementary specification document can correspond to the list.

Table 8.2 Supplementary specification

Brief description	Expanded description
Functionality	This section of the document is the only one addressing functional requirements (behaviors). It typically presents functional requirements that cut across multiple use cases and are therefore not captured in use case documents. For example, the security features of the system may be discussed here
Usability	The requirements and constraints that define what the actors perceive as the usability of the system. Usability includes issues such as the ease of use of the system, its documentation and help facilities; the training required before the system can be effectively and efficiently used; the aesthetics and consistency of the graphical user interface, and similar considerations.
Reliability	Reliability determines the demanded availability of the system on the 24-hour timescale, acceptable mean time between failures, expected recoverability from failures of different severity, accuracy of system outputs, and similar issues
Performance	This section includes expectations regarding the response time of the system (on average and at peak times), transaction throughput, resource consumption, possible number of concurrent users, etc. Performance demands may vary between use cases, so this section may need to refer to specific use cases
Supportability	This section could be better called **maintainability and scalability**. It defines the features of the system that enhance its maintainability and scalability, i.e. the ease with which the system can be modified, extended, tested, performance-tuned, reconfigured, migrated to other platforms, internationalized, etc.
Other constraints	This section includes anything of significance to the project that is not already captured in the previous five sections. It lists policy decisions regarding the project's infrastructure, legal issues that may affect the project, considerations regarding integration with legacy systems existing in the organization, etc.

The first five sections of the supplementary specification document are commonly known as **FURPS** features – the acronym created from the first letters of section names. With the addition of 'other constraints', the issues addressed in the document are referred to as **FURPS**+ features of the system.

The supplementary specification document should be started in the early stages of the project to identify the key issues that may affect the project's budget and feasibility. However, the full definition of most supplementary features is not expected to be determined until later in the project. Like many other project artifacts, the supplementary specification grows with the project.

Accordingly, the supplementary specification for Iteration 1 of the case-study is quite basic. The main issues are as follows:

- Functionality
  - EM is a multi-user application.
  - User authorization and privileges to access various features of the application are controlled centrally from a database to which the application program connects.

- Usability
  - There is no training required for a computer-literate user to be able to use the Iteration 1 program. Simple explanation of the aim and basic features of the application will suffice to use the program.
  - Iteration 1 is a console-based program that guides the user by providing the uniform list of menu options. Only one option at a time may be requested. The options are not interdependent in the sense that all options are available all the time.
  - Being a console-based program, the application can be run from any desktop user-interface.

- Reliability
  - The application must be available 24 hours a day every day of the week. There must be no database-related downtime. Any scheduled email-server downtimes due to maintenance must be notified to EM users by email with at least 24-hours' warning.
  - Failure of the program must not compromise the correctness and integrity of the database. A user must be able to restart the program after failure and find the database information to be consistent and not affected by the failure.

- Performance
  - There is no upper limit on the number of concurrent users.
  - The response time of the system may not be affected if the number of concurrent users is 100 or less.
  - The response time for subflows S1 and S2 (Section 8.2.3) must be less than 5 seconds 90 percent of the time.
  - The response time for subflow S3 (Section 8.2.3) must be less than 10 seconds 90 percent of the time for email messages not exceeding 1 MB in size (including any attached documents). Note, however, that Iteration 1 does not allow email attachments.

- Supportability
  - The system architectural design must conform to the PCMEF framework to allow proper maintainability and scalability (Chapter 9).

- Test-driven development is used for code production. Acceptance testing is used for code validation. Test units obtained from test-driven development and from acceptance tests are used for regression testing when Iteration 2 code is changed. The aim of **regression testing** is to ensure that the code already tested and accepted has not been broken as a result of successive development and programming.
- Other constraints
  - The project must use an Oracle database, but it must be easily portable to other relational databases.
  - Iteration 1 must use Java and JDBC to access the Oracle database from the program.

Summary

1. The case study explored in the textbook is called EM (Email Management). EM is a function with the CM (Contact Management) domain, discussed in Chapter 7. EM is similar in functionality to commercial software packages known as Email Marketing.

2. The use cases of EM addressed in Iteration 1 are: `View Unsent Messages`, `Display Message Text`, and `Email Message`.

3. The sections of a use case document are: brief description, actors, preconditions, postconditions, basic flow, subflows, and exception flows.

4. Like a domain class referred to in Chapter 7, a *conceptual class* is a definition for a set of business objects. In an implemented application, conceptual classes constitute one group (package) of *application classes*.

5. *Supplementary specification* document defines *FURPS+ features* of the system. FURPS stands for functionality, usability, reliability, performance, and supportability. The plus (+) stands for constraints other than FURPS features.

Key Terms

application class	242	FURPS	244
association attribute	243	FURPS+	244
basic flow	237	performance	243
conceptual class	242	regression testing	245
Email Management	234	reliability	243
Email Marketing	235	subflow	239
EM	*See* Email Management	supplementary specification	243
exception flow	241	supportability	243
flow of events	237	usability	243
functionality	243	use case document	236

Review Questions

Discussion Questions

1. What is a use case model, a use case diagram, and a use case document?

2. How does the concept of alternative flow, used frequently in the literature, relate to the various flow notions presented in this chapter?

3. Which FURPS+ feature defines the system's maintainability and scalability?

4. Which FURPS+ feature defines legal implications for the system, such as potential breaches of personal privacy law?

Case Study Questions

1. What could be good alternative names for the three EM use cases in Figure 8.2?

2. Refer to Figure 8.7 and to the defintion of exception flows in Section 8.2.4. Is there a possibility for an exception occurring in the scenario in Figure 8.7 that is not accounted for in the defined exception flows?

3. The explanation of Figure 8.8 contains the following observation: 'The association named `sender` identifies `Employee` who is scheduled to email the `OutMessage`. This association links to zero `Employees` if the sender for `OutMessage` is not scheduled yet.' Is this observation semantically credible? If you can see some semantic imprecision, how would you rectify it?

4. Does the Iteration 1 model permit storing employees in the EM database who have only a group account in the database? Explain.

Problem-Solving Exercises

Case Study Exercises

1. The use case model for the case-study (Figure 8.2) makes it clear that the EM application uses a production database that is shared by many AEM applications (and EM is just one of these applications). Yet, the conceptual model for EM (Figure 8.8) has been created without consideration of any existing database structure (schema). This is acceptable practice because the conceptual model is an application's view on the database schema, which will eventually be used for mapping between the database tables and the application's domain classes.

   Granted, reflect on the situation in which the conceptual model has to be adapted and extended to include the following requirements (or perhaps to consider the existing database schema). Modify the conceptual class diagram in Figure 8.8 to consider the following issues:

   (a) There is a need to distinguish between `PersonContact` and `OrganizationContact` as two categories of `Contact`. Although `OutMessage` is always destined for a `Contact`, the contact may be a generic organization's email address. In some cases, this may be the only email address that EM has to any contact in that organization. It is also possible that a `PersonContact` can be an individual whose organization is not known.

   (b) There is a need to distinguish between an employee who is scheduled to send an outmessage and the actual sender of it.

(c) In some cases an outmessage is scheduled to a department, not to any particular employee. Any employee working for that department can send such an outmessage.

(d) In some cases an outmessage can only be sent by authorized employees according to seniority in the managerial hierarchy of employment.

Minicase – Time Logging

1. Refer to the Time Logging minicase in Chapter 7. Write a part of the use case document (Section 8.2) for Time Logging. Write only the basic flow section of the document. Include sketches or prototypes of the graphical user interfaces (i.e. user–computer interaction screens).

Chapter

9

Architectural Design

The system's architectural design begs an analogy from the building industry. A house cannot be built unless an architect designed it (perhaps a shed – yes, but not a house). Similarly, any reasonably large software system cannot be built without a prior architectural design. Software architecture is a foundation on which all other design and programming solutions must be based.

Architecture of the system should be addressed early in the process. Booch *et al.* (1999) consider architecture as one of only three main characteristics of any development process favoring the UML. The three characteristics of the process are:

1. iterative and incremental
2. use case driven
3. architecture-centric.

What is software architecture? The definitions are abundant and multifaceted. A succinct definition may be that **software architecture** is the organization of software elements into a system aiming to achieve some purpose. More detailed investigation reveals that software architecture addresses a large number of concerns, such as organization of specific software modules (classes, packages, components), interconnections between modules, assignment of behaviors to modules, scalability of modules to larger solutions, etc.

What is architectural design? Again, definitions vary but the intent is clear. **Architectural design** is the set of decisions aiming at efficient and effective software architecture together with the rationale for these decisions. The rationale emphasized in this book is the *understandability, maintainability, and scalability* of the system. Larman (2002) identifies four concerns of architectural design, namely that it:

1. relates to non-functional requirements (see the supplementary specification in Section 8.4)
2. involves large-scale, system-level fundamental decisions
3. tackles interdependencies and tradeoffs, and
4. provides for generation and evaluation of alternative solutions.

Architectural Layers and Dependency Management

Like all software production, architectural design is a continuing, iterative, and incremental effort. Early architectural decisions take a broad view on the software architecture. One of the first decisions to be taken relates to structuring the system into layers of modules and establishing principles of inter-module communication. This is the concern of this chapter. More detailed architectural solutions, such as intra-module communication, are discussed in relevant places later in the book.

A sound architectural design calls for:

- a hierarchical **layering** of software modules that reduces complexity and enhances understandability of module dependencies by disallowing direct object intercommunication between non-neighboring layers, and

- an enforcement of programming standards that make module *dependencies* visible in compile-time program structures and that forbid muddy programming solutions utilizing just runtime program structures.

These observations are particularly, and painfully, true for modern object-oriented software production. The object paradigm equips a software engineer with a multitude of very powerful programming abstractions, which – when used unwisely – result in programs impossible to understand and maintain, even by the programmers who wrote them.

Architectural Modules

9.1.1

Architectural design is an exercise in managing module dependencies. Module A depends on module B if changes to module B may necessitate changes to module A. It is important that dependencies do not cross **dependency firewalls** (Martin, 2003). In particular, dependencies should not propagate across non-neighboring layers and must not create cycles.

Architectural design takes a **proactive approach** to managing dependencies in software. It does so by deciding early in the process on hierarchical layers of software modules and on dependency firewalls between the modules. This is a *forward engineering* approach – from design to implementation. The aim is to deliver a software design that minimizes dependencies by imposing an architectural solution on programmers.

Eventually, the proactive approach to managing dependencies must be supported by the **reactive approach** which aims to measure dependencies in implemented software. This is a *reverse engineering* approach – from implementation to design. The implementation may or may not conform to the desired architectural design. If it does not, the aim is to compare the metric values in the software with the values that the desired architecture would have delivered. The troublesome dependencies must be pinpointed and addressed.

Design classes

Previous chapters in Part 2 concentrated on modeling 'business objects' classified as business entities (Chapter 6), domain classes (Chapter 7), and conceptual classes (Chapter 8). However 'business objects' are but one set of classes in an object-oriented program.

A typical program needs classes responsible for presenting information on the user's computer screen, classes to access the database, classes to perform algorithmic calculations, etc. There are different names used to signify the entire set of classes that need to be designed and implemented in a computer program. They are called interchangeably design classes, software classes, application classes, program classes, system classes, or implementation classes. The term used here is **design classes** or simply *classes*, but other terms may be more suitable elsewhere in the book (design classes is also the term favored by the UP).

Packages

Design classes are grouped into packages according to an architectural framework adopted for the development project. A **package** (UML, 2002) is a grouping of modeling elements under an assigned name. A package may contain other packages. Packages can be grouped and structured into hierarchical **layers** supportive of the chosen software architecture.

In the UML, package is a logical design concept. Eventually, packages must be implemented and mapped to programming language concepts. Modern languages, most notably Java and C#, provide for a direct mapping that uses the notion of the package on the implementation end. Support for the implementation package is in the form of a namespace for classes and for importing other packages.

A package owns its *members* (elements) – removing the package from the model removes also its members. It follows that a member (usually a class) can belong to one package only.

A package may have package *imports* to other packages. This means that package A or element of package A can refer to package B or to its elements. Consequently, a class is owned by only one package but it can be imported to other packages. Imports introduce dependencies between packages and their elements.

Figure 9.1 presents an example of the UML package notation. A package can be presented with no members (elements) revealed (Package A). A package can depend on another package (Package A depends on Package B).

The **dependency relationship** means that some members of Package A refer in some way to some members of Package B (this can mean that Package A imports some elements of Package B). The implications are twofold:

- Changes to Package B may affect Package A, normally leading to the need to recompile and retest Package A.
- Package A can only be used (reused) together with Package B.

Package elements can be revealed by including their graphical representations within the borders of the owner package or by using the circle-plus notation. In Figure 9.1, Package B owns Class X, Package C owns Package D, Package E owns Package F, and Package F owns Class Y and Class Z.

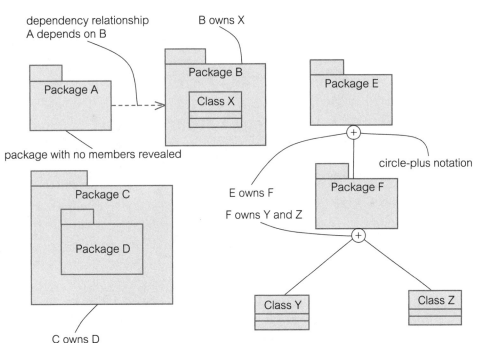

Figure 9.1
Package notation

Package Dependencies 9.1.2

Objects must intercommunicate for a system to perform its tasks. Objects depend on each other for services. Dependency management does not mean that dependencies as such are a problem. It means that dependencies should be minimized and unnecessary dependencies should be eliminated from architectural design.

Particularly troublesome are **circular dependencies** between objects. Fortunately, most of the time circular packages can be avoided or made relatively harmless through careful *refactoring* (redesign) or through programming techniques (Martin, 2003). Figure 9.2 shows two examples of circular dependencies between packages.

In Figure 9.2, Package A depends on Package B and vice versa. This means that a dependency-related change in Package B will demand a change in Package A, which may in turn demand a change in Package B, etc. The final outcome is that the two packages are inseparable with regard to the program's understanding, maintainability, and scalability.

Similarly, a change in Package E may demand a change in Package D, and then in Package C. The change in Package C may in turn demand a change in Package E, etc. The path is longer, but the problem is the same.

Adding a new package, as shown in Figure 9.3, can break circular dependencies between packages (Figure 9.2). In Figure 9.3, elements in Package A, on which Package B depended, were factored out into their own Package A2. Package B does not depend any more on Package A – it depends on Package A2. Understandably enough, Package A depends now on Package A2. Similarly in the second example, elements in Package C, on which Package E depended, were factored out into their own Package C2.

Figure 9.2
Circular
dependencies
between
packages

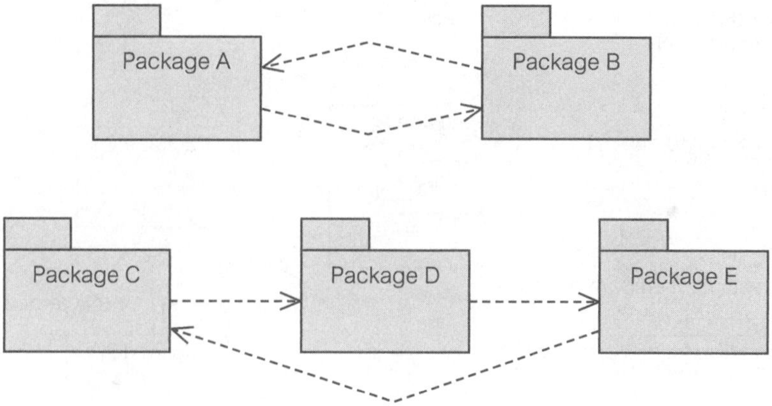

Figure 9.3
Eliminating circular
dependencies
between
packages

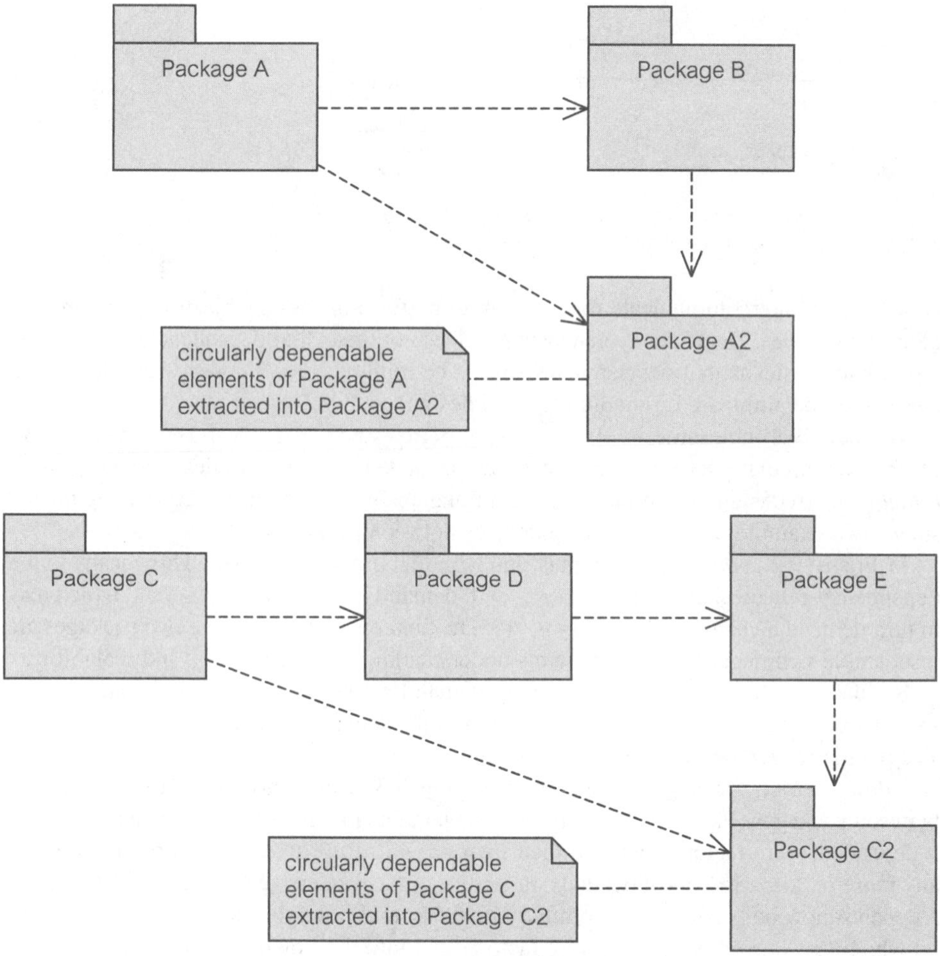

The horizontal structures of packages as in Figure 9.3 are called **partitions**. When circular dependencies between partition packages are broken, by adding new packages as explained in Section 9.1.2, the dependency structure within a partition becomes a hierarchy (rather than a linear horizontal structure).

Layer Dependencies   9.1.3

As stated before, packages can be grouped and structured into hierarchical layers supportive of the chosen software architecture. Since a package may contain other packages, a layer is a package itself. In the UML a layer package can be stereotyped as «layer».

From the architectural design perspective, layers are vertical structures (Figure 9.4). Vertical layers consist of *partitions* of packages (Section 9.1.2). Superimposing vertical structures of layers on horizontal structures of partitions creates a hierarchy of package dependencies. Three critical objectives of good architectural design of layers are that:

- the layer hierarchy does not disintegrate to a network structure (where a package can potentially depend on any other package in the system)

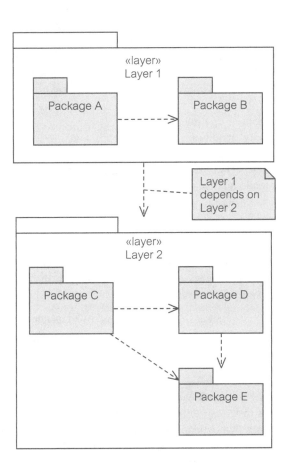

Figure 9.4
Layers as packages

- the layer hierarchy minimizes dependencies between packages
- the layer hierarchy establishes a *stable* framework for the lifecycle of system development.

The first objective is intuitively obvious. The complexity of networks grows exponentially with addition of new elements to the structure. In practice, all complex structures that work, including living organisms and human-made systems, are *hierarchies*.

The second objective states that the layer hierarchy should *minimize dependencies* between packages. The widely accepted method of achieving this is by making higher layers depend on lower layers but not vice versa. Unfortunately, the top-down-only dependency structure is not quite realistic. In reality, the bottom-up dependencies will exist, but they can be made relatively harmless by skillful design and programming. A desired outcome is that higher layers depend on lower layers whereas lower layers can still communicate with higher layers without exerting undue (unmanageable) dependencies.

The third objective is that the layer hierarchy is a **stable framework**. **Stability** means that something is resistant to change and steadfast of purpose. A stable architectural framework, once designed, is not receptive of changes. A stable framework determines the fixed set of rules for 'the game' of software development. Within these rules, the moves of the 'game' are flexible.

Note that the stability of vertical layers increases in the top-down direction. Higher layers depend on lower layers. Lower layers are required to be stable because any changes to them may have a ripple effect on higher layers (Martin, 2003).

`Layer 2` in Figure 9.4 is **stable** and `Layer 1` is **unstable**. `Layer 1` depends on `Layer 2`. `Layer 2` is independent and can therefore be replaced by a new one without a ripple-effect on the rest of the system. This is the principle and the reason behind allowing a high dependency (**high coupling**) in the top-down direction and ensuring a low dependency (low coupling) in the bottom-up direction.

Note that the stability condition of layers means that the technique of eliminating circular dependencies between layers by adding new layers is not acceptable. Fortunately, there exist programming techniques to ensure that circular dependencies between layers can be eliminated or made relatively harmless.

9.1.4 Class Dependencies

The programming techniques that allow eliminating or incapacitating circular dependencies between layers (and packages at large) have to do with the architectural design of classes rather than packages. The point is that:

- dependencies between layers translate to (are caused by) dependencies between packages
- dependencies between packages translate to dependencies between classes
- dependencies between classes translate to dependencies between class members, predominantly between methods.

In Figure 9.5, `Layer 1` depends on `Layer 2` because there is some class in `Layer 1` that depends on a class in `Layer 2`. `Package A` depends on `Package B` because there is some class in `Package A` that depends on a class in `Package B`. The consequence is that if offending class dependencies (i.e. class dependencies that introduce cycles) can be

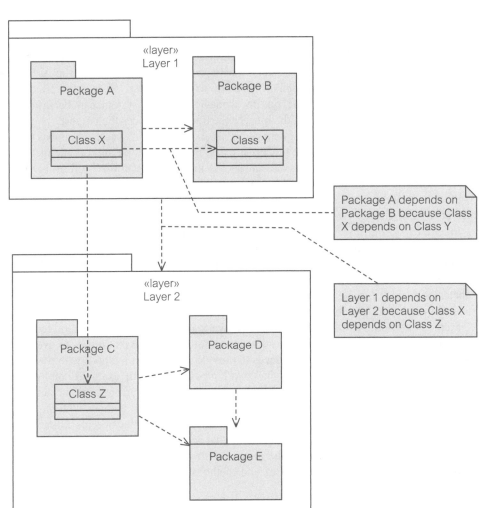

Figure 9.5
Class
dependencies
and the resulting
layer and package
dependencies

eliminated or made harmless then the overall software architecture of layers and packages can be that much more stable.

The main programming technique to break cycles between classes, and therefore contribute to the elimination of cycles between packages and between layers, involves the use of the *interface* concept. A supporting technique is targeted use of *event processing*, possibly on top of the use of interfaces. The two techniques are explained in Sections 9.1.7 and 9.1.8, after the dependencies between methods are described.

Inheritance Dependencies   9.1.5

One of the most troublesome problems in dependency management is the class and method dependencies caused by implementation inheritance. **Implementation inheritance** is a means of structural and behavioral sharing between a base class (or superclass) and its derived classes (subclasses), such that runtime service invocations can be given a subclass object in place of a superclass object. A subclass object *is a kind of* superclass object, which inherits all the superclass's features but it can change (override) some of these features and it can add new functionality specific to the subclass. As a result, from the viewpoint of the client object, the runtime behaviour of the system can be different depending on a particular object in the inheritance tree that services the request.

This notion of getting a different behaviour, depending on an object that happens to be servicing the request, is called **polymorphism**. The invocation of an appropriate method, conditional on the instantiated class at runtime, is known as **dynamic binding** (or **late binding**). It is a late binding since the method invocation (binding from the base class's method declaration to the subclass's method declaration) is determined at runtime rather than at compile-time.

Inheritance is not always accompanied by polymorphism. A set of classes could be arranged into a hierarchy from the general to the specific and yet they may not override any methods provided by their superclasses. Therefore, they would not produce polymorphic behavior. Polymorphic behavior is provided by **method overriding**. This is when subclasses provide a more context-specific implementation of a method declared by the superclass and therefore change its original behavior.

Method overriding is different from method overloading. Overriding a method requires the subclass to provide the exact same signature as for the method that it tries to override. **Method overloading** is when a class needs to provide a number of methods with the same name but different set of signatures. Java API provides a lot of examples of method overloading. Take, for example, the method `println()` from `System.out` object. The `println()` method is an overloaded method. It is in fact a set of methods with the same name and different parameters. There is a version of `println()` that accepts an integer, a version that accepts a `String` object, a version that accepts a character, etc.

It is clear that implementation inheritance, while useful for **code reuse**, introduces worrying dependencies between classes and methods. Inheritance dependencies can be classified into two groups:

- compile-time dependencies between classes in an inheritance tree
- runtime dependencies involving client objects accessing services of classes in an inheritance tree.

Figure 9.6 is a simple example demonstrating *compile-time dependencies* between classes in an inheritance tree and opening up the possibility for runtime dependencies. When interpreting this example only in the context of information explicitly provided in the figure, A inherits `Object`, *but* it does not provide its own overridden version of the `wait()` service. Therefore, it could be argued that there is no runtime inheritance dependency between A and `Object`. There is, however, a compile time dependency, as any changes to the `wait()` method in `Object` will be statically inherited by A.

In general, all generalization relationships in the diagram introduce compile-time dependencies in the direction of the arrows (C depends on B, B depends on A, A depends on `Object`). The dependencies are *transitive*, which means that if C depends on B and B depends on A then C depends on A, etc.

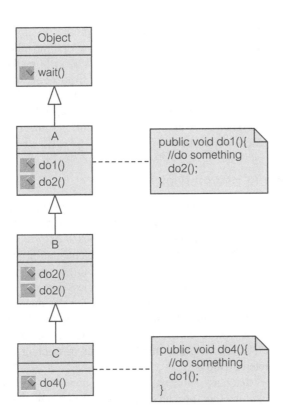

Figure 9.6
Compile-time
inheritance
dependencies

However, there are further runtime complications lurking in Figure 9.6. B inherits A and B overrides A's do2(). This creates potential polymorphic behavior on do2() and introduces a likely runtime dependency in the opposite direction, from A to B. A would depend on B if A's do1() method needs to call the do2() method of B, rather than its own. These kinds of inheritance-based circular dependencies are very difficult to control and they create maintenance hassle.

Figure 9.7 exemplifies runtime dependencies involving a client object accessing services of classes in an inheritance tree. An interesting (and peculiar) aspect of the presented

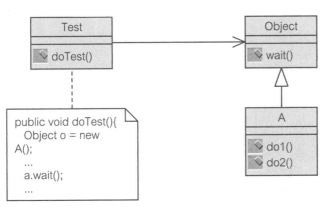

Figure 9.7
Runtime
inheritance
dependencies

model is that although `Test` has instantiated `A` (to represent its `Object` association), it does not use `A`'s services. As a result, `Test` does not have runtime inheritance dependency on `A`. Moreover, the dependency of `Test` on `Object`'s `wait()` method is really a static dependency manifested by the existence of association from `Test` to `Object`.

Note that runtime dependencies would resurface the moment `A` overrides the `wait()` method. If `A` overrode the `wait()` method, then runtime dependencies would exist from `Test` to `Object` and `A`. The following sections illustrate the most frequent contexts in which runtime inheritance dependencies occur.

Inheritance without polymorphism

Implementation inheritance, despite its reuse power, has been given troublemaker status by many software development 'shops'. This status is deserved only to the point to which implementation inheritance has been overused and abused by programmers (Maciaszek *et al.*, 1996a; Maciaszek, 2001). If used properly, implementation inheritance remains a powerful and very useful technique.

The simplest way of using inheritance is when a subclass does not override the inherited methods (does not provide its own implementations for the methods). This results in inheritance without polymorphism. Although **inheritance without polymorphism** is not terribly useful, it is the easiest to understand and manage. In reality, a subclass may be overriding some but not all inherited methods, thus restricting inheritance without polymorphism to selected methods.

Figure 9.8 illustrates that class `B` inherits `do2()` and does not override it. Therefore, the `B`'s `do3()` uses the `do2()` method provided entirely by the parent class `A`.

Extension and restriction inheritance

Extension inheritance is the proper use of implementation inheritance. It states that the subclass inherits the properties of its superclass and provides extra features to enhance the class definition. The subclass is *a kind of* its superclass. Overridden methods, if they are overridden by the subclass, should be made to enforce the definition of the methods and make them work in the context of the subclass.

Figure 9.8

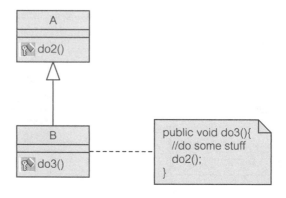

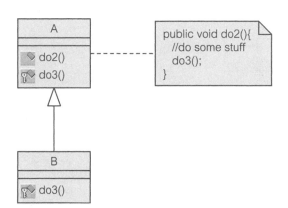

Figure 9.9
Extension
inheritance

Figure 9.9 is an example of extension inheritance, where subclass B inherits do2() and do3() from A, and it then overrides do3(), presumably by extending the functionality obtained from the inherited method. Method do3() can be invoked on A or on B object. It will perform differently depending on which object it is called.

Implementation inheritance other than extension inheritance is problematic. Problematic inheritances range from various forms of restriction inheritance to bluntly unacceptable convenience inheritance (Maciaszek, 2001). **Restriction inheritance** happens when a class inherits a method and then overrides it by just suppressing some of the inherited functionality. As a result, the subclass is no longer *a kind of* superclass. In some cases, restriction results in complete suppression of the inherited method. This happens when the method is implemented as empty (i.e. doing nothing).

Down-calls

Overriding, and therefore polymorphism, gives way to **down-calls** in method invocations. This is illustrated in Figure 9.10. Even though class X is associated with class A, when X executes do2(), it actually executes B's implementation of do2(). This happens because do2() is executed on the myA object, which is an instance of B.

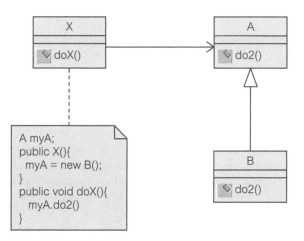

Figure 9.10
Down-calls

Figure 9.11
Up-calls

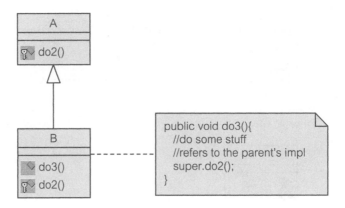

The down-call in Figure 9.10 introduces a runtime inheritance dependency from X to B, which is not visible in static compile-time program structure. X has an association to A, but not to B. Such runtime dependencies are very difficult to manage (precisely because they are not visible in static program definition).

Up-calls

Overriding, and therefore polymorphism, succumbs also to **up-calls** (or **callbacks**) in method invocations. This is illustrated in Figure 9.11. This time, the subclass B uses the parent's implementation of do2() explicitly when it in fact has its own overridden version of do2(). Although such a call to super may be explained, the combination of down-calls and up-calls introduces a nasty circular dependency issue on the classes involved.

Inheritance dependencies can be seen as a form of method dependencies. In general, apart from ordinary method dependencies, other kinds of method dependency include those that are due to delegation and those that are due to inheritance.

9.1.6 Method Dependencies

Dependencies between classes translate to dependencies between class members (features, in the UML parlance). Usually, dependencies between data members can be managed relatively easily (although implementation inheritance of data members may blur the picture). Dependencies between methods create a real challenge, in particular that in practice many method dependencies cannot be tracked down by just analyzing the static compile-time structure of the program.

Figure 9.12 illustrates method dependencies and how they propagate to class dependencies (and, therefore, also to package and layer dependencies). There are two packages called control and entity (the names are not capitalized to follow the usual practice). Class names start with a capital letter signifying the immediate package to which the class belongs. Hence, CActioner denotes that the class is owned by the control package.

CActioner uses method do1() to send a message do(3) to EEmployee. Therefore, do1() depends on do3(). The dependency propagates up on owning classes and

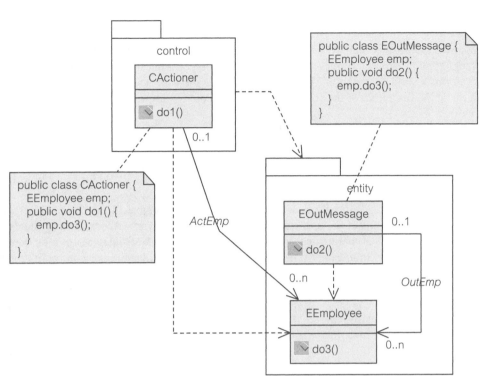

Figure 9.12
Method dependencies and the resulting class and package dependencies

packages. CActioner depends on EEmployee, and control depends on entity. Similarly, do2() in EOutMessage invokes method do3() on EEmployee. Hence, EOutMessage depends on EEmployee.

Note that method dependencies are made explicit in the model on the level of classes by establishing *unidirectional associations* between dependent classes. Both CActioner and EOutMessage have data members emp of type EEmployee, which implemented unidirectional associations to EEmployee, called ActEmp and OutEmp, respectively.

Making method dependencies statically visible in the code by means of explicit associations between classes is a strongly recommended practice (Lee and Tepfenhart, 2002). This is important because method dependencies are frequently not discoverable from the analysis of the source code. In the presence of inheritance and polymorphism and because of the demands of the layered architecture, a message originator (**client object**) frequently does not know the specific receiver of the message (**supplier object**) until runtime.

If the analysis of the program behavior discovers a method dependency between classes with no explicit association then the program may be considered to be in violation of the architectural design. However, in some cases, creating an association to legitimize the method dependency may itself be in violation of the architectural design. The introduction of interfaces (Section 9.1.7) and event processing (Section 9.1.8) into the design can solve this dilemma. More complex runtime method dependencies (called *acquaintance dependencies*) may require even more radical design decisions as discussed in Section 9.1.9.

Method dependencies in the presence of delegation

Message passing is realized as a **synchronous communication** between the client and supplier of a service. A message from a *client object* requests that a *supplier object* performs a service (method). The interpretation of a message and the means of executing it are at the discretion of the supplier object. This could be the **delegation** of the work to another object.

As in a military chain of command, an object can delegate the authority to perform the work to another object. What is perceived by the client object to be the supplier object is in reality a **delegator object**. Although the work is delegated, the supplier object – alias the delegator object – is not relieved from a contractual responsibility (to the client object) for the work.

The delegation is normally necessary to allow a client object in one layer to get a service from an object in a distant (non-neighboring) layer. Otherwise, the stable framework of vertical hierarchical layers (Section 9.1.3) would disintegrate to a random network of intercommunicating objects with no hope of understanding or controlling the system complexity and evolution.

Figure 9.13 demonstrates method dependencies in the presence of delegation when the layer framework consists of packages named `control`, `entity`, `mediator`, and `foundation`. For clarity, the unidirectional associations to signify message passing are not drawn (but they are programmed in the Java code presented in the UML notes).

In Figure 9.13, `CActioner` and `EOutMessage` request a `do3()` service from `EEmployee`. However, `EEmployee` delegates the execution of the service to `MBroker` and `MBroker` delegates it further down to `FUpdater`. `FUpdater` performs the service. This is communicated back to the client objects following the same path but upwards. Note that the delegation is frequently necessary to conform to the vertical layer architecture that disallows direct communication between non-neighboring layers.

The consequence of delegation is that a *client* might not know its real *supplier* (and it might not even care to know as long as the 'goods' are supplied). Unlike in Figure 9.13, knowledge of the real supplier may not be available from a static analysis of the program code and may be hidden behind the dynamicity of inheritance (in particular interface inheritance) and polymorphism.

As the discovery of the program's runtime behavior is 'not much fun' for a system maintainer or a project manager, the practice of *explicit associations* between classes engaged in message passing is so much more important. Without explicit associations, the **impact analysis** due to a change in the supplier code may be unachievable.

Method dependencies in the presence of implementation inheritance

As observed in Section 9.1.5, **implementation inheritance** dependencies are to a large degree a special kind of message (method) dependency. Method dependencies due to implementation inheritance are difficult to manage. Many of such dependencies happen dynamically at runtime and are not visible in the compile-time program structure.

However, there are pros and cons. The dynamic behaviour due to method overriding allows complex behavior to be achieved with less work. A subclass needs only to override

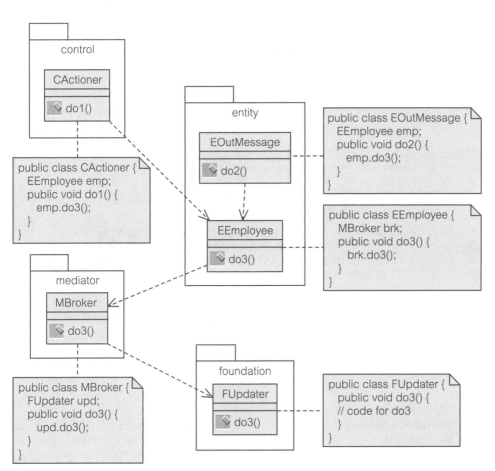

Figure 9.13
Method
dependencies
in the presence
of delegation

certain methods in order to achieve different behavior. Additional methods could be added to extend the functionalities already provided by a superclass.

Not only are many method dependencies due to implementation inheritance not discoverable from the analysis of the source code, but they are also likely to create cycles. The main reason for cycles is a combined use of down-calls and up-calls between client and supplier objects. Figure 9.14 illustrates possible complications when message passing is performed on objects participating in implementation inheritance.

Figure 9.14 shows that `Client` has a reference (`class1`) to `SubClass` but keeps that reference as a `SuperClass` type instead (Sequence 1). In practice, the assignment of a `SubClass` instance to a `SuperClass` reference is likely to be done at runtime, rather than as a simple assignment in Figure 9.14. When `do1()` is called, it executes `doA()` on the `SuperClass` (Sequence 2). It appears that `doA()` calls `manualA()`. However, `SuperClass`'s `manualA()` has been overridden and therefore the overridden method is called instead (Sequence 3). Execution of Sequences 2 and 3 is an example of a **down-call** method call.

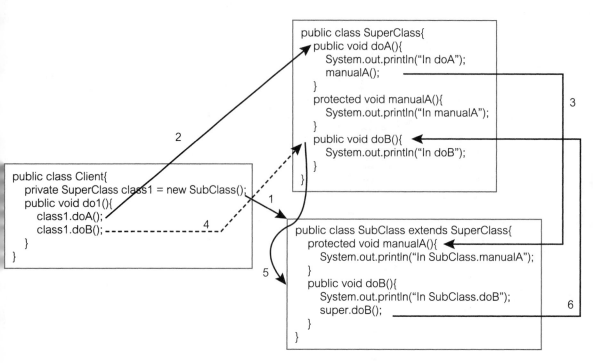

Figure 9.14 Down-call and up-call

It then follows that `do1()` further executes `doB()` from `SuperClass`. Again, `doB()` has been overridden by `SubClass` and therefore `SubClass`'s `doB()` is executed in place of the `SuperClass`'s method (Sequence 5). Interestingly, `SubClass`'s `doB()` provides an extension of the parent's `doB()`. It executes its parent's `doB()` for completeness of the operation (Sequence 6). Sequence 6 is an example of an **up-call** method call.

Polymorphic behavior involving a combination of down-calls and up-calls gives maintenance problems. Up-calls and down-calls link classes and their methods into an irregular network of interconnecting objects, where even the distinction between client and supplier objects becomes blurred. An error in one of the methods in the execution sequence is difficult to trace as the real instance of the class can only be determined at runtime.

9.1.7 Interfaces

In the UML 2.0, **interface** is a declaration of a set of *features* (Section 9.1.1) that is not directly instantiable, i.e. no objects of it can be directly created. An interface is realized (implemented) by an object of a class, which promises to deliver the structure and behavior of the interface to the rest of the program. The object that implements the interface provides 'a public *façade* that conforms to the interface specification' (UML, 2002, p.123).

The UML 2.0 interface concept expands the notion of interface used in popular programming languages (and in earlier versions of the UML). An interface can declare attributes, not just operations. By contrast, in Java an interface can contain data members but they must be constants (defined as `static` and `final`).

As a consequence of allowing attributes in interfaces, it is possible to create associations between interfaces and between an interface and a class. Attributes typed as another interface or class represent associations. In the UML 2.0 it is possible to navigate from an interface to a class via an association. This is not possible in Java.

Interface is sometimes said to be a 'pure' abstract class. Not quite (although that is the best one can do in languages that do not support interfaces, such as C++). An **abstract class** is a class that contains at least one method which is not (or cannot be) implemented by that class, and therefore it cannot be instantiated. In a **pure abstract class** no method is implemented.

Pure or not, a class is a class is a class. In languages that support only **single implementation inheritance**, such as Java, a class can only extend one base class (abstract or concrete), but it can implement multiple interfaces. This is a huge practical difference.

The related difference is that interfaces allow passing objects typed as interfaces in method calls. The exact class of that interface does not need to be determined until runtime. For the client object it does not matter what the supplier class is. It matters only that it implements the method called (Lee and Tepfenhart, 2002).

When used as the main entry points to concrete classes in packages, interfaces in particular, but also abstract classes, provide mechanisms to hide the internal complexity of the package and to permit package extensions without affecting client objects in other packages. The notion of a **dominant class** can be used to realize these mechanisms within the package. A dominant class implements the main interfaces and abstract classes of a package. In the words of Rumbaugh *et al.* (1999, p.219), 'A dominant class subsumes the interface of the component'.

Figure 9.15 shows the UML notations for an interface, an abstract class (italic font), and a class. The interface notation differs in the way the stereotype «`Interface`» is displayed. It can be displayed, from left to right, as an explicit label, an icon, or a 'decoration'.

The UML 2.0 introduced another iconic variation where a circle (called a ball) can be supplemented by a half-circle (called a socket). However, both the ball and the socket notation in particular, do not seem to scale up gracefully to larger models. Therefore, these icons will be avoided in this book in favor of the decoration notation (not really directly advised in the UML 2.0 but widely used in practice).

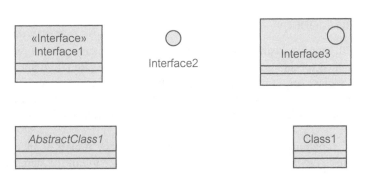

Figure 9.15
UML notations for interface, abstract class, and class

Figure 9.16
Implementation
dependency

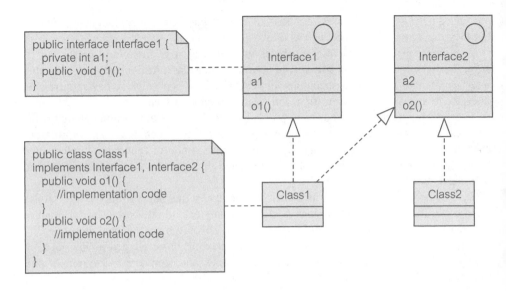

Implementation dependency

More than one class may implement an interface and a class may implement more than one interface. The set of interfaces implemented by a class is called its **provided interface**. This is the class's promise to its clients that its instances will provide the interface features. Provided interfaces are specified in the UML 2.0 by a dependency relationship between the class and the interface implemented by that class. This is called an **implementation dependency**.

Figure 9.16 shows the UML notation for implementation dependency. A class at the tail of the arrow implements the interface at the head of the arrow (note that the arrows are shown here on dotted lines, but the UML 2.0 uses solid lines). Class1 implements both interfaces. Class2 implements only Interface2.

Classes provide implementation (the code) for all operations of their interfaces. In the case of attributes, the class promises that any of its instances will maintain information about the type and multiplicity of the attribute and that it will deliver that attribute to any client object, but the class itself does not have to have that attribute in its implementation (UML, 2002).

Usage dependency

Once declared, interfaces can be used by classes (or other interfaces) that require them. It is said that a class (or an interface) uses **required interfaces**. Required interfaces specify services that a class (or an interface) needs so that it can perform its own services to its clients. Required interfaces are specified in the UML 2.0 by a dependency relationship between the class (or the interface) and the interface that is required. This is called a **usage dependency**.

Figure 9.17 shows the UML notation for usage dependency. A class or interface at the tail of the arrow uses the interface at the head of the arrow (the use of the stereotype «uses»

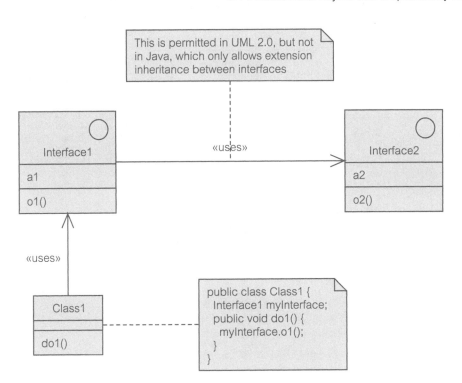

Figure 9.17
Usage
dependency

is not compulsory in the UML 2.0, but it is customary). `Class1` uses `Interface1`, which in turn uses `Interface2`.

`Class1` contains method `do1()`, which calls the services of operation `o1()`. In the static code it is not clear which implementation of the required interface will do the service. This can be an instance of any class which implements `Interface1`. The exact instance will be resolved at runtime when an executing instance of `Class1` sets the value of data member `myInterface` to refer to a concrete object of a concrete class.

Breaking circular dependencies with interfaces

Interfaces can be used with great success to reduce dependencies in the code. Programming with interfaces allows client objects to be unaware of the specific classes of objects they use and of the classes that actually implement these interfaces. One of the most important principles of reusable, maintainable, and scalable object-oriented design is: 'Program to an interface, not an implementation' (Gamma *et al.*, 1995, p.18).

Previous discussion made it clear that circular dependencies in the system must be eliminated at any cost. It turns out that interfaces introduce the most powerful weapon in dealing with circular dependencies (Martin, 2003). To understand why this is the case, consider an example of circular dependency between the `presentation` and `control` packages in Figure 9.18.

The cycle in Figure 9.18 is caused by `CInit` using the services of `PPrimaryWindow` and by `PDialogBox` using the services of `CActioner`. Two explicit unidirectional

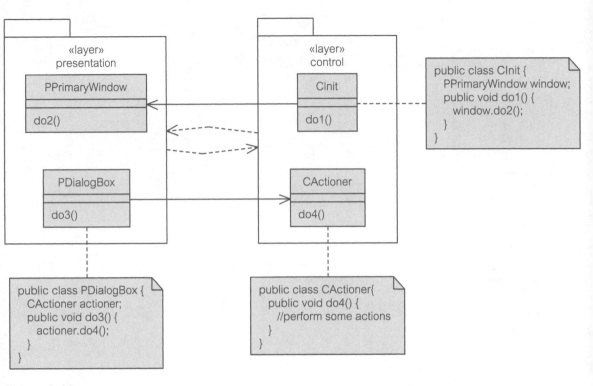

Figure 9.18 Circular dependency

associations ascertain the message passing between these classes. The cycle is particularly troublesome because it is between «layer» packages and this harms the principle of the top-down dependencies between layers discussed in Section 9.1.3.

A solution to the dilemma comes from the skillful introduction of an interface into the design (Martin, 2003), as shown in Figure 9.19. In the example, the cycle is broken by adding interface ICPresenter in the control package. The interface defines method do2() needed by CInit, which is in the same package. But the interface is actually implemented by PPrimaryWindow in the presentation package. CInit uses the interface and PPrimaryWindow implements it.

Note that to break the cycle, the interface and the class that implements it are in different packages. This may be a surprise to a novice programmer, but it should not be a revelation to a designer responsible for the architectural design of the system. It is frequently more desirable to put interfaces in the package that uses them, not in the package that implements them (Martin, 2003). Fowler calls this the **Separated Interface pattern** (Fowler, 2003). Alternatively, interfaces may be extracted into a separate package.

9.1.8 Event Processing

Method dependencies (Section 9.1.6) apply to a *synchronous communication* between the client and the supplier of a service. A message from a client object requests that a supplier

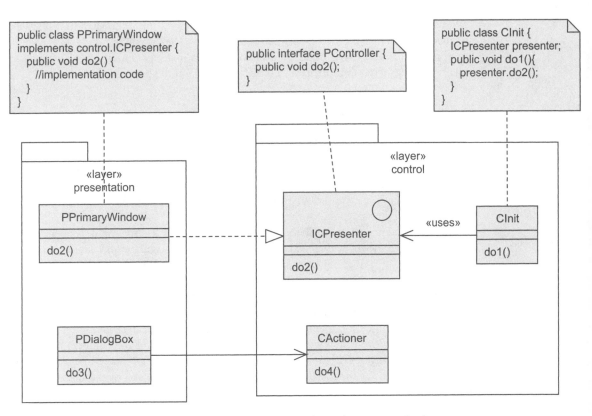

Figure 9.19 Using an interface to eliminate circular dependency between methods

object performs the service (method). The interpretation of a message and the means of executing it are at the discretion of the supplier object (this could be the *delegation* of the work to another object).

In architectural design, synchronous messages need to be considered separately from **asynchronous communication** where methods are 'fired' to service asynchronous **events**. In event processing there is a separation between an event originator (**publisher object**) and various event **listeners/observers** (known as **subscriber objects**) that want to be informed of an event occurrence and take their own, presumably different, actions.

In large systems, a separate **registrator object** may perform the subscription, i.e. the 'handshaking' between the publisher and subscribers. To register a subscriber with the publisher object, the registrator object acting on the subscriber's behalf calls the publisher's `addActionListener()` method with the subscriber object as an argument. If no registrator object is used, the subscriber object will directly call the `addActionListener()` method.

A method that intercepts an event (such as a mouse click on a `JButton` object) sends a 'fire event' message to the *publisher object*. Typically the 'fire event' message and the method that services it are in the same publisher object. However, the method housing the 'fire event' message depends only loosely on the method that services it. It may even be possible that no subscriber object listens to the event and there is no dependency at all.

Usually, the publisher object creates an **event object** – the publisher translates the intended meaning of the event into an event object (called something like BCommand-ButtonEvent). The event object is passed (in a *callback* operation) to all subscriber objects that registered their interest in the mouse click on the button.

Event processing and layer dependencies

In *synchronous message passing*, if client object A sends a message to supplier object B, then A depends on B because A expects some results out of the execution of B. In *asynchronous event processing*, the sender of the message is the publisher object but the message passing is handled as a *callback*. In a callback, the publisher has no knowledge or interest in how the subscriber processes the event. The dependency exists but it is negligible from the viewpoint of the architectural design.

The handshaking of subscribers and publishers causes a stronger dependency. If a registrator object mediates the handshaking, then it depends on both the publisher and the subscriber. If a subscriber object registers itself, then it depends on the publisher. To loosen dependencies due to handshaking, subscribers can be passed to the registration methods in arguments typed as interfaces (see below). The dependencies are then lowered, but further program analysis will be required to determine the class of a subscriber. The analysis will involve the determination of classes that implement a subscriber interface.

For readability, the following examples adhere to two naming conventions. Firstly, the methods performing registration of subscribers to a publisher are named beginning with the phrase add and ending with the phrase Listener. The name of the event object is placed between these two phrases, e.g. addXXXListener, where XXX is the name of the event object.

The second convention applies to methods that fire events in a publisher class. A publisher class will normally house 'normal' methods as well as methods that fire events. To distinguish between these two kinds of method, each event method begins with the phrase fire, such as fireCommandButtonEvent().

A fire method goes through the list of subscribers and, for each subsciber, calls its associated process method. As a matter of convenience (rather than a rule), a name of a process method may begin with the phrase process, such as processCommand-ButtonEvent(). A fire method does not normally perform excessive calculation or program logic.

Figure 9.20 illustrates event processing involving the presentation and control «layer» packages. CActioner is the only subscriber to PConsole's events (PDisplayEvent). PDisplayEventRegistrator does the handshaking of PConsole and CActioner. The doI() method intercepts and interprets the events, and it fires fireDisplayEvent(). PConsole creates PDisplayEvent. Note that placing PDisplayEventRegistrator in the presentation package creates an acceptable downward dependency between the presentation and control «layer» packages (Section 9.1.3).

Event processing and interfaces

In Figure 9.20, the registrator class was placed strategically in the presentation «layer» package, and not in the control «layer» package, to avoid undesirable

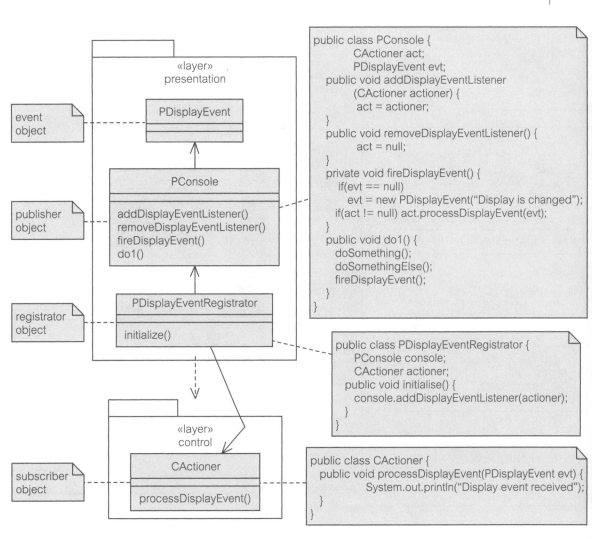

Figure 9.20 Event processing and layer dependencies

upward dependency between layers (Section 9.1.3). But strategic placement of classes has its limits and in a large design the circular dependencies due to message passing and event processing are increasingly likely. For example, classes in the `presentation` package may also want to subscribe to publishers in other packages, possibly even non-neighboring packages.

The resolution to cycles in event processing comes again from the skillful use of interfaces (Section 9.1.7). Figure 9.21 illustrates how even a downward dependency in Figure 9.20 can be reduced to oblivion. The dependency in Figure 9.20 was caused by a method call in `PConsole`'s `fireDisplayEvent()` to `processDisplayEvent()` in `CActioner`. In Figure 9.21, a new interface `IPDisplayEventSubscriber` separates `PConsole` from `CActioner`. `PConsole` uses `IPDisplayEventSubscriber`, which `CActioner` implements.

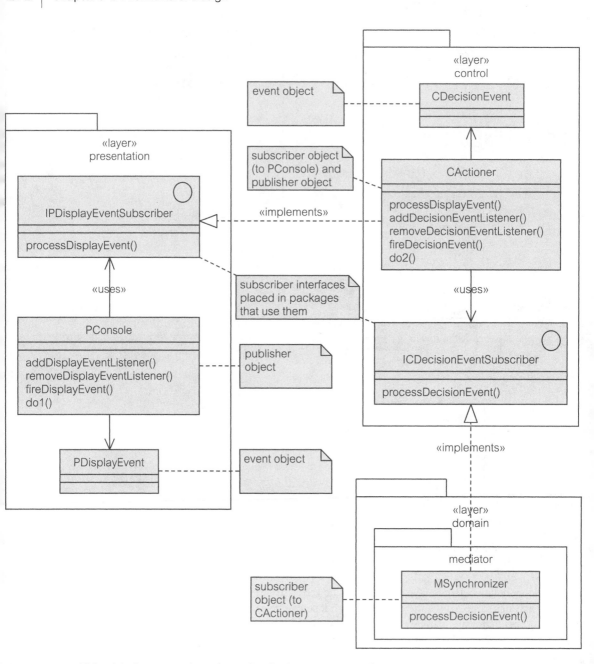

Figure 9.21 Using interfaces to reduce dependencies in event processing

Figure 9.21 shows also how event processing can be linked together to accomplish a complex system. `PConsole` creates a `PDisplayEvent` object and uses the `IPDisplayEventSubscriber` interface to notify `CActioner` of the `PDisplayEvent` object. `CActioner` pre-processes `PDisplayEvent` with its `processDisplayEvent()` method and creates a `PDecisionEvent` object.

`CActioner`, now in its capability as a publisher, uses the `ICDecisionEventSubscriber` interface to notify `MSynchronizer` of the `PDecisionEvent` object. `MSynchronizer` processes the `PDecisionEvent` with its `processDecisionEvent()` method.

Acquaintance

9.1.9

As explained in the opening paragraphs of Section 9.1, good architectural design requires the creation of dependency firewalls so that dependencies between neighboring layers are minimized, circular dependencies are eliminated, and direct dependencies between non-neighboring layers are disallowed. The use of delegation, interfaces, and event processing greatly contributes to these objectives.

However, there are situations when objects in non-neighboring layers may communicate without breaking the principles of good architectural design. This can happen when an object gets acquainted at runtime with another object (in a non-neighboring layer) and wants to take advantage of this acquaintance by requesting services of that object.

Acquaintance defines a situation when an object is passed another object in an argument to its method. More precisely, an object A gets acquainted with object B if another object C passes B to A in an argument of the message to A. Object communication due to acquaintance is one of the programming techniques legitimized in the Law of Demeter (Lieberherr and Holland, 1989).

Figure 9.22 illustrates acquaintance. `CActioner` uses `retrieveEmployee()` to retrieve an `EEmployee` object from the database. The retrieval process is not explained, but presumably `CActioner` delegates the request down to a layer responsible for communication with the database. Once the employee information is retrieved, the `EEmployee` object is instantiated. `CActioner` passes `EEmployee` to `PEmpBrowser` in the message `displayEmployee(emp)`. `PEmpBrowser` is now acquainted with `EEmployee` and sends the message `getName()` to it to get the employee name for display.

Acquaintance dependencies and interfaces

As shown in Figure 9.22, acquaintance introduces dependencies. **Acquaintance dependencies** are *method dependencies* acquired dynamically at runtime. The highly dynamic nature of acquaintance dependencies distinguishes them from 'regular' method dependencies discussed in Section 9.1.6.

From an architectural perspective, dynamic means difficult to see and understand. Dynamic means also that it is not possible to use explicit associations between classes to visualize (and therefore legitimize) acquaintance dependencies in the code. Sometimes an acceptable solution can come from the introduction of interfaces into the design.

The design in Figure 9.22 has two architectural flaws:

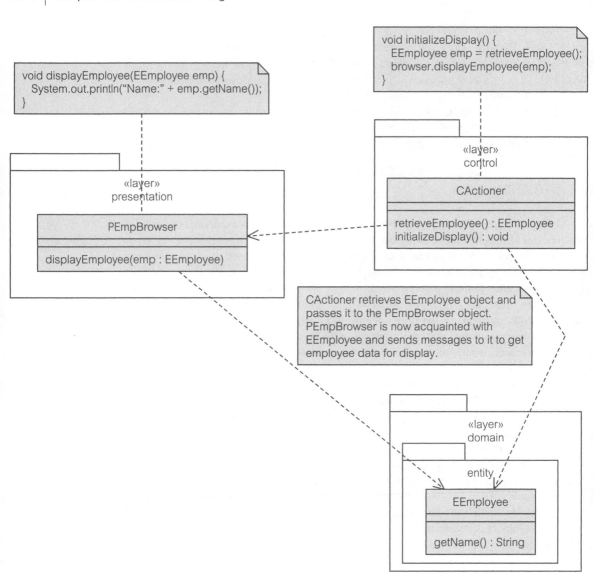

Figure 9.22 Acquaintance

- The `control` package is upward-dependent on the `presentation` package (because `CActioner` calls `browser.displayEmployee(emp)` on `PEmpBrowser`).
- The `presentation` package depends on the non-neighboring `domain` package (because `PEmpBrowser` calls `emp.getName()` on `EEmployee`).

Both flaws can be resolved with interfaces, as shown in Figure 9.23. The technique is similar to the one used to break circular dependencies with interfaces (Section 9.1.7). `ICEmpBrowser` breaks the upward dependency from `control` to `presentation`. `IPEmployee` breaks the acquaintance dependency from `presentation` to `domain`.

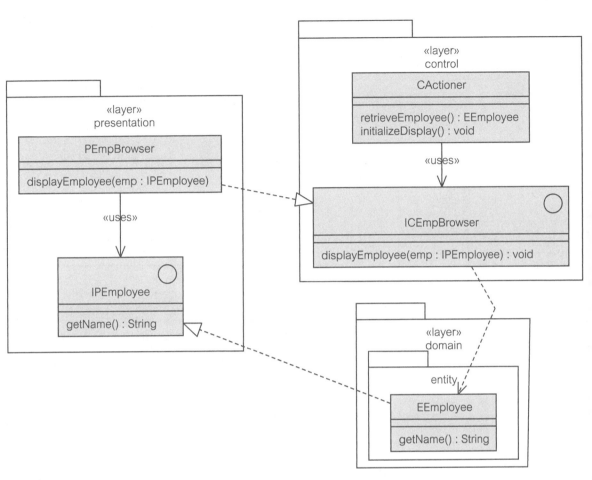

Figure 9.23 Using interfaces to reduce dependencies

Acquaintance package

In more complex scenarios, the use of interfaces and event processing (within the scope discussed in Sections 9.1.7 and 9.1.8) may not provide an obvious architectural solution to acquaintance dependencies. Even the solution in Figure 9.23 is rather unsatisfactory because the implementation dependency (Section 9.1.7) from EEmployee to IPEmployee spans non-neighbouring packages.

A better solution comes from addressing the acquaintance as a problem in its own right that requires separate management. To this end, a separate acquaintance package may be introduced. The **acquaintance package** is a stand-alone package consisting of interfaces only. The package is not a layer and is not a part of the layer hierarchy.

Figure 9.24 demonstrates how the acquaintance package separates acquaintance dependencies into an isolated problem that can be managed independently. The model exemplifies the separation of concerns principle that should feature in any good architectural

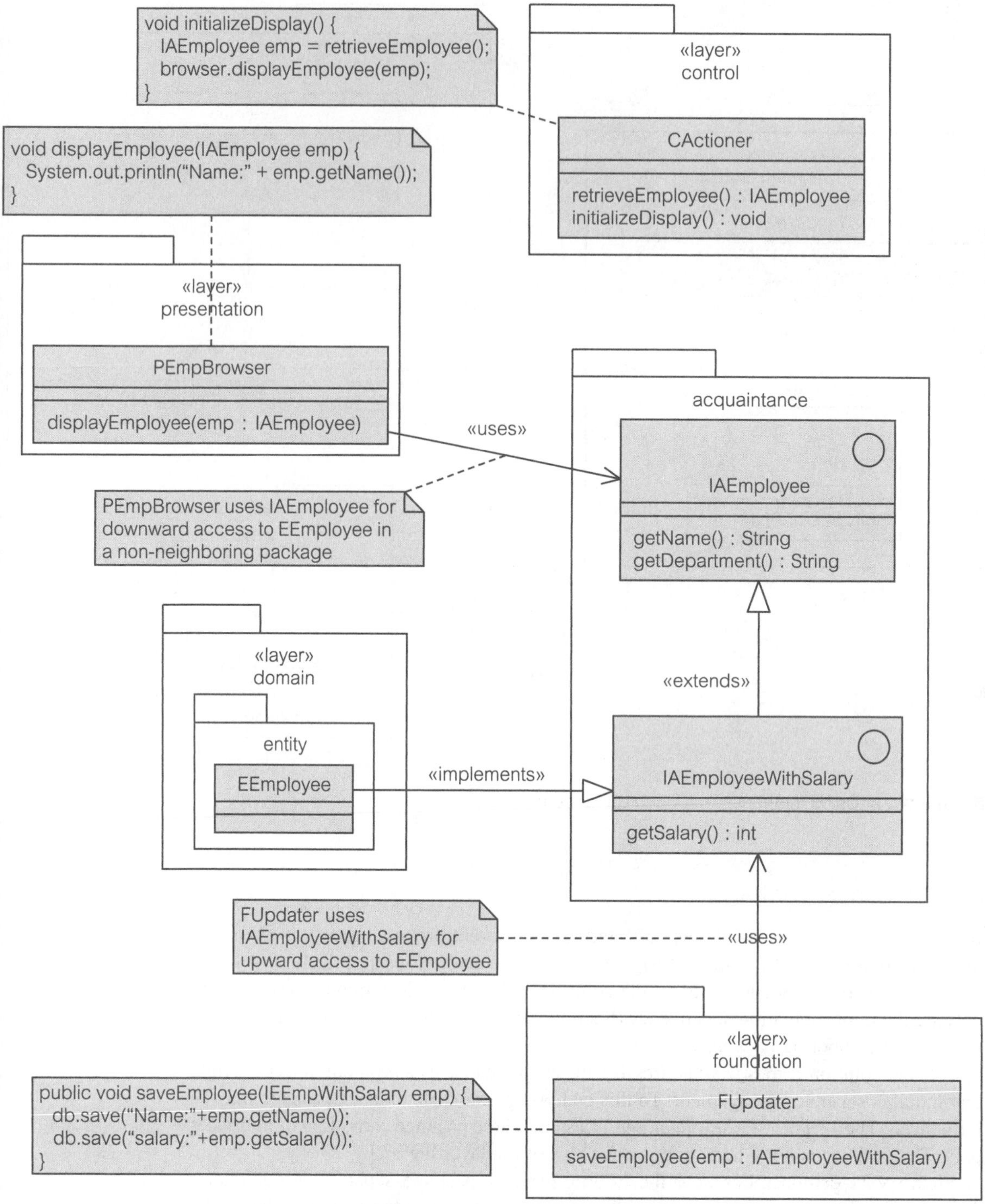

Figure 9.24 Using the acquaintance package

design (Larman, 2002). The `acquaintance` package consists only of interfaces. `IAEmployee` is extended by `IAEmployeeWithSalary`, which in turn is implemented by `EEmployee`.

As in Figures 9.15 and 9.16, `CActioner`'s method `initializeDisplay()` uses `retrieveEmployee()` to retrieve from the database and instantiate an `EEmployee` object (this process engages other objects not shown on the diagram). Although the `EEmployee` *provided interface* (Section 9.1.7) is `IAEmployeeWithSalary`, `CActioner` requires only the `IAEmployee` interface (i.e. all employee information except salary).

The retrieved object (typed as `IAEmployee`) is passed to `displayEmployee(emp: IAEmployee)` in `PEmpBrowser`. `PEmpBrowser` is now acquainted with `EEmployee` and uses it to `getName()` – the service that is part of the `PEmpBrowser`'s *required interface* (Section 9.1.7). If the layer hierarchy is `presentation – control – domain (entity) – foundation`, then `PEmpBrowser` uses `IAEmployee` for *downward* access to `EEmployee` in a *non-neighboring package*.

In the bottom part of Figure 9.24, `FUpdater` requires the `IAEmployeeWithSalary` interface in the method `saveEmployee(emp : IAEmployeeWithSalary)`. If some client passes to this method an `EEmployee` object, then the `saveEmployee()` method can `getSalary()`, as well as `getName()`, prior to saving employee information in the database. `FUpdater` uses `IAEmployeeWithSalary` for *upward* access to `EEmployee`.

Architectural Frameworks

9.2

Framework is a construction on which the solution to a problem is built. In object technology, a framework is a reuse technology (Maciaszek, 2001). The technology applies to the reuse of the design, as opposed to the reuse of the code. Framework provides a skeleton solution to the problem, which needs to be customized and extended to serve a useful function. The customization involves writing the specific code which 'fills the gaps' in the framework (i.e. which implements various elements of the framework while conforming to the overall structural and behavioral framework design).

The best-known reuse frameworks are enterprise resource planning (ERP) systems, such as SAP or JDEdwards. ERP systems offer both design and code reuse. They are generic software packages. The software is customized and extended to suit the customer's needs. The customization must be done within the skeleton design imposed by the framework.

Framework imposes an architectural design on the system. In this sense, every framework is an **architectural framework**, whether or not it is a software product such as an ERP system or just a design idea and prerogative imposed on the development team. The latter is the subject of the discussion that follows.

Model–View–Controller

9.2.1

One of the best-known architectural frameworks is the **Model–View–Controller** (MVC) framework developed as part of the Smalltalk-80 programming environment (Krasner and Pope, 1988). MVC made a huge footprint on object-oriented design. It is a classic example of the use of the principle of separation of concerns in object-oriented design. In Smalltalk-80, MVC forces the programmers to divide application classes into three groups that specialize and inherit from three Smalltalk-provided abstract classes: Model, View and Controller.

Model objects represent data objects – the business entities and the business rules in the application domain. Changes to model objects are notified to view and controller objects via event processing. This uses the publisher/subscriber technique. Model is the publisher and it is therefore unaware of its views and controllers. View and controller objects subscribe to the Model, but they can also initiate changes to model objects. To assist in this task, Model supplies necessary interfaces, which encapsulate the business data and behavior.

View objects represent GUI objects and present the state of the Model in the format required by the user, typically on a graphic display. View objects are decoupled from model objects. View subscribes to the Model so that it is notified of Model changes and it can update its display. View objects can contain subviews, which display different parts of the Model. Typically, each view object is paired with a controller object.

Controller objects represent mouse and keyboard events. Controller objects respond to the requests that originate from View and that are the results of user interactions with the system. Controller objects give meaning to keystrokes, mouse clicks, etc. and convert them into actions on the model objects. They mediate between view and model objects. By separating user input from visual presentation, they allow the system response to user actions to be changed without changing the GUI presentation, and vice versa – changing GUI without changing system behavior.

Figure 9.25 illustrates an actor's (user's) perspective on communication between MVC objects. The lines represent communication between objects. The user GUI events are intercepted by view objects and passed to controller objects for interpretation and further action. Mixing the behavior of View and Controller in a single object is considered bad practice in MVC.

Figure 9.25
MVC framework

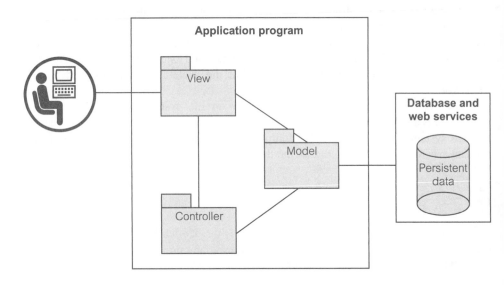

Consider a scenario where a user activates a menu option to display customer details on the presentation screen. A view object receives the event and passes it to its controller object. The controller object requests Model to provide customer data. The model object returns the data to the controller object, which supplies it to View for display. Alternatively, the model object can pass the data to View directly. Any future changes to the state of the Model can be notified to view objects that subscribe to these changes. This way, View can refresh its display to reflect the current business data values.

The MVC separation of concerns has numerous advantages. The most important are (Gamma *et al.*, 1995; Larman, 2002):

- permitting the separate development of the GUI and the business data and logic of the model layer
- replacing or migrating to a different GUI without any radical changes needed in the model
- reorganizing or redesigning the model while retaining the GUI presentation to the user
- allowing multiple views on the same model state
- changing the way the GUI responds to user events without changing the GUI presentation (a view's controller can even be changed at runtime)
- enabling execution of the model without the GUI (e.g. for testing or for batch-mode processing).

Presentation–Control–Mediator–Entity–Foundation 9.2.2

The MVC principles underpin most modern architectural frameworks and related patterns. The Unified Process (UP) uses the MVC principles when separating classes into boundary, control, and entity objects – the concepts derived from the Objectory method (Jacobson, 1992). Boundary objects correspond to MVC view objects, control objects are MVC controller objects, and entity objects represent MVC model objects.

The MVC approach has influenced virtually all architectural frameworks that emphasize the need for hierarchical layers of objects (Buschmann *et al.*, 1996; Fowler, 2003) in order to manage object dependencies (Section 9.1). This section introduces one such framework used in the book's case-study. The framework is called **Presentation–Control–Mediator–Entity–Foundation** (PCMEF). The principles of PCMEF are similar to other popular layering schemes (Fowler, 2003).

PCMEF is a layered architectural framework organized as a vertical hierarchy. Each *layer* is a package that can contain other packages. Packages within each layer are known as *partitions* (Sections 9.1.2 and 9.1.3). In other words, the architecture consists of vertical layers, which can be partitioned. When the system grows, partitions can be organized into a system of sublayers, i.e. partitions can be layered. Layering of partitions is outside the scope of the book.

In a strict layered architecture, higher layers utilize the services (and therefore depend on) lower layers, but not vice versa. A strict layered architecture is not fully possible in practice (Section 9.1.3). Nevertheless, with careful design of layers, it is possible to devise an architectural framework where higher layers are *unstable* and lower layers are increasingly more *stable* (Section 9.1.3). Such a framework opens up to downward dependencies and limits upward dependencies in bottom-up object collaboration.

PCMEF Layers

The PCMEF framework consists of four layers: presentation, control, domain, and foundation. The domain layer contains two predefined packages: entity and mediator. With reference to the MVC framework, presentation corresponds to MVC View, control to Controller, and entity to Model. mediator and foundation do not have MVC counterparts.

The PCMEF main dependencies are downward, as shown by the arrows in Figure 9.26 – presentation depends on control, control depends on domain (on mediator and, possibly but not necessarily, on entity), mediator depends on entity and on foundation. Upward dependencies are realized through loose coupling facilitated by

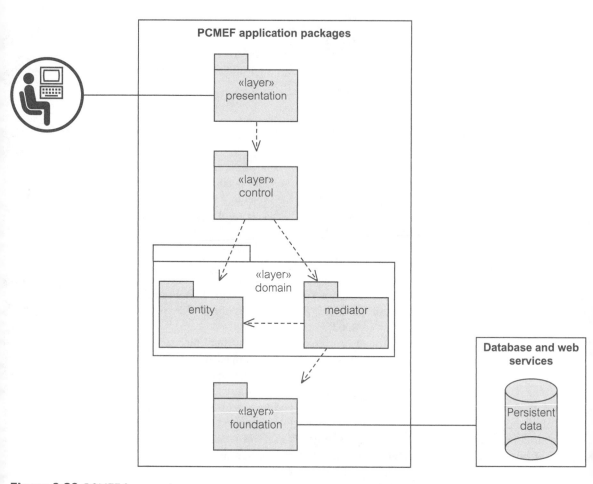

Figure 9.26 PCMEF framework

interfaces, event processing, acquaintance package and similar techniques discussed in Section 9.1. Dependencies are only permitted between neighboring layers.

The **PCMEF** vertical layers preset the system architecture – invariant for all iterations of the incremental development process. The downward dependencies are made apparent by the requirement of setting unidirectional associations between dependent classes in neighboring layers. The horizontal dependencies within layers are relatively unrestricted as long as circular dependencies are eliminated.

In Java, the dependencies between packages convert to `import` statements (Section 9.1.1). The dependencies shown in Figure 9.26 correspond to the import statements in Listing 9.1:

Listing 9.1 Package imports

```
package presentation;
import control.*;

package control;
import domain.entity.*;
import domain.mediator.*;

package entity;
package mediator;
import entity.*;
import foundation.*;

package foundation;
```

The `presentation` **layer** contains classes that define GUI objects. In a Microsoft Windows environment, many `presentation` classes would be subclassed from the MFC (Microsoft Foundation Classes) library. In a Java environment, `presentation` classes can be based on the classes and interfaces of the Java Swing library. The user communicates with the system via presentation classes. Accordingly, the class containing the program's `main` function is typically housed in the `presentation` package (alternatively it can reside in the `control` package).

The `control` **layer** handles `presentation` layer requests. It consists of classes responsible for processing the user's interactions (passed to `control` from `presentation` objects). As a result, `control` is responsible for the bulk of the program's logic, algorithmic solutions, main computations, and maintaining session state for each user.

The `entity` **package** of the `domain` **layer** handles `control` layer requests. It contains classes representing 'business objects'. They store (in the program's memory) objects retrieved from the database or created in order to be stored in the database. Many entity classes are container classes.

The `mediator` **package** of the `domain` layer establishes a channel of communication that mediates between `entity` and `foundation` classes. Mediation serves two main purposes: firstly, to isolate the two packages so that changes in any one of them can be introduced independently, and secondly, to eliminate a need for `control` classes to communicate directly with `foundation` classes whenever new `entity` objects need to be retrieved from the database (such requests from `control` classes are then channeled via `mediator` classes).

The `foundation` **layer** is responsible for all communications with database and web services, which manage persistent data required by the application program. This is where the connections to database and web servers are established, queries to persistent data are constructed, and the database transactions are instigated.

PCMEF principles

Apart from the layered architecture, the PCMEF framework defines design principles (Section 9.1) and advocates design patterns (Section 9.3) necessary to properly manage object dependencies and deliver solutions that are understandable, maintainable, and scalable. The primary PCMEF principles are:

- Downward Dependency Principle (DDP)
- Upward Notification Principle (UNP)
- Neighbor Communication Principle (NCP)
- Explicit Association Principle (EAP)
- Cycle Elimination Principle (CEP)
- Class Naming Principle (CNP)
- Acquaintance Package Principle (APP).

The **Downward Dependency Principle** states that the main dependency structure is top-down. Objects in higher layers depend on objects in lower layers. Consequently, lower layers are more stable than higher layers. They are difficult to change, but (paradoxically) not necessarily difficult to extend (Martin, 2003). Interfaces, abstract classes, dominant classes and similar devices (Section 9.1.7) should encapsulate stable packages so that they can be extended when needed.

The **Upward Notification Principle** promotes low coupling in bottom-up communication between layers. This can be achieved by using asynchronous communication based on event processing (Section 9.1.8). Objects in higher layers act as subscribers (observers) to state changes in lower layers. When an object (publisher) in a lower layer changes its state, it sends notification to its subscribers. In response, subscribers can communicate with the publisher (now in the downward direction) so that their states are synchronized with the state of the publisher.

The **Neighbor Communication Principle** demands that a package can only communicate directly with its neighbor package. This principle ensures that the system does not disintegrate to an incomprehensible network of intercommunicating objects. To enforce this principle, message passing between non-neighboring objects uses delegation (Section 9.1.6). In more complex scenarios, `acquaintance` package (Section 9.1.9) can be used to group interfaces to assist in collaboration that engages distant packages.

The **Explicit Association Principle** visibly documents permitted message passing between classes (Section 9.1.6). The principle is used predominantly on classes with downward dependencies (see Downward Dependency Principle above) and on classes engaged in frequent collaboration. Associations that are results of this principle are unidirectional (otherwise they would create circular dependencies). It must be remembered, however, that not all associations between classes exist because of message passing between these classes. For example, bidirectional associations may be needed to implement referential integrity between classes.

The **Cycle Elimination Principle** ensures that circular dependencies between layers, between packages, and between classes within packages are broken. Circular dependencies violate the separation of concerns guideline and are the main obstacle to reusability. Cycles can be resolved by creating a new package specifically for the purpose (Section 9.1.2) or by forcing one of the communication paths in the cycle to communicate via the interface (Section 9.1.7.3).

The **Class Naming Principle** makes it possible to recognize in the class name to what package it belongs. To this aim, each class name is prefixed in PCMEF with the first letter of the package name (e.g. `EInvoice` is a class in the `entity` package). The same principle applies to interfaces. Each interface name is prefixed with two capital letters – the first is the letter 'I' (signifying that this is interface) and the second letter identifies the package (e.g. `ICInvoice` is an interface in the `control` package).

The **Acquaintance Package Principle** is the consequence of the Neighbor Communication Principle. The `acquaintance` package consists of interfaces that an object passes, instead of concrete objects, in arguments to method calls. The interfaces can be implemented in any PCMEF package. This effectively allows communication between non-neighboring packages while centralizing dependency management to a single `acquaintance` package. The need for the `acquaintance` package was explained in Section 9.1.9 and is discussed again below in the PCMEF context.

Acquaintance in PCMEF+

Acquaintance happens when, within a method, a message is sent to the object that is a parameter of the method (Section 9.1.9). Because acquaintance is acquired dynamically at runtime, special care must be exercised to avoid excessive coupling of objects due to acquaintance. The Acquaintance Package Principle ensures that the Neighbor Communication Principle is satisfied in the presence of acquaintance.

In PCMEF, acquaintance in the *downward* direction to objects in neighboring packages is never necessary because associations link such objects (which means that a message can be sent to an attribute in the client object (`this`) that links to the supplier object). Acquaintance in the *upward* direction to objects in neighboring packages should employ interfaces to eliminate cycles (Section 9.1.9). Acquaintance which in effect spans *non-neighboring* objects should be channeled through interfaces grouped in the `acquaintance` package. Figure 9.24 provides a good example.

Figure 9.27 shows how the **`acquaintance package`** effectively extends the PCMEF framework into the **PCMEF+** framework. Interfaces of the `acquaintance` package can be implemented and/or used by classes of any PCMEF package (see the explanation of the implementation and usage dependencies in Section 9.1.7). The external package containing PCMEF packages in Figure 9.27 is only for visualization purposes; it does not exist in practice.

Note again that the `acquaintance` package groups interfaces for upward communication and for downward communication to non-neighboring objects. Altogether, there are five possibilities for channeling the object communication via `acquaintance` interfaces:

Figure 9.27
Acquaintance
package in
PCMEF+

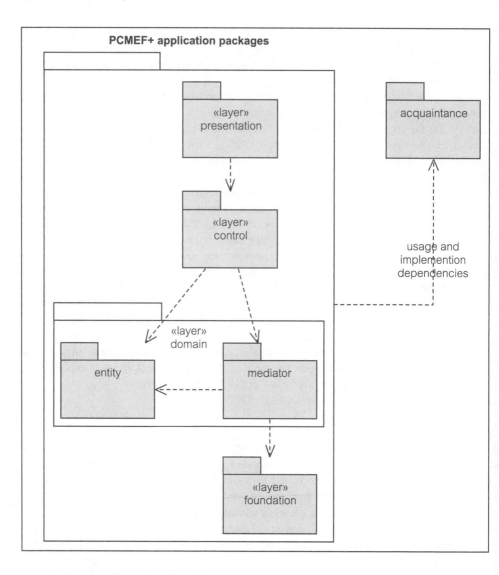

1. F uses A interfaces implemented in D, C, or P
2. D uses A interfaces implemented in C or P
3. C uses A interfaces implemented in P
4. P uses A interfaces implemented in D or F
5. C uses A interfaces implemented in F.

The acquaintance package can be seen as an application-specific library of interfaces. Like any library, the acquaintance package should be designed with stability in mind. As mentioned above in the context of the Downward Dependency Principle, a stable package is not easily amenable to changes but it can be extended to accommodate system growth.

The same rule applies to external libraries used by the application program, such as Java API packages. PCMEF packages using Java data types depend on `java.util`, PCMEF packages engaged in event processing depend on `java.awt.event`, etc. The (relative) stability of Java libraries ensures that coupling PCMEF packages to them is unlikely to create a maintenance nightmare in the future.

Deployment of PCMEF layers

The PCMEF architectural framework does not make a statement about the deployment of layers on computer nodes. The layers are intended to be deployable independently as components. **Component** is defined in the UML 2.0 as 'a modular part of a system that encapsulates its contents and whose manifestation is replaceable within its environment' (UML, 2002, p.322). The UML 2.0 provides also a component deployment diagram to show deployment of components in an execution environment.

Deployment of PCMEF layers as components results in some kind of **client/server architecture**. As a minimum, the architecture consists of an application client and a database/web server. This is a **two-tier architecture**, where the application program on one computer node controls all PCMEF software objects and the database/web server on another computer node manages persistent data (Figure 9.26). The two-tier architecture applies to multi-user database applications as well as to single-user desktop applications. Desktop applications run the client and the server processes on the same machine.

A two-tier architecture as described above is a **thick-client** setup. In more complex deployments, PCMEF layers – with the exception of the `presentation` layer – can be moved to server computers. This results in **thin-client** architectures. A thin-client architecture can be two tiers or many tiers. For example, the database server can be deployed on two nodes to separate database business and integrity rules (programmed with stored procedures and triggers) from the more mundane database responsibility of storing and managing the data. This results in a **three-tier architecture**, where PCMEF software objects are still running on a client tier, or possibly some domain and foundation objects are moved to the middle tier.

Multi-tier architectures are also possible. In a distributed system, some PCMEF layers can be mapped to EJB or .NET components and deployed separately. In applications that have to display and process large volumes of data from a database, the domain layer can be deployed on an object server. An Object Storage API then provides the mapping between the persistent object server, the remaining PCMEF application layers, and the corporate relational database server.

Architectural Patterns

9.3

The discussion of architectural design is not complete without identifying, naming, and explaining tradeoffs of the design patterns advocated for architectural frameworks, such as PCMEF. A **design pattern** names and explains the best and widely acknowledged practice and knowledge to solve a design problem. Ever since the seminal work by Gamma *et al.* (1995), the study of design patterns has flourished and evolved into an important branch of knowledge within software engineering at large. The Gamma *et al.* (1995) book was written by four prominent authors. Hence, these patterns are commonly known as **Gang of Four** (GoF) patterns.

Patterns increase awareness of the proper application of common techniques for managing dependencies, for reusing functionality, for information hiding, for working with abstraction, etc. The study of patterns makes it possible to avoid 'reinventing the wheel'. The previous discussion in this chapter applied many patterns without identifying and describing them. This section revisits the previous discussion and explains what patterns have been used. All patterns discussed below are GoF patterns.

9.3.1 Façade

The intent of the **Façade pattern** is described in Gamma *et al.* (1995, p.185) as to define 'a higher-level interface that makes the subsystem easier to use'. The goal is to 'minimize the communication and dependencies between subsystems'.

A 'higher-level interface' is not necessarily the concept of interface as introduced in Section 9.1.7. This can be an abstract class or concrete dominant class, also explained in Section 9.1.7. The point is that a higher-level interface encapsulates the main functionality of the subsystem (package) and provides the main or even the only entry point for the clients of the package.

Client objects communicate with the package via the façade object. The façade object delegates the work to other package objects as needed. The consequence is the reduction of communication paths between packages and the reduction of the number of objects that clients of the package deal with. In essence, the package gets hidden behind the façade object.

Figure 9.28 demonstrates the `EEntity` class as the façade to the entity package. Clients of the package, such as `CActioner` and `MBroker`, send requests to `EEntity`, which forwards them to the appropriate objects within the package. `EEntity` is a concrete dominant class. This could be an *outer class* and the three remaining classes could be **inner classes**. (In Java, inner classes have their definitions placed within the outer class definition.) Making `EEntity` an interface or abstract class could further reduce the clients' dependencies on the entity package.

9.3.2 Abstract Factory

The **Abstract Factory pattern** provides 'an interface for creating families of related or dependent objects without specifying their concrete classes' (Gamma *et al.*, 1995, p.87). As opposed to the Façade pattern where a 'higher-level interface' could mean a concrete class, an interface in Abstract Factory is a true interface (preferably) or an abstract class (Section 9.1.7).

Abstract Factory enables the application to behave differently by accessing one of several families of objects hidden behind the abstract factory interface. A configuration parameter value can control which family should be accessed.

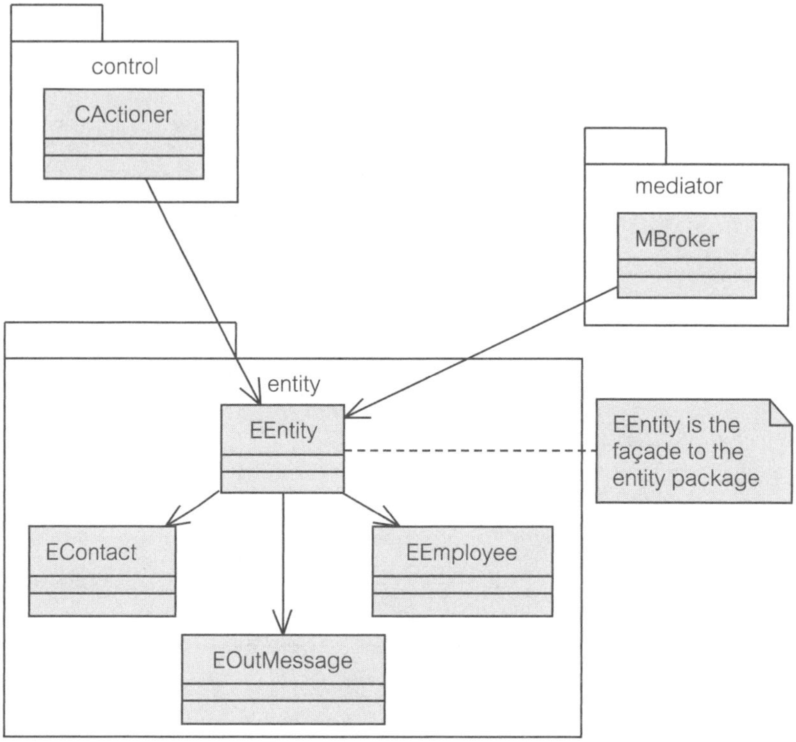

Figure 9.28
Façade pattern

Figure 9.29 gives an example where the application can execute using either a console display family of objects or a GUI window family of objects. IPPresentation is an abstract factory that defers creation of concrete objects to PConsole or PWindow concrete factories, depending on how the system is configured. Client objects (such as PInit) access concrete objects via their interface (IPPresentation).

Because Abstract Factory is an interface which gets implemented in entire families of classes, extending it to support new families may have a ripple effect on existing concrete classes. Gamma *et al.* (1995) discuss a few implementation solutions to address this problem.

On closer inspection, the Abstract Factory pattern can be seen as a variation of the Façade pattern. The abstract factory interface can be used as a 'higher-level interface' through which the communication to a package is channeled, a set of concrete classes is produced and the classes that do real work inside the package are encapsulated.

Chain of Responsibility 9.3.3

The intent of the **Chain of Responsibility pattern** is to 'avoid coupling the sender of a request to its receiver by giving more than one object a chance to handle the request' (Gamma *et al.*, 1995, p.223). The chain of responsibility is really just another name for the concept of **delegation** (Section 9.1.6).

Figure 9.29
Abstract Factory
pattern

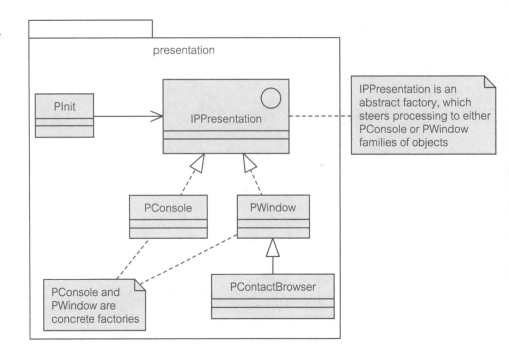

If a chain of responsibility is involved, a client object that sends a message does not have a direct reference to an object that ultimately supplies the service. This pattern is necessary to enforce the Neighbor Communication Principle in the design (Section 9.2.2).

Figure 9.30 gives an example for the Chain of Responsibility pattern. `PWindow` gets a `displayContact()` request and sends a `retrieveContact()` message to `CActioner`. `CActioner` cannot satisfy the request and forwards it to `EContact` (if the requested `EContact` object has been instantiated before and exists in the program's memory) or to `MBroker` (if the `EContact` object has to be retrieved from the database). If the object is in memory, `EContact` will provide the service and the object will be returned to `PWindow` for display. Otherwise, `MBroker` will delegate the request to `FReader` so that the object can be retrieved from the database and instantiated as `EContact` before it is passed to `PWindow`.

9.3.4 Observer

The intent of the **Observer pattern** is to 'define a one-to-many dependency between objects so that when one object changes state, all its dependents are notified and updated automatically' (Gamma *et al.*, 1995, p.293). Also known as the **Publish–Subscribe pattern**, the Observer pattern is built into the handling of asynchronous communication in event processing (Section 9.1.8).

The pattern relates two types of object: **subject** (the object that is observed) and **observer**. In Section 9.1.8, subject was called a *publisher* object and observer was called

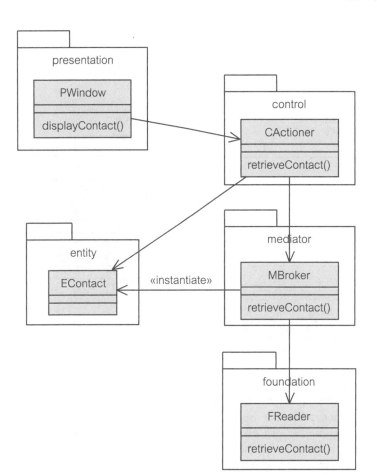

Figure 9.30
Chain of
Responsibility
pattern

a *subscriber* object. A subject may have many observers, which subscribe to it. All observers are notified of subject state changes and can then perform the processing necessary to synchronize their states with the subject state. Observers are not related to each other and can do different processing in response to notifications of subject state changes.

Although the definition of the Observer pattern mentions dependencies, the pattern promotes low coupling between subjects and observers. The notifications are broadcast automatically to observers. The subject does not know the concrete classes of observers, provided the notifications are based on interfaces that observers implement (Section 9.1.8). Subjects and observers execute in separate threads, thus further enhancing the low coupling. The low coupling of the Observer pattern can be (and should be) taken advantage of in layered architectural frameworks to support upward communication between layers.

The PCMEF framework sanctions the Observer pattern in the Upward Notification Principle (Section 9.2.2). The inter-layer chain of notifications is bottom-up. The `foundation` layer notifies its state changes to the `mediator` package, which passes them further to the `entity` package and to the `control` layer. The `control` layer sends the notifications up to the `presentation` layer.

Figure 9.31
Observation
pattern

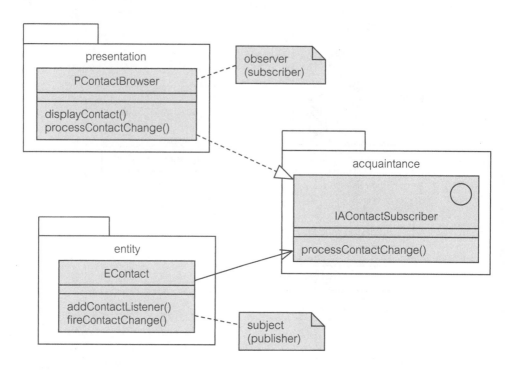

Figure 9.31 shows how the Observer pattern is engaged in upward notification from the `entity` package to the `presentation` layer. `PContactBrowser` subscribes to `EContact`. Because the two classes are in non-neighboring packages, the `acquaintance` package is used as per the Acquaintance Package Principle (Section 9.2.2). The `acquaintance` package contains the `IAContactSubscriber` interface.

There is no dedicated *registrator object* (Section 9.1.8) in Figure 9.31. `EContact` uses `addContactListener()` to register `IAContactSubsriber` as its observer. In reality, the observer is `PContactBrowser`, which implements the `IAContactSubsriber` interface. When the state of `EContact` changes in some way, `fireContactChange()` notifies the change to `PContactBrowser` by calling `processContactChange()` on `IAContactSubscriber`. `processContactChange()` can then request `displayContact()` to display the new state of `EContact` in the browser window.

9.3.5 Mediator

The **Mediator pattern** defines objects that encapsulate intercommunication between other objects, possibly from different layers. The pattern 'promotes loose coupling by keeping objects from referring to each other explicitly, and it lets you vary their interaction independently' (Gamma *et al.*, 1995, p.273).

The Mediator pattern is given its rightful place in the PCMEF framework, where the `mediator` layer mediates between the `foundation` layer and the `entity` package (Section 9.2.2). The `control` layer is another example of the Mediator pattern in its capability to mediate between the `presentation` layer and the `entity` package.

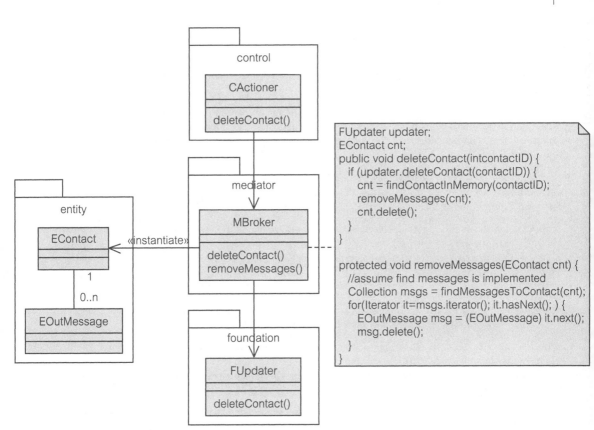

Figure 9.32 Mediator pattern

In PCMEF, the `mediator` package decouples the `entity` objects and the `foundation` objects. It acts also as a façade (Section 9.3.1) between the `entity` and `foundation` objects, thus reducing the number of interconnections between them. Façade differs from Mediator in that the Façade interconnection protocol is unidirectional and one-to-many. By contrast, Mediator replaces many-to-many interconnections with one-to-many interconnections to the *colleagues* that it mediates.

Moreover, the `mediator` package maintains synchronization between subjects (`foundation`) and observers (`entity`), thus promoting an enhanced form of the Observer pattern (Section 9.3.4). In the Observer pattern, the mediator object that encapsulates complex update semantics between subjects and observers is known as a Change Manager (Gamma *et al.*, 1995).

Figure 9.32 is an example. `CActioner` delegates `deleteContact()` to `MBroker`. The `MBroker` task is twofold. Firstly, it needs to delegate `deleteContact()` further down to `FUpdater`, which is responsible for deleting the contact in the database (the database will also delete any outmessages still in the database to that contact).

Secondly, if the deletion in the database is successful, `MBroker` needs to check if `EContact` is in the program's memory, together with any `EOutMessages` that are destined for it. If it is, then `MBroker` sends a `removeMessages(cnt)` message to delete `EOutmessages`, followed by `cnt.delete()` to delete `EContact`.

Summary

1. *Software architecture* is defined as the organization of software elements into a system aiming at achieving some purpose.

2. *Architectural design* is a set of decisions aiming at efficient and effective software architecture together with the rationale for these decisions. A sound architectural design uses hierarchical *layering* of software objects (*design classes*) and ensures that *dependencies* between objects are minimized and visible in compile-time program structures.

3. Architectural layers are constructed from *packages*, which contain design classes. Packages can be nested. Accordingly, three levels of structural dependencies must be considered: *layer dependencies*, *package dependencies*, and *class dependencies*.

4. From the behavioral perspective, *method dependencies* are the main category of dependencies in a program. Method dependencies result from message passing between objects. A *client object* depends on a *supplier object*. In the presence of delegation, a supplier object can be a *delegator object*, which merely delegates the service to a real supplier of it.

5. *Interface* is a declaration of a set of features (attributes and operations) that is not directly instantiable. *Java interface* allows only attributes that are constants. *UML interface* allows any attributes, including attributes that create associations to classes and associations between interfaces.

6. An interface is different from an *abstract class* or *pure abstract class*. In languages with single implementation inheritance, a class can be a subclass of at most one class (and that one class can be abstract or purely abstract). However, a class can implement multiple interfaces (and the same interface may be implemented by many classes).

7. The use of interfaces results in two kinds of dependency: *implementation dependency* (when a class implements an interface) and *usage dependency* (when a class uses an interface). Interestingly, and in contrast to other dependencies, implementation and usage dependencies can be quite beneficial in software architectures. In particular, they can be used to break circular dependencies between classes, packages, and layers.

8. *Event dependencies* are the second main category of dependencies in a program (apart from method dependencies). To be precise, event dependencies are a kind of method dependencies such that the message passing is asynchronous. In event processing, the dependency is between a *publisher object* and a *supplier object*. Unlike in synchronous method dependencies, event dependencies are weaker, more resistant to program changes, and easier to manage.

9. Combining event processing and interfaces creates the most powerful mechanism to facilitate *dependency management* in software architectures.

10. *Acquaintance* defines a situation when an object is passed another object in an argument to its method. The object passed can be (and frequently is) an interface. *Acquaintance dependencies* are method dependencies acquired dynamically at runtime. Acquaintance is a very useful programming practice, but its invisibility in compile-time program structures is a problem. One way of addressing the problem is to place interfaces used in acquaintances in a separate *acquaintance package*.

11. *Architectural framework* is a skeleton solution to a software development, which forces a broad architectural design on developers. One of the best-known architectural frameworks is MVC.

12. This book applies the architectural framework called PCMEF. PCMEF defines a number of strict software design principles. The aim is to minimize dependencies between software objects and facilitate

understandability, maintainability, and scalability in the resultant system. The framework is called PCMEF+ when the existence of the acquaintance package needs to be emphasized.

13. *Design pattern* names and explains the best and widely acknowledged practice and knowledge to solve a design problem. When a pattern serves the purpose of architectural design, it is called an *architectural pattern*.

14. Patterns that most prominently feature in the PCMEF framework are: Façade, Abstract Factory, Chain of Responsibility, Observer, and Mediator. These are all GoF patterns.

Key Terms

«layer» package	253
abstract class	265
Abstract Factory pattern	286
acquaintance	273, 283
acquaintance dependency	273
acquaintance package	275, 283
Acquaintance Package Principle	283
APP	*See* Acquaintance Package Principle
architectural design	248
architectural framework	*See* framework
asynchronous communication	269
callback	*See* up-call
CEP	*See* Cycle Elimination Principle
Chain of Responsibility pattern	287
circular dependencies	251
Class Naming Principle	283
client object	261
client/server architecture	285
CNP	*See* Class Naming Principle
code reuse	256
component	285
control layer	281
controller object	278
coupling	254
Cycle Elimination Principle	283
DDP	*See* Downward Dependency Principle
delegation	262, 287
delegator object	262
dependency firewall	249
dependency relationship	250
design class	250
design pattern	285
domain layer	281
dominant class	265
down-call	259, 263
Downward Dependency Principle	282
dynamic binding	256
EAP	*See* Explicit Association Principle
entity package	281
event	269
event object	270
Explicit Association Principle	282
extension inheritance	258
Façade pattern	286
foundation layer	282
framework	277
Gang of Four	286
GoF	*See* Gang of Four
impact analysis	262
implementation dependency	266
implementation inheritance	255, 262
inheritance without polymorphism	258
inner class	286
interface	264
late binding	*See* dynamic binding
layer	250, 253
layering	249
listener object	*See* subscriber object
mediator package	281
Mediator pattern	290
method overloading	256
method overriding	256

model object	278	registrator object	269
Model–View–Controller	277	required interface	266
multi-tier architecture	285	restriction inheritance	259
MVC	*See* Model–View–Controller	Separated Interface pattern	268
NCP	*See* Neighbor Communication Principle	single implementation inheritance	265
Neighbor Communication Principle	282	software architecture	248
observer	288	stability	254
observer object	*See* subscriber object	stable framework	254
Observer pattern	288	stable layer	254
package	250	subject	288
partition	253	subscriber object	269
PCMEF+	283	supplier object	261
PCMEF	*See* Presentation–Control–	synchronous communication	262
	Mediator–Entity–Foundation	thick-client	285
polymorphism	256	thin-client	285
presentation layer	281	three-tier architecture	285
Presentation–Control–Mediator–Entity–		two-tier architecture	285
Foundation	279	UNP	*See* Upward Notification Principle
proactive dependency management	249	unstable layer	254
provided interface	266	up-call	260, 264
publisher object	269	Upward Notification Principle	282
Publish–Subscribe pattern	*See* Observer pattern	usage dependency	266
pure abstract class	265	view object	278
reactive dependency management	249		

Review Questions

1. Dependencies between software objects can be analyzed from different viewpoints and at various levels of abstraction. Which of these viewpoints or level of abstraction is most relevant for the notion of *dependency firewall*?

2. The book uses the term *design class* to mean – depending on the context – any of the following related terms: software class, system class, application class, implementation class, and program class. Explain differences in emphasis of these related terms.

3. There are two main methods to eliminate circular dependencies between packages. What are they?

4. If you were to classify various dependencies according to the impact on architectural design, what would this classification be? By impact, we mean the degree to which they ought to be minimized. Assume that the impact can be troublesome, neutral, or helpful.

5. What would be good alternative names for PCMEF packages?

6. Which of the GoF patterns discussed in this chapter is the best match for the Upward Notification Principle (UNP)? Explain.

7. Which of the GoF patterns discussed in this chapter can be used to implement a dominant class? Explain.

Problem-Solving Exercises

Case Study Exercises

1. Consider the subflow *S1 – View Unsent Messages* in Section 8.2.3. Think about design classes that may be needed to implement this subflow. Draw a class diagram with PCMEF packages and assign design classes to these packages. You may need to use interfaces to ensure PCMEF principles.

   Think about the sequence of operations needed to perform the subflow. Add these operations to classes in the diagram.

2. Consider the subflow *S1 – View Unsent Messages* in Section 8.2.3. Refer also to Exercise 1 above. Draw an alternative class diagram for this subflow. Use the PCMEF naming convention to name classes. Do not show packages. You may need to use interfaces to ensure PCMEF principles.

   The alternative diagram should consider a scenario where viewing unsent messages is obtained by asking an employee object for outmessages allocated to that employee. If these outmessages are not in the memory cache, the program has to make a 'trip' to the database.

   Think about the sequence of operations needed to perform this scenario. Add the operations to classes in the diagram.

3. Consider the subflow *S3 – Email Message* in Section 8.2.3. Think about design classes that may be needed to implement this subflow. Use the PCMEF naming convention to name classes. Do not show packages. You may need to use interfaces to ensure PCMEF principles.

   Consider a scenario where the outmessage to be emailed has to be retrieved from the database only if it is not already in the memory cache. In the control package, use separate classes to retrieve the outmessage and to send it.

   Think about the sequence of operations needed to perform this scenario. Add the operations to classes in the diagram.

Minicase – Contact Information Management

One of the use cases related to the EM case-study is `Manage Contact Information` (Figures 7.4 and 8.1). Like EM, `Manage Contact Information` is a subset of CM (Figure 7.1). CM is a subset of AEM.

CIM (Contact Information Management) is concerned with maintaining current information about contacts. As per the definition of contact in the domain glossary (Table 7.1), contact is a person or organization that AEM communicates or does business with. In practice, all contacts are people. It is just that in some cases a person that AEM communicates with is anonymous to AEM (or the personal details may be of no interest to AEM). Also, in some cases, a contact may not represent an organization but a private person (and yet, AEM wants to keep information about this person). For these reasons, CIM distinguishes between `PersonContact` and `OrganizationContact` as two kinds of `Contact`.

The functionality of CIM consists of four standard operations that can be performed on a business object – Create it, Read it, Update it, and Delete it. This is nicknamed the CRUD functionality. Figure 9.33 shows a use case diagram for CIM. The four main use cases are all modeled as abstract because of the differences in handling `PersonContacts` and `OrganizationContacts`.

`Read Contact` in Figure 9.33 is extended by two other use cases because a contact has to be read (retrieved) from the database before the application program can update it or delete it. `Update OrganizationContact` is extended by `Create PersonContact` to signify the fact that a `PersonContact` can be created in the process of updating

Figure 9.33
Use case diagram
for CIM

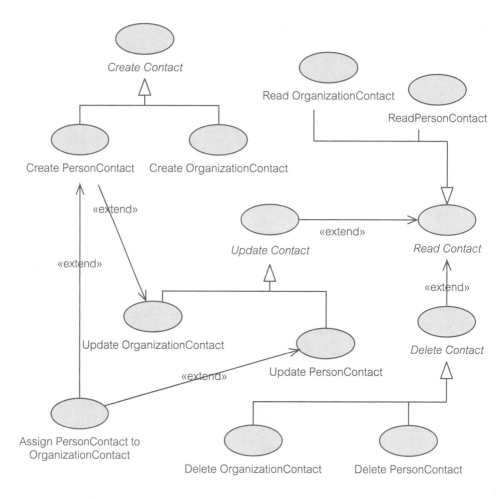

OrganizationContact. Once created, PersonContact can be assigned to OrganizationContact by extending the use case Update PersonContact.

Create PersonContact is extended by Assign PersonContact to Organization-
Contact. This means that PersonContact can be (but does not have to be) added to
OrganizationContact when it is created.

The abstract use case Read Contact retrieves contact information from the database and
presents a list of contacts in browser window, as shown in Figure 9.34. The window is for the concrete use case Create OrganizationContact. Recall from the domain glossary (Table 7.1)
that there are six predefined organization types: advertisers, advertiser groups, agencies, agency
groups, outlets, and providers. An organization can be one, many, or none of these types.

The columns called Date Created, Cr Emp [CR], Date Modified, and Emp [MD]
contain dates and initials of employees who created and last modified contact information. For
each OrganizationContact, CIM can identify many, one, or zero PersonContacts.
PersonContacts can be retrieved and displayed in a separate browser window (not shown).

The use case Read Contact displays only basic information about contacts. Complete
information about contacts includes other details, such as address, telephone, etc. This
information is addressed by other use cases, as discussed next.

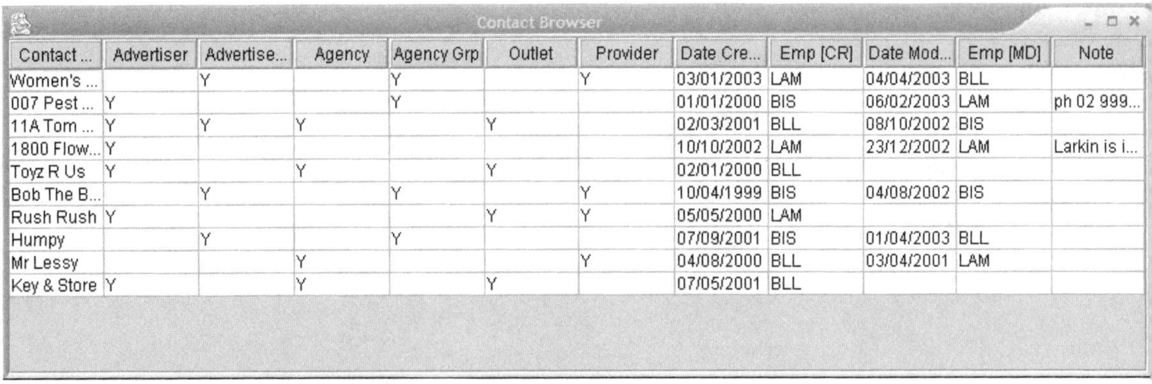

Contact ...	Advertiser	Advertise...	Agency	Agency Grp	Outlet	Provider	Date Cre...	Emp [CR]	Date Mod...	Emp [MD]	Note
Women's ...	Y			Y		Y	03/01/2003	LAM	04/04/2003	BLL	
007 Pest ...	Y			Y			01/01/2000	BIS	06/02/2003	LAM	ph 02 999...
11A Tom ...	Y	Y	Y		Y		02/03/2001	BLL	08/10/2002	BIS	
1800 Flow...	Y						10/10/2002	LAM	23/12/2002	LAM	Larkin is i...
Toyz R Us	Y		Y		Y		02/01/2000	BLL			
Bob The B...		Y		Y		Y	10/04/1999	BIS	04/08/2002	BIS	
Rush Rush	Y				Y	Y	05/05/2000	LAM			
Humpy		Y		Y			07/09/2001	BIS	01/04/2003	BLL	
Mr Lessy			Y			Y	04/08/2000	BLL	03/04/2001	LAM	
Key & Store	Y		Y		Y		07/05/2001	BLL			

Figure 9.34 Browser window for OrganizationContact

The use case `Create Contact` presents to the actor 'entry windows' (dialog boxes) to insert details about `OrganizationContact` or `PersonContact`. The functionality of this use case can be derived from the examples of entry windows presented in Figures 9.28 and 9.29. Note that windows are prototypes only and subject to changes during detailed design. For example, the use case `Create Contact` should allow for four main action buttons:

- `OK` (i.e. save the entered details in the database, dismiss the window, and return to the browser window)
- `Cancel` (i.e. cancel all entered information and return to the browser window)
- `Clear` (i.e. clear all entered information, do not dismiss the window, and allow to re-enter)
- `Save` (i.e. save the entered details in the database, do not dismiss the window, and allow to enter next contact).

Figure 9.35 shows the window prototype with three tab pages for `Create Organiza-tionContact`. This facility allows organization details to be entered, including postal and courier address (by using separate tabs). The window does not provide for entering `Person-Contacts` associated with `OrganizationContact`. The assignment of `PersonContacts` to `OrganizationContact` can be done via the use cases `Create PersonContact` or `Update OrganizationContact`.

Figure 9.36 shows the window prototype for `Create PersonContact`. The use case allows `PersonContact` to be assigned to `OrganizationContact`. `Organization-Contact` must exist before `PersonContact` can be assigned. Action buttons are missing from the prototype window.

Figure 9.37 presents the window prototype for the use case `Update Organization-Contact`. As modeled in the use case diagram (Figure 9.33), this use case can be extended by two other use cases: `Create PersonContact` and `Assign PersonContact to Organ-izationContact`. For this reason, the window has one more tab page called `Contacts`.

Figure 9.38 shows the update window for `OrganizationContact` with the `Contacts` tab page opened. This tab page allows the existing `PersonContact` to be assigned to the `ContactList` (by activating the use case `Assign PersonContact to Organization-Contact`) or a new `PersonContact` (Figure 9.36) to be created before assigning it. Creating a new `PersonContact` involves the use case `Create PersonContact`.

The use case `Update PersonContact` presents the same window as the use case `Create PersonContact` (Figure 9.36). The difference is that the fields in the window for `Update`

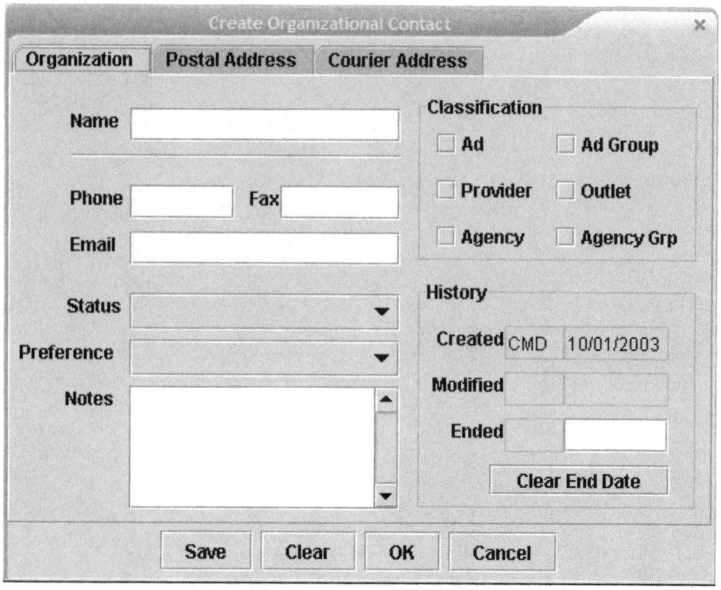

Figure 9.35
Entry window for
Organization-
Contact

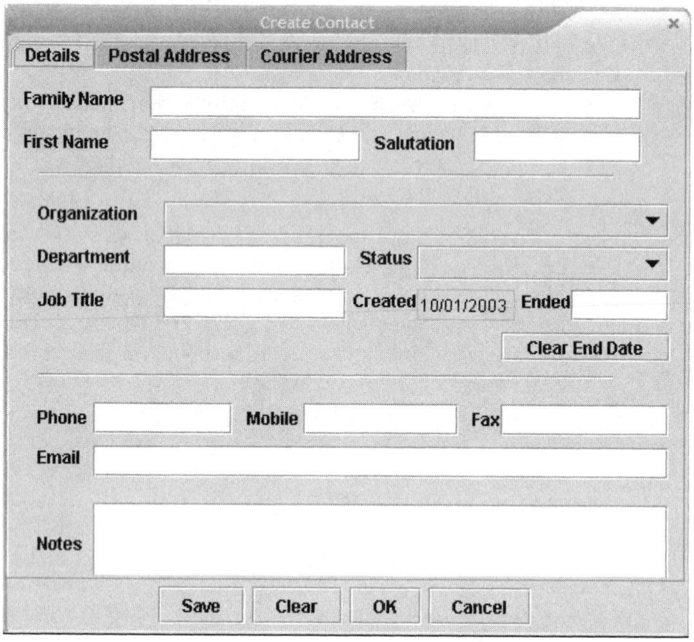

Figure 9.36
Entry window for
PersonContact

PersonContact contain values. There are also differences with regard to business rules and allowed actions (e.g. the set of action buttons may be different).

The use case Delete OrganizationContact allows OrganizationContact to be deleted after relevant information is displayed (Figure 9.39). There is no Contacts tab page in the window. This means that CIM does not allow OrganizationContact and all its

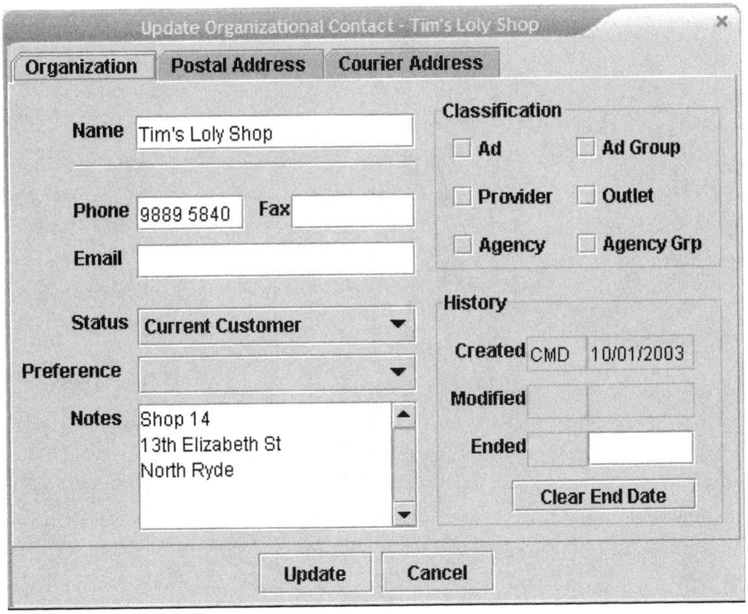

Figure 9.37
Update window
for Organization-
Contact

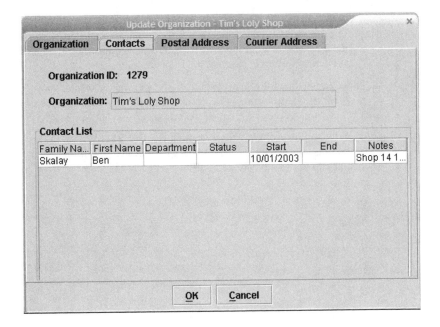

Figure 9.38
Tab page to assign
PersonContacts to
Organization-
Contact

associated `PersonContacts` to be deleted in one action. Also, `OrganizationContact` cannot be deleted if it still has `PersonContacts` associated.

Deleting `PersonContacts` is conducted by the use case `Delete PersonContact`. The window prototype for it is not shown here, but the window fields are the same as in `Create PersonContact` (Figure 9.36).

Figure 9.39
Delete window
for Delete
Organization-
Contact

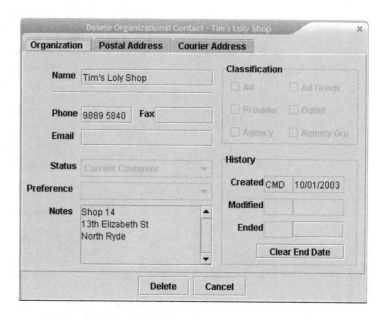

Figure 9.39
Delete window
for Delete
Organization-
Contact

Exercises

1. Based on the minicase specifications, develop a conceptual class diagram. Use the informational content of prototype windows to discover classes and their attributes. Define multiplicity and participation of associations. Explain the model.

2. Based on the minicase specifications, develop a design class diagram conforming to the PCMEF+ framework. Name classes according to PCMEF+ conventions. Show only the most important operations. Explain the model.

3. Refer to your solution for Question 2 above. Discuss the use in your model of the five GoF patterns introduced in Chapter 9. If some patterns have not been used, modify your class diagram to take advantage of all five patterns. Explain the model.

10

Database Design and Programming

Virtually all information systems process data stored in a **database**. Application programs access the database for data, bring the data to the program's memory for processing, and record any changes to data back in the database. Typically, many different programs access a database at the same time. Each program can have many instances running from different *client* workstations and accessing the same database. The database is a *server* providing services to many programs concurrently.

The software responsible for the storage and manipulation of data in the database is called the **database management system** (DBMS). A DBMS provides an abstraction that presents the server data to the client programs in more understandable terms than the bits and bytes. The abstraction is known as a **database model** (or **data model**). The dominant database model for business information systems is the **relational model**. **Structured Query Language** (SQL) is the relational language that the application programs must use to gain access to the database.

The database is all of the following:

- *Large* – its size is frequently measured in gigabytes or terabytes. An application program can only fit a small part of the database data in the memory allocated to it within the random access memory (RAM) of the computer.

- *Persistent* – the database resides on the non-volatile (persistent) secondary storage, such as magnetic and optical disks. The data stays on the disks permanently, whether or not the disk drives are powered and operational.

- *Multi-user shareable* – many users and many application programs can access the database concurrently. A large software chunk of the DBMS, called the **transaction manager**, provides the support for concurrency.

- *Recoverable* – apart from the concurrency control, the transaction manager is responsible for ensuring that the database can always recover from software and hardware failures. In the case of some hardware failures, recovery may require using database *backups* (persistent copies of the database taken at specified time intervals).

- *Consistent* – the DBMS guarantees the integrity (consistency) of its database by ensuring that no user or application program can break the business rules defined on the data. The business rules are implemented by the programming mechanisms known as *referential integrity constraints* and the *triggers*.

- *Secure* – the DBMS guarantees security of its database by ensuring that only authenticated and authorized users and application programs can access the data and execute internal database programs (*stored procedures*).

- *Extensible* – the database provides a degree of logical and physical data independence. The data independence means that changes (extensions) to the database design do not invalidate existing application programs (existing programs are not interested in new changes and they should run as before). Extensibility relates to logical changes in database definitions (such as adding a new column to a table) and to the physical changes in database storage (such as modifying indexes).

As the central repository of enterprise information and the key strategic resource, the database must be designed very carefully. The main difficulty stems from the demand for multi-user access to data. If many users and programs access the database then the database design must be a skillful compromise between individual demands and pressures. This means that the database design is normally a central activity independent from the development of individual applications and systems (something that cannot be given its deserved consideration in a book that evolves around a single case study dedicated to one application program).

10.1 Quick Tutorial in Relational Databases from a Software Engineering Viewpoint

The relational database model dominates the corporate database market. The model is now more than thirty years old and some relational DBMSs (most notably Oracle) have been used to store enterprise data for about twenty years. Commercial pressures and business inertia will see the relational databases as the dominant force for many years to come.

The relational model presents data as **records** (i.e. **rows**) in **tables** (i.e. **relations**). The records in different tables (or in the same table) cannot be linked by user-visible **navigational links**. The concept of *referential integrity*, based on the notion of the *foreign key*, is used for that purpose (Section 10.1.2). SQL statements are compiled to relational algebra operations. Three of these operations – `select`, `project`, and `join` – are compulsory in the model (Codd, 1982). No navigational links or other physical access paths must be required for these operations to produce the results from the database.

Clearly, the relational model imposes various constraints on system development and software engineering. The quick tutorial, presented below, aims to explain the most essential of these constraints. The tutorial uses a simple `MovieActor` database. This database is referred to later with relation to Java application programming.

Table

The relational database model is based on the strong formal foundations of the theory of mathematical sets and predicate logic. The relational concept of a **table** is considered to be a mathematical set (a mathematical relation, to be precise), although with a few imperfections to make the concept practical (let's admit – real life is more complex than the theory).

The table consists of a fixed number of **columns** and a varying number of **records** (*rows*). Columns must be **primitive data types**, such as numbers or strings of characters. Listing 10.1 shows a table named `movie`, which is made up of three columns and two rows. The table content was retrieved from the database by the SQL `select` statement.

Listing 10.1 Select statement to get table content

```
Select statement to get table content

SQL> select * from movie;

MOVIE_CODE MOVIE_TITLE                     DIRECTOR
---------- ------------------------------ -------------------------
        10 Interview with the Vampire     Neil Jordan
        11 The Birdcage                   Mike Nichols
```

The asterisk (*) in the `select` statement requests that all columns defined for the table should be retrieved. The `select` statement in Listing 10.1 represents an **interactive SQL** query. SQL queries must also be used within programs, such as Java programs, to access the database. This is a **programmatic** use of SQL (as opposed to the interactive use). Programmatic SQL is known as **embedded SQL** because some form of SQL (this could be JDBC or SQLJ) is embedded within application program statements.

In robust programs, the asterisk must not be used in `select` statements because the future changes to table definitions (such as adding a column) will break the application programs. The programmer should list all requested columns in the `select` statement, as below:

```
SQL> select movie_code, movie_title, director from movie;
```

SQL statements are not case sensitive. The following statement, although not pretty, is equivalent to the statement above:

```
SQL> SELECT movie_code, MOVIE_title, DIRECTOR from Movie;
```

Figure 10.1 shows the design of the table structure for the table content in Listing 10.1. The table design uses two compartments – the upper contains the table name, the lower lists the columns, the data types of the columns, key indicators, and whether or not the column accepts `null` values.

movie			
movie_code	NUMBER(5)	<pk>	not null
movie_title	VARCHAR2(30)		null
director	VARCHAR2(20)		null

Figure 10.1
Structure of the movie table

The design in Figure 10.1 uses Oracle *data types*. The `movie_code` column accepts integer values up to five digits. The other two columns accept varying-length strings of characters up to 30 and 20 characters, respectively.

Purists could argue that `movie_code` is not a number because it does not make sense to use `movie_code` for any mathematical computations. However, making `movie_code` a number allows using the DBMS facility to automatically generate sequential numbers for `movie_code` when `movie` rows are inserted into the table. This benefit outweighs any puritan opinion on the issue, in particular for large tables.

If a table is a mathematical set, then a table content must not have duplicate elements, i.e. duplicate rows. The notion of a unique key guarantees that. A **unique key** (called also **candidate key** or **alternate key**) consists of one or more columns that are not allowed to have duplicate values in any row of the table. One such unique key is arbitrarily chosen as more relevant in the table design and is called a **primary key**. This is indicated by <pk> in Figure 10.1.

In most practical situations, it is essential that each table has a primary key to identify its rows. This is equivalent to using *object identifiers* in object systems to identify each object of a class (Maciaszek, 2001). Even though that is the case, most relational DBMSs permit tables without a unique identifier, which means that duplicate rows can be inserted. The duplicate rows have exactly the same values in all columns visible to the user. Internally, however, the DBMS would maintain the unique identification by means of a special pseudo-column called `row_id` or similar.

By definition, a primary key does not allow `null` values. A **null** value, if allowed for a column, means that the column may have no value in some rows. There may be two reasons for it: the value is not currently known or the value is not allowed (does not apply) for a given row.

Once the table structure is defined within a CASE tool, the tool can automatically generate the SQL `create table` statement. For Figure 10.1, this will result in a SQL script that will contain the `create table` statement as shown in Listing 10.2 (the informational comment in the last line has been added after the script was generated). If the CASE tool is connected to the database, the developer can request that the script be automatically run on the database so that the table is immediately created. If not, the script can be saved in a file and executed at a later time. The table definitions created in this process are known as a **database schema**.

Listing 10.2 Create table statement

```
Create table movie

create table movie (
    movie_code          NUMBER(5)                   not null,
    movie_title         VARCHAR2(30),
    director            VARCHAR2(20),
    constraint PK_MOVIE primary key (movie_code)
)
/ -- Oracle permits using / instead of ; to terminate SQL statements
```

Referential Integrity   10.1.2

Because the relational model explicitly disallows **navigational links** (Section 10.1), relational databases represent conceptual relationships between records of tables by means of the principle of referential integrity. **Referential integrity** uses the notion of a foreign key to link records in one table to records in another (or even the same) table.

A **foreign key** is a set of columns (frequently just one column), whose values correspond to the values of the primary key in another (or the same) table. This correspondence of foreign and primary key values establishes links between records.

Figure 10.2 provides an example of tables linked by referential integrity. The graphical notation used in Figure 10.2 is known as a **logical database model**. When extended with the storage and other physical properties of the underlying DBMS, the model is called a **physical database model**.

The model in Figure 10.2 links actors and movies. Each record in the table `listed_as` links one actor to one movie and gives the position number at which the actor is listed (in order to distinguish between the leading and supporting actors). The primary key of `listed_as` consists of two columns: `actor_code` and `movie_code`. `actor_code` alone is a foreign key `<fk1>` to the records in actor, and `movie_code` alone is a foreign key `<fk2>` to `movie`. Note that in this case no `null` values can be allowed for `actor_code` and `movie_code` although, in general, null values may be permitted for a foreign key (to capture the fact that a foreign key record is not linked to any record in the primary table).

The arrows show the direction of the foreign-to-primary key mapping. They also represent one-to-many relationships between the tables. The same actor can play in multiple movies and he/she will then be listed multiple times in `listed_as`. Similarly, one movie links to many `actors`. The relationships are annotated with the referential integrity equality constraints. Each value of `movie_code` in `listed_as` must have the corresponding `movie_code` value in `movie`. The same principle applies to `actor _code`.

Listing 10.3 provides sample database content for the database schema in Figure 10.2. Analysis of the content can help in understanding the referential integrity principle.

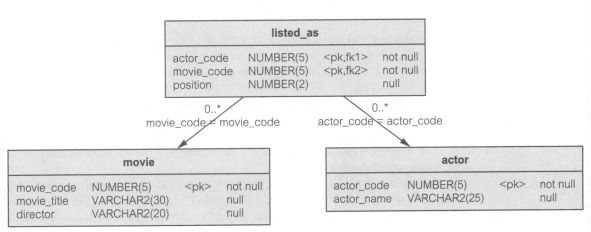

Figure 10.2 Logical database model for MovieActor

Listing 10.3 MovieActor database content

```
Select statements to display MovieActor database content
SQL> select * from movie;
MOVIE_CODE MOVIE_TITLE                     DIRECTOR
---------- --------------------------      ----------------
        10 Interview with the Vampire      Neil Jordan
        11 The Birdcage                    Mike Nichols

SQL> select * from actor;

ACTOR_CODE ACTOR_NAME
---------- --------------------------
       100 Brad Pitt
       101 Tom Cruise
       102 Antonio Banderas
       105 Robin Williams
       106 Gene Hackman

SQL> select * from listed_as;

ACTOR_CODE MOVIE_CODE POSITION
---------- ---------- --------
       100         10        1
       101         10        2
       102         10        3
       105         11        1
       106         11        2
```

10.1.3 Conceptual versus Logical Database Models

Database modeling can be performed at various levels of abstraction. Working with **abstraction** means that modeling decisions are taken about the level of detail at which the model is presented. Details considered irrelevant to the abstraction level are omitted from the model.

A logical database model, such as in Figure 10.2, makes a commitment to the relational database technology, which links data objects by referential integrity. In fact, the model in Figure 10.2 also makes a commitment to a particular DBMS (Oracle). A model at a higher level of abstraction, which does not make a commitment to the database technology, is called a **conceptual database model**.

The **entity–relationship** (ER) modeling technique is the best-known technique for conceptual database modeling (Section 2.1.2). Figure 10.3, used before as Figure 2.5, uses the ER notation to represent the conceptual model that corresponds to the logical model in Figure 10.2.

A conceptual database model can also be presented using the UML class diagram. This capability of class diagrams has already been taken advantage of in Chapter 7 (when

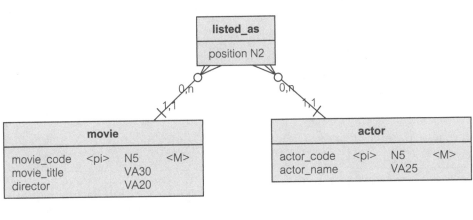

Figure 10.3
Conceptual
ER model for
MovieActor

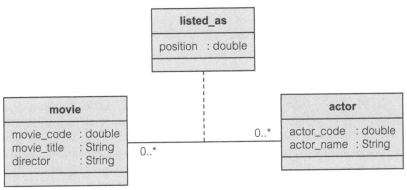

Figure 10.4
Conceptual UML
class model for
MovieActor

discussing domain class modeling) and Chapter 8 (when presenting the conceptual class model for Iteration 1 – Figure 8.8).

The class diagram in Figure 10.4 corresponds to the ER diagram in Figure 10.3. An interesting aspect of this example is that it leads to the UML concept of association class. An **association class** is a class that represents an association relationship between other classes. Modeling with an association class is needed when an association itself has attributes and a class is required to store these attributes. `listed_as` is an association class in Figure 10.4, illustrated by a dashed line from it to the association relationship.

Implementing Business Rules   10.1.4

A database is a collection of records related by referential integrity. These relationships between records must be valid from the business perspective. They must follow the **business rules**. The enforcement of business rules in the database requires that database modification operations must pass the rules before they can be allowed to proceed. SQL provides three modification operations: `insert`, `update`, and `delete`. Therefore the completion of each of these operations is subject to passing the business rules programmed into the database.

Some rules are simple and apply in a similar way to many records in the database. For example: 'If a `movie` record is deleted then all linked `listed_as` records must also be

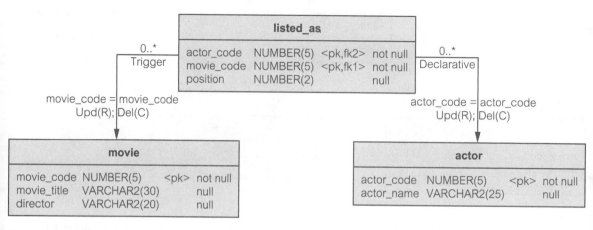

Figure 10.5 Logical database schema with business rule indicators for MovieActor

deleted'. Other rules are more complex and are exclusive to particular tables and to particular relationships between records. For example: 'Brad Pitt is always the leading actor (listed as position number one) in all Neil Jordan's movies in which he appears'.

Declarative referential integrity can be used in a relational database to implement many simple and repetitive business rules. Declarative referential integrity is implemented as a simple declaration in a SQL `create table` (or `alter table`) statement, which states what to do when a record in that table is to be deleted, updated, or inserted (the last possibility is not available in many DBMSs). The exact implementation of declarative referential integrity is up to the DBMS.

More complex and exclusive business rules require **procedural referential integrity** enforcement. This involves the use of a database programming language, unique to each DBMS. Programs written in such language to enforce the business rules are known as **triggers**. A separate trigger may be written for each of the three modification operations on each table. In this scenario, each table can have up to three triggers. Some DBMSs (e.g. Oracle) allow splitting of these three triggers according to various conditions, thus allowing for more than three triggers on a table.

Figure 10.5 shows how a logical database schema can be graphically enhanced to indicate declarative or procedural integrity enforcement. The model shows that the referential integrity on the right-hand relationship is declarative and that it is procedural (trigger) on the left-hand relationship. The deletion of an actor or a movie must cascade – `Del(C)` – to the linked records in `listed_as` (i.e. they must also be deleted). The updates are restricted – `Upd(R)`. This means that an attempt to update `actor_code` in `actor` or `movie_code` in `movie` to a different value will be disallowed by the DBMS because this is likely to break the referential integrity (for example, updating `movie_code` in `movie`, without at the same time updating that `movie_code` in `listed_as`, will produce incorrect database content).

In most DBMSs, the support for the declarative referential integrity of delete and update operations allows for three options: `cascade`, `restrict`, and `nullify` (set null). The last option means that if a primary key is updated or a record is deleted from a primary table, then the corresponding foreign key values will be set to `null`. Some DBMSs allow a fourth option – to set foreign key values to some `default` value, instead of `null`.

Listing 10.4 illustrates declarative referential integrity. The integrity is enforced in the `alter table` statement. Although the `add constraint` option is allowed in the `create table` statement, it will result in error in this case. This is because the table `actor` does not exist when the table `listed_as` is created, therefore the `add constraint` option would not be able to reference it.

Listing 10.4 Declarative referential integrity with on delete cascade in MovieActor

```
Declarative referential integrity with on delete cascade in MovieActor

SQL> CREATE TABLE listed_as (
  2     actor_code    NUMBER(5),
  3     movie_code    NUMBER(5),
  4     position      NUMBER(2),
  5     PRIMARY KEY (actor_code, movie_code)
  6  ) ;

SQL> CREATE TABLE actor (
  2     actor_code    NUMBER(5),
  3     actor_name    VARCHAR2(25),
  4     PRIMARY KEY (actor_code)
  5  ) ;

SQL> ALTER TABLE listed_as
  2     ADD CONSTRAINT fk_const3 FOREIGN KEY  (actor_code)
  3     REFERENCES actor
  4     ON DELETE CASCADE;
```

Listing 11.5 illustrates procedural referential integrity. The trigger program performs a simple delete of all `listed_as` records with the `movie_code` values corresponding to the `movie_code` value in the just deleted `movie` record. This trigger does a similar job to the declarative integrity presented in Figure 10.4 and it could be replaced by a declarative integrity. CASE tools are able to automatically generate trigger programs as a replacement for any declarative integrity. For more complex business rules, the triggers must be programmed manually.

Listing 10.5 Procedural referential integrity with delete trigger in MovieActor

```
Procedural referential integrity with delete trigger in MovieActor

create trigger tda_movie after delete
on movie for each row
begin
    -- Delete all children in "listed_as"
    delete listed_as
    where movie_code = :old.movie_code;
end;
/
```

10.1.5 Programming Database Application Logic

Triggers demonstrate that relational databases are not just passive containers of data. Relational databases are active – they can be programmed and the programs are stored in the database and can be executed from it. This introduces an important system development question. Should the database application logic be programmed in the application program on the client process or in the database on the server process?

The answer is typical: it depends. Programming the database application logic in the client program requires using a programmatic variant of SQL (this is called **embedded SQL**). Each SQL statement in the program (such as shown in Listing 10.6) is transmitted to the database where it can be parsed, validated, optimized, compiled, and executed. If the program has many SQL statements and frequently accesses the database, the process is costly and can impact on the performance of the whole system. However, there are many situations where SQL statements to the database are constructed dynamically at runtime during the program's execution and require the user's input before they can be constructed. These kinds of SQL statement may have to stay in the client program.

Listing 10.6 Embedded SQL select in MovieActor application program

```
Embedded SQL select in MovieActor application program

-- Display the leading actor for each movie
EXECUTE SELECT movie_title, actor_name
        FROM movie m, listed_as l, actor a
          WHERE m.movie_code = l.movie_code
            AND l.actor_code = a.actor_code
            AND l.position = 1;
```

In most other situations, the database application logic should be programmed in the database server as a **stored procedure** (i.e. a program that is stored in the database and can be invoked from there). Each DBMS has its own variant of the programming language for stored procedures and triggers (triggers are special kinds of stored procedures, which cannot be directly called because they 'fire' automatically when a table is modified).

Listing 10.7 is an example of an Oracle stored procedure that searches for movies with a given string in `movie_title`. Following the `create procedure` statement, there are two calls to it with `execute` statements. In this case, the execute statements are run from the SQL interactive programming environment, but normally they will be part of the client application program. Note that stored procedures can have input and output arguments. Note also the use of the `upper` function to account for the fact that column values in the database are case sensitive (but SQL statements are not case sensitive, as mentioned in Section 10.1.1).

Stored procedures can take not only input parameters, but also output and input/output parameters. Although the output parameters return values to the caller, it may be more convenient to use a stored function instead of a stored procedure. A **stored function** is a block of code stored in a database, which always returns a single value of a specified type.

Listing 10.7 Stored procedure in MovieActor database

```
Stored procedure in MovieActor database
```
```
SQL> -- String search for a movie using stored procedure
SQL> CREATE OR REPLACE PROCEDURE string_search (string IN VARCHAR2) AS
  2         CURSOR c1 IS
  3              SELECT movie_title AS found
  4              FROM movie
  5              WHERE UPPER(movie_title) LIKE '%'||UPPER(string)||'%';
  6         BEGIN
  7           FOR c1rec IN c1 LOOP
  8                dbms_output.put_line
                   ('Found movie title: '||LPAD(c1rec.found,30));
  9           END LOOP;
 10         END string_search;
 11  /

Procedure created.

SQL> EXECUTE string_search('vamp');
Found movie title:     Interview with the Vampire

SQL> EXECUTE string_search('the');
Found movie title:     Interview with the Vampire
Found movie title:               The Birdcage
```

In some DBMSs stored procedures and functions can be grouped into packages. A **database package** is made up of two parts: a specification and a body. The specification contains declarations and signatures of procedures and functions included in the package. The body contains the implementations of procedures and functions.

Listing 10.8 shows a database package called MovieSearch with two functions. The string_search function has the same functionality as the string_search stored procedure in Listing 10.7. The leading_actors function performs the task of the select statement in Listing 10.6.

Indexes

Relational databases do not support pointer-based navigational paths between records. As a consequence, in most relational databases, indexes are the only access paths to records in a table other than a sequential scan of the entire table.

An **index** is a data structure, separate from data pages that store table records, which consists of a hierarchical tree of index nodes. The nodes contain key–pointer pairs. The index keys hold values extracted from one or more columns of the table for which the index has been constructed. The key values are kept in sorted order. The index pointers in non-leaf nodes (i.e. not at the bottom of the tree) point to the nodes in the next lower level

Listing 10.8 Package and functions in MovieActor

```
Package and functions in MovieActor

create or replace package MovieSearch as
    type ref_cursor is REF CURSOR;
    function string_search(string in VARCHAR2) return ref_cursor;
    function leading_actors return ref_cursor;
end MovieSearch;
/


create or replace package body MovieSearch is
    function string_search(string in VARCHAR2) return ref_cursor is
    cur ref_cursor;
    begin
        open cur for
            SELECT *
            from movie where UPPER(movie_title) like
                                    '%'||UPPER(string)||'%';
        return cur;
    end;
    function leading_actors return ref_cursor is
    cur ref_cursor;
    begin
        open cur for
            SELECT *
            FROM movie m, actor a, listed_as l
            WHERE m.movie_code = l.movie_code AND l.actor_code =
                                                a.actor_code
AND l.position = 1
        return cur;
    end;
end MovieSearch;
/
```

of the tree. The index pointers in leaf nodes point to (or directly contain) table records, which have the same key value as in the index node.

Relational databases permit the dynamic creation and dropping of indexes with SQL `create index` and `drop index` statements. The process supports **physical data independence**. The application programs can perform their database tasks with or without indexes. However, the performance of programs can vary significantly depending on the current setup of indexes in the database.

In general, the applications depend entirely on a DBMS with regard to whether or not an index will be used for a given operation on a database. Clearly, a DBMS can use an index only if a database programmer created the index. This does not mean, however, that a large number of indexes should be created just in case a DBMS elects to use them. Indexes introduce a significant maintenance cost for a DBMS.

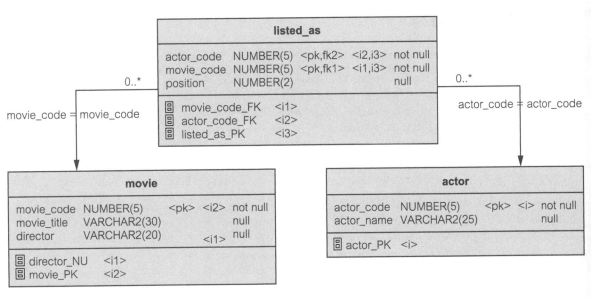

Figure 10.6 Indexes in a physical database model for MovieActor

The changes to database records necessitate making corresponding changes in indexes. These changes to indexes (index rebuilding) are done automatically, in the background, by a DBMS, but the performance of all applications currently 'talking to' the database may suffer. The tradeoff is clear. Intensive modifications of a database with many indexes may slow down the response time of applications, but extensive searches in a database with many indexes can demonstrate performance boosts. The task of a database developer is to create an index mix that delivers the best performance for the whole set of application programs accessing the database.

Apart from performance, indexes are a DBMS vehicle to guarantee **uniqueness** of records in tables. Since a primary key defines such uniqueness, a DBMS constructs an index for each primary key defined in a database. If not explicitly requested by a programmer, the primary key indexes are created implicitly by a DBMS.

Typically, a programmer should create indexes on foreign keys in support of referential integrity (Section 10.1.2). In most cases, foreign key indexes are **non-unique** (i.e. a table can have many records with the same foreign key value). The `create index` statement provides an option to request a unique index. Otherwise, the index is created as non-unique.

Figure 10.6 shows a physical database model obtained by adding indexes to the logical database model in Figure 10.2. The `actor` table has only the primary key index. The `movie` table has the primary key index and the index called `director_NU` specified as a non-unique (NU) index on the `director` column. The `listed_as` table has the primary key index (unique) and two foreign key indexes (non-unique). The `listed_as_PK` index is defined jointly on the two primary key columns: `actor_code` and `movie_code`.

Once a physical database model is defined within a CASE tool, the tool can automatically generate a script to create all database tables and indexes. Listing 10.9 demonstrates such script for the design in Figure 10.6. Note that, depending on the setting of the generation options, primary key indexes can be created explicitly (as for the `actor` table) or implicitly (as for the `movie` table). The latter option is normally preferred.

Listing 10.9 SQL statements to create tables and indexes in MovieActor database

```
SQL statements to create tables and indexes in MovieActor database
```

```
/*===============================================================*/
/* Table: actor                                                  */
/*===============================================================*/
create table actor (
   actor_code              NUMBER(5)                        not null,
   actor_name              VARCHAR2(25)
)
/
/*===============================================================*/
/* Index: actor_PK                                               */
/*===============================================================*/
create unique index actor_PK on actor (
   actor_code ASC
)
/
/*===============================================================*/
/* Table: movie                                                  */
/*===============================================================*/
create table movie (
   movie_code              NUMBER(5)                        not null,
   movie_title             VARCHAR2(30),
   director                VARCHAR2(20),
   constraint PK_MOVIE primary key (movie_code)
)
/
/*===============================================================*/
/* Index: director_NU                                            */
/*===============================================================*/
create index director_NU on movie (
   director ASC
)
/
/*===============================================================*/
/* Table: listed_as                                              */
/*===============================================================*/
create table listed_as (
   actor_code              NUMBER(5)                        not null,
   movie_code              NUMBER(5)                        not null,
   position                NUMBER(2),
   constraint PK_LISTED_AS primary key (actor_code, movie_code),
   constraint FK_LISTED_A_REFERENCE_ACTOR foreign key (actor_code)
        references actor (actor_code)
   on delete cascade
```

```
)
/
/*================================================================*/
/* Index: movie_code_FK                                           */
/*================================================================*/
create index movie_code_FK on listed_as (
    movie_code ASC
)
/
/*================================================================*/
/* Index: actor_code_FK                                           */
/*================================================================*/
create index actor_code_FK on listed_as (
    actor_code ASC
)
/
```

Mapping Transient Objects to Persistent Records

The mapping between **transient objects** in an application program and **persistent records** in a database used by the application has a number of dimensions of increasing level of intricacy. Moreover, depending on whether or not the database is in existence before an application is developed, the mapping starts as either a forward engineering or a reverse engineering activity.

The mapping can take the following forms:

1. Forward mapping of conceptual classes (Section 8.3) to tables.

2. Reverse mapping of tables to conceptual classes is normally replaced by two concurrent steps:
   (a) reverse mapping of tables to design classes (Section 9.1.1), and
   (b) forward mapping of conceptual classes to design classes.

3. Forward mapping of design classes to tables. Because design classes specify both attributes and operations, the mapping involves also the active aspects of tables, namely triggers and stored procedures.

4. Reverse mapping of tables to design classes. This includes a resolution of such issues as how the application is affected by trigger activations and stored procedure invocations.

5. Caching of table records as class objects in the program's memory. This includes adherence to the success or failure of database transactions, and the resulting commits or rollbacks of database changes.

The mapping can also be influenced by the presence of database middleware software and APIs between the client application programs and the corporate relational database server. The middleware can in effect lead to a three-tier architecture with a persistent object data store between an application and the relational database. A bit of history of object database model is in place.

10.2.1 Object Databases, SQL:1999, and Impedance Mismatch

The object database model is a competitor of the relational model. The Object Data Management Group (ODMG) develops the standards for object databases. Object DBMSs gained considerable attention in the mid 1990s, in particular in niche database applications concerned with multimedia and workgroup processing.

In recent years, the ODMG standards have made a shift from specifying an object DBMS to defining an Object Storage API. The task of an Object Storage API is to provide a layer of software between the application program and the relational (or other) database in order to map the application's objects to relational records and vice versa. The mapping may involve the use of a persistent object database. The main purpose of such an object database is to do the mapping and rely on the relational database for more routine database functions, such as transaction management.

From the perspective of the PCMEF framework (Section 9.2.2), placing an Object Storage API between an application and a relational database results in moving many of the tasks performed by the domain and foundation classes to the Object Storage API. The design of these classes must now conform to the Object Storage API and it is partly subsumed by the API.

The rise and demise of object databases has been marked by the emergence of a new object-relational database standard, SQL:1999. The new standard attempts to add object-oriented features to the relational model. The task is very difficult because of the underlying philosophical disparities between the object and the relational model, such as that regarding the use of navigational links. The task of making tables look like objects results in a complex layer of supporting software, which has so far failed to gain significant take up by the developers. This includes the object-oriented features in Oracle, starting from Oracle8.

SQL:1999 does not eliminate one of the main stumbling blocks in communication between application programs and relational databases – the impedance mismatch. This refers to the impossibility of using the application language (such as Java) to directly manipulate the data in the database without the need to engage SQL. The declarative nature of SQL manipulates data as sets of records. All popular application languages are procedural in nature and manipulate data as individual records. They are record-at-a-time languages, as opposed to the SQL set-at-a-time processing. SQL provides the cursor mechanism (Listing 10.7) to address the mismatch.

The impedance mismatch is a reason to develop a mapping strategy from classes to tables and vice versa. But it is not the only reason. The other reason is a necessary separation between the persistent records in a database and transient entity objects in an application program's memory cache. In most large systems, caching of records retrieved from the database as objects accessible to the program is a major design undertaking. This issue is partly addressed in Chapter 12 and in more depth in Part 4. The following section discusses only the mapping of conceptual classes to tables.

Object-Relational Mapping

10.2.2

Section 10.1.3 contains an example of the mapping of tables in a logical database model to conceptual classes in a UML class model. To the extent of the limits of logical database modeling, the example is quite far-reaching.

This section is concerned with the mapping of conceptual classes (in an object-oriented program) to tables (in a relational database). This is frequently called object-relational mapping (Martin, 2003) – a bit of an 'overloaded' term, not to be confused with the notion of an object-relational database. The mapping is bidirectional. It can be *from objects to tables*, when a database is not in existence during application design. It can be *from tables to objects*, when a database pre-exists and when an application program maintains an in-memory cache of database data (Chapter 12).

The semantic power of logical database modeling is limited in comparison with the semantic expressiveness of class modeling. This reflects the underlying simplicity of the relational model – table and referential integrity are the only two modeling primitives. Object-oriented concepts, such as type inheritance, interfaces, aggregation, etc., are not part of the relational model. Frequently, procedural solutions need to be programmed into the relational database to fully express the semantics of a declarative model presented in a class diagram.

Conceptual classes are merely containers of data. Operations are normally not considered in conceptual classes. This makes the mapping to tables simpler. The main challenge is in the mapping of relationships between classes. The relationships to consider include associations with various multiplicities, aggregations, and generalizations.

Except for the simplest class models, there is more than one possible outcome for mapping of each relationship. The following sections present the most likely outcomes. There is only one mapping provided for each scenario, but major alternative solutions are raised in the discussion that follows. To facilitate understanding and comparison of the mechanics of mappings, all examples apply to identical class structures and use symbolic class and attribute names. A CASE tool was used to generate all mapping results.

Mapping a one-to-many association and aggregation

One-to-many associations between conceptual classes are the most frequently used, and also the easiest to understand and to map to tables. A class on the one-end of the association is mapped to a table without any changes other than applying relational data types to the columns. A class on the many-end of the association is mapped to another table with a foreign key added to implement the association in terms of the relational referential integrity.

As discussed briefly in Section 7.4.2, aggregation is used infrequently in conceptual class modeling. Despite its great modeling potential, the UML underplays the importance of aggregation and treats it as just a special kind of association. Consequently, the mapping of associations and aggregations to tables brings similar or identical outcomes.

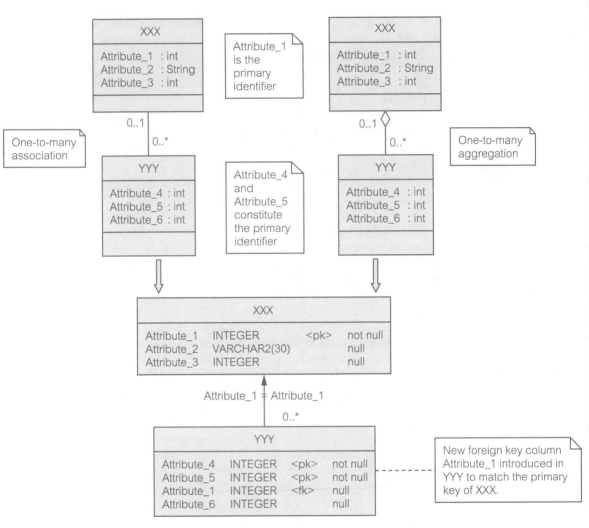

Figure 10.7 Mapping a one-to-many association and aggregation

Figure 10.7 gives an example where a one-to-many association, and an identical one-to-many aggregation, are mapped to a table structure. Clearly, any extra semantics of the aggregation, in comparison with the association, are lost in the mapping. Any such semantics will need to be implemented separately in the procedural logic of the database.

The mapping assumes that identifiers were defined on the conceptual classes as indicated in the notes in Figure 10.7. The UML does not have a visual way of showing class identifiers except as auxiliary stereotypes or notes. This is consistent with the object-oriented philosophy that objects are identified by automatically generated immutable object identifiers (OIDs) (Maciaszek, 2001), rather than by using user-defined attributes. However, most CASE tools allow identifiers to be defined by entering them as additional properties of class attributes.

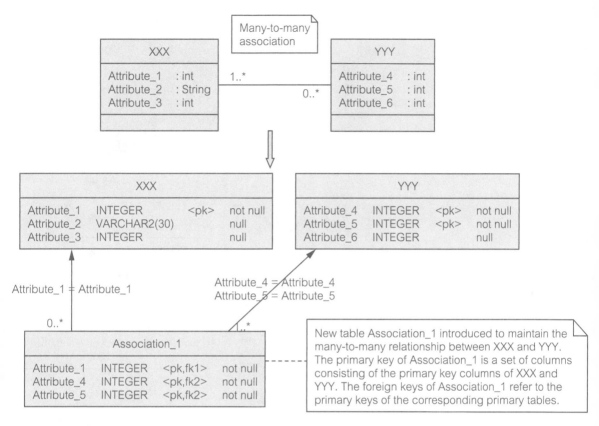

Figure 10.8 Mapping a many-to-many association

`Attribute_1` introduced in YYY as the foreign key permits `null` values. This reflects the optional participation of YYY objects in the association with XXX. If the multiplicity were defined as `1..1`, thus signifying mandatory participation, then `Attribute_1` would be defined as `not null`.

Mapping a many-to-many association

The relational database model is unable to directly maintain a many-to-many relationship between tables. This is because a foreign key value in any record can refer to at most one primary key value in another record. To capture a many-to-many relationship, the relational model is forced to introduce a "relationship table" to convert one many-to-many association on classes to two one-to-many relationships on tables.

Figure 10.8 shows an example. The attached note explains the mapping principle. Observe that `Attribute_1` in `Association_1` is defined as `not null` even though it is the foreign key to XXX, as in Figure 10.7 where it was allowing `null` values. A simple explanation is that `Attribute_1` is also part of the `Association_1` primary key and no part of a primary key can accept `null` values. A deeper explanation is that any YYY record with `null` value in `Attribute_1` in Figure 10.7 can still appear as a YYY record

Figure 10.9
Mapping a one-to-
one association

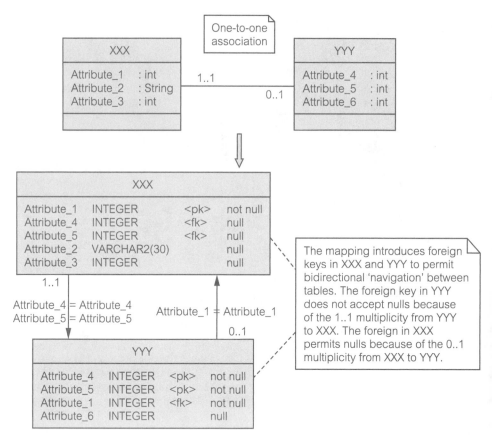

in Figure 10.8, but YYY does not host Attribute_1 values. YYY, which does not link to XXX, will simply have no record in Association_1.

Mapping a one-to-one association

One-to-one associations between classes may be the simplest to understand but they are certainly not the simplest to convert to a relational model. The mapping offered in Figure 10.9 is the most direct but introduces excessive duplication of columns and circular dependencies.

Depending on circumstances, a better solution may be to combine both classes into a single table. Alternatively, a solution like that in Figure 10.8, which extracts foreign keys into a 'relationship table', may be preferred. Observe also that a 'relationship table' is necessary in all cases where an association class (cf. Figure 10.4) is defined on any association between classes, including one-to-one association.

Mapping a one-to-many recursive association

Recursive (that is, **self-referential**) associations set up on a single class are not infrequent in modeling. A classic textbook example of a one-to-many recursive association is an

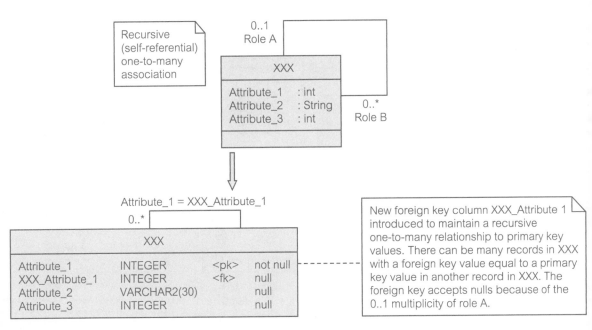

Figure 10.10 Mapping a one-to-many recursive association

association to capture the hierarchical structure of employees in an organization. In such a structure, an employee who is a manager manages other employees who are subordinates. A subordinate employee is responsible to only one managing employee.

Figure 10.10 shows a UML notation for recursive associations and the mapping to a relational structure. The mapping introduces a foreign key column, which is obtained from the definition of the primary identifier. Foreign key values in XXX match a primary key value in XXX (except when a foreign key value is `null`).

Mapping a many-to-many recursive association

A classic textbook example for a many-to-many recursive association is the 'bill of materials' problem, known also as explosion and implosion of parts. Products consist of parts (a computer consists of a processor, memory, etc.). Each part can consist of smaller parts (subparts). The same subpart (as a concept, not an instance) can be used in the production of various products. In fact, the product itself is a part in this approach. Clearly, the association on parts is recursive and many-to-many.

As shown in Figure 10.11, the mapping of a recursive many-to-many association is reminiscent of the mapping of a many-to-many association on two classes (Figure 10.8). A "relationship table" is required to express such an association.

Mapping generalization

As discussed in Section 7.4.2, the use of **generalization** for conceptual class modeling is not particularly encouraged. Moreover, the mapping target, i.e. the relational database

Figure 10.11
Mapping a many-
to-many recursive
association

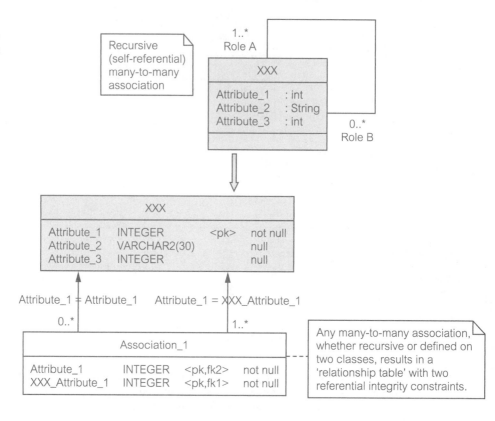

model, does not understand the inheritance of attributes that underpins the notion of generalization.

Inheritance can only be imperfectly simulated in the relational model. One solution is a straight duplication of superclass attributes in a 'subclass table'. Another solution is not to have a 'superclass table' at all and to make a 'subclass table' to represent both generic (superclass) and specific (subclass) types. A solution that seems most appealing is shown in Figure 10.12. The primary identifier of a superclass is duplicated in the 'subclass table' and used as its primary key (or part of its primary key) and as the foreign key to the 'superclass table'.

10.3 Database Design and Creation for Email Management

Iteration 1 of the EM case study assumes that the database pre-exists and is loaded with data about employees, contacts, and outmessages. The EM application program retrieves this information from the database, prepares and sends emails (outmessages), and updates the database to mark which outmessages have already been sent. The next

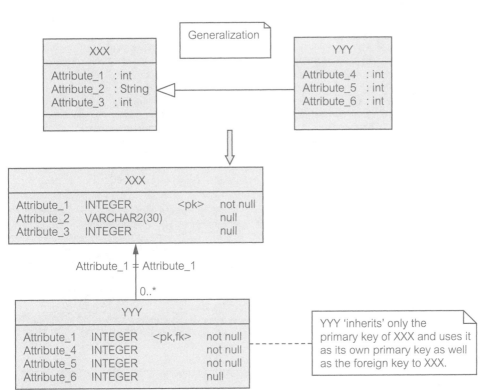

Figure 10.12
Mapping
generalization

iterations will allow outmessages and related information from the application program to be inserted.

The conceptual class diagram for EM was defined as part of the Iteration 1 requirements in Chapter 8 (Figure 8.8). The diagram is repeated below in Figure 10.13 for convenience.

Database Model   10.3.1

Figure 10.14 presents a physical database model obtained from the conceptual model in Figure 10.13. The model is physical, not just logical, because it defines physical characteristics (indexes) and it applies data types of a particular DBMS (Oracle). The mapping from the conceptual model is very direct and self-explanatory.

Apart from implicit indexes on primary keys, an extra unique index is defined on `login_name` in the `Employee` table (`login_UN`). This index is used to authenticate that the user of the program works under the database `login_name` that is listed in the `Employee` table. Such a user is then considered a legitimate employee who is authorized to use the EM system.

There are no indexes defined on foreign keys. It is considered that the tables will contain a relatively small number of records (in thousands rather than millions) and foreign key indexes will rarely be used by the DBMS while still creating a maintenance cost.

Figure 10.13
Conceptual class
diagram for EM

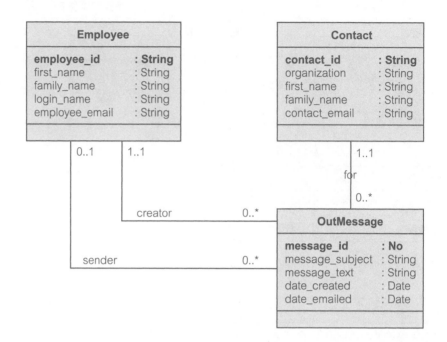

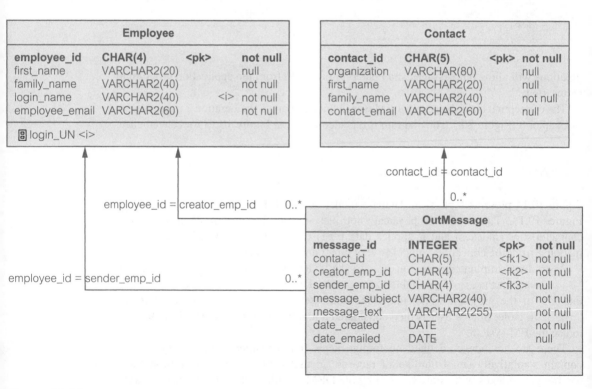

Figure 10.14 Logical database schema for EM

Creating the Database Schema

A CASE tool can automatically generate SQL create statements from a physical database model. These statements can be run on a database to create a database schema (database table structure). Listing 10.10 presents such an automatically generated SQL script for creating the schema for EM.

Listing 10.10 SQL script to create the EM database schema

```
Script to create the EM database schema

/*===============================================================*/
/*Table: Contact                                                 */
/*===============================================================*/
create table Contact (
   contact_id           CHAR(5)                           not null,
   organization         VARCHAR(80),
   first_name           VARCHAR2(20),
   family_name          VARCHAR2(40)                      not null,
   contact_email        VARCHAR2(60),
   constraint PK_CONTACT primary key (contact_id)
)
/
/*===============================================================*/
/*Table: Employee                                                */
/*===============================================================*/
create table Employee (
   employee_id          CHAR(4)                           not null,
   first_name           VARCHAR2(20),
   family_name          VARCHAR2(40)                      not null,
   login_name           VARCHAR2(40)                      not null,
   employee_email       VARCHAR2(60)                      not null,
   constraint PK_EMPLOYEE primary key (employee_id)
)
/
/*===============================================================*/
/* Index: login_UN                                               */
/*===============================================================*/
create unique index login_UN on Employee (
   login_name ASC
)
/
/*===============================================================*/
/* Table: OutMessage                                             */
/*===============================================================*/
```

```
create table OutMessage (
   message_id            INTEGER                          not null,
   contact_id            CHAR(5)                          not null,
   creator_emp_id        CHAR(4)                          not null,
   sender_emp_id         CHAR(4),
   message_subject       VARCHAR2(40)                     not null,
   message_text          VARCHAR2(255)                    not null,
   date_created          DATE                             not null,
   date_emailed          DATE,
constraint PK_OUTMESSAGE primary key (message_id),
constraint FK_OUTMES_REF_CONTACT foreign key (contact_id)
      references Contact (contact_id),
constraint FK_OUTMES_REF_CREATOREMP foreign key (creator_emp_id)
      references Employee (employee_id),
constraint FK_OUTMES_REF_SENDEREMP foreign key (sender_emp_id)
      references Employee (employee_id)
)
/
```

10.3.3 Sample Database Content

After the schema is created on a database, the table structures can be loaded (populated) with data. Iteration 1 of EM assumes that the database is loaded and that the loading occurs from many points of the overall AEM system. For the purpose of this book, a SQL script with insert statements to load the database will suffice (the script, like all other code for the case study, is available from the book website).

Listing 10.11 presents sample database content for EM after the insert script was run to load the data. The analysis of the database content can be useful for better understanding of the processing requirements of the EM system.

Listing 10.11 Sample content of EM database

Sample content of EM database

```
SQL> select * from Employee;


EMPLOYEE_ID FIRST_NAME FAMILY_NAME LOGIN_NAME EMPLOYEE_EMAIL
---------- --------- ---------- --------- ----------------------
E011        Leszek     Maciaszek   leszek11   leszek@ics.mq.edu.au
E012        Bruc Lee   Liong       bruc11     bliong@ics.mq.edu.au
E013        Stephen    Bills       steve11    sbills@acnielsen.com.au
```

```
SQL> select * from Contact;

CONTACT_ID ORGANIZATION FIRST_NAME FAMILY_NAME CONTACT_EMAIL
---------- ------------------ ---------- ----------- ------------------
C1234      SBS Sydney   Pablo      Romero      promero@sbs.com.au
C4321      Channel 9    Vincent    Buckley     vbuckley@chnine.com.au
C2233      ABC Radio    Dorothy    Norris      dnorris@abc.com.au
C5887      Ford         Agatha     Sommer      asommer@ford.com.au
           Australia

SQL> select contact_id, creator_emp_id, sender_emp_id,
message_subject, message_text
  2  from OutMessage
  3  order by contact_id;

CONTACT_ID CREATOR_EMP_ID SENDER_EMP_ID MESSAGE_SUBJECT
---------- -------------- ------------- --------------------
MESSAGE_TEXT
-----------------------------------------------------------------
----------------------
C1234      E011                         Product missing
The Product name for your ad CI223375XY is missing. Can you please
supply it?

C2233      E012                         Log incomplete
Log LG02JUN20 does not contain any ad instances between 1 and 4 pm.
Please re-send a corrected log.

C2233      E011                         Log incorrect
Log SZ020620B contains ad instances that overlap with program times
between 9:30 and 11:00 am. Looks like durations of some ad instances
are incorrect.

C4321      E011                         Agency missing
What is the agency which booked the advertisement DL5FG88779, please?

C5887      E013                         Contract renewal
Your contract with us is due for renewal next month. We will mail
the new contract to you for your signing at the beginning of next
month. Please inform us if you require changes to the existing
contract details.

C5887      E011                         Are you satisfied?

This is just a courtesy email to ask if you are satisfied with the
quality and timeliness of the advertising expenditure reports that
we supply to you as per our current contract. Please let me know if
our service can be improved in any way.
```

Summary

1. A *database* is large, persistent, multi-user shareable, recoverable, consistent, secure, and extensible.

2. The dominant database model for business information systems is the *relational model*. The relational model presents data as *records* (rows) in *tables* (relations).

3. *SQL* is the language for processing data in relational databases. There are two main variants of SQL: *interactive SQL* and *embedded SQL*.

4. A relational *database schema* is a set of table definitions for a particular domain. Tables are linked and integrated by means of *referential integrity* constraints.

5. A database schema can be presented at different levels of abstraction – as a *conceptual* database model, *logical* database model, or *physical* database model.

6. Business rules, that a database must obey, can be programmed by means of *declarative referential integrity* and *procedural referential integrity* (*triggers*).

7. Application logic can be programmed with *embedded SQL* and as *stored procedures*.

8. *Indexes* are a database technique to improve system performance and to guarantee the uniqueness of records in tables.

9. An important software engineering task is to map between *transient objects* in an application program and *persistent records* in a database. This is called *object-relational mapping*. The mapping is made difficult by the *impedance mismatch*.

Key Terms

abstraction	306	embedded SQL	303, 310
alternate key	*See* unique key	entity–relationship model	306
association class	307	ER	*See* entity–relationship model
business rule	307	foreign key	305
candidate key	*See* unique key	generalization	321
column	303	impedance mismatch	316
conceptual classes	317	index	311
conceptual database model	306	inheritance	322
cursor	316	interactive SQL	303
data model	*See* database model	logical database model	305, 317
database	301	navigational link	302, 305
database management system	301	non-unique index	313
database model	301	null	304
database package	311	Object Data Management Group	316
database schema	304	object database model	316
DBMS	*See* database management system	Object Storage API	316
declarative referential integrity	308	object-relational mapping	317

ODMG	*See* Object Data Management Group	row	*See* record
persistent record	315	self-referential association	*See* recursive association
physical data independence	312	SQL	*See* Structured Query Language
physical database model	305	SQL: 1999	316
primary key	*See* unique key	stored function	310
primitive data type	303	stored procedure	310
procedural referential integrity	308	Structured Query Language	301
programmatic SQL	*See* embedded SQL	table	302, 303
record	302, 303	transaction manager	301
recursive association	320	transient objects	315
referential integrity	305	trigger	308
relation	*See* table	unique index	313
relational database model	301	unique key	304
relational model	*See* relational database model		

Review Questions

Discussion Questions

1. What is the most characteristic difference between relational data structures and object structures? Explain the consequences.

2. Explain how interactive and embedded SQL are used in database application development.

3. Can a foreign key column allow null values? Explain by example.

4. What is the most popular technique for modeling conceptual database structures?

5. Compare declarative and procedural referential integrity. Are they competing or cooperating technologies?

6. Compare the use of embedded SQL and stored procedures in database application development.

7. Discuss the main pros and cons of database indexes.

8. Do object and relational database technologies compete or cooperate? Why do you think this is the case?

Case Study Questions

1. Consider the EM database schema in Figure 10.14. Why is `sender_emp_id` in `OutMessage` allowed `null` values?

2. The design of the `Employee` table in the EM database schema in Figure 10.14 would create problems if applications other than EM wanted to access the same table. What are the problems? How can they be rectified for these other applications and how can the issue be readdressed in EM?

3. The design of the `Contact` table in the EM database schema in Figure 10.14 allows `null` values in columns `organization` and `contact_email`. What are the reasons for allowing null values in these two columns?

Problem-Solving Exercises

Case Study Exercises

1. Consider the EM database schema in Figure 10.14. There is a need to distinguish between an employee who is scheduled to send an outmessage and the actual sender of it. Modify the schema to accommodate this new requirement.

2. Consider the EM database schema in Figure 10.14. There is a need to distinguish between PersonContact and OrganizationContact as two categories of Contact. Although OutMessage is always to a Contact, the contact may be a generic organization's email address. In some cases, this may be the only email address that EM has to any contact in that organization. It is also possible that a PersonContact can be an individual whose organization is not known. Modify the schema to accommodate this new requirement.

Minicase – Contact Information Management

Refer to the CIM (Contact Information Management) minicase in Chapter 9. Answer the following questions whether or not you have a solution to the Chapter 9 minicase questions.

1. Develop a logical database model for CIM.

2. Write a trigger code for the following business rule. If the contact 'is ended', information about its postal and courier address should be deleted from the database. Inserting values into the columns end_date and emp_id_ended 'ends' the contact. Contact is not deleted – it is only marked as ended. The trigger code can be pseudo-code.

3. The trigger requested in Question 2 does not check whether emp_id_ended or date_ended has values or not. It is, therefore, possible to update emp_id_ended and/or date_ended with null values. This means that CourierAddress and PostalAddress can be deleted even if the update is incorrect (i.e. update the column values to null). Provide an improved version of the trigger code that addresses the null issue.

4. In some DBMSs, such as Oracle, the trigger action (e.g. deleting PostalAddress and CourierAddress) can be performed *before* or *after* the trigger event (e.g. updating emp_id_ended and date_ended). When is it appropriate for the trigger to fire *before* or *after* the event?

Chapter

11

Class and Interaction Design

Class design is the process of ensuring that the classes deliver the behavior specified in the use case model (Chapter 8) while conforming to the architectural framework chosen for the system (Chapter 9). Class design starts with the identification of classes (and interfaces) and with their allocation to packages. This is followed by the determination of class features (Section 9.1.1) required by the use case realizations. As a consequence, the class dependencies and relationships are established.

In practice, class design is inseparable from interaction design, so it makes sense to discuss both in one chapter. Once initial classes are chosen, interaction models provide a useful guide for the determination of the class features, in particular for class operations. This chapter begins with the class design and refines it later to accommodate the concerns of the interaction design.

Class design is concerned with the design classes (Section 9.1.1), as opposed to the analysis classes. Class design takes into account the implementation platform. This includes the database solution (Chapter 10) and the programming environment.

The notion of class design includes the design of interfaces (Section 9.1.7). Many interfaces are the consequence of principles and mechanisms required by the architectural framework. They enhance the program's understandability, maintainability, and scalability.

At runtime, an object-oriented system is a set of collaborating objects. Each object provides services as defined by its class. Finding classes is therefore a crucial task of object-oriented analysis and design. System analysis concentrates on finding *conceptual classes* (Section 8.3). Other application classes (Section 8.3) may or may not be addressed in any detail during analysis. During design, application classes are labeled *design classes* – to better reflect their place in the software lifecycle. The adjectives (conceptual, application, design, etc.) may be omitted when they are obvious from the context.

Finding design classes involves two main forces: the demands of use case realizations and the engineering concerns motivated by the architectural design. The flows of events in use case documents (Section 8.2) can guide the designer to focus each class on a single purpose (a class should do one thing). The architectural framework – PCMEF+ in this book (Section 9.2.2) – dictates the allocation of classes to packages, the naming conventions, and the architectural principles that the classes must obey.

Classes must have a reason to exist, a responsibility to fulfill. UML defines **responsibility** as 'a contract or obligation of a classifier' (UML, 2002, p.E-625). The concept of classifier includes classes as well as interfaces. Understandably, interfaces can and should be identified in the process of finding classes.

The main guideline for assigning a responsibility to a class is that the class, which has the relevant data, should perform the responsibility. If all the data is in one class, the problem is solved. If the data is spread across multiple classes, the possible solutions are as follows (Riel, 1996; Larman, 2002):

- Put the responsibility in one class (frequently presentation class) and delegate parts of the work to other classes with data.
- Create a 'third party' class (frequently control or mediator class), assign the responsibility to it, and make it delegate parts of the work to other classes as needed.
- Use an existing class as a 'third party' class.

The following discussion splits the process into finding classes from use case requirements and elaborating the initial design by applying architectural considerations to it. In reality, these two considerations, as well as any other class design considerations, are tackled in parallel. The sequence adopted here is from concretion to abstraction. Use case requirements demand concrete functionality with concrete classes. Abstract classes and interfaces are not a major consideration. The emphasis changes when architectural requirements are taken into account. Non-functional requirements demand interfaces.

Interaction design serves both the purpose of verifying the existing class design and augmenting it with further details. In particular, **signatures** (the argument list) of class operations (methods) can be specified. Two main UML modeling techniques in support of the interaction design are **sequence diagrams** and **communication diagrams** (known as **collaboration diagrams** prior to UML 2.0).

11.1 Finding Classes from Use Case Requirements

Classes must satisfy and deliver the behavior specified in use case requirements. These are **functional requirements** defined in the use case document (Section 8.2). Finding classes from use case requirements involves extracting requirements from the use case document and conceiving of classes and collaborations between classes needed to fulfill these requirements.

The process of finding classes from use case requirements must ensure that classes and collaborations adhere to the architectural framework for the project. Issues to be considered include the interactions between actors and the presentation layer, the control logic of the system and the informational (database) needs of the system. Remember that actors can only communicate with the system via presentation classes.

Conceptual classes, which define business objects in the database, have been identified beforehand (Section 8.3). Conceptual classes become entity classes in the design. There is no immediate need to reconsider them now. Note also that most entity classes are not specific to one use case but apply to the enterprise system as a whole. The issue of the entity package – and its responsibility to *cache* business objects in the program's memory – will be readdressed later (starting from the very next step of finding classes from architectural design).

A systematic approach to finding classes from use case requirements can use a table to list requirements and identify classes. The table can consist of five columns headed as follows:

- *Requirement number* – This is a sequential number for ease of reference. If the requirements management within a project is done properly then requirements are already numbered and stored in the project's CASE repository (Maciaszek, 2001).

- *Requirement definition* – This is the text of the requirement with references to models, diagrams, and figures making up the complete requirement definition.

- *Responsible package and class name* – This column 'finds the class' for the requirement. It identifies the package name and the class name responsible for fulfilling the requirement. If the class name is prefixed with a letter that identifies its package then the listing of the package name is not compulsory. Alternatively, package names can be listed in a separate column.

- *Responsible operation name* – This column gives names to class operations responsible for the requirement. Only the main operations are identified. Secondary operations assisting in completing the service will be defined during interaction design (Chapter 12).

- *Collaborating package, class or interface* – This column identifies the main collaborators of the responsible operation, if the operation is not able to provide the service on its own. The column can contain only the name of a collaborating package, but frequently the class or interface name is also provided.

Finding Classes from Use Case Requirements for Email Management   11.1.1

Table 11.1 assists in finding classes from the use case document for Email Management (Section 8.2). The requirements have been copied from the use case document into the Requirement Definition column. Since EM requirements for Iteration 1 are quite simple, the resulting responsibilities can be combined in a small number of classifiers. In some

Table 11.1 Finding classes from use case requirements

Req. no.	Requirement definition	Responsible package and class name	Responsible operation name	Collaborating package and class or interface
R1	The system displays an informational message and requests that the Employee provides a username and password	presentation PConsole	displayLogin	presentation PConsole
			getUserInput	control CActioner
		control CActioner	login	foundation FConnection
R2	The system attempts to connect the Employee to the EM database	foundation FConnection	getConnection	acquaintance IAConstants, foundation FReader
		foundation FReader	readEmployee	
R3	Upon successful connection, the application displays a menu list of possible options that the Employee can request	presentation PConsole	displayMenu	
R4	If the Employee chooses to exit the EM application by typing 4, the use case ends	presentation PConsole	getUserInput	control CActioner
		control CActioner	exit	foundation FConnection
R5	*S1 – View Unsent Messages*: The information displayed in the console window is as per example in Figure 8.5	presentation PConsole	getUserInput	presentation PConsole
			viewMessages	acquaintance IAConstants, mediator MBroker
		mediator MBroker	retrieveMessages	foundation FReader
		foundation FReader	readMessages readContact	
R6	*S2 – Display Message Text*: The Employee is prompted for a message_id before the text of that message is displayed. A message text is displayed as shown in Figure 8.6	presentation PConsole	getUserInput	presentation PConsole
			displayMessageText	mediator MBroker
R7	*S3 – Email Message*: The Employee is prompted to specify which message_id should be emailed. The Employee types in the message_id, and the email is sent and the database is updated	presentation PConsole	getUserInput	presentation PConsole
			prepareMessage	control CActioner MAPI,
		control CActioner	sendMessage	acquaintance IAConstants, foundation FWriter
		foundation FWriter	updateMessage	

Table 11.1 (cont'd)

Req. no.	Requirement definition	Responsible package and class name	Responsible operation name	Collaborating package and class or interface
R8	*S3 – Email Message*: An informational message is displayed in the console window after successful emailing as shown in Figure 8.7	presentation PConsole	displayConfirmation	
R9	*E1 – Incorrect username or password*: If, in the basic flow, the actor provides an incorrect username or incorrect password (Figure 8.3), the system displays an error message. The system permits the actor to re-enter the username and password or to quit the application. The actor is given three chances of providing correct username and password. If three-times unsuccessful, the system cancels the login and the use case terminates	ref. R1 presentation PConsole control CActioner	displayLoginError exit	presentation PConsole ref. R1, control CActioner foundation FConnection
R10	*E2 – Incorrect option*: If, in the basic flow, the actor provides an incorrect option number (Figure 8.4), the system ignores the entered value and re-displays the list of menu options. If three-times unsuccessful, the system logs the actor out and restarts the use case (by displaying the login prompt – Figure 8.3)	presentation PConsole control CActioner ref. R1	getUserInput displayMenu logout	presentation PConsole foundation FConnection
R11	*E3 – Too many messages*: If, in the S1 subflow, the number of unsent messages scheduled for the actor exceeds a parameter-predefined number of how many messages can be viewed at a time, the system displays an informational message stating that there are more messages in the database. The informational message is displayed after the predefined number of unsent messages is shown to the actor and before the menu list is re-displayed.	ref. R5 presentation PConsole	tooManyMessages	
R12	*E4 – Email could not be sent*: If, in the S3 subflow, the mail server returns an error that the email could not be sent, the system informs the actor that the email was not sent and the use case continues by displaying the menu list	ref. R7 control CActioner presentation PConsole	handleEmailException displayEmailFailure displayMenu	presentation PConsole

cases, a single design class per package is sufficient in initial iterations (this is particularly true for the control and mediator packages). Undoubtedly, the steps of finding classes from architectural requirements and from test-first design will suggest more classes and interfaces.

Requirement R1 is taken care of by PConsole's displayLogin service. The service requires getUserInput to obtain user login information. This information is passed to the login operation of CActioner. The FConnection class in the foundation layer performs the login.

Requirement R2 engages the getConnection operation of the FConnection class. getConnection uses the interface IAConstants (placed in acquaintance package) to find out the database to which the program should connect. IAConstants represents all *constant values* used in the application. readEmployee verifies that the user being connected is one of the employees allowed to use the EM system (i.e. the employee's login name and email address are in the Employee table).

The full responsibility for displaying the menu list, as per requirement R3, is placed in the displayMenu operation of PConsole. If the user chooses to exit the application at any stage, as per requirement R4, the user's exit request is read by PConsole's getUserInput and passed to CActioner to perform the exit operation. The exit operation requires the collaboration of the foundation layer.

Requirement R5 of the subflow *S1 – View Unsent Messages* is expressed visually in Figure 8.5. The user's request to display unsent messages in the console window is intercepted by PConsole's getUserInput and passed to its own operation named viewMessages. viewMessages uses IAConstants to obtain the maximum number of messages that can be displayed at a time. It then engages MBroker to retrieveMessages. MBroker delegates this task to FReader, which accesses the database with operations readMessages and readContact.

The subflow *S2 – Display Message Text* is shown as equivalent to the requirement R6. It begins with PConsole's getUserInput. The user input, recognized as the request to display outmessage text, is passed to displayMessageText in the same class (PConsole). To display the outmessage text, the application has to find out if the outmessage is in the program's memory cache (as an instance of EOutMessage of the entity package) or it has to be accessed from the database using FReader of the foundation package. The task of finding out which way to proceed requires the collaboration of MBroker. Because this task has more to do with the architectural design than with use case requirements, the explanation of it is left to the next step of finding classes from architectural requirements.

Requirements R7 and R8 are concerned with the emailing of outmessages, according to the subflow *S3 – Email Message*. To start with, getUserInput requests the collaboration of prepareMessage, which in turn passes the work to CActioner's sendMessage. At this point, there is a need to use JavaMail™ API library (called MAPI – Messaging API – in jargon), which provides the functionality of composing and sending electronic messages (MAPI is discussed in Section 13.4.1). sendMessage requires the collaboration of IAConstants to obtain the address of the mail server. Assuming that the email was sent successfully, FWriter's updateMessage will update the OutMessage table (Figure 8.8) by setting up the date_emailed value.

Requirement R8 concludes subflow S3. The responsibility for displaying an informational message about a successfully sent email is given to the `displayConfirmation` operation of the `PConsole` class.

The remaining requirements relate to the exception flows. The flow *E1 – Incorrect username or password* is presented as the requirement R9. It starts with responsibilities defined for requirement R1. On incorrect login entry, the `displayLoginError` of `PConsole` displays an informational message and allows the user to retry up to three times. If the user is unable to provide correct login information, `CActioner`'s `exit` operation provides a graceful clean-up and exit.

The responsibility for requirement R10 (*E2 – Incorrect option*) is assigned to `PConsole`. If `getUserInput` discovers that the provided menu option is incorrect, it requests `displayMenu` to re-display the menu list. If three-times unsuccessful, `CActioner`'s `logout` operation logs the user out and provides another login possibility as per requirement R1.

The exception flow *E3 – Too many messages* is represented as the requirement R11. It restricts the number of outmessages that can be displayed simultaneously on the screen. This is important because of the limited size of the program's memory and because of the usability of the user interface (see FURPS in Section 8.4). `viewMessages` (see R5 above) obtains the limit for the number of outmessages from `IAConstants`. If there are still unretrieved outmessages left in the database, `viewMessages` informs `tooManyMessages` in `PConsole` that this is the case. `tooManyMessages` displays information to this effect.

Requirement R12 is defined by the exception flow *E4 – Email could not be sent*. If email could not be sent for whatever reason, `CActioner`'s `sendMessage` (see R7 above) requests `handleEmailException` to interpret the problem. `PConsole`'s `displayEmailFailure` operation then displays appropriate information. The successive `displayMenu` operation allows the use case to continue.

Initial Class Design for Email Management 11.1.2

Table 11.1 provides enough information to attempt to draw an initial class model for Email Management. Because the table lists responsible operations, they can be shown in the model. However, the table was not meant to provide step-by-step message passing scenarios and to show all collaborators. The initial class diagram can fill some gaps, but in general the model will not be complete yet.

Figure 11.1 presents the mapping from Table 11.1 to a class diagram. There are a few additional pieces of information but there are also 'missing links' due to the gaps in the table (in particular, many operations are missing). The associations for downward communication are shown but the model does not explain how upward communication is conducted. Due to the simplicity of Iteration 1, the responsibilities of three packages (`presentation`, `control`, and `mediator`) are cumulated in three single classes, one for each package. The design of the entity classes is not present yet.

The constants in `IAConstants` are named. They identify the database (used by `FConnection`) and the mail server (used by `CActioner`) to which the application

Figure 11.1
Class diagram
for Email
Management

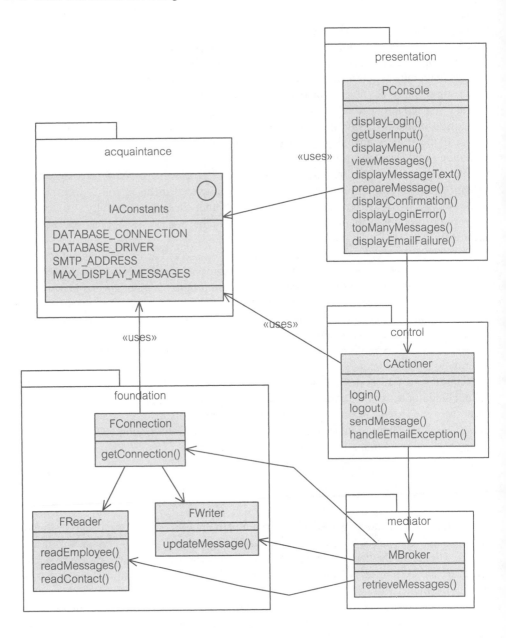

connects. The last constant informs the application about the maximum number of outmessages that can be displayed on the screen (used by PConsole) (see below).

The model includes associations between collaborating classes. As per the PCMEF architecture, all associations are downward. Most associations could be tracked down to collaborations directly visible in Table 11.1. However, because the table does not show step-by-step message passing, some collaborations (as analyzed from the table) seem to be between non-neighboring packages, which is disallowed by PCMEF. In practice, all such collaborations will use associations (as shown in Figure 11.1) and other means of communication permitted by PCMEF.

Constants in interface

A **Java interface** is a convenient way of storing *constants*. Data members in the Java interface, as opposed to the UML interface (Section 9.1.7), are implicitly public, static, and final (Eckel, 2000). Hence, they are constants. The classes that use `IAConstants` need only to import the interface:

```
import acquaintance.IAConstants;
```

The values for the constants are not shown in the diagram, but of course every constant must have a value when the program is compiled and that value cannot be changed. Because an interface does not have instances, the runtime program environment stores constant values in the static storage area allocated to the interface.

Consequently, constants can be used to *parameterize* a program's behavior. Parameterization is at compile time, not at runtime, but it has the advantage that it is clearly visible in the source code and it is confined to one interface in the code. When a more sophisticated parameterization is required, such that it is decided at runtime and still visible in the source code, then a singleton class can be used. A *singleton class* is allowed to instantiate only one object.

Architectural Elaboration of Class Design **11.2**

Classes (and interfaces) must satisfy architectural constraints imposed by the architectural framework chosen for the project. The constraints include **non-functional requirements** (FURPS+) defined in the supplementary specification document (Section 8.4).

Architectural constraints introduce a need for the **elaboration** of the initial class design. Elaboration is the improvement process based on architectural decisions. Elaboration of class design is a narrower concept than the one defined in the **Unified Process**. In the UP, elaboration is elevated to one of the four major system development phases (Chapter 1). The UP phases are (Booch *et al.*, 1999; Kruchten, 1999):

1. inception
2. elaboration
3. construction
4. transition.

Elaborating the design from architectural requirements results in modifications and additions to classes found from user requirements. Therefore, the process can start with a vertical subset of the table used for finding classes from use case requirements and then extend the table to include columns that introduce modifications and additions. The new table (Table 11.2) can consist of the following columns:

Table 11.2 Architectural elaboration of class design

Req. no.	Responsible class and operation	Collaborating package and class or interface	Architectural principle and/or pattern and/or other reason for change	New/updated responsible class and operation	New/updated collaborating package and class or interface
R1	PConsole displayLogin PConsole getUserInput CActioner login	presentation PConsole control CActioner mediator MBroker	DDP and Chain of Responsibility	MBroker login	foundation FConnection
R2	FConnection connect	acquaintance IAConstants, foundation FReader			
	FReader readEmployee		employee retrieved from the database	MBroker createEmployee	entity EEmployee
R3	PConsole displayMenu				
R4	PConsole getUserInput CActioner exit	control CActioner mediator MBroker	DDP and Chain of Responsibility	MBroker logout	foundation FConnection
R5	PConsole getUserInput PConsole viewMessages	presentation PConsole acquaintance IAConstants	DDP and Chain of Responsibility when EOutMessage and EContact objects instantiated (ref. the last row for R5); NCP and APP contact details must be retrieved together with the messages	CActioner retrieveMessages PConsole displayMessages	mediator MBroker acquaintance IAEmployee IAOutMessage IAContact, entity EEmployee EOutMessage EContact
	MBroker retrieveMessages			MBroker retrieveContacts	foundation FReader
	FReader readMessages FReader readContact		messages and contacts retrieved from the database	MBroker createContacts MBroker createMessages	entity EContact entity EOutMessage
R6	PConsole getUserInput PConsole displayMessageText	presentation PConsole	DDP and Chain of Responsibility to decide where to look for the message	CActioner retrieveMessage MBroker isInCache	mediator MBroker entity EOutMessage foundation FReader

Table 11.2 (*cont'd*)

Req. no.	Responsible class and operation	Collaborating package and class or interface	Architectural principle and/or pattern and/or other reason for change	New/updated responsible class and operation	New/updated collaborating package and class or interface
			once the instance of EOutMessage is in cache; NCP and APP	PConsole displayMessageText	acquaintance IAEmployee IAOutMessage IAContact, entity EEmployee EOutMessage EContact
R7	PConsole getUserInput PConsole prepareMessage CActioner sendMessage	presentation PConsole control CActioner MAPI, acquaintance IAConstants, foundation FWriter	DDP and Chain of Responsibility Mediator; to flag the cache is dirty	MBroker updateMessage MBroker flagCache	foundation FWriter
	FWriter updateMessage				
R8	PConsole displayConfirmation				
R9	ref. R1	presentation PConsole ref. R1, control CActioner			
	PConsole displayLoginError				
	CActioner exit		DDP and Chain of Responsibility	MBroker logout	foundation FConnection
R10	PConsole getUserInput PConsole displayMenu	presentation PConsole			
	CActioner logout		DDP and Chain of Responsibility	MBroker logout	foundation FConnection
	ref. R1				
R11	ref. R5 PConsole tooManyMessages				
R12	ref. R7 CActioner handleEmailException PConsole displayEmailFailure PConsole displayMenu	presentation PConsole			

- *Requirement number* – As in Table 11.1.
- *Responsible class and operation* – This column combines columns 2 and 3 of Table 11.1 into one column.
- *Collaborating package, class or interface* – This column is originally the same as the last column in Table 11.1. However, if changes are introduced in the row with an entry in that column, then this entry may change in comparison with Table 11.1.
- *Architectural principle and/or pattern and/or other reason for change* – This column refers to Chapter 9, and in particular to Sections 9.2 and 9.3 in which the principles and patterns for the PCMEF framework are defined.
- *New/updated responsible class and operation* – This column lists new or updated classes and operations to carry out or complete responsibilities not fully resolved in the step of finding classes from use case requirements.
- *New/updated collaborating package, class or interface* – This column identifies collaborators for newly introduced or updated classes and operations.

11.2.1 Architectural Elaboration of Class Design for Email Management

Table 11.2 presents the class design for Email Management after the architectural elaboration. The first three columns reiterate Table 11.1 findings. The remaining three columns are the product of elaboration. The elaboration resulted in the introduction of the entity classes, extensions to the acquaintance package, and additions of methods to classes in all PCMEF packages except the foundation classes.

MBroker gained the login operation as a result of the elaboration of requirement R1. This is because the PCMEF framework forbids direct collaboration between the control layer and the foundation layer (due to the Downward Dependency Principle and the Chain of Responsibility pattern). Hence, CActioner delegates login to MBroker.

Requirement R2 is addressed when MBroker's login calls connect on the FConnection object. connect sends the readEmployee message to FReader. Assuming that the user of the EM application is recognized as an authorized employee in the database, the employee details are returned to MBroker. MBroker uses the createEmployee operation to instantiate the EEmployee object in the program's memory cache.

Requirement R3 does not lead to any changes due to the architectural elaboration. However, MBroker handles the exit operation in requirement R4 on the way from CActioner to FConnection.

The elaboration with regard to requirement R5 (*View Unsent Messages*) is significant. The Downward Dependency Principle and the Chain of Responsibility pattern result in the introduction of the retrieveMessages operation in CActioner. CActioner delegates this operation to MBroker. MBroker recognizes that the contact details must be retrieved together with the outmessages for that contact. To this aim, it engages the retrieveContacts operation and it delegates the work of retrieving outmessages and contact details to FReader's readMessages and readContact.

The outmessages and contacts are returned to MBroker, which then uses the operations createContact and createMessages (in this sequence) to instantiate the EContact and `EOutMessage` objects. `MBroker` ensures also that during the instantiation of `EOutMessages`, the association links are created between the `EOutMessage` and `EContact` objects.

At this point, `PConsole`'s `viewMessages` can invoke the `displayMessages` operation to obtain details of each outmessage and its associated contact and to present this information on the computer screen. According to the Neighbor Communication Principle and the Acquaintance Package Principle, `displayMessages` uses appropriate interfaces in the `acquaintance` package to get access to the `EOutMessage` and `EContact` objects, which implement these interfaces.

The class design for requirement R6 (*Display Message Text*) is also extensively augmented in the process of the architectural elaboration. Firstly, `PConsole`'s `displayMessageText` is channeled via `CActioner`'s `retrieveMessage` on the way to `MBroker`. `MBroker` can get the outmessage text from the relevant `EOutMessage` object, if that object is in the memory cache and it is not 'dirty' (i.e. its informational content is the same as in the database). Otherwise, `MBroker` must engage `FReader` to bring the `EOutMessage` object to the cache. The `MBroker`'s operation `isInCache` decides which way to proceed.

Once an instance of `EOutMessage` is in cache, `PConsole`'s `displayMessageText` can access this instance via `IAOutMessage` interface, which `EOutMessage` implements. In practice, the other entity interfaces (`IAEmployee` and `IAContact`) must also be used because the access to `EOutMessage` follows the association links from `EEmployee` and `EContact` to `EOutMessage` objects.

Requirement R7 (*Email Message*) is augmented by two operations in `MBroker`: `updateMessage` and `flagCache`. `updateMessage` enforces the Downward Dependency Principle and the Chain of Responsibility pattern. Once `FWriter`'s `updateMessage` updates the `OutMessage` table, `MBroker` uses `flagCache` to flag the cache as dirty. The details of how this is done are not resolved yet. The point of this operation is that the program knows that the objects in the entity package become dirty as soon as an outmessage is emailed and the database is updated.

The design for requirement R8, which concludes the work initiated by requirement R7, is not affected by the architectural elaboration. Similarly, the architectural elaboration has not introduced significant changes to the class design for requirements R9–R12, which define the exception flows of the use case. Only the `MBroker`'s `logout` operation has been used in requirements R9 and R10 to allow `CActioner` to delegate `logout` to `FConnection`.

Class Design for Email Management after Architectural Elaboration 11.2.2

The findings of Table 11.2 lead to the creation of an improved class model for Email Management, as shown in Figure 11.2. The `entity` package is added to the model. The `entity` and `mediator` packages constitute the `domain` package, as one of the PCMEF layers. The `acquaintance` package has three new interfaces implemented by the classes in the entity package. New operations discovered during the architectural elaboration are shown in the pertinent classes.

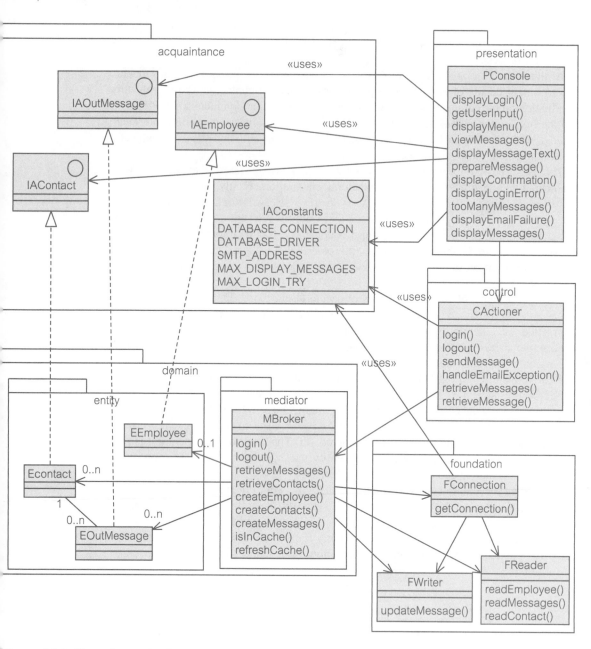

Figure 11.2 Class diagram for Email Management

11.2.3 Class Instantiation

An important side effect of the architectural elaboration is the realization of who (i.e. which class) should be made responsible for creating a new instance of another class. In other words, who should send a message to the *constructor* method of another class so that a new object of that class is instantiated.

Some classes may be instantiated on the program's startup by some initialization method. Other classes are created dynamically at runtime but their creators are known statically (at compile time). In more complex cases, the exact creator of an object is determined at runtime. However, for the bulk of objects in the program their creators can be known at design time. This means that class instantiation can be carefully designed and the architectural considerations can be at the forefront of this design effort.

Class instantiation must adhere to the principles of the architectural framework chosen for the project. Instantiation can cross architectural layers as long as the Downward Dependency Principle of the PCMEF framework is followed. This means that classes in the higher layers instantiate classes in the (neighboring) lower layers, but not vice versa.

Who instantiates the first object?

An object-oriented system at runtime resembles a football match. The players pass the ball like the classes that pass messages. A player takes decisions about whom to pass the ball to 'at runtime'. The responsibilities are distributed among players and no one player can control the game. Similarly, no object is in control of the course of the game in an object-oriented program.

Just about the only 'ball passing' that can be controlled with some degree of certainty is at the kickoff of the match. A football match has a start, and an object-oriented program must start somehow. The first object must be instantiated at the start of the program. The start point of a computer program is in the **main method**. The main method instantiates the first object – this is an object of the class which contains the main method.

In Email Management, the class containing the `main` method is in the `presentation` package and is called `PMain`. Java requires an array of `String` objects as an argument to the `main` method (Figure 11.3). The `args` hold the arguments, if any, invoked on the command line when starting the program (not used in Iteration 1). In Java, the name of the class that contains the `main` method must have the same name as the program file that is run. The constructor method to instantiate `PMain`, i.e. `PMain()`, provides the second 'kick' by instantiating one or more other classes and passing the 'ball' to one of these newly created objects.

Instantiation diagram for Email Management

The UML class diagramming technique can be used to show who creates new instances of other classes. This can be achieved by drawing dependency relationships between classes stereotyped as «`instantiate`».

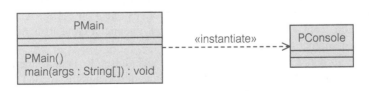

Figure 11.3
The PMain class in EM

Figure 11.4
Instantiation
diagram for EM

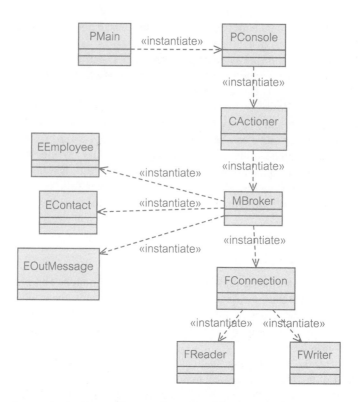

When a class A instantiates class B then the object A requires the reference to the object B. If this reference ought to be used for future message passing from A to B (as is frequently the case), then a unidirectional association link should be established from A to B.

Figure 11.4 shows the instantiation diagram for Email Management. Association links are not modeled in Figure 11.4. They are shown in Figure 11.2. Note that there is no need to associate PMain and PConsole because the control does not return to PMain after leaving it at the 'kickoff'.

11.3 Interactions

UML 2.0 defines an **interaction** as 'a unit of behavior that focuses on the observable exchange of information between parts' (UML, 2002, p.140). 'A **part** represents a set of instances that are owned by a containing classifier instance' (UML, 2002, p.161). In effect, a part is an object that exists during an interaction. The existence of an object at a particular time is called the **lifeline**.

An interaction is realized as a sequence of messages between lifelines. Messages can be synchronous (Section 9.1.6) or asynchronous (Section 9.1.8). A **message** is a communication from a *sending event occurrence* on one lifeline to a *receiving event occurrence* on another lifeline.

UML 2.0 provides a number of graphical techniques to depict interactions. The techniques include sequence diagrams, communication diagrams (called collaboration diagrams prior to UML 2.0), and interaction overview diagrams.

Sequence Diagrams

A **sequence diagram** defines the sequencing of messages and their event occurrences on lifelines. Since the lifelines represent parts and the parts represent objects, a sequence diagram shows message interchanges between objects in an interaction. The scope of the interaction is at the designer's discretion – this could be a use case, a part of it, a number of use cases, a single requirement, an action from a user, etc.

A rectangular frame with a name in a compartment in the upper left corner depicts an **interaction** (Figure 11.5). The points on the frame can serve as **gates** to signify the beginnings or ends of the messages. Gates represent the conceptual interface of an interaction. They can simulate events from/to an actor. The gate in Figure 11.5 tells us that the interaction starts when the message `doIt()` is called on the `:Client` lifeline.

Messages are shown as horizontal arrows between lifelines. The part name for the lifeline consists of three elements: `partName:ClassName[multiplicity]`. The multiplicity can be used to represent a collection of objects. If not specified, the multiplicity is deemed to be one.

Either the name of the `partName` or the name of the `ClassName` may be omitted. If both names are present, an object (`partName`) is a specific instance of the class (`ClassName`). If `partName` is omitted, an object is instatiated and it represents any or all instances of the `ClassName` class. If `ClassName` is omitted, an object is not instantiated.

The emphasis in a sequence diagram is on the sequence of messages. Placing messages one under another shows this. The optional numbering of messages also indicates the sequence. An object receiving a message activates the relevant method. The time when the flow of control is focused in an object is called **activation**. Activations are shown as narrow rectangles on object lifelines.

Hierarchical numbering of messages shows activation dependencies between messages. In particular, as shown in Figure 11.5, a message to self (i.e. a method call on the same

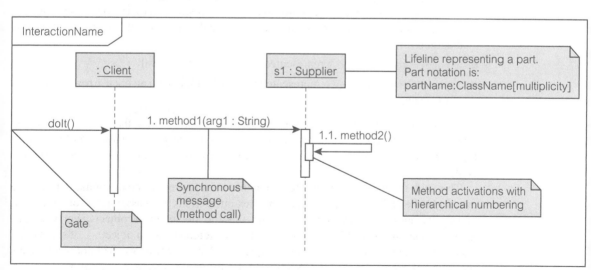

Figure 11.5 Sequence diagram – notation

Figure 11.6
Messages in a
sequence diagram

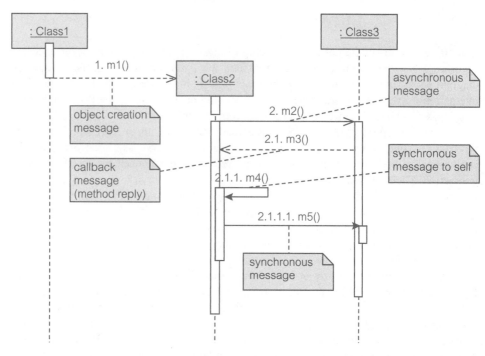

object) within one activation results in a new activation. This is shown both by the hierarchical numbering and graphically by the attachment of a new narrow rectangle.

As shown in Figure 11.6, UML 2.0 distinguishes among:

- **synchronous message** – represented by a filled arrow head
- **callback message** – represented by a dashed line with an open arrow; this is called a **method reply** in the UML 2.0 (not to be confused with a **return** from a message call, which is implicit at the end of the activation and normally not shown on interaction diagrams)
- **asynchronous message** – represented by an open arrow head
- **object creation message** – represented by a dashed line with an open arrow to an object (part) rectangle

Interactions focus on sequences of messages, not on the data that the messages pass around. Therefore, the signatures of messages do not need to be shown and the return types are normally not visualized. The return types are frequently understood from the context.

This said, the incapability of interaction diagrams to present the manipulations on data can hinder the understanding of more complex interactions that pass objects (or collections of objects) and that may use association links to obtain these objects. For example, assuming that in Figure 11.5 the object s1 holds a reference to an object x1 of some other class, a message from :Client to s1, requesting that s1 returns x1, will not result in any message link from s1 to x1 (see Section 11.4.3 for a more concrete example).

Communication Diagrams

Communication diagrams were known as collaboration diagrams prior to UML 2.0. The name change makes it clear that the UML notion of collaboration means more than the semantics produced by a communication diagram.

A **collaboration** 'describes how an operation or a classifier is realized by a set of classifiers used and related in a specific way' (UML, 2002, p.304). The definition of collaboration has two aspects: structural and behavioral (Maciaszek, 2001). UML 2.0 introduces a new diagram called an **internal structure diagram**. The internal structure diagram treats a collaboration as a kind of classifier. An internal structure diagram exposes the structure and the behavior of that classifier.

Internal structure diagrams and interaction diagrams share the concept of a part. An internal structure diagram shows how the parts deliver the behavior of the classifier that contains them. This objective of an internal structure diagram is not different from the main objective of interaction diagrams.

Terminological elucidation aside, a communication diagram is merely a visual variation of a sequence diagram. Most CASE tools can freely convert between the two diagrams. Figure 11.7 is a communication diagram that corresponds to the sequence diagram in Figure 11.6, with the notes suppressed.

Messages in a communication diagram are shown with a solid line and an arrow with the message name. The solid line can be used to make a statement about how an object sending the message acquired the 'handle' on the receiving object (this could be, for example, by an association link or by acquaintance). The current version of UML 2.0 does not address this issue but many CASE tools do.

A communication diagram does not illustrate lifelines (but the objects (parts) represent the lifelines). Activations are implicit in the hierarchical numbering of messages. An object creation message is also implicit (to some degree) in the numbering – the newly created object continues the numbering from the next sequential value. Apart from that, there is no visual distinction between an object creation and callback messages.

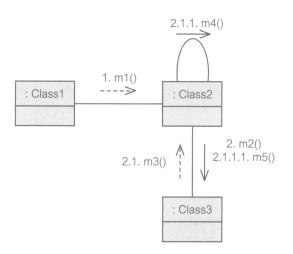

Figure 11.7
Messages in a communication diagram

Figure 11.8
Sequence
diagram with
interactions and
interaction
occurrences

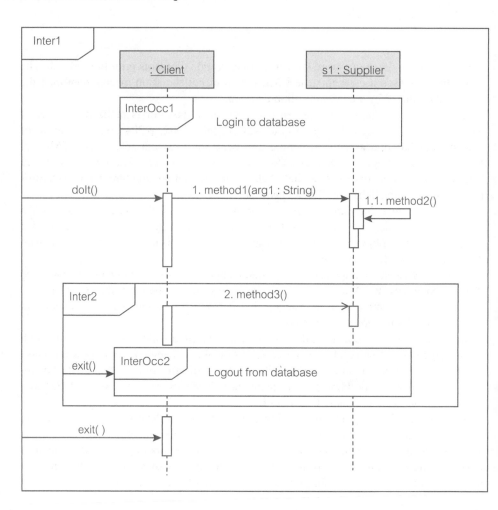

Figure 11.9
Interaction
overview diagram

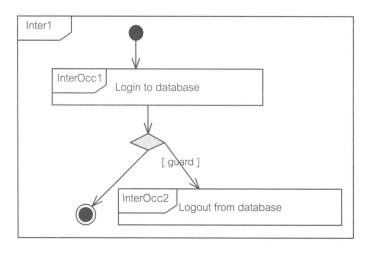

In practice, developers tend to use sequence diagrams much more than communication diagrams. From the visual perspective, sequence diagrams have an advantage for presenting more complex models in which the explicit visualization of message sequences is essential – even though they may require printing on large paper formats using printers (plotters) capable of taking large formats.

Communication diagrams may be more useful for the analysis of messages from/to a given object. They may be more convenient when drawing initial draft interactions and doing 'iterative' trial-and-error modeling. Because of this, they are quite handy for brainstorming sessions.

Interaction Overview Diagrams 11.3.3

Interactions can contain smaller interactions, called interaction fragments. An interaction fragment is a semantic notion that uses the same syntactic notation as an interaction – a frame with a name in a compartment in the upper left corner.

An interaction that has been completely defined, presumably by an interaction diagram, is called an interaction occurrence. Interaction occurrences have their gates resolved and they can, therefore, be combined to show the flow of control between them and within larger interactions. This capability is applied in UML 2.0 on top of activity diagrams (yet another UML modeling technique) to deliver interaction overview diagrams.

Figure 11.8 shows how a sequence diagram can refer to interactions and interaction occurrences. The diagram is an extension of that in Figure 11.5. The interaction `Inter1` uses the functionality of an interaction occurrence `InterOcc1` to log into the database. It then does some work on its own before combining the message called `method(3)` and `InterOcc2` into `Inter2`. `Inter2` is fully contained in `Inter1`. `Inter2` sends the `exit` message to `InterOcc2`, which results in the logout from the database. After the logout, the `Inter1` gate sends the `exit` message to `:Client`.

An interaction overview diagram is a restricted variation of an activity diagram (Maciaszek, 2001) in which object nodes are replaced by interactions and interaction occurrences. Figure 11.9 presents a simple example. The transition from the initial state (black circle) 'fires' `InterOcc1`. On exit from `InterOcc1`, the decision is taken either to end the interaction or, if the guard constraint is satisfied, to start `InterOcc2`.

Interactions for Email Management 11.4

The identification of interactions for EM is quite straightforward. Iteration 1 of EM is the console-based menu-driven application with a limited number of actions that a user can take. The simplest way to identify interactions is therefore to associate an interaction with each main action that a user can take. These are 'happy path' interactions (Section 8.2). After that, the 'unhappy path' interactions, corresponding to the exception flows in the use case specification, may be added.

There is no need to produce an interaction overview diagram. The list of interactions, as below, will suffice:

- 'happy path' interactions:
  - login
  - exit
  - view unsent messages
  - display message text
  - email message
- 'unhappy path' interactions:
  - incorrect username or password
  - incorrect option
  - too many messages
  - email could not be sent.

The following presents interaction diagrams for EM. The 'happy path' interactions are presented as sequence diagrams. They represent distinct interaction occurrences. These interaction occurrences are referred to in 'unhappy path' interactions, which are modeled as communication diagrams.

Consistent with good modeling practice, completeness of the models takes second place behind abstraction needs. The diagrams emphasize important points and omit less relevant modeling decisions if they would obscure the models. Some of the omitted aspects are trivial or obvious, but others may be tricky. The latter are re-addressed during programming and refactoring (Chapter 12).

The diagrams are largely self-explanatory when analyzed in the context of the previous discussion in this chapter. These 'happy path' interactions to which exception flows apply are used as interaction fragments in the diagrams presenting the 'unhappy path' interactions. However, the enclosing interaction frames (Figure 11.8) are not presented to save space.

To a significant degree, the diagrams are visual representations of messages presented in Table 11.2. The signatures of messages furnish additional explanation. In most cases, the instantiation of objects is assumed because it was discussed before (Figure 11.4).

11.4.1 The 'Login' Interaction

The 'Login' interaction starts with the `displayLogin()` from `:PMain` to `:PConsole` (Figure 11.10). This message is part of the `PMain()` constructor method, which instantiates `PConsole` before sending `displayLogin()` to it (Figure 11.3). `:PConsole`'s `getUserInput()` obtains the username and password from the user and sends the `login()` request to `:CActioner`.

`:CActioner` delegates the `login()` request to `:MBroker`, which in turn delegates it in the `connect()` message to `:FConnection`. `:FConnection` instantiates `:FReader` (not shown) and the two objects get associated in the process.

`:MBroker` builds a SQL string and passes it in the `query()` message to `:FReader`. `:FReader` executes a SQL search on the database by sending the following `select` statement on its database connection (in practice, the asterisk (*) ought to replaced by the `employee` column names):

```
select * from employee where login_name = ?;
```

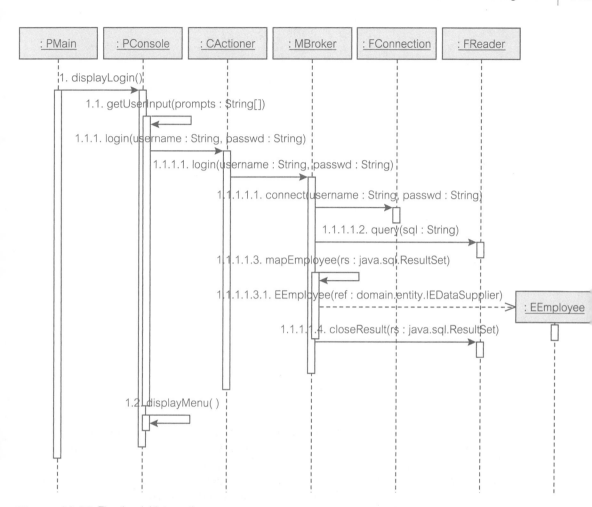

Figure 11.10 The 'Login' interaction

The loginName provides the unique identification of an employee in the database.
:FReader returns the result set to :MBroker. :MBroker uses the result set to map
employee raw data to the newly created :EEmployee object. It then asks :FReader to
close the result set.

The outcome is that :EEmployee is populated with values on all its data members (not
shown). The 'Login' interaction is now concluded and :PConsole uses displayMenu()
to display the application menu to the user.

The 'Exit' Interaction 11.4.2

The 'Exit' interaction is a simple sequence of delegations from :PConsole to :FCon-
nection (**Figure 11.11**). Once :FConnection closes the connection to the database,
:CActioner exits from the system.

Figure 11.11
The 'Exit'
interaction

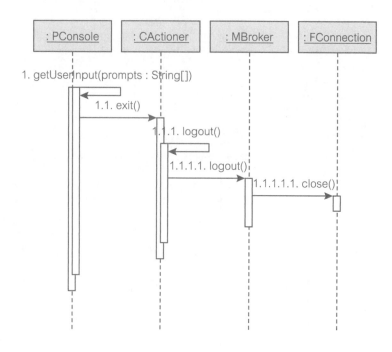

11.4.3   The 'View Unsent Messages' Interaction

The 'View Unsent Messages' interaction begins with the user's request on :PConsole (Figure 11.12). viewMessages() creates a new (empty) Java collection object (e.g. ArrayList) and passes it in retrieveMessages() to :CActioner. :CActioner delegates the request to :MBroker after supplying its :EEmployee object to the argument list (:CActioner is linked to :EEmployee in the 'Login' interaction).

:MBroker asks :FReader to execute the following query() on the database:

```
select * from OutMessage
          where sender_emp_id = ? and date_emailed is null";
```

The result set from query() is used to create a collection of :EoutMessage objects in the cache and establish appropriate hash maps. The constructor of :EOutMessage objects uses the IEDataSupplier interface. This interface defines the collection into which the :EOutMessage objects can be placed.

The fact that the collection of outmessages is returned to :MBroker and the fact that the instantiated :EOutMessage objects are placed within that collection cannot be properly shown in the UML interaction diagrams (Section 11.3.1). Interaction diagrams are not intended to present the manipulations on data. Messages on the diagrams do not show return data types. Moreover, in sequence diagrams it is not possible to make a clear indication that a message uses an association link (a variable holding a reference to an object or a collection of objects) in order to return an object (or collection thereof) to the client. Communication diagrams can be more flexible in this regard.

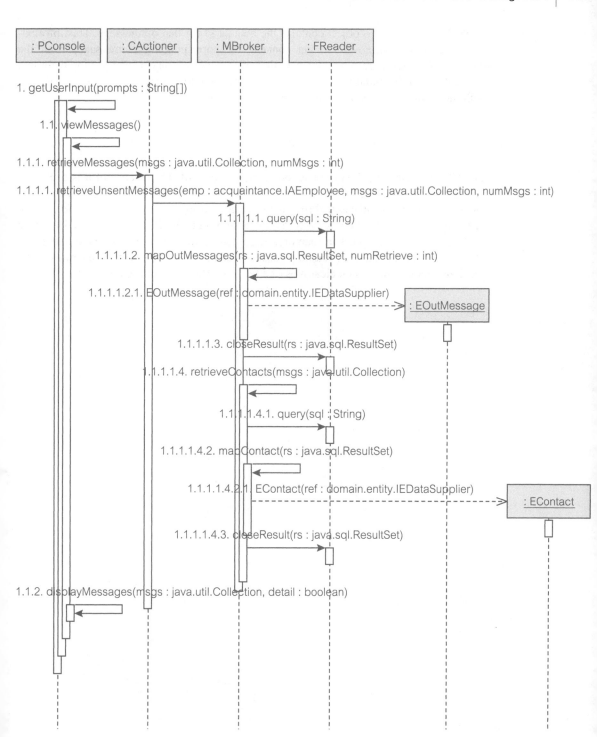

Figure 11.12 The 'View Unsent Messages' interaction

Each :OutMessage object contains the contact id for that outmessage. This information is used by :MBroker to get contacts for corresponding outmessages from the database. This action results in instantiation of :EContact objects and placing them in a Java collection. Eventually, :PConsole is in a position to display outmessages together with the contact information using displayMessages().

11.4.4 The 'Display Message Text' Interaction

The 'Display Message Text' interaction is straightforward. The essence of it is explained in the note in Figure 11.13. :MBroker checks whether :EOutMessage is already in memory and, if not, it has to bring it to memory using query() on :FReader. The instantiation of :EOutMessage is assumed and not shown in Figure 11.13. Once :EOutMessage is mapped in memory, :MBroker returns it to the ultimate client, i.e. :PConsole. As per the explanation regarding inadequacies of interaction diagrams in the previous section, there is no clear message to :EOutMessage in Figure 11.13.

Figure 11.13
The 'Display
Message Text'
interaction

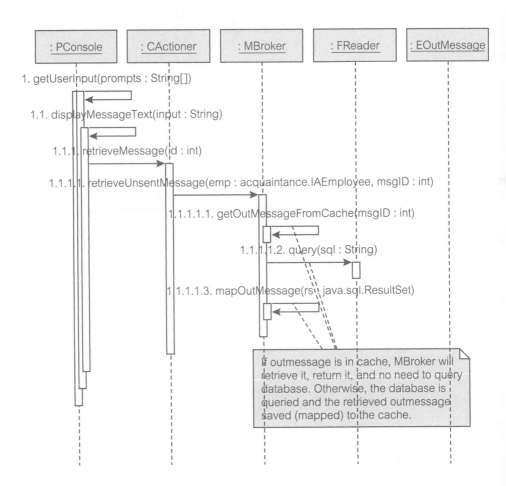

The 'Email Message' Interaction   11.4.5

The 'Email Message' interaction starts when the user chooses to send an email containing an outmessage text found in the database (Figure 11.14). Once this request is made, :PConsole starts preparing the email for sending using prepareMessage(). First, prepareMessage() uses :CActioner to retrieveMessage(), as explained in the interaction 'Display Message Text'. Once the outmessage details are returned, :PConsole instructs :CActioner to sendMessage().

:CActioner uses the functionality of the JavaMail library to email the outmessage with the send() method. If send() succeeds, then the sendMessage() method activates updateMessage() on :MBroker. :MBroker delegates the job to :FWriter, which constructs and executes the following SQL update statement on the database:

```
update OutMessage set date_emailed = ? where message_id = ?";
```

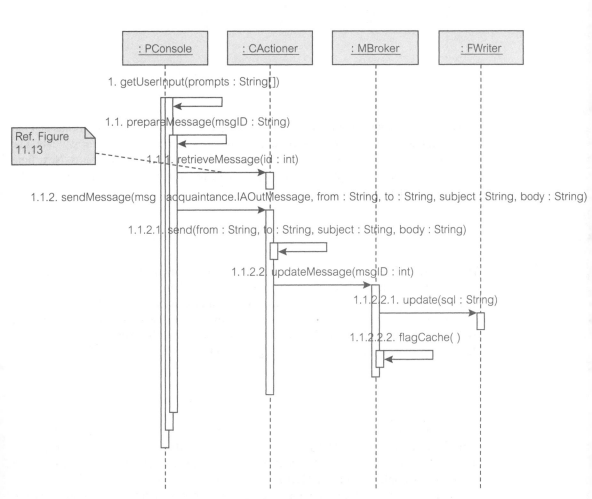

Figure 11.14 The 'Email Message' interaction

Figure 11.15
The 'Incorrect
User Name or
Password'
Interaction

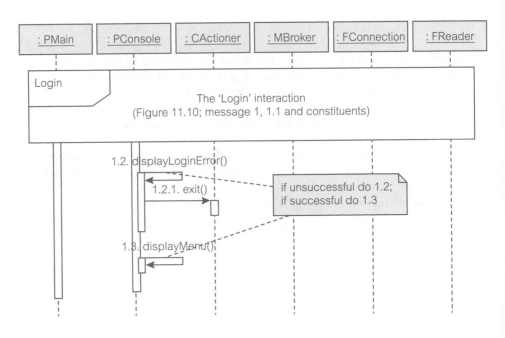

The update statement modifies a record in the OutMessage table. This means that the corresponding :EOutMessage object in the program's cache contains incorrect data. For that reason, :MBroker uses flagCache() to set the cache to the dirty status. Next time :MBroker is asked to supply an entity object to the program's logic, it will re-retrieve the data from the database.

11.4.6 The 'Incorrect User Name or Password' Interaction

The 'Incorrect User Name and Password' interaction is an alternative execution path of the 'Login' interaction, as shown in Figure 11.15. When :PConsole is returned an 'unsuccessful login' from the sequence of operations activated by getUserInput() (Figure 11.10), it uses displayLoginError() to give the 'unsuccessful login' feedback to the user. If this is the third time in row that such feedback is given, the program sends the exit() message to :CActioner (Figure 11.11).

11.4.7 The 'Incorrect Option' Interaction

If the user's login is successful, :PConsole uses displayMenu() to present the menu options to the user (Figure 11.16). getUserInput() reads the option number typed in by the user. If the entered value is incorrect, the program ignores the value and re-displays the menu (this is implicit in Figure 11.16).

The user is allowed three attempts to enter a valid option number (this is not shown in Figure 11.16). The program obtains the number of permitted attempts from a constant

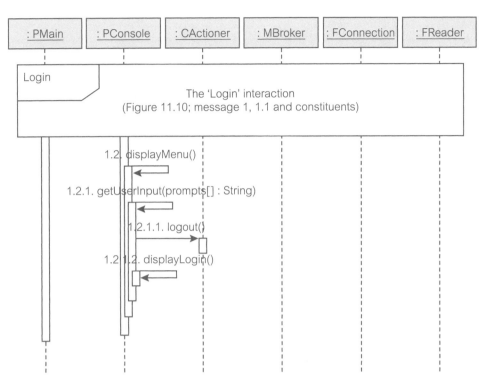

Figure 11.16
The 'Incorrect
Option' interaction

value `MAX_LOGIN_TRY` in `IAConstants` (**Figure 11.2**). After three mistakes, `:PConsole` initiates `logout()` and, when the control is returned to it, invites the user to log in again (`displayLogin()`).

The 'Too Many Messages' Interaction 11.4.8

A constant value `MAX_DISPLAY_MESSAGES` in `IAConstants` (**Figure 11.2**) controls the maximum number of outmessages that the program is prepared to display on the user's console screen. This is necessary for the usability reasons and because of the limited memory available to the program.

As shown in Figure 11.17, the 'Too Many Messages' interaction is an extension of the 'View Unsent Messages' interaction. As can be seen in Figure 11.12, the message from `:PConsole` to `:CActioner` called `retrieveMessages()` has the number of out-messages (`numMsgs`) in its argument list. This ensures that only that many outmessages will be retrieved from the database and returned to `:PConsole` in the container passed also as an argument (`msgs`).

The outmessages are displayed with `displayMessages()`. Following the display, the method `tooManyMessages()` will inform the user how many outmessages have not been retrieved from the database. In Iteration 1, the user can only see these remaining outmessages after emailing some of the outmessages currently visible on the screen.

Figure 11.17
The 'Too Many
Messages'
interaction

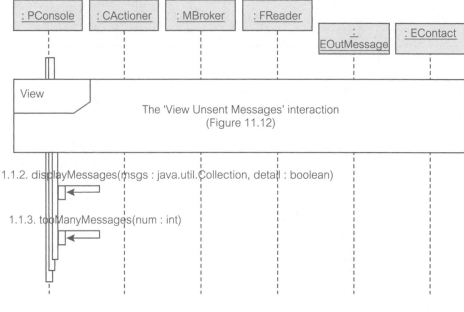

Figure 11.18
The 'Email Could
Not Be Sent'
interaction

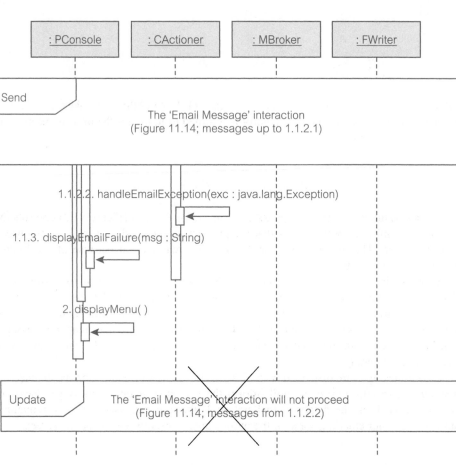

The 'Email Could Not Be Sent' Interaction 11.4.9

The 'Email Could Not Be Sent' interaction divides the 'Email Message' interaction into two fragments, as shown in Figure 11.18. When :CActioner gets a Java exception that the email has not been sent, the method handleEmailException() interprets the problem so that :PConsole's displayEmailFailure() can inform the user that the emailing failed. After that :PConsole re-displays the menu in the displayMenu() operation. The interaction fragment to update the database will not proceed.

Summary

1. *Class design* and *interaction design* are two sides of the same coin. They need to be conducted in parallel.

2. *Finding classes* from use case requirements involves extracting requirements from the use case document and conceiving of classes and collaborations between classes needed to fulfill these requirements.

3. Classes must conform to the chosen architectural framework. Architectural constraints introduce a need for the *elaboration* of the initial class design.

4. A *Java interface* is a convenient way of storing constants and parameterizing a program's behavior.

5. Architectural elaboration includes decisions about *instantiation* of classes.

6. *Interactions* are modeled in sequence diagrams and communication diagrams.

7. A *sequence diagram* defines the sequencing of messages and their event occurrences on lifelines.

8. A *communication diagram* (known as a collaboration diagram prior to UML 2.0) is merely a visual variation of a sequence diagram.

9. Synchronous, asynchronous, callback, and object creation messages should be distinguished when modeling interactions.

10. Interactions focus on sequences of messages, not on the data that the messages pass around. Therefore, the signatures of messages do not need to be shown and the return types are normally not visualized.

11. An interaction defined in an interaction diagram is called an *interaction occurrence*. An *interaction overview diagram* is a restricted variation of an *activity diagram* in which object nodes are replaced by interactions and interaction occurrences.

Key Terms

«instantiate» relationship 345
activation 347
activity diagram 351
application class 331
asynchronous message 348
callback message 348
class design 331
class instantiation 345
collaboration 349
collaboration diagram *See* communication diagram
communication diagram 332, 349
design class 331
elaboration 339
functional requirements 332
gate 347
interaction 346, 347, 351
interaction design 331
interaction fragment 351
interaction occurrence 351

interaction overview diagram 351
interface 331
internal structure diagram 349
Java interface 339
lifeline 346
main method 345
message 346
method reply *See* callback message
method return 348
non-functional requirements 339
object creation message 348
part 346
responsibility 332
sequence diagram 332, 347
signature 332
synchronous message 348
Unified Process 339
UP *See* Unified Process

Review Questions

Discussion Questions

1. Class design includes interface design. Which requirements, functional or non-functional, are the driving force behind interface design? Explain. (Caveat – interface design in this question is about design of UML/Java interfaces, not about user interface design.)

2. The table device to find classes from use case requirements (Table 11.1) is not designed to be complete and correct with regard to an architectural framework and in conformance with all PCMEF principles (Section 9.2.2). Which PCMEF principles are not followed or cannot be confirmed by studying Table 11.1? Is this acceptable?

3. Interaction diagrams, and sequence diagrams in particular, are widely used to present the detailed logic of program behavior. However, they are not able to express a certain kind of object intercommunication, and this can result in unexplained gaps in the flow of logic. What is this limitation of interaction diagrams? Is it justified?

Case Study Questions

1. Refer to R11 in Table 11.1, which addresses the exception flow *E3 – Too many messages*. How is this exception implemented in Iteration 1? Does this implementation ensure that the program memory will not overflow when reading outmessages from the database?

2. Refer to the 'Display Message Text' sequence diagram in Figure 11.13. What assumption is made and how could you have done it differently if such assumption is not made? Hint: The assumption relates to the 'View Unsent Messages' interaction.

3. One approach to cleaning up the objects in the memory is by utilizing the Java `finalize()` method during garbage collection. Explain when this could be used in the EM case study program.

4. Can the 'Too Many Messages' interaction be thought as a type of programming exception? Can it be implemented using a Java exception?

Problem-Solving Exercises

Case Study Exercises

1. Refer to the design of the class `PMain` (Figure 11.3) and to the instantiation diagram for EM (Figure 11.4). Can `PMain` instantiate more than one class and still comply with the PCMEF framework? Draw a relevant fragment of the instantiation diagram. Optionally, write the code for `PMain.java`. Explain.

2. Refer to the design of the class `PMain` (Figure 11.3) and to the instantiation diagram for EM (Figure 11.4). Assume so called 'eager instantiation' such that `PMain` is given the responsibility to instantiate in its constructor many (or even a majority of) application classes. This will not comply with the PCMEF framework, but may be allowed as a justified exemption. Draw a relevant fragment of the instantiation diagram. Optionally, write the code for `PMain.java`. Explain.

3. Consider the 'Exit' interaction (Section 11.4.2). Convert the sequence diagram in Figure 11.11 to a communication diagram.

4. Consider the 'Email Message' interaction (Section 11.4.5). Convert the sequence diagram in Figure 11.14 to a communication diagram.

Minicase – Time Logging System

This minicase assumes that you have solutions to the TLS minicase questions in Chapters 7 and 8. These solutions are included in the Instructor's Manual for the textbook and are available to instructors from the book website.

1. Find design classes for TLS using the tabular approach as in Chapter 11, Table 11.1. Describe the table entries requirement by requirement in the style similar to Chapter 11. For the sake of simplicity, assume that two entity classes are sufficient – `EEmployee` and `ETimeLogRecord`.

2. Develop a design class diagram for TLS reflecting your solution to Question 1 above. Show classes, interfaces and method names (no need to specify methods' signatures). Explain your main assumptions and simplifications.

3. In Questions 1 and 2 above, we assumed a simplified version of the entity layer. In reality, the domain object model for TLS (Chapter 7, Minicase – Time Logging, Question 2) would have defined other entities such as `Activity`, `Task`, `Calendar`, and `Contact`. Based on the domain object model for TLS (provided by your instructor), present a more complete design class diagram specifically for the entity layer. Introduce interfaces and explain why they are needed. Show important methods. Do not show data members.

4. Develop a sequence diagram for the interaction 'Display Login Window'.

5. Develop a communication diagram for the interaction 'Login and Retrieve Timelog Entries'. The model should not display timelog entries, just retrieve them to memory. Provide a brief explanation.

6. Develop a sequence diagram for the interaction 'Display Timelog Entries'. The model should assume that timelog entries have already been retrieved to memory. Provide a brief explanation.

7. Develop a sequence diagram for the interaction 'Display Timelog Entry for Update'. This interaction should present a dialog box window for a selected timelog entry, presumably because the employee wants to update the entry. Provide a brief explanation.

8. Develop a sequence diagram for the interaction 'Save Timelog Entry after Update'. This interaction saves to the database changes made in the update dialog box. Provide a brief explanation.

9. Develop a sequence diagram for the interaction 'Synchronize Timelog'. This interaction is needed to allow the employee to log on to TLS from different workstations at the same time. TLS should be able to periodically synchronize the displayed timelog entries with the latest data available in the database.

10. Develop a communication diagram for the interaction 'Create New Timelog Entry'.

11. Develop a communication diagram for the interaction 'Delete Timelog Entry'.

Minicase – Contact Information Management

This minicase assumes that you have solutions to the CIM minicase questions in Chapters 9 and 10. These solutions are included in the Instructor's Manual for the textbook and are available to instructors from the book website.

1. Find design classes for CIM using the tabular approach as in Chapter 11, Table 11.1. Describe the table entries, requirement by requirement, in the style similar to Chapter 11.

2. Develop a design class diagram for CIM reflecting your solution to Question 1 above. Show classes and interfaces (no need to show methods). Explain your main assumptions and simplifications.

3. Develop a sequence diagram for the interaction 'Display Login Window'.

4. Develop a communication diagram for the interaction 'Do Login'.

5. Develop a sequence diagram for the interaction 'List All Contacts'.

6. Develop a sequence diagram for the interaction 'Display Contact Details'.

7. Develop a communication diagram for the interaction 'Create New PersonContact'.

8. Develop a sequence diagram for the interaction 'Update Contact'.

Chapter

12

Programming and Testing

A constant feedback between *programming and testing* is the focus of any system development. The purpose of system development is a software product – a program that works and meets stakeholders' requirements. Requirements analysis is necessary to document and organize the requirements. System design is necessary to 'divide and conquer' the complexity of the problem domain and enable proper project management. But the real crunch is in programming and testing.

In agile software development (Martin, 2003), testing takes a front seat and drives programming. This is known as **test-driven programming**. Test code is written before application code. The responsibility of the application programmer is to produce the code that passes the test program. The tests determine what is programmed. They also determine the detailed design of classes. For that reason, test-driven programming is sometimes generalized to mean **test-driven development**.

A program is a response to a test. A program asserts and verifies its test. If so, what verifies the test? The answer lies in yet another kind of testing – acceptance testing. **Acceptance testing** verifies if the application code (and, therefore, the tests passed by the application) satisfies stakeholders' requirements.

No testing can be complete and exhaustive. Acceptance testing cannot prove a program correct. Even in a small system, the number of possible execution paths in a program is too many to test them all. Similarly, in test-driven development, writing a test program to test each function and each combination of functions is not feasible, and may not even be useful.

There is a tradeoff between the cost and benefit of tests. The tradeoff determines the amount of test effort with relation to the amount of programming effort. A similar tradeoff, albeit from an educational viewpoint, has to be considered when discussing programming and testing in a book. This chapter explains test-driven development, programming, and acceptance testing. The EM case study serves to exemplify the techniques and processes.

Prior to presenting the case study, a quick tutorial in Java prepares the reader for more intricate code in the case study implementation. The tutorial takes a software engineering angle. It emphasizes the importance of maintaining class associations in programs, handling collections, managing object caches, and accessing the database.

12.1 Quick Tutorial in Java from a Software Engineering Viewpoint

Section 10.1 contained a quick tutorial in relational databases from a software engineering viewpoint. The tutorial used a simple `MovieActor` database to explain the principal database design and programming concepts. The Java tutorial presented below develops a simple `MovieActor` application program that accesses the `MovieActor` database.

The tutorial introduces selected Java concepts fundamental for engineering and developing Java systems. Unlike the EM case study, no attempt is made to place the discussed solutions within a design and architectural framework. All code resides in just five classes, three of which are entity classes corresponding to three tables in the `MovieActor` database.

Complete Java and Oracle source code and the UML model for this tutorial can be downloaded from the book website. The code excerpts presented below retain the line numbers for programming statements as in the complete solution and the program documentation on the website. For these reasons, there are gaps in line numbers in the listings of the code excerpts below.

12.1.1 Class

A *Java class* is a template for object creation. As such, it defines the following concepts (Lee and Tepfenhart, 2002):

- its name and visibility
- member variables (data members)
- member functions (methods)
- constructors
- visibility of members
- its superclass (if any) and interfaces (if any).

A class and its members must be assigned a level of visibility. The visibility of a class determines what other objects in the program can access its instances and properties. Class visibility is normally declared as *public* so that all other objects can freely access class instances.

Visibility of members can be public, protected, private, or package. Most data members are private (accessible only to the class instances) and most methods are public (accessible to instances of any class). The set of all public methods of a class defines the class interface. Because a class interface is a different concept from a *Java interface* or *UML interface*, it is sometimes called a class protocol to avoid terminology confusion (Lee and Tepfenhart, 2002). Visibility is discussed in more depth later in the book.

There are two categories of data members (or fields): instance variables and class variables. An instance variable belongs to an object (instance). It can be typed with a primitive data type or with a class data type. A variable with a primitive data type stores directly a value of that type. A **class data type** is a user-defined type signifying a previously defined class in the program. A variable of that type stores a reference (handle) to an object of a class. It is, therefore, sometimes called a **reference data type**.

In an object-oriented world, 'everything is an object'. Storing of data can only be done in an object. Method executions can only be performed on an object. Because 'everything is an object', a class itself must sometimes be treated as an object that can store data and perform methods. A *class variable* belongs to a class and is accessible to all objects of that class. All objects share the same class variable. Class variables are defined with the `static` keyword.

A **local variable** used 'locally' within a method body of the class is not a data member. Data members can store constant or non-constant values. Constants cannot be defined for local variables. Constants are defined with the `final` keyword.

Like data members, **methods** can be instance methods or class methods. An **instance method** belongs to an object. A **class method** belongs to a class (i.e. all objects of that class). Class methods are defined with the keyword `static`. They can be accessed either with an object of the class (`objectVariable.classMethod()`) or without an object by referring to the class name (`ClassName.classMethod()`).

Java supports **method overloading** by allowing many methods of a class to have the same name. Overloaded methods vary by having different signatures. A **method signature** is the method's list of arguments (parameters). A data type of the value that a method returns to a client object is called the return type. **Argument types** and **return types** can be primitive data types or class data types. A **method prototype**, sometimes called a *header* (Lee and Tepfenhart, 2002), consists of a method name, its signature and the return type. A method prototype can be either used in interfaces or declared as abstract, because it does not define an implementation.

A **constructor** is a special method that is used to instantiate a class (i.e. to create an object of the class). A constructor can take arguments and can be overloaded so that objects can be created in a variety of ways. A constructor name is the same as the name of the class for which it is defined.

Figure 12.1 shows the UML design of the `Movie` class. The `Movie` class is an entity class that corresponds (maps) to the movie table in Figure 10.1. The class consists of three

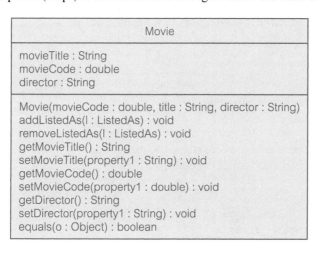

Figure 12.1
Design of the Movie class

Listing 12.1 Movie.java

```
Movie.java
7:    public class Movie {
8:        private String movieTitle;
9:
10:       private double movieCode;
11:
12:       private String director;
13:
14:       private Collection listedAs;
15:
16:       public Movie(double movieCode,String title,String director){
17:           this.movieCode = movieCode;
18:           this.director = director;
19:           this.movieTitle = title;
20:           listedAs = new ArrayList();
21:       }
22:
23:       public void addListedAs(ListedAs l){
24:           listedAs.add(l);
25:       }
26:
27:       public void removeListedAs(ListedAs l){
28:           listedAs.remove(l);
29:       }
30:
35:       public String getMovieTitle() {
36:           return movieTitle;
37:       }
38:
43:       public void setMovieTitle(String title) {
44:           this.movieTitle = title;
45:       }
46:
51:       public double getMovieCode() {
52:           return movieCode;
53:       }
54:
59:       public void setMovieCode(double code) {
60:           this.movieCode = code;
61:       }
62:
67:       public String getDirector() {
68:           return director;
```

```
69:       }
70:
75:       public void setDirector(String director) {
76:           this.director = director;
77:       }
78:
79:       public boolean equals(Object o){
80:           try{
81:               Movie m = (Movie) o;
82:               if(m.movieCode == movieCode) return true;
83:           }catch(Exception exc){}
84:           return false;
85:       }
86:
87:   }
```

data members (all of them instance variables), a constructor, and a number of instance methods with their signatures. Data members defined with a class (reference) data type are not visible in the UML middle class compartment because they are represented as role names on the association lines (Section 12.1.2).

Listing 12.1 is a complete definition (implementation) of the Java class `Movie.java` for the design in Figure 12.1. The definition includes visibility properties (suppressed from the visual display in Figure 12.1). The type of `listedAs` is a `Collection`, discussed in Section 12.1.2.

Class Associations and Collections   12.1.2

As discussed throughout Chapter 9, the understandability, maintainability, and scalability of systems is preconditioned on making object collaboration paths clearly visible in the code. One way of enforcing this visibility is by means of setting up association links between classes, which collaborate by passing messages. The PCMEF architectural framework encourages this.

As indicated before, associations between classes are typically represented by instance variables, which store references to the associated objects – only one reference in the case of an association with a multiplicity of one, or a collection of references in the case of a multiplicity of many.

From conceptual to design class model

Most large systems implement some kind of caching of table records as class objects in the program's memory (Section 10.2). Figures 10.2 and 10.4 show the mapping between a relational database model and a conceptual class model for `MovieActor`. The conceptual

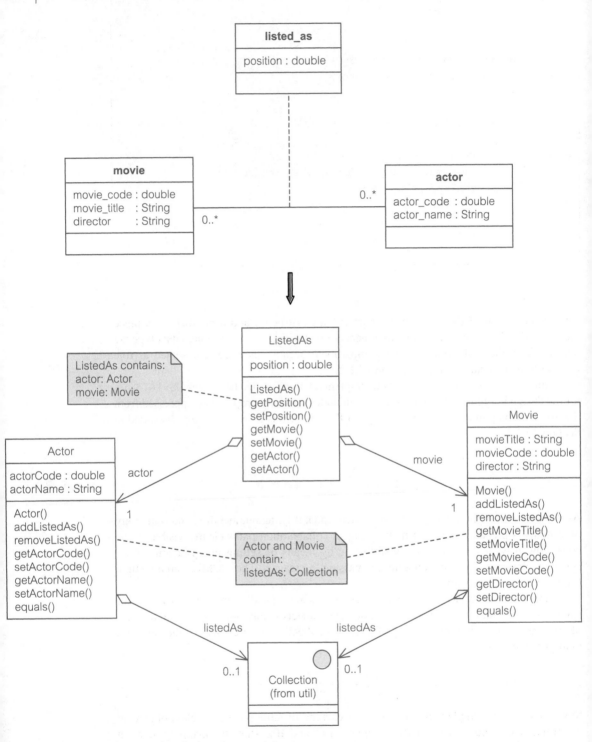

Figure 12.2 From conceptual to design class model

class model can serve as a starting point for the design of classes in the entity package of a MovieActor program that conforms to the PCMEF framework.

The conceptual class model for MovieActor used the association class listed_as to store the position attribute. A many-to-many association linked the classes movie and actor. This was a succinct and expressive model.

The transformation of the MovieActor conceptual model to a design model must clearly retain the three entity classes, as shown in Figure 12.2. By a Java convention, the class names start with capital letters and attribute names have underscores replaced with the capital letters of successive words. Method names are added, as the design of entity classes must be placed in the overall context of the design of interactions (Section 11.3).

What may come as a surprise in Figure 12.2 is that the many-to-many association was not converted to two one-to-many associations, following the principle discussed in Section 10.2.2 (albeit discussed in the context of a mapping to tables). Instead, a slightly convoluted design emerged with four unidirectional associations with the multiplicities of one. The understanding of this design requires that the notion of Java collection is explained (next section).

Java collections

Unlike object-oriented databases, object-oriented programming languages do not provide explicit support for implementing and maintaining associations between objects. It is a programmer's responsibility to program associations into classes and to maintain the integrity of association links. The task can become quite tricky, in particular in the case of bidirectional associations in which a modification of a link in one object necessitates a corresponding modification of a link in an associated object.

From a data structure perspective, an **association link** is stored in an instance variable. In the case of a multiplicity of one, the instance variable is typed with a class data type. A value of the variable is a reference to an object of that class. In the case of a multiplicity of many, the instance variable is typed with the Collection interface from a Java library java.util.Collection. A value of the variable is a reference to some object that implements the Collection interface. Figure 12.3 shows the Collection interface.

The Collection interface represents a **container** for objects (called *elements*). Its methods allow adding new elements, removing existing elements, finding if it contains a specific element, checking if the collection is not empty, checking its size (the number of elements), placing the elements in an array, and iterating over its elements using an Iterator object.

The java.util.Collection library delivers three categories of containers: List, Set, and Map. These categories are interfaces themselves with only two or three implementations of each one (Eckel, 2000).

The concrete classes that implement the List functionality are ArrayList, LinkedList, and Vector. ArrayList is an ordered list of elements implemented with an array. It provides rapid direct access to elements but it may be slow when adding and removing elements. LinkedList is superior for sequential traversing through elements but it is slow for random access to individual elements. Vector is considered to be a

Figure 12.3
The Collection
interface

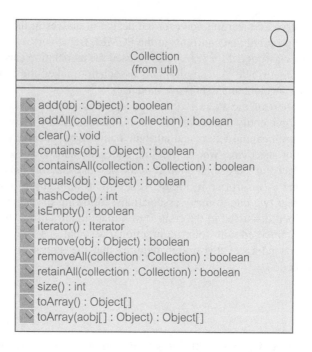

legacy class, but it remains a popular choice for storing association links (Lee and Tepfenhart, 2002).

There are two concrete classes with the Set functionality: HashSet and TreeSet. Both ensure that the elements are unique (as a set does not permit duplicate elements). HashSet uses a hashing function to deliver quick access to individual elements. TreeSet implements a tree structure, which keeps the elements in a sorted order. This benefits traversals based on a sorted order, producing a sorted subset, or finding the first or last object.

The Map interface maintains key-value pairs that allow finding a value using a key. Indexes of relational databases use the same principle (Section 10.1.6). There are two implementations of the Map interface: HashMap and TreeMap. HashMap uses a special value called hash code, which allows rapid access to the object key and, therefore, quick retrieval of the object value. TreeMap allows viewing object values in the order sorted by object keys.

Returning to Figure 12.2, the aggregation relationships from Actor and Movie to the Collection interface have multiplicities 0..1. An optional participation (i.e. the multiplicity of zero) means that an Actor or Movie object may not be listed at all in a ListedAs object. The multiplicity of one means that an Actor or Movie object may be linked to an object that holds a collection of references to many ListedAs objects. The collection represents, therefore, the multiplicity of many in the conceptual model.

Java collections are not aware of a class of objects that they contain. In reality, they contain references to objects typed with the Object class, which is the root of all Java classes. In effect, a Java collection will allow references to objects of any class to be stored. To ensure a degree of safety, Java forces *casting* objects to a correct type when they are extracted from a collection. From the viewpoint of the type safety, the C++ solution to use parameterized types is superior for implementing association links.

Associations on entity objects

Listing 12.1 presents the Movie class. Listing 12.2 is an excerpt from the Actor class that shows its data members. The listedAs variable defines the collection of references to ListedAs objects. The collection is an ArrayList created within the Actor() constructor. The addListedAs() and removeListedAs() methods are used to add or remove ArrayList elements. This changes (indirectly, via ListedAs) the association links between actors and movies.

Listing 12.2 Actor.java

```
Actor.java

7:    public class Actor {
8:         private double actorCode;
9:
10:        private String actorName;
11:
12:        private Collection listedAs;
13:
14:        public Actor(double code, String name){
15:            this.actorCode = code;
16:            this.actorName = name;
17:            listedAs = new ArrayList();
18:        }
19:
20:        public void addListedAs(ListedAs l) {
21:            listedAs.add(l);
22:        }
23:
24:        public void removeListedAs(ListedAs l) {
25:            listedAs.remove(l);
26:        }
66:    }
```

Listing 12.3 is an excerpt from the ListedAs class. It shows how each ListedAs object maintains links to its Movie object and Actor object. The references to Movie and Actor objects are passed in arguments of a call to the ListedAs() constructor. Once a ListedAs object is created, it passes itself as an argument in calls to the addListedAs methods on the Movie and Actor objects. These calls ensure enforcement of the 'referential integrity' between ListedAs and Movie and between ListedAs and Actor.

Listing 12.3 ListedAs.java

```
ListedAs.java
5:    public class ListedAs {
6:        private double position;
7:
8:        private Movie movie;
9:
10:       private Actor actor;
11:
12:       public ListedAs(Movie m, Actor a, double position){
13:           this.movie = m;
14:           this.actor = a;
15:           this.position = position;
16:
17:           //register this ListedAs to the Movie and Actor
18:           movie.addListedAs(this);
19:           actor.addListedAs(this);
20:       }
69:
70:   }
```

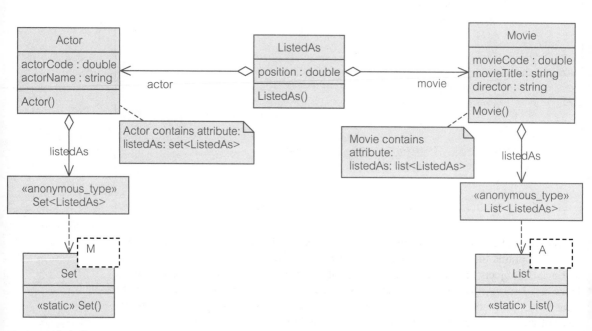

Figure 12.4 C++ parameterized types

C++ parameterized types

Ideally, an instance variable that stores a collection of references to other objects should be typed with a collection class that defines everything in the collection in terms of a type parameter. Such a class is called variously a **parameterized type**, a **class template**, or a **generic class**. Before a parameterized type can be used, the type parameter must be replaced with an existing class.

Parameterized types are not supported in Java, although an experimental Java compiler with such support is available from Sun. Parameterized types exist in C++ (Ege, 1992). Figure 12.4 shows how parameterized types could be used in a C++ application for `MovieActor`.

Figure 12.4 shows two parameterized types: `Set<M>` and `List<A>`. The `Set` class is defined as a class template based on a parameter class `M`, and the `List` class is based on a parameter class `A`. All member variables and member functions of the `Set` and `List` classes must be defined in terms of the parameters `M` and `A`, respectively.

Before such variables or functions can be used, the parameterized types must be replaced with specific classes. These classes are stereotyped in Figure 12.4 as «anonymous_type». The «anonymous_type» classes replace the type parameter with a class name. They depend on the corresponding parameterized types for their functionality.

For example, `Actor` contains a variable `listedAs`. The type of this variable is `Set<ListedAs>`. This, in effect, establishes an aggregation/association link from `Actor` to a collection (`Set`) of references pointing to objects of the `ListedAs` class.

Listing 12.4 shows C++ syntax corresponding to the model in Figure 12.5. Class definitions for parameterized types specify class parameters on which they are defined. Similarly, implementations of all methods, such as constructors `Set()` and `List()`, point to a class parameter. The parameterized type is then used to instantiate collection objects, such as `Set<ListedAs> listedAs`.

A comparison of Figures 12.2 and 12.4 and related code listings shows how C++ parameterized types are superior to using the Java `Collection` interface for the implementation of associations with a multiplicity of many. The creation of new types based on other types makes it possible to define variables typed with collection classes that can contain only objects of specific class.

Listing 12.4 Programming C++ parameterized types

```
Programming C++ parameterized types

template <class M> class Set
{
   public:
       static Set();

       ...
};
template <class M> Set<M>::Set() {...}

#include "Set.h"
class Actor
```

```cpp
{
   public:
      Actor();
   private:
      double actorCode;
      string actorName;
      Set<ListedAs> listedAs;
};
Actor::Actor() { }

template <class A> class List
{
   public:
      static List();

      ...
};
template <class A> List<A>::List() {...}

#include "List.h"
class Movie
{
   public:
      Movie();
   private:
      double movieCode;
      string movieTitle;
      string director;
      List<ListedAs> listedAs;
};
Movie::Movie(){ }

#include "Actor.h"
#include "Movie.h"
class ListedAs
{
   public:
      ListedAs();
   private:
      double position;
      Movie movie;
      Actor actor;
};
ListedAs::ListedAs(){
   position = -1;
}
```

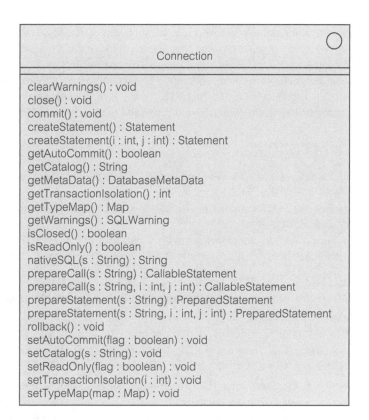

Figure 12.5
The Connection
interface

Database Access in Java

12.1.3

As discussed in Chapter 10, the only way to access data in a relational database is by means of some kind of SQL. Java applications and applets can access a database using **Java Database Connectivity** (JDBC) or **SQL for Java** (SQLJ). JDBC and SQLJ allow Java to call embedded SQL and to call stored procedures (Section 10.1.5). The JDBC standard is part of the **Java Development Kit** (JDK) class library (the `java.sql` package).

A DBMS can provide a technology to use Java for coding stored procedures into the database (i.e. a Java method can be stored and run in a database). Oracle supports such technology under the name **Java Stored Procedures** (Bonazzi and Stokol, 2001; Lakshman, 2002). This is an example of a two-way integration environment where Java can call a stored procedure and vice versa. The technology has limitations and it is not discussed further in this book.

Database access in Java can also be achieved from reusable Java components such as **JavaBeans, Enterprise JavaBeans** (EJB), or **Business Components for Java** (BC4J) (Bonazzi and Stokol, 2001; Lakshman, 2002). The latter is an Oracle technology. JavaBeans allows the use of JDBC calls in Bean methods. EJB allows building components that execute in a server-side environment. EJB delivers a middle tier of a three-tier or multi-tier architecture (Section 9.2.2). An EJB component can contain JDBC and SQLJ statements. BC4J is part of Oracle JDeveloper's integrated programming environment.

Whereas EJB provides database-like services to support persistency, transactions, and security, BC4J concentrates on encapsulating the business logic in a separate tier. In Oracle, a BC4J component can be deployed as an EJB server object.

Java has been designed for web environments. The technologies involved include Java applets, Java servlets and Java Server Pages (JSP). As any Java technology, the technologies for Web environments can access a database through the means discussed in this section.

Comparison of JDBC and SQLJ

JDBC and SQLJ are two standard ways to embed SQL statements in Java code in order to communicate with a database. SQLJ runs on top of JDBC and requires a translator that replaces the embedded SQL statements with calls to SQLJ runtime environment. This runtime library uses JDBC.

JDBC provides an API to communicate with a database and uses a JDBC driver to connect to a database. There are four types of JDBC drivers (White *et al.*, 1999):

1. JDBC/ODBC bridge plus ODBC driver – this requires an Open Database Connectivity (ODBC) driver to be installed on a client machine before being able to use JDBC to access the database.
2. Native API – a vendor-specific driver that converts JDBC calls into DBMS-specific API, such as Oracle Call Interface (OCI); it requires some DBMS binary code to be loaded on a client machine.
3. Open Protocol Net – this translates JDBC calls into a database-independent net protocol allowing access to many different databases from the same Java client; the translation to a DBMS protocol is done on a server, making the connectivity transparent to the client.
4. Native Protocol Net – like a type 3 driver but uses a proprietary net protocol to access a specific vendor's database.

Once a Java program loads a database driver, a database connection (Connection object) can be established. JDBC or SQLJ statements and calls to stored procedures can then be created (Statement objects) and executed on that connection. Result sets returned from the execution of queries and stored procedures require the involvement of a ResultSet object. When processing is completed, the program closes the Statement, ResultSet and Connection objects.

JDBC and SQLJ code can be mixed in a program sharing the same connection and result sets. SQLJ consists of a SQLJ translator and a SQLJ runtime environment. The translator is a preprocessor that converts a SQLJ source program (with a .sqlj extension) into a Java source (.java extension), before compiling the source to produce a class file (.class extension). The runtime consists of a SQLJ library, which implements, in pure Java, the SQLJ statements embedded in the program. Typically, a SQLJ runtime uses a JDBC driver to access a database.

SQLJ is a higher-level programming environment than JDBC. Normally, it allows programming the same functionality with less code. The syntax and semantics of SQL embedded in a program are validated and optimized at compile time. The resulting code is more robust and can deliver better performance. However, JDBC has an advantage of directly supporting the construction and execution of dynamic SQL. In dynamic SQL, the details of database objects, such as table and column names, do not need to be known at compile time and can be provided to the program at runtime.

Establishing a database connection

Establishing a database connection involves the use of a JDBC class `DriverManager` and a JDBC interface `Connection` (from the `java.sql` library). There are several ways of loading a JDBC/ODBC bridge driver. The simplest uses the method `Class.forname()` (Line 16 in Listing 12.5). The method comes from `java.lang.Class`. It implicitly creates an instance of a driver and registers it with the `DriverManager` object.

Listing 12.5 Making the database connection

```
Making the database connection

11:   public class Connection {
12:       private java.sql.Connection conn;
13:
14:       public Connection() throws Exception {
15:           //establish connection
16:           Class.forName("oracle.jdbc.driver.OracleDriver");
17:           conn =
18:               DriverManager.getConnection(
19:                   "jdbc:oracle:thin:@localhost:1521:oracle8i",
20:                   "pse1",
21:                   "pse1");
22:       }
136: }
```

A connection object (`conn` – Line 17) is created with a call to `getConnection()` on the `DriverManager` object (Line 18). `getConnection()` requires three parameters: a URL connect string pointing to a database instance (Line 19), a database username (Line 20), and a database password (Line 21).

Figure 12.5 shows the methods of the `Connection` interface. The interface includes methods returning three kinds of interface that can be used to execute SQL statements. These interfaces are `Statement`, `PreparedStatement`, and `CallableStatement`.

Executing SQL statements

A statement object needs to be created to perform a SQL query on a database. A statement object must conform to one of the three JDBC interfaces: `Statement`, `PreparedStatement`, or `CallableStatement`.

A `Statement` object is used to execute simple SQL statements that do not have parameters. A `PreparedStatement` object can be used to execute the same SQL statement repeatedly but each time with different search conditions or values. A `CallableStatement` object is used to call stored procedures in the database.

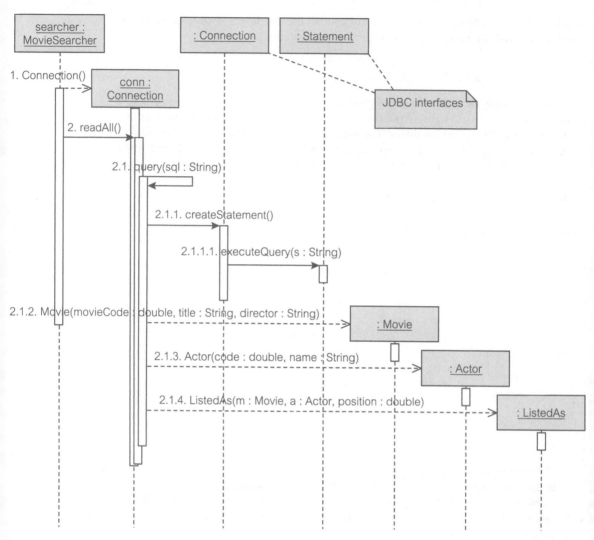

Figure 12.6 Sequence diagram for accessing the database and creating entity types

To load entity objects to memory, the MovieActor application needs to query the database and to create entity objects from result sets returned by queries. For simplicity, the MovieActor application consists of only five classes: three entity classes, the MovieSearcher class, and the Connection class. The MovieSearcher class initiates processing and displays the results of database access to the screen. The Connection class interacts with the database.

Figure 12.6 (also Figure 2.13) presents a sequence diagram for the process of populating the entity cache upon retrieving the data from the database. The searcher :MovieSearcher object instantiates the conn:Connection object and then sends to it the `readAll()` message. The `readAll()` method constructs a SQL query string and passes it to the `query()` method.

The `query()` method sends the `createStatement()` message on the `conn` object. This is shown in Figure 12.6 as a message to the JDBC Connection interface. The `createStatement()` returns a `Statement` object. The `executeQuery()` message on the `Statement` object produces a `ResultSet` object that is returned to the `readAll()` method.

A `ResultSet` object (implementing the JDBC `ResultSet` interface) is not shown in Figure 12.6. It represents the set of records returned from the execution of the query. The object allows iterating over the records and accessing the data values of individual items (columns) in a record. Because the SQL query is a join query, which retrieves in one go all records from the three tables in the `MovieActor` database, iterating over the `ResultSet` can result in creating the `Movie`, `Actor`, and `ListedAs` objects in the application memory cache.

Listings 12.6 and 12.7 provide the code details that the sequence diagram in Figure 12.6 could not capture. The code for the `MovieSearcher` class in Listing 12.6 does not require further explanation. The most interesting method is `readAll()` within the `Connection` class in Listing 12.7.

Listing 12.6 MovieSearcher.java

```
MovieSearcher.java

8:     public class MovieSearcher {
13:        private Connection conn;
14:        private Collection listedAs;
15:
16:        public MovieSearcher() throws Exception {
17:            conn = new Connection();
18:            retrieveAll();
19:        }
204:
205:       public static void main(String args[]) {
207:               MovieSearcher searcher = new MovieSearcher();
249:       }
250: }
```

The `readAll()` is presented on Lines 23–42 in Listing 12.7. It first creates an `ArrayList` collection on Line 24. The SQL statement is placed in a string (Line 26) and then passed as an argument to the `query` method. The `query` method is shown on Lines 45–48. It creates an object conforming to the `Statement` interface that can be used to run SQL queries against the database connected to. The `st` statement object is created by executing `createStatement()` on the `conn` object (Line 46). On Line 47, the SQL query string is executed on the `st` object and the records retrieved from the database are stored in an instance of the `ResultSet` object called `rs` (Line 25).

Listing 12.7 Connection.java

```
Connection.java
11:   public class Connection {
12:       private java.sql.Connection conn;
13:
14:       public Connection() throws Exception {
15:           //establish connection
16:           Class.forName("oracle.jdbc.driver.OracleDriver");
17:           conn =
18:               DriverManager.getConnection(
19:                   "jdbc:oracle:thin:@localhost:1521:oracle8i",
20:                   "pse1",
21:                   "pse1");
22:       }
23:       public Collection readAll() throws Exception{
24:           Collection c = new ArrayList();
25:           ResultSet rs =
26:               query("SELECT * FROM movie m, actor a, listed_as l
                        WHERE m.movie_code = l.movie_code
                           AND l.actor_code = a.actor_code");
27:           while (rs.next()) {
28:               double movieCode = rs.getDouble("movie_code");
29:               String movieTitle = rs.getString("movie_title");
30:               String director = rs.getString("director");
31:
32:               double actorCode = rs.getDouble("actor_code");
33:               String actorName = rs.getString("actor_name");
34:
35:               double position = rs.getDouble("position");
36:
37:               Movie m = new Movie(movieCode, movieTitle, director);
38:               Actor a = new Actor(actorCode, actorName);
39:               ListedAs la = new ListedAs(m, a, position);
40:               c.add(la);
41:           }
42:           return c;
43:       }
44:
45:       private ResultSet query(String sql) throws Exception {
46:           Statement st = conn.createStatement();
47:           return st.executeQuery(sql);
48:       }
136: }
```

On Line 27, the `next()` method of the `ResultSet` object loops through the records one record at a time. The data is fetched in the assignments statements in Lines 28–35. From the data in each record fetched, three entity objects are instantiated in the memory cache: `Movie`, `Actor`, and `ListedAs` (Lines 37–39).

Each `ListedAs` object contains three data members. Two of them are a `Movie` and an `Actor` object. In effect, the collection of `ListedAs` objects contains all `MovieActor` database records. The objects are placed in the collection using the `add()` method on Line 40.

Calling stored procedures and functions

The `preparedCall()` method, defined in the `Connection` interface (Figure 12.5), returns a `CallableStatement` object that can be used to call a stored procedure or function. Listings 12.8 and 12.9 illustrate the code needed to call, execute, and display results returned by the stored function `string_search` described in Chapter 10 in Listing 10.8.

The `displaySearchMoviesByStoredFunction()` method in the `MovieSearcher` class in Listing 12.8, requests that the `conn` object performs the `searchMoviesByStoredFunction()` method (Line 62). The search string (`"vamp"`) is hard-coded in the call from the main method to `displaySearchMoviesByStoredFunction()` (Line 244).

Listing 12.8 displaySearchMoviesByStoredFunction() – method in MovieSearcher

```
displaySearchMoviesByStoredFunction() - method in MovieSearcher

8:    public class MovieSearcher {
59:
60:      public void displaySearchMoviesByStoredFunction(String str)
                throws Exception{
61:        System.out.println("Searching movies on specified
                                          string:" +str);
62:        Collection c = conn.searchMoviesByStoredFunction(str);
63:        Iterator it = c.iterator();
64:        while(it.hasNext()){
65:            displayMovie((Movie) it.next());
66:            System.out.println();
67:        }
68:      }
194:     private void displayMovie(Movie movie) {
195:       System.out.println("Movie Code: " + movie.getMovieCode());
196:       System.out.println("Movie Title: " + movie.getMovieTitle());
197:       System.out.println("Movie Director: " + movie.getDirector());
198:     }
205:     public static void main(String args[]) {
244:            searcher.displaySearchMoviesByStoredFunction("vamp");
249:     }
250: }
```

Listing 12.9 searchMoviesByStoredFunction( ) – method in Connection

```
searchMoviesByStoredFunction() - method in Connection

11:  public class Connection {
115:

116:     public Collection searchMoviesByStoredFunction(String searchStr)
                        throws Exception{
117:         Collection c = new ArrayList();
118:

119:         CallableStatement st =
        conn.prepareCall("{ ? = call MovieSearch.string_search (?)}");
120:         st.registerOutParameter(1, OracleTypes.CURSOR);
                                    //we are expecting cursor
121:         st.setString(2,searchStr);
122:         st.execute();
123:         ResultSet rs = (ResultSet) st.getObject(1);
124:         while (rs.next()) {
125:             double movieCode = rs.getDouble("movie_code");
126:             String movieTitle = rs.getString("movie_title");
127:             String director = rs.getString("director");
128:             Movie m = new Movie(movieCode, movieTitle, director);
130:             c.add(m);
131:         }
132:         closeResult(rs);
133:

134:         return c;
135:     }
136: }
```

MovieSearcher expects a Collection of Movie objects to be returned by the call on Line 62. Once returned, the Iterator object (Figure 12.3) is used to iterate through Movie objects (Lines 63–67) and requests the displayMovie() method (Lines 194–198) to perform the display of the results to the screen. Figure 12.7 is an execution screenshot that shows the outcome of a search for movies containing the string "vamp" in the movie title (cf. the execution in Listing 10.7).

Figure 12.7
Display of string search results using a stored function

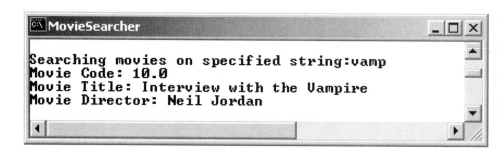

To perform the service of finding the `"vamp"` string in movie titles (Listing 12.9), the `Connection` object needs to activate the `string_search` stored function (Listing 10.8). First an `ArrayList` is instantiated to hold the `Collection` returned by the search (Line 117). The `prepareCall()` method calls the stored function and qualifies the call with the name of the containing database package (Line 119). The question marks signify parameters – they are known as *bind parameters* or *placeholders*. The first question mark before the equals sign represents the return value of the function. The question mark at the end refers to the input `searchStr` parameter.

The call to the stored function creates an object of the `CallableStatement` class. The return value of the stored function is registered to this object as an output parameter using the `registerOutParameter()` method. Because the return value (signified by number 1) is expected to be a collection of objects, the database cursor mechanism is used (Line 120). The input parameter (signified by number 2) is bound to the `Connection` object using the `setString()` method (Line 121). This completes the construction of the `CallableStatement` object and the `execute()` method is called to activate the `string_search` stored function (Line 122).

On Line 123, the `CallableStatement` object is cast to a `ResultSet` object. This cast allows using the `getObject()` method in place of a `getCursor()` method. The program can now iterate over `ResultSet` objects and add them into the `Collection` (Line 130), which is returned to `MovieSearcher` (Line 62 in Listing 12.8).

Test-Driven Development

Test-driven development is a practice popularized by the agile software development (Martin, 2003) of which the main representative is eXtreme Programming (XP) (Newkirk and Martin, 2001). However, test-driven development can be and should be embraced by other development processes, including the Unified Process (UP) (Kruchten, 1999).

Test-driven development means both test-first programming and test-first design. The test-driven development invites developers to write test specifications and programs before deciding on the final design and before starting 'cutting the application code'. The application code is written as a response to a test code, not vice versa.

If a test code is written before the application code, then clearly the test program will fail when run. That is precisely the point. A test code is written to fail the application code. The application code should be implemented so that the test will succeed next time it is run. This will assert the existence of the functionality demanded by the test. The essence of test-driven development is to drive software development, not software verification.

Test-driven development is an iterative and incremental process intermixed with writing the application code. The idea is to write a test case for a tiny problem, followed by just enough code to run the test, followed by extensions to the test case, and a bit more code, etc.

Test-driven development requires that a suite of unit tests be programmed for white box testing of individual classes and main collaborations between classes. The conventional understanding of white box testing is 'testing to code' (Maciaszek, 2001). The idea is to study the code, understand it, and test (exercise) possible execution paths. However, in the test-driven development the real code does not exist yet. The code can only be imagined based on the existing design and the paths can be exercised in 'dry-runs' (i.e. running the code mentally, without the computer).

Test-driven development starts as a unit-based testing. The notion of a **test unit** has two interpretations: a test unit can be seen either as a target of the test or as a resource of the test. A target of a test unit is typically a single class in the application code, but it can also be just selected methods of a class or a few cooperating classes. As a resource, a test unit is a piece of code – a class or a set of classes that perform the testing. Methods within a test unit class are called **test cases**.

Test cases can be combined in **test suites** to run a collection of test cases that target many classes or even the whole system. An interesting question is where to place the test code with regard to the application code to be tested. There are a number of possibilities.

As observed by Eckel (2000), a test case can be written within a main() method of each class to be tested (i.e. within each test unit). As described in Section 11.2.3, one of the main() methods instantiates the first object in the application and starts the program. This is the main() for the class invoked on the command line. The main() methods in other classes can be conveniently used for unit testing.

An alternative to placing the test case within the main() methods is to put them in a static inner class within a class to be tested (Eckel, 2000). An **inner class** in Java is a class definition of a class placed within another class definition (**outer class**). Since an inner object can freely access all elements of an enclosing outer object, it can be advantageously used to contain a test case. During compilation, an inner class is generated as a separate class. If the outer class is named X and the inner class is named Y, then the generated class will be called X$Y. The X$Y class can be used for testing, but it can be excluded from any code distributed to the users.

Using a main() method or an inner class are viable approaches to unit testing but they do not give any support to the overall testing framework. The framework is a sole responsibility of the developers and programmers. A comprehensive and systematic approach to the test-driven development is better served by generic testing frameworks, which are libraries of classes and interfaces aimed at facilitating test implementations. JUnit (JUnit, 2003) is a Java framework recommended by the agile software development and XP in particular.

12.2.1 JUnit Framework

JUnit defines the framework for creating test cases, test suites, and the tools for running them. The principal classes of the JUnit framework are TestCase and TestSuite. Both implement an interface called Test. Test defines the methods to run a test.

TestSuite is a composite class that can contain (conceptually) more than one Test. Because Test is just an interface implemented as either TestCase or TestSuite, a TestSuite object can contain multiple TestCase objects and/or another TestSuite object. So a TestSuite object can be composed into more complex TestSuite objects, which in turn can be composed, and so on recursively.

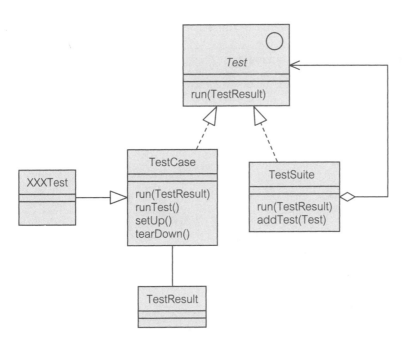

Figure 12.8
JUnit in terms of
the Composite
pattern

Figure 12.8 shows an overview structure of the JUnit framework. The model uses one of the most fundamental and most useful patterns in object-oriented design and programming – the **Composite pattern** (Gamma *et al.*, 1995). The pattern allows objects to be recursively composed. Individual TestCase objects and compositions (aggregations) of them (TestSuite objects) are treated uniformly. Test is an interface that represents both individual objects and compositions of them. Client objects, such as XXXTest, manipulate the concrete objects in the composition through the Test interface.

A test unit can be implemented as a subclass that extends TestCase. If the scope of a test unit is the XXX class, then the test class can be named XXXTest. XXXTest is defined as a subclass of TestCase that adds various test methods to the methods inherited from TestCase. XXXTest is usually placed in the same package as the XXX class.

Testing of the XXX class presumes that objects of that class are created during a test run and interacted with to perform the test. These objects – known as a **fixture** of the test unit – establish the context for the XXXTest class. Fixture objects provide the target for the testing code. The testing code 'exercises' the objects in the fixture and produces the test results.

The setUp() method is used to initialize the fixture objects, and the tearDown() method is used to clean up the fixture at the end of each test case. If a test unit runs multiple test cases, then the setUp() and tearDown() methods are called multiple times so that each test case is given a 'clean sheet' to start from.

The runTest() method is used to run a test unit by calling the desired test cases (e.g. within the XXXTest class). JUnit supports static and dynamic modes of running test cases. The static mode has two variants. The first variant of the static mode is shown in Listing 12.10. When invoked by one of the few TestRunner classes of the JUnit framework, the runTest() method calls the test cases listed in it.

Listing 12.10 runTest( ) within a TestCase class

```
runTest() - method in XXXTest

public class XXXTest extends TestCase {
   public XXXTest(String testName) {
      super(testName);
   }
   public void testSomething() {
      ...
   }
   public void testSomethingElse() {
      ...
   }
   public void runTest() {
      testSomething();
      testSomethingElse();
   }
}
```

Listing 12.11 runTest( ) within anonymous inner class

```
runTest() within anonymous inner class within YYYTestUnit

public class YYYTestUnit extends TestCase {
   public static Test suite() {
      TestSuite suite = new TestSuite();
      TestCase test = new XXXTest("my test") {
         public void runTest() {
            testSomething();
            testSomethingElse();
            testSomethingDifferent();
         }
         public void testSomethingDifferent(){
            ...
         }
      };
      suite.addTest(test);
      suite.addTest(new YYYTestUnit("another test"));
      return suite;
   }
   public static void main(String args[]){
      junit.textui.TestRunner.run(suite());
      //junit.swingui.TestRunner.run(YYYTestUnit.class);
   }
}
```

The second variant of the static mode takes advantage of an anonymous inner class. An **anonymous inner class** is an inner class with no name that is represented by the return value obtained from the creation of a new object of some class. Assuming that the runTest() method is not included within XXXTest as in Listing 12.10, the runTest() method can be defined within an anonymous inner class, shown in bold type in Listing 12.11. The string, such as 'my test', is required to identify the test if it fails.

Note that an anonymous inner class calls test cases explicitly. It does not have to call all test cases defined within XXXTest and it can introduce and implement new test cases, such as testSomethingDifferent() in Listing 12.11. Note also that a test unit can be run in a text user interface (in the console window) or in a GUI (swing) window.

The dynamic mode of preparing a test unit and running it uses Java reflection to implement the runTest() method at runtime. **Reflection** is a mechanism allowing the discovery of class and method information at runtime and providing the ability to create and execute objects, classes of which are not known at compile time.

Listing 12.12 shows how a test method is found and invoked dynamically. The dynamic mode assumes that an argument string provided to the XXXTest constructor is the name of the test case to call with the runTest() method.

Listing 12.12 runTest( ) implemented dynamically

```
runTest() implemented dynamically

   public static Test suite() {
      TestSuite suite = new TestSuite();
      TestCase test1 = new XXXTest("testSomething");
      TestCase test2 = new XXXTest("testSomethingElse");
      suite.addTest(test1);
      suite.addTest(test2);
      return suite;
   }
   public static void main(String args[]){
      junit.textui.TestRunner.run(suite());
   }
```

JUnit provides a visual interface to run test cases and test suites. The interface simplifies invoking the tests, it shows the test progress, and it indicates successful tests with a green progress bar. If a test fails, a red progress bar is displayed and the names of failed tests are listed.

Test-Driven Development in Email Management — 12.2.2

As pointed out by Martin (2003), test-driven development forces the design of the resulting software to be conveniently callable and testable. This objective is achieved by minimizing coupling between classes. In test-driven development, the primary mechanism of decoupling classes is by surrounding them with interfaces (Section 9.1.7).

In Iteration 1 of the EM case study, the decoupling of classes is the main motivation of the PCMEF+ architectural framework (Section 9.2.2). The framework itself, prior to test-driven development, forces the design that is conveniently callable and testable. In doing so, interfaces are given proper consideration. Most interfaces are grouped in the `acquaintance` package, which is used to break circular dependencies and to ensure observance of the Downward Dependency Principle (Section 9.2.2).

Test-driven development in Iteration 1 assumes the existence of a *prior architectural design*. Test-driven development is no substitute for a lack of architecture. Additionally, for educational reasons, Iteration 1 minimizes the number of classes in PCMEF packages. The targets of the test-driven development in Iteration 1 are the internal structuring of classes, the discovery of methods, and the establishment of message passing in support of interactions. Test-driven development is performed concurrently with the class and interaction design (Chapter 11) and it guides the programming.

The 'Login' interaction is one of nine interactions identified for Iteration 1 (Section 11.4). Being a relatively simple interaction, it can be used to explain the process, philosophy, and outcomes of test-driven development.

The PCMEF architecture requests that inter-layer message passing is *downward* from a higher package to a lower package. Any *upward* communication needs to go through interface or event propagation. In the login scenario, a user is prompted to perform login. This is easily captured as the following code in the PMain class:

```
PConsole console;
console.displayLogin();
```

Test-driven development, similarly to other kinds of testing, does not stipulate testing everything all the time. It does not make sense to write test cases that are not useful. There is not much testing that can be done on the `PConsole` implementation of login. `PConsole` merely delegates the login service to a lower layer, to the `CActioner` class.

The EM case study is a database application. The login verification requires a database connection as well as checking that the user is an employee in the `Employee` table. `PConsole` acquires the username and password and passes this information to `CActioner`, as follows:

```
class PConsole{
      CActioner actioner;
      void displayLogin(){
          ...
          actioner.login(username,password);
      }
}
```

The above code section clearly shows that there is a need to test `CActioner`'s login implementation. `CActioner` is a concrete class that represents the `control` layer (as per the Façade pattern). The test case for it is as in Listing 12.13.

Listing 12.13 Method testLogin( ) in CActionerTest

Method testLogin() in CActionerTest

```
void testLogin(){
   CActioner actioner = new CActioner();
   try{
      IAEmployee emp = actioner.login("user","passwd");
      assertEquals(emp.getLoginName(), "user");
   }catch(Exception exc){
      fail("Exception occurs during login");
   }
}
```

JUnit comes with a variety of `assert` methods to assert the test outcomes, such as `assertTrue()`, `assertSame()`, `assertNull()`, `assertEquals()`. The `assertEquals()` tends to be most useful. It is used in Listing 12.13 to assert that the username provided to `login()` is equal to the login name of that user, as stored in the `Employee` table and obtained by calling `getLoginName()` on the `EEmployee` object.

The `testLogin()` method stated the intent with regard to `CActioner`. `CActioner` must implement that intent. This is sometimes called **intentional programming** (Martin, 2003). Clearly, `CActioner`'s login method must return an `EEmployee` object (`IAEmployee` interface) to assert that the employee's login name is equal to the username provided. Going backwards, intentional programming shows also how the client (`PConsole`) methods should be constructed. The resulting code section in `CActioner` is shown in Listing 12.14.

Listing 12.14 Method login( ) in CActioner

Method login() in CActioner

```
private IAEmployee emp;
...
public Object login( String username, String passwd ) {
   emp = broker.login( username, passwd );
}
```

`CActioner` is now able to return an `EEmployee` object but the fulfillment of the `login()` service is delegated further down to `MBroker`. The `emp` object is the representation of the `EEmployee` concrete object, but there is no necessity or reason at this stage to bother about concrete implementation of the `EEmployee` object. Therefore, the `login()` method expects an `IAEmployee` interface instead. Using an interface is sufficient for the `assertEquals()` call in Listing 12.13.

The `testLogin()` method in Listing 12.13 helped in the implemenation of `CActioner`, but it is still not very useful for conducting regular tests of `CActioner`. `CActioner` delegates the `login()` service to `MBroker`, and it is `MBroker` that returns an `emp` object to `CActioner`. In most situations, it is more practical to do testing at its source.

Listing 12.15 presents the `testLogin()` method implemented in the `MBrokerTest` class. The code allows testing for success and failure by blocking/unblocking the statements in Lines 39 and 43. Assuming that the username and password are 'pse1' and 'pse1', the unblocking of Line 39, and simultaneous blocking of Line 43, will result in a successful test run.

Listing 12.15 Method testLogin( ) in MBrokerTest

```
Method testLogin() in MBrokerTest

35:     public void testLogin(){
36:         System.out.println("Mediator: Login Testing");
37:         try{
38:             MBroker broker = new MBroker();
39:             //IAEmployee emp = broker.login("pse1","pse1");
43:             IAEmployee emp = broker.login("wrong","wrong");
44:             assertNotNull(emp);
45:             assertEquals(emp.getLoginName(),"pse1");
46:         }catch(Exception exc){
47:             exc.printStackTrace();
48:             fail("Fail to login:"+exc.getMessage());
49:         }
50:     }
```

The intentional programming based on the test case in Listing 12.15 may result in the `login()` method shown in Listing 12.16. The code clearly shows a need to connect to a database to retrieve the employee information. `FConnection` manages the connection and `FReader` does the retrieval. Separate test cases are needed to test these two classes. Retrieval of the `emp` object is performed by the query message in Lines 83–85. A result set from the retrieval is mapped to the `emp` object (Line 86). The `mapEmployee()` method is the only method that knows how to create an `EEmployee` object.

Listing 12.16 does not reveal how `FConnection` and `FReader` objects are instantiated. The instantiation may be done within a dedicated test case for `MBroker`, such as `MBrokerTest`. However, the instantiation may also be done as part of a test suite implementation in which `MBrokerTest` is but one of many test cases. Figure 12.9 shows the `TestRunner` window, executing the `EMSSuite`. The screenshot was taken when `TestRunner` reported a failure of the `testLogin()` method shown in Listing 12.15.

The execution of `EMSSuite` in Figure 12.9 must include additional test cases that will involve the `FConnection` and `FReader` objects. The construction of these test cases reveals a tight coupling between these two classes. An `FReader` instance can only be acquired through an `FConnection` instance. This is acceptable, at least for the time being, because they belong to the same package (`foundation`).

Listing 12.16 Method login( ) in MBroker

```
Method login() in MBroker

76:     public IAEmployee login(String username, String passwd) {
77:         try {
78:             if (!connection.isConnected()) {
79:                 //fail connecting
80:                 if (!connection.connect(username, passwd))
81:                     return null;
82:             }
83:             java.sql.ResultSet rs =
84:                 reader.query(
85:                     "select * from employee where login_name = '" +
                                                username + "'");
86:             IAEmployee emp = mapEmployee(rs);
87:             reader.closeResult(rs);
88:             return emp;
89:         } catch (Exception exc) {
90:         }
91:         return null;
92:     }
```

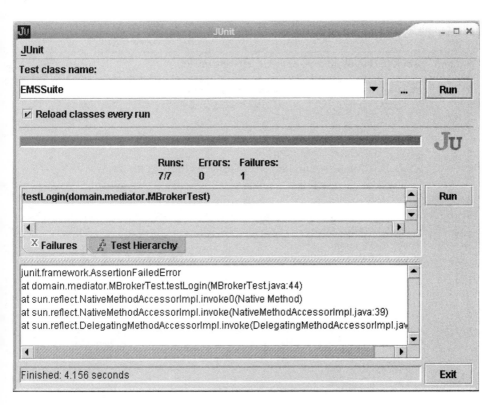

Figure 12.9
A failed
MBrokerTest( ) test

Listings 12.17 and 12.18 show test cases in `FConnectionTest` and `FReaderTest`, which, when combined with the `testLogin()` method in `MBrokerTest`, allow for relatively complete testing of the 'Login' interaction.

Listing 12.17 Method testConnecting( ) in FConnectionTest

```
Method testConnecting() in FConnectionTest

43:     public void testConnecting(){
44:         System.out.println("Foundation: Connection Testing");
46:         try{
48:             FConnection conn = new
                FConnection(IAConstants.DB_DRIVER,IAConstants.DB_URL);
49:             conn.connect("pse1","pse1");
51:             assertTrue(conn.isConnected());
52:         }catch(Exception exc){
53:             exc.printStackTrace();
54:             fail("Fail to connect: "+exc.getMessage());
55:         }
56:     }
```

Listing 12.18 Method testRetrieveEmployee( ) in FReaderTest

```
Method testRetrieveEmployee() in FReaderTest

56:     public void testRetrieveEmployee(){
57:         System.out.println("Foundation: Retrieval Employee
                                                    Testing");
58:         try{
59:             FConnection conn =
                    new FConnection(IAConstants.DB_DRIVER,
                                                IAConstants.DB_URL);
60:             FReader reader = conn.getReader();
61:             conn.connect("pse1","pse1"); //connect to database
62:             java.sql.ResultSet rs = reader.query
                    ("Select * from employee where login_name
                                                    = 'pse1'");
63:             IAEmployee emp = mapEmployee(rs);
64:             assertEquals(emp.getLoginName(), "pse1");
65:         }catch(Exception exc){
66:             fail("Exception in requesting emp data:
                                        "+exc.getMessage());
67:         }
68:     }
```

Acceptance and Regression Testing

Test-driven development drives software design decisions, supplies software documentation and facilitates software evolution. Test-driven development targets smaller implementation units – test units tend to be individual classes. Even if a test unit targets multiple classes, the nature of it is a white box test. Test-driven development does not ensure that the functional requirements of the system are met. White box testing cannot, for example, detect 'missing functionality' – a piece of functionality that was not implemented for whatever reason.

Acceptance testing fills the gap (Martin, 2003). The project stakeholders, customers and users, drive acceptance tests. These are **black box tests**, which verify if the use case requirements are met, with no consideration given to the internal workings of the software. Test-driven development dictates implementation. Acceptance testing verifies and approves implementation.

Figure 12.10 outlines the place and role of testing in the development lifecycle. The starting point to test-driven development is a set of documents: the use case document, conceptual class model and supplementary specifications (Chapter 8). The place and role of an architectural design framework (Chapter 9) with regard to test-driven development is a slightly controversial issue. Agile development does not assume that an architectural framework is imposed on programmers. However, in large-scale developments, new projects are extensions of prior solutions and the management of such developments demands that a clear architectural design exists and is scalable. In this book, architectural design (the PCMEF framework) is assumed prior to test-driven development.

Interestingly enough, the fact that acceptance testing is a black box testing makes it possible to write acceptance tests quite independently of the system design and programming efforts. Acceptance tests are written as **test scripts**. An expectation is that most of these test scripts will be automated by using *capture/playback tools*, by programming with a *scripting language* (that comes with a capture/playback tool), or even by programming in the language used for application development (in some cases, test code is an inherent part of the application code).

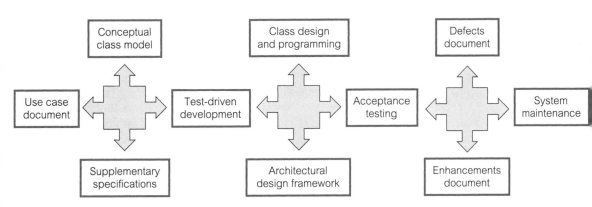

Figure 12.10 Testing in the development lifecycle

The test scripts that cannot be automated will be used for manual testing by a human tester. Any system failures discovered by acceptance testing are classified as **defects** (to be fixed in the current iteration) or **enhancements** (that are left aside for consideration in future iterations).

Like test cases and test suites of test-driven development, most acceptance tests should be in the form of programs that execute against the implementation code and either pass the implemented program or fail it. In fact, implemented acceptance tests are frequently organized in **test cases** and **test suites** in a way similar to that shown in Figure 12.8. There are two main differences.

Firstly, a unit of an acceptance test is a piece of functionality that normally spans multiple classes. Secondly, acceptance tests contain **verification points**, which check whether the expected functionality is met by the implementation. Verification points define the expectations of stakeholders with regard to the system behavior under the input conditions, business rules, expected outcomes of business transactions, anticipated changes in the database, desired ways of presenting computation and processing results, etc.

Regression testing is the re-execution of relevant acceptance tests on successive code iterations. The aim of regression testing is to ensure that iterative extensions (increments) to the code have not resulted in unintended side effects and errors in the old parts of the code that were not supposed to change during the iteration.

Since regression tests should be re-executed at least prior to product release at the end of each iteration, they should be automated as much as possible. Manual regression testing by human testers is impractical for large systems.

An acceptance/regression test unit consists of:

■ a test script

■ implementation of the test script (if an automatic execution of the script is possible)

■ specification of data input to be used for testing

■ a test result document.

12.3.1 Test Scripts in Email Management

A test script can be written as a table (Table 12.1) showing **test steps** and *verification points*. Steps and verification points are numbered consecutively. The letter S or V after the number identifies a step or verification point (moreover, the rows with verification points are written in italics).

Each **verification point** is formulated as a question. Depending on how the question is formulated, either a positive (*true*) or a negative (*false*) answer to the question can mean successful verification. The Verify column is specified with **automated verification** in mind. The expected answers to verification points can be: *false*, *true*, or *unknown*. If automated the verification alone cannot assert the verification outcome, the verification point is verified *unknown*. **Manual verification** by a human tester must be used to complete an *unknown* verification and conclude if the test passed or failed this verification point.

Test scripts are aimed at testing selected functionality identified by the project stakeholders – users, managers, sponsors, but also developers. The test script in Table 12.1.

Table 12.1 Test script document

Line	Verify	Description
1S		Enter the 'login' directive – incorrect username and password
2V	false	Did login succeed?
3S		Enter the 'login' directive – correct username and password
4V	true	Did login succeed?
5S		Enter the 'get employee' directive – correct username
6V	true	Does the employee identified by login name exist?
7S		Enter the 'count of outmessages' directive
8V	true	Is the count displayed?
9S		Enter the 'list of outmessages' directive. Optionally, provide the maximum number of outmessages to be displayed. Display outmessage ids and subjects only
10V	true	Is the list displayed?
11S		Enter the 'get outmessage' directive. Provide outmessage id. Display outmessage id, subject and text of the outmessage according to the provided outmessage id
12V	true	Is the message information displayed?
13S		Enter the 'email outmessage' directive. Email to yourself the outmessage displayed in Step 12
14V	unknown	Has the email arrived at your address?
15S		Enter the 'get outmessage' directive for the outmessage id just emailed in Step 14. Display outmessage id, subject and text of this outmessage
16V	false	Is the message information displayed?
17S		Enter the 'reset testbed' directive. Reset the database to the state it was before this test script has been executed
18S		Enter the 'get outmessage' directive for the outmessage id emailed in Step 14. Display outmessage id, subject and text of this outmessage
19V	true	Is the message information displayed?
20S		Enter the 'close EM application' directive
21V	true	Did logout succeed?
22S		Quit or re-execute this test script

- tests for unsuccessful (2V) and successful (4V, 6V) login
- retrieves and displays outmessages for the connected employee (8V, 10V, 12V)
- emails a specified outmessage (14V)
- attempts to retrieve and display the outmessage just emailed (16V)
- resets the testbed, i.e. resets the database to the original state, and retrieves and displays the outmessage previously emailed (19V)
- tests for successful logout (21V) and quits the test run.

12.3.2 Test Input, Output, and Regression Testing in Email Management

Iteration 1 of EM is a console-based application. It is, therefore, not possible to take advantage of capture/playback tools, because they require a GUI application. Acceptance

Listing 12.19 Input file for testing

```
Input file for testing

1s:   login
          pse1
          pse10
2v:   false
3s:   login
          pse1
          pse1
4v:   true
5s:   getemployee
6v:   true
7s:   countmessages
8v:   true
9s:   listmessages
          20
10v:  true
11s:  getmessage
          14
12v:  true
13s:  sendmessage
          14
          bliong@ics.mq.edu.au
          leszek@ics.mq.edu.au
          Product missing
          The Product name for your ad CI223375XY is missing.
          Can you please supply it?
14v:  unknown
15s:  getmessage
          14
16v:  false
17s:  resetTestbed
18s:  getmessage
          14
19v:  true
20s:  closeEM
21v:  true
22s:  quit
```

tests for Iteration 1 are implemented in Java. One such test class is called `CEMSAccept-anceTest` and is placed in the EM `control` package of Iteration 1. The class implements the test script in Table 12.1.

Complete code for `CEMSAcceptanceTest` is available from the book website. For ease of reference, the line numbers for code excerpts discussed in the book are kept identical to the line numbers in the complete code on the website.

The test input to `CEMSAcceptanceTest` can be provided either interactively or in a file. The interactive mode permits execution of test steps in any sequence, but for frequent testing, and for regression testing in particular, the file input should be used.

Listing 12.19 is an example of the input file for testing. The input file contains directives for all steps and verification points in the test script in Table 12.1. Directives obeyed by `CEMSAcceptanceTest` are implemented as constant fields as shown in Listing 12.20. The values for directives constitute part of an invariant testbed. A *testbed* defines an invariant set of input data (any input files and the expected database content) that must not change between tests.

For example, the message id equal to `14` provided in directive `11s` (Listing 12.18) implies that the outmessage in the database with that id must remain unchanged between various executions of the test program. In effect, that particular record should be marked in the database as *test data*, never to be changed in the process of normal (production) use of the database.

When the outmessage `14` is retrieved from the database, its content id displayed and verified (`12v`). This content is then supplied to step `13s`, which assumes that message id, as well as email instructions 'from', 'to', 'subject', and 'body', are given in an argument list to the `SendMessage` directive. The expected verification of `SendMessage` is unknown (`14v`) because there is no way that the test program, or the EM program, can check that the outmessage has actually reached the recipient. This has to be verified separately by the recipient.

Listing 12.20 Directives for testing

```
       Directives for testing

46:        public static final String DIRECTIVES[] =
47:           new String[] {
48:              "Login",
49:              "GetEmployee",
50:              "GetMessage",
51:              "ListMessages",
52:              "SendMessage",
53:              "CountMessages",
54:              "ResetTestbed",
55:              "CloseEM",
56:              "Quit" };
```

Listing 12.21 is an output file from a 'successful' testing, i.e. a test run where all verification points in the input file were asserted as passed. **Regression testing** can be done

Listing 12.21 Output file from successful testing

```
Output file from successful testing

2v:   OK
4v:   OK
6v:   OK
8v:   OK
10v:  OK
12v:  OK
14v:  UNKNOWN
16v:  OK
19v:  OK
21v:  OK
```

Listing 12.22 Method main( ) in CEMSAcceptanceTest

```
Method main() in CEMSAceptanceTest

293:    public static void main(String args[]) throws Exception {
294:        String inputFilename = null;
296:        CEMSAcceptanceTest at = new CEMSAcceptanceTest();
297:
298:        if (args.length == 0) {
299:            BufferedReader in =
300:                new BufferedReader(new InputStreamReader(System.in));
301:            String s =
302:                "Do you want to go interactive (I) or
                     provide input filename (F):";
303:            System.out.print(s);
304:            s = in.readLine().trim().toLowerCase();
305:            if (s.equals("i"))
306:              at.performTesting(goInteractiveMode(), inputFilename);
307:            else {
308:                System.out.print("Filename: ");
309:                inputFilename = in.readLine().trim();
310:                at.performTesting(
311:                    goFileMode(new File(inputFilename)),
312:                    inputFilename);
313:            }
314:        } else {
315:            inputFilename = args[0].trim();
316:            at.performTesting(goFileMode(new File(inputFilename)),
                                                       inputFilename);
317:        }
319:    }
```

by providing an input file that has a corresponding output file generated earlier by the test program. If the program detects that such an input/output pair already exists, it will perform regression testing against the input file and check whether the test results in the previous and the current output files are the same. The check is performed by simply taking the difference between the first output file and the second. If the second output file already exists when the program starts, it will replace its content with the new content.

Implementation of Test Script in Email Management

12.3.3

The `main()` method of the `CEMSAcceptanceTest` class instantiates an `CEMSAccept-anceTest` object (Listing 12.22, Line 296) and it then expects either interactive input from the user or a test input file (Line 302). If an output file from a previous test run exists, it is replaced by a new one (Line 316).

The only thing that the `CEMSAcceptanceTest()` constructor does (Listing 12.23) is to create a new `CActioner` object (Line 61). The `control` package of Iteration 1 is the only layer that `CEMSAcceptanceTest` communicates with to do the testing.

Given a directive and a list of arguments, the `test()` method (Listing 12.22) performs the test according to the directive. Each directive knows what to expect as its arguments. Insufficient arguments trigger `IllegalArgumentException`, which then causes the test to fail.

Listing 12.23 Constructor CEMSAcceptanceTest( )

```
Constructor CEMSAceptanceTest()

60:       public CEMSAcceptanceTest() {
61:           actioner = new CActioner();
62:       }
```

Listing 12.24 Method test( ) in CEMSAcceptanceTest

```
Method test() in CEMSAceptanceTest

253:      public void test(String directive, List args) throws Exception {
254:          if ("Login".equals(directive))
255:              doLogin(args);
256:          else if ("Getemployee".equals(directive))
257:              doGetEmployee();
258:          else if ("Listmessages".equals(directive))
259:              doListMessages(args);
260:          else if ("Getmessage".equals(directive))
```

```
261:              doGetMessage(args);
262:          else if ("Sendmessage".equals(directive))
263:              doSendMessage(args);
264:          else if ("Countmessages".equals(directive))
265:              doCountMessages();
266:          else if ("Resettestbed".equals(directive))
267:              doResetTestbed();
268:          else if ("Closeem".equals(directive))
269:              doCloseEM();
270:          else
271:              throw new IllegalArgumentException("Wrong directive is
                                                         given");

272:      }
```

As an example, the GetMessage directive (11s) causes the test() method to call the doGetMessage() method (Line 261 in Listing 12.24). The doGetMessage() method assumes that a message id is provided in the argument list (Listing 12.25). It then asks CActioner to retrieve the outmessage (Line 152) and constructs the outmessage content in preparation for this outmessage to be emailed by directive 13s.

Listing 12.25 Method doGetMessage( ) in CEMSAcceptanceTest

```
Method doGetMessage() in CEMSAceptanceTest

149:    private void doGetMessage(List args) {
150:        try {
151:           lastAction =
152:               actioner.retrieveMessage
                            (Integer.parseInt(args.get(0).toString()));
153:           if (lastAction == null)
154:               throw new IllegalArgumentException
                            ("No such message retrieved");
156:           IAOutMessage msg = (IAOutMessage) lastAction;
157:           StringBuffer buf = new StringBuffer();
158:           buf.append("Message id:
                            ").append(msg.getMessageID()).append("\n");
159:           buf.append("Message subject: ").append(msg.getSubject());
160:           buf.append("Message text:").append(msg.getMessageText());
161:           buf.append("\n\n");
163:           recordData(buf.toString());
164:        } catch (Exception exc) {
165:           throw new IllegalArgumentException("Wrong messageid is
                                                         given.");
166:        }
167:    }
```

The code of a test execution is shown in Listing 12.26. The execution passed the test – its output corresponds to the expected output in Listing 12.21. The outcome of verification point 14v has still to be verified manually.

Listing 12.26 Execution listing

```
Execution listing

1s: login
pse1
pse10
2v: false
--> 2v: OK
3s: login
pse1
pse1
4v: true
--> 4v: OK
5s: getemployee
6v: true
--> 6v: OK
7s: countmessages
8v: true
==================================
Total messages: 2
==================================
--> 8v: OK
9s: listmessages
20
10v: true
==================================
List of messages
Message id: 14
Message subject: Product missing

Message id: 45
Message subject: Are you satisfied?
==================================
--> 10v: OK
11s: getmessage
14
12v: true
==================================
Message id: 14
Message subject: Product missing
Message text:The Product name for your ad CI223375XY is missing. Can
you please supply it?
==================================
```

```
--> 12v: OK
13s: sendmessage
14
bliong@ics.mq.edu.au
leszek@ics.mq.edu.au
Product missing
The Product name for your ad CI223375XY is missing. Can you please
supply it?
14v: unknown
--> 14v: UNKNOWN
15s: getmessage
14
16v: false
--> 16v: OK
17s: resetTestbed
18s: getmessage
14
19v: true
=====================================
Message id: 14
Message subject: Product missing
Message text:The Product name for your ad CI223375XY is missing. Can
you please supply it?
=====================================
--> 19v: OK
20s: closeEM
21v: true
--> 21v: OK
22s: quit
```

12.4 Iteration 1 Runtime Screenshots

Iteration 1 is a non-GUI console-based application. The program can be run in a 'DOS window', as shown in Figure 12.11. The DOS execution does not visually separate the program's output from the user's input. Executing the application in an integrated development environment (IDE) can provide such separation. Figure 12.12 shows an execution in an IDE window.

Listing 12.27 is the Iteration 1 execution 'screen dump'. The dump was obtained by a copy/paste from one run session on a DOS screen. The session demonstrates the 'happy path' scenario of the use case document, i.e. the basic flow and the subflows (Sections 8.2.2 and 8.2.3).

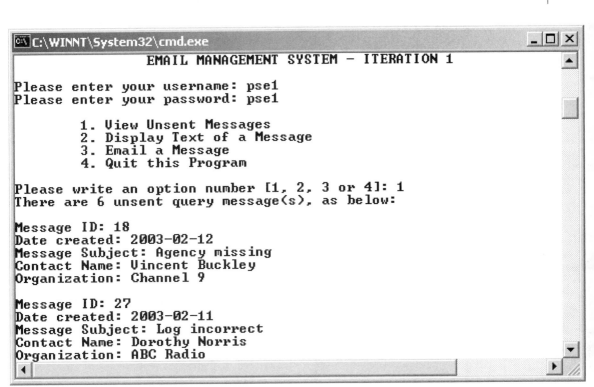

Figure 12.11 Iteration 1 executing in a DOS screen

Source: Screenshot of Microsoft® DOS, reprinted by permission from Microsoft Corporation, Copyright © 1990–2003 Microsoft Corporation

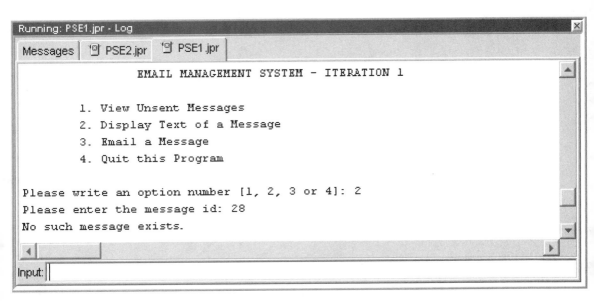

Figure 12.12 Iteration 1 executing in an IDE screen

Listing 12.27 Iteration 1 execution screen dump – 'happy path'

```
Iteration 1 execution screen dump - "happy path"

                EMAIL MANAGEMENT SYSTEM - ITERATION 1

Please enter your username: pse1
Please enter your password: pse1

        1. View Unsent Messages
        2. Display Text of a Message
        3. Email a Message
        4. Quit this Program

Please write an option number [1, 2, 3 or 4]: 1
There are 2 unsent query message(s), as below:

Message ID: 14
Date created: 2003-02-12
Message Subject: Product missing
Contact Name: Pablo Romero
Organization: SBS Sydney

Message ID: 45
Date created: 2003-02-11
Message Subject: Are you satisfied?
Contact Name: Agatha Sommer
Organization: Ford Australia

        1. View Unsent Messages
        2. Display Text of a Message
        3. Email a Message
        4. Quit this Program

Please write an option number [1, 2, 3 or 4]: 2
Please enter the message id: 14
Message ID: 14
Date created: 2003-02-12
Message Subject: Product missing
Contact Name: Pablo Romero
Organization: SBS Sydney
Message Text:
The Product name for your ad CI223375XY is missing. Can you please
supply it?

        1. View Unsent Messages
        2. Display Text of a Message
```

```
        3. Email a Message
        4. Quit this Program

Please write an option number [1, 2, 3 or 4]: 3
Please enter the message id you want to email: 14
The message is successfully sent and updated.

        1. View Unsent Messages
        2. Display Text of a Message
        3. Email a Message
        4. Quit this Program

Please write an option number [1, 2, 3 or 4]: 1
There are 1 unsent query message(s), as below:

Message ID: 45
Date created: 2003-02-11
Message Subject: Are you satisfied?
Contact Name: Agatha Sommer
Organization: Ford Australia

        1. View Unsent Messages
        2. Display Text of a Message
        3. Email a Message
        4. Quit this Program

Please write an option number [1, 2, 3 or 4]:
```

Listing 12.28 is the Iteration 1 execution 'screen dump' for the 'unhappy path' scenario of the use case document, i.e. the exception flows (Section 8.2.4).

Listing 12.28 Iteration 1 execution screen dump – 'unhappy path'

```
Iteration 1 execution screen dump - "unhappy path"

            EMAIL MANAGEMENT SYSTEM - ITERATION 1

Please enter your username: pse1
Please enter your password: wrong_password
Invalid login. Please try again. This will be your second try.
Please enter your username: pse1
Please enter your password: pse1

        1. View Unsent Messages
        2. Display Text of a Message
        3. Email a Message
        4. Quit this Program
```

```
Please write an option number [1, 2, 3 or 4]: 5
Invalid option. Please choose 1,2,3, or 4.


        1. View Unsent Messages
        2. Display Text of a Message
        3. Email a Message
        4. Quit this Program

Please write an option number [1, 2, 3 or 4]:
Please write an option number [1, 2, 3 or 4]: 1
There are 20 unsent query message(s), as below:

Message ID: 50
Date created: 2003-02-12
Message Subject: Your competitors
Contact Name: Pablo Romero
Organization: SBS Sydney

Message ID: 27
…

There are 22 unsent query messages left unretrieved in database.

        1. View Unsent Messages
        2. Display Text of a Message
        3. Email a Message
        4. Quit this Program

Please write an option number [1, 2, 3 or 4]: 3
Please enter the message id you want to email: 50
Failed in sending message. Verify the mail properties or message's
addresses.
Failure info: no network connection or mail address invalid.

               EMAIL MANAGEMENT SYSTEM - ITERATION 1

        1. View Unsent Messages
        2. Display Text of a Message
        3. Email a Message
        4. Quit this Program

Please write an option number [1, 2, 3 or 4]:
```

Iteration 1 performs some basic formatting of an email before sending it to its destination. Figure 12.13 shows an example of one such email. Before sending, the outmessage is given a 'salutation' header to the recipient, greetings line, and the name of the sender.

Figure 12.13
Iteration 1 email
after reaching its
destination

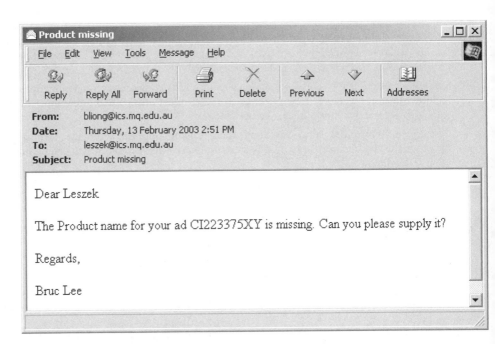

Summary

1. The definition of *Java class* consists of the class name and visibility, data members and methods, constructors, members' visibility, and any class's superclasses and interfaces.

2. *Class interface* (its protocol) is not the same as a Java interface or UML interface.

3. There are two categories of *data members*: instance variables and class variables. There are also two categories of *methods*: instance methods and class methods.

4. *Overloaded methods* have the same name but different signature.

5. A *Java collection* represents a container for objects. It can store multiple references to objects and is, therefore, used to store association links with a multiplicity of many.

6. In C++, a *parameterized type* is used to implement association links with a multiplicity of many.

7. JDBC and SQLJ are two standard ways to embed SQL statements in Java code in order to communicate with a database.

8. Establishing a database connection involves the use of a JDBC class `DriverManager` and a JDBC interface `Connection` (from the `java.sql` library).

9. A statement object needs to be created to perform a SQL query on a database. A statement object must conform to one of the three JDBC interfaces: `Statement`, `PreparedStatement`, or `CallableStatement`.

10. The `preparedCall()` method returns a `CallableStatement` object which can be used to call a stored procedure or function.

11. *Test-driven development* requires writing test programs prior to writing the application code to pass the test program. This is an example of *white box testing*. Test-driven development is supported by the JUnit framework.

12. *Acceptance testing* is used to test application code after it has been written. This is an example of *black box testing*. Acceptance test are written as *test scripts* with *verification points*. Failures discovered by acceptance testing are classified into *defects* and *enhancements*.

13. *Regression testing* is the re-execution of acceptance tests on successive code iterations. Regression testing requires stable testbeds. A *testbed* defines an invariant set of input data (any input files and the expected database content) that must not change between tests.

14. Test-driven development, successive application programming, and acceptance testing result in an executable program. The Iteration 1 program is a *console-based application*, which can be run in a DOS window or an IDE window.

Key Terms

«anonymous_type» class	375	Java Stored Procedures	377
acceptance testing	365, 395	JavaBeans	377
agile software development	385	JDBC	*See* Java Database Connectivity
anonymous inner class	389	JDK	*See* Java Development Kit
argument type	367	JUnit	386
association link	371	local variable	367
automated verification	396	manual verification	396
BC4J	*See* Business Components for Java	method	367
black box testing	395	method overloading	367
Business Components for Java	377	method prototype	367
class data type	367	method signature	367
class interface	366	outer class	386
class method	367	overloading	*See* method overloading
class protocol	*See* class interface	parameterized type	375
class template	*See* parameterized type	primitive data type	366
collection	371	reference data type	*See* class data type
composite pattern	387	reflection	389
constructor	367	regression testing	396, 399
container	*See* collection	return type	367
data member	366	signature	*See* method signature
defect	396	SQL for Java	377
EJB	*See* Enterprise JavaBeans	SQLJ	*See* SQL for Java
enhancement	396	test case	386, 396
Enterprise JavaBeans	377	test script	395
eXtreme Programming	385	test step	396
field	*See* data member	test suite	386, 396
fixture	387	test unit	386
generic class	*See* parameterized type	test-driven development	365, 385
inner class	386	test-driven programming	365
instance method	367	verification point	396
instance variable	366	visibility	366
intentional programming	391	white box testing	385
Java Database Connectivity	377	XP	*See* eXtreme Programming
Java Development Kit	377		

Review Questions

1. Explain the difference between class interface (class protocol), Java interface, and UML interface.

2. Private data members (attributes) are accessible only to the class instances, i.e. to any object of the class, not just to the object that contains these data members. Provide an example in Java with two objects of the same class and such that one of these objects accesses directly an attribute value in the other object. Are there any interesting observations resulting from this question?

3. Provide a Java example illustrating that a local variable within a method body of the class is not a data member.

4. Provide a Java example illustrating that a class method can be accessed either with an object of the class or without an object by referring to the class name.

5. Provide a Java example illustrating method overloading.

6. In Java, associations with multiplicity of many are implemented using Java collections. There are three main kinds of collection: `List`, `Set`, and `Map`. Discuss the pros and cons of these collections for implementing associations.

7. Compare collections and parameterized types as two techniques for implementing associations.

8. Compare JDBC and SQLJ for accessing a database from an application program.

9. List the classes/interfaces of the `java.sql` library that are most useful for programming database access in Java.

10. Test-driven development results in two categories of code – test code and application code. The book explains three approaches to where the test code can be contained with respect to the application code. What are these approaches?

11. JUnit supports static and dynamic modes of running test cases. What Java language mechanisms are used in implementing each mode?

12. Analyze the code in Listing 12.29 below. What is the output of the program? Step through and explain what happens.

13. Refer to Section 12.2.2 and Listing 12.18. How is the 'retrieve employee' tested in the listing? There seems to be no explicit part in the listing that checks if the retrieval is successful. Explain how this testing is done.

14. Refer to Section 12.3.1 and Listing 12.19. Comment on the assumptions made for the `sendmessage` directive (Line `13s`).

Problem-Solving Exercises

Tutorial and Case Study Exercises

1. Refer to Section 12.1.3 and Listing 12.5. Suppose that you had developed such a `Connection` class and would like to write a `TestCase` as a unit test on this class. How could you test it?

2. Refer again to Section 12.1.3 and Listing 12.5. Continuing from the previous question, suppose that the `Connection` class does not declare that it throws an exception. Is it possible to develop a `TestCase` to test this constructor? If so, show how.

3. Refer to Section 12.2.2 and Listing 12.13. How would you develop a stub for the listing? That is, suppose that you have not implemented `CActioner`'s `login()` method but you would like to have a `TestCase` corresponding to the one shown in Listing 12.13. How would you achieve this?

Listing 12.29 Sample program

```
Sample Program

7:    public class TestMe{
8:        private String field1;
9:
10:        private TestMe anotherMe;
11:
12:        public static void main(String args[]){
13:            TestMe me = new TestMe();
14:            me.field1 = "Hello1";
15:            me.anotherMe = me;
16:            me.anotherMe.field1 = "Hello2";
17:            System.out.println(me.field1);
18:            System.out.println(me.anotherMe.field1);
19:            me.convertMe(me);
20:            System.out.println(me.field1);
21:            System.out.println(me.anotherMe.field1);
22:        }
23:        private void convertMe(TestMe anotherMe){
24:            anotherMe.field1 = "Hello3";
25:            anotherMe.anotherMe = new TestMe();
26:            anotherMe.anotherMe.field1 = "Hello4";
27:            anotherMe = anotherMe;
28:            anotherMe = new TestMe();
29:            anotherMe.field1 = "Hello5";
30:            anotherMe.anotherMe = new TestMe();
31:            anotherMe.anotherMe.field1 = "Hello6";
32:        }
33:    }
```

4. Refer to Section 12.1.3 and Listing 12.8. This listing is modified as shown in Listing 12.30 below. The modifications are shown in underlined text. Complete the `TestCase` for the `MovieActor` application to test the client code in Listing 12.8. What needs to be done to ensure that `testDisplaySearchMoviesByStoredFunction()` is successful? Show the code. (Hint: Create a stub.)

Minicase – Time Logging System

This minicase assumes that you have solutions to previous TLS minicase questions, in particular those in Chapter 11. These solutions are included in the Instructor's Manual for the book and are available to instructors from the book website.

1. Write a test unit class in support of the test-driven development aimed at the interaction 'Delete Time Record'.

2. Develop an acceptance test case for 'Delete Time Record'.

Listing 12.30 Sample test program

```
testSearchMoviesByStoredFunction()

 8:    public class MovieSearcherTest {
59:
60:        public void testDisplaySearchMoviesByStoredFunction(
                   String str)
                   throws Exception{
61:            System.out.println(
                   "Searching movies on specified string:" +str);
62:            Collection c = conn.searchMoviesByStoredFunction(str);
63:            Iterator it = c.iterator();
64:            while(it.hasNext()){
65:                displayMovie((Movie) it.next());
66:                System.out.println();
67:            }
68:        }
194:       private void displayMovie(Movie movie) {
195:           System.out.println("Movie Code: " +
                                  movie.getMovieCode());
196:           System.out.println("Movie Title: " +
                                  movie.getMovieTitle());
197:           System.out.println("Movie Director: " +
                                  movie.getDirector());
198:       }
205:       public static void main(String args[]) {
244:           searcher.displaySearchMoviesByStoredFunction("vamp");
249:       }

           ...
250: }
```

Minicase – Contact Information Management

This minicase assumes that you have solutions to previous CIM minicase questions, in particular those in Chapter 11. These solutions are included in the Instructor's Manual for the book and are available to instructors from the book website.

1.   Write an acceptance test case in Java for the interaction 'Read OrganizationContact'.

Chapter

13

Iteration 1 Annotated Code

The EM case study discussed in this book is sufficiently small to allow presentation of most of the resulting code. Previous chapters used the EM code to exemplify discussed topics. Although special care was taken not to present the code outside of its wider context, the only way to completely deliver this context is by presenting the code en bloc.

Accordingly, the last chapters in Parts 2, 3 and 4 of this book demonstrate the majority of the code obtained in successive iterations of the EM case study. Any code not presented in these chapters for reasons of space can be downloaded from the book website.

This chapter contains the Java code for Iteration 1. The database code is not included here because it is offered in Chapter 10. The code is presented according to typical Java documentation practices. The code overview explains the hierarchies of packages, interfaces, and classes. A class diagram gives a visual code overview. Most fields and methods are listed and annotated. All significant methods are discussed in more detail. Some supporting, less important, or trivial methods are omitted from this chapter's discussion.

Code Overview

The Java code for Iteration 1 conforms strictly to the PCMEF architectural framework introduced in Section 9.2.2. More accurately, it conforms to the PCMEF+ framework, which adds the `acquaintance` package to the other PCMEF packages. The **package hierarchy** is therefore:

- `acquaintance`
- `presentation`
- `control`
- `domain.entity`
- `domain.mediator`
- `foundation`

The `acquaintance` package contains all interfaces necessary for communication between objects in non-neighboring packages. For simplicity, Iteration 1 curtails the use of other kinds of interface. There is only one interface outside of the `acquaintance` package. There are five interfaces in the **interface hierarchy**. According to the PCMEF convention, the interface names begin with the capital letter 'I'.

- `interface acquaintance.IAConstants`
- `interface acquaintance.IAContact`
- `interface acquaintance.IAEmployee`
- `interface acquaintance.IAOutMessage`
- `interface domain.entity.IEDataSupplier`

To emphasize the clarity and highlight the simplicity of the PCMEF framework, Iteration 1 restrains the number of classes in each package. This leads to some classes being too large and doing too much. Such an approach penalizes the cohesion of classes in exchange for better (lower) coupling. In successive iterations, the cohesion of classes is readdressed and incohesive classes are split into smaller classes. The **class hierarchy** in Iteration 1 is as follows:

- `presentation.PMain`
- `presentation.PConsole`
- `control.CActioner`
- `domain.entity.EContact`
  - `implements acquaintance.IAContact`
- `domain.entity.EEmployee`
  - `implements acquaintance.IAEmployee`
- `domain.entity.EOutMessage`
  - `implements acquaintance.IAOutMessage`
- `domain.mediator.MBroker`

- ∎ implements acquaintance.IAConstants,
  domain.entity.IEDataSupplier
- ∎ foundation.FConnection
- ∎ foundation.FReader
- ∎ foundation.FWriter

Figure 13.1 shows the final class model for Iteration 1. The model extends slightly the class diagram presented in Figure 11.2. The IEDataSupplier interface is added in the final solution. Also, the existence of the PMain class is made explicit in Figure 13.1.

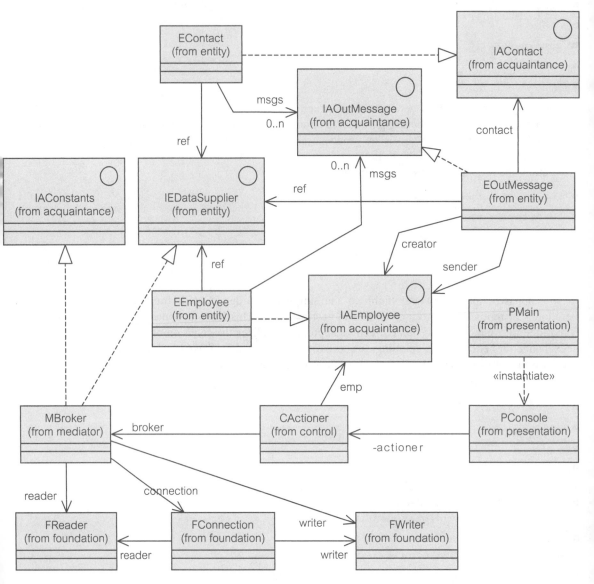

Figure 13.1 Class diagram for Iteration 1 of EM

Package Acquaintance

The `acquaintance` package consists of four interfaces:

- `IAConstants`
- `IAContact`
- `IAEmployee`
- `IAOutMessage`

Interface IAConstants

As explained in Section 11.1.2, an interface can be used to store system constants. Grouping the constants in a single interface enables customizing (parameterizing) of program behavior for deployment and for different uses. An alternative to using the interface could be to create a resource file to store all the initialization information. An interface that houses system constants makes the initialization task more transparent. A user needs only to modify the constant values and rebuild prior to deployment.

Listing 13.1 explains the meaning of constant fields in the `IAConstants` interface. Listing 13.2 shows the code.

Listing 13.1 IAConstants field summary

static String	**DB_DRIVER** Driver in the format specified by database supplier. We use Oracle.
static String	**DB_URL** JDBC database URL.
static int	**MAX_MESSAGE** Limit of messages to be displayed. Note that this is not the limit for retrieving.
static String	**SMTP_ADDRESS** SMTP address for emailing.

Listing 13.2 IAConstants.java

```
IAConstants.java

11:  public interface IAConstants {
16:     String DB_DRIVER      = "oracle.jdbc.driver.OracleDriver";
19:     String DB_URL = "jdbc:oracle:thin:@localhost:1521:oracle8i";
23:     String SMTP_ADDRESS   = "mail.ics.mq.edu.au";
26:     int MAX_MESSAGE = 20;
27:  }
```

Listing 13.3 IAEmployee method summary

String	**getEmail**()
	Get the employee's email address.
String	**getEmployeeID**()
	Get the employee id.
String	**getFamilyName**()
	Get the family name of the employee.
String	**getFirstName**()
	Get the first name of this employee.
String	**getLoginName**()
	Get the employee's login name.
Collection	**getUnsentOutMessages**(int numMsgRetrieve)
	Get all messages (up to numMsgRetrieve) assigned to this employee.
void	**removeSentOutMessage**(IAOutMessage msg)
	Remove a message from this employee's assignment, perhaps because it is already sent.
void	**setEmail**(java.lang.String email)
	Set the employee's email address.
void	**setEmployeeID**(java.lang.String id)
	Set employee id.
void	**setFamilyName**(java.lang.String familyName)
	Set the family name of the employee.
void	**setFirstName**(java.lang.String fname)
	Set first name of this employee.
void	**setLoginName**(java.lang.String login)
	Set login name for the employee.

Listing 13.4 IAEmployee.java

```
IAEmployee.java

9:   public interface IAEmployee {
11:      public void setEmployeeID( String id );
14:      public String getEmployeeID();
17:      public void setFirstName( String fname );
20:      public String getFirstName();
23:      public void setFamilyName( String familyName );
26:      public String getFamilyName();
29:      public void setEmail( String email );
32:      public String getEmail();
35:      public void setLoginName( String login );
38:      public String getLoginName();
41:      public java.util.Collection getUnsentOutMessages(int
            numMsgRetrieve);
44:      public void removeSentOutMessage(IAOutMessage msg);
46:   }
```

Interface IAEmployee 13.2.2

Listings 13.3 and 13.4 define the `IAEmployee` interface. The `EEmployee` class implements this interface. An `EEmployee` object represents the current user of the EM application.

Interface IAContact 13.2.3

Listings 13.5 and 13.6 define the `IAContact` interface. The `EContact` class implements this interface. An `EContact` object represents a business entity to which an outmessage can be sent.

Listing 13.5 IAContact method summary

String	**getContactID**() Get contact id.
String	**getEmail**() Get the contact's email address.
String	**getFamilyName**() Get family name of the contact.
String	**getFirstName**() Get first name of the contact.
String	**getOrganization**() Get the organization of this contact.
Collection	**getUnsentOutMessages**(int numMsgToBeRetrieved) Get all outmessages destined for this contact.
void	**removeSentOutMessage**(IAOutMessage msg) Remove an outmessage destined for this contact, perhaps because it is already sent.
void	**setContactID**(java.lang.String contactID) Set contact id.
void	**setEmail**(java.lang.String email) Set the contact's email address.
void	**setFamilyName**(java.lang.String familyName) Set family name of the contact.
void	**setFirstName**(java.lang.String fname) Set the first name of the contact.
void	**setOrganization**(java.lang.String org) Set the contact's organization.

Listing 13.6 IAContact.java

```
IAContact.java

8:    public interface IAContact {
10:       String getContactID();
13:       void setContactID( String contactID );
16:       String getFirstName();
19:       void setFirstName( String fname );
22:       String getFamilyName();
25:       void setFamilyName( String familyName );
28:       String getEmail();
31:       void setEmail( String email );
34:       String getOrganization();
37:       void setOrganization( String org );
40:       java.util.Collection getUnsentOutMessages(int
             numMsgToBeRetrieved);
43:       void removeSentOutMessage(IAOutMessage msg);
44:    }
```

13.2.4 Interface IAOutMessage

Listings 13.7 and 13.8 define the `IAOutMessage` interface. This interface represents outgoing messages from the company to various contacts.

Listing 13.7 IAoutmessage method summary

`IAContact`	**`getContact()`**
	Get the contact for this outmessage.
`java.sql.Date`	**`getCreationDate()`**
	Get the creation date of this outmessage.
`IAEmployee`	**`getCreatorEmployee()`**
	Retrieve employee who created this outmessage initially.
`int`	**`getMessageID()`**
	Get the outmessage id.
`String`	**`getMessageText()`**
	Get the outmessage body.
`IAEmployee`	**`getSenderEmployee()`**
	Retrieve the employee who is responsible for sending this outmessage.
`java.sql.Date`	**`getSentDate()`**
	Get the sent date of this outmessage.

java.lang.String	**getSubject**()
	Get the outmessage subject.
void	**setContact**(IAContact contact)
	Set the contact for this outmessage.
void	**setCreationDate**(java.sql.Date date)
	Set the creation date of this outmessage.
void	**setCreatorEmployee**(IAEmployee emp)
	Set employee who creates this outmessage.
void	**setMessageID**(int id)
	Set the outmessage id.
void	**setMessageText**(java.lang.String text)
	Set the outmessage text.
void	**setSenderEmployee**(IAEmployee emp)
	Set employee who is responsible for sending this outmessage
void	**setSentDate**(java.sql.Date date)
	Set the sent date of this outmessage.
void	**setSubject**(java.lang.String subject)
	Set the outmessage subject.

Listing 13.8 IAOutMessage.java

IAOutMessage.java

```
11:   public interface IAOutMessage {
14:       int getMessageID();
17:       void setMessageID( int id );
20:       IAEmployee getSenderEmployee();
23:       void setSenderEmployee(IAEmployee emp);
26:       IAEmployee getCreatorEmployee();
29:       void setCreatorEmployee(IAEmployee emp);
32:       IAContact getContact();
35:       void setContact(IAContact contact);
37:       String getSubject();
40:       void setSubject( String subject );
43:       String getMessageText();
46:       void setMessageText( String text );
49:       java.sql.Date getCreationDate();
52:       void setCreationDate( java.sql.Date date );
55:       java.sql.Date getSentDate();
58:       void setSentDate( java.sql.Date date );
60:   }
```

13.3 Package Presentation

The presentation package contains two classes:

- PMain
- PConsole

13.3.1 Class PMain

The main function is trivial (and rightly so), as Listings 13.9 and 13.10 demonstrate. The main method contains only one function – new PMain() on Line 23. This invokes the PMain() constructor, which then invokes the constructor on PConsole. The reference to the PConsole object is stored in the console variable. The variable is used to send the dislayLogin() message to PConsole and in effect to pass the control to PConsole, thus putting the application in full swing.

Listing 13.9 PMain method summary

```
PMain()
        Construct the PMain object on application start.
static void    main(java.lang.String[] args)
                      Main method, the start of the application.
```

Listing 13.10 PMain.java

```
PMain.java
9:    public class PMain {
11:       public PMain() {
12:          try {
13:             PConsole console = new PConsole();
14:             console.displayLogin();
15:          }
16:          catch ( Exception exc ) {
17:             exc.printStackTrace();
18:          }
19:       }
22:       public static void main( String[] args ) {
23:          new PMain();
24:       }
25:    }
```

Class PConsole

The PConsole class represents a console window that Iteration 1 provides to a user to interact with the application. Listing 13.11 is a summary of methods in PConsole.

Listing 13.11 PConsole method summary

```
PConsole()
```
        Create a new console object.
```
PConsole(CActioner actioner)
```
        Create a new console object by specifying the actioner.

private void	`display(java.lang.String s)`	
	Display a string to screen.	
private void	`displayConfirmation()`	
	An email is successfully sent, inform the user about this.	
private void	`displayEmailFailure(java.lang.String msg)`	
	Failed sending the email.	
void	`displayLogin()`	
	Display the login screen, loop until the user gets the login right or until the limit of allowed attempts to login is exceeded.	
private boolean	`displayLoginError(java.lang.Object status)`	
	Inform the user about wrong login information.	
void	`displayMenu()`	
	Display the main menu of the application.	
private void	`displayMessages(java.util.Collection msgs, boolean detail)`	
	Display an outmessage to the screen and if the detail variable is set, display the outmessage body as well.	
private void	`displayMessageText(java.lang.String input)`	
	Display the content of an outmessage.	
private java.lang.Object	`getUserInput(java.lang.String[] prompts)`	
	Accept user input according to the state the program is in.	
private boolean	`prepareMessage(java.lang.String msgID)`	
	Prepare the outmessage as indicated by the msgID for sending.	
private java.lang.String	`readInput()`	
	Read a line of input.	
private void	`tooManyMessages(int num)`	
	Display that there are too many outmessages to be displayed. Not all are retrieved	
private void	`viewMessages()`	
	View the list of unsent outmessages.	

The data members declared in PConsole are shown in Listing 13.12. Note the association from PConsole to CActioner.

Listing 13.12 Fields in PConsole.java

```
Fields in PConsole.java

17:   public class PConsole {
18:       private BufferedReader in;
19:       private PrintStream out;
20:       private static final String VIEW_MESSAGE = "1";
21:       private static final String VIEW_TEXT_MESSAGE = "2";
22:       private static final String SEND_MESSAGE = "3";
23:       private static final String QUIT = "4";
24:
25:       /** Ask login information */
26:       private static final int LOGIN_STATE = 1;
27:
28:       /** Display menu and ask user choice */
29:       private static final int NORMAL_STATE = 2;
30:
31:       /** The state we are in */
32:       private int state;
33:
34:       /** Association to control layer */
35:       private CActioner actioner;
36:
```

Constructing a PConsole object

Iteration 1 contains two constructors for creating a PConsole object (Listing 13.13). The PMain object (Listing 13.10, Line 13) invokes the default constructor (Lines 38–40). The constructor that creates PConsole by specifying a CActioner object (Lines 43–47) is not used in Iteration 1 – it is referred to in one of the case study questions at the end of the chapter.

Listing 13.13 Constructors PConsole( )

```
Constructors PConsole()

38:       public PConsole() {
39:           this(new CActioner());
40:       }
41:
43:       public PConsole(CActioner actioner) {
44:           in = new BufferedReader(new InputStreamReader(System.in));
45:           out = System.out;
46:           this.actioner = actioner;
47:       }
```

Listing 13.14 Method displayLogin( ) in PConsole

```
Method displayLogin() in PConsole

58:     public void displayLogin() {
59:         display("\t\tEMAIL MANAGEMENT SYSTEM - ITERATION 1\n\n");
60:         state = LOGIN_STATE;
61:
62:         //loop 'forever' till the user gets it right
63:         while (true){
64:             Object status = getUserInput(new String[] {
65:             "Please enter your username: ",
66:             "Please enter your password: " });
67:
68:             if(displayLoginError(status)) break;//apparently the
                    login is OK
69:         }
70:
71:         display("\n");
72:         state = NORMAL_STATE;
73:
74:         //continue the normal execution of the program
75:         //if the login is successful
76:         displayMenu();
77:     }
```

Listing 13.15 Method displayLoginError( ) in PConsole

```
Method displayLoginError() in PConsole

295:    private boolean displayLoginError(Object status) {
296:        if(status == CActioner.LOGIN_OK) return true;
297:        else if(status == CActioner.LOGIN_FAIL_1){
298:            display("Invalid login. Please try again.
                        This will be your second try.\n");
299:            return false;
300:        }else if(status == CActioner.LOGIN_FAIL_2){
301:            display("Invalid login. Please try again.
                        This will be your last try.\n");
302:            return false;
303:        }else if(status == CActioner.LOGIN_FAIL_3){
304:            display("You have failed 3x to login. Program will
                    quit.\n");
305:            actioner.exit();
306:            return false;
307:        }
308:        return false;
309:    }
```

Displaying login and menu

Upon launching the application, the user is presented with a login request. This is performed by the `displayLogin()` method (Listing 13.14). Incorrect logins are handled by the `displayLoginError()` method (Listing 13.15) called on Line 68. A correct login results in a message to `displayMenu()` (Line 76). The `displayMenu()` method is shown in Listing 13.16.

Listing 13.16 Method displayMenu( ) in PConsole

```
Method displayMenu() in PConsole

160:    public void displayMenu() {
161:        state = NORMAL_STATE;
162:        StringBuffer sb =
163:            new StringBuffer
                    ("\t\tEMAIL MANAGEMENT SYSTEM - ITERATION 1\n\n");
164:        sb.append("\t1. View Unsent Messages\n");
165:        sb.append("\t2. Display Text of a Message\n");
166:        sb.append("\t3. Email a Message\n");
167:        sb.append("\t4. Quit this Program\n\n");
168:        sb.append("Please write an option number [1, 2, 3 or 4]: ");
169:
170:        while (true)
171:            getUserInput(new String[] { sb.toString()});
173:    }
```

Viewing outmessages

Listings 13.17 to 13.20 explain how outmessages are presented in the console window. The `viewMessages()` method in Listing 13.17 requests `CActioner` to retrieve messages (Line 179). To actually display the retrieved outmessages to a screen, the call to the `displayMessages()` method is made (Line 193). The `displayMessages()` method is shown in Listing 13.18. The call to `tooManyMessages()` on Line 196 aims to inform the user whether the outmessages displayed represent all outmessages held in the database. The `tooManyMessages()` method is presented in Listing 13.20.

The `displayMessages()` method (Listing 13.18) iterates through the collection of `EOutMessage` objects and displays one outmessage at a time to the screen. If the argument variable called `detail` is set, then an outmessage text is also displayed (Lines 224–231). This happens when the user activates option 2 on the menu list (Listing 13.16, Line 165). This options leads to the `displayMessageText()` method (Listing 13.19).

Listing 13.17 Method viewMessages( ) in PConsole

```
Method viewMessages() in PConsole

176:    private void viewMessages() {
177:        Collection msgs = new ArrayList();
178:        int remainder =
179:            actioner.retrieveMessages(msgs,
                    IAConstants.MAX_MESSAGE);
180:        Iterator it = msgs.iterator();
181:        IAOutMessage msg;
182:        StringBuffer buf = new StringBuffer();
183:        if (msgs.size() == 0)
184:            buf.append("No unsent query messages.");
185:        else {
186:            buf.append("There are ").append(msgs.size()).append(
187:                " unsent query message(s), as below:\n\n");
188:        }
190:        display(buf.toString());
191:        buf = null;
192:
193:        displayMessages(msgs, false);
194:
195:        if (remainder > 0)
196:            tooManyMessages(remainder);
198:    }
```

Listing 13.18 Method displayMessages( ) in PConsole

```
Method displayMessages() in PConsole

206:    private void displayMessages(java.util.Collection msgs,
                                boolean detail) {
207:        for (Iterator it = msgs.iterator(); it.hasNext();) {
208:            IAOutMessage msg = (IAOutMessage) it.next();
209:                IAContact contact = msg.getContact();
210:            StringBuffer buf = new StringBuffer();
211:            buf.append
                    ("Message ID:").append(msg.getMessageID())
                                                .append("\n");
212:            buf.append
                    ("Date created: ").append(msg.getCreationDate())
213:                .append( "\n");
214:            buf.append
                    ("Message Subject: ").append(msg.getSubject())
                                                .append("\n");
215:            buf.append("Contact Name: ")
216:                .append(contact.getFirstName())
```

```
217:                    .append(" ")
218:                    .append(contact.getFamilyName())
219:                    .append("\n");
220:              buf.append("Organization: ").append(
221:                  contact.getOrganization()).append(
222:                  "\n");
223:
224:              if (detail)
225:                  buf.append
                          ("Message Text: \n").append(msg.
226:                          getMessageText()).append("\n");
228:              buf.append("\n"); //extra blank line to separate each
                      message
229:              display(buf.toString());
230:              buf = null;
231:              }
232:      }
```

The `displayMessageText()` method (Listing 13.19) displays the full content of an outmessage. Because the database state could have changed between the time the outmessage was listed on the screen and the time the user requested its display, the method asks `CActioner` to do a fresh retrieval of the outmessage from the database (Line 146). Following successful retrieval, the `displayMessages()` method is called with the `detail` argument set to true.

Listing 13.19 Method displayMessageText() in PConsole

```
Method displayMessageText() in PConsole

143:     private void displayMessageText(String input) {
144:         try {
145:             int i = Integer.parseInt(input);
146:             IAOutMessage msg = actioner.retrieveMessage(i);
147:             if (msg == null) {
148:                 display("No such message exist.\n\n");
149:                 return;
150:             }
151:             displayMessages(java.util.Collections.singleton(msg),
                     true);
152:         } catch (NumberFormatException exc) {
153:             display("Invalid Message ID.\n\n");
154:         } catch (Exception exc2) {
155:             display("Could not retrieve the message\n\n");
156:         }
157:     }
```

Listing 13.20 Method tooManyMessages( ) in PConsole

```
Method tooManyMessages() in PConsole

280:     private void tooManyMessages(int num) {
281:         if (num == 0)
282:             return;
283:         if (num == 1)
284:             display("There is "
285:                 + num
286:                 + " unsent outmessage left unretrieved in
                    database.\n\n");
287:         else
288:             display(
289:                 "There are "
290:                     + num
291:                     + " unsent outmessages left unretrieved in
                        database.\n\n");
292:     }
```

Requesting to email an outmessage

The user requests emailing an outmessage by choosing option 3 on the menu list (Listing 13.16, Line 166). This activates the prepareMessage() method (Listing 13.21). The method re-retrieves data from the current state of the database (Lines 242–243), then builds the outmessage content, and instructs CActioner to send the email (Line 257). Depending on the outcome, the method invokes collaborating methods to display confirmation (Line 260) or failure (Line 262) to the user.

Listing 13.21 Method prepareMessage( ) in PConsole

```
Method prepareMessage() in PConsole

239:     private boolean prepareMessage(String msgID) {
240:         try {
241:             int id = Integer.parseInt(msgID);
242:             IAOutMessage msg = actioner.retrieveMessage(id);
243:             IAEmployee emp = actioner.getEmployee();
244:             IAContact contact = msg.getContact();
245:
246:             String subject = msg.getSubject();
247:             String from = emp.getEmail();
248:             String to = contact.getEmail();
249:
250:             StringBuffer body = new StringBuffer();
```

```
251:            body.append
                    ("Dear ").append(contact.getFirstName()).
                                               append("\n\n");
252:            body.append(msg.getMessageText());
253:            body.append("\n\nRegards,\n\n").append(

254:                emp.getFirstName()).append("\n");
255:
256:            boolean b =
257:                actioner.sendMessage(msg, from, to, subject,
                                               body.toString());
258:
259:            if (b)
260:                displayConfirmation();
261:            else
262:                displayEmailFailure
                        ("no network connection or mail address
                        invalid.\n");
263:
264:            return b;
265:        } catch (Exception exc) {
266:            displayEmailFailure(exc.getMessage());
267:        }
268:        return false;
269:    }
```

13.4 Package Control

The `control` package contains one class only – `CActioner`. This class encapsulates all activities known to Iteration 1 of the EM case study.

13.4.1 Class CActioner

Listing 13.22 is a summary of methods in the `CActioner` class. Fields in `CActioner` are listed in Listing 13.23.

The data members declared in `PConsole` are shown in Listing 13.12. Note the association from `PConsole` to `CActioner`.

Listing 13.22 CActioner method summary

```
CActioner()
        Create a new CActioner object.
CActioner(MBroker broker)
        Create a new CActioner object by specifying an MBroker object.
void                    exit()
                        Quit the application.
IAEmployee              getEmployee()
                        Retrieve the currently logged-in employee.
private void            handleEmailException(java.lang.Exception exc)
java.lang.Object        login(java.lang.String username,
                        java.lang.String passwd)
                        Log the user in with the given username and password.
void                    logout()
                        Log the user out without quitting application.
IAOutMessage            retrieveMessage(int id)
                        Retrieve an outmessage based on its id.
int                     retrieveMessages(java.util.Collection msgs, int
                        numMsgs)
                        Retrieve the numMsgs unsent outmessages into msgs.
private boolean         send(java.lang.String from, java.lang.String to,
                        java.lang.String to, java.lang.String subject,
                        java.lang.String body)
                        Send the message.
boolean                 sendMessage(IAOutMessage msg)
                        Send message and request the database update when successful.
boolean                 sendMessage(IAOutMessage msg,
                        java.lang.String from, java.lang.String to,
                        java.lang.String subject, java.lang.String body)
                        Send the message, update it if successfully sent.
```

Listing 13.23 Fields in CActioner.java

```
Fields in CActioner.java

15:    public class CActioner {
16:        /** Login succeeded */
17:        public static final Object LOGIN_OK = "LOGIN OK";
18:
19:        /** First attempt for login failed */
20:        public static final Object LOGIN_FAIL_1 = "LOGIN FAIL 1";
21:
22:        /** Second attempt for login failed */
23:        public static final Object LOGIN_FAIL_2 = "LOGIN FAIL 2";
24:
```

```
25:        /** Final attempt for login failed */
26:        public static final Object LOGIN_FAIL_3 = "LOGIN FAIL_3";
27:
28:        /**
29:         * Allowed maximum of unsuccessful login attempts before
30:         * the program will exit.
31:         */
32:        private static final int MAX_LOGIN_TRY = 3;
33:
34:        /** Association with the broker */
35:        private MBroker broker;
36:
37:        /** The one and only EEmployee object we have */
38:        private IAEmployee emp;
39:
40:        /** Login attempts so far */
41:        private volatile int loginTry = 0;
42:        //volatile because we don't hold it for much longer than
               necessary
```

Constructing a CActioner object

Iteration 1 contains two constructors for creating a CActioner object (Listing 13.24). The PConsole object (Listing 13.13, Line 39) invokes the default constructor (Lines 45–52). The constructor that creates CActioner by specifying an MBroker object (Lines 55–57) is referred to in the problem-solving exercises.

Listing 13.24 Constructors CActioner( )

Constructors CActioner()
| ```
45:    public CActioner() {
46:       try {
47:          broker = new MBroker();
48:       }catch ( Exception exc ) {
49:          exc.printStackTrace();
50:          exit(); //quit app if this happens
51:       }
52:    }
55:    public CActioner( MBroker broker ) {
56:       this.broker = broker;
57:    }
``` |
```

Initiating login

PConsole makes CActioner responsible for logging the user into the database, and therefore for permitting the user to continue with the application. The login() method (Listing 13.25) accepts the username and passwd String objects (Line 65) and passes them in a call to MBroker (Line 67). The status of the login is returned to PConsole as a constant value.

Listing 13.25 Method login( ) in CActioner

```
Method login() in CActioner

60:            * Log the user in with the given username and passwd.
61:            * @param username the name of the user to login
62:            * @param password the password to the database
63:            * @return the status of the login: LOGIN_OK, LOGIN_FAIL_1, etc
64:            */
65:         public Object login( String username, String passwd ) {
66:             loginTry++;
67:             emp = broker.login( username, passwd );
68:
69:             if(emp != null){
70:                 loginTry=0; //reset
71:                 return LOGIN_OK;
72:             }else{
73:                 switch(loginTry){
74:                     case 1: return LOGIN_FAIL_1;
75:                     case 2: return LOGIN_FAIL_2;
76:                     default: return LOGIN_FAIL_3;
77:                 }
78:             }
79:         }
```

Listing 13.26 Method retrieveMessages( ) in CActioner

```
Method retrieveMessages() in CActioner

160:       public int retrieveMessages( Collection msgs, int numMsgs ) {
161:           return broker.retrieveUnsentMessages( emp, msgs, numMsgs );
165:       }
```

Routing retrieval of outmessages

The request to retrieve outmessages from the database arrives to CActioner from PConsole (Listing 13.17, Line 179). CActioner delegates this service to MBroker. The retrieveMessages() method (Listing 13.26) requests that MBroker retrieves up to numMsgs of outmessages and places them in the msgs collection (Line 161). Only

Listing 13.27 Method retrieveMessage( ) in CActioner

Method `retrieveMessage()` in `CActioner`
| ```
172:    public IAOutMessage retrieveMessage( int id ) {
173:        return broker.retrieveUnsentMessage( emp, id );
174:    }
``` |

Listing 13.28 Overloaded methods sendMessage( ) in CActioner

Overloaded Methods `sendMessage()` in `CActioner`
| ```
97:     public boolean sendMessage(IAOutMessage msg){
98:         return sendMessage(msg, msg.getSenderEmployee().getEmail(),
99:                       msg.getContact().getEmail(),
                         msg.getSubject(),
                         msg.getMessageText());
100:    }
103:    public boolean sendMessage(IAOutMessage msg, String from,
104:    String to, String subject, String body ) {
106:        try{
107:            if ( send( from, to, subject, body ) ) {
108:                return broker.updateMessage( msg.getMessageID() );
109:            }
110:        }catch(Exception exc){
111:            handleEmailException(exc);
112:        }
113:        return false;
114:    }
``` |

outmessages created for handling by the employee passed in the argument `emp` are to be retrieved. `CActioner` maintains an association to `emp` (Listing 13.23, Line 38). The `retrieveMessages()` method returns the `int` number of outmessages left unretrieved in the database (Line 160).

The `displayMessageText()` method in `PConsole` requests the retrieval of all details of a single outmessage (Listing 13.19, Line 146). The service for this request is provided by the `retrieveMessage()` method in `CActioner` (Listing 13.27). `CActioner` delegates the request further to `MBroker` (Line 173). The `retrieveMessage()` method returns an `EOutMessage` object (Line 172). This must be an `EOutMessage` object (or null if nothing is retrieved) because `EOutMessage` is the only class that implements the `IAOutMessage` interface.

Emailing an outmessage

`CActioner` is responsible for emailing an outmessage, as requested by the user. `CActioner` has two overloaded methods called `sendMessage()` to perform this service (Listing 13.28). Only one of these methods is used in Iteration 1. `PConsole` requests the services of the second method (Lines 103–114). This method is called from `PConsole`

(Listing 13.21, Line 257). If the outmessage is successfully sent, MBroker is directed to update the outmessage record in the database (Line 108). The actual act of emailing is performed by the send() method (Line 107), which uses the JavaMail™ API library to do the job (see next section).

Using JavaMail™ API

JavaMail™ API – commonly known as **MAPI** (Mail API) – is a library for reading, composing, and sending email messages. JavaMail™ API supports various email delivery protocols, including SMTP, POP, and IMAP. Iteration 1 uses JavaMail™ API to send emails through the Simple Mail Transfer Protocol (SMTP). The SMTP server of the email sender transports the email to the SMTP server of the email recipient. The recipient can acquire the email through POP or IMAP protocols.

JavaMail™ API depends on JavaBeans Activation Framework (JAF). JAF is used to handle the Multipurpose Internet Mail Extensions (MIME) format. The MimeMessage class is used to create objects that understand MIME types and headers.

In Iteration 1, the emailing is done by the send() method (Listing 13.29) invoked by the sendMessage() method (Listing 13.28, Line 107). On invocation, the send() method obtains the from and to email addresses as well as the message subject and body. The from and to strings are passed to the constructor of the InternetAddress class so that address objects for the message's from and to fields are instantiated (Lines 123–125).

The Properties object (Lines 128–131) is used to hold information such as the email server address, username, and password. This object is passed to the constructor of the Session object (Line 134). In Iteration 1, a single default email session is sufficient. The Session object is then passed along to the MimeMessage constructor to create a Message object (Line 137). Lines 139–146 set the components of the Message object. Finally, the Message object is passed to the send() method of the Transport object, which performs the sending of the email.

Package Entity

13.5

The entity package consists of one interface and three classes:

- IEDataSupplier
- EContact
- EEmployee
- EOutMessage

Interface IEDataSupplier

13.5.1

The IEDataSupplier interface is responsible for providing data to entity objects and for enabling them to maintain association links to each other. As a result, the entity objects currently cached in memory represent an exact snapshot of a subset of the database state.

Listing 13.29 Private method send( ) in CActioner (JavaMail™ API)

```
Private Method send() in CActioner (JavaMail™ API)
121:    private boolean send( String from, String to, String subject,
                                String body )
122:    throws Exception{
123:        InternetAddress fromAddr = new InternetAddress( from );
124:        InternetAddress[] toAddr = new InternetAddress[ 1 ];
125:        toAddr[ 0 ] = new InternetAddress( to );
126:
127:        //construct mapi classes
128:        java.util.Properties props = new java.util.Properties();
129:
130:        //we assume that we use smtp here
131:        props.put( "mail.smtp.host", IAConstants.SMTP_ADDRESS );
132:
133:        //instantiate a new email session
134:        javax.mail.Session session =
                 javax.mail.Session.getDefaultInstance( props, null );
135:
136:        //construct the email message
137:        javax.mail.Message msg1 =
                        new javax.mail.internet.MimeMessage( session );
138:
139:        msg1.setRecipients( javax.mail.Message.RecipientType.TO,
                                toAddr );
140:        msg1.setFrom( fromAddr );
141:
142:        msg1.setSubject( subject );
143:        msg1.setSentDate( new java.util.Date() );
144:
145:        // If the desired charset is known, you can use
                                           setText(text, charset)
146:        msg1.setText( body );
147:
148:        //finally send the email message
149:        javax.mail.Transport.send( msg1 );
150:
151:        return true;
152:    }
```

The IEDataSupplier interface provides also a decoupling of the entity and mediator packages so that a circular dependency is eliminated (Section 9.1.7). The interface is implemented by MBroker from the mediator package and it is used by all three entity classes.

Listings 13.30 and 13.31 show the details of the IEDataSupplier interface.

Listing 13.30 IEDataSupplier method summary

```
IAContact      getContact(int contactOID)
                  Not to be used externally, only for entity classes.
IAEmployee     getEmployee(int empOID)
                  Not to be used externally, only for entity classes.
int            retrieveUnsentMessages(IAContact contact,
               java.util.Collection msgs, int numMsgRetrieve)
                  Retrieve the numMsgRetrieve number of outmessages for a particular
                  contact and place them in the msgs collection.
int            retrieveUnsentMessages(IAEmployee emp,
               java.util.Collection msgs, int numMsgRetrieve)
                  Retrieve the numMsgRetrieve number of outmessages for a particular emp
                  and place them in the msgs collection.
```

Listing 13.31 IEDataSupplier.java

```
IEDataSupplier.java

12:  public interface IEDataSupplier {
13:      /**
17:       * @param emp - the employee responsible for these outmessages
18:       * @param msgs - the collection into which these outmessages
                          will be placed
19:       * @param numMsgRetrieve - the max number of outmessages
                          retrieved
20:       * @return int - the number of outmessages still left
                          unretrieved in the database
21:      */
22:      public int retrieveUnsentMessages(IAEmployee emp, Collection
                                           msgs, int numMsgRetrieve);
23:
24:      /**
28:       * @param contact - the contact to whom the outmessages are
                          addressed
32:      */
33:      public int retrieveUnsentMessages(IAContact contact,
                                  Collection msgs, int numMsgRetrieve);
34:
36:      public IAEmployee getEmployee(int empOID) throws Exception;
37:
39:      public IAContact getContact(int contactOID);
40:  }
```

Object identifiers and identity field pattern

The `IEDataSupplier` interface makes it clear that each entity object is given a unique **object identifier** (OID) (Maciaszek, 2001). Object identifiers are then used for association links between objects cached in memory. In the EM implementation, each entity object is allocated a globally unique OID when it is first created. This OID is guaranteed to be unique for the duration of program execution.

The use of object identifiers for in-memory objects has been perfected in object database systems (Maciaszek, 2001). In EM, a less sophisticated technique is implemented. Various ways of implementing object identifiers are the subject of the **Identity Field pattern** (Fowler, 2003).

The Identity Field pattern states that an identify field 'saves a database ID field in an object to maintain identity between an in-memory object and a database row' (Fowler, 2003, p.216). In other words, the identify field ensures proper mapping between in-memory transient objects and database persistent objects. In the simplest case, the Identity Field pattern allows the primary key of a database record to be used as an OID for the corresponding in-memory object. This makes the pattern less demanding than object database implementations, or even the EM implementation.

Using the primary key as an OID is problematic on at least the following grounds:

- Frequently, primary keys have a well-understood business meaning and are used as such in business dealings. This means that they can change over time. Also, they are guaranteed to be unique only within the records of one table, which can create problems when used for in-memory objects. In-memory objects use identity fields as object handles, whether or not they know the class of these object handles.

- Even if primary keys can serve the OID purpose for objects created as a result of reading database records, the application is likely to create new entity objects in memory and then store them persistently in the database. Most databases have their own mechanisms to automatically generate primary key values when a new record is inserted into a table (this mechanism is even called *identity* in SQL*Server and Sybase; in Oracle it is called *sequence*). Having an in-memory primary key, which has to be replaced by the database-generated primary key when writing data to the database, is awkward, to say the least.

- 'Table-unique' primary keys are bound to create problems when used as object identifiers in classes that are involved in implementation inheritance.

- Implementing object identifiers as globally unique identity fields can prove very useful later if a decision is taken to deploy the `entity` package into an object data store in a middle tier of the multi-tier architecture.

Identity fields in EM are implemented by combining the first three letters of the entity name (excluding the first letter that identifies the package – e.g. `EMP` in case of `EEmployee`) with a randomly generated unique integer value. Identity fields are therefore 'execution-unique' object identifiers, i.e. they are unique within a program execution.

Note finally that identify fields are used in addition to any situation when an object also holds another object or contains a reference to a container of other objects. As pointed out by Fowler (2003), the fact that object systems ensure the correct 'containment' identity under the covers (in Java) or by memory pointers (in C++) does not replace the need for identity fields.

Class EEmployee   13.5.2

The `EEmployee` class implements the `IAEmployee` interface (Section 13.2.2). This class maintains association links to all outmessages (`EOutMessage` objects) assigned to it and currently loaded in memory.

A client object is able to retrieve outmessages by various criteria, such as: querying the `EEmployee` object regarding its outmessages, querying an `EContact` object about outmessages addressed to it, or asking the `MBroker` object to find required outmessages. Listing 13.32 shows the data members of `EEmployee`.

Listing 13.32 EEmployee field summary

```
private java.lang.String      email
private java.lang.String      employeeID
private java.lang.String      familyName
private java.lang.String      firstName
private java.lang.String      loginName
private java.util.Collection  msgs
private int                   OID
private IEDataSupplier        ref
```

Listing 13.33 explains the main methods of `EEmployee`. The get and set methods for the `EEmployee` primitive data types are omitted.

Listing 13.33 EEmployee method summary

```
EEmployee(IEDataSupplier ref)
     Default empty constructor.
java.util.Collection   getUnsentOutMessages(int maxMsgsRetrieve)
                             Get all messages (up to numMsgRetrieve) assigned to this
                             employee.
void                   removeSentOutMessage(IAOutMessage msg)
                             Remove a message from this employee's assignment, perhaps
                             because it is already sent.
```

Constructing an EEmployee object

An `EEmployee` object is instantiated by the `MBroker` class, which implements the `IEDataSupplier` interface. The constructor for `EEmployee` is shown in Listing 13.34.

Listing 13.34 Constructor EEmployee( )

```
Constructor EEmployee()
28:      public EEmployee(IEDataSupplier ref) {
29:          this.ref = ref;
30:      };
```

Getting unsent outmessages

EEmployee can use the ref variable, which points to the MBroker object, to request the retrieval of outmessages that have not been sent yet. The number of retrieved outmessages is limited by the value of the maxMsgsRetrieve argument. The getUnsentMessages() method is shown in Listing 13.35.

Listing 13.35 Method getUnsentMessages( ) in EEmployee

```
Method getUnsentMessages() in EEmployee
90:      public Collection getUnsentOutMessages(int maxMsgsRetrieve) {
91:          if (msgs == null)
92:              ref.retrieveUnsentMessages( this, msgs,
                                              maxMsgsRetrieve );
93:          return msgs;
94:      }
```

In Iteration 1, all requests from CActioner to bring unsent messages to the cache and to remove sent messages from the cache are addressed to MBroker. This is because MBroker controls the state of the cache. The getUnsentMessages() method, and the removeSentOutMessages() presented in the next section, are not used in Iteration 1. If invoked by CActioner, they would need to engage MBroker. The same principle applies to similar methods in EContact, explained in Section 13.5.3.

Removing sent outmessages

An EEmployee object has the msgs collection variable to hold all OutMessage objects assigned to that EEmployee and currently in memory cache. Similarly, each OutMessage object has a variable linking it to EEmployee. Once an outmessage is successfully emailed, the relevant OutMessage object must be removed from the collection (Line 105 in Listing 13.36) and it must be asked to set its reverse link to EEmployee to null (Line 106).

Listing 13.36 Method removeSentOutMessage( ) in EEmployee

```
Method removeSentOutMessage() in EEmployee

99:       public void removeSentOutMessage(IAOutMessage msg) {
100:          if (msgs == null) return;
103:          //detach from the list of messages
104:          //also detach this emp from the message
105:          if (msgs.remove(msg))
106:             msg.setSenderEmployee(null);
107:      }
```

Class EContact   13.5.3

The EContact class implements the IAContact interface (Section 13.2.3). Each EContact object maintains association links to all outmessages (EOutMessage objects) addressed to it and currently loaded in memory.

Listing 13.37 shows the data members of EContact. The use of the OID and ref fields is similar to that discussed in the previous section in the context of EEmployee.

Listing 13.37 EContact field summary

```
private java.lang.String        contactID
private java.lang.String        email
private java.lang.String        familyName
private java.lang.String        firstName
private java.util.Collection    msgs
private int                     OID
private java.lang.String        organization
private IEDataSupplier          ref
```

Listing 13.38 explains the main methods of EContact. The get and set methods for the Econtact primitive data types are omitted.

Listing 13.38 EEmployee method summary

```
EContact(IEDataSupplier ref)
    Default empty constructor.
java.util.Collection   getUnsentOutMessages(int numMsgToBeRetrieved)
                           Get all messages destined for this contact.
void                   removeSentOutMessage(IAOutMessage msg)
                           Remove a message destined for this contact, perhaps because it is
                           already sent.
```

Constructing an EContact object

An EContact object is instantiated by the MBroker class, which implements the IEDataSupplier interface. The constructor for EContact is shown in Listing 13.39.

Listing 13.39 Constructor EContact( )

```
Constructor EContact()

24:     public EContact(IEDataSupplier ref) {
25:         this.ref = ref;
26:     }
```

Getting unsent outmessages

The method to get unsent outmessages for EContact (Listing 13.40) is identical to that presented in Listing 13.35 for EEmployee. EContact uses the ref variable, which points to the MBroker object, to request the retrieval of outmessages that have not been sent yet. The number of retrieved outmessages is limited by the value of the maxMsgsRetrieve argument.

Listing 13.40 Method getUnsentMessages( ) in EContact

```
Method getUnsentMessages() in EContact

88:     public Collection
                    getUnsentOutMessages(int numMsgToBeRetrieved) {
89:         if (msgs == null)
                ref.retrieveUnsentMessages(this,msgs,
                                            numMsgToBeRetrieved);
90:         return msgs;
91:     }
```

Removing sent outmessages

In a similar way to an EEmployee object, an EContact object has the msgs collection variable to hold all OutMessage objects assigned to that EContact and currently in memory cache. Similarly, each OutMessage object has a variable linking it to EContact. Once an outmessage is successfully emailed, the relevant OutMessage object must be removed from the collection (Line 102 in Listing 13.41) and it must be asked to set its reverse link to EContact to null (Line 103).

Listing 13.41 Method removeSentOutMessage( ) in EContact

```
Method removeSentOutMessage() in EContact
96:     public void removeSentOutMessage(IAOutMessage msg) {
97:         if (msgs == null) return;
100:            //detach from the list of messages
101:            //also detach this contact from the message
102:            if (msgs.remove(msg))
103:                msg.setContact(null);
104:    }
105: }
```

Class EOutMessage
13.5.4

The EOutMessage class implements the IAOutMessage interface (Section 13.2.4). Each EOutMessage object maintains association links to its EEmployee and EContact, provided these objects are currently loaded in memory.

In Iteration 1, the employee who creates an outmessage (creator_emp_id in the OutMessage table) is also responsible for emailing this outmessage. Upon sending, the columns sender_emp_id and date_emailed in the OutMessage table are updated (Figure 10.14 in Section 10.3.1).

Listing 13.42 shows the data members of EOutMessage. The use of the OID and ref fields is similar to that discussed previously in the context of EEmployee and EContact. The fields contactOID, creatorOID, and senderOID provide links to EContact and EEmployee. In Iteration 1, creatorOID and senderOID link to the same EEmployee object.

Listing 13.42 EOutMessage field summary

```
private IAContact           contact
private int                 contactOID
private java.sql.Date       creationDate
private IAEmployee          creator
private int                 creatorOID
private int                 messageID
private java.lang.String    messageText
private int                 OID
private IEDataSupplier      ref
private IAEmployee          sender
private int                 senderOID
private java.sql.Date       sentDate
private java.lang.String    subject
```

Apart from the constructor, all methods in `EOutMessage` are `get` and `set` methods. Listing 13.43 shows these `get` and `set` methods which handle non-primitive types (i.e. classes). Other `get` and `set` methods are omitted.

Listing 13.43 EOutMessage method summary

EOutMessage (IEDataSupplier ref)	
Default empty constructor.	
IAContact	**getContact**()
	Get the contact for this message.
IAEmployee	**getCreatorEmployee**()
	Retrieve employee who created this message initially.
IAEmployee	**getSenderEmployee**()
	Retrieve the employee who is responsible for sending this message.
void	**setContact**(IAContact contact)
	Allows the assignment of contact.
void	**setCreatorEmployee**(IAEmployee emp)
	Set employee who creates this message.
void	**setSenderEmployee**(IAEmployee emp)
	Set employee who is responsible for sending this message.

Constructing an EOutMessage object

An `EOutMessage` object is instantiated by the `MBroker` class, which implements the `IEDataSupplier` interface. The default empty constructor for `EOutMessage` is shown in Listing 13.44.

Listing 13.44 Constructor EOutMessage( )

```
Constructor EOutMessage()

27:     public EOutMessage(IEDataSupplier ref) {
28:         this.ref = ref;
29:     }
```

Getting and setting a contact for outmessage

As shown in Listing 13.42, `EOutMessage` has a field (`contactOID`) that can be used to find an `EContact` object for a particular `EOutMessage` object. However, the `contactOID` can only point to `EContact` already in the memory cache. If `EContact` is not in the cache, then it must be retrieved from the database and assigned to `EOutMessage`. The assignment results in setting up the `contact` and the `contactOID` fields. Clearly, making `EOutMessage` hold the `EContact` object and a reference to the same object is redundant in Iteration 1.

The task of getting and setting `EContact` for `EOutMessage` is given to the `getContact()` and `setContact()` methods presented in Listing 13.45. `EOutMessage` calls on `MBroker` (represented by the `ref` variable) to `getContact()` and passes to it a `contactOID` (Line 123 in Listing 13.45). When the `EContact` object is returned from `MBroker`, `EOutMessage` is in a position to `setContact()` (Lines 106–108) and return it to the client of `getContact()` (Lines 121–125).

Listing 13.45 Methods getContact( ) and setContact( ) in EOutMessage

```
Methods getContact() and setContact() in EOutMessage

121:    public IAContact getContact() {
122:        if (contact == null)
123:            setContact(ref.getContact(contactOID));
124:        return contact;
125:    }
106:    public void setContact(IAContact contact) {
107:        this.contact = contact;
108:    }
```

Getting and setting a creator employee for outmessage

The task of getting and setting an `EEmployee` object as a creator employee for an `EOutMessage` object is analogous to getting and setting `EContact` for `EOutMessage`, as discussed in the previous section. This is shown in Listing 13.46.

Listing 13.46 Methods getCreatorEmployee( ) and setCreatorEmployee( ) in EOutMessage

```
Methods getCreatorEmployee() and setCreatorEmployee() in
EOutMessage

130:    public IAEmployee getCreatorEmployee() {
131:        try {
132:            if (creator == null)
133:                setCreatorEmployee(ref.getEmployee(creatorOID));
139:            return creator;
140:        }
161:    public void setCreatorEmployee(IAEmployee emp) {
162:        creator = emp;
163:    }
```

Getting and setting a sender employee for outmessage

The task of getting and setting an `EEmployee` object as a sender employee for an `EOutMessage` is shown in Listing 13.47. Note again that in Iteration 1 the creator and the sender of an outmessage are the same employee.

Listing 13.47 Methods getSenderEmployee( ) and setSenderEmployee( ) in EOutMessage

Methods getSenderEmployee() and setSenderEmployee() in EOutMessage

```
145:    public IAEmployee getSenderEmployee() {
146:        try {
147:            if (sender == null)
148:                setSenderEmployee(ref.getEmployee(senderOID));
155:            return sender;
156:        }
168:    public void setSenderEmployee(IAEmployee emp) {
169:        sender = emp;
170:        }
```

13.6 Package Mediator

The mediator package consists of one class:

■ MBroker

The MBroker class implements two interfaces: IAConstants (in the acquaintance package) and IEDataSupplier (in the entity package).

Listing 13.48 MBroker field summary

private FConnection	**connection**	
	The connection used by reader/writer	
private java.util.Map	**contacts**	
	Cache of contacts	
private boolean	**dirty**	
	Does the cache need re-retrieval	
private java.util.Map	**emps**	
	Cache of employees	
private java.util.Map	**msgs**	
	Cache of messages	
private FReader	**reader**	
	Reader of database	
private int	**remainder**	
	How many messages remain in database	
private FWriter	**writer**	
	Writer to database	

Class MBroker

Being the sole class in the mediator package, MBroker has quite a bit of work to do. It bridges and decouples the three PCMEF packages (control, entity, and foundation) from tight dependencies. MBroker is aware of the entity objects currently in the memory cache. It is responsible for extracting data from SQL query results (of foundation layer) and for maintaining the main logic of entity creations. MBroker handles the mapping from raw data (query results) to entity objects and vice versa.

The main responsibilities of MBroker are indirectly visible in the data members that it maintains, as shown in Listing 13.48.

Listing 13.49 presents the methods defined in MBroker.

Listing 13.49 MBroker method summary

MBroker()	
Construct a broker.	
MBroker(FConnection connection)	
Create a new broker with a particular connection.	
private IAContact	**createContact**()
	Create a new contact object.
private IAEmployee	**createEmployee**()
	Create a new employee object.
private IAOutMessage	**createOutMessage**()
	Create a new outmessage object.
private java.util.Collection	**doRetrieveMessagesAndContacts**(IAContact contact, int numMsgs)
	Perform the retrieval of outmessages from database.
private IAOutMessage	**doRetrieveUnsentMessageAndContact** (IAEmployee em, int msgID)
	Perform a message retrieval for a particular msgID directly from database.
private java.util.Collection	**doRetrieveUnsentMessagesAndContacts** (IAEmployee emp, int numMsgs)
	Perform the retrieval of unsent outmessages from database.
private void	**flagCache**()
	Change the flag to indicate whether the entity cache is dirty or not.
IAContact	**getContact**(int contactOID)
	Not to be used externally, only for entity classes.
IAEmployee	**getEmployee**(int empOID)
	Not to be used externally, only for entity classes.
private int	**getOID**(java.lang.Object o)
	Create an OID for the object given.
private IAOutMessage	**getOutMessageFromCache**(int msgID)
	Pull an outmessage out of the cache, if one exists.
private boolean	**isDirty**()
	Is the cache flagged as dirty?

private boolean	**isInCache**(java.lang.Integer msgID)
	Is the outmessage in cache already?
IAEmployee	**login**(java.lang.String username, java.lang.String passwd)
	Perform a login and return the employee details.
void	**logout**()
	Log the user out, clean all connections.
private IAContact	**mapContact**(java.sql.ResultSet rs)
	Map contact raw data to EContact.
private IAEmployee	**mapEmployee**(java.sql.ResultSet rs)
	Map employee raw data to EEmployee.
private IAOutMessage	**mapOutMessage**(java.sql.ResultSet rs)
	Map outmessage raw data to EOutMessage.
private java.util.Collection	**mapOutMessages**(java.sql.ResultSet rs, int numRetrieve)
	Retrieve only numRetrieve messages from the result set.
private void	**retrieveContacts**(java.util.Collection msgs)
	Retrieve contacts for given messages.
IAOutMessage	**retrieveUnsentMessage**(IAEmployee emp, int msgID)
	Retrieve a single message either from cache or directly from database.
int	**retrieveUnsentMessages**(IAEmployee emp, java.util.Collection msgs, int numMsgs)
	Retrieve unsent outmessages from the cache or database.
boolean	**updateMessage**(int msgID)
	Indicate that the message has been sent.

Constructing an MBroker object

There are two constructors defined in MBroker (Listing 13.50). The constructor actually used in Iteration 1 is shown on Lines 48–50. The constructor that creates MBroker by specifying an FConnection object (Lines 52–68) is referred to in the problem-solving exercises.

Requesting login connection

When instructed by CActioner to login() (Section 13.4.1), MBroker requests FConnection to connect the user to the database (Listing 13.51, Lines 78–81). The login process checks whether the user is an employee in the Employee table. This is done by means of the SQL query (Section 12.1.3) in Lines 83–85. A successful login allows MBroker to create a new EEmployee object in memory cache using the mapEmployee() method (Line 86), as explained in the next section.

Listing 13.50 Constructors MBroker( )

```
Constructors MBroker()

48:    public MBroker() throws ClassNotFoundException {
49:        this(new FConnection(DB_DRIVER, DB_URL));
50:    }
51:
52:    /** Create a new broker with a particular connection */
53:    public MBroker(FConnection connection) {
54:        try {
55:            dirty = true; //retrieve the outmessages first time
56:            this.connection = connection;
57:            reader = connection.getReader();
58:            writer = connection.getWriter();
63:        }
64:        msgs = new HashMap();
65:        contacts = new HashMap();
66:        emps = new HashMap();
67:        remainder = 0;
68:    }
```

Listing 13.51 Method login( ) in MBroker

```
Method login() in MBroker

76:    public IAEmployee login(String username, String passwd) {
77:        try {
78:        if (!connection.isConnected()) {
79:            //fail connecting
80:            if (!connection.connect(username, passwd))
81:                return null;
82:        }
83:        java.sql.ResultSet rs =
84:            reader.query(
85:                "select * from employee where login_name = '" +
                                                username + "'");
86:            IAEmployee emp = mapEmployee(rs);
87:            reader.closeResult(rs);
88:            return emp;
89:        } catch (Exception exc) {
90:        }
91:        return null;
92:    }
```

Creating Employees Cache

Although an index on the `Employee` table guarantees that login names of employees are unique (Section 10.3.1), the SQL query in Listing 13.51 (in Lines 83–85) permits a set of records (`ResultSet`) to be returned. When called, the `mapEmployee()` method (Listing 13.52) iterates through the result set and creates an `EEmployee` object (Line 413). Once created, the raw data is mapped to `EEmployee` fields (Lines 415–424). The `OID` field of `EEmployee` is set in Line 426 and used as an index of the `emps Map` collection (cache of employees) (Line 427).

Listing 13.52 Method mapEmployee( ) in MBroker

```
Method mapEmployee() in MBroker

409:     private IAEmployee mapEmployee(java.sql.ResultSet rs) {
410:         EEmployee emp = null;
411:         try {
412:             if (rs.next()) {
413:                 emp = (EEmployee) createEmployee();
414:
415:                 String empid = rs.getString("employee_id");
416:                 String fname = rs.getString("first_name");
417:                 String familyname = rs.getString("family_name");
418:                 String email = rs.getString("employee_email");
419:                 String loginName = rs.getString("login_name");
420:                 emp.setEmployeeID(empid);
421:                 emp.setFirstName(fname);
422:                 emp.setFamilyName(familyname);
423:                 emp.setEmail(email);
424:                 emp.setLoginName(loginName);
425:
426:                 emp.setOID(getOID("EMP" + empid));
427:                 emps.put(new Integer(emp.getOID()), emp);
428:             }
429:         } catch (Exception exc) {
430:         }
431:         return emp;
432:     }
```

Retrieving unsent outmessages

When asked by `CActioner` (Section 13.4.1), `MBroker` undertakes to retrieve outmessages for a given employee (user). `MBroker` can retrieve outmessages from the cache or, if the cache is empty or dirty, it can perform the retrieval of outmessages from the database. The first task belongs to the `retrieveUnsentMessages()` method (Listing 13.53,

Lines 192–209). The second task is undertaken by the doRetrieveUnsentMessages-
AndContacts()method (Lines 211–247).

Listing 13.53 Methods retrieveUnsentMessages() and
doRetrieveUnsentMessagesAndContacts() in MBroker

```
Methods retrieveUnsentMessages() and
doRetrieveUnsentMessagesAndContacts() in MBroker
```

```
192:          * @param emp the employee assigned for these messages
193:          * @param msgs the collection into which the messages will
                                                        be filled
194:          * @param numMsgs the number of messages to be retrieved.
195:          * @return int the number of messages still unretrieved
196:          */
197:       public int retrieveUnsentMessages(
198:          IAEmployee emp,
199:          Collection msgs,
200:          int numMsgs) {
201:          if (msgs.isEmpty()) {
202:             try {
203:                msgs.addAll(doRetrieveUnsentMessagesAndContacts(emp,
                                                             numMsgs));
204:             } catch (Exception exc) {
205:                exc.printStackTrace();
206:             }
207:          }
208:          return remainder;
209:       }
210:
211:       /** Perform the retrieval of outmessages from database. */
212:       private Collection doRetrieveUnsentMessagesAndContacts(
213:          IAEmployee emp,
214:          int numMsgs)
215:          throws Exception {
222:
223:          java.sql.ResultSet rs =
224:             reader.query(
225:                "Select * from outmessage where sender_emp_id = '"
226:                   + emp.getEmployeeID()
227:                   + "' and date_emailed is null");
228:
230:          Collection msgs = mapOutMessages(rs, maxRetrieve);
231:          reader.closeResult(rs);
232:          retrieveContacts(msgs);
233:
```

```
234:         dirty = false;
235:
236:         //calculate the remainder of messages on the server
237:         rs =
238:            reader.query(
239:              "Select count(*) from outmessage where
                                               sender_emp_id = '"
240:                  + emp.getEmployeeID()
241:                  + "' and date_emailed is null");
242:         rs.next();
243:         int count = rs.getInt(1);
244:         reader.closeResult(rs);
245:         remainder = count - msgs.size();
246:         return msgs;
247:     }
```

MBroker is also responsible for retrieving a single outmessage for a given employee using the retrieveUnsentMessage() method. This method is usually called in order to display the outmessage body just before the user emails it. The code for this method, and for the method invoked by it called doRetrieveUnsentMessageandContact(), are similar to shown above and are, therefore, not presented here.

Creating an outmessages cache

The retrieval of outmessages from the database results in the need to put EOutMessage objects into the cache. This task is requested by the mapOutMessages() call in the doRetrieveUnsentMessagesAndContacts() method (Listing 13.53, Line 230).

Listing 13.54 Method mapOutMessages( ) in MBroker

```
Method mapOutMessages() in MBroker

493:    private Collection mapOutMessages(
494:        java.sql.ResultSet rs,
495:        int numRetrieve) {
496:
497:        Collection c = new ArrayList(numRetrieve);
498:        for (int i = 0; i < numRetrieve; i++) {
499:            IAOutMessage msg = mapOutMessage(rs);
500:            if (msg == null)
501:                return c;
502:            c.add(msg);
503:        }
504:        return c;
505:    }
```

The `mapOutMessages()` method is given in Listing 13.54. The `mapOutMessage()` method, called in Line 499, is similar to the `mapEmployee()` method in Listing 13.52, and not shown for reasons of space.

Creating a contacts cache

The retrieval of outmessages from the database results also in the need to put `EContacts` objects into the cache. This task is requested by the `retrieveContacts()` call in the `doRetrieveUnsentMessagesAndContacts()` method (Listing 13.53, Line 232).

The `retrieveContacts()` method is given in Listing 13.55. The `mapContact()` method, called in Line 268, is similar to the `mapEmployee()` method in Listing 13.52, and not shown for reasons of space.

Listing 13.55 Method retrieveContacts( ) in MBroker

```
Method retrieveContacts() in MBroker

250:    private void retrieveContacts(Collection msgs) {
251:        Iterator it = msgs.iterator();
252:        EOutMessage msg;
253:        while (it.hasNext()) {
254:            msg = (EOutMessage) it.next();
255:            IAContact contact = null;
256:            Object cntObj = contacts.get(new
                                    Integer(msg.getContactOID()));
257:            try {
258:                contact = (IAContact) cntObj;
259:            } catch (ClassCastException exc) {
260:            }
261:            if (contact == null) {
262:                try {
263:                    java.sql.ResultSet rs =
264:                        reader.query(
265:                            "Select * from contact where
                                            contact_id = '"
266:                                + cntObj.toString()
267:                                + "'");
268:                    contact = mapContact(rs);
269:                    reader.closeResult(rs);
270:                } catch (Exception exc) {
271:                    exc.printStackTrace();
272:                }
273:            }
274:        }
275:    }
```

Updating outmessages after emailing and restoring the cache

Upon successful emailing of an outmessage, the CActioner's sendMessage() method (Section 13.4.1) calls on MBroker to updateMessage(). This operation has a double purpose: to update the OutMessage table in the database and to restore the program's entity cache by removing the emailed EOutMessage object from its EEmployee and EContact objects.

Listing 13.56 presents the updateMessage() method. In Line 292, the method gets the EOutMessage object (just emailed) from the cache. In Line 299, it sets the sentDate field (Listing 13.42) of this object to the current date. It then calls the unmapOutMessage() method (Line 301) to update the database (Listing 13.57). When this is done, the flagCache() call in Line 305 flags the cache as dirty. The statements in Lines 308–315 remove the emailed EOutMessage object from its EEmployee and EContact objects (not really implemented in Iteration 1).

Listing 13.56 Method updateMessage( ) in MBroker

```
Method updateMessage() in MBroker

287:    public boolean updateMessage(int msgID) {
292:        EOutMessage msg = (EOutMessage)
                                    getOutMessageFromCache(msgID);
299:        msg.setSentDate(new
                        java.sql.Date(System.currentTimeMillis()));
300:        try {
301:            java.sql.PreparedStatement st = unmapOutMessage(msg);
302:            if (st.executeUpdate() != 1)
303:                return false;
304:
305:            flagCache();
306:
308:            msgs.remove(new Integer(msg.getOID()));
309:            EContact contact = (EContact) msg.getContact();
310:            contact.removeSentOutMessage(msg);
311:            EEmployee emp = (EEmployee) msg.getCreatorEmployee();
312:            emp.removeSentOutMessage(msg);
313:            emp = (EEmployee) msg.getSenderEmployee();
314:            emp.removeSentOutMessage(msg);
315:            return true;
319:        }
321:        return false;
322:    }
```

Listing 13.57 Method unmapOutMessage( ) in MBroker

```
Method unmapOutMessage() in MBroker

508:      private java.sql.PreparedStatement unmapOutMessage(EOutMessage
                                                                     msg)
509:        throws Exception {
510:        java.sql.PreparedStatement st =
511:          writer.update(
512:            "Update OutMessage set date_emailed = ? where
                                              message_id = ?");
513:        st.setDate(1, msg.getSentDate());
514:        st.setInt(2, msg.getMessageID());
515:        return st;
516:      }
```

Package Foundation

13.7

The foundation package consists of three classes:

- FConnection
- FReader
- FWriter

Class FConnection

13.7.1

The FConnection class performs typical tasks of establishing a database connection, as discussed in Section 12.1.3. It solicits the assistance of the FReader and FWriter classes to perform the database retrieval and the database modification, respectively.

Listing 13.58 shows the data members in FConnection, including associations to FReader and FWriter.

Listing 13.58 FConnection field summary

```
private java.sql.Connection    conn
private java.lang.String       dbDriver
private java.lang.String       dbUrl
private FReader                reader
private FWriter                writer
```

Listing 13.59 is the summary of methods in FConnection, including associations to FReader and FWriter.

Listing 13.59 FConnection method summary

```
FConnection (java.lang.String driver, java.lang.String dbUrl)
     Construct a new FConnection object.
void       close()
           Close the connection.
boolean    connect(java.lang.String username,
           java.lang.String passwd)
               Get a connection to database with the given username and passwd. If the
               connection is successfully made, and there exists an old connection, the old
               connection will be closed and replaced with the new connection.
FReader    getReader()
           Retrieve default reader implementation supported by this connection.
FWriter    getWriter()
           Retrieve default writer implementation supported by this connection. Ideally this
           class could be implemented as AbstractFactory or AbstractMethod but we opt for
           simplicity for the moment.
boolean    isConnected()
           Have we connected to database?
```

Constructing an FConnection object

The constructor of a new FConnection object is shown in Listing 13.60. The constructor initializes its dbDriver and dbUrl data members. The FConnection class shares its java.sql.Connection object with its FReader and FWriter objects.

Listing 13.60 Constructor FConnection()

```
Constructor FConnection()

33:       public FConnection( String driver, String dbUrl ) throws
                                              ClassNotFoundException {
34:           this.dbDriver = driver;
35:           Class.forName( driver );
36:           this.dbUrl = dbUrl;
37:       }
```

Obtaining database connection

The connect() method in Listing 13.61 establishes a connection to the database with the given username and password. If the connection is successfully made, and there exists an old connection, the old connection will be closed and replaced with the new connection. The method returns true if there is only one connection established (either old or new).

Listing 13.61 Method connect( ) in FConnection

```
Method connect() in FConnection

79:     public boolean connect( String username, String passwd ) {
80:         if ( conn != null ) { //we had an old connection, we may
                                                need to close it
81:             if ( ( username != null && username.length() != 0 ) &&
                     ( passwd != null && passwd.length() != 0 ) ) {
82:                 Connection con = null;
83:                 try {
84:                     con = DriverManager.getConnection( dbUrl,
                                                username, passwd );
85:                 }catch ( Exception exc2 ) {
86:                     exc2.printStackTrace(); //debugging
87:                 }
88:                 if ( con != null ) { //switch connection
89:                     try {
90:                         conn.close();
91:                     }catch ( Exception exc ) {}
92:                     conn = con;
93:                 }
94:             }
95:         }
96:         else { //no connection has been made, make a new one
97:             try {
98:                 conn = DriverManager.getConnection( dbUrl,
                                                username, passwd );
99:             }catch ( Exception exc ) {
100:                exc.printStackTrace(); //debugging
101:            }
102:        }
104:        getReader().setConnection( conn );
105:        getWriter().setConnection( conn );
106:        try {
107:            return conn != null && !conn.isClosed();
108:        }
109:        catch ( Exception exc ) {
110:            return false;
111:        }
112:    }
```

The `getReader()` and `getWriter()` methods in Lines 104–105 are used to create new FReader and FWriter objects and to establish corresponding association links to these objects from the FConnection object. These two methods are not shown here.

13.7.2 Class FReader

The FReader class is responsible for executing SQL query strings, returning the result sets to the client, and cleaning up the result set after it has been processed. Listing 13.62 is the summary of FReader's methods. The methods are not discussed further. The principles of executing SQL statements are explained in detail in Section 12.1.3.

Listing 13.62 FReader method summary

```
FReader(java.sql.Connection conn)
      Create an FReader object on the provided connection.
void                    closeResult(java.sql.ResultSet rs)
                        MBroker calls this method after processing the result set.
java.sql.ResultSet   query(java.lang.String sql)
                        Query database based on the SQL string.
void                    setConnection(java.sql.Connection conn)
                        Change the connection for this reader.
```

13.7.3 Class FWriter

The Fwriter class is responsible for executing SQL update strings provided to it by MBroker (Listing 13.57), and cleaning up the result set after it has been processed. Listing 13.63 is the summary of FWriter's methods. The methods are not discussed further. The principles of executing SQL statements are explained in detail in Section 12.1.3.

Listing 13.63 FWriter method summary

```
FWriter(java.sql.Connection conn)
      Create an FWriter object that writes all updates and data to the connection provided.
void                         closeStatement(java.sql.
                                                PreparedStatement st)
void                         setConnection(java.sql.Connection conn)
                             Change the connection for this writer.
java.sql.PreparedStatement   update(java.lang.String sql)
```

Summary

1. The Java code for Iteration 1 conforms strictly to the PCMEF architectural framework.

2. To emphasize the clarity and highlight the simplicity of the PCMEF framework, Iteration 1 restricts the number of classes in each package.

3. The `acquaintance` package consists of four interfaces: `IAConstants`, `IAContact`, `IAEmployee`, and `IAOutMessage`.

4. The `presentation` package contains two classes: `PMain` and `PConsole`.

5. The `control` package contains one class only: `CActioner`. This class encapsulates all activities known to Iteration 1 of the EM case study.

6. JavaMail™ API – commonly known as MAPI (Mail API) – is a library for reading, composing and sending email messages.

7. The `entity` package consists of one interface and three classes: `IEDataSupplier`, `EContact`, `EEmployee`, and `EOutMessage`.

8. The `mediator` package consists of one class: `MBroker`. `MBroker` bridges and decouples the `control`, `entity`, and `foundation` packages from tight dependencies.

9. The `foundation` package consists of three classes: `FConnection`, `FReader`, and `FWriter`.

Key Terms

class hierarchy	415	MAPI	*See* JavaMail
Identity Field pattern	438	object identifier	438
interface hierarchy	415	OID	*See* object identifier
JavaMail	435	package hierarchy	415

Iteration 1 Questions and Exercises

Below is a small set of questions and exercises with regard to the EM Iteration 1 code. More questions and exercises are available from the book's website.

1. Iteration 1 uses the Java collection library to implement associations between entity classes. What are these associations? Which Java concrete container is used? What class and which method instantiates this container? What class and which method populates (loads) this container? How are association links to this container initialized?

2. What is the purpose of the interface `IAConstants`? Can the same purpose be achieved differently? How?

3. Listing 13.13 contains two constructors for `PConsole`. The second constructor `PConsole (CActioner actioner)` is not used in Iteration 1. How could it be used? Similarly,

Listing 13.50 contains two constructors for `MBroker` and the second constructor is not used in Iteration 1. How could it be used? Are these two constructors in `PConsole` and `MBroker` related in any way?

4. Explain the code behind the first `SendMessage()` method in `CActioner` (Listing 13.28, Lines 97–99).

5. The method `getUnsentMessages()` (Listings 13.35 and 13.40) is not used in Iteration 1. What are the consequences?

6. What is the reason in Iteration 1 for replacing the old database connection with a new one, as implemented in `FConnection`'s `connect()` (Listing 13.61)?

7. A resource file could replace the interface `IAConstants` in Iteration 1 (Section 13.2.1). Show the content of such a file. Explain how the application will use the file.

8. Consider the method `displayLoginError()` in Listing 13.15. What could be an obvious alternative implementation?

9. Explain the code changes if a decision were taken to remove the interface `IEDataSupplier` from Iteration 1. What would be the impact on the PCMEF framework?

Part

3

Software Refactoring and User Interface Development

Chapter 14   Iteration 2 Requirements and Object Model   463

Chapter 15   Architectural Refactoring   478

Chapter 16   User Interface Design and Programming   509

Chapter 17   Web-Based User Interface Design and Programming   541

Chapter 18   Iteration 2 Annotated Code   584

I teration 1 of the case study produced a software product that was simplified in a number of ways. The main objective was to deliver a *release* of the project demonstrating a clear architectural design and amenability to extensions. The secondary objective was to base the solution on only the most fundamental software engineering practices and to explain these practices in a way that streamlined the book's educational mission.

Perhaps the most obvious shortcomings of the Iteration 1 product are the lack of a *graphical user interface* (GUI) and the design failing to take advantage of some most powerful aspects of object technology. Iteration 2 discussed in this part of the book aims to rectify these shortcomings.

The techniques and methods of software engineering uncovered in Iteration 2 of the EM case study include refactoring, in-memory caching, implementation inheritance, composition, GUI design, web-enabled GUI design, visibility, polymorphism, exception handling, concurrency, threads, etc. The architectural framework of Iteration 1 is retained and reinforced to ensure continuing understandability, maintainability, and scalability of the product. The *agile software development* remains the center of gravity in the case study.

The main learning objectives of Part 3 and Iteration 2 of the case study are to gain knowledge of:

- code refactoring and how the sound initial design architecture facilitates refactoring
- the relationship between refactorings and design patterns
- refactoring patterns for the middle tier of the system so that the future deployment of the software domain layer on an application server is facilitated
- the principles of user interface design
- the practice of user interface design based on standard components and a standard event model
- technologies in support of web-based user interface design
- enabling technologies for the web server tier and managing transactions on stateless Internet systems
- design patterns for the application's presentation layer with regard to desktop and web-based user interfaces.

Iteration 2 Requirements and Object Model

The focus of Iteration 2 of the Email Management (EM) case study is on building a GUI front-end to the application and on providing web-enabled versions of the system. According to the PCMEF framework, the majority of changes in this iteration are in the presentation layer, which encapsulates interaction with the user. The new Iteration 2 functionality is added on top of the Iteration 1 functionality.

The typical practice of **agile software development** is to iterate every two weeks (Martin, 2003). At the end of each two-week effort, a running executable for the current iteration is demonstrated to the customers and it undergoes acceptance testing. Two weeks of work of a team of developers produces an outcome of significant size.

The sizes of EM iterations conform to the principles of agile software production. While it is not possible to explore in a textbook every detail of the application code, it is possible to build up the explanations by concentrating on new aspects of each iteration. The new aspects of Iteration 2 are refactoring of the application domain layer and replacing the presentation layer for both the desktop GUI and the web-based access to the system.

Adding a GUI/web-enabled front-end to an application addresses a FURPS+ feature of *usability*, documented in supplementary specifications for the project (Section 8.4). Iteration 2 adds extra *functionality* features. These are captured in a use case model and in an associated use case document.

    Figure 14.1 is a use case model for Iteration 2. The boundary of the project, and the actors, which determine this boundary, are unchanged from Iteration 1. The actors are, therefore, not shown in the model. The diagram presents use cases and main relationships between them. The Iteration 2 new functionality is embraced by a rectangle. Some new use cases are merely specializations (subtype use cases) of the abstract use case `View Unsent Messages`. There are four new use cases related to filtering of currently viewable

Figure 14.1
Use case diagram
for Iteration 2

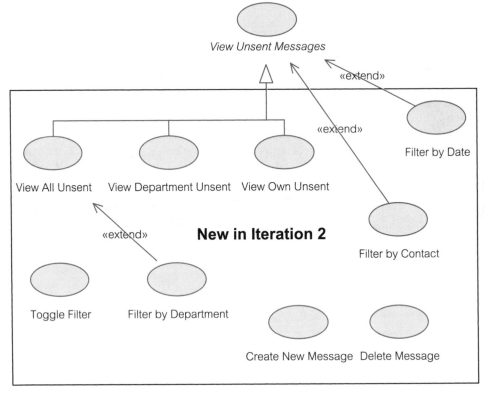

outmessages. Finally, there is a use case to `Create New Message` and a use case to `Delete Message`.

In Iteration 1, the use case `View Unsent Messages` was responsible for displaying all outmessages not sent yet and still in the database (i.e. with `date_emailed` equal to `null` in the `OutMessage` table). In Iteration 2, this use case is specialized into three subtypes. `View All Unsent` provides the functionality of the Iteration 1 `View Unsent Messages`.

The use case `View Department Unsent` displays all outmessages scheduled for emailing by any employee of the department in which the current user (i.e. the logged-in EM employee) works. This implies that the conceptual classes (resulting in a database schema) must have knowledge of employees' departments and of 'scheduled departments' for outmessages.

The use case `View Own Unsent` displays outmessages scheduled for emailing by the current employee (i.e. the logged-in EM employee). This implies that the conceptual classes must have knowledge of 'scheduled employees' for outmessages.

Since the use case `View Unsent Messages` specializes completely into three subtype use cases, it itself becomes an **abstract use case**. It is also a *base use case* for two use cases to filter in or filter out currently visible outmessages. These two use cases are `Filter By Date` and `Filter by Contact`. The third major filter, `Filter by Department`, extends only the use case `View All Unsent`. This filter has been added to the case study for educational value; its practical usefulness is doubtful because the use case `View Department Unsent` achieves a similar outcome.

The use case `Toggle Filter` sets on or off a filter on a currently displayed list of unsent outmessages. As per the `View Unsent Messages` use case, the current list can be all messages, department messages or own messages. Initially the filter is off. The filter can be set on a scheduled date (i.e. date scheduled for emailing) and/or on a contact (i.e. email destination) and/or on a department (i.e. emails that the department is responsible for). The date filter is not by a specific date but by the date in comparison to today's date. This means that the date filter can find past, today's, and future outmessages.

The use cases `Create New Message` and `Delete Message` extend the functionality of Iteration 1 by allowing creation and deletion of outmessages in the database. The Iteration 1 assumption that all outmessages are created by a separate 'production' system (and given to the EM application) is waived in Iteration 2. It is now possible to manipulate the content of the database directly from the EM application.

The two remaining use cases are `Display Message Text` and `Email Message`. These use cases have the same functionality as in Iteration 1, but the presentation of this functionality uses desktop and/or web-enabled GUI.

Use Case Document   14.2

The scope of the use case document for Iteration 2 is a straight union of the old Iteration 1 requirements and the new Iteration 2 requirements. The parent use case, which absorbs both iterations, is `Manage Email` (Figure 8.1). As demanded by the iterative and incremental development, Iteration 2 delivers an increment on top of Iteration 1.

14.2.1 Brief Description, Preconditions, and Postconditions

Brief description

Iteration 2 of the `Manage Email` use case allows an employee to create, delete, display, and email messages to contacts. The use case handles only outgoing messages. Hence, for the sake of precision, the messages are called outmessages.

The use case can display and email outmessages previously stored in the database by other processes. It also allows a new outmessage to be created, displayed or emailed, as required. Stored messages can also be deleted when they are no longer applicable. The display of outmessages can be constrained by a number of display conditions (search criteria). The current display can be further filtered on a number of filter conditions.

Preconditions

1. A user (actor) is an Employee who works for the Customer Department or is otherwise authorized by the System Administrator to access the EM application.
2. The EM database contains outmessages to be emailed to contacts. The creation of new outmessages is no replacement for outmessages stored in the database by other processes of the AEM system (Chapter 6).
3. An Employee is connected to the email server and is an authorized database user.

Postconditions

1. The program updated the EM database to reflect any successful emailing of outmessages.
2. The EM database is left in an intact state if any exception or error occurred.
3. Upon the Employee quitting the application, all database connections are closed and all application desktop or web-enabled GUI windows are closed.

14.2.2 Basic Flow

Consistently with the approach taken in Iteration 1, the description of flow of events includes prototypes of GUI windows. The prototypes allow 'picturing the situation' and facilitate understanding of textual specifications.

Basic flow

The use case starts when an Employee wishes to create, view, and/or email outmessages to contacts.

The system displays an informational message and requests that the Employee provides a username and password (Figure 14.2).

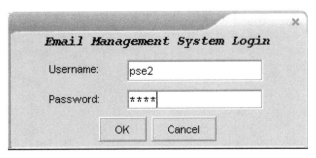

Figure 14.2
Prototype of login window

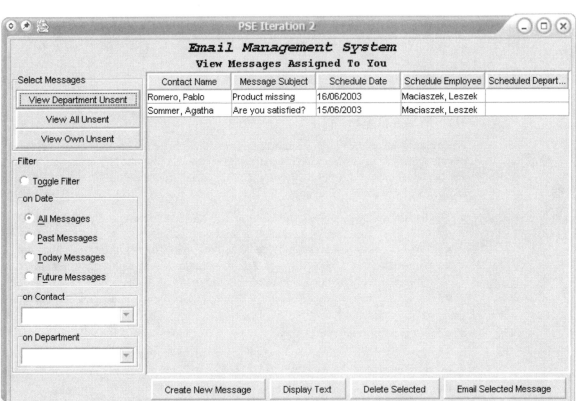

Figure 14.3 Prototype of main application window

1. The system attempts to connect the Employee to the EM database.

2. Upon successful connection, the application displays the main application window through which the user can interact with the system (Figure 14.3).

3. A user can perform the following tasks:
   - (a) view unsent outmessages to contacts (see '*S1 – View Unsent Messages*', below)
   - (b) filter the display of outmessages on various criteria (see '*S2 – Filter Messages*', below)
   - (c) display text of selected outmessage (see '*S3 – Display Message Text*', below)

(d) email selected outmessage (see '*S4 – Email Message*', below)

(e) create new outmessage (see '*S5 – Create New Message*', below)

(f) delete selected outmessage (see '*S6 – Delete Message*', below)

(g) quit the application, upon which the use case terminates.

14.2.3 Subflows

S1 – View Unsent Messages

This subflow consists of three options available as a group of three toggle buttons or similar devices (Figure 14.3):

- S1.1 – View All Unsent
- S1.2 – View Department Unsent
- S1.3 – View Own Unsent.

S1.1 – View All Unsent

When a user selects the option `View All Unsent`, the application presents a complete list of unsent outmessages. There is a clear indication on the window that all unsent outmessages are displayed. The indication is by means of a pressed toggle button `View All Unsent`, and by means of a clear label above the list. The label reads: `All unsent outmessages`.

- The list shows the columns entitled: `Contact Name`, `Message Subject`, `Scheduled Date`, `Scheduled Employee` and `Scheduled Department`:
  - `Contact Name` displays family name and first name of a contact
  - `Scheduled Employee` displays family name and first name of an employee or nothing (if the scheduled employee is not known)
  - `Scheduled Department` displays department name or nothing (if the scheduled department is not known).
- The list can be sorted, at least by `Contact Name` and `Scheduled Date`.
- The list is scrollable to accommodate situations when the retrieved number of rows exceeds the size of the window.
- Outmessages in the list are selectable with the mouse. The usual functionality of `Ctrl-Click` to select multiple non-adjacent outmessages and `Shift-Click` to select a range of adjacent outmessages should be supported, although this functionality is not needed for the functionality of Iteration 2.

S1.2 – View Department Unsent

When a user selects the option `View Department Unsent`, the application presents a list of outmessages scheduled to be emailed by employees in the department of the current employee (i.e. the current user). There is a clear indication on the window that only outmessages scheduled for a particular department are displayed. The indication is by means of a pressed toggle button `View Department Unsent`, and by means of a clear label above the list. The label reads: `Outmessages assigned to your department`.

S1.3 – View Own Unsent

When a user selects the option `View Own Unsent`, the application presents a list of outmessages scheduled to be emailed by the current employee (i.e. the current user). There is a clear indication on the window that only outmessages scheduled for a logged-in employee are displayed. The indication is by means of a pressed toggle button `View Own Unsent`, and by means of a clear label above the list. The label reads: `Outmessages assigned to you`.

S2 – Filter Messages

This subflow consists of four options:

- S2.1 – Toggle Filter
- S2.2 – Filter by Date
- S2.3 – Filter by Contact
- S2.4 – Filter by Department.

S2.1 – Toggle Filter

The filters panel provides a set of controls to constrain the items selected for display after they have been retrieved from the database by the `View Unsent Messages` subflow. The panel is not active unless a list of outmessages is displayed by `View Unsent Messages` and `Toggle Filter` has been clicked.

By default, the option `Toggle Filter` is turned off. The user can turn this filter on to apply the other filter options: `Filter by Date`, `Filter by Contact`, and/or `Filter by Department`. A radio button or a check box can implement the option `Toggle Filter` (Figure 14.3).

The filter is shown as active when the list of displayed outmessages is restricted by the conditions specified by `Filter by Date`, `Filter by Contact`, and/or `Filter by Department`. When the filter is set on, applying the Toggle Filter action can turn it off. This in effect re-displays the list of outmessages as requested by the `View Unsent Messages` subflow, before any filter was applied.

S2.2 – Filter by Date

The `Filter by Date` panel provides a set of radio buttons to filter on outmessages with a scheduled date (i.e. scheduled for emailing) in the past, future, today, or all (any date). Only one of these buttons can be active at any time. By default, the button `All` is active when the panel is active.

S2.3 – Filter by Contact

The filters panel provides a combo box, which allows a contact to be selected from the dropdown list of contact names or which can be left blank (Figure 14.3). The filter is automatically performed when the contact is selected. This has the effect of modifying the list of outmessages displayed to show only outmessages destined for that contact, excluding any outmessages filtered out by the current scheduled date filter.

Figure 14.4
Dialog box window
showing the
message text
of the currently
selected message

S2.4 – Filter by Department

A combo box is also provided to allow the user to filter the list of outmessages by a department picked from a dropdown list of department names (Figure 14.3). Only those outmessages belonging to a particular department (as chosen from the combo box) are listed. A blank entry in the combo box means no filtering on department has been performed. This filter is automatically performed when the department name is selected. This has the effect of modifying the list of outmessages displayed to show only outmessages assigned to a particular department or, to be precise, to outmessages assigned to employees from the selected department. The list excludes any outmessages filtered out by the current scheduled date and contact filters.

S3 – Display Message Text

An outmessage currently selected (highlighted) in the outmessage list window can be displayed in full in a separate dialog box window (Figure 14.4). The window presents the complete text of the outmessage together with other descriptive information. The text pane is scrollable. The window contains two buttons:

- `Email this Message` – see subflow S4, below.
- `Return to List of Messages` – to dismiss this window and return to the main application window.

S4 – Email Message

The dialog box in Figure 14.4, which allows an outmessage to be emailed, can be produced by the subflow S3 or by this subflow. In subflow S3, double-clicking on a selected

Figure 14.5
Informational
message after
emailing

outmessage produces the dialog box. In subflow S4, the same effect is achieved by pressing the `Email Selected Message` button.

A successful emailing results in updating the database and in an informational message displayed to the user (Figure 14.5).

S5 – Create New Message

Iteration 2 provides an option to create a new outmessage and save it in the database. Pressing the button `Create New Message` in the main application window results in the dialog box shown in Figure 14.6.

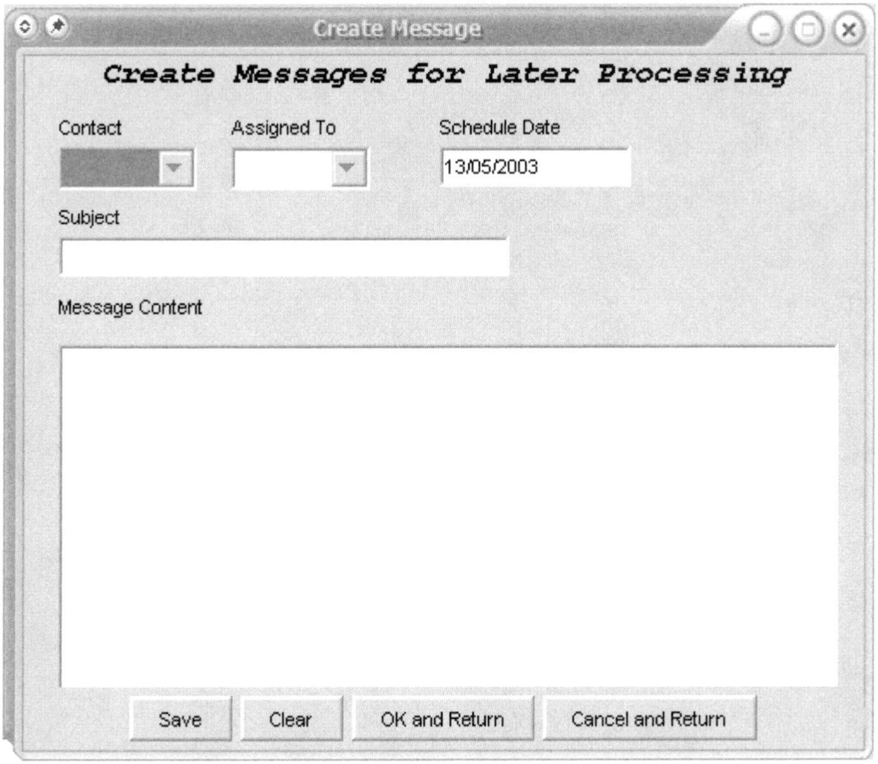

Figure 14.6
Dialog box for
creating a new
outmessage

Figure 14.7
Delete message
confirmation

The dialog box allows a contact to be selected and a scheduled employee and/or a scheduled department to be assigned. The subject and the outmessage content can be typed in the provided fields. The window contains four action buttons:

- `Save` – to save the new outmessage in the database, but keep the dialog box open to allow creating the next outmessage.
- `OK and Return` – to save the new outmessage in the database, and then dismiss this window and return to the main application window.
- `Clear` – to clear the current content of the dialog box and permit the user to create a new outmessage from scratch.
- `Cancel and Return` – to cancel the operation, dismiss this window, and return to the main application window.

S6 – Delete Message

When outmessages are no longer applicable, perhaps due to corrections made by other employees, then they can be deleted from the database. Pressing the `Delete Message` button when an outmessage is selected in the main window activates this subflow. A simple window to ask the user for confirmation about the deletion is then displayed, as shown in Figure 14.7.

If the user opts to cancel the deletion, then nothing happens.

14.2.4 Exception Flows

Any exception occurring during runtime should be caught and relayed to the user by means of an informational message box. The program must not crash on any exception from the database, from the network email failure, or from the application.

E1 – Incorrect username or password

If, in the basic flow, the actor provides an incorrect username or incorrect password, the system displays an error message (Figure 14.8). The message reads: 'Invalid login. Please

Figure 14.8
Message box for
incorrect login

try again. This will be your second attempt.' The use case continues and allows the user to
re-enter the username and password. The second unsuccessful attempt results in the error
message: 'Invalid login. Please try again. This will be your last attempt.' The use case
continues and allows the user to re-enter the username and password.

   The user is given three chances to provide correct username and password. If three-
times unsuccessful, the system displays the message: 'Exceeded the maximum of three
attempts to login. Application will quit' (Figure 14.9). The use case terminates.

Figure 14.9
Message box after
three unsuccessful
attempts to log in

E2 – Email could not be sent

If, in the S4 subflow, the mail server returns an error that the email could not be sent, the
system informs the actor that the email was not sent (Figure 14.10). The use case continues
after the user acknowledges the error message by pressing the OK button.

Figure 14.10
Message box
upon email failure

14.3 Conceptual Classes and Relational Tables

The conceptual class model for Iteration 2 contains four classes: Employee, Department, Contact, and OutMessage (Figure 14.11). Association lines are given association names, and association roles and multiplicities on both ends of associations. Primary attributes (identifiers) are typed in bold font.

Employee may be employed_by at most one Department. Department employs many Employees, but it may exist even if it does not employ any Employee. Department may have scheduled OutMessages. There is at most one Department for each OutMessage. There is precisely one Contact for each OutMessage. Contact may be linked to zero or many OutMessages.

The association named outmsg_creator links OutMessage to Employee who created that OutMessage in the database. The association named outmesg_scheduled identifies Employee who is scheduled to email the OutMessage. This association links to zero Employees if the OutMessage is not scheduled for any particular Employee. The association named outmesg_sender identifies the Employee who emailed the OutMessage. This association links to zero Employees before the OutMessage is emailed.

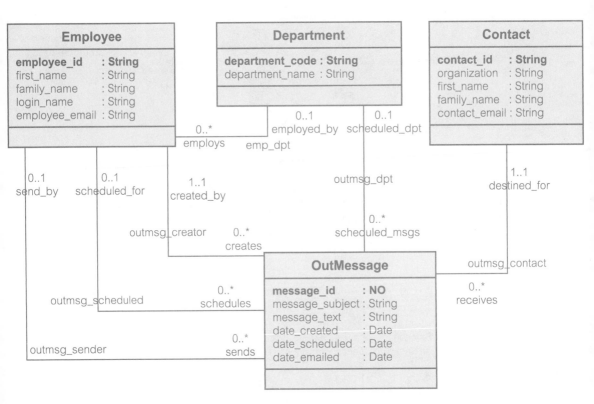

Figure 14.11 Conceptual classes for Iteration 2

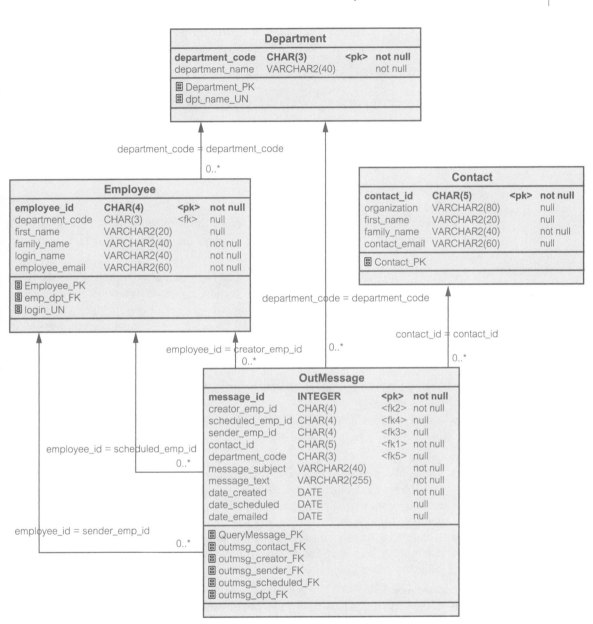

Figure 14.12 Relational tables for Iteration 2

Most attributes are typed as `strings`. The type of `message_id` is a `number` (signified by NO). The three date attributes are typed as `dates`.

According to object-relational mapping rules explained in Chapter 10, a conceptual class model can be automatically converted to a relational database model. Figure 14.12 shows a relational model derived from the conceptual model in Figure 14.11. The model should be self-explanatory. The index compartment identifies the indexes created on primary keys (PK), on foreign keys (FK), and on unique columns (UN).

14.4 Supplementary Specification

Supplementary specifications are largely unchanged from Iteration 1. The changes result from the move to a desktop/web-enabled GUI interface and from additional functionality.

- Functionality
  - EM is a multi-user application.
  - User authorization and privileges to access various features of the application are controlled centrally from the database to which the application program connects.

- Usability
  - There is no training required for a computer-literate user to be able to use the Iteration 2 program. Simple explanation of the aim and basic features of the application will suffice to use the program.
  - Iteration 2 is a desktop/web-based GUI program that provides an intuitive way of using various application options. Only one option at a time may be requested. Making all secondary windows **modal** with regard to the application primary window enforces this requirement. (A *modal window* does not allow switching to other windows of the application without first completing processing in this window and closing it.)
  - Iteration 2 executable can be deployed on a Windows **desktop GUI** or as a **web-based GUI**.

- Reliability
  - The application must be available 24 hours a day every day of the week. There must be no database-related downtime. Any scheduled email server downtimes due to maintenance must be notified to the EM users by email with at least 24 hours' warning.
  - A failure of the program must not compromise the correctness and integrity of the database. A user must be able to restart the program after failure and find the database information to be consistent and not affected by the failure.

- Performance
  - There is no upper limit on the number of concurrent users.
  - The response time of the system may not be affected if the number of concurrent users is 100 or less.
  - The response time for subflows S1 and S5 must be less than 10 seconds 90 percent of the time.
  - The response time for subflows S2 and S3 must be less than 5 seconds 90 percent of the time.
  - The response time for subflow S4 must be less than 10 seconds 90 percent of the time for email messages not exceeding 1 MB in size (including any attached documents). Note, however, that Iteration 2 does not allow email attachments.

- Supportability
  - The system architectural design must conform to the PCMEF framework to allow proper maintainability and scalability.
  - Test-driven development is used for code production. Acceptance testing is used for code validation. Test units obtained from test-driven development and from acceptance tests are used for regression testing when Iteration 2 code is changed.
- Other constraints
  - The project must use the Oracle database, but it must be easily portable to other relational databases.
  - Iteration 2 must use Java and JDBC or SQLJ to access the Oracle database from the program.

Summary

1. Iteration 2 adds a GUI front-end to the EM system. Apart from a desktop GUI, there are applet and servlet versions of Iteration 2 permitting accessing the system with an Internet browser.

2. Iteration 2 introduces additional criteria, including filters, by which outmessages can be viewed. It also allows the user to create new outmessages interactively.

3. The conceptual class model for Iteration 2 contains one new class (Department) and a number of new associations.

Key Terms

abstract use case	465	modal window	476
agile software development	463	web-based GUI	476
desktop GUI	476		

Review Questions

1. Explain the implementation dependencies between the use cases View Unsent Messages and Filter Messages.

2. What does the control *Toggle Filter* do?

3. Explain the need for four action buttons in subflow *S3 – Create New Message*?

4. The attribute scheduled_emp_id in OutMessage (Figure 14.11) is not mandatory (i.e. accepts null values). Could this attribute be modeled as mandatory? Explain.

5. Explain the interdependencies between the subflows *View Department Unsent* and *Filter by Department*.

Chapter

15

Architectural Refactoring

Iteration 1 of the EM case study resulted in a running executable that could be demonstrated to the project customers and other stakeholders. Clear and robust PCMEF architecture (Chapter 9) is a special strength of Iteration 1 deliverable. Consequently, the software is *supportable*, i.e. it is understandable, maintainable, and scalable.

It is fair to say, however, that of these three features, Iteration 1 emphasizes understandability, represented in the minimization of object coupling. Minimization of object coupling can easily lead to low cohesion of objects and, therefore, to difficulties with maintainability and scalability. There is a need for a better balance between all three features. This better balance can be achieved by refactoring.

'**Refactoring** is the process of changing a software system in such a way that it does not alter the external behavior of the code yet improves its internal structure' (Fowler, 1999, p.XVI). Refactoring is about cleaning up the code after it has been written. Refactoring targets are potential problem areas in the design so far. Fowler calls these problem areas 'bad smells in code'.

Refactoring integrates very well with **agile development** (Martin, 2003). It can be conducted at any point during iteration, but it is most effective towards the end of the current iteration or at the beginning of the next iteration. Refactoring can significantly improve the internal structure of the code without changing its external behavior.

It can be argued that the practice of test-driven development (Section 12.2) is a partial substitution for refactoring. In reality, test-driven development uses a variation of refactoring – a variation that applies to cleaning up the design rather than the code. Test-driven development is an iterative and incremental process intermixed with writing the application code. Refactoring can anticipate 'bad smells in code' and eliminate them before they happen.

In this book, refactoring is used at the beginning of Iteration 2 in order to restructure Iteration 1 code for maintainability and scalability, and to prepare it for the Iteration 2 increment. The main changes will be in the domain layer; less so in the control and foundation layers. The presentation layer is not refactored because Iteration 2 effect-ively replaces Iteration 1 presentation (and any refactoring would be immediately lost).

Note also, that the development and code of Iteration 1 is suboptimal for pedagogically motivated reasons. Many important object-oriented technologies were not used in Iteration 1 because of the book's pedagogy and the adopted sequence of topic presentation. Accordingly, the discussion of refactoring in this chapter is suboptimal as well.

Refactoring Targets

15.1

Fowler (1999) identifies and names the whole range of 'bad smells in code'. This is one kind of **refactoring targets**. Other targets are not that much the result of 'bad smells', but the result of a desire to further improve the code, in particular to improve the architecture of the code (Fowler, 2003).

Some more interesting refactoring targets triggered by 'bad smells' are:

- duplicated code – the same pieces of code in multiple places
- long method – a method that does too much
- large class – a class that does too much and/or has too many data members
- long parameter list – too much data passed in parameters (rather than asking other objects for the data)
- divergent change – when a class has to be changed as a result of more than one kind of change
- shotgun surgery – when the same change affects many classes
- feature envy – a method that accesses many other objects with `get` messages in order to get data for its own computation
- data clumps – data items (data members, parameters) that tend to be used together in many places and should be made into an object.

A refactoring target has a number of *refactoring methods* or *refactoring patterns* to eliminate 'bad smells' or to introduce architectural improvements. Sometimes, the same refactoring method or refactoring pattern can be used to resolve (or partly resolve) more than one refactoring target.

Refactoring Methods

15.2

In the software lifecycle, the time and effort put into code maintenance significantly outweighs the time and effort put into writing the code in the first place. Code maintenance is reading it and trying to understand it in order to modify or extend it. Any refactoring of code during its production, no matter how small, can significantly benefit software maintainers.

Refactoring methods (or simply **refactorings**) are basic principles and best practices of changing the code to improve its understandability, maintainability, and scalability. The code changes are small, one step at a time, but the improvements can be quite dramatic. Unfortunately, so can be deteriorations of code if refactorings are not done properly.

In contemporary practice, CASE and programming development tools can effectively assist in performing refactorings. Many tools contain catalogs of supported refactorings. Fowler (1999) is a principal source of reference that lists and documents in excess of sixty refactoring methods. The following discussion illustrates the use of refactoring methods by discussing just three of them:

- *Extract Class*
- *Subsume Method*
- *Extract Interface*

15.2.1 Extract Class

One of the refactoring targets is called *large class* – a class that does too much and/or has too many data members. Large classes can result from excessive minimization of coupling between classes. In the case of the large class target, two methods relevant to Iteration 1 code are: *Extract Class* and *Extract Interface* (Fowler, 1999).

Extract Class refactoring is defined as: 'Create a new class and move the relevant fields and methods from the old class into the new class' (Fowler, 1999, p.149). The main difficulty is in deciding how to split a large class into a number of smaller classes. The idea is to extract consistent and integrated pieces of functionality into a separate class (classes).

Once fields and methods are relocated to new class (classes), an association link should be established from the old to the new class. This can be a one-way link unless there is an obvious need for backward message passing. Of course, the relocation of methods has an impact on client classes that depended on these methods. This necessitates changes to method invocations in these classes.

Figure 15.1 shows how the *Extract Class* refactoring could be applied to the CActioner class (Section 13.4.1). CActioner is involved in two quite disparate tasks: in retrieving outmessages requested by the user and in sending (emailing) outmessages. It is logical to extract these two tasks into separate classes: CMsgSeeker and CMsgSender. To avoid terminological confusion, CActioner is renamed to CAdmin. Constructor and non-public methods are not considered.

As expected by *Extract Class* refactoring, CAdmin maintains association links to the new classes. The links are supported by two methods: getMsgSeeker() and getMsg-Sender(). The former gets the CMsgSeeker object, the one responsible for retrieving outmessages for the presentation layer. The latter gets the CMsgSender object responsible for emailing outmessages.

Refactoring results in one new method (setEmployee()). setEmployee() is used to establish an association from CMsgSeeker to EEmployee. This is required because

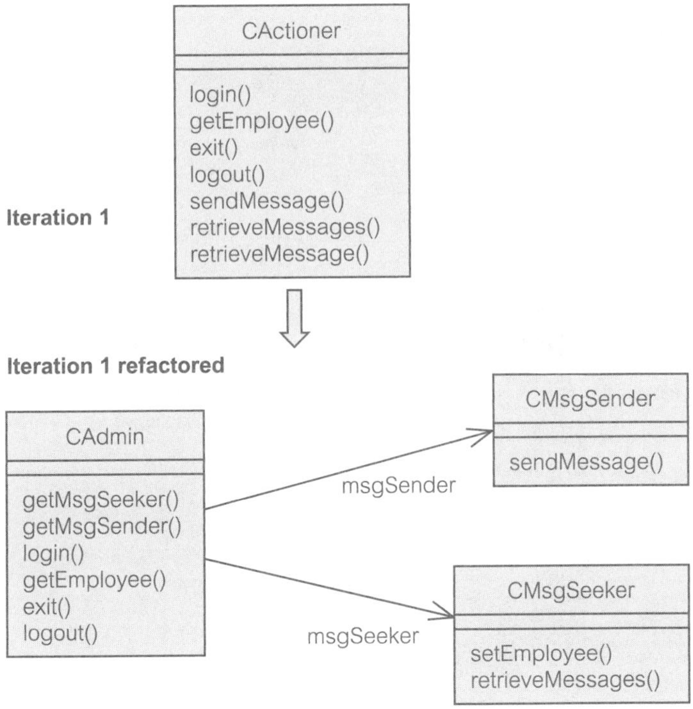

Figure 15.1
Extract Class
refactoring

outmessage retrievals require an employee's data. setEmployee() gets an EEmployee object from CAdmin's login() method.

Subsume Method

Duplicated code (the same pieces of code in multiple places) is a frequent refactoring target. Depending on its the nature, duplicated code can be addressed in a number of different ways. A typical refactoring for duplicated code is *Extract Method*, i.e. turning code duplicated in several methods into a separate method (Fowler, 1999). Another suitable refactoring, not listed by Fowler, is the Subsume Method. **Subsume Method refactoring** eliminates a method by including its functionality into another existing method.

The *Extract Class* refactoring in Figure 15.1 reveals that a CActioner's method retrieveMessage() is not present in the refactored code. The elimination of retrieveMessage() is not due to *Extract Class*. It is due to *Subsume Method* that combines retrieveMessage() into retrieveMessages().

The Iteration 1 code is unduly influenced by two separate menu options available to the user: *View Unsent Messages* and *Display Text of a Message* (Figure 12.12). The first option results in retrieving and displaying many outmessages; the second, in retrieving and displaying one outmessage that the user intends to email. In both cases, complete data content of EOutMessage objects is retrieved but the display of information to the user varies.

Figure 15.2
Subsume Method
refactoring

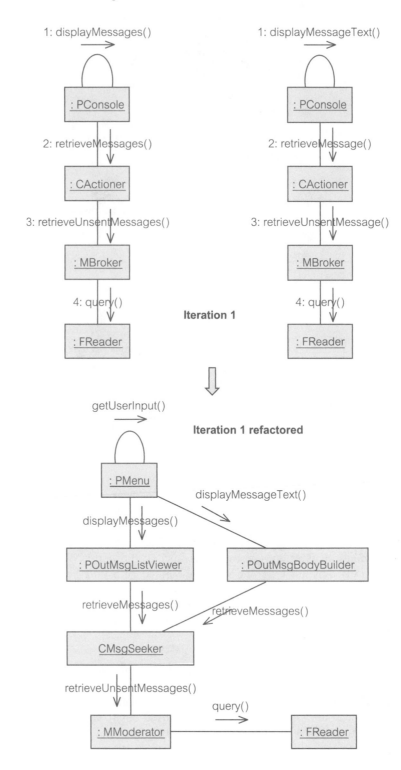

The truth of the matter is that there is lots of duplicated code resulting from independent processing of these two menu actions, as observed in Section 13.6.1. Surely, retrieving many outmessages and retrieving a single outmessage involves very similar processing. Figure 15.2 demonstrates the two sequences of message passing for Iteration 1 and how they are combined into a single path starting from the `control` layer. The distinction between many outmessages and a single outmessage is evident only in the `presentation` layer.

Extract Interface 15.2.3

The refactoring target of Extract Interface is twofold and defined as 'Several clients use the same subset of a class's interface, or two classes have part of their interfaces in common' (Fowler, 1999, p.341). The **Extract Interface refactoring** method is to 'extract the subset into an interface' (ibid.). The idea of this refactoring is related to the very nature of interfaces (Section 9.1.7).

Like *Extract Class* (Section 15.2.1), *Extract Interface* is frequently a response to a large class target. This is a recurrent refactoring target in Iteration 1. PConsole is a large class that does too much. Depending on the menu option selected by the user, PConsole performs distinct tasks. For example, it may need to display a list of outmessages or details of a single outmessage.

In Iteration 1, the execution of these different tasks is encapsulated by the method `displayMenu()` (Section 13.3.2, Listing 13.16). This method contains a private method `getUserInput()`, which accepts the user's request and decides on a task by invoking the appropriate PConsole method, such as `displayMessages()`. PConsole has only two public methods: `displayLogin()` and `displayMenu()`. Everything else is encapsulated. Encapsulation has advantages but 'smells' of a large class which may not be easy to maintain and scale.

Refactoring of PConsole can first use the *Extract Class* method to create, for example, two separate classes to handle the display of a list of outmessages and the display of a single outmessage (Figure 15.3). The two new classes POutMsgListViewer and POutMsgBodyBuilder take pertinent responsibilities from PConsole (renamed now PMenu).

A natural next step is to acknowledge that two new presentation classes in the refactored code use the same `display()` method to display a string to screen. Clearly, the code will gain in readability and documentability if the `display()` method is extracted into an interface, implemented by PMenu and used, as needed, by the new `presentation` classes.

Figure 15.3 represents design refactored by using *Extract Class* and *Extract Interface* on the `presentation` layer. Refactoring of this layer has limited value for Iteration 2. The move in Iteration 2 to the graphical user interface signifies quite radical reorganization of the `presentation` layer. Even so, the existence of the interface and new classes will facilitate the transition. In some way, more radical refactoring would be justified. For example, POutMsgBodyBuilder can be split into two classes to separate displaying the outmessage from preparing it for emailing.

Figure 15.3
Extract Interface
refactoring

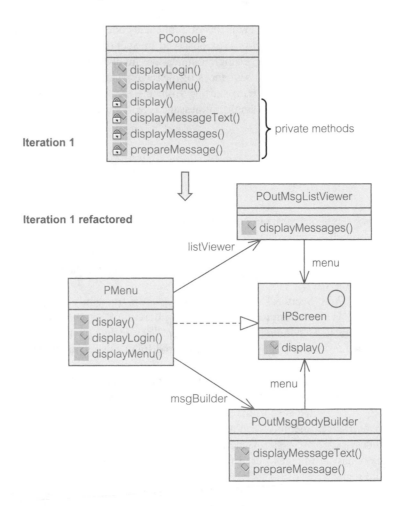

15.3 Refactoring Patterns

Refactoring is inseparable from architectural design and framework development. Significant architectural improvements can be achieved by coordinated application of multiple refactoring methods. Initial system design is guided by architectural patterns, as discussed in Section 9.3. Architectural patterns are also instrumental in refactorings aimed at more significant code corrections or extensions.

Refactoring patterns are architectural patterns used in code refactoring. Fowler (2003) calls them patterns of enterprise application architecture. They target those aspects of the system that make it an enterprise application, as opposed to small-scale desktop applications. They address such issues as communication with the database, in-memory caches of persistent objects, transaction and concurrency management, web presentation, working with distributed objects, etc.

Refactoring patterns position the system for easy scalability when it grows to a large-scale solution. Iteration 1 of the EM case study emphasizes the database presence in the application while retaining a quite primitive text-based user interface. Iteration 2 makes a move to a graphical user interface. Refactoring patterns discussed in this chapter apply still to Iteration 1 and concentrate therefore on issues other than the user interface.

The following discussion illustrates the architectural patterns used for refactoring of the Iteration 1 code within the `domain` layer. Most of these patterns are documented in Fowler (2003) – a state-of-the-art source of reference that lists and documents more than fifty architectural patterns. The patterns are presented in the following groups:

- *Identity Map*
- *Data Mapper*
- *Lazy Load*
- *Unit of Work.*

Identity Map 15.3.1

Iteration 1 acknowledges the importance of assigning object identifiers (OIDs) to `entity` objects (Section 13.5) and the importance of maintaining entity caches by the `mediator` package (Section 13.6). This is good, but currently `MBroker` 'smells' of a large class and a number of *refactoring patterns* can be used to improve identity management and caching. One such pattern is **Identity Map** (Fowler, 2003).

The *Identity Map* pattern 'ensures that each object gets loaded only once by keeping every loaded object in a map. Looks up objects using the map when referring to them' (Fowler, 2003, p.195). An *Identity Map* object maintains one or more maps (e.g. hash maps) that map an object identifier to an object (Section 12.1.2). *Identity Map* has two principal objectives:

- To ensure that the same database record is not loaded many times into different application objects (this would create havoc if the application modified one of these objects, but not the others).
- To avoid unnecessary loading of the same data many times (this would impact on the application's performance).

Fowler (2003) distinguishes between explicit and generic identity maps. Objects in an *explicit identity map* are accessed (`get`), registered (`put`), and unregistered (`remove`) with distinct methods for each class of cached objects. For example, to access an object:

```
getEEmployee (new Integer(empOID));
```

Objects in a *generic identity map* are accessed (`get`), registered (`put`), and unregistered (`remove`) with a single method for all classes. A parameter of the method determines the class. For example, to access an object:

```
get ("EEmployee", new Integer(OID));
```

A generic map can only be used if all object identifiers are generated by the same algorithm and are globally unique for all objects across all classes. A generic map allows easy creation and maintenance of a single registry of object identifiers that other objects can use to find an object by its OID.

An explicit map has the advantage of readability and documentability. All available maps are statically stated in the code. Additions and deletions of maps are localized to a single class, so adding and deleting new methods is not a problem.

Fowler (2003) distinguishes further between one map per class and one map per session. *One map per session* requires globally unique object identifiers. In this sense, it goes hand in hand with a generic identity map. *One map per class* can use object identifiers unique within a class, but it faces the problem of how to handle classes in an inheritance tree. In both cases, identity maps on updatable objects must be given transactional protection and marked as dirty whenever identity objects get out of sync with the corresponding database records.

In the case of Iteration 1, the benefits of the *Identity Map* pattern, as well as the motivations behind the *Extract Class* method, give rise to a refactoring that leads to a new class `EIdentityMap` (Listing 15.1). `EIdentityMap` defines two maps (Lines 19–20). One maps `OIDs` to `entity` objects and the other maps `msgID` to the `OID` of the `EOutMessage`. Iteration 1 does not require other maps, but they can be added whenever needed. The example shows methods needed to handle mapping of `EContact` objects.

Listing 15.1 Class EIdentityMap – fragment

```
Class EIdentityMap - fragment

18:   public class EIdentityMap {
21:       private Map OIDToObj; //OID -> Obj
22:       private Map msgPKToOID; //msgPK -> OID
23:
24:       public EIdentityMap() {
25:           OIDToObj = new HashMap();
28:           msgPKToOID = new HashMap();
29:       }
30:
31:       /** Get the stored contact */
32:       public IAContact findContact(int contactOID) {
33:           return (IAContact) OIDToObj.get(new Integer(contactOID));
34:       }
35:       /** Store a contact with the OID indicated */
36:       public void registerContact(IEObjectID oidObject) {
37:           OIDToObj.put(new Integer(oidObject.getOID()), oidObject);
41:       }
42:       /** Unregister a registered contact */
43:       public void unregisterContact(IEObjectID oidContact) {
44:           OIDToObj.remove(new Integer(oidContact.getOID()));
46:       }
113: }
```

EIdentityMap is an *explicit identity map* – it has separate methods for each entity class. The class represents the strategy of *one map per session* – it uses globally unique OIDs.

Data Mapper

The **Data Mapper pattern** is defined as 'a layer of *Mappers* that moves data between objects and a database while keeping them independent of each other and the mapper itself' (Fowler, 2003, p.165). The generic *Mapper* pattern, referred to in the definition, is 'an object that sets up a communication between two independent objects' (Fowler, 2003, p.473). *Mapper* differs from the *Mediator* pattern (Section 9.3.5) in that objects decoupled by a mapper object are blissfully unaware of each other, whereas objects using mediator are aware of it.

In the PCMEF framework, *Data Mapper* belongs to the mediator package. In Iteration 1, the MBroker class (Section 13.6.1) is responsible, among other things, for knowing of entity objects in the cache and for requesting data from the database if an object is not in the cache or if the cache is dirty. These responsibilities of *Data Mapper* need to be extracted from MBroker into separate class(es), using the *Extract Class* refactoring (Section 15.2.1). MDataMapper is one such new class in the refactored Iteration 1 code.

Figure 15.4 is a UML **activity diagram** (Section 2.2.5) that shows how MDataMapper decouples the entity package (responsible for the cache) from the foundation package (responsible for accessing the database). The activity diagram is used here for convenience rather than as a demonstration of its normal applicability.

The semantics of the activity model in Figure 15.4 is easy to follow. The meaning of graphical objects is explained in UML notes. To start with, a control object (CAdmin) requests MDataMapper to obtain an entity object. CAdmin may guide this request in a number of ways:

■ CAdmin can know an OID of an object and pass it to MDataMapper, or

■ CAdmin can know some attribute values of an object, perhaps the primary key value, and pass this information to MDataMapper as a search condition, or

■ CAdmin can request a referential search by asking MDataMapper to find objects that are linked to the object known by CAdmin.

MDataMapper needs to establish where the object(s) is. Is it in memory cache or has it to be retrieved from the database? If in memory cache, is it clean? If not, it must be retrieved from the database. EIdentityMap (Listing 15.1) knows if an object is in cache. If EIdentityMap has the objects and they are clean, they will be returned to MData-Mapper and then to CAdmin. If not, MDataMapper constructs relevant SQL queries and passes them to FReader for access to the database.

Load – check-out

Figure 15.4 is not a complete account of MDataMapper responsibilities. Once data records are retrieved from the database, MDataMapper makes them into objects (i.e. MDataMapper

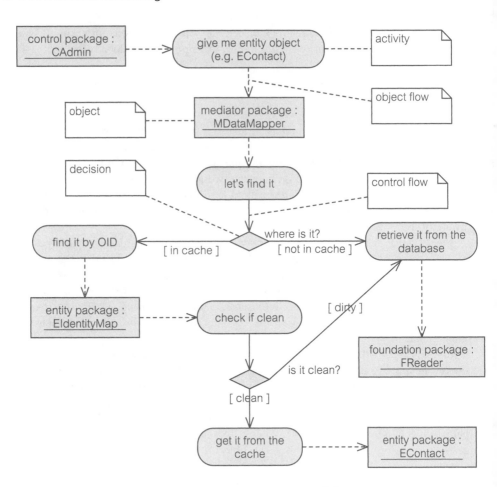

creates new `entity` objects). The new objects are then registered in `EIdentityMap`. This is a **load** operation – database records are retrieved (loaded) and transformed to memory objects. From the database perspective, the load is a **check-out** operation (records are checked out to the program). The load process is also called **materialization** (Larman, 2002).

A fragment of the sequence diagram in Figure 15.5 illustrates a possible scenario for object loading in the refactored Iteration 1 code. The diagram relates to the 'Login' interaction (Section 11.4.1). It shows how `MDataMapper` retrieves and creates a new `EEmployee` object when asked to get it by employee name. This operation includes generation of an OID for `EEmployee`, which is then passed to `EIdentityMap` in the parameter of `registerEmployee()`.

Unload – check-in

Naturally enough, if *Data Mapper* is responsible for loading objects from the database, it should also be responsible for the opposite activity of unloading objects to the database.

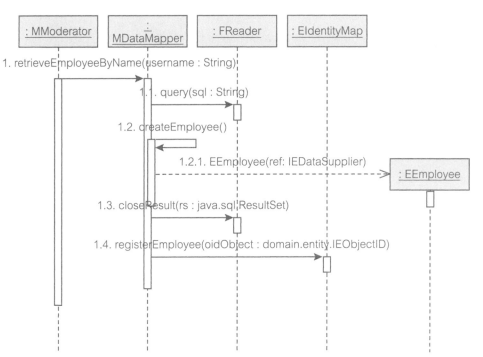

Figure 15.5
Sequence
diagram for
object loading

From the database perspective, this is a **check-in** operation. The **unload** process is also known as **passivation** and **dematerialization** (Larman, 2002). The unload operation is required when:

- a new `entity` object is created by the application and it needs to be persistently stored in the database, or
- an `entity` object gets updated by the application and the changes need to be persistently stored in the database, or
- an `entity` object is deleted by the application and, therefore, the corresponding database record must be deleted from the database.

Unloading is subject to the scrutiny of business transactions and the database `commit` and `rollback` operations. The topic of transaction management is discussed in detail in Part 4 of the book in the context of Iteration 3 of the case study.

Iteration 1 does not create or delete `entity` objects, but it does update `EOutMessage` objects to indicate that they have been emailed. This is the task of the 'Email Message' interaction (Section 11.4.5). A fragment of the sequence diagram in Figure 15.6 illustrates how an 'update' unload can be implemented in the refactored Iteration 1 code.

`CMsgSeeker` sends an outmessage and it then asks `MModerator` to `updateMessage()`. `MModerator` delegates this task to `MDataMapper`, which constructs a SQL update statement. `FWriter` makes the change in the database. This permits `MDataMapper` to `unregisterMessage()` in `EIdentityMap`. Part of this operation is to `flagCache()` as dirty. The example assumes that `MDataMapper` has its own map of `OIDs`.

Figure 15.6
Sequence
diagram for
MDataMapper
activity of check-in

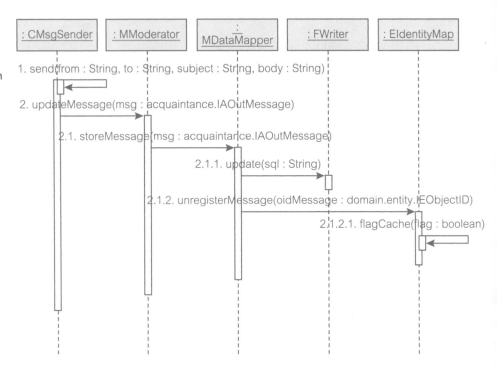

15.3.3 Alternative Data Mapper Strategies

In the refactored Iteration 1, a single *Data Mapper* class (`MDataMapper`) is used to map and unmap raw data into all `entity` objects known to the application (`EEmployee`, `EContact`, and `EOutMessage`). `MModerator` serves as a façade for the mediator package. `MDataMapper` maintains associations to `EIdentityMap` on the one hand, and to `FReader` and `FWriter` on the other hand. This is shown in Figure 15.7.

More complex systems or successive iterations may demand alternative solutions based on various refactoring patterns. The following list pinpoints common alternative strategies (Larman, 2002; Fowler, 2003):

■ Many *Data Mappers*, perhaps one for each entity class.

■ Using metadata and Java reflection to dynamically generate *Data Mappers* as needed by the application.

■ Lazy check-in that maps only data currently needed by the application and, as one possibility, creates empty objects (proxies) for data not retrieved from the database but linked to the data already retrieved.

Many data mappers

`MDataMapper` in the refactored Iteration 1 has separate methods for managing client requests targeting different `entity` objects. This is needed because there are many

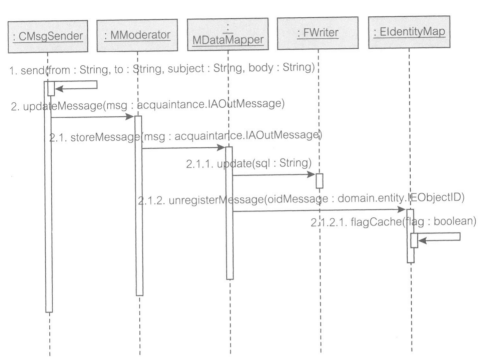

Figure 15.7
MDataMapper in
the refactored
Iteration 1

different ways in which *Data Mapper* is asked to find `entity` objects. Additionally, each `entity` object has its own unique data members and associations to other objects. In the case of a larger number of `entity` classes managed by the application, a single *Data Mapper* can become a bloated class.

Figure 15.8 shows an alternative Iteration 1 solution with many data mappers – one *Data Mapper* per `entity` class. The three mappers implement, in their unique ways, the `IMDataMapper` interface. `MModerator` maintains a one-to-many association to `IMDataMapper` objects (Larman, 2002).

The meanings of the methods are:

- `getByOID()` – get an entity object if given its OID; retrieve it from database if cache is dirty.

- `retrieve()` – retrieve an entity object from the cache (if it is there) or from the database; if the latter, create a new entity object and put it in the cache.

- `insert()` – convert a new entity object (created by the application) to raw data and insert it into the database.

- `update()` – save the changes to an entity object to the database.

- `delete()` – delete an entity object from the database and remove it from the cache.

Note that if a separate *Data Mapper* is used for each entity class, then it may also be desirable to have one *Identity Map* (Section 15.3.1) per entity class. Each mapper maintains then its own cache.

Figure 15.8
Many Data
Mappers

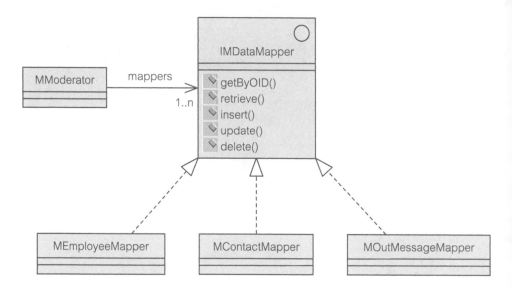

Figure 15.8 Many Data Mappers

Metadata mapping

The aim of the **Metadata Mapping pattern** (Fowler, 2003) is to dynamically generate the object-relational mapping based on **metadata** (data about data). Metadata stores the knowledge about mappings between tables and classes, columns and data members (fields), foreign keys and associations links, etc. Section 10.2.2 describes the kinds of mappings that can be stored in metadata.

The program can interrogate the metadata at runtime and dynamically construct SQL statements on the one hand and getters/setters on `entity` objects on the other hand. From the scalability perspective, *Metadata Mapping* permits easy adaptation of the application to database schema changes and to data-definitional changes, in particular additions, of `entity` classes.

An important decision related to *Metadata Mapping* is where to keep the metadata. There are three possibilities (Fowler, 2003):

- Directly in the *source code* of the application (in the `mediator` package in the case of the **PCMEF** framework).

- In an *external file*, preferably an XML file (the application reads the file during initialization and creates corresponding mappings in the program structure).

- In the *database* (this allows sharing of the same metadata by multiple applications and enables automatic checking for the latest changes to the database schema).

There are two main strategies to embed the mapping information into the running code (Fowler, 2003):

- *Code generation*, which reads metadata information and generates classes to do the mapping (this is done in the build process prior to program compilation).

- *Reflective program*, which allows customizing the application to any new metadata information at runtime.

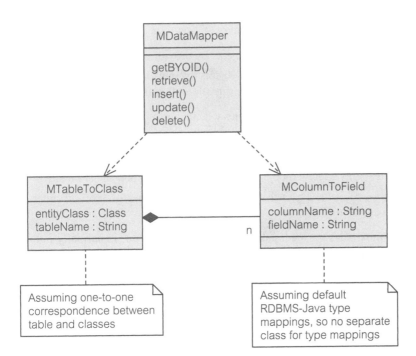

Figure 15.9
Metadata Mapping
pattern

In PCMEF, classes that could do *Metadata Mapping* belong to the `mediator` package. Figure 15.9 presents a simple class model for *Metadata Mapping*. The model is not implemented in the EM case study.

`MDataMapper` depends on the two metadata classes for finding the mapping information necessary to perform its methods. Methods that retrieve the database, such as `retrieve()`, will ask `MTableToClass` to get `entityClass` corresponding to the `tableName` from which data is being retrieved. Methods that write to the database, such as `insert()`, will ask `MTableToClass` to get `tableName` and `MColumnToField` to get `columnNames`.

Lazy Load   15.3.4

Database records and the corresponding entity objects in the application are very interrelated. A request to load an entity object may result in a need to load a long series of interrelated entity objects. These interrelated entity objects correspond to database records linked by referential integrity constraints (i.e. foreign key mappings to primary key records in other tables).

In most cases, an application must not be allowed to try to load all interrelated objects. Firstly, this may not be possible because of the limited size of the memory cache. Secondly, this may not be permissible because of the concurrency requirement of the database, which must allow many applications to use the same records in a conflict-free way. Thirdly, loading objects that may not be needed by the application has a negative impact on performance.

There are two main kinds of retrieval operation to be considered:

- **Identity load** – retrieves specific objects by providing an `OID` or a primary key value.
- **Predicate load** – retrieves many objects by performing a query search based on predicate conditions, possibly following referential integrity constraints.

There are three main loading strategies which control how many objects from the result set returned by a retrieval operation will actually be stored in the cache:

- **Closure load** – all objects reachable from the specified object are loaded.
- **Flat load** – only specified objects, with no component objects, are loaded.
- **n-levels load** – objects reachable within given number of levels from the specified object are loaded.

As explained, closure load, called sometimes *eager load*, is normally not acceptable. Remaining strategies are variants of *lazy load*. The **Lazy Load** pattern is defined as 'an object that doesn't contain all of the data you need but knows how to get it' (Fowler, 2003, p.200). Some approaches to implement *Lazy Load* are:

- Lazy Initialization
- Virtual Proxy
- OID Proxy.

Lazy Initialization

The **Lazy Initialization pattern** (Beck, 1997) is the simplest variant of the *Lazy Load* pattern. On request from a client object, *Data Mapper* – which is responsible for maintaining the `entity` cache – searches the cache for data and, if the data is not there, loads it from the database.

The implementation of *Lazy Initialization* differs depending on several factors. *Data Mapper*'s attempt to obtain data from the cache can be done by looking at the value of a data member in an `entity` object. If the value is `null` (and `null` is not expected according to business rules), then *Data Mapper* has to initialize the data member by making a trip to the database. But there may be several complications.

Data member may be a primitive data type, a class reference, or a collection of class references. Each case requires different implementation machinery. Also, a `null` value can be a legitimate value rather than a placeholder for a missing object yet to be loaded. Finally, the dependency structure of the adopted architectural framework may not allow `entity` objects to depend on `foundation` objects to get database data (PCMEF uses `MDataMapper` to solve this problem but there is still the issue of dependency between `entity` and `mediator`).

Listing 15.2 demonstrates how *Lazy Initialization* can be applied within `EOutMessage` assuming that the application contains a data mapper with `contactOID` to loaded `EContact` object and a data member with `contactID` corresponding to a foreign key in the database. When `EOutMessage` is asked to `getContact()`, it checks whether `contactOID` is null. If it is, then `EContact` is not loaded. To load it, `EOutMessage` sends a `retrieveContact()` message to `MDataMapper`.

Listing 15.2 Method getContact( ) in EoutMessage

Method getContact()in EOutMessage

```
public IAContact getContact() {
    if (contactOID == null)
        contact = MDataMapper.retrieveContact(contactID);
    return contact;
}
```

Virtual Proxy

The **Virtual Proxy pattern** (Gamma *et al.*, 1995) is a more powerful alternative to *Lazy Initialization*. Proxy is a placeholder object that stands in for the real object. It receives messages destined for a real object (called real subject in *Virtual Proxy*) and creates the real object if it does not already exist. In *Lazy Load*, proxy stands for an object that may need to be loaded on an attempt to access it.

Figures 15.10 and 15.11 show how *Virtual Proxy* can be used in the context of Iteration 1 code. MDataMapper is responsible for the entity cache. In the EM case study, entity objects are identified by the application-allocated OIDs. To illustrate *Virtual Proxy*, let entity objects be identified by their primary keys (PKs). Assume that EOutMessage has been loaded and that EContactProxy knows the PK of its real subject. When MData-Mapper creates EContactProxy, it initializes its contactID field with its corresponding foreign key (FK) value in EOutMessage.

As seen in Figure 15.10, EOutMessage maintains an association to contact. The association is typed with the IAContact interface. In reality, the link is to EContact-Proxy. When MDataMapper asks for contact (getContact()), EOutMessage returns EContactProxy.

When, in the next step, MDataMapper asks, for example, for contact's firstName (Figure 15.11), EContactProxy checks if its real subject (EContact) exists. If it does not, it requests MDataMapper to instantiate it. EContactProxy can then return first-Name. The next request, for familyName, follows the same routine except that EContact is already loaded.

An interface in the entity package, implemented by MDataMapper and used by the proxies, would eliminate the cycle between MDataMapper and EContactProxy (Section 9.1.7). In general, there can be many proxies for the same real subject. Making all these proxies use the same interface will be an extra bonus.

OID Proxy

The *Virtual Proxy* pattern is a popular way to implement *Lazy Load*, but potentially redundant in systems that assign object identifiers (OIDs) to entity objects when loading them. Object programming environments have internal mechanisms to ensure the identity of objects loaded to memory and use these mechanisms to link objects. The mechanisms vary between languages.

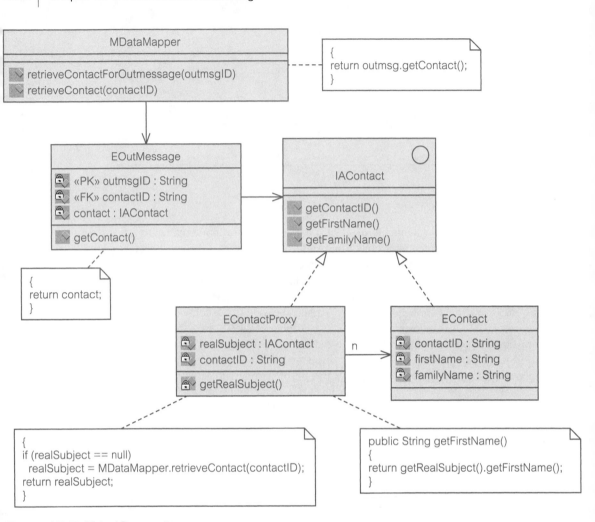

Figure 15.10 Virtual Proxy pattern

In Java, the mechanism is hidden from the programmer. A link between objects appears to the programmer as containment. For example, if EOutMessage has a field contact, then the programmer can use this field to access the linked EContact object as if EContact were physically contained in EOutMessage. In C++, the contact would be a memory pointer to EContact.

None of these mechanisms is a replacement for OIDs assigned explicitly by the program to entity objects when they are instantiated in memory. In all but trivial situations, complex transfers of entity objects between the application and the database call for programs to explicitly assign OIDs to in-memory objects. This introduces duplication between internal mechanisms of programming environments to ensure identity of objects and explicit allocation of OIDs.

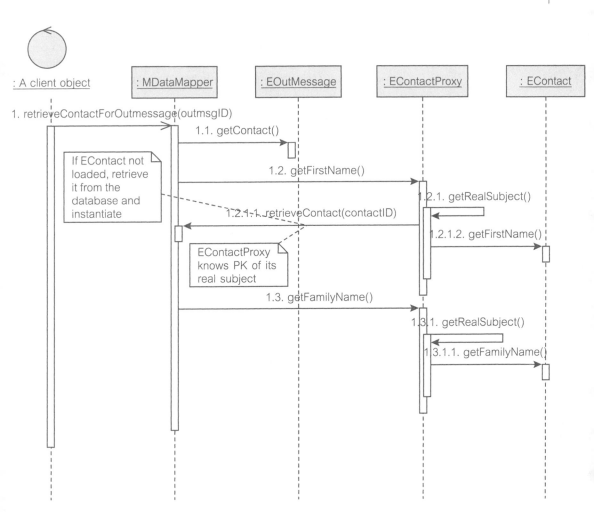

Figure 15.11 Virtual Proxy – sequence diagram for retrieveContactForOutmessage()

Duplication is not always bad. The fact that both techniques link in-memory objects can be taken advantage of in *Lazy Load*. The result is that *Lazy Load* can be fully implemented with proxy-like indirection but without a need for separate proxy classes. A singleton class that maintains maps of OIDs to objects (called EIdentityMap in the refactored Iteration 1 code) replaces proxy classes. The approach can be documented in a pattern – the **OID Proxy pattern**.

EIdentityMap knows if an entity object is loaded. Upon loading, the object is provided with an OID and all its data members are initialized. Initialization includes foreign key (FK) values obtained from the database. OID-based association links corresponding to foreign keys are initialized to null if the linked object has not been loaded yet.

An additional advantage of *OID Proxy* over *Virtual Proxy* is the ease with which the dirty/clean status of an entity object can be determined. When first loaded, the entity object is flagged as clean. If the data content of the object gets out of sync with its corresponding content in the database, the `flag` is set to dirty. At all times, the `entity` object knows its status and can trigger reloading to refresh its content from the database.

There are two variations of *OID Proxy* that differ in how the program navigates between associated entity objects:

- Navigation in Identity Map
- Navigation in Entity Classes.

Navigation in Identity Map

An identity map keeps every loaded `entity` object in a map. The mapping maintains a relationship between an `OID` and its object. Other maps that relate primary key values to `OID`s can also be maintained in order to support requests to search for objects based on their field values. These maps are in general sufficient to navigate between objects that are linked in the database by referential integrity constraints.

Navigation in Identity Map requires that an *Identity Map* interrogate `entity` objects to establish association links. An association link in an `entity` object is represented in two ways:

- by a foreign key (`FK`) value obtained from the database
- by an `OID` to a related object in memory.

Figure 15.12
OID Proxy pattern
– Navigation in
Identity Map

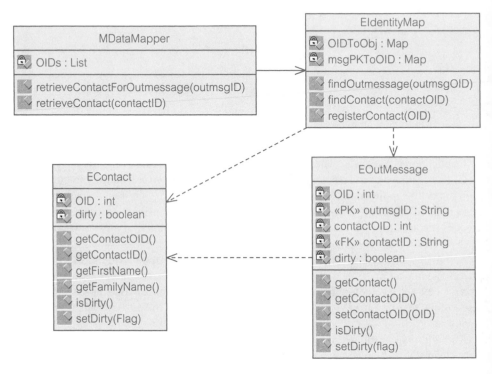

Both FK and OID data members can be null. A null in the foreign key has the same meaning as in the database – the object is not linked. A null in the OID means that the associated object is not loaded.

Figure 15.12 shows a class model that uses *OID Proxy* instead of *Virtual Proxy*. The class EOutMessage contains a data member contactOID that serves as a proxy for the EContact object it links to. As per the *Lazy Load* pattern, EOutMessage does not contain the data requested when getContact() is called on it, but it knows how to get it.

MDataMapper keeps a list of OIDs of all objects loaded in memory. When passed an OID of any object, it can immediately verify if such object is loaded. When passed a primary key (PK) value of an object (e.g. outmsgID), it can ask EIdentityMap for the corresponding OID.

Figure 15.13 explains the sequence of messages for the same scenario as in Figure 15.11. With *Identity Map* in place, each entity object knows its state (if it is clean or dirty). The state is checked by isDirty(). Assuming that EOutMessage is clean,

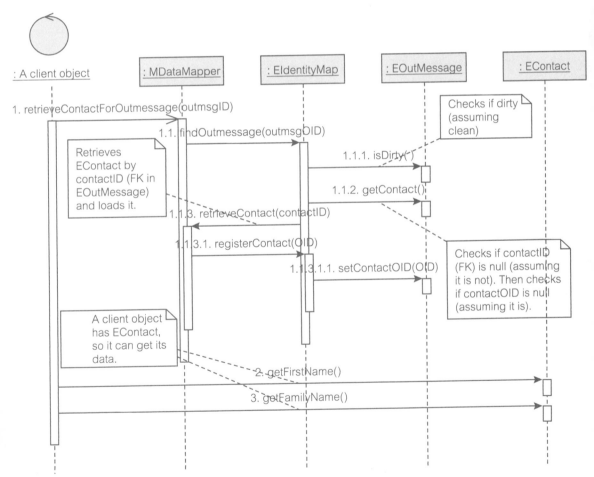

Figure 15.13 OID Proxy: Navigation in Identity Map – sequence diagram for retrieveContactForOutmessage()

EIdentityMap asks EOutMessage to getContact(). EOutMessage checks whether the foreign key value to EContact is null (it should not be because in Iteration 1 contactID is not allowed to be null in the database). It then checks whether contactOID is null.

EContact may or may not be loaded in memory. EOutMessage has this knowledge in contactOID. If contactOID is null, then EContact has not been loaded. The sequence diagram in Figure 15.13 assumes that this is the case. EIdentityMap asks MDataMapper to retrieve the EContact based on the foreign key value.

The outcome will be that EContact is loaded (lazily), MDataMapper will update its list of OIDs, EIdentityMap will update its maps, and contactOID in EOutMessage gets set. EContact is now loaded and returned to the client object, which can now ask it directly for data (getFirstName(), getFamilyName(), etc.).

EIdentityMap is in charge of all navigations between entity objects. In this approach, entity objects do not have to contain associated objects. Entity objects are contained in maps of EIdentityMap. Entity objects themselves have only OIDs to other objects.

Navigation in Entity Classes

Navigation in *Identity Map* obscures object-relational mapping. Referential integrity constraints are visible in entity objects and they are enhanced (duplicated) by OIDs to linked objects. However, an entity object cannot navigate these links directly. *Identity Map* is the only place that knows how to get an object given its OID. In a system with a large number of entity classes, *Identity Map* is doing too much.

The responsibility to navigate between entity objects can be placed on these objects. **Navigation in Entity Classes** requires that an entity object does not just contain an OID to another object, but that it also contains that object (like in the *Virtual Proxy* example presented in Figure 15.10).

Figure 15.14 presents a sequence diagram, corresponding to Figure 15.13, but which uses Navigation in Entity Classes. Much of the processing logic to findContact-ForOutmessage() is shifted from MDataMapper and EIdentityMap to EOutMessage.

Upon determining that EOutMessage is clean, MDataMapper instructs to get-Contact(). If EContact is not loaded, EOutMessage initiates the load. It passes its outmsgOID to MDataMapper so that a new EContact can be associated with it once registered in EIdentityMap.

In the scenario in which a client object asks MDataMapper for the whole EContact, the client object can directly get data from EContact (getFirst-Name(), getFamilyName(), etc.). However, if EContact has been loaded before, EOutMessage would get the data from EContact (it would also check that EContact is not dirty before obtaining the data).

Navigation in Entity Classes provides more intuitive and more elegant implementation of the *OID Proxy* pattern. The semantics of relationships between persistent business objects is implemented directly in these objects. Navigation in Identity Map requires going back and forth to entity objects to find data in related objects. Navigation in Entity Classes allows linear movement between entity objects. *Identity Map* is only needed to find the initial object from which further navigation can continue.

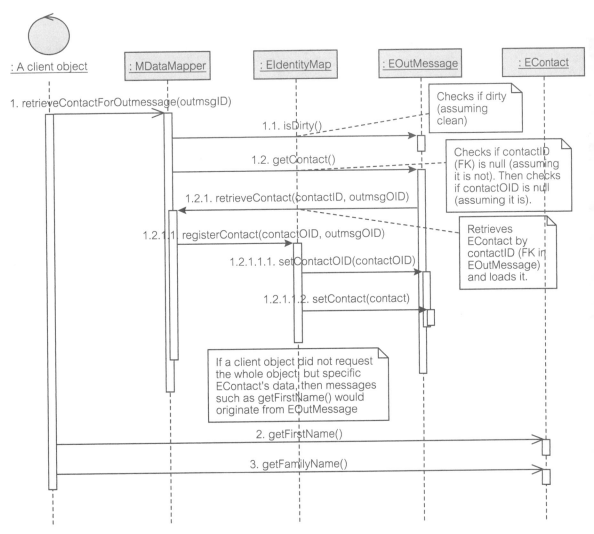

Figure 15.14 OID Proxy: Navigation in Entity Classes – sequence diagram for retrieveContactForOutmessage()

Unit of Work

15.3.5

Entity objects need to be loaded (checked out) from the database for two reasons. Firstly, because the application needs them and they have not been loaded. Secondly, because the application finds that they have become dirty (i.e. inconsistent with the database state).

In Iteration 1, the only objects that may need to be flagged as dirty after they have been emailed are the EOutMessage objects. Iteration 1 does not make any changes to EContact and EEmployee objects. To simplify things, Iteration 1 makes the whole cache (all `entity` objects) dirty as soon as any `EOutMessage` is emailed (Section 13.6.1, Listing 13.56). The `dirty` flag is maintained in the `MBroker` class.

The refactored Iteration 1 code introduces significant flexibility to cache management. One improvement is the introduction of a dirty flag in each `entity` object. When loaded, the object is flagged as clean. The flag is changed to dirty when it is modified. This is illustrated in Listing 15.3. After `EOutMessage` is emailed, `MModerator` sends a `setDirty()` message to the affected `EOutMessage` object (Line 99).

Listing 15.3 Method updateMessage( ) in MModerator

```
Method updateMessage()in MModerator
87:      public boolean updateMessage(IAOutMessage msg) {
91:          msg.setSentDate(new java.sql.Date(System.
                                          currentTimeMillis()));
92:
93:          boolean b = mapper.storeMessage(msg);
94:          if (b) {
96:              msg.setContact(null);
97:              msg.setCreatorEmployee(null);
98:              msg.setSenderEmployee(null);
99:              msg.setDirty(true);
100:         }
```

The approach where each entity object knows if it is dirty or not allows individual loading and unloading of objects. However, many business transactions managed by the application do multiple changes to a variety of objects in the cache before attempting to write these changes to the database. The changed objects need to be marked dirty in unison when the database confirms that the transaction successfully committed. These issues get very complex quickly.

The **Unit of Work pattern** 'maintains a list of objects affected by a business transaction and coordinates the writing out of changes and the resolution of concurrency problems' (Fowler, 2003, p.184). The changes can be due to three modification operations: inserting a new entity object to the database, deleting an object from the database, or updating of object's data members.

The *Unit of Work* pattern requires a new class in the `mediator` package. The class can be called `MWorkUnit` or similar. *Unit of Work* is introduced in Iteration 2, but its full applicability is demonstrated in Iteration 3 (Chapter 21).

15.4 Refactored Class Model

The refactored Iteration 1 code consists of an increased number of classes as compared with the original design (Section 13.1, Figure 13.1). New classes improve design cohesion

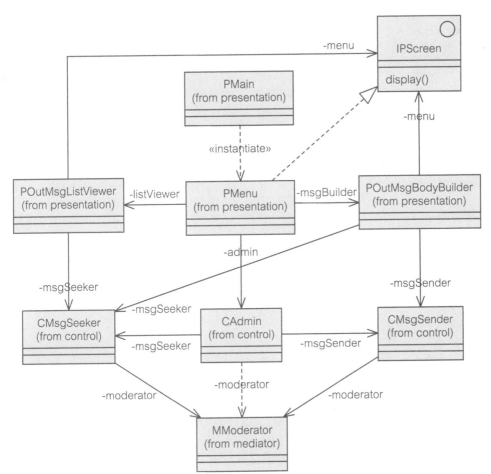

Figure 15.15
Presentation and control layers in refactored Iteration 1

while not impacting adversely on design coupling. Dependencies between classes in the refactored code conform to the **PCMEF** framework.

The refactored class model is presented here in three class diagrams. The first diagram (Figure 15.15) presents classes in the presentation and control layers. Section 15.2 explains refactorings that resulted in the model in Figure 15.15.

The second diagram for the refactored model (Figure 15.16) concentrates on the domain layer. The notes in the diagram provide basic explanations. The details of refactoring patterns used in the domain layer are discussed in Section 15.3. The use of Java collection interfaces in modeling associations is as discussed in Section 12.1.2.

The foundation layer is the only PCMEF layer that is not affected by refactoring of Iteration 1. However, the dependencies from mediator to foundation change slightly due to replacing MBroker by two classes: MModerator and MDataMapper. This is shown in Figure 15.17.

Figure 15.16
Domain layer in
refactored
Iteration 1

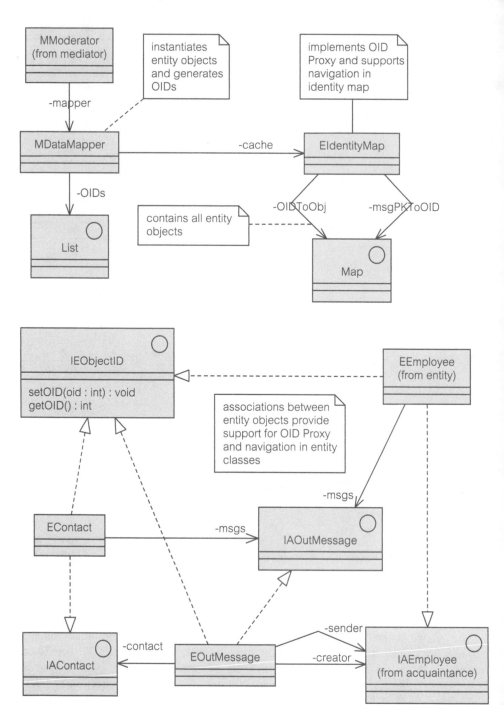

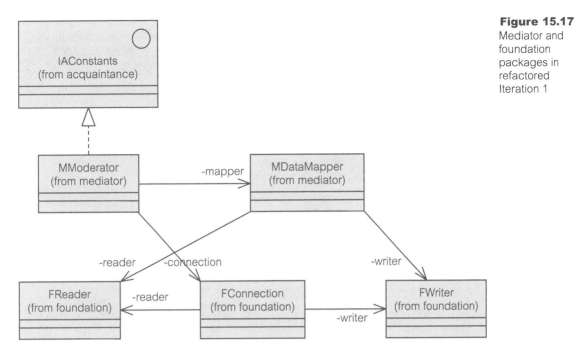

Figure 15.17
Mediator and
foundation
packages in
refactored
Iteration 1

Summary

1. *Refactoring* is the process of cleaning up and improving the internal structure of the code without changing its external behavior.

2. There are two main *refactoring targets*: elimination of 'bad smells in code' (cleaning up) and structural improvements to the code resulting in a better code architecture.

3. *Refactoring methods* (or simply *refactorings*) are basic principles and best practices of changing the code to improve its supportability (understandability, maintainability, and scalability).

4. *Extract Class* refactoring splits a large class into a number of smaller classes.

5. *Extract Method* refactoring turns duplicated code into a separate method.

6. *Subsume Method* refactoring eliminates a method by including its functionality in another existing method.

7. *Extract Interface* refactoring extracts a set of method signatures duplicated in several classes or used by several clients into an interface.

8. *Refactoring patterns* are architectural patterns used in code refactoring.

9. The *Identity Map* pattern assigns object identifiers to objects and maintains maps to find in-memory objects based on their object identifiers.

10. The *Data Mapper* pattern decouples in-memory entity objects from their persistent representation in the database and is responsible for maintaining memory caches of entity objects.

11. UML activity diagrams serve as a behavior specification technique able to depict control and data flows.

12. *Load* (check-out, materialization) is the process of retrieving records from the database and transforming them to memory objects. The opposite operation is called *unload* (check-in, passivation, dematerialization).

13. The *Lazy Load* pattern loads only selected objects from database to memory but it can load remaining and related objects when needed. Approaches to *Lazy Load* are Lazy Initialization, Virtual Proxy, and OID Proxy.

14. The *Lazy Initialization* pattern loads the objects on specific request from a client object responsible for maintaining the entity cache. The load is not transparent to the clients.

15. The *Virtual Proxy* pattern uses a placeholder object (proxy) that stands-in for the real object and can load the real object in a way that is transparent to the client.

16. The *OID Proxy* pattern is a handy replacement for the *Virtual Proxy* pattern in applications that maintain maps of OIDs to objects. The maps can be used instead of proxy classes to load objects in memory in a way that is transparent to the client. There are two variations of *OID Proxy* that differ in how the program navigates between associated entity objects: Navigation in Identity Map and Navigation in Entity Classes.

17. *Navigation in Identity Map* uses an Identity Map class every time the application needs to navigate to a linked entity object (i.e. linked by referential integrity). If object X is linked to object Y, Identity Map would interrogate X to obtain the link to Y and it will then access Y.

18. *Navigation in Entity Classes* uses an Identity Map class to get the first entity object in a navigation sequence but it then relies on entity classes to navigate to related classes. If object X is linked to object Y, Identity Map would allow the client to access X but it will then pass control to X to continue navigation to Y.

19. The *Unit of Work* pattern makes the application aware of business transactions and concurrency issues. It keeps track of changes to entity objects and whether or not the changes have been committed to the database.

Key Terms

activity diagram	487	metadata	492
agile development	478	Metadata Mapping pattern	492
check-in	*See* unload	Navigation in Entity Classes	500
check-out	*See* load	Navigation in Identity Map	498
closure load	494	n-levels load	494
Data Mapper pattern	487	OID Proxy pattern	497
dematerialization	*See* unload	passivation	*See* unload
Extract Class refactoring	480	predicate load	494
Extract Interface refactoring	483	refactoring	*See* refactoring method
flat load	494	refactoring method	480
identity load	494	Refactoring pattern	484
Identity Map pattern	485	refactoring target	479
Lazy Initialization pattern	494	Subsume Method refactoring	481
Lazy Load	494	Unit of Work pattern	502
load	488	unload	489
materialization	*See* load	Virtual Proxy pattern	495

Review Questions

Discussion Questions

1. Compare the applicability of refactoring in agile development and in Unified Process?

2. Compare refactoring targets of *Extract Class* and *Extract Interface*. Use examples, different from those in the text, to show similarities and differences.

3. *Subsume Method* refactoring is not frequently used. Why? Compare it with *Extract Method*.

4. Explain the objectives of the *Identity Map* pattern? How is Identity Map related to object-relational mapping?

5. Objects are characterized as having state, behavior, and identity. Discuss how well different kinds of identity map support the notion of object identity (OID). Discuss the four kinds of identity map: explicit identity map, generic identity map, one map per session, and one map per class.

6. Discuss advantages and disadvantages of the data mapping strategy based on many data mappers.

7. The *Metadata Mapping* pattern does not specify where the metadata should be kept (stored). What are the possibilities? How do they compare?

8. Provide an example to explain the three lazy load options: closure load, flat load, and n-levels load.

9. Compare *Virtual Proxy* and *OID Proxy*.

10. Compare *Navigation in Identity Map* and *Navigation in Entity Classes*.

Case Study Questions

1. Consider the *Extract Class* refactoring in Figure 15.1. Refer to the `setEmployee()` method. What would be a likely prototype of this method? (Recall that the method prototype is more than method signature as it includes the return type.)

2. Consider the *Extract Class* refactoring in Figure 15.1 and the *Subsume Method* refactoring in Figure 15.2. Refer to the `retrieveMessages()` method. What would be a likely prototype of this method?

3. What needs to be done in the `control` layer if we do not want to expose many of the `control` layer's classes to the `presentation` layer?

4. Suppose that the EM application allows the user to filter outmessages. This means that the user can apply filter criteria to display only selected subsets of outmessages, e.g. outmessages scheduled for emailing in the future, outmessages scheduled for a particular department, etc. How could we model this?

Problem-Solving Exercises

1. Refer to the *Extract Interface* refactoring in Figure 15.3. Could you refactor the code differently? Show the new model.

2. Refer to Case Study Question 4 above. Consider that a `MessageFilter` object is used to implement filtering of outmessages by the application passing the object to appropriate classes

in the `domain` layer. Draw a fragment of sequence diagram that modifies the model for the 'View Unsent Messages' interaction (Figure 11.12) to include filtering with a `MessageFilter` object.

3. Most of the EM activities are initiated by `control` layer and delegated to `mediator`. `Mediator` further manipulates `entity` objects as it sees fit. We can model this differently by using the Publish–Subscribe pattern on `entity` objects. When an `entity` object is modified, it notifies its subscribers of this fact. Present a sequence diagram for this.

4. As shown in Figure 15.4, `MDataMapper` is responsible for finding `entity` objects and if necessary loading them into memory. Show an alternative design whereby `MModerator` plays a more important role in the process. What refactoring methods and patterns, if any, drive this modification?

Chapter

16

User Interface Design and Programming

The principal 'increment' of Iteration 2 over Iteration 1 of the EM case study is the replacement of a text-based console interface by a graphical and web-based user interface. Iteration 1 focused on setting up the system on a robust architectural design. The architecture defines the internal structure and the internal workings of the system. However, what sells the software is its look and feel, not its internal organization. Iteration 2 concentrates on giving the EM system a proper look-and-feel.

As observed in the introductory comments to Chapter 9, architectural design begs for the analogy from the building industry. A house cannot be built unless an architect designed it first. A house cannot be sold unless a buyer likes its look and feel. The user interface (UI) design and programming efforts aim at delivering an attractive and usable look-and-feel to a system by defining the UI objects and actions that enable a user to perform the system's functions.

Enterprise applications are invariably client/server (C/S) solutions. Frequently, they are multi-tier solutions. The tiers define multiple levels of servers, such as web server, application server, and database server. A client can be a desktop, laptop, palmtop, mobile phone, dumb terminal, etc. An application can support multiple clients.

One way of classifying clients is to divide them into programmable clients and browser clients (Singh *et al.*, 2002). A programmable client assumes that a program resides and executes on the client and it has access to client storage resources. Equally importantly, a programmable client can load the data from a server, disconnect from the data source if so required, cache data locally, process it, and render it in its UI. A programmable client is sometimes called a thick client or rich client.

A browser client needs a server to download the requested data and to obtain instructions for rendering the data in a web-based UI. Except for simple validations of user input, a browser client does not have processing capability on its own. The data is presented as a web page formatted in HyperText Markup Language (HTML). A browser client is also called a thin client, web client, or HTML client.

An application, such as the EM case study, can be deployed:

- *locally* with a programmable client (a Java client in case of EM)
- on a **web server** with a browser client and accessed by servlets and Java Server Pages (JSP)
- on an **application server**, such as an Enterprise JavaBeans (EJB) server, with a programmable or browser client.

The EM case study assumes a programmable Java client deployed locally. However, to explain browser clients and various deployment options, parts of Iterations 2 and 3 of the EM solution have been reprogrammed. This chapter discusses UI design and programming for a Java application client that uses the Java Foundation Classes (JFC) with Swing API. It also presents a UI for an application developed using business components and such that the business logic is 'derived' from the underlying database design. Such an application would be normally deployed on an application server.

16.1 User Interface Design Guidelines

Interface is an overloaded term in systems development. In object technology, an *interface* is a declaration for a set of features that is not directly instantiable. A class's **provided interface** is a set of interfaces implemented by the class. A set of interfaces required by a class from other classes is known as a **required interface**. A set of public methods in a class is called its **public interface** (or protocol). **Interface design** means also anything that has to do with establishing communication between software/hardware components. Clearly, the notion of *user interface* is unrelated to these other notions of interface.

The lifecycle of a UI design is an integral part of the system development lifecycle. The days are gone when a UI design was an afterthought of system/program design. They are gone with the extinction of the procedural programming paradigm epitomized by Cobol systems. Modern systems made a paradigm switch from program-in-control to user-in-control, i.e. the user decides what a program does, which actions it performs, and when they are performed.

Accordingly, the UI design made a move from being a predominantly system design/implementation task to being an activity starting in the very early stages of requirements analysis. In contemporary practice, abided by in this book, sketches of UI windows are frequently included in use case documents (Chapters 8 and 14). These early sketches assist enormously in documenting and validating functional user requirements.

Inclusion of UI sketches in use case documents assists in defining functional requirements for a system under development. This is only an initial and complementary aspect of UI design. The **UI design** delivers the system functionality to a user, but, as a stand-alone activity, it concentrates on the **usability** of the system. Usability is one of the FURPS+ features (Section 8.4).

The definition of *usability* includes the UI look-and-feel, but its main characteristics are the system's ease of use, ease of learning, support the UI provides towards the user's efficiency, speed of actions, error resilience and recoverability, adaptability of the UI environment. In a nutshell, and risking some imprecision, a usable system is a user-friendly system.

The design of the UI must conform to a set of overriding guidelines (principles) for what is considered to be a 'good design'. The guidelines override detailed technical considerations. The usability is at the forefront of the guidelines.

Historically, more technically oriented UI design guidelines were presented in the context of a particular look and feel. The aim was to show how a guideline could be fulfilled in the look and feel of Win32 (Windows), Macintosh, Motif (Unix), etc. In contemporary practice of cross-platform and runtime-customizable look and feel, the guidelines can be presented for their merits and the underlying look and feel can be chosen later.

The UI design guidelines can be explained with various degrees of granularity and overlap (Lethbridge and Laganiere, 2001; Maciaszek, 2001; Sommerville, 2001). In this book, the guidelines are grouped into the following categories:

- user in control
- interface consistency
- interface forgiveness
- interface adaptability.

User in Control 16.1.1

The **user-in-control** guideline is like a commandment that rises over and above all other guidelines. The guideline captures the nature of interactions between a user and a program. With modern graphical and web-based user interfaces, a user instructs the program about each next step to be taken. Even at a time when the program is busily doing some processing and a user is awaiting the outcome, the user should retain the perception of control.

For the sake of precision, the user-in-control guideline is really about the user's perception of control. This is sometimes called the *no mothering* principle. A user should not have a feeling of being constantly told by the program what to do. At any time, a user should be able to instruct the program what to do – to take the next step, to change the course of action, to interrupt the current task, etc.

The user-in-control guideline is directly assisted by object technology. In fact, the current popularity of object technology can be attributed to the match that it provided for the emerging graphical user interfaces in the 1980s. An object-oriented program consists of a large number of collaborating objects. Each object is a small programming module with a set of services ready to be performed when asked by other objects or when activated by a direct user event. Behind each user–program interaction there is an object that understands the user's request.

For the user to have the perception of control, the program has to be designed accordingly. The UI has to be easy to use. It should use the terminology of the business domain, not computer jargon. It should minimize interface changes as a result of changes in the system's state. The user must not be constantly surprised by unavailability of menu items, command buttons, and other controls in situations when these controls were available when doing similar tasks in similar windows. Any guidance provided by the program to the user should be restrained and discreet.

The user-in-control guideline assumes proper and timely feedback from a program when the program performs a task that cannot be interrupted. This is predominantly the performance issue. A user gets anxious if the program does some processing that takes longer than usual and the user is not informed of what is going on. There may be good reasons why the program is slow. This may be due to unusual workload or to a need to undertake an administrative task by the system, such as the reorganization of indexes in a relational database. None of these factors frees a UI designer from providing timely informational feedback to the user.

16.1.2 Interface Consistency

Consistency in interface design means conformance to industry and organization standards with regard to naming, coding, abbreviations, placement of visual objects, use of controls, including menus, buttons, keyboard functions, etc. Interface consistency is not a feature of a single isolated application program. Interface consistency refers to consistency across many applications within an enterprise system and/or across many applications executing on the same UI platform.

Individual creative urges, ingenuity inclinations, departures from standards for the sake of making things more attractive, etc. are not welcome in UI design. They only confuse users and impact negatively on the user-in-control guideline. The standards may not be the best reflection of the state of the art, but a designer must remember that just about the only thing a user cares about is to get the job done in the simplest, quickest, and most familiar way.

However, consistency does not mean repeating the same mistakes over and over again. There are limits to consistency and to standards. Standards have the tendency to legitimize both good and bad practices and to hinder progress. Improvements in system software and hardware, new computing capabilities, emerging applications, and even social, political, legal, or economic factors can necessitate innovation and nonconformity in new applications.

Interface consistency subsumes interface aesthetics. It can be assumed that a consistent interface conforming to standards will result in an aesthetic interface – an interface attractive visually, with a sense of balance and symmetry, good use of color, appealing alignment and spacing of elements, pleasing grouping of related elements, no special demands on movements of the human eye, etc.

16.1.3 Interface Forgiveness

An application should be forgiving of its users doing unusual things, activating unusual events, entering erroneous data, etc. A **forgiving interface** implies a resilient interface – an interface that can gracefully accommodate exceptions and errors. A forgiving interface implies an interface easy to explore – an interface that encourages the user to explore unknown options and that enforces the user-in-control principle.

A forgiving interface delivers proper feedback to a user and friendly exception handling. A program's perspective on a user must be that of a vendor's perspective on a customer: no matter what, the customer is right. A user can make any error of judgment, perform any action, activate any menu option, press any command button, and yet the program must not fail. A silly action must be undoable. An unacceptable action must be handled.

Undoing a user action seems, at first, a simple task of forgetting what the user did. This is indeed the case in a single-user stand-alone application, like Microsoft Word. The 'Undo Typing' option in Microsoft Word permits undoing not just the latest, but a large number of recent actions on a Word document. Not so in the case of a typical enterprise application accessing a database and committing business transactions to persistent database storage. A committed transaction cannot be undone. At best, it can be compensated.

How to compensate a transaction? Imagine that a user has withdrawn money from a bank account. Clearly, once committed, this transaction cannot be undone. But it can be compensated. A user must have a possibility to put the money back into the account. A compensating transaction is not an automatic system's action. A user must instigate it. Even then, a compensating transaction may fail.

Imagine a reverse banking transaction in which a user deposited money into a joint account. Imagine then that the user decides to 'undo' the transaction soon after and withdraw the deposited money. The withdrawal transaction may fail if, in the meantime, the other account holder accessed the account from another location and withdrew the money just deposited.

Forgiveness includes the UI reaction to an unacceptable action by a user. Firstly, an unacceptable action must not cause the system to fail. Secondly, an unacceptable action must not be allowed. Thirdly, an unacceptable action must be handled gently. The user must be informed about the nature of the problem, must be 'educated' why the system cannot perform the action, and must be told how to correct the problem and what alternative action may be allowed.

Interface Adaptability 16.1.4

A user interface should be able to accommodate any user. User diversity has a number of dimensions. Firstly, a user can be a novice user or an experienced user. Secondly, users can come from different locales. Thirdly, a user may be a person with disabilities.

The UI design should be **adaptable** so that its features can be changed depending on the user's familiarity with it. Familiarity has two aspects. The first aspect relates to familiarity with using the UI as the mechanism of interacting with the system and being able to 'move around' and 'move forward'. The second aspect relates to familiarity with 'getting things done' in a business sense. This aspect assumes a user with a good knowledge of the application's business domain.

A good UI should provide customization and personalization facilities to allow a user to change the UI features depending on the level of computer and/or business knowledge. Customization is an act of declaring to the program a level of the user's familiarity with it so that the UI can change its appearance and behavior. Personalization has less to do with a user's familiarity and more with a user's preferred ways of doing things.

The UI design should be adaptable so that its features can be changed depending on a user's locale (Lethbridge and Laganiere, 2001). Locale-specific information is a feature of modern Internet-age systems. An application can query an operating system on which it executes to obtain locale information and it can then adapt to that locale. Adaptation includes a change of user language (e.g. from English to Italian), change of character set and fonts, change of currency, change of time, change of sorting order, change of date format, change of formats for postal addresses and telephone numbers, change in the way people are named and referred to, change of icons and metaphors (such as meaning of color in different cultures), etc.

The UI design should be adaptable so that people with disabilities can use its features. Different disabilities ask for different adaptability measures. Blind people require an application to accept Braille or speech. Deaf people require visual substitution for any sound output. Physically disabled people may require a voice recognition capability to be built into the system. An adaptable UI should support alternative input and output devices such as Braille terminals, screen readers, screen magnifiers, and similar.

16.2　User Interface Components

User interface programming takes advantage of widely available **class libraries** that provide GUI 'windowing' components and determine an application's look and feel. In the world of Java, the class library is called Java™ Foundation Classes (JFC). The majority of JFC consists of a GUI component kit called Swing. The kit provides GUI components for use in Java applications and applets.

The **Swing component kit** enables delivery of applications with *pluggable look-and-feel*. Pluggable has several meanings. It can mean the conformance to the GUI platform on which the program executes (Windows, Unix, etc.). It can mean a uniform cross-platform look-and-feel that has identical manifestation on any execution platform. Swing calls this the Java look-and-feel. Finally, it can mean a programmer-customizable look-and-feel unique to an application.

To achieve **pluggability**, most Swing components are themselves platform-independent or **lightweight**, sometimes called peerless. A lightweight component is programmed without any use of platform-specific (peer) code. Unfortunately, not all Swing components are lightweight – some are **heavyweight**. In most cases where heavyweight components are used, Swing provides workarounds to hide the peer code so that pluggable look-and-feel is still achievable.

In Swing, most concrete classes representing UI components are named starting with the letter J, e.g. `JDialog`, `JMenuBar`, `JButton`. The components are very intertwined. They can be composed in various ways to deliver a required UI design. It is not easy to classify UI components into coherent groups. One crude classification can be:

- containers (e.g. `JInternalFrame`, `JTabbedPane`)
- menus (e.g. `JPopupMenu`, `JRadioButtonMenuItem`)
- controls (e.g. `JRadioButton`, `JScrollBar`).

Containers

Containers are rectangular areas on a GUI desktop that contain other components, including other containers, menus, and controls. Depending on their intended purpose and role with regard to other containers, they are called windows, dialogs, panes, panels, and similar terms. They determine the prime look and feel of an application.

Swing has a variety of classes able to produce container objects. Four of these classes are **heavyweight classes**: JWindow, JFrame, JDialog, and JApplet. In most situations, a top-level container of a program is an instance of a heavyweight container. Lightweight container classes need heavyweight components for screen painting and event handling. **Lightweight classes** include: JInternalFrame, JDesktopPane, JOptionPane, JPanel, JTabbedPane, JScrollPane, JSplitPane, JTextPane, and JTable.

Frequently an application has only one top-level **primary window**, and a number of **secondary windows** (i.e. windows that depend on other windows; they need a parent window) (Maciaszek, 2001). A JWindow is a top-level container with no 'decorations' – no borders, title, menu bar, or scroll bar. Because of these deficiencies, a subclass of JWindow, such as JFrame or JPanel, is normally used to implement a popup window. A JFrame object has 'decorations'. A JPanel can be used to implement a **dialog box** – a secondary window to display a message and/or obtain input from the user.

Figure 16.1 is an example of a primary and a secondary window. The primary window named Figure 16.1 is a JFrame. The secondary window named About is a JPanel.

The primary window in Figure 16.1 has a menu bar (JMenuBar), toolbar (JToolBar), and buttons in the upper right corner to iconify and close the window. The menu bar items are instances of JMenuItem. The toolbar buttons are instances of JButton. The primary window can be resized from any side or a corner of its border and it can be dragged (moved) from the title bar. The secondary window would normally have a fixed size.

JWindow, JFrame, and JPanel are heavyweight components. To be able to add lightweight components to a heavyweight container object, the container must use a special method getContentPane(), e.g.

```
aFrame.getContentPane().add(toolBar, BorderLayout.NORTH);
```

JDialog is another heavyweight component for creating *dialog windows* (dialog boxes). Yet another Swing component – JOptionPane – provides a number of standard dialog windows. All standard dialogs are *modal*. When a modal window is active (currently visible), a user cannot use other windows until the processing in the modal window is completed and the window is dismissed. A modeless window allows information to be entered in that window as well as in the primary window just by bringing a desired window to the top.

An application can request a dialog window by invoking the appropriate method in JOptionPane, e.g.:

```
void helpAbout_ActionPerformed(ActionEvent e)
  {
    JOptionPane.showMessageDialog(this, new
      Frame1_AboutBoxPanel1(),
      "About", JOptionPane.PLAIN_MESSAGE);
  }
```

Figure 16.1
Primary and
secondary
windows

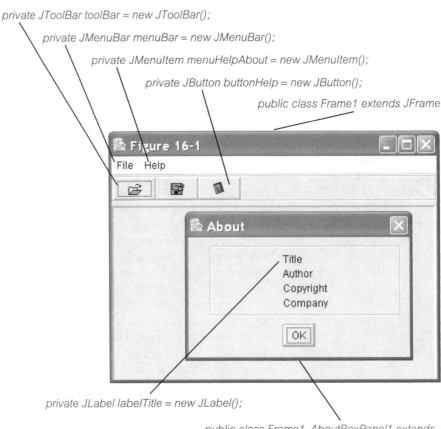

private JToolBar toolBar = new JToolBar();

private JMenuBar menuBar = new JMenuBar();

private JMenuItem menuHelpAbout = new JMenuItem();

private JButton buttonHelp = new JButton();

public class Frame1 extends JFrame

private JLabel labelTitle = new JLabel();

public class Frame1_AboutBoxPanel1 extends JPanel

JApplet is a heavyweight component for creating **applets** – programs that execute inside a web page (Chapter 17). Applets are downloaded from a server and can be cached in a web browser for execution. JWindow, JDialog, and JApplet depend on a JFrame. Hence, minimizing JFrame minimizes its window, dialog, or applet. Destroying JFrame destroys also its window, dialog, or applet etc.

Swing provides a large number of lightweight panes to use in other containers. One of them is a JOptionPane, which implements a standard set of message boxes, such as to give a warning, to request a confirmation for an action, to explain an event, etc. Other very useful panes include JTabbedPane, JScrollPane, JTextPane, and JSplitPane.

A **JTabbedPane** object results in a window with many 'tabbed pages/panels'. **Tabbed pages** overlap each other, so at any point in time only one page can be seen. Pressing a tab brings its tabbed page to the front. Tabbed pages are very useful to handle a large volume of data in a single dialog window. They have a special place in applet programming, which discourages the use of popup dialogs (Eckel, 2000).

Figure 16.2 demonstrates a tabbed pane with two panels named Movie and Actor. Adding a JPanel object to the JTabbedPane object creates each tabbed pane.

A **JScrollPane** object provides horizontal and vertical scrolling capabilities to a window. A variety of **scroll bars** is available to select from. A **JTextPane** object displays

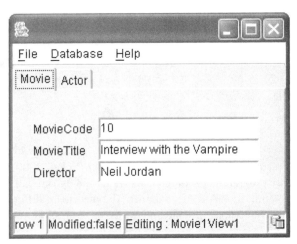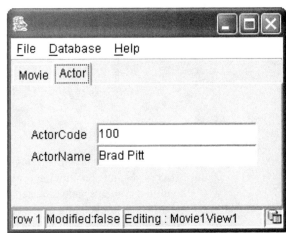

Figure 16.2 Tabbed pane

text. This is a good candidate to be a 'scrollable client', i.e. it can obtain scrolling capabilities from JScrollPane. By extending (inheriting from) JEditorPane, JTextPane acquires basic editing capabilities.

A **JSplitPane** object delivers a *split window* with two or more dependent panes, i.e. an action on one pane results in visual or other changes in the dependent pane. The panes can be separated vertically or horizontally. Windows Explorer is a 'split pane' window.

One important Swing component that resists easy classification is **JTable**. Although not quite a window or a pane, a JTable object is a container of data. JTable delivers a table of rows and columns. It can be used for all sorts of complex tabular manipulations, including spreadsheet-like functionality. However, a primary use of JTable is as a grid to display data records obtained from a relational database.

Figure 16.3 is an example of a window containing a JTable object. The scrolling facility is provided by a JScrollPane object. JScrollPane uses a JViewport object

Figure 16.3
Table

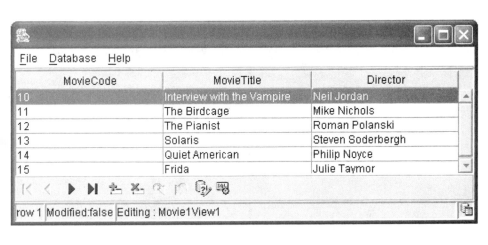

to provide a 'viewport' onto a data source – the content of the database `Movie` table, as indicated in the following code excerpt:

```
private JTable tableMovie1View1 = new JTable();
private JScrollPane scroller = new JScrollPane();
scroller.getViewport().add(tableMovie1View1, null);
```

Layout management

Swing applies a **layout manager** to place components within a container (Eckel, 2000). Unless absolute positioning is explicitly programmed, components are placed dynamically within a container and adjusted to the dimensions of the container. The placement differs significantly depending on the chosen layout manager. A method `setLayout()` allows the desired layout manager to be chosen, e.g.

```
aFrame.getContentPane().setLayout(new GridLayout(6,5));
```

The **layouts** provided by Swing include `BorderLayout`, `FlowLayout`, `GridLayout`, `BoxLayout`, and `GridBagLayout`. **BorderLayout** is a default layout scheme for most

Figure 16.4
Layout managers applied to the same set of components

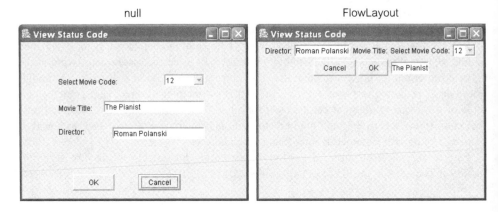

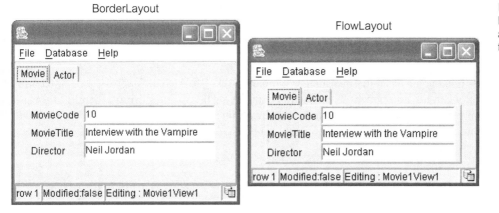

Figure 16.5
Layout managers
applied to a
tabbed pane

containers, except `JPanel` (which uses `FlowLayout` by default). Manual positioning of graphical components within containers can be programmed with a layout manager set to `null`:

```
aContainer.getContentPane().setLayout(null);
```

Explanation of detailed characteristics of these layouts is beyond this book (Eckel, 2000). Figure 16.4 shows how the layouts differ when different layout managers are applied on the same set of components. The layout in the top left corner is a `null` layout set manually. The remaining layouts were obtained by applying different schemes to the initial `null` layout.

Figure 16.4 may give an impression that some popular layouts, such as `BorderLayout`, are inferior to others. That is not the case. The choice of layout should be picked to match the container. Figure 16.5 shows `BorderLayout` and `FlowLayout` applied to a tabbed pane.

Layering management

An application can open multiple windows, which then overlap windows behind them. A Swing class called `JLayeredPane` adds depth to containers by supporting layering of windows and other components. This class provides methods to move components to front, to back, or to reposition them relative to each other.

Most components go to a standard (default) layer. Components in a **default layer** overlap properly based on user's selections of these components (e.g. clicking a window makes it a top-level window). `JLayerPane` allows also declaring special characteristics of layers, which make them behave in a predefined way with regard to other layers. The special cases are:

- **palette layer** which floats above the default layer (e.g. a floating toolbar)
- **modal layer** which appears on top of all other active windows, toolbars and palettes in the application and does not allow switching to these other windows unless it itself is dismissed (e.g. a modal dialog window)

- **popup layer** which displays temporarily in its own layer above other layers (e.g. a combo box, tooltip)
- **drag layer** that makes the component visible when it is dragged before it is dropped on a destination layer.

Each layer has a distinct integer number (from 1 to 5). The layer for a component is set when the component is added to a container. The current position (depth) of a component within a layer is also indicated by an integer value. This value can be specified directly (setLayer()). The position can be changed by invoking moveToFront() and moveToBack().

16.2.2 Menus

Windows and some other components can hold **menus**. Swing's classes in support of menus include JMenuBar, JMenu, JMenuItem, JCheckBoxMenuItem, and JRadioButtonMenuItem. A class model for menu-related Swing components is shown in Figure 16.6.

JPopupMenu, JMenuBar, JMenu, and JMenuItem implement the same interface MenuElement. JMenuItem extends AbstractButton – this makes it clear that JMenuItem is a control (Section 16.2.3). JCheckBoxMenuItem and JRadioButtonMenuItem are two kinds of JMenuItem.

The Swing class model for menus distorts the fact that a JMenuItem object is contained in a JMenu object, and a JMenu object is contained in a JMenuBar object. No containment (aggregation) relationships are used in the model to represent this fact. Arguably, the representation where JMenu is a subclass of JMenuItem is an example of improper use of implementation inheritance (Section 9.1.5).

Figure 16.7 provides a visual representation of Swing menus. A menu bar (JMenuBar) contains JMenu objects. An item on a dropdown JMenu object can be a JMenuItem object

Figure 16.6
Swing menus

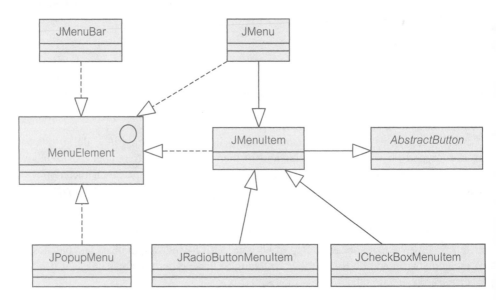

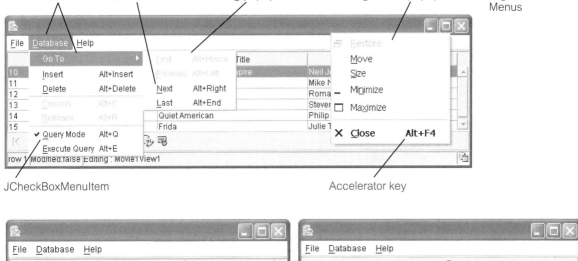

Figure 16.7
Menus

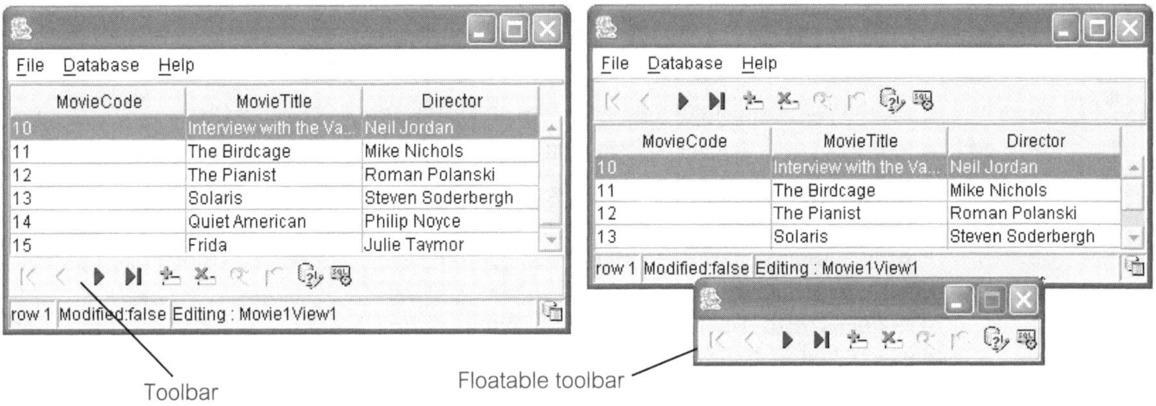

Figure 16.8 Toolbars

(e.g. `Insert`) or another `JMenu` object (e.g. the `Go To` menu item). The latter results in a **cascading** ('pull-right') *popup* menu (`JPopupMenu`). Another example of a `JPopupMenu` is a **right-click popup** menu. A `JMenuItem` object can be a checkmark of `JCheckBoxMenuItem` (e.g. `QueryMode` item) or a selection of `JRadioButtonMenuItem`. Each menu can have an accelerator key.

Figure 16.8 explains the use of toolbars in UI design. Typically, a **toolbar** contains actions and controls that duplicate the functionality of some most useful menu items. This allows a quicker activation of these menu items. A Swing container called `JToolBar` assists in designing toolbars into the UI. Toolbars can have a fixed location in the window frame or they can be floatable, i.e. can be undocked from the frame into a separate window.

Controls   16.2.3

Controls are the heart of the Swing event model. They intercept, understand, and implement user actions. Broadly speaking, they divide into:

Figure 16.9
Swing controls

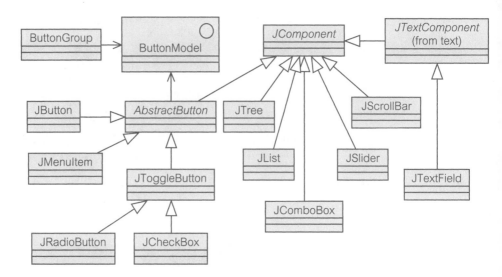

- action *buttons* that are inherited from an abstract class called `AbstractButton`
- *other controls* that are inherited directly from a root abstract class called `JComponent`.

Figure 16.9 is a class model for Swing controls. The model shows that there are four categories of buttons: `JButton`, `JRadioButton`, `JCheckBox`, and `JMenuItem` explained in the previous section. To implement an interrelated behavior of a set of buttons, they need to be added to a `ButtonGroup` (Eckel, 2000).

Figure 16.10 visualizes buttons and other controls listed in Figure 16.9. Controls are implemented with the Swing event model. Each control can have one or more subscriber

Figure 16.10
Buttons and other controls

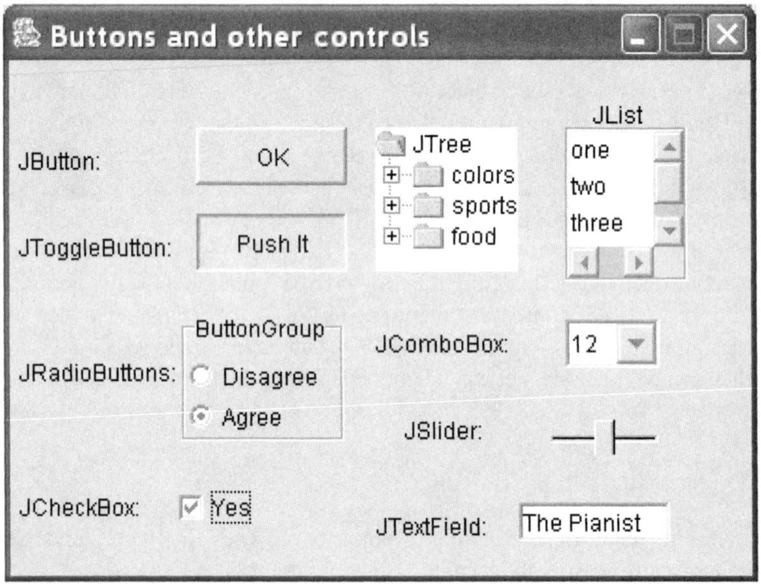

objects that listen to it. For example, a JTextField object may publish events such as a change in the text, pressing a Delete key on the keyboard, or selecting a Copy item from a menu.

JButton is a simple push button. Unlike JButton, JToggleButton once pushed remains pushed (set to true) until it is pressed again. The pushed JToggleButton indicates that it is active. Two categories of JToggleButton are JCheckBox and JRadioButton.

JCheckBox is a square box that can be set to either true or false. The true value of a **checkbox** is indicated by a checkmark in it. JRadioButton is used to select one and only one button in the set of buttons, as for example in Iteration 2 filters (Figure 14.3). As in many mechanical devices, when one **radio button** is 'pushed in', all other buttons 'pop out'. This functionality is achieved by adding each radio button to ButtonGroup.

JComboBox permits selection from a **dropdown list** (**combo box**). A combo box is frequently called a **picklist** in the jargon. A JComboBox object can be editable or not (if not, it does not permit typing in a user's own selection). By default, a JComboBox object is not editable. JComboBox allows only one selection.

JList supports multiple selections (with typical Ctrl-click and Shift-click actions). Multiple selections in JList are possible because JList is a fixed-size but scrollable **list box** of items (note that scrolling is not an automatic feature of JList; it can be achieved by wrapping JList in a JScrollPane).

The meaning and applicability of Swing's JScrollBar and JSlider are as expected. Scroll bars can be added to most containers. Sliders allow input adjustments, such as in volume control.

Last but not least, JTree is a very useful control and one of the most powerful in Swing (Eckel, 2000). In most situations, a simple tree view showing a hierarchy of various items and containers, as in Windows Explorer, is sufficient. However, if an application requires more sophisticated implementation of a tree, the Swing library is likely to meet the challenge.

User Interface Event Handling 16.3

The user interface is all about **event processing** (Section 9.1.8) and the **Observer pattern** (Section 9.3.4). The PCMEF framework recommends using event processing for upward notification between layers – the UNP principle (Section 9.2.2). Event processing in user interface design relates to only one PCMEF layer – the presentation layer.

The Swing **event model** is derived from the MVC framework (Section 9.2.1). In Swing, view and controller aspects of MVC are combined in a separate component (such as JButton). For each such component, Swing defines a separate model interface (such as ButtonModel) (Figure 16.7). All the application has to do to change a predefined component behavior is to implement its model interface in its own way.

Any user action via available user input devices (mouse, keyboard, etc.) triggers a program event that needs to be intercepted by an event source object – a **publisher** object. Event source notifies an occurrence of an event to any object interested in that event. These target objects are **subscriber** (listener, observer) objects. Each event source can have many subscribers and each subscriber can listen to many event sources.

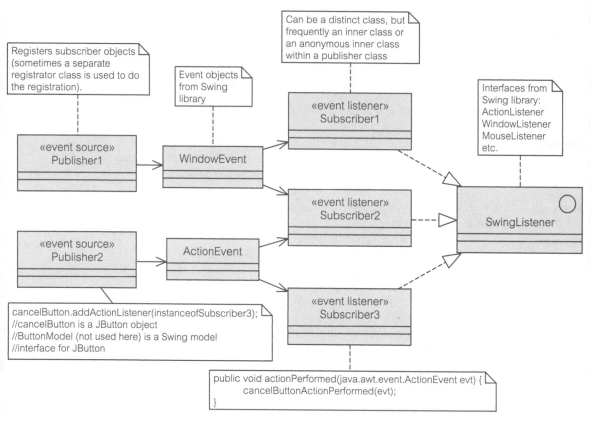

Figure 16.11 Swing event handling

Figure 16.11 is an abstract example of event handling. Each subscriber class implements a Swing listener interface (such as `ActionListener`) or it extends a class that implements such an interface. The code that registers a subscriber object as a listener can be included in the publisher class or this responsibility can be given to a separate registrator object (Figure 9.20).

In the example, when the user presses the `cancelButton` with the mouse, the button triggers an action event. This will invoke `actionPerformed()` in `Subscriber3` – the only method of a Swing `ActionListener` interface that `Subscriber3` implemented. The argument to `actionPerformed()` is an `ActionEvent` object. `ActionEvent` informs a `Subscriber3` object about the event and the source of it (a `Publisher2` object).

As noted in Figure 16.11, a *subscriber class* can be a distinct class. This may be a good option in more complex event handling. In PCMEF, a distinct subscriber class is likely to reside in the `control` layer and listen to a publisher in the `presentation` layer. In simpler cases, a subscriber class can be an **inner class** of the publisher class, or even an **anonymous inner class**. Listings 16.1, 16.2, and 16.3 are three examples that lead to the same outcome: they implement an `ActionListener` on the publisher object.

Listing 16.1 Subscriber as separate class

```
Subscriber as separate class

public class ShowTitleListener implements ActionListener{
   TitleChanger host; //reference to the object that changes the title
   public ShowTitleListener(TitleChanger host){
      this.host = host;
   }
   public void actionPerformed(ActionEvent evt){ //a request to
                                            change the title comes
      System.out.println("The title is now changed to " +
                                            host.changeTitle());
   }
}
public class TitleChanger{
   public void show(){
      Button b = new Button("Change Title");
      …
      b.addActionListener(new ShowTitleListener(this));
                                  //this is where it is used
      …
   }
}
```

Listing 16.2 Subscriber as inner class

```
Subscriber as inner class

public class TitleChanger{
   public void show(){
      Button b = new Button("Change Title");
      …
      b.addActionListener(new ShowTitleListener());
      …
   }
   //inner class declaration
   private class ShowTitleListener implements ActionListener{
      public void actionPerformed(ActionEvent evt){
                         //a request to change the title comes
         System.out.println("The title is now changed to " +
         TitleChanger.this.changeTitle());
                              //direct reference to outer class
      }
   }
}
```

Listing 16.3 Subscriber as anonymous inner class

```
Subscriber as anonymous inner class
public class TitleChanger{
   public void show(){
      Button b = new Button("Change Title");
      ...
      b.addActionListener(new ActionListener(){
                                     //creating anonymous inner class
         public void actionPerformed(ActionEvent evt){
            System.out.println("The title is now changed to " +
            TitleChanger.this.changeTitle());
                                     //direct reference to outer class
         }
      });
      ...
   }
}
```

All Swing components have a **model interface** defined in the library. For example, a model interface for buttons is called `ButtonModel`, for `JList` is called `ListModel`, for `JTable` is called `TableModel`, etc. Model interfaces can be implemented in the application's unique way according to the required application logic. However, for components not requiring a unique model implementation, the interaction with the standard model is hidden behind the methods of the component class. This is done by a component's method delegating a message to its model, e.g.:

```
public String getTitle() {
   return getModel().getTitle();
}
```

Figure 16.12 shows a sequence diagram illustrating how a `TableModel` is used in the EM case study. In the figure, `TableModel` is implemented by `PMessageTableModel`. It shows how `PMEssageTableModel` is used to store outmessages and perform filtering on outmessages displayed by a `JTable` object. Sorting and filtering operations are placed in `PMessageTableModel`. This is because `PMessageTableModel` is responsible for storing data that can then be sorted and filtered. Filter requests come from `PWindow` as indicated in the figure. `PMessageTableModel` filters the data by delegating the request to its `PDisplayList`. Subsequent operations from `JTable` to request the data from its model (in this case `PMessageTableModel`) will result in the return of the filtered data.

Figure 16.12 illustrates how the `PWindow` requests `PMessageTableModel` to perform a filter on certain criteria (only `datefilter` and `contactfilter` shown). `PMessage-TableModel` then requests its data, `PDisplayList`, to eliminate those `PDisplayData` that do not satisfy the criteria. Once the filtering is finished, `PWindow` triggers the screen to be repainted and forces `JTable` to display the modified subset of data. `JTable` queries its model, `PMessageTableModel`, for the *new* list of messages to be displayed on the screen.

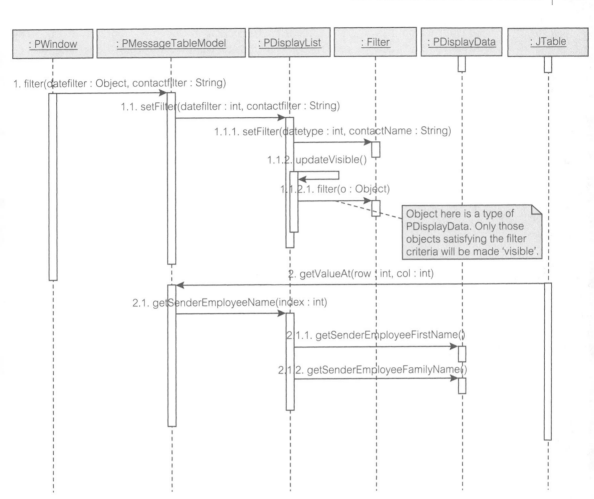

Figure 16.12 Sequence diagram involving PMessageTableModel

JTable queries the data on a per row and column basis. PMessageTableModel translates this request to the appropriate fields stored in the model. This process is accomplished by the getSenderEmployeeName() message to PDisplayList. PDisplayList then constructs the name of the sender employee by combining his/her first name and family name.

Patterns and the User Interface

16.4

Graphical user interfaces (GUIs) are largely responsible for the changeover from procedural to object-oriented software. Although object-oriented software and programming languages have been known since the 1960s, the introduction of GUIs has necessitated the move to event-driven programming inherent in object-orientation. GUIs move the center of control from the program to the user. The user is in charge of program's execution by deciding which actions should be executed next. These actions translate to input events. Each input event requires an object to service it.

Graphical user interfaces are also largely responsible for the popularity of **patterns** in system design. 'Look and feel' sells the software. Users demand early UI prototypes to evaluate the system's look and feel. Integrated development environments (IDEs) and Rapid Application Development (RAD) techniques allow quick production of such prototypes. All these demands lead to advances in GUI component reuse. Such advances are documented in GUI-related patterns and vice versa – most of the highly influential **Gang of Four** (GoF) patterns (Gamma *et al.*, 1995) can be found in GUI component design.

This section covers only a small subset of commonly used patterns in UI development. The patterns discussed are Observer, Decorator, Chain of Responsibility, and Command. Observer and Chain of Responsibility have been discussed before in other contexts.

16.4.1 Observer

Various components in the UI observe model (entity) objects (as per the Model–View–Controller framework (Section 9.2.1)). They change UI behaviors or representations based on received notifications that the model has changed. Such a relationship of observing the model is conveniently called the **Observer pattern** (Section 9.3.4).

Consider an example of the relationship between JTable and its JTableModel, as shown in Figure 16.13. The table registers for its model's events. Upon modification of the model, the table is notified and it is therefore able to respond accordingly. Figure 16.13 shows observers implemented on the interaction between a JTable and its model. The figure does not include all components related to JTable, as there are many of those. It shows only JTableModel and TableCellEditor.

The table is constructed with an instance of JTableModel. The table registers its interest on the model via the addTableModelListener() method. This ensures that the table will be notified when the model has changed.

When the user decides to modify a cell in the table, by double-clicking on the cell, the table constructs a CellEditor. The CellEditor (or rather its editable component) is set with the value retrieved from the model via getValueAt() (message 2.1). To make the matter more interesting, TableCellEditor itself is actually a model to JTable. JTable is a subscriber (listener) to TableCellEditor (message 2.2.1).

Figure 16.13 uses the Observer pattern for:

- JTable observing JTableModel (message 1)
- JTable observing TableCellEditor (message 2.2.1).

When a modification is done on an editable component, such as a checkbox or textfield (message 3), the TableCellEditor notifies the table via its editingStopped() method (implementation of Observer from message 2.2.1). The table is then able to process the modified value retrieved from getCellEditorValue() and change its JTableModel's value (message 3.1.2 setValue()).

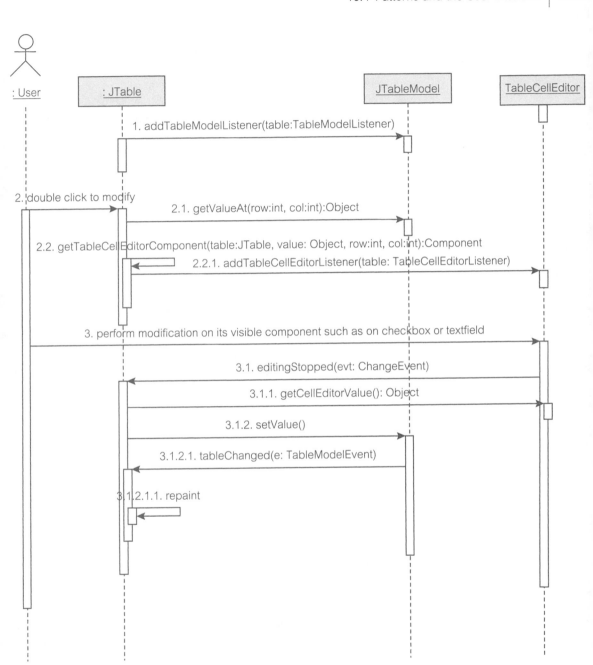

Figure 16.13 Observers

`JTable` acts as a mediator between the value modified in `TableCellEditor`'s component and the value saved in `JTableModel`. The modification on `JTableModel` forces it to notify all interested parties (`JTable` and other classes that register via `addTableModelListener()`, message 1). The notification is done by calling their `tableChanged()` method. Finally the observer, `JTable`, repaints itself (message 3.1.2.1.1) by querying the model for its data to be shown on the screen.

The Observer pattern is used extensively in UI design. It allows development of UI component compositions and rich component interactions (complex event notifications). The Observer pattern addresses a requirement of event-driven systems that the model can be modified at any time and the UI has to be aware of such modifications.

16.4.2 Decorator

The **Decorator pattern** (Gamma *et al.*, 1995) dictates that a set of wrapper classes can be used to *decorate* the appearance of a component. This happens, for example, when a set of scrollbars is used to decorate a `JList` to form a scrollable list. Another example is a `Frame` decorated by scrollbars, menubar, toolbar, and borders.

Figure 16.10 illustrates the use of decorators. It shows a `Panel` decorated with a titled-border '`ButtonGroup`'. It also shows a `JList` placed inside a `JScrollPane`. `JScroll-Pane` is a scrollable panel.

Decorator pattern is used to beautify and enhance usability (user-friendliness) of the UI. The sole purpose of some UI components, such as borders, is to be used as decorators.

16.4.3 Chain of Responsibility

When a component is incapable of providing service for a particular request, the component could opt to delegate such responsibility to its subcomponents until one of the subcomponents is able to respond to the request. The related pattern is called **Chain of Responsibility** (Section 9.3.3).

Windows implements this pattern to aid its *Help* system. Whenever a Windows user does not understand the purpose of certain control in the GUI, s/he can right-click on the component to seek clarification of its purpose. Figure 16.14 shows how the current component (slider for screen resolution) responds on user's right-click and selecting the 'What's this?' menu item.

The current component will figure out whether it can respond to the request. If not, it will delegate the request to the next object in the chain of responsibility. Eventually, some component should be found that is able to display appropriate information on screen and stop the *chain*.

In Figure 16.14, the current component will delegate the request to its container component. The container component is the panel with titled-border '`Screen Resolution`'. If the panel has the answer, it will display the information on the screen and stop the request propagation. The chain of requests continues to the topmost container component that is able either to provide information (could be specific information or generic information) or to stop the chain without answer.

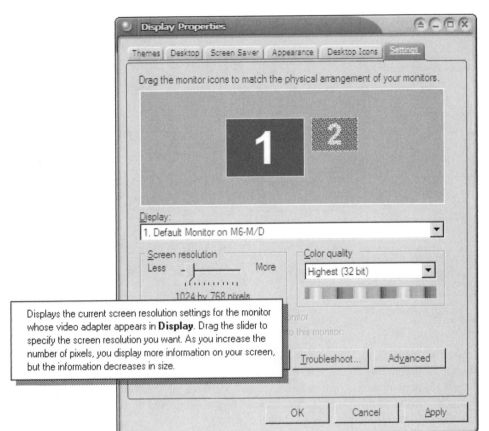

Figure 16.14
Help: Chain of Responsibility

This pattern simplifies the design of commonly required delegation sequences, such as the *Help* system. However, there is a drawback to this pattern. It requires all contributing containers to implement the pattern. The container or component has to be able to decide whether it can respond to the request or needs to propagate it further. Moreover, the components are growing in size if they would like to participate on many different *help* contexts, i.e. more than one chain of responsibility contexts.

Command   16.4.4

The **Command pattern** (Gamma *et al.*, 1995) is similar to the Chain of Responsibility pattern. Command delegates the request to the next component until one of them can service the request. Slightly different from Chain of Responsibility, where the request is delegated to a parent container and can go to the top of the hierarchy, components in the Command pattern delegate the request to a well-known interface.

Consider, for example, a drawing application. The application needs to provide an undo–redo mechanism. Each activity performed in the application needs to be *recorded* to

Figure 16.15
Command Pattern
example: Undo

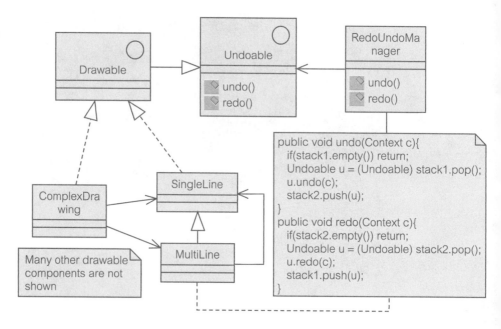

allow the application to revert to its previous states. However, the activities performed in the application are so diverse that they have different *undo* meanings. For example, a box drawing is treated as a set of four sets of single-line strokes. The command pattern dictates that irrespective of this diversity, the contributing components must implement a simple interface and therefore they can be treated equally.

Figure 16.15 shows a design of undo that follows the Command pattern. RedoUndo-Manager does not know how each of its components stored in the stack performs undo or redo actions. When an undo is required, it pops the recent value from stack1 and calls its undo() method. The undo itself could be a very complex operation, but this is left for the component to perform.

A complex component, such as the MultiLine class, could further use the Undoable property to perform its undo(), as shown in Figure 16.15.

16.5 User Interface for Email Management

In Iteration 2, the user interfaces are not much different from the prototype shown in Chapter 14. Minor variations are due to removing or adding certain widgets to clarify and simplify the GUI. For example, the text on command buttons has been changed in Figure 16.16 from its prototype in Figure 14.3. Single-word labels on buttons, such as *Insert*, replace longer text proposed in the prototype such as *Insert New Message*. The all-important *Exit* button is added.

The display of outmessages in Figure 16.16 is sorted in descending order by Scheduled Dpt. Clicking on the column name does the sorting. The filter options are

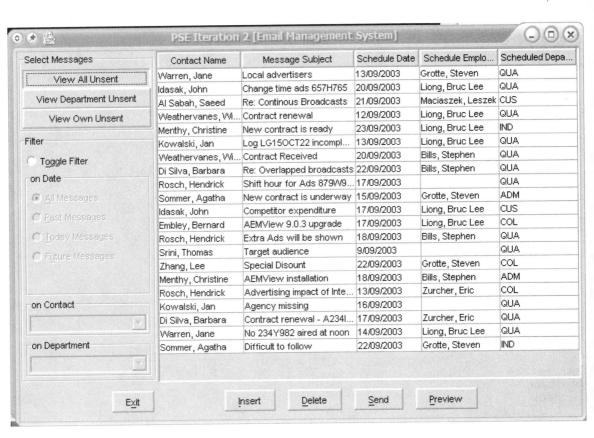

Figure 16.16 Iteration 2 main GUI

disabled by default in the initial display of outmessages. Clicking at the `Toggle Filter` button makes the filter options underneath enabled.

Additional messages are displayed to inform the user about incomplete information provided in the GUI, such as shown in Figure 16.17. The example refers to the *Create New Message* subflow presented in Chapter 14 in Figure 14.6.

Outmessage insertion, supported by the dialog box in Figure 14.6, triggers a series of interesting actions. Before the dialog box can be shown on the screen, the program needs to construct the outmessage placeholder and ensure that the outmessage is registered in `EIdentityMap`. Figure 16.18 shows that the creation of an OID for the new outmessage is handled by `MDataMapper`.

Furthermore, the new outmessage is automatically flagged as dirty to indicate that it needs to be included in the next cycle of update (or reloading) performed by `EIdentityMap`. Once the outmessage placeholder is obtained, the outmessage can be modified and updated by `PMessageDetailWindow` (Figure 14.6).

Update of the newly created outmessage is performed at the end of execution of subflow *S5 – Create New Message* (Figure 14.6). Figure 16.19 shows that the saving mechanism is consistent with the *Identity Map* and *Data Mapper* patterns, discussed in Chapter 15.

Figure 16.17
Error messages for
Create New
Message

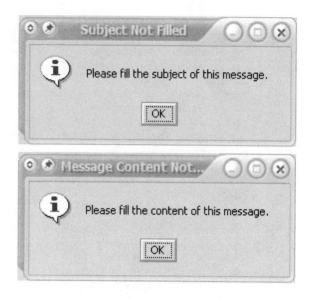

Figure 16.18
Obtaining a new
outmessage
placeholder

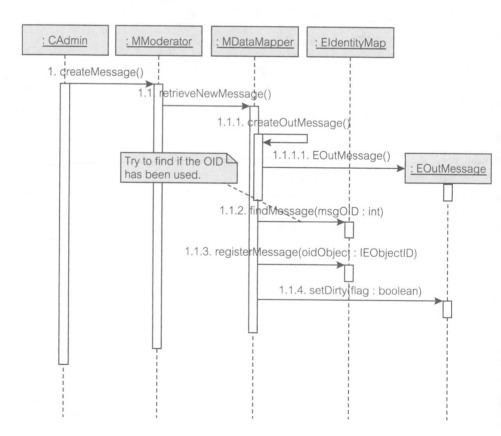

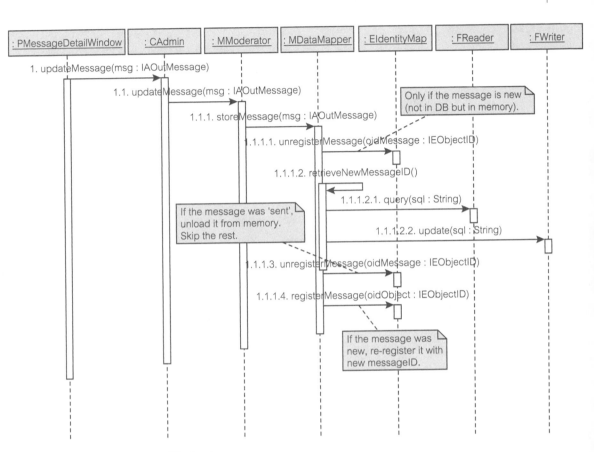

Figure 16.19 Updating a modified outmessage

Figure 16.19 illustrates the scenario where the user has finished editing the outmessage in the PMessageDetailWindow and chooses to save it in the database. Saving the outmessage requires MDataMapper to synchronize the content of the cache with the content of the database (as far as that outmessage is concerned). First, MDataMapper needs to un-register the outmessage from EIdentityMap if the outmessage has just been created, i.e. it exists only in memory, not yet in database.

This un-registering is required because MDataMapper initially registered the outmessage in EIdentityMap using an automatically generated OID rather than the one computed based on the real outmessage's properties. Once the outmessage is unregistered, its proper messageID is obtained from the database before the outmessage is saved in the database. Obtaining messageID for the new outmessage completes all the required data needed by an EOutMessage. Updating of the newly created message can now be concluded by re-registering it to EIdentityMap with its OID and messageID.

Other changes from the GUI prototype used in Chapter 14 relate to the use of a proper dialog to confirm that the user wants to delete the message. A dialog box shown in Figure 16.20 now replaces Figure 14.7.

Figure 16.20
Window to delete
an outmessage

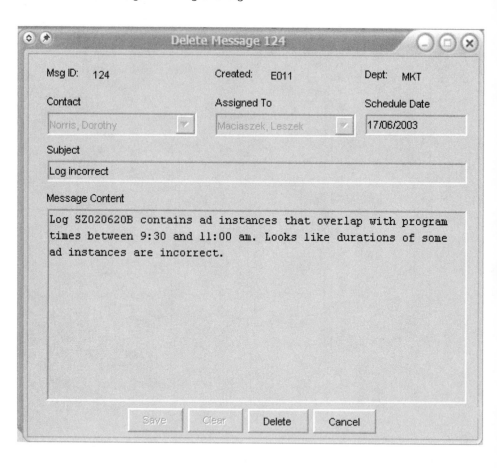

Figure 16.21
Error 'Unable to
Send'

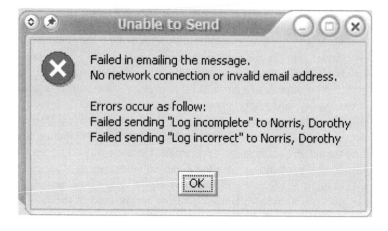

With this new window, the user is informed which outmessage is about to be deleted and therefore mistakes can be avoided. Fields in the dialog box are not editable.

There are other minor improvements in the UI design for Iteration 2. For example, an error message to show that particular outmessages have not been sent is now illustrated in Figure 16.21.

Summary

1. User interface (UI) design must consider two main kinds of client: a programmable client and a browser client. A *programmable client* assumes that a program resides and executes on the client and it has access to client storage resources. A *browser client* needs a server to download the requested data and to obtain instructions for rendering the data in a web-based UI.

2. Apart from delivering the system functionality to a user, the UI must satisfy a range of other requirements known under the term of *usability*. The main UI design guidelines are: (1) user in control, (2) interface consistency, (3) interface forgiveness, and (4) interface adaptability.

3. *Class libraries* for UI provide 'windowing' components and determine an application's look-and-feel. In the world of Java, the class library is called Java™ Foundation Classes (JFC). The majority of JFC consists of a UI component kit called Swing. The Swing components can be grouped into containers, menus, and controls.

4. *Containers* determine the prime look and feel of an application. They represent rectangular areas on a UI desktop and contain other components, including other containers, menus, and controls. Windows, dialogs, panes, and panels are examples of containers. Swing applies a 'layout manager' to place components within a container.

5. Windows and some other components can hold *menus*. Menu components are used to implement menu bars and their menu items. Checkboxes and radio buttons can be considered as kinds of menu items. Toolbars can also be classified as menus.

6. *Controls* represent the UI event model. They divide into actions buttons and other controls. Normal 'push' buttons, radio buttons, checkboxes and menu items are all kinds of action buttons. Other controls include list boxes of items to select multiple or just single item (combo box), scroll bars and sliders. One of the most versatile and useful controls is a tree view of containers and items.

7. The Swing *event model* is derived from the MVC framework. The UI event handling should conform to the Observer pattern.

8. The commonly used patterns in UI development are: Observer, Decorator, Chain of Responsibility, and Command.

9. The UI for the EM Iteration 2 consists of a primary window with various controls but without a menu bar and menu items. The UI includes also a number of secondary windows (dialog and message boxes).

Key Terms

AbstractButton	522
anonymous inner class	524
applet	516
application server	510
BorderLayout	518
browser client	509
C/S	*See* client/server
cascading popup menu	521
Chain of Responsibility pattern	530
checkbox	523
class library	514
client/server	509
combo box	523
Command pattern	531
containers	515
controls	521
Decorator pattern	530
default layer	519
dialog box	515
drag layer	520
dropdown list	*See* combo box
event model	523
event processing	523
Gang of Four patterns	528
GoF	*See* Gang of Four patterns
heavyweight classes	515
heavyweight Swing components	514
HTML client	*See* browser client
inner class	524
interface	510
interface adaptability	513
interface consistency	512
interface design	510
interface forgiveness	512
JApplet	516
JButton	522
JCheckBox	522
JCheckBoxMenuItem	520
JDialog	515
JFrame	515
JLayeredPane	518
JList	523
JMenu	520
JMenuBar	520
JMenuItem	520, 522
JOptionPane	515
JPanel	515
JRadioButton	522
JRadioButtonMenuItem	520
JScrollBar	523
JScrollPane	516, 523

JSlider	523
JSplitPane	517
JTabbedPane	516
JTable	517
JTextPane	516
JToolBar	521
JTree	523
JWindow	515
layout manager	518
layouts	518
lightweight classes	515
lightweight Swing components	514
list box	523
look and feel	509
menus	520
modal layer	519
model interface	526
multi-tier system	509
Observer pattern	523, 528
palette layer	519
patterns	528
picklist	*See* combo box
pluggability	514
popup layer	520
primary window	515
programmable client	509
provided interface	510
public interface	510
publisher	523
radio button	523
required interface	510
rich client	*See* programmable client
right-click popup menu	521
scroll bar	516
secondary window	515
split window	517
subscriber	523
Swing component	514
tabbed page	516
TableModel	526
thick client	*See* programmable client
thin client	*See* browser client
toolbar	521
UI design	510
UI	*See* user interface
usability	510
user interface	509
user-in-control	511
web client	*See* browser client
web server	510

Review Questions

1. A programmable client or a browser client may represent an application UI. What are these clients? What deployment options do they offer?

2. The notion of interface is used in software engineering in multiple contexts and with different meanings. What are popular uses of the word 'interface' in software engineering?

3. Which of the four UI design guidelines has been, according to you, most fundamental in the shift from procedural to object-oriented programming? Justify your standpoint.

4. Programming a Swing UI requires cooperation of lightweight and heavyweight components. How does this affect portability of Java applications?

5. What are the differences between a primary and a secondary window? Can an application have multiple primary windows? Can a primary window be modal?

6. What are the layout management and the layering management? Are these two concepts related? Explain.

7. What is the difference between checkboxes and radio buttons? Explain with examples.

8. What is the difference between a combo box and a list box? Explain how and when these two components are used?

9. Explain the pros and cons of the various implementation options for subscriber classes.

10. Explain the differences between the Chain of Responsibility and Command patterns. How do these patterns apply to the UI design?

11. Discuss the usage of patterns in the window design in Figure 16.10 (duplicated below for convenience as Figure 16.22). Consider the following patterns: Observer, Mediator, Decorator, and Command.

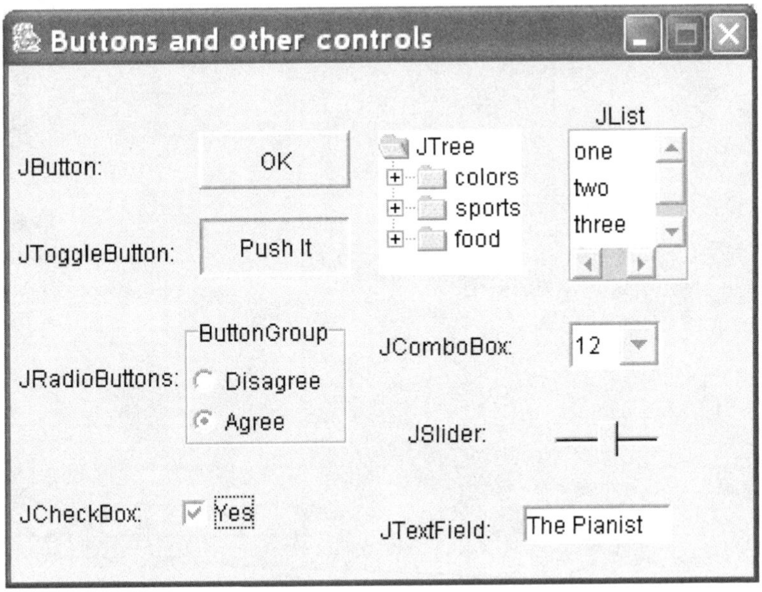

Figure 16.22
Buttons and other controls

Problem-Solving Exercises

1. Draw a sequence diagram to show how `Toggle Filter` (Figure 16.16) could be implemented. Assume you have one table model to store all the required data for display.

2. Draw a sequence diagram for deleting an outmessage in the EM application. Apply the `Identity Map` and `Data Mapper` patterns explained in Chapter 15. What are the interesting issues discovered?

3. Explain why Figure 16.15 'Obtaining a new outmessage placeholder' does not show how the OID and PK (`messageID`) of the new message are acquired. How is this done?

4. Draw a sequence diagram to show how `PMessageTableModel` could achieve the EM functionality of `Filter by Contact`.

5. The EM Iteration 2 specifies that the data displayed in the main window should be sorted by certain columns. Suppose it is allowed to perform the sorting by clicking on the table header. How could this be implemented? Use the Observer pattern (Section 9.3.4). Draw a sequence diagram and show a relevant code excerpt.

6. Figure 16.23 is the window implemented to satisfy the 'Create New Message' use case from the subflow S5, Figure 14.6. From the UI perspective, what is wrong with it? How could it be improved?

Figure 16.23
'Insert New
Message' window

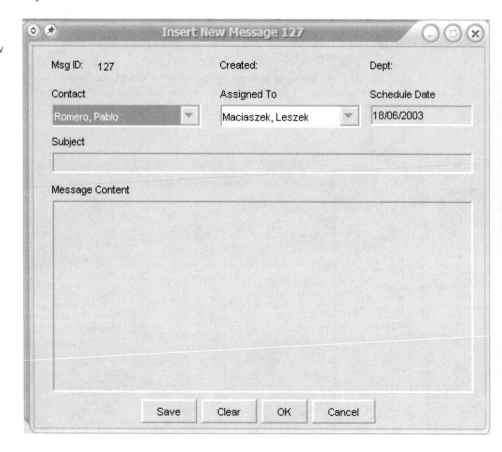

Chapter

17

Web-Based User Interface Design and Programming

An obvious trend in enterprise application development is to make applications web-enabled. A web-based application is ubiquitous – it can be used at any time from anywhere. Clearly, there are very few situations where availability of a web application is not an attractive proposition. Unfortunately, the challenges in building such applications are considerable. Most serious challenges are with the server software, not addressed in this chapter. This chapter concentrates on the client software.

A **web-based application** means that an Internet browser manages the rendering of UI content, but the business logic and database state exists on a server. This means, to begin with, that the **HyperText Markup Language** (HTML) is used. An HTML-formatted **web page** is a mix of the presentation content (e.g. some text) and rendering instructions (e.g. font size). HTML can be used to apply rendering instructions on a text in standard UI components, including Swing components. This can improve the presentation in applications that are not necessarily web-enabled.

A `JApplet` component in Swing provides a UI container that can be placed in a web page. Java applets and JavaScript are but two technologies that make the UI dynamic within a browser. This means that a web-based UI can be changed dynamically in both layout and content. HTML uses the <object> tag to download an object that lives in the URL space to the client. An **applet** can be such an object within an HTML page and retrieved from a web server.

For security reasons, an applet can be digitally signed. Applet lives in a **sandbox** environment. It is termed *sandbox* as it has limited and restricted access to system resources. An applet cannot access system resources unless an explicit permission is given to it. In technical terms, a Java applet consists of one or more *JavaBeans*, reusable components that are stored in a compressed form in a **Java Archive file** (JAR). This improves the download time.

The server technologies for web-based applications include servlets and Java Server Pages. A **servlet** is a Java code which creates HTML pages on the fly and which is managed by a web server. The code may be supported by Java Server Pages (JSPs). A web server provides a channel of communication between HTML client browsers and the database server. Once loaded in a web server, a servlet can connect to a database and maintain its connection for more than one client. *Servlet chaining* permits a servlet to pass a client request to another servlet.

If a servlet is a Java code with embedded HTML elements, then a **Java Server Page** (JSP) is the opposite – an HTML page with embedded Java code (*tags* or *scriptlets*) to manage the dynamic content of the page and to supply data to it. A JSP is dynamically compiled to a servlet prior to running.

Tags are really placeholders for Java code designed so that they are reusable (Section 17.4.8). Tags are a better proposition than scriptlets. **Scriptlets** mix Java code with web page content and sit, therefore, on the boundary of the presentation and control layers. As a result, they are not really reusable.

Modern technology for web-based user interfaces ensures a more strict separation of the presentation and control layers. Tags and metadata-driven frameworks based on XML provide this separation on the presentation (view) end. Jakarta **Struts** technology (Section 17.4.9) supported by XML enhances this separation on the control (controller) end, while at the same time offering a range of reusable tags for the presentation layer.

Related emerging technology on the presentation end (not discussed here) is **JavaServer Faces** (JSF) (JSF, 2003). The idea is to define in J2EE something like a Swing library (Chapter 16) for web-based user interfaces.

With simple **thin web clients** all business logic for the application is executed on a server. A web page request is sent to a web server. The web server performs the request and sends the result back to the client. At this point, in most cases, the connection between the client and the server is terminated.

With **thick web clients** it is possible to execute some business logic on the client. A good, albeit undemanding, example of executing business logic on a client is a validation of user input.

Components of a typical web-based system are deployed on at least three *tiers*: web client, web server, and database server. In some cases, a separate application server is desired. This chapter concentrates on enabling technologies for the web client tier and the web server tier. It also explains transactions on stateless Internet systems, but other technologies for the database server are discussed elsewhere in the book (Chapters 10, 20, and 21). Technologies for the application server are described in Chapter 22.

Technologies are a moving target. Principles and patterns are of more lasting value. This chapter revisits patterns explained earlier in the book and discusses them from the viewpoint of web-based applications. Some patterns that specifically apply to web systems are also introduced. The chapter concludes with a description of the servlet variant of the EM case study.

Enabling Technologies for the Web Client Tier

From the user's perspective, a **client** is what the user sees executing on the workstation. A user may not need to be aware whether the execution is in fact happening inside the workstation or remotely on some server machine. The software engineer's perspective on the client/ server separation is of course different. Either way, the **client/server** (C/S) is a logical division. The *client* requests services of a server and the **server** provides these services to authorized clients. The deployment of client and server components is secondary.

The technologies discussed in this section as the enablers for the web client tier are HTML, scripting languages, and applets. Explanations of other interesting technologies can be found in books dedicated to the topics (e.g. Singh *et al.*, 2002).

Basic HTML

The **HyperText Markup Language** (HTML) is the most common format found to represent web pages on the net. Pages stored in the HTML format use standard *formatting tags* and, as a result, allow the proper display by web browsers.

HTML follows the specification of the **World Wide Web Consortium** (W3C) (W3C, 2003). This consortium releases various specifications to ensure standardization of web technologies and their implementations. Despite the standardization efforts, web browser developers (vendors) may implement their own slightly modified versions of the specification. The term 'slightly' is perhaps understated, as it is commonly known that a web page will have different look and feel if viewed in different web browsers.

Figure 17.1 shows an HTML document displayed by a web browser. It is a simple example that is implemented to access the MovieActor database. The example shows

Figure 17.1
HTML document displayed by a browser

that the user can select a search condition (such as Title) and type in a search string value (such as Birdcage) in order to find details of a movie.

Listing 17.1 contains an example of an HTML document corresponding to the rendering of it shown in Figure 17.1. The listing includes basic *tags* for input processing.

Listing 17.1 Sample HTML document

```
Sample HTML document

1:        <html>
2:        <head>
3:        <!-- comment: just an example of a title -->
4:        <title> Testing MovieSearcher Servlet </title>
5:        <body>
6:           <form method="post" action="/SearchMovie">
7:           <table border=0 width="70%">
8:              <tr><td>Search movies by:</td>
9:                 <td><select name="searchBy">
10:                    <OPTION value="TitleV">Title
11:                    <OPTION value="ActorV">Actor
12:                    <OPTION value="DirectorV">Director
13:                 </select></td>
14:                 <td><input name=searchField type=text></td>
15:              </tr>
16:              <tr><td></td><td><input type="submit" value="Submit">
17:              <input type=reset value="Clear"</td></tr>
18:           </table>
19:           </form>
20:        </body>
21:        </html>
```

An HTML document has to be started with the `<html>` tag and closed by the `</html>` tag (Lines 1 and 21). Optionally, an HTML document may use a *heading section* `<head>` to inform the web browser about its *metadata* (data about data, i.e. informational data about the document itself). The `<title>` tag can be used in the heading section as indicated by Line 4. *Comments* can appear anywhere in the document provided they are placed inside `<!--` and `-->` tag (Line 3).

Most **HTML tags** have to be enclosed by placing / on the tag name such as in `</html>`. Some tags do not have to be explicitly closed, such as `<p>`, which stands for the start of a paragraph, or `<option>` (Line 10). A tag may have many attributes to allow *tag customization*, for example `method` and `action` are attributes of the `form` tag (Line 6).

The *body*, `<body>`, of an HTML dictates what data is to be displayed inside the web browser frame. Most HTML tags are applicable only within this tag.

A common tag, used to represent data in a tabular format, is `<table>` (Lines 7–18). The *table* on Line 7 defines the attribute `border` with size 0 indicating that no border should be drawn. This can be observed in Figure 17.1. Data in the table is arranged by its *rows* (`<tr>`, Line 8). Each row may have many *columns* (`<td>`, Line 8), but usually the same number of columns for all rows.

This chapter discusses only the HTML tags necessary when accepting user inputs into a *form*. This is indicated by the `<form>` tag on Lines 6–19. Fields in the form will be transmitted to a server or external sources when the user finishes processing the form.

The form has two types of the `method` tag – a `post` to indicate that the data collected in the form is to be posted to the server, and a `get` to indicate that it acquires the data from the server. Line 6 shows that the data will be posted to the server.

The *server URL*, which the form will call, is placed in the `action` attribute. This is usually a CGI script, servlet/JSP, or other web page program capable of processing the data. Line 6 in Listing 17.1 shows that the form processor is handled by a *servlet* called `SearchMovie`, located on the root of the server (indicated by `/`).

Inputs can be collected by means of dropdown lists (the `<select>` tag (Line 9) and the `<input>` tag (Lines 14, 16, 17). Each of the chosen and filled input is transferred to the server. The server identifies the input by its name. For example, the dropdown list has the name `searchBy`. In the case of the list in Listing 17.1, only the user's selected value, as indicated by the `<option>` tag, will be sent to the server. For example, if the user selects `Actor` from the dropdown list, then `searchBy` is bound to the `Actor`'s list of values.

There are other types of input. Listing 17.1 only shows `text`, `submit`, and `reset`. The `text` type indicates that the input has to be placed in a text field. The `submit` type indicates that a button is required to be shown in place of this `input` tag. The `submit` button will trigger the submission of data provided in the form to the form's `action` web address. The `reset` type allows the fields in the form to be reset to their original values, usually either empty or default selection.

Other input types are `button`, `radio`, `hidden`, etc. The `button` type displays a button on the screen ready for the user to click on. The `radio` type represents a radio button with unselected state. The `hidden` type is an attribute in which the server can remember certain user non-modifiable values. A hidden value is simply passed to the server for storage.

This chapter does not show how the elements in a web page can be organized into a nicely viewed page. This could have been done by optimizing attributes of various tags (such as the `align` attribute) as well as by formatting the tags (such as `<center>`). The usage of the `frame` tag is also not demonstrated here. The `Frame` tag allows a collection of web pages to be displayed together within a single frame.

Scripting Language 17.1.2

Scripting languages are used in HTML documents to enrich user interactions. Scripts such as VBScript and JavaScript are used to perform quick validation of inputs, simple animations, and other activities to make the web page 'alive'. Scripts, when they are used, need to be declared in the heading of the HTML document. This chapter provides an example of a JavaScript to perform input validation.

JavaScript was introduced by Netscape. The JavaScript specifications are available in a compressed zip file on Netscape (2003). Microsoft provides variations to this script known as **JScript**. The third scripting language supported by the HTML specification is

VBScript. This is a variation of Visual Basic (VB) from Microsoft. Both JScript and VBScript documentation can be found at the Microsoft website (Microsoft, 2003a).

Listing 17.2 shows a `JavaScript` (Lines 3–16) to validate whether the input given by the user (Line 20) is within the range of 0–100 (Line 18). The script is placed in the heading section of the document. It is 'fired' once the user clicks on the submit button, as indicated by the `onSubmit` event handler (Line 18). *Events* are part of attributes within various form elements. They can be placed in any of input elements that can be modified by the user. Script types are declared in web pages with the `script language` attribute (Line 3).

Listing 17.2 Sample JavaScript

```
Sample JavaScript

1:          <HEAD>
2:              <TITLE> Form Validation </TITLE>
3:              <SCRIPT LANGUAGE="JavaScript">
4:                  <!--
5:                      function checkIt(int lower, int upper) {
6:                          var strval = document.sampleForm.percent.value;
7:                          var intval = parseInt(strval);
8:                          if ( lower < intval && intval < upper ) {
9:                              return( true );
10:                         } else {
11:                             alert("Input " + strval + " is out of "+
                                    lower+"-"+upper+" range");
12:                             return( false );
13:                         }
14:                     }
15:                 <!-- end script -->
16:             </SCRIPT>
17:          </HEAD>
18:          <FORM NAME="sampleForm" METHOD="post"
                    ACTION="/SearchMovie" onSubmit="checkIt(0,100)">
19:              <P>Percentage given:
20:              <INPUT TYPE="text" NAME="percent" VALUE="1">
21:              <BR><INPUT TYPE="submit">
22:          </FORM>
```

As with most scripting languages, a JavaScript is *statically parsed* to check for syntactic errors. However, a JavaScript is not compiled as per Java or C/C++ compilation. In compiled languages, the **static binding** is commonly used to resolve all program references at compile time.

References in a JavaScript are dynamically bound. They are resolved at runtime as needed. An example of the **dynamic binding** in scripting is the modification of `onSubmit="checkIt(0,100)"` (**Line 18**) to `onSubmit="checkItWrong(0,100)"`. The web page will be displayed exactly the same, but the error will be displayed on the page when the button is clicked.

The flexibility of dynamic binding makes JavaScript a lightweight device that can avoid excessive checking of code. Adding and removing code can be done freely, thus facilitating incremental development of the code. On the negative side, some errors may not be discovered until runtime, when the user activates the script statements (e.g. when clicking on a button as in Listing 17.2, Line 21).

Web browser vendors provide slightly different implementations of scripts, even though they all claim 'conformance' to the standard. This makes it difficult for web developers to develop web pages with confidence that they will run properly on various browsers.

Embedding of JavaScript is also tricky. For example, older versions of web browsers (that support the older HTML specifications) do not understand the `<script>` tag and therefore ignore it and proceed to the next available tag. This is the reason why the body of the script in Listing 17.2 is 'protected' by a *comment* tag (Lines 4 and 15). When an older browser finds the comment tag, it will ignore the script's body and therefore will not cause parse errors. A newer browser will find that the comment tag (Line 4) does not have its matching comment-close tag and it will ignore Line 4 altogether.

The script in Listing 17.2 will only be executed when the user clicks on the submit button (the `onSubmit` action). The script is executed via calls to `checkIt()` on Line 18. The `checkIt` function (Line 5) checks the value of input text, presented by Line 20, to see if it has the correct value (as demanded by the `lower` and `upper` parameters of `checkIt()`).

JavaScript can access the current web page via its objects. This is shown on Line 6 where the script checks the `value` of the text field named `percent` (declared on Line 20). The `value` is returned as a string which needs to be converted into an integer via the call to a built-in function `parseInt()`. If the input value is valid (Lines 8–9), then the script returns `true` (Line 9), otherwise it displays a message box indicating the wrong input and returns `false` (Line 12).

When the event handler `onSubmit` finishes calling the script, it decides whether to continue execution of the event as planned or to stop the execution. This is the main reason why the script has to return a `true` or `false` value. The `true` value indicates that everything is checked and the execution may continue, which in this case will send the data, obtained from the form, to `SearchMovie`, as indicated by the `action` attribute (Line 18). The `false` value cancels the calling of `SearchMovie`.

Applet: Thin and Thick   17.1.3

Applets can be categorized into thin and thick. Both are sets of classes that make up an application. The distinction is based on how much code resides on the client and how much on the server (Figure 17.2). Both thin and thick applets have their server counterpart. However, a **thin applet** performs most of its activities on the server, and a **thick applet** performs most of its activities on the client.

A *thin applet* implies that the minimal set of code will be loaded into a client computer. It requires heavy support from the server end to achieve its full functionality. Due to a smaller size of the client code, a thin applet loads much faster and it is therefore preferable for a slow connection Internet.

The advantages of a thin applet are usually the disadvantages of a thick applet, and vice versa. The following are some characteristics of a thin applet:

Figure 17.2
Applet–server
communication

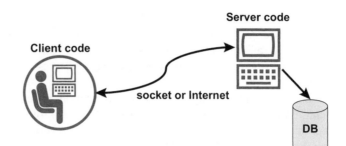

- It loads the client machine faster since the client code consists only of the presentation layer classes.
- It requires heavy processing on the server as the presentation classes do not do much calculation/logic (accordingly, extra classes are needed on the server).
- It decouples the presentation layer classes from those located on the server. Changes on either side (client or server code) usually do not affect the other side, unless the changes are dramatic and affect the application functionality.
- Thin applets are more difficult to maintain as there are possibly two places of modification: server and client code.
- It is more difficult to detect errors since they could come from the client code as well as from the server code. It may be difficult to establish if the server code has the difficulties (server unavailability, for example) or the socket/Internet connection is unreliable.

Listing 17.3 explains a subset of *applet methods*. The init() method is the place to put all the GUI-related methods. The start() method activates the program and responds to user's activities (start threads, for example). The stop() method stops the execution of applet's activities, such as stopping the UI painting threads. The destroy() method releases all resources and prepares the applet to be unloaded from the system.

Listing 17.3 Applet method summary

```
void    destroy()
            Called by the browser or applet viewer to inform this applet that it is being reclaimed and
            that it should destroy any resources that it has allocated.
void    init()
            Called by the browser or applet viewer to inform this applet that it has been loaded into
            the system.
void    start()
            Called by the browser or applet viewer to inform this applet that it should start its
            execution.
void    stop()
            Called by the browser or applet viewer to inform this applet that it should stop its execution
```

Figure 17.3
Applet state
transition mode

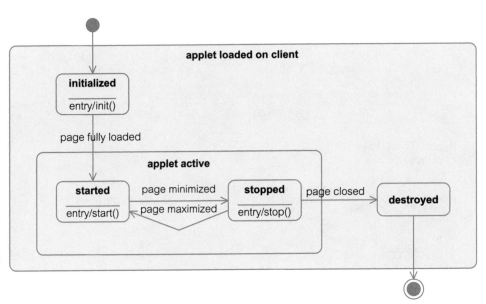

Figure 17.3 shows an applet state transition model. An applet goes through the state transitions as required by the browser. Initially the browser ensures that the applet's `init()` method is called to initialize the applet after its constructor is called. Once it is `initialized`, the applet can enter the `active` state. It is activated via the call to its `start()` method. The applet construction is done before its initialization. This is the main reason why the UI constructions cannot be placed on an applet's constructor. At this point, the applet is not fully loaded to the system yet. When the applet is in the `started` state, it will remain in this state as long as the web page is open.

There are times when an applet changes its state to `stopped`. This depends on the way the applet is implemented, but it is usually when the applet is minimized or when it is not visible on the screen. The `stopped` state allows the application to save the system's resources acquired by inactive applets. When the applet is no longer needed, such as when the web page is closed, it gets into the `destroyed` state. At this point, the applet releases all the system resources it has acquired.

Figure 17.4 shows an example of an applet. This applet is a chat engine applet whereby users connect to a central server and chat with their friends. More sophisticated variants of such an applet are implemented by ICQ, MSN and other chat engines that plug to the web. A combination of applet and scripting language seems to be a perfect match for this type of application. Other examples of common applications that use applets are banking applications, stock monitoring via the Internet, and similar applications that require extensive processing on a server and less on a client.

An applet executing in a web page is placed in a very restrictive environment called the sandbox model. The sandbox model is a set of rules to restrict an applet's access to its host system. It prevents the applet from accessing vulnerable host system resources. If an applet were allowed to have unlimited memory access and operating system resources, someone with malicious intent could harm the system. All applets are placed in a sandbox in which they are created and executed. They can only access resources in the confined limits of the

Figure 17.4
Simple applet
example

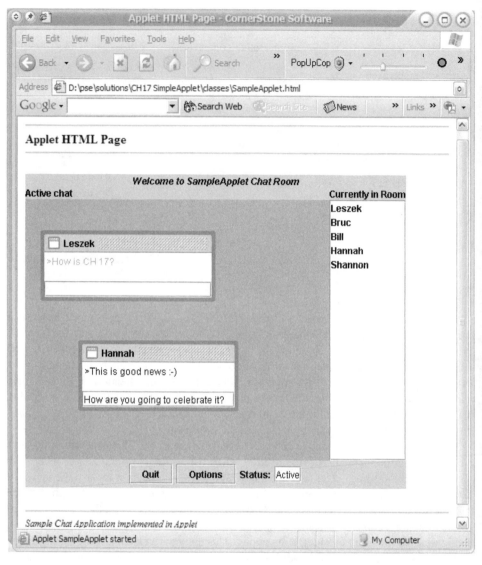

Figure 17.4
Simple applet
example

sandbox. So-called **trusted applets** are executed outside the sandbox according to the privileges given.

The Java sandbox model relies on a three-tier defense system, as follows:

1. *The bytecode verifier* – all Java code is compiled and verified during compilation; this ensures that only the code that conforms to the Java language specification is allowed to run in a Java Virtual Machine.

2. *The applet class loader* – an applet class loader loads the applet code; the class loader prevents other classes from replacing important Java API classes.

3. *The security manager* – a security manager restricts activities performed by an applet; it permits certain operations and restricts dangerous ones.

In short, an applet is not allowed to:

- read from a file system of the host machine (including files, properties, etc.)
- write or delete a file
- connect to a network port on any machine except the HTTP server it comes from
- execute or load another programs/library/DLL code.

The only way for an applet to access the host system resources is if the developer grants *permission* to the applet. When **signed applets** are downloaded, the user will be prompted to allow the applet to get the permissions required. The applet will not be executed if the user does not allow it. This chapter does not cover applet signing, as it is dependent on the browser's implementation. Steps to sign an applet are slightly different among Internet Explorer, Sun, and Netscape.

An applet version of Iteration 2 of the EM case study is a **thick applet**. Transforming the already existing Iteration 2 code into a thick applet is easy under the PCMEF architectural design. Transformation is done on the PWindow class so that it inherits from JApplet instead of JFrame. Figure 17.5 shows an applet running on an AppletViewer. The functionality of this applet is the same as for the Iteration 2 Java application discussed in this part of the book.

Enabling Technologies for the Web Server Tier

17.2

The **web server** tier manages the communication between web clients and the application's business logic. The *business logic* itself can be implemented within the web server or within a dedicated application server using, for example, the EJB technology. Other typical functions of the web tier include (Singh *et al.*, 2002):

- presentation of the dynamic content in web pages, including HTML, graphics, images, sound, and video
- controlling the screen flow in web clients (i.e. the sequences in which screens can be displayed)
- maintaining transactional states of clients.

An early web server technology, to supply dynamic content to the clients, was the *Common Gateway Interface* (CGI). This technology is now superseded by more capable J2EE technologies of servlets and JSP pages. These two technologies are discussed next.

Servlet

17.2.1

The difference between an applet and a servlet is that a **servlet** is fully located on the server. There is no client code as such in the servlet. The client is an HTML page or other pages, such as JSP or ASP. A servlet is a dedicated service running on a server machine to

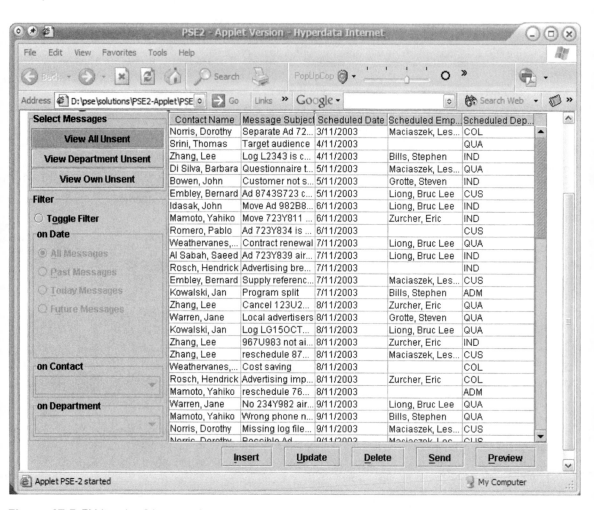

Figure 17.5 EM Iteration 2 in an applet

serve multiple clients. It is a Java code that has been compiled and deployed on a web server.

'Servlet' is a derivation of the term 'server applet'. It awaits requests from clients, be it HTML client or JSP, and replies accordingly. Figure 17.6 shows how a web server responds to a request from a client computer (HTML). The web server houses the **servlet container** (or *web container*) that is responsible for finding, loading, and executing the requested servlet.

The servlet is able to access the server's resources, including the database (DB). It then usually returns HTML format output. In fact, the output could be another form, but for this chapter's purposes, it is assumed to be HTML.

The following list presents advantages of a servlet as compared with other technologies, such as CGI:

Web server

Figure 17.6
Servlet
communication

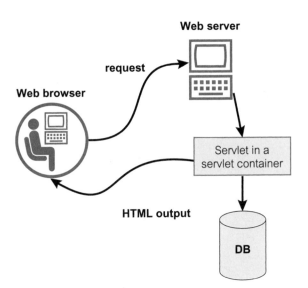

request

Web browser

Servlet in a
servlet container

HTML output

DB

- Stronger type checking (the servlet needs to be compiled and deployed, whereas CGI is parsed only when needed).
- Late binding of any references (the servlet container is free to implement strategies to improve the servlet invocation speed by late binding of references, i.e. binding at runtime when really needed).
- Richer interaction with the server (the servlet technology allows multiple concurrent execution paths with its server, as opposed to CGI that allows only a single path).
- Efficient (the servlet pool is maintained by a web container and the pool is usually fully optimized, whereas CGI processes are created only when a CGI request occurs; they use operating system threads and are therefore more expensive to create).
- More powerful in input and output handling (the servlet technology provides extensive functionalities to process and parse inputs/outputs; the developers can use standard Java API to achieve the appropriate outcome).
- Portable (the servlet can be moved between different web servers and containers as long they conform to the J2EE specification).
- Secure from buffer overflow and other attacks (Java provides checking for various security issues, such as 'array out of bounds' checking, which would have to be done manually by a CGI developer).

The **servlet active state model** is shown in Figure 17.7. Servlet states are fully controlled by its container. The servlet container ensures that enough servlets are in the pool to serve the clients. If the pool may overflow then the container removes servlets not currently needed in order to conserve resources. The servlet goes into the `active` state when the server container (the web server) invokes its `init()` method. When it is `active`, various requests (HTTP requests) can be handled by the servlet as well as by HTTP posts. When the servlet is no longer in use, it is usually destroyed by the container by calling its `destroy()` method. This allows the servlet to release all its resources.

Figure 17.7
Servlet active state
model

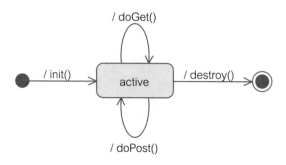

Figure 17.8
Servlet invocation

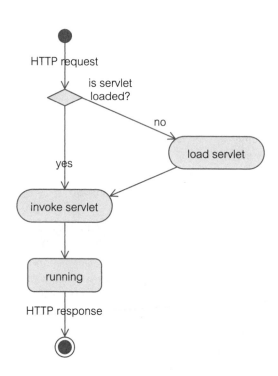

The **servlet container** (web server) supports various strategies to maintain the pool of active servlets. One servlet can serve multiple clients and does not maintain the state of individual clients. Figure 17.8 illustrates how a request is intercepted by the server and redirected to the servlet container. The servlet container ensures that the servlet is loaded (the activity `load server`) and initialized (the activity `invoke server`). At this point, the servlet is in the `running` state. Requests to a running servlet return an output via HTTP response. As previously mentioned, the output can be of any type, typically it is HTML output.

A servlet can handle requests from various clients, such as HTML, applet, JSP, etc. Figure 17.9 is an example of the servlet output for a request shown in Figure 17.1. It lists the details of a requested movie in a table format.

Figure 17.9
SearchMovie
servlet

JSP

The second J2EE technology commonly used is **Java Server Pages** (JSP). JSP is a variation of the servlet technology. JSP separates the business logic from the presentation. The business logic is represented by a servlet whereas the presentation is the JSP. The JSP communication path between a client and the server (Figure 17.10) is not much different from that shown for the servlet in Figure 17.6.

The main difference is that a *JSP request* requires a couple of additional preparatory steps before it can be invoked. A JSP page needs to be parsed by a servlet engine (a servlet container). This generates the servlet code that needs to be compiled and instantiated by the container. Once the servlet is ready, a normal invocation happens, similar to the servlet invocation in Figure 17.8.

JSP shares most of the servlet advantages. JSP does not provide any new capabilities that could not be accomplished with a servlet. However, separating the presentation from the content provides a separation of concerns. In a typical scenario, the dynamic content can be achieved by a servlet, which is then *formatted* by a JSP page to be displayed on the client.

Listing 17.4 shows an example of a JSP page. Lines 1–4 contain *directive tags*. A JSP page could extend, import, or set particular system properties using directive tags. The page is capable of using Java API as in a servlet or in a Java application. Lines 5–54 show typical HTML tags intermixed with JSP tags.

Figure 17.10
JSP
communication

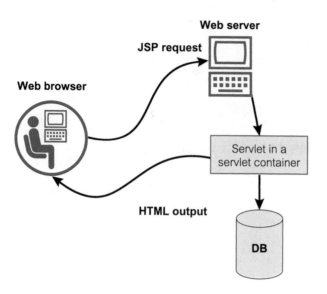

Web server

JSP request

Web browser

1) Send request to JSP
   Servlet engine will then
   • parse the JSP
   • generate servlet code
   • compile the servlet
   • instantiate the servlet
2) Invoke the servlet

Servlet in a
servlet container

HTML output

DB

The JSP declarations can be placed within a *declaration tag* `<%! %>` (Lines 9–44).
Alternatively, the same declaration can be placed in a *scriptlet tag* `<% %>`.

Listing 17.4 provides functions to initialize and destroy a JSP page (`jspInit()` and
`jspDestroy()`, respectively). The necessary connection is created in `jspInit()`

Listing 17.4 Sample JSP

```
Sample JSP page

 1:   <%@page contentType="text/html"%>
 2:   <%@page import="movie.*" %>
 3:   <%@page import="java.util.*" %>
 4:   <%@page import="java.io.*" %>
 5:   <html>
 6:   <head><title>Movie JSP</title></head>
 7:   <body>
 8:   <%-- declare and put basic function --%>
 9:   <%!
10:       movie.Connection conn;
11:       Exception error = null;
12:       public void jspInit(){ //override initialization of the JSP
13:           try{
14:               conn = new Connection();
15:           }catch(Exception exc){
16:               error = exc;
17:           }
```

```
18:        }
19:        public void jspDestroy(){ //ensure proper resource release
20:            conn.close();
21:            conn = null;
22:        }
23:        public void displayMoviesByLeadingActors(ServletResponse
                                                    response)
24:            throws Exception{
25:            PrintWriter out = response.getWriter();
26:            if(error != null){
27:                out.println("<h1>Error has occurred</h1>");
28:                error.printStackTrace(out);
29:                return;
30:            }
31:            out.println("<h1>The database content</h1>");
32:            out.println("<table border=2>");
33:            out.println("<tr><th>Movie Title</th><th>Main actor</th>
                         <th>Director</th></tr>");
34:            Collection listedAs = conn.getLeadingActorsByQuery();
35:            Iterator it = listedAs.iterator();
36:            while(it.hasNext()){
37:                ListedAs la = (ListedAs) it.next();
38:                Movie m = la.getMovie();
39:                Actor a = la.getActor();
40:                out.println("<tr><td>"+m.getMovieTitle()+"</td><td>"+
                         a.getActorName()+"</td><td>"+m.getDirector()+
                         "</td></tr>");
41:            }
42:            out.println("</table>");
43:        }
44:    %>
45:
46:    <%-- use below to include javabeans --%>
47:    <%--<jsp:useBean id="listedAs" scope="session"
        class="movie.ListedAs" /> --%>
48:    <%-- <jsp:getProperty name="listedAs"
             property="getLeadingActorsByQuery" /> --%>
49:    <%--<jsp:include page="/DisplayMessageContent.jsp"
        flush=true /> -->
50:    <%-- this requested the display of all movies --%>
51:    <% displayMoviesByLeadingActors(response); %>
52:    <p>Click <a href="index.html">here</a> to go to main page.
53:    </body>
54:    </html>
```

(Lines 12–18) and closed in `jspDestroy()` (Lines 19–22). The function `display-MoviesBy LeadingActors()` retrieves data from the connection created during the servlet initialization and displays the data in a table format (Lines 32–42) to an HTTP response parameter (Line 23).

JSP is able to use **JavaBeans** and **Enterprise JavaBeans** (EJB) as indicated by Lines 47 and 48 (provided the `<!--` and `-->` comment tag is removed). JavaBeans are a set of Java classes that follow predefined rules to allow inspections and modifications on their properties. EJB is similar to JavaBeans but it supports the capability of accessing shared business logic and a shared database. EJB is fully managed by a server container (usually an *application server*).

The `id` attribute on Line 47 is treated as a reference name (variable name) in the current page. The `class` attribute dictates the full class name of the JavaBeans. The `scope` attribute dictates circumstances under which the JavaBeans is active. As a result, it defines the web application *state*. The scope can have the following values:

- page – the bean is only valid for the current page
- request – the bean is active for the current request only
- session – the bean is active for the current session
- application – the bean is active from the start until the finish of the application, including multiple sessions if necessary.

The `scope` attribute is used by the servlet container to effectively calculate the proper strategy to maintain the number of servlets for client requests. The servlet container has to ensure that the servlet's state is obeyed according to the scope. If the servlet scope is a session, then the container has to ensure that the particular servlet exists for the full extent of the session.

Figure 17.4 Line 48 shows that a JavaBeans property can be queried and changed via a JSP tag as well as by a common Java function invocation. Line 48 is equivalent to a single Java call `listedAs.getLeadingActorsByQuery();`.

Line 48 shows the `include` directive in JSP. This `include` directive can be used to embed another page into the current page. This is useful in developing complex web pages. JSP encourages page reuse through this approach.

Line 51 calls the function declared on Line 23. If the function on Line 23 returns a string instead of displaying directly to the HTTP response, then the scriptlet (`<% %>`, Line 51) needs to be modified to an expression tag (`<%= %>`). The expression tag would allow the output of a method to be displayed as part of its HTML code.

Global variables can be accessed in a JSP page. These variables must be referenced from JSP tags, as mentioned above. One such variable is `response` that corresponds to the HTTP response of the current page (Line 51). Global variables allow the current JSP page to interact with its server environment. Other variables, such as `exception`, are used to maintain the states or events that occur between JSP pages.

Figure 17.11 shows the result of the execution of the code from Listing 17.4. JSP is tag-based and as such its power is realized in the reuse of tags. The JSP specification provides a standard library, called *Custom Tag Library*, which can be used to develop and reuse pre-existing tags for different web pages.

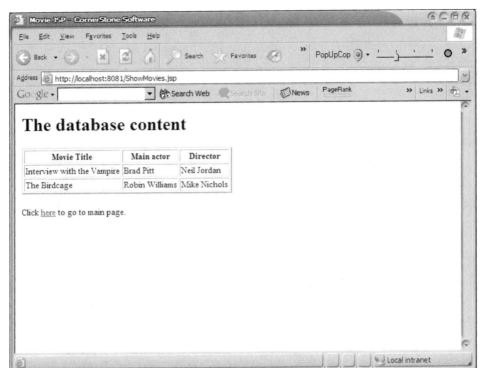

Figure 17.11
HTML output of
JSP code

Transactions on Stateless Internet Systems   17.3

Systems developed for the Internet are constrained by the way the Internet is implemented. Internet systems are **stateless systems**. They are based on server applications that service requests without connecting (distinguishing between) successive requests from the same client.

Internet systems are built to be stateless since they are purely based on the **pull technology**. Data needs to be requested (pulled) from the server. The server runs continuously awaiting client requests. There are numerous advantages of stateless systems; some of them are:

- simpler server application programming – server application does not need to remember all possible states of interactions that it may have with every client

- simpler server application maintenance and duplication – server application and its data could easily be the subject of server load-balancing; multiple servers could serve the same application clients without the clients knowing the originating server identity

- robust – most Internet systems are deployed on many servers rather than a single server; the same service could be received from different servers thus making the clients less dependent on a particular server.

There are, however, many web applications where it is essential to maintain the transaction states of the clients. Consider a typical e-business application where the buyers can place multiple items in a to-buy basket (a shopping cart) and keep browsing for additional items before eventually placing the order (or not placing it). There is a need in such applications to remember the content of the basket until the decision to order is taken. The states of the basket need to be known between different interactions.

The question is, then, how could a stateless Internet system maintain states? Are there any ways to change the stateless system to a stateful one? Not quite, but it is possible to require the client to remember the states.

There are two principal approaches to remembering the states. The first approach is *by passing the state* acquired in an initial request to successive requests. The second approach is by storing the states in a *session object* that the client has when it initiates the first request to the server. It is also common that the Internet system will combine both approaches to maximize the amount of data that it can remember.

The HTTP request in Listing 17.5 corresponds to the output for the SearchMovie servlet shown in Figure 17.9. The listing illustrates the state passing approach. In the code, previously acquired states are passed to the server as *parameters* to be maintained for the next request. The server responds to the requests according to the values of parameters. As the lists of parameters change and grow in size, the server application is getting more complex.

Listing 17.5 States passed as parameters

```
States passed as parameters

http://localhost:8081/SearchMovie?searchBy=ActorV&searchField
=Birdcage
```

Parameters in Listing 17.5 are separated by an ampersand (&). The start of the parameter is indicated by the question mark (?). The HTTP request is sent to SearchMovie with two parameters, searchBy is assigned to ActorV and searchField is assigned to Birdcage.

Listing 17.5 has limitations that could be addressed by a session-based state storage:

- It is getting awkward when there are many states to maintain. The web address is getting too long and error-prone in programming.

- User interactions are complex in the sense that many pathways can result from any particular page. Removing a parameter not required in the parameter list in the next request may cause difficulties later when this parameter needs to be used in future requests. It is frequently not possible to acquire the same information again.

- It is not possible to store a composite or complex state, such as states of multimedia objects. Such states are usually non-convertible to a simple text format that can be passed as parameters.

- Some parameters must not be displayed due to security reason, such as a tax file number or pin number.

A **session object** can be used to remember states and address the shortcomings of the state passing approach. A session object is created when the client connects to the server and it is maintained for the duration of the connection. The server can query and change the states stored in the session object and it is therefore able to provide stateful responses to the client.

Listing 17.6 Line 1 shows how the client state, identified by a previously stored userID, can be retrieved from the session object. In this example, the application checks whether the user reaches the page through its normal path, i.e. the userID is known to the session object. The application will not continue if it determines that the userID is null (Lines 2–5).

Listing 17.6 States stored in session

```
States stored in session

1:   Object userID = request.getSession().getAttribute("userid");
2:   if(userID == null){
3:       reportError();
4:       return;
5:   }
6:   request.getSession().setAttribute("root_page","/SearchMovie");
7:
8:   String prevPage = (String) request.getParameter("ref_page");
```

An active session object can be acquired from an HTTP request as shown on Lines 1 and 6. The states stored in the session object are identified by their names. Line 6 shows that the attribute root_page with the value /SearchMovie is stored in the session.

Listing 17.6 also shows an example of the parameter retrieval (Line 8). The parameter ref_page is acquired from the HTTP request. The server can only acquire parameters passed by clients. It cannot set the parameters to be passed back to the client.

As opposed to the way databases handle transactions (Chapter 21), the J2EE specification does not demand that a session state must be recoverable after a crash or failure (Singh *et al.*, 2002). Therefore, applications using J2EE implementations that supply recoverability extensions risk being less portable.

Patterns and the Web

17.4

There is an overwhelming amount of software pattern documentation and literature available today. Separating 'the wheat from the chaff' among this jungle of patterns is not easy. The approach to explaining patterns taken in this book is to introduce them within the context of software engineering topics discussed and to address only the most established and influential patterns.

The patterns discussed so far included Façade, Abstract Factory, Chain of Responsibility, Observer, Decorator, Command, Mediator, Identity Map, Data Mapper, Lazy Load and

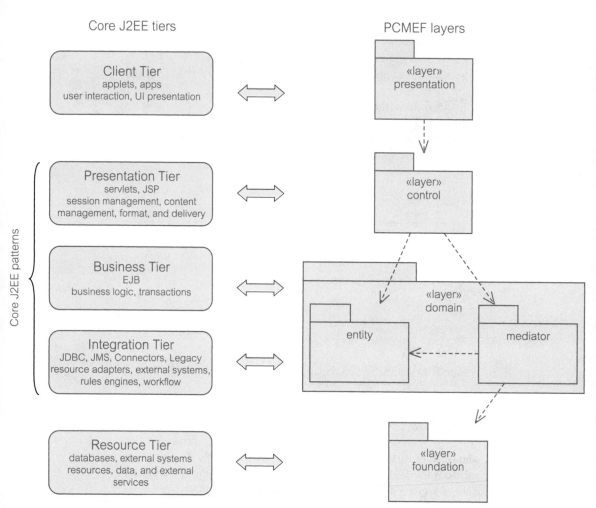

Figure 17.12 J2EE tiers and PCMEF layers

a few more. These are popular patterns from the **GoF** and **PEAA** sets of patterns, i.e. **Gang of Four** (Gamma *et al.*, 1995) and **Patterns of Enterprise Application Architecture** (Fowler 2003). In the web context, the most significant is the set of patterns known as *Core J2EE* patterns (Alur *et al.*, 2003).

The Core J2EE patterns define best software engineering practices for the development with J2EE technologies, including servlets, JSP and EJB, web services, XML. Core J2EE patterns are classified by tiers. The Core J2EE tiers (Alur *et al.*, 2003) map nicely to the PCMEF layers used in this book. This is illustrated in Figure 17.12.

Rather than introducing the whole new range of patterns for the web, this section brings in only one new J2EE pattern (Front Controller) and concentrates on discussing how some of the previously introduced patterns can be used with web technologies. New technologies such as JSP tags and Struts are also explained to illustrate the usage of these patterns.

Patterns discussed in this section are Observer, Composite, Factory Method, Strategy, Decorator, MVC, and Front Controller.

Observer

The **Observer pattern**, discussed already in Sections 9.3.4 and 16.4.1, is a set of *observers* that are notified automatically about changes in the *subject*. The pattern seems to suit web-based applications, but this is, perhaps surprisingly, not always true. Consider a web-based application consisting of a servlet/JSP code (subject) and a set of client pages (observers). It may be expected that client pages should be notified when the server has new updates. This, however, cannot be done on stateless Internet systems, as the server has no control over its clients.

There are ways to get around the *statelessness* of the Internet system (Section 17.3), but they do not let the Observer pattern play a role because of the browser's limitation. The statelessness nature of web applications makes the state change notification process a difficult task. To receive the changes, web browsers need to re-query the subject's state.

Java applications using applets are normally a good match for the Observer pattern. Consider a stock exchange applet that is used to monitor the ups and downs of a particular stock price. This particular system will have a server application that has a list of stock ids and a set of applets connected to the server. The applets are observers to the server. The server is the subject. The server maintains the list of connected applets and informs the applets of changes in stock prices.

A common implementation of such applications is by forcing the client's applets to query the server in fixed time intervals. A contrasting implementation would be to make the server continuously transfer the stock data to applets. The tradeoff is in the efficiency and implementation difficulty. The latter approach forces the server to work hard endlessly as long as the applet is connected. Data is transferred to applets irrespective of whether the user is monitoring the particular stock price or other stock prices. The former is more efficient in that only the stock data monitored currently by the user is requested from the server. The server does not need to keep applets' states and to launch dedicated threads to serve every applet. The applet does the hard work of polling the server in preset intervals.

Composite

The **Composite pattern** (Gamma *et al.*, 1995) specifies that an object can be constructed as a composition of other objects. This forms a hierarchical tree of objects. The feature of this pattern is that the user treats both individual objects as well as composite objects uniformly. Message passing using *delegation* down the composition tree can be efficiently used to service user's requests. The composite object delegates received requests to a component object that can perform the service.

Composite is a natural match for the organization of pages displayed on the web. A web page can be composed of multiple pages thanks to the HTML *frame tag*. However, this is somewhat different from the common usage of Composite in development of more conventional software systems. Because the client is aware of the composition, it does not need to direct the request to the *composite object* (frame page). It can send the message directly to an individual object contained in the frame.

Composite can be used for the creation of single web pages, such as those developed by JSP. The developer can use the JSP `<jsp:include>` directive, such as in Listing 17.4. The reuse of web pages is achieved through the usage of this `include` directive. However, unlike in a typical application of Composite where the composite objects are rendered on the screen, the JSP `include` directive combines multiple pages into a single web page. This way, the JSP `include` directive allows a common *look and feel* to be achieved across the website.

Composite is commonly used with other patterns such as the GoF Template and Factory Method patterns. The *Template* pattern rules the placement of web pages. It can ensure that a common web page, such as a company heading or logo, is shown consistently on all web pages. The *Factory Method* pattern can be used to generate or embed the content of web pages into a composite web page, thus providing dynamic behavior on this web page.

17.4.3 Factory Method

The **Factory Method pattern** (Gamma *et al.*, 1995) defines that subclasses of the base class are responsible for creating the *product*. A client only knows the existence of the base class. It calls the base class's method to create certain objects (the product). However, the base class does not know how to create the product and it delegates the call to an overridden method implemented by its subclass. Figure 17.13 is an example of Factory Method. It shows that only subclasses `Sub1` and `Sub2` know how to create `ProductA` and `ProductB`, respectively.

This pattern is used extensively in web applications for situations where the client requests a web page and the server creates the web page dynamically. The server

Figure 17.13
Factory Method pattern

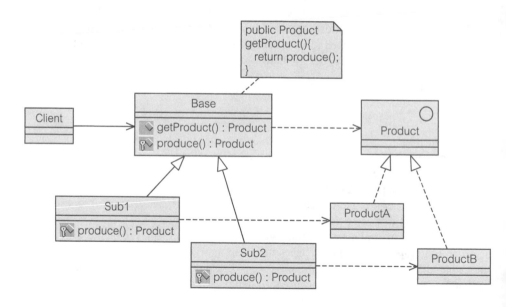

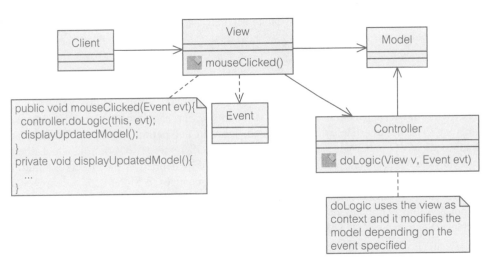

Figure 17.14
Strategy pattern

application (`Base` class in this case) decides which web page to display. The decision what page to display depends on the logic contained in the subclasses of Factory Method (`Sub1` or `Sub2` in Figure 17.13). This allows the server to create web pages dynamically. The client knows only one entry point to those web pages, through the `Base` class.

Strategy

17.4.4

The **Strategy pattern** (Gamma *et al.*, 1995) is a slight variation on Factory Method. Strategy can be used to define a web page (`View`) that delegates its work to a `Controller` (Figure 17.14). The `Controller` object knows the *strategies* for the list of actions that can be performed on the `Model`. The `View` and `Event` objects provide the actions to `Controller`.

In web applications, the view could be a web page or an applet. This pattern is used by the SearchMovie servlet (Figure 17.9).

Decorator

17.4.5

Another variation of the Composite pattern is known as the **Decorator pattern** (Gamma *et al.*, 1995). This pattern specifies that other objects decorate an object. In a typical GUI the main window is *decorated* by scroll bars, menus, toolbars, and other widgets. The existence of decorations is an option in the `Window` class.

The main difference between the Decorator and Composite patterns is that the main object (`Window`) and its decorations are aware of each other whereas such awareness is unidirectional in the Composite pattern. The composite object knows its component objects (and delegates to them) but not vice versa.

The application of Decorator in web systems involves the use of a scripting language within HTML. The standard HTML specification does not allow decorations. With the help of a scripting language, it is possible to decorate a web page with scroll bars and other widgets not found in HTML.

17.4.6 Model–View–Controller

The **MVC pattern** (Section 9.2.1) has a slightly different usage in web applications. Internet systems are stateless and, as such, they do not permit traditional MVC. The traditional MVC pattern requires View to redirect all requests to Control, which then modifies the Model. View and Model have a relationship, defined by the Observer pattern, such that View observes the Model and is notified of changes to Model.

In web applications, however, MVC cannot get the benefit of Model's notifications. It is not possible to implement the Observer pattern in HTML (unless the application is an applet) (Section 17.4.1). This forces some modification on the use of the MVC pattern as shown in Figure 17.15. A mixture of JSP and EJB can achieve this type of MVC implementation.

The `Control` class in Figure 17.15 is an HTTP servlet (hence, it is stereotyped as HS). `Model` is represented by JavaBeans or Enterprise JavaBeans (EJB). `Views` (stereotyped as client pages) are a set of JSP files that display the data retrieved from `Model`. The user events or commands are represented in the form of HTTP `post` or `get` methods handled by `Control`. `Control` is a servlet that serves multiple `Views`.

The classic one-to-one relationship between `Control` and `View` does not apply in this modified MVC pattern. `Control` is implemented as the `Front Controller` pattern discussed in the next section. The `Control` class itself can implement either the `Strategy` or `Factory Method` pattern to decide what to do with the requests or which `View` to display.

Figure 17.15
Web MVC

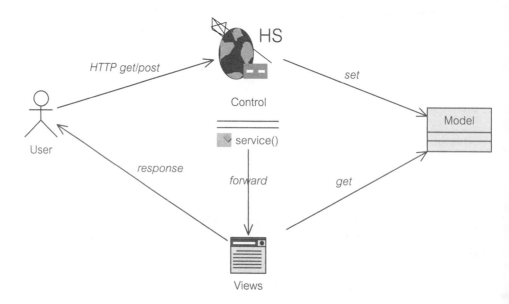

Figure 17.16
Front Controller

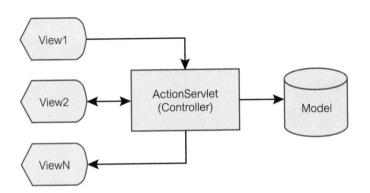

Front Controller

17.4.7

A typical web application has a single point of entry served by a servlet. The user only needs to know one single web address rather than many. Developers are free to implement the navigation from this single entry point. The pattern to support this style of work is called the **Front Controller pattern** (Alur *et al.*, 2003). The principles of Front Controller are illustrated in Figure 17.16.

A servlet that acts as Front Controller decides what views to display based on the state of the user session. This is where Strategy or Factory Method patterns are used. The Front Controller pattern allows the centralization of code related to system services, security services, content retrieval, view management, and navigation. The pattern promotes reuse of application code across requests (instead of embedding the same code in multiple views).

Reuse of Tags in JSP

17.4.8

As the JSP technology advances, developers would like to reuse components from previously implemented web pages. JSP provides such reuse via the **Custom Tag Library**. Page developers, such as JSP developers, focus on developing web pages by using custom tags. **Custom tags** provide a simple view of much more complex low-level functionality, such as database access, network access, or internationalization. The core software developers implement these low-level functionalities. Custom tags, therefore, allow the 'knowledge transfer' from the core software developers to page developers.

The following is the sequence of activities to use custom tag libraries (`taglib` for short):

1. Add `taglib` directive to JSP files.

2. Create tag library descriptor (`.tld`) describing the tags and declare it on `web.xml`.

3. Implement tag handlers to support the tag.

Listing 17.7 shows how a tag library is used in JSP. A tag library known as `SampleTags` is referenced as `mytag` in the JSP (Line 6). This reference occurs in the heading section of HTML. From then on, the `mytag` tag is made available in the body of HTML. Line 15 shows how `mytag`'s `openConnection` is used to open the connection to the database called `myDatabaseName`. Once the database is open, a query to search all employee details is launched (Line 16). The result of the query is displayed in a table format (Lines 18–22).

Listing 17.7 TagLib directive in JSP

```
Add taglib directive to JSP files (sample.jsp)

 2:    <head>
 6:       <%@ taglib uri='SampleTags' prefix='mytag' %>
 7:    </head>
11:    <body>
15:       <mytag:openConnection db="myDatabaseName">
16:          <mytag:query> select * from employee </mytag:query>
17:          <table>
18:          <mytag:rows>
19:             <tr><mytag:columns columnVal='cVal' >
20:                <td><%= cVal %> </td>
21:             </mytag:columns></tr>
22:          </mytag:rows>
23:       </mytag:openConnection>
```

Custom tags, once developed, need to be deployed on a web server that supports JSP, such as Tomcat (Tomcat, 2003). Tag declarations need to be placed in the deployment descriptors, or they can be referred to by the filename `web.xml`. Listing 17.8 shows how the `taglib` in Listing 17.7 is declared.

Listing 17.8 TagLib declaration in web.xml

```
Declare the taglib directive on deployment (web.xml)

10:    <taglib>
11:       <taglib-uri>SampleTags</taglib-uri>
12:       <taglib-location>/WEB-INF/tlds/SampleTags.tld</
                                                  taglib-location>
13:    </taglib>
```

Listing 17.8 shows how Listing 17.7, Line 6, is able to figure out the existence of the tag. This is possible because the tag is declared in Listing 17.8, Line 11. The real location of the tag descriptor is provided on Line 12.

XML is the most commonly used standard nowadays for web development. This includes the development of taglibs. A taglib descriptor is declared in XML to follow format specified in JSP standard. Listing 17.9 shows selected tags declared in `SampleTags.tld`.

Lines 1–2 specify the standard implemented by the custom tag. The document type is a `taglib` (Line 3) that follows XML format (Line 1). `SampleTags` is in version 1.0 (Line 4) and is implemented according to the JSP specification 1.2 (Line 5). Lines 6–9 serve the taglib documentation purpose.

Listing 17.9 SampleTags.tld

```
SampleTags.tld

 1:   <?xml version="1.0" encoding="ISO-8859-1" ?>
 2:   <!DOCTYPE taglib PUBLIC
         "-//Sun Microsystems, Inc.//DTD JSP Tag Library 1.2//EN"
         "http://java.sun.com/dtd/web-jsptaglibrary_1_2.dtd">
 3:   <taglib>
 4:      <tlibversion>1.0<tlibversion>
 5:      <jsp-version>1.2</jsp-version>
 6:      <short-name>My Sample Tags</short-name>
 7:      <uri>http://somewhere.com/tlds/SampleTags</uri>
 8:      <display-name>SampleTags</display-name>
 9:      <description>Sample Tags To Illustrate TabLib </description>
15:      <tag>
16:         <name>openConnection</name>
17:         <tag-class>sample.OpenConnectionTag</tag-class>
18:         <body-content>JSP</body-content>
19:         <description>
20:            Capable of nesting database connection from which
                queries can be executed
21:         </description>
22:         <attribute>
23:            <name>db</name>
24:            <required>true</required>
25:            <rtexprvalue>false</rtexprvalue>
26:         </attribute>
27:      </tag>
28:      <tag>
29:         <name>query</name>
30:         <tag-class>sample.QueryTag</tag-class>
31:         <body-content>JSP</body-content>
32:         <description> Execute query defined in its body
                                                  </description>
32:         <attribute>
33:         <name>var</name>
34:            <required>true</required>
35:            <rtexprvalue>false</rtexprvalue>
36:         </attribute>
37:      </tag>
```

The most interesting parts of Listing 17.9 are Lines 15–27 and 29–37 where two tags are declared. Lines 15–27 specify the openConnection tag (Line 16) that has been implemented by a class openConnectionTag in sample package (Line 17). This tag has one attribute called db that has to be filled and that does not return any values (Line 22–25). Similarly, the query tag has been declared on Line 29 to refer to the sample.QueryTag class implementation.

It is left to a software developer to implement the tags described above. *Tag handlers* can be implemented by inheriting from javax.servlet.jsp.tagext.Tag. Only three methods need to be implemented from this interface: doStartTag(), doEndTag(), and release(). They are shown in Listing 17.10. When the JSP engine encounters a start of a tag, it calls the doStartTag() method. Once the tag is fully processed, its doEndTag() is executed to allow the tag to perform other necessary activities. Finally, when the tag is no longer needed and just about to be garbage-collected, its release() method is called to allow the tag to perform *clean* exit.

Listing 17.10 javax.servlet.js.tagext.Tag Method Summary

int	**doEndTag()**
	Process the end tag for this instance.
int	**doStartTag()**
	Process the start tag for this instance.
Tag	**getParent()**
	Get the parent (closest enclosing tag handler) for this tag handler.
void	**release()**
	Called on a Tag handler to release state.
void	**setPageContext(PageContext pc)**
	Set the current page context.
void	**setParent(Tag t)**
	Set the parent (closest enclosing tag handler) of this tag handler.

Sun's documentation (Sun, 2003) illustrates a tag lifecycle in a state model shown in Figure 17.17. Setting its parent and page context values initializes the tag. After initialization, the tag can Process tag content following doStartTag() invocation. Once the tag is ended by doEndTag(), it can be released via the call to the release() method. Only then can the tag be reused, provided all its values are reset to known default values.

Note, however, that the path cycle between the states Property initialized and Process tag content can only be executed if the tag invocation of doStartTag() does not throw any exceptions. Errors can be thrown as JspException instances by any of doStartTag(), doEndTag(), and release() methods.

A quick snapshot of OpenConnectionTag is shown in Listing 17.11. The class extends TagSupport which has the entire skeleton required to create a standard tag, including an empty implementation of the Tag interface. The db attribute declared in Listing 17.9, Line 23, is taken advantage of by the method setDb() (Lines 6 and 20–22).

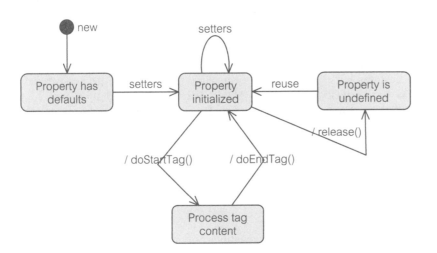

Figure 17.17
Tag lifecycle

Listing 17.11 OpenConnectionTag implementation

```
OpenConnectionTag.java

 1:   package sample;
 2:   import javax.servlet.jsp.*;
 3:   import javax.servlet.jsp.tagext.*;
 4:   import javax.servlet.http.*;
 5:   public class OpenConnectionTag extend TagSupport{
 6:       String dbName;
20:       public void setDb(String db){
21:           dbName = db;
22:       }
23:       public int doStartTag() throws JspException{
24:           performOpenConnection();
25:           return SKIP_BODY; //don't evaluate the body with this tag
26:       }
27:       public int doEndTag() throws JspException{
28:           if(conn != null) conn.close();
29:       }
```

The method `doStartTag()` opens a new connection to the named database via the call
to `performOpenConnection()` (Lines 23–24). The method `performOpenConnec-`
`tion()` is assumed to be a privately implemented method and it is not shown here.
`return SKIP_BODY` (Line 25) indicates that if there is more data embedded in the usage
of the tag in JSP, it needs to be skipped (not processed by the current tag). `doEndTag()`
simply closes the open connection.

17.4.9 Decoupled Control: Struts

Struts (Goodwill, 2002) provides an additional level of decoupling between the presentation and business logic. Struts is an open-source project from Apache (Apache, 2003). Struts has been developed from the MVC design pattern and then evolved towards incorporating the Front Controller pattern. This section concentrates on MVC aspects of Struts.

Most Struts implementations follow the diagram shown in Figure 17.18. The Front Controller is represented by `ActionServlet (Controller)` and `ActionA-Z`. `ActionServlet` is a singleton. Collaboration between `Controller` and its `Actions` takes advantage of the Strategy, Factory Method, Service to Worker, Dispatcher, and Navigator patterns.

`ActionServlet` decides which `Action` class should be executed (Strategy and Navigator). It delegates the service execution (Service to Worker). It dispatches events to `Action` classes (Dispatcher). `Action` classes need to inform `ActionServlet` which `View` to display as the result of executions via Factory Method or Navigator patterns.

The sequence of execution begins with `View1-N` requesting modification on data to be performed by `ActionServlet`. `ActionServlet` dynamically finds the appropriate actions to be performed (`ActionA-Z`). The action instance performs activities on the model and returns the result back to `ActionServlet`. `ActionServlet` presents this result in one of the `View1-N`.

Figure 17.18
Struts overview
Source: Adapted from *Mastering Jakarta Struts* by James Goodwill. Copyright © 2002 by Ryan Publishing Group. Reproduced here by permission of Wiley Publishing, Inc. All rights reserved

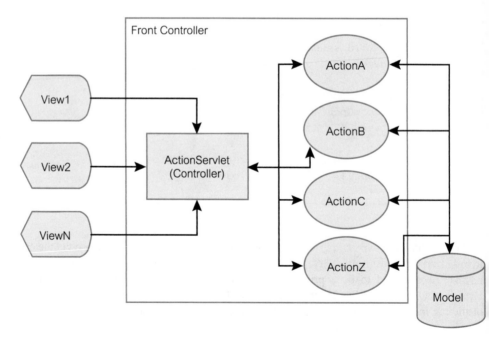

As in the case of the custom tag library in JSP, Struts requires the developer to implement a servlet and to provide appropriate mapping between the implemented class and its published name. The steps are as follows:

1. Create views (usually JSP pages (Listings 17.7, 17.9, 17.11)).

2. Create controller and action classes.

3. Define relationships between views and controller (`struts-config.xml`).

4. Describe all Struts components in `web.xml` (Listing 17.8).

Struts provides a higher level of abstraction than JSP. The presentation layer is treated in Struts as a separate unit in its own right. Struts permits web developers to decouple the presentation from the actions performed on business logic and data.

Servlet Implementation of Email Management

17.5

Figure 17.19 shows an overall state transition model for the servlet implementation of the EM Iteration 2. The login, display outmessage, and send outmessage use cases are handled by the `EMS` servlet. The `EMSEdit` servlet handles the outmessage viewing and editing. The servlets are in fact called `PEMS` and `PEMSEdit` servlets. However, the servlets may have name aliases that are different from their original names. This allows the web administrators to customize the servlets to their needs. This chapter and Chapter 18 refer to the names `EMS` and `PEMS` interchangeably. Similarly, `EMSEdit` and `PEMSEdit` are equivalent.

The servlet version of the EM Iteration 2 is a complete web-based implementation of the EM case study. After a successful login, the user is presented with the main page where the unsent outmessages allocated to that user are displayed. From this page, the user can click on any of the following links:

■ a link to the 'Department Outmessages' page

■ a link to the 'All Unsent Outmessages' page

■ a button to view/edit the details of outmessages shown on the 'Selected Outmessages' page

■ a button to send an outmessage from the 'Selected Outmessages' page.

When the user is in any of the above pages, s/he can navigate to other pages via the links. The usual login screen for Iteration 2 has been converted into standard HTML format as shown in Figure 17.20.

The servlet is loaded from the local web server. The login window is generated by the `EMS` servlet as indicated by its web address. The login verification process is shown in Figure 17.21. `CAdmin` is responsible for performing the login sequence, as per the normal GUI implementation of Iteration 2.

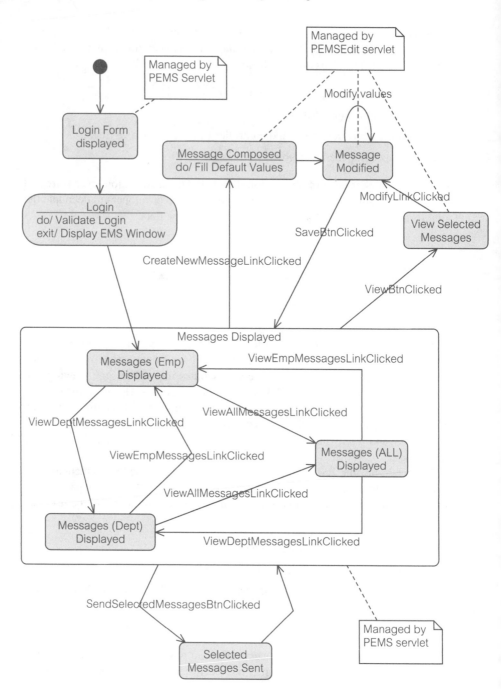

Figure 17.19
EM Iteration 2
servlet version –
state model

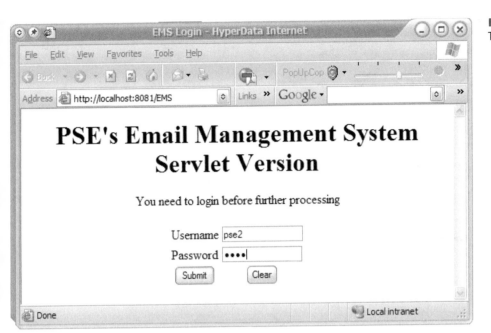

Figure 17.20
The login screen

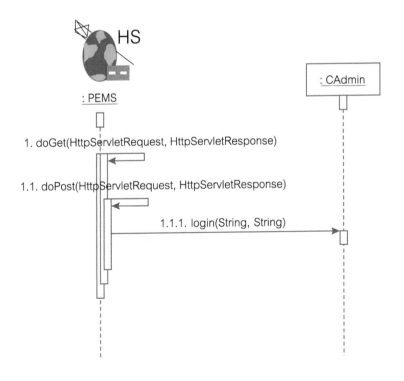

Figure 17.21
Login verification

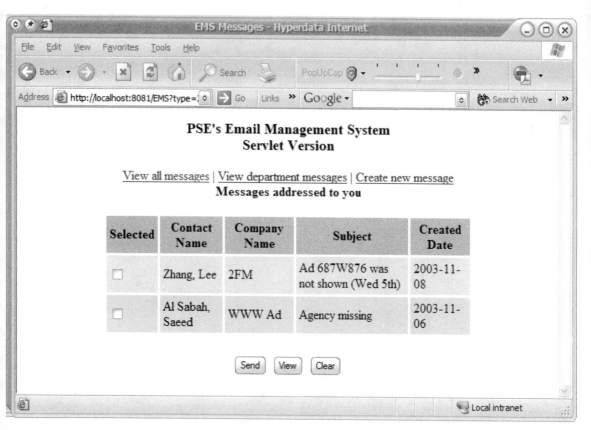

Figure 17.22 View Own Outmessages

`doGet()` is requested when the servlet is called the first time to initiate the login process (Figure 17.20). Upon pressing the `Submit` button, the `doPost()` method is executed and the login verification continues.

Once the login is fully verified, the next page that lists all outmessages assigned to the current employee is shown (Figure 17.22). The user is able to view and send outmessages through this window.

Note that Figure 17.22 shows exactly the same web address as the login page. This indicates that the same servlet serves the two pages. In this case, EMS servlet serves these pages. This approach requires the EMS servlet to remember the states of the user's connection on a session-by-session basis.

A sequence diagram for listing outmessages assigned to current employee is illustrated in Figure 17.23. An outmessage retrieval request is intercepted by the EMS servlet, which further redirects it to `CMsgSeeker`. Retrieved outmessages are then displayed on the screen for the user to view and manipulate.

When the user decides to view some selected outmessages, the content of those outmessages is displayed on the screen shown in Figure 17.24.

Figure 17.23
Retrieve Own
Outmessages
sequence diagram

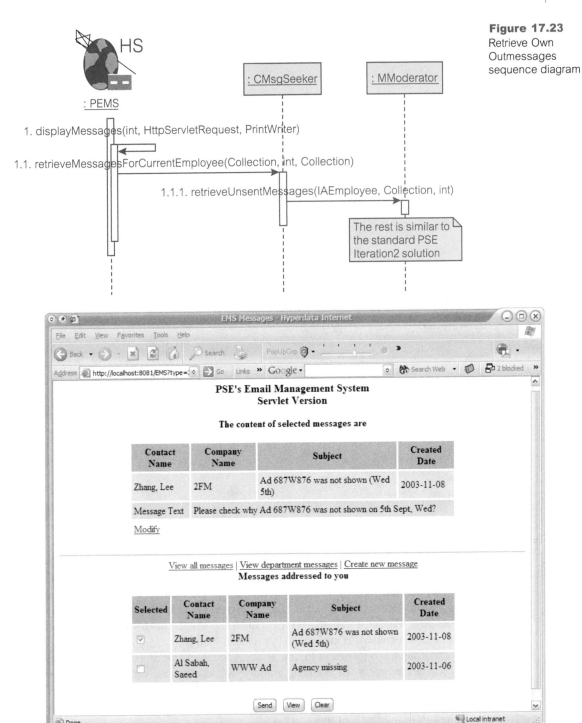

Figure 17.24 View Selected Outmessages

Figure 17.25
Edit Selected
Outmessages

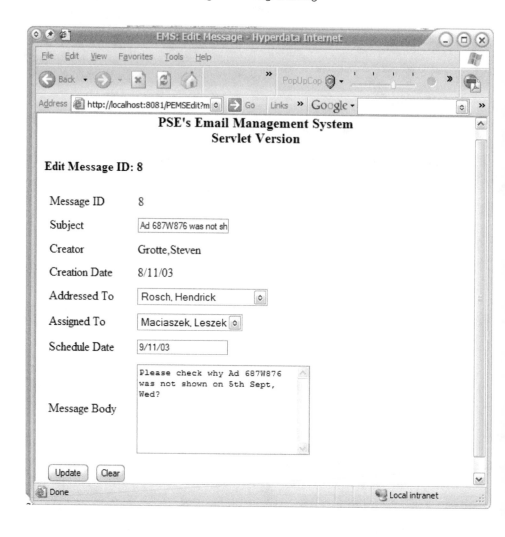

Figure 17.24 shows how summarized content of selected outmessages is displayed. Note that the lower part of the window contains the list of outmessages as in Figure 17.22. Note also that the table provides a link to Modify the viewed outmessage. The message editing is supplied by the EMSEdit servlet. Figure 17.25 indicates in the Address bar that the EMSEdit servlet is called with a parameter, msg=1. This parameter is not shown in Figure 17.24 because it is embedded in the Modify link.

Each of the fields shown in Figure 17.25 is editable. The dropdown lists are selectable and contain the lists of all available employees and contacts. The sequence of execution for message editing involves the two servlets shown in the sequence diagram in Figure 17.26. The sequence diagrams emphasize interactions between the EMS and EMSEdit servlets required by outmessage editing.

The EMS servlet processes requests to view a selected outmessage text. It then invokes EMSEdit with the proper parameter to display the outmessage on the screen. This results in

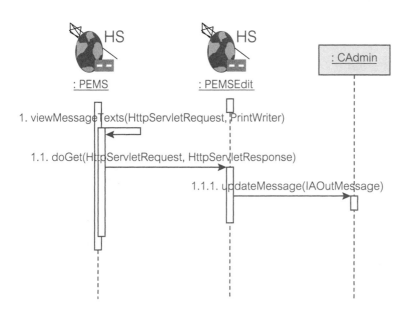

Figure 17.26
Interactions for
outmessage
editing

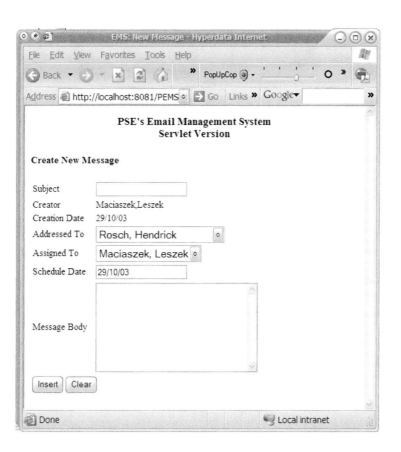

Figure 17.27
Insert New
Outmessage

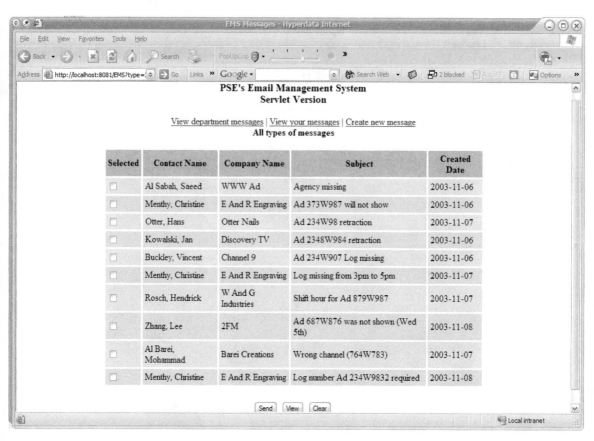

Figure 17.28 View All Outmessages

the window shown in Figure 17.25. Once the user clicks on the `Update` button in Figure 17.25, the outmessage is updated on the server via the call to `CAdmin`'s `updateMessage()`.

Figure 17.27 shows another usage of the `EMSEdit` servlet. A request to show a new outmessage creation page results in Figure 17.27. Dropdown lists and other fields are initialized to default values. Note that `Creator` and `Creation Date` are non-modifiable fields. This prevents data corruption and illegal manipulation of outmessages.

Slightly different from Figure 17.22, Figure 17.28 shows a list of all unsent outmessages available from the database.

Summary

1. A *web-based application* means that an Internet browser manages the rendering of UI content, but the business logic and database state exists on a server. The client technologies for web-based applications include *applets*. The server technologies include *servlets* and *Java Server Pages*. Other related technologies are *tags*, *scriptlets*, *Struts*, and *JavaServer Faces*.

2. Components of a typical web-based system are deployed on at least three *tiers*: web client, web server, and database server. In some cases, a separate application server is desired.

3. The *client/server* (C/S) is a logical division. The *client* requests services of a server and the *server* provides these services to authorized clients.

4. The *HyperText Markup Language* (HTML) is the most common format found to represent web pages on the net. Pages stored in the HTML format use standard *formatting tags* and, as a result, allow their proper display by web browsers.

5. *Scripting languages* are used in HTML documents to enrich user interactions. *Scripts* can perform quick validation of inputs, simple animations, and other activities to make the web page 'come alive'.

6. *Applets* can be categorized into thin and thick. Both thin and thick applets have their server counterpart. A *thin applet* performs most of its activities on the server, and a *thick applet* performs most of its activities on the client.

7. *Servlet* is a dedicated service running on a server machine to serve multiple clients. It is a Java code that has been compiled and deployed on a web server. There is no client code as such in the servlet. The client is an HTML page or other pages, such as JSP or ASP.

8. *Java Server Pages* (JSP) is a variation of the servlet technology. JSP separates the business logic from the presentation. The business logic is represented by a servlet whereas the presentation is the JSP. JSP is able to use *JavaBeans* and *Enterprise JavaBeans* (EJB).

9. Internet systems are *stateless systems*. Two approaches to implementing a *stateful system* on the Internet are by using *state passing* and by using a *session object*.

10. The *Core J2EE patterns* define best software engineering practices for the development with J2EE technologies, including servlets, JSP and EJB, web services, XML. Other well-known patterns, such as the *GoF* and *PEAA* sets of patterns, also apply to web-based systems. Applicable patterns include Observer, Composite, Factory Method, Strategy, Decorator, MVC, and Front Controller.

11. JSP supports reuse of components from previously implemented web pages via the *Custom Tag Library*. Custom tags provide a simple view of much more complex low-level functionality, such as database access, network access, or internationalization.

12. *Struts* – an open-source project from Apache – provides an additional level of decoupling between the presentation and business logic.

13. The servlet version of the EM Iteration 2 is a complete web-based implementation of the EM case study. The thick-applet implementation of the EM Iteration 2 is also available (and runnable) from the book's website.

Key Terms

applet	541, 547	pull technology	559
applet state transition model	549	sandbox	541, 549
C/S	*See* client/server	script	545
client	543	scripting language	545
client/server	543	scriptlet	542
Composite pattern	563	server	543
Custom Tag Library	567	servlet	541, 551
custom tags	*See* tags	servlet active state model	553
Decorator pattern	565	servlet container	552, 554
dynamic binding	546	session object	561
EJB	*See* Enterprise JavaBeans	signed applet	551
Enterprise JavaBeans	558	state passing	560
Factory Method pattern	564	stateful system	560
Front Controller pattern	567	stateless system	559
Gang of Four patterns	562	static binding	546
GoF	*See* Gang of Four patterns	Strategy pattern	565
HTML	*See* HyperText Markup Language	Struts	542, 572
HTML tags	544	tags	542, 567
HyperText Markup Language	541, 543	thick applet	547, 551
JAR	*See* Java Archive file	thick web client	542
Java Archive file	541	thin applet	547
Java Server Page	542	thin web client	542
Java Server Pages	555	transaction states	560
JavaBeans	558	trusted applet	550
JavaServer Faces	542	VBScript	545
JScript	545	W3C	*See* World Wide Web Consortium
JSF	*See* JavaServer Faces	web page	541
JSP	*See* Java Server Page	web server	551
MVC pattern	566	web-based application	541
Observer pattern	563	World Wide Web Consortium	543
Patterns of Enterprise Application Architecture	562	XML	568
PEAA patterns	*See* Patterns of Enterprise Application Architecture		

Review Questions

1. Some HTML tags do not require an enclosing tag, for example `<p>`. What is the reason for this 'inconsistency'? What if you put an enclosing tag for such an HTML tag?

2. What is the meaning of the `<br />` tag? Keep in mind that the `<br>` tag causes the browser to insert a line break.

3. What happens if a tag is not closed or when the matching open/close tags are out of order?

4. What does the `width` attribute mean when it is specified in a table tag (as shown in Listing 17.1, Line 7)? What will happen when its value is too large or too small?

5. Listing 17.2 line 20 has the following entry:

   ```
   <INPUT TYPE="text" NAME="percent" VALUE="1">
   ```

   What is the purpose and meaning of setting the `value` attribute?

6. Discuss the pros and cons of thin and thick applets. Give examples of applications suitable for thin and for thick applets.

7. Explain the connection between the sandbox model and signed applets.

8. What are typical responsibilities of the web server tier in a multi-tier web system?

9. What are typical responsibilities of the application server tier in a multi-tier web system?

10. Explain different ways of a combined use of servlet and JSP technologies for building web systems.

11. Explain different ways of achieving a stateful implementation on the stateless Internet.

12. Explain the correspondence between the Core J2EE tiers and the PCMEF framework.

13. Explain how the Observer and MVC patterns can be (should be) used for designing various variants of web-based systems. The variants to consider include thin applet, thick applet, and servlet/JSP. What other patterns can be used to address any shortcomings of the Observer and MVC patterns?

14. Provide critical evaluation of Figures 17.25 and 17.27 from the perspective of the UI design.

Problem-Solving Exercises

1. Refer to Figure 17.20. The implementation of the login window uses the servlet technology. Implement the same login window using HTML. Assume that the EMS servlet can handle the HTTP post request of this HTML.

2. Suppose you need to develop a web page as in Figure 17.24. How would you achieve the display of the content of a selected oumessage followed by the listing of outmessages addressed to the current user? What JSP tags can be used to achieve this? Use the include directive `<jsp:include>` in the solution. There is no need to demonstrate JSP files that deliver the web page.

3. Figure 17.24 shows a table that does not have the same number of columns for the rows. How would you program this functionality in an HTML table tag?

4. List the changes required to convert the servlet version of the EM Iteration 2 to a Struts-based application.

Chapter

18

Iteration 2 Annotated Code

The EM case study discussed in this chapter does not cover code that had been presented in Part 2 in the context of Iteration 1. This chapter continues the presentation style as seen in *Iteration 1 Annotated Code* in Chapter 13. However, an additional technology is used in this chapter to present the EM API. The documentation produced by Javadoc is enhanced by snapshots of class diagrams produced by the software tool called yDoc from yWorks – the diagramming company (yWorks, 2003).

The chapter concentrates on explaining the code changes between Iteration 1 and Iteration 2. Any code not presented in this chapter for space reasons is available on the book's website. The chapter begins with the code overview for Iteration 2. The code overview explains the hierarchies of packages, interfaces and classes. A relevant class diagram gives a visual code overview. Most fields and methods are listed and annotated. Significant methods are discussed in detail but less important or trivial ones are omitted from the discussion.

A web version of the EM Iteration 2 is discussed after the presentation of the desktop version of Iteration 2. The web version represents Iteration 2 in the form of applet as well as servlet implementations. Understandably, most discussion on the web implementation of Iteration 2 relates to the `presentation` package.

Code Overview

Continuing from Iteration 1, the EM Iteration 2 code conforms strictly to the **PCMEF+ architectural framework** discussed in Section 9.2.2. The package hierarchy and classes within each package are shown in Figure 18.1.

There are noticeable differences between the Iteration 2 class model (Figure 18.2) and the Iteration 1 model presented in Chapter 13. Many of these changes have already been discussed in the refactoring chapter (Chapter 15). Some important changes are:

- the `presentation` package is overhauled to support graphical and web-based user interfaces
- `CActioner` has been split into `CAdmin`, `CMsgSeeker`, and `CMsgSender` (and related changes have been made in the `mediator` package)
- `domain.entity.IEDataSupplier` is no longer used
- `EIdentityMap` and `MDataMapper` are introduced to handle caching of `entity` objects.

The discussion in this chapter is trimmed down due to space constraints. Readers interested in more details are encouraged to check the resources on the book's website, which include the source code for all iterations of the EM case study.

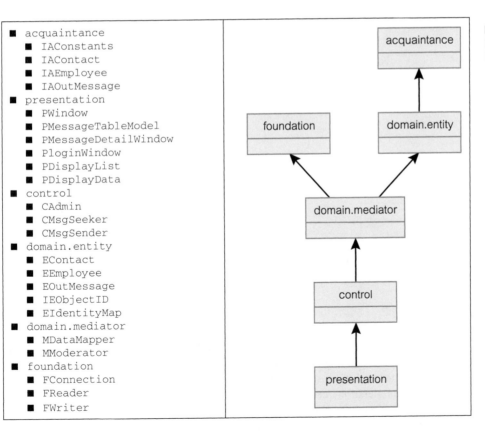

- acquaintance
  - IAConstants
  - IAContact
  - IAEmployee
  - IAOutMessage
- presentation
  - PWindow
  - PMessageTableModel
  - PMessageDetailWindow
  - PloginWindow
  - PDisplayList
  - PDisplayData
- control
  - CAdmin
  - CMsgSeeker
  - CMsgSender
- domain.entity
  - EContact
  - EEmployee
  - EOutMessage
  - IEObjectID
  - EIdentityMap
- domain.mediator
  - MDataMapper
  - MModerator
- foundation
  - FConnection
  - FReader
  - FWriter

Figure 18.1
Packages in EM Iteration 2

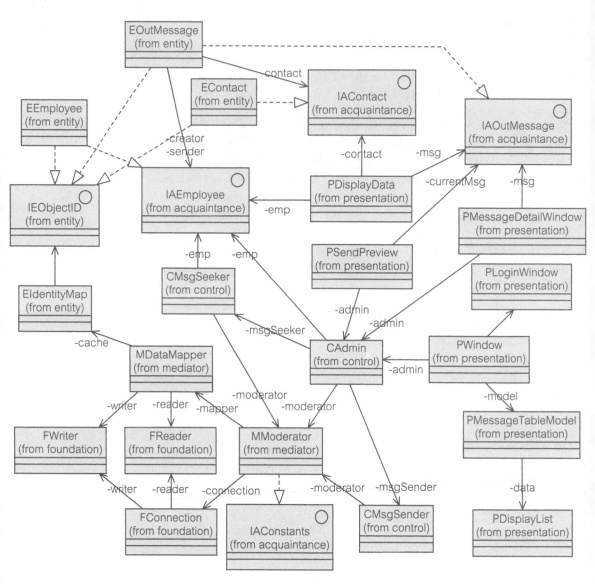

Figure 18.2 Class diagram for EM Iteration 2

18.2 Package Acquaintance

The acquaintance package consists of four interfaces (Figure 18.3). IAConstants is not modified in Iteration 2 and therefore is not discussed in this chapter.

Although the acquaintance package consists of the same number of interfaces as in the previous iteration, each interface introduces new properties to support object maintenance by a memory manager. The interfaces allow an *Identity Map* (Section 15.3.1) to store objects represented by these interfaces.

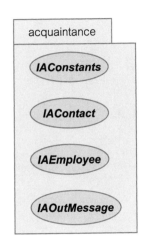

Figure 18.3
Package
Acquaintance and
its classes in EM 2

Interface IAEmployee

A notable modification on `IAEmployee` is the addition of the methods `isDirty`, `get/setDepartmentCode` and, `add/removeOutMessage` (Figure 18.4). The latter allow proper maintenance of associations between an employee and his/her outmessages.

Iterators of `java.util.iterator` are used to iterate over outmessages. This is a convenient way of allowing the application to search for an employee's outmessages. Two distinct types of outmessage are recognized: the outmessages allocated to the employee as a sender and outmessages created by the employee. `EEmployee` is the only class that

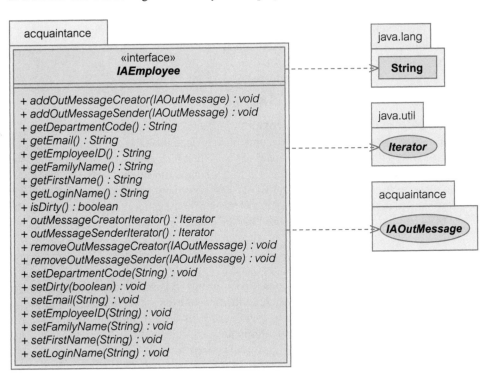

Figure 18.4
Interface
IAEmployee
in EM 2

Figure 18.5
Package
Presentation and
its classes in EM 2

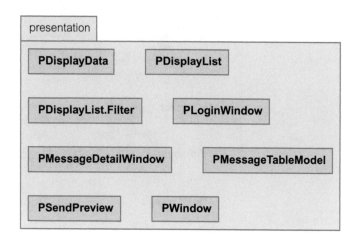

implements the IAEmployee interface. Two other interfaces related to entity objects, namely IAOutMessage and IAContact, follow the same trend as IAEmployee.

18.3 Package Presentation

The presentation package contains seven classes and one inner class (Figure 18.5). According to the object-oriented principle of 'uniform distribution of intelligence', the behavior found in the presentation package of Iteration 1 has been dispersed among a number of new classes introduced in Iteration 2.

18.3.1 Class PWindow

PWindow (Figure 18.6) is a replacement for PConsole. The class also houses the main() method to start the application that was previously placed in PMain.

The PWindow class contains references to CAdmin, which is the **dominant class** of the control layer, and to PMessageTableModel, which is the sole reference to the model of the JTable used in the GUI. Simple JTable construction is shown in Figure 16.3. PLoginWindow is used to acquire the login information for the connection to the database. The javax.swing library is extensively used but the details are cut out from Figure 18.6.

Constructing and launching PWindow

Java fires various events during the construction of the widgets. When in the GUI design mode, the programmer may want to ignore these Java events and concentrate on events initiated by the user. For this purpose, designMode is used to indicate that the GUI is under construction. When the construction is finished, designMode is set to false (Line 35 in Listing 18.1).

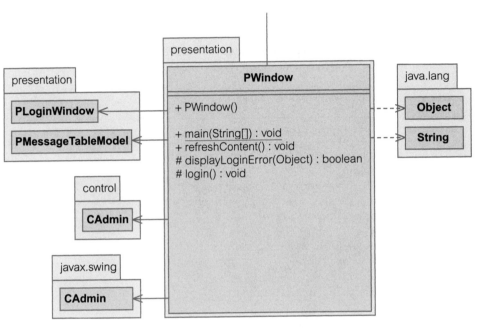

Figure 18.6
PWindow in EM 2

Listing 18.1 Constructing PWindow

```
Constructors PWindow()

23:     public PWindow() throws Exception{
24:         designMode = true;
25:         admin = new CAdmin();
28:         login();
29:         model = new PMessageTableModel(retrieveData(1));
30:         initComponents();
31:         model.attachSortHeading(viewTable); //activate the sorting
32:         populateContact();
33:         populateDepartment();
34:         setButtonsEnable(false);
36:         designMode = false;
37:     }
```

Iteration 2 follows the requirement of Iteration 1 that the user has to login() (Line 28) to the database before s/he is allowed to use the system. Once the user is verified, the data stored in PMessageTableModel is retrieved by the retrieveData() call (Line 29). The model also supports sorting of its columns. This is achieved by calling the attachSortHeading() method (Line 31). Various other items in the GUI need to be populated such as contact combo box as well as department combo box (Lines 32–33). These combo boxes allow the user to pick a value from a dropdown list. This is used for example for filtering outmessages (explained later).

The application is started from PWindow's main() method (Listing 18.2). Line 569 requests UIManager to present the Java application with the look and feel of the current operating system. By default, Java will use the look and feel known as *Metal*. Then a new instance of PWindow is created and shown (Lines 572–573).

Listing 18.2 Launching PWindow – main( )

```
Launching PWindow the first time - main()

567:    public static void main(String args[]){
568:        try{
569:            UIManager.setLookAndFeel(
                    UIManager.getSystemLookAndFeelClassName());
570:        }catch(Exception exc){}
571:        try{
572:            PWindow w = new PWindow();
573:            w.show();
574:        }catch(Exception exc){
575:            exc.printStackTrace();
576:        }
577:    }
```

Data retrieval in PWindow

There are three different types of data retrieval supported by PWindow (Listing 18.3). The first is the retrieval of all unsent outmessages (subflow S1.1 described in Section 14.2.3). The second is the retrieval of all unsent outmessages scheduled to the employee's department only (subflow S1.2). The last type is the retrieval of all unsent outmessages allocated to the current employee (subflow S1.3).

Listing 18.3 Method retrieveData( ) in PWindow

```
Method retrieveData() in PWindow

72:     private Collection retrieveData(int type){
73:         Collection data = new ArrayList();
75:         int remainder =0;
76:         switch(type){
77:             case 1: remainder = admin.getMsgSeeker()
                    .retrieveAllMessages(data,
                    IAConstants.MAX_MESSAGE,null);
                    break;
78:             case 2: remainder = admin.getMsgSeeker()
                    .retrieveMessagesForDepartment(
                    admin.getEmployee().getDepartmentCode(),
                    data,IAConstants.MAX_MESSAGE,null);
                    break;
```

```
79:              case 3: remainder = admin.getMsgSeeker()
                     .retrieveMessagesForCurrentEmployee(
                     data,IAConstants.MAX_MESSAGE,null);
                     break;
80:              default: throw new IllegalArgumentException(
                     "Unknown type:"+type);
81:          }
85:          return data;
86:      }
```

Whenever the user clicks on any of the three action buttons named 'View department messages' or 'View own messages' or 'View all messages', there is a need to refresh the display of outmessages shown on the screen. The method responsible for changing the list of outmessages on the screen is changeModel() (Listing 18.4). The method retrieves the data via retrieveData() call (Line 424) and then further filters the data according to the previously selected filter options. Initially the outmessages are filtered by the dates as indicated on Lines 426–428. The outmessages can be further filtered by their contact information as shown on Lines 430–431. Finally, if the user requested a filter on department, the outmessages will be filtered as on Lines 433–434. As the outmessages are different from previous values, there is a need to repopulate the contact and department combo boxes (Lines 436–437).

Listing 18.4 Method changeModel() in PWindow

```
Method changeModel() in PWindow

423:     private void changeModel(int type){
424:         model.setModel(retrieveData(type));
425:         if(filterOnOffBtn.isSelected()){
426:             model.filter(todayChk.isSelected()?
                     PMessageTableModel.TODAY_FILTER:
427:                 (futureChk.isSelected()?
                         PMessageTableModel.FUTURE_DAYS_FILTER:
428:                     (pastChk.isSelected()?
                         PMessageTableModel.LAST_DAYS_FILTER:
429:                     PMessageTableModel.ALL_DAYS_FILTER)));
430:             String cont = contactCmb.getSelectedItem().
                                                     toString().trim();
431:             model.filter(cont.length() == 0?
                         PMessageTableModel.NO_CONTACT_FILTER:cont);
433:             String dep=departmentCmb.getSelectedItem().
                                                     toString().trim();
434:             model.filterDepartment(dep.length() == 0? null: dep);
435:         }
436:         populateContact();
437:         populateDepartment();
438:     }
```

Listing 18.5 shows the implementation of subflows S1.1, S1.2, S1.3. All these methods utilize the `changeModel()` method by providing it with a different parameter. Again, if the GUI is in `designMode`, the button event is ignored.

Listing 18.5 Methods ownBtnActionPerformed( ), deptBtnActionPerformed( ), and allBtnActionPerformed( ) in PWindow

Methods ownBtnActionPerformed(), deptBtnActionPerformed(), and allBtnActionPerformed() in PWindow

```
416:     private void ownBtnActionPerformed(ActionEvent evt) {
418:             if(designMode) return;
419:             changeModel(3);
420:     }
439:     private void deptBtnActionPerformed(ActionEvent evt) {
441:             if(designMode) return;
442:             changeModel(2);
443:     }
445:     private void allBtnActionPerformed(ActionEvent evt) {
447:             if(designMode) return;
448:             changeModel(1);
449:     }
```

Populating contact and department combo boxes are similar opoations. Listing 18.6 shows how this is done for department combo boxes. Department names are read from the model (Line 98) and the combo box is populated (Line 102). Department is treated somewhat differently in that there is a need to check whether an outmessage has been assigned to the department. If the outmessage has not been assigned to the department concerned, then there is no need to add such a department to the combo box, as shown on Line 101.

Listing 18.6 Method populateDepartment( ) in PWindow

Method populateDepartment() in PWindow

```
95:      private void populateDepartment(){
96:          departmentCmb.removeAllItems();
97:          departmentCmb.addItem("");
98:          Iterator it=model.getDepartmentNames().iterator();
99:          while(it.hasNext()){
100:             Object d = it.next();
101:             if(d != null && d.toString().trim().length() != 0)
102:                 departmentCmb.addItem(d);
103:         }
104:     }
```

When the user decides to preview the content of a selected outmessage, a new PSendPreview window with the outmessage content is displayed (Listing 18.7). In this window, the user can see the outmessage as it will be displayed on the recipient's email reader. As can be seen, many of the windows in the presentation layer implement the setTarget() function accordingly.

Listing 18.7 Method previewBtnActionPerformed( ) in PWindow

```
Method previewBtnActionPerformed() in PWindow

389:     private void previewBtnActionPerformed(ActionEvent evt) {
390:         int []rows=viewTable.getSelectedRows();
391:         if(rows.length == 0) return;
392:         for(int i=0;i<rows.length;i++){
393:             PSendPreview msgWin = new PSendPreview(this,true,
                                                         admin);
394:             msgWin.setTarget((IAOutMessage)model.
                 getRawObject(rows[i]));
395:             msgWin.show();
396:         }
397:         refreshContent();
398:     }
```

Filter activation

The filtering capability can be turned on and off according to the state of a radio button (filterOnOffBtn). However, the Java radio button implementation is not deselectable. This means that once a radio button is selected, there is no way to deselect it. To achieve a deselect state for the radio button, the code in Listing 18.8 is assisted by another radio button (invisibleBtn). Both invisibleBtn and filterOnOffBtn are grouped by a ButtonGroup. ButtonGroup allows a single selection on any of the components in the group (therefore deselecting the others). This way, whenever a deselect state is required, the invisibleBtn needs to be selected as shown on Lines 462–464. Method setButtonsEnable is used to make all other filtering fields and buttons enabled or disabled based on the state of filterOnOffBtn.

Whenever the user needs to filter the outmessages on his/her contact or department information, s/he can do so by clicking on department combo box or contact combo box. Filtering is done in the model's filterDepartment() (Line 404 in Listing 18.9) or a corresponding filter method for contact filtering. Before filtering can be done, there is a need to check that the GUI is not in designMode and that the filterOnOffBtn is enabled. The filtering will not be performed if the GUI is in design mode or the filter button is off.

Listing 18.8 Method filterOnOffBtnActionPerformed( ) in PWindow

Method filterOnOffBtnActionPerformed() in PWindow
450:       boolean prevSelected = false;
451:       private void filterOnOffBtnActionPerformed(ActionEvent evt) {
453:           if(designMode){
454:               setButtonsEnable(false);
455:               return;
456:           }
458:           if(!prevSelected){
459:               prevSelected = true;
460:               setButtonsEnable(true);
461:           }else{
462:               setButtonsEnable(false);
463:               invisibleBtn.setSelected(true);
464:               prevSelected = false;
465:           }
466:       }

Listing 18.9 Method departmentCmbActionPerformed( ) in PWindow

Method departmentCmbActionPerformed() in PWindow
400:       private void departmentCmbActionPerformed(ActionEvent evt) {
402:           if(designMode || !filterOnOffBtn.isSelected()) return;
404:           model.filterDepartment(departmentCmb.getSelectedItem().
toString());
405:       }

Listing 18.10 shows one example of date filtering. PMessageTableModel's filter method is called with a proper parameter as shown on Line 543. A similar approach is used for futureChkActionPerformed(), pastChkActionperformed(), and allChkActionPerformed().

Listing 18.10 DateFiltering in PWindow

DateFiltering in PWindow: Method todayChkActionPerformed()
539:       private void todayChkActionPerformed(ActionEvent evt) {
541:           if(designMode) return;
543:           model.filter(PMessageTableModel.TODAY_FILTER);
544:       }

Class PMessageDetailWindow

PMessageDetailWindow is used to display the details of an outmessage (Listing 18.11). It can also display blank outmessage data as shown by showNewMessage() method. The outmessage displayed can be modified via the call to setEditable().

Collection of employees and contacts is required in case the user chooses to modify an outmessage (Listing 18.12). If the outmessage is editable, then the user has the ability to reassign another employee to handle the outmessage and/or to change the contact of the outmessage. These two collections are also used in the creation of a new outmessage.

The setTarget() method causes the PMessageDetailWindow to show the IAOut-Message information given to the method (Listing 18.13). The title of the window depends on whether or not the window is editable. When it is editable and the out-message contains a reference to contact, then the title is changed to *Update Message*; otherwise it is set to *Insert New Message*. When it is not editable, then the title is changed to *Delete Message* (Lines 85–87). Various other properties such as contact field, employee field, etc. are filled based on the information retrieved from the outmessage (Lines 89–94).

Listing 18.11 PMessageDetailWindow method summary

static void	**main**(java.lang.String[] args)
	Testing.
void	**setEditable**(boolean editable)
	Make the fields editable/disabled
void	**setTarget**(IAOutMessage msg)
	Change what to display on the screen
void	**showNewMessage**()
	Clear all fields and show empty message

Listing 18.12 Fields in PMessageDetailWindow

Fields in PMessageDetailWindow.java

```
19:     private control.CAdmin admin;
20:     private boolean editable;
21:     private acquaintance.IAOutMessage msg;
23:     private java.util.Collection employees;
25:     private java.util.Collection contacts;
```

Listing 18.13 Method setTarget( ) in PMessageDetailWindow

```
Method setTarget() in PMessageDetailWindow

82:        public void setTarget(acquaintance.IAOutMessage msg){
83:            this.msg = msg;
84:            if(editable){
85:                if(msg.getContact() != null)
                        setTitle("Update Message "+msg.getMessageID());
86:                else setTitle("Insert New Message "+msg.getMessageID());
87:            }else setTitle("Delete Message "+msg.getMessageID());
89:            assignContact(msg.getContact());
90:            assignTo(msg.getSenderEmployee());
91:            msgIDLbl.setText(""+msg.getMessageID());
92:            creatorLbl.setText(msg.getCreatorEmployeeID());
93:            deptCodeLbl.setText(msg.getDepartmentCode());
94:            fillMessageDetails(msg);
95:        }
```

The saveMessage() method saves the information contained in the fields of PMessage-
DetailWindow after modification by the user (Listing 18.14). Initially the fields are
checked for their entries (Lines 339–344 and cut lines). Once all the fields' entries are
verified then the outmessage is modified appropriately (Lines 397–399). An attempt to
update the outmessage is performed in Line 404. If this attempt fails then an error message
is shown and the method returns false, indicating the failure.

Listing 18.14 Method saveMessage( ) in PMessageDetailWindow

```
Method saveMessage() in PMessageDetailWindow

338:       private boolean saveMessage(){
339:           IAContact contact =
                   findContact(contacts,contactCmb.getSelectedItem().
                                                               toString());
340:           if(contact == null){
341:               JOptionPane.showMessageDialog(this,
                        "Please select contact information.",
                        "Contact Not Selected",JOptionPane.
                                               INFORMATION_MESSAGE);
342:               contactCmb.requestFocus();
343:               return false;
344:           }
               ... [cut to save space]
397:           msg.setSenderEmployee(employee);
398:           msg.setSubject(subject);
403:           try{
```

```
404:              admin.updateMessage(msg);
405:          }catch(Exception exc){
406:              exc.printStackTrace();
407:              JOptionPane.showMessageDialog(this,
                     "Fail to save message, please check that all fields
                     are filled.","Fail to Save",JOptionPane.
                                                   ERROR_MESSAGE);
408:              return false;
409:          }
410:          return true;
411:      }
```

Listing 18.15 Method okBtnActionPerformed( ) in PMessageDetailWindow

Method okBtnActionPerformed() in PMessageDetailWindow
| ```
413:      private void okBtnActionPerformed(ActionEvent evt) {
414:          if("Delete".equals(okBtn.getText())) admin.
                                                   deleteMessage(msg);
415:          closeDialog(null);
416:      }
``` |

The OK button serves two purposes (Listing 18.15). The first is as an indication that the user has finished with his/her activities on the outmessage, such as viewing it. The second is an indication that the user would like to delete the current message, if the PMessage-DetailWindow is uneditable (Line 414).

Listing 18.16 Method populateContact( ) in PMessageDetailWindow

Method populateContact() in PMessageDetailWindow
| ```
434:      private void populateContact(){
435:          contactCmb.removeAllItems();
438:          contacts = admin.listContacts();
439:          java.util.Iterator it = contacts.iterator();
440:          while(it.hasNext()){
441:              IAContact c = (IAContact) it.next();
442:              contactCmb.addItem(c.getFamilyName()+",
                                           "+c.getFirstName());
443:          }
444:      }
``` |

Populating the content of various widgets such as the contact or employee combo boxes is shown in Listing 18.16. The list of contacts is retrieved from CAdmin on Line 438. It is then iterated and added to the contactCmb combo box (Line 442).

Figure 18.7
PMessageTable-
Model.java

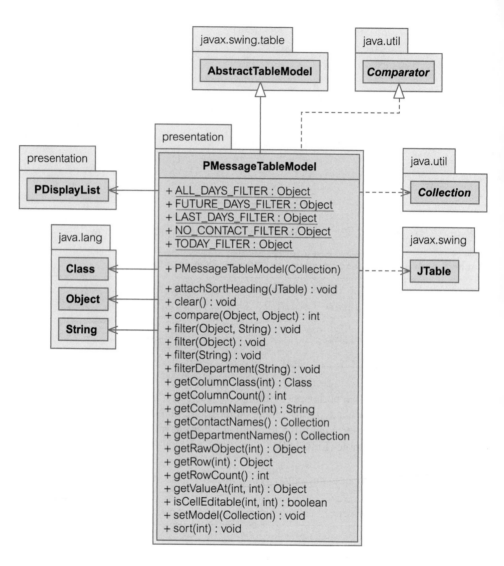

18.3.3 Class PMessageTableModel

The PMessageTableModel class represents the model for JTable (Figure 18.7). The model is used to store outmessages, filter the outmessages, provide services to JTable for the data to be displayed, and finally to perform sorting.

Methods such as getColumnCount(), getColumnName(), getColumnClass(), isCellEditable(), getRowCount(), getRow(), getValueAt(), clear() are overridden methods used to provide services for JTable. Please read Java documentation for their descriptions.

Listing 18.17 Fields in PMessageTableModel.java

```
Fields in PMessageTableModel.java

16:      public static final Object LAST_DAYS_FILTER = new Integer(0);
17:      public static final Object TODAY_FILTER = new Integer(1);
18:      public static final Object FUTURE_DAYS_FILTER = new
                                                        Integer(2);
19:      public static final Object ALL_DAYS_FILTER = new Integer(3);
20:      public static final Object NO_CONTACT_FILTER = "No contact
                                                        filter";

22:      private PDisplayList data;
23:      private int columnCount = 5;
24:      private boolean[] ascending = {true,true,true,true,true};
25:      private String[] columnName ={"Contact Name",
                "Message Subject",
                "Schedule Date",
                "Schedule Employee", "Scheduled Department"};
26:      private Class[] types = new Class [] {
27:          java.lang.String.class, java.lang.String.class,
             java.util.Date.class, java.lang.String.class,
             java.lang.String.class
28:      };
29:      boolean[] canEdit = {false,false,false,false,false};
```

Some static variables are defined in the `PMessageTableModel` class to provide filtering capabilities to the clients of the class (Listing 18.17). The class stores its data in `PDisplayList` (Line 22). Currently there are only five columns (Line 23) with defined names (Line 25) and sorting (Line 24). The types of the columns, needed by `getColumn-Class()`, are defined on Lines 26–27. All the columns are uneditable (Line 29).

The parameters of the `filter()` method provide information on whether the filtering is to be performed on contacts or dates (Listing 18.18). Depending on the type of filter required, the `setFilter()` method is called on the `data` object (which is an instance of `PDisplayList`). Once the filtering is done, the table needs to be updated via a call to `fireTableDataChanged()`.

However, if the filtering needs to be done on a contact only, there is a much simpler method `setFilterContact()` to call (Listing 18.19, Line 63). The data is filtered only on the specified contact and the table is updated accordingly. A similar approach applies to department filtering (not discussed in this chapter).

Sorting messages in the `PMessageTableModel` is quite an interesting task (Listing 18.20). First of all, the model is capable of handling multiple sorting columns as indicated by its `ascending` variable (Line 153). It uses the `java.util.Collections` class to perform the sorting (Line 154) and provides its own `compare()` method (implementation of `Comparable`). The `compare()` method gets the appropriate values from the input parameters (which are instances of `PDisplayData`, to be explained later). `PDisplayList`'s

Listing 18.18 Method filter( ) in PMessageTableModel – date and contact

Method filter() in PMessageTableModel - Date and Contact
| ```
44:    public void filter(Object datefilter, String contactfilter){
45:        if(contactfilter == NO_CONTACT_FILTER) contactfilter = null;
48:        if(ALL_DAYS_FILTER.equals(datefilter)){
49:          data.setFilter(3,contactfilter);
50:        }else if(LAST_DAYS_FILTER.equals(datefilter)){
51:          data.setFilter(0,contactfilter);
52:        }else if(TODAY_FILTER.equals(datefilter)){
53:          data.setFilter(1,contactfilter);
54:        }else if(FUTURE_DAYS_FILTER.equals(datefilter)){
55:          data.setFilter(2,contactfilter);
56:        }
58:        fireTableDataChanged();
59:    }
``` |

Listing 18.19 Method filter( ) in PMessageTableModel – contact only

Method filter() in PMessageTableModel - Contact Only
| ```
60:    public void filter(String contactfilter){
61:        if(contactfilter == NO_CONTACT_FILTER) contactfilter = null;
63:        data.setFilterContact(contactfilter);
64:        fireTableDataChanged();
65:    }
``` |

static methods, such as getContactName() (Lines 166–167), are used to acquire the appropriate values from v1 and v2. Once the values are acquired, they are compared to see whether o1 is greater than o2 or vice versa (Line 186). In the case when an exception occurs, the comparison is done based exclusively on whether the current column is ascending or descending (Lines 187–189).

Listing 18.20 Method sort( ) in PMessageTableModel

Method sort() in PMessageTableModel
| ```
149:   int sortColumn;
150:   public void sort(int column){
151:       if(data == null) return;
152:       sortColumn = column;
153:       ascending[column] = !ascending[column];
154:       Collections.sort(data.getData(), this);
155:       fireTableDataChanged();
156:   }
``` |
```

```
161:    public int compare(Object v1, Object v2) {
162:        Comparable o1= null, o2 = null;
163:        try{
164:            switch(sortColumn){
165:                case 0:
166:                    o1 = PDisplayList.getContactName(v1);
167:                    o2 = PDisplayList.getContactName(v2);
168:                    break;
               ...[cut to save space]
185:            }
186:            return ascending[sortColumn]?
                    o1.compareTo(o2):o2.compareTo(o1);
187:        }catch(Exception exc){
188:            return o1 == null?
                (ascending[sortColumn]?-1:1):(ascending
                                        [sortColumn]?1:-1);
189:        }
190:    }
```

Class PDisplayList

18.3.4

PDisplayList (Figure 18.8) is a class used to represent a list of outmessages. It has some common utitilities to extract information regarding the outmessages. Data stored in PDisplayList is in the format of PDisplayData. Methods such as getContactName(), getCreatorEmployeeName(), getScheduleData(), getScheduledDepartment(), getSenderEmployeeName(), getSubject() are some of the static utility methods. The return values of the above methods are of Comparable instance, which means that they can be compared against each other.

To fully support the filtering mechanism, PDisplayList needs to store data in two different containers (Listing 18.21). The first is called data (ArrayList, Line 16). The second is called invisibleData (Collection, Line 17). The usage of ArrayList versus Collection is arbitrary. ArrayList allows direct indexed access, whereas Collection does not. PDisplayData stored in data contains the *visible* outmessages displayed on the screen, whereas the ones in invisibleData are *not visible* on the screen.

Listing 18.21 Fields in PDisplayList.java

```
Fields in PDisplayList.java

16:        private ArrayList data;
17:        private Collection invisibleData;
18:        private int visibleSize = 0;
19:        private Filter filter;
```

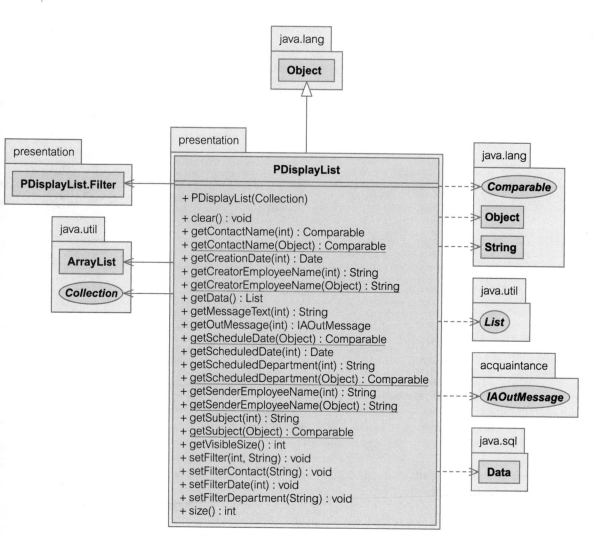

Figure 18.8 PDisplayList.java

The PDisplayList object is constructed by providing a list of outmessages (Listing 18.22). It iterates over the outmessages one after another (Line 29) and converts them into PDisplayData to be added into the data array list (Line 34). A filter object is created on Line 41. This provides generic filter functionalities discussed below in the context of the PDisplayList.Filter class.

'Getter' methods such as getOutMessage() are passed to the PDisplayData from the data collection (Listing 18.23, Line 71). Many other 'getter' methods work in similar fashion.

Listing 18.22 Constructor in PDisplayList

```
Constructor in PDisplayList

22:     public PDisplayList(Collection msgs) {
24:         data = new ArrayList(msgs.size());
25:         IAOutMessage msg = null;
26:         IAContact contact;
27:         IAEmployee emp;
28:         Iterator it=msgs.iterator();
29:         while(it.hasNext()){
30:             try{
31:                 msg = (IAOutMessage) it.next();
32:                 emp = msg.getSenderEmployee();
33:                 contact = msg.getContact();
34:                 data.add(new PDisplayData(msg,emp,contact));
35:             }catch(Exception exc){
36:                 exc.printStackTrace();
37:             }
38:         }
39:         visibleSize = data.size();
41:         filter = new Filter();
42:         invisibleData = new ArrayList();
43:     }
```

Listing 18.23 Method getOutMessage( ) in PDisplayList

```
Method getOutMessage() in PDisplayList

70:     public synchronized IAOutMessage getOutMessage(int index){
71:         PDisplayData d = (PDisplayData) data.get(index);
72:         return d.getOutMessage();
73:     }
```

Filtering on department or contact is done as shown in Listing 18.24 on Line 148. Once the filtering is done, the display needs to be updated to reflect visibility of data via updateVisible().

Listing 18.24 Method setFilterDepartment( ) in PDisplayList

```
Method setFilterDepartment() in PDisplayList

147:    public synchronized void setFilterDepartment(String deptCode){
148:        filter.setFilterDept(deptCode);
149:        updateVisible();
150:    }
```

The following rule is applied to perform filtering. All `data` is placed in the `invisible-Data` collection and removed from the visible collection (Listing 18.25, Lines 158–159). The data is then iterated row after row (Line 163) and passed to the `filter()` method of the `PDisplayList.Filter` class (Line 165). If the `filter()` method returns `true`, then the outmessage is added to the `data` collection and removed from `invisibleData`.

Listing 18.25 Method updateVisible( ) in PDisplayList

```
Method updateVisible() in PDisplayList

156:      private void updateVisible(){
158:          invisibleData.addAll(data);
159:          data.clear();
160:          visibleSize = 0;
162:          Iterator it = invisibleData.iterator();
163:          while(it.hasNext()){
164:              Object o = it.next();
165:              if(filter.filter(o)){
166:                  data.add(o); //put into visible
167:                  it.remove(); //remove from invisible
168:                  visibleSize++;
169:              }
170:          }
171:      }
```

18.3.5 Class PDisplayList.Filter

`Filter` is an inner class of `PdisplayList`. It provides filtering on outmessages (Listing 18.26). Method signatures show that each `setFilter()` method supports a different category, such as filter on date, filter on contact as well as on department.

Listing 18.26 PDisplayList.Filter method summary

```
boolean   filter(java.lang.Object o)
void      setFilter(int datetype)
void      setFilter(int datetype, java.lang.String contactName)
void      setFilter(java.lang.String contactName)
void      setFilterDept(java.lang.String deptCode)
```

Depending on the type to be filtered, the `filter()` method chooses different comparison strategies (Listing 18.27). If the `datetype` is set, then the messages are filtered based first on the date (Line 213). The outmessage's date (Line 211 in `getScheduled-Date()`) is compared with today's date to determine whether the outmessage is *past*, *current*, or *future* (Lines 215–219, not everything shown). Once the outmessage is filtered on date, it is further checked against the department code filter (Line 239). At the end of the process, the method declares whether the outmessage passes the filter (`selected`) or not.

Listing 18.27 Method filter( ) in Filter

```
Method filter() in Filter
207:          public boolean filter(Object o){
208:              PDisplayData d = (PDisplayData) o;
209:              Calendar today = new GregorianCalendar();
210:              Calendar oCal = new GregorianCalendar();
211:              oCal.setTime(d.getScheduledDate());
212:              boolean selected = false;
213:              switch(datetype){
214:                  case 0: //past
215:                      selected = oCal.before(today) &&
                             !isToday(today,oCal);
216:                      break;
                     ...[cut to save space]
223:                  case 3: //all
224:                      selected = true;
225:                      break;
226:                  default:
227:                      selected = true;
228:                      break;
229:              }
232:              if(selected && contactName != null){
233:                  try{
234:                      selected=contactName.indexOf(
                             d.getContactFamilyName().toLowerCase())
                                                       != -1 ||
235:                          contactName.indexOf(
                             d.getContactFirstName().toLowerCase()) != -1;
237:                  }catch(Exception exc){}
238:              }
239:              if(selected && deptCode != null){
240:                  try{
241:                      selected = d.getScheduledDepartmentCode()
                             .toLowerCase().equals(deptCode);
242:                  }catch(Exception exc){}
243:              }
244:              return selected;
245:          }
```

Figure 18.9
Classes in the
Control package

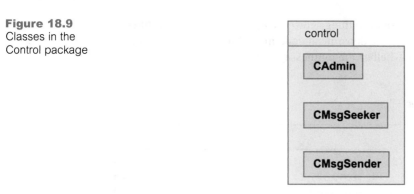

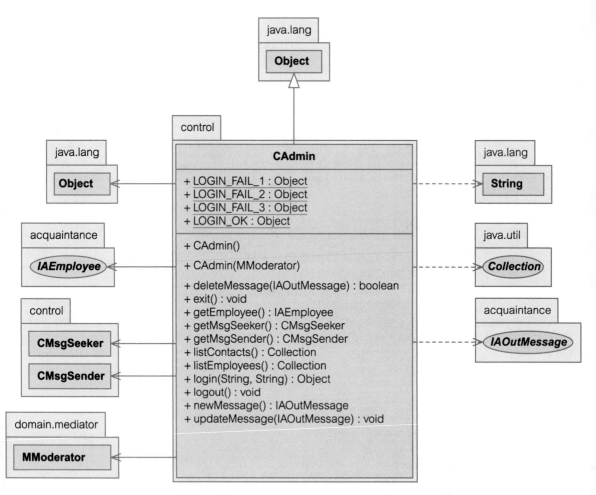

Figure 18.10 Class CAdmin in EM 2

Package Control

The `control` package consists of three classes (Figure 18.9). Much of the behavior of `CAdmin`, `CMsgSeeker`, and `CMsgSender` has been covered before in Chapters 13, 14, and 15.

Class CAdmin

As mentioned, the `CAdmin` class (Figure 18.10) carries no significant changes from Iteration 1 (Chapter 13). Additional methods are `newMessage()`, `getMsgSeeker()`, `getMsgSender()`, `listContacts()`, and `listEmployees()`. The employee and contact lists are required to populate various combo boxes in the `presentation` package. The method `newMessage()` is used to create a new outmessage to be stored in the database.

Class CMsgSeeker

The services of the `CMsgSeeker` class (Figure 18.11) were analyzed in Chapter 15 where a refactoring decision was taken to divide `CActioner` into `CMsgSeeker` and `CMsgSender`. There are three distinct methods to search for outmessages: outmessages for current employee, for the employee's department, or all outmessages irrespective of employee or department.

Listing 18.28 presents the code excerpts related to the three retrieval methods. Note that outmessages already contained in the `msgs` collection will not be re-retrieved (Lines 64–68).

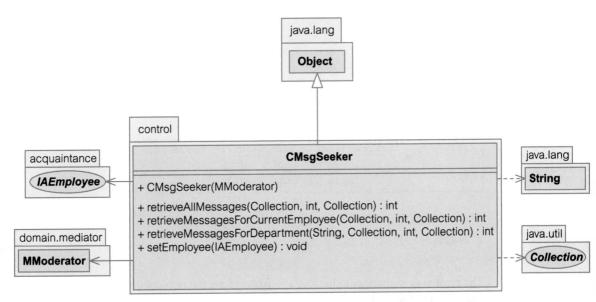

Figure 18.11 Class CMsgSeeker in EM 2

Listing 18.28 Message retrieval methods in CMsgSeeker

Method `retrieveMessagesForCurrentEmployee()`,`retrieveMessagesFor-Department()`, and `retrieveAllMessages()` in CMsgSeeker

```
48:    public int retrieveMessagesForCurrentEmployee(
49:        Collection msgs,
50:        int numMsgs,
51:        Collection msgIDs) {
53:        int remainder = moderator.retrieveUnsentMessages(
                emp, msgs, numMsgs);
56:        if (msgIDs == null || msgIDs.isEmpty())
57:            return remainder;
60:        Iterator it = msgs.iterator();
61:        while (it.hasNext()) {
62:            IAOutMessage msg = (IAOutMessage) it.next();
63:            Integer id = new Integer(msg.getMessageID());
64:            if (!msgIDs.contains(id)) {
65:                it.remove();
66:                remainder++;
68:            }
69:        }
70:        return remainder;
77:    }
91:    public int retrieveMessagesForDepartment(String departmentCode,
92:        Collection msgs,
93:        int numMsgs,
94:        Collection msgIDs) {
96:        int remainder = moderator.retrieveUnsentMessages(
                    departmentCode, msgs, numMsgs);
            ...[same as Line 56-77]
134:   public int retrieveAllMessages(
135:        Collection msgs,
136:        int numMsgs,
137:        Collection msgIDs) {
139:        int remainder = moderator.retrieveUnsentMessages(msgs,
                numMsgs);
            ...[same as Line 56-77]
```

18.5 Package Entity

The most visible changes in the `entity` package are the introduction of the `IEObjectID` interface and the `EIdentityMap` class (Figure 18.12). Changes to other `entity` objects are minimal. The changes relate to the inclusion of necessary code to help `EIdentityMap`

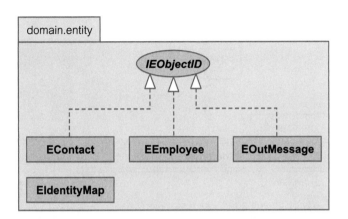

Figure 18.12
Classes in the
Entity package

manage the **cache** (the dirty property of objects) and the establishment of proper references between entity objects, i.e. **Navigation in Entity Classes** as opposed to Navigation in Identity Map (Section 15.3.4). There is an association from `EIdentityMap` to `IEObjectID`, but the association is maintained in maps and therefore not properly shown in Figure 18.12. Refer to Section 18.2 'Package Acquaintance' for descriptions of methods implemented in this package.

`IEObjectID` provides a simplified interface to specify the property of an OID. `IEObjectID` carries two methods: `getOID()` and `setOID(int)`. Other `entity` objects support the notion of OID by ensuring that the association links are traversable through the sequence of OIDs in each entity object. For example, it is possible for an `EOutMessage` object to be queried (via `getContactOID()`) for its `EContact` since it stores the `contactOID` as the reference. The real `IAContact` may or may not yet be loaded into the memory. This is the implementation of the **OID Proxy** pattern explained in Section 15.3.4. The use of OID is explained in Section 13.5.1 'Object Identifiers and Identity Field Pattern'.

Apart from the above additional methods, the `EEmployee` class supports a new `department` property. This property is used in the Iteration 2 specification to identify outmessages that are assigned to a particular employee's department (the subflow *S1.2– View Department Unsent*, Section 14.2.3).

Class EIdentityMap 18.5.1

The `EIdentityMap` (Figure 18.13) class is explained in Section 15.3.1. Its purpose is to store the cache of entity objects to be used by the application.

`EIdentityMap` stores entity objects via various mappings between each entity's PK, its OID, and the entity object itself. Lines 20–22 in Listing 18.29 are only used internally by the `EIdentityMap` to ensure that entity objects are not loaded more than once. The main map is the `OIDToObj` map. This map is used to fetch an object identified by the OID.

Figure 18.13
Class
EIdentityMap
in EM 2

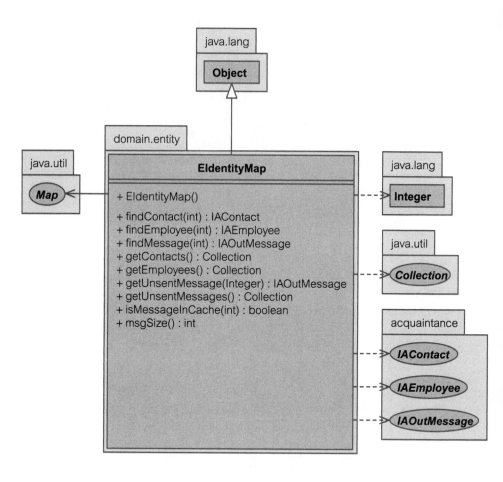

Listing 18.29 Fields in EIdentityMap

```
Fields in EIdentityMap

19:      private Map OIDToObj; //OID -> Obj
20:      private Map msgPKToOID; //msgPK -> OID
21:      private Map empPKToOID; //empPK -> OID
22:      private Map ctcPKToOID; //ctcPK -> OID
```

The `registerContact()` method (Listing 18.30) gets the given `oidObject`'s OID and puts it into the contact map (Line 38) and finally to `OIDToObj` (Line 39). Replace `ctcPKToOID` with `empPKToOID` or `msgPKToOID` to perform registration for employee and message objects. The only modification required to unregister the objects (either employee, contact, or outmessage) is the change of method calls from *put* to *remove* on the mappers.

Listing 18.30 Method registerContact( ) in EIdentityMap

```
Method registerContact() in EIdentityMap

36:    public void registerContact(IEObjectID oidObject) {
37:        Integer oid = new Integer(oidObject.getOID());
38:        ctcPKToOID.put(((IAContact)oidObject).getContactID(),oid);
39:        OIDToObj.put(oid, oidObject);
40:    }
```

Listing 18.31 shows how an `EOutMessage` object is retrieved from the cache. A similar technique is used for `findContact()`, `findEmployee()`, `getContact()`, and `getEmployee()`. The `findContact()`, `findEmployee()`, and `findMessage()` methods are examples of `OIDToObj` map usage.

Listing 18.31 Method getUnsentMessage( ) and findMessage( ) in EIdentityMap

```
Method getUnsentMessage() and findMessage() in EIdentityMap

67:    public IAOutMessage getUnsentMessage(Integer msgID) {
68:        Integer oid = (Integer) msgPKToOID.get(msgID);
70:        if (oid == null)
71:            return null;
72:        return findMessage(oid.intValue());
73:    }
62:    public IAOutMessage findMessage(int msgOID) {
63:        return (IAOutMessage) OIDToObj.get(new Integer(msgOID));
64:    }
```

Listing 18.32 shows how the `getUnsentMessages()` method iterates through the list of outmessages' PKs in the cache and requests `findMessage()` to get the entity object. The other methods to obtain employees and contacts (`getEmployees()` and `getContacts()`) are similar. Whereas `getUnsentMessages()` retrieves from the `msgPKToOID` map, `getContacts()` retrieves from the `ctcPKToOID` map and `getEmployees()` from the `empPKToOID` map.

Listing 18.32 Method getUnsentMessages( ) in EIdentityMap

```
Method getUnsentMessages() in EIdentityMap

76:    public Collection getUnsentMessages() {
77:        Collection c = new ArrayList();
78:        Iterator it = msgPKToOID.values().iterator();
79:        while (it.hasNext()){
80:            Object o = findMessage(((Integer) it.next()).intValue());
81:            if(o != null) c.add(o);
82:        }
83:        return c;
84:    }
```

Figure 18.14
Classes in the
Mediator package
of EM 2

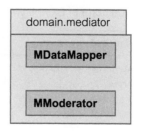

18.6 Package Mediator

The `mediator` package (Figure 18.14) is extensively discussed in Chapter 15. Here, it is included for completeness.

Major changes in the `mediator` package between Iteration 1 and Iteration 2, as explained in Chapter 15, include the following:

■ `MDataMapper` is introduced as the class that is responsible for the mapping between raw data in database and their entity objects in the cache.

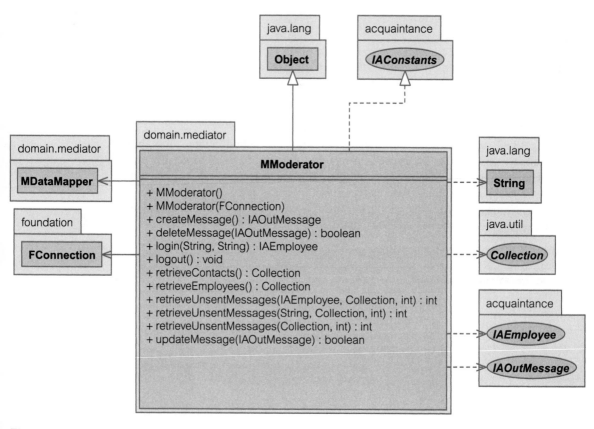

Figure 18.15 Class MModerator in EM 2

- MDataMapper collaborates with EIdentityMap. EIdentityMap is used as a cache manager for entity objects.
- All requests to loading and unloading of entity objects are moderated by MModerator.

Class MModerator

The MModerator class (Figure 18.15) intercepts all entity object retrievals and redirects these requests to EIdentityMap or to MDataMapper. Message retrievals are divided into three categories: retrieval by employee details, by department details, and finally all unsent outmessages irrespective of their employee or department details.

Listing 18.33 shows how the login is done in MModerator. Initially the FConnection is queried to check if the user is connected to the database (Line 72) and, if not, the connection is made (Line 74). Once the connection is established, the employee's data is retrieved from MDataMapper (method retrieveEmployeeByName() on Line 80).

Listing 18.33 Method login( ) in MModerator

```
Method login() in MModerator
70:      public IAEmployee login(String username, String passwd) {
71:          try {
72:              if (!connection.isConnected()) {
74:                  if (!connection.connect(username, passwd))
75:                      return null;
76:              }
80:              IAEmployee emp = mapper.retrieveEmployeeByName
                                                        (username);

82:              return emp;
83:          } catch (Exception exc) {
84:          }
85:          return null;
86:      }
```

Class MDataMapper

The MDataMapper class provides services to load raw data into entity objects and to unload them into the database (Figure 18.16). Entity object retrievals are achieved via calls such as retrieveEmployeeByID(), retrieveContactByID(), etc. The unload-Messsage() method unloads outmessage objects into the database. Currently there is no need to have other unload methods, for contact or employee, as they are never changed by the application.

Associations to FReader and FWriter are required to allow MDataMapper to interact with the database (Listing 18.34). EIdentityMap serves as the cache manager for all entity objects. A list of OIDs is maintained only for the purpose of ensuring that newly

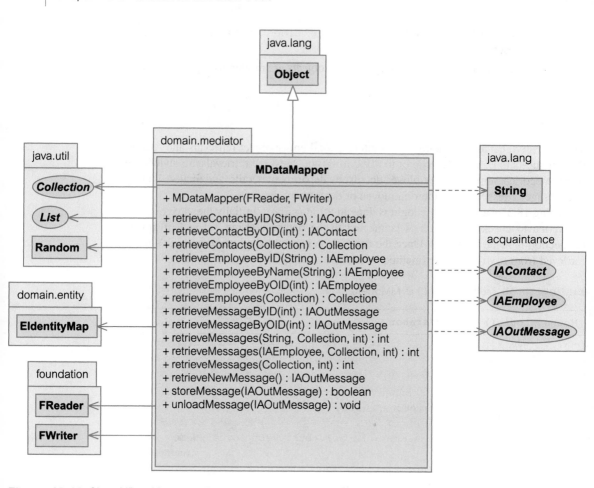

Figure 18.16 Class MDataMapper in EM 2

Listing 18.34 Fields in MDataMapper

```
Fields in MDataMapper.java

33:      private FReader reader;
34:      private FWriter writer;
35:      private EIdentityMap cache;
36:      private List OIDs;
37:      private boolean contactFullyRetrieved,employeeFullyRetrieved;
38:      private Random rand;
39:      private Collection newMsgOIDs;
```

created OIDs do not conflict with pre-existing ones. A random number, represented by
rand, is used to generate new OIDs for new outmessages not yet saved in the database.
Once an entity object is saved in the database, it is assigned a proper OID. Finally, newly
created outmessages are stored in collections of their own, newMsgOIDs. This is because
they require special treatment in terms of entity deletion or saving. A deletion of newly
created entity objects does not require the deletion of corresponding records in the
database, provided they are not saved in the database yet. Otherwise, they are to be
removed from memory and deleted from the database.

Outmessage retrievals and loading

There are times when an outmessage becomes **dirty** and needs to be reloaded. Listing 18.35
shows how outmessage re-retrieval is done by calling retrieveMessageByID()
(Line 62). A special case needs to be applied if the input parameter, msg, is a newly
created outmessage (not yet saved in the database, Line 60). If it is a newly created outmessage, then it is not reloaded from the database (there is no record of it in the database
anyway).

Listing 18.35 Method reretrieveMessage() in MDataMapper

```
Method reretrieveMessage() in MDataMapper

57:     private IAOutMessage reretrieveMessage(IAOutMessage msg) {
60:         if(newMsgOIDs.contains(
                new Integer(((EOutMessage)msg).getOID())))) return null;
62:         return retrieveMessageByID(msg.getMessageID());
63:     }
```

Iteration 2 provides three different types of outmessage retrieval. The first one is the
retrieval of outmessages assigned to a particular employee, the second is for outmessages
assigned to employees of a particular department, and the third for all unsent outmessages
irrespective of their assigned employees or departments (Listing 18.36).

The retrievals acquire the outmessages from EIdentityMap (cache on Line 171). The
iterated outmessages are re-retrieved if they are found dirty (Lines 175–176). Only a
subset of outmessages is returned. This depends on the value of numMsgs as given to
fillArrayUpto() (Line 180). The retrieveMessages() method returns the number
of outmessages in the cache (and database) so that the caller knows the number of
outmessages that could further be retrieved. This number is calculated on Line 185.
fillArrayUpto() returns zero if the total number in the collection is less than numMsgs,
otherwise it returns the total size of outmessages in the collection.

The retrieval of outmessages from the database is the main responsibility of do-
RetrieveMessages() (Listing 18.37). This method executes a retrieval query from
FReader (Line 200), finds out the total number of objects that exist in the database
(Line 201), and populates the cache (Line 209) with the created outmessage objects
(Lines 207–208). The outmessages are inserted into the results collection (Line 210).

Listing 18.36 Method retrieveMessages( ) in MDataMapper

Method retrieveMessages() in MDataMapper - irrespective of dept and emp

```
169:    public int retrieveMessages(Collection msgs, int numMsgs) {
171:         Collection cc = cache.getUnsentMessages();
172:         ArrayList c = new ArrayList(cc.size());
173:         for (Iterator it = cc.iterator(); it.hasNext();) {
174:             IAOutMessage m = (IAOutMessage) it.next();
175:             if (m.isDirty()) //re-retrieve the message if dirty
176:                 m = reretrieveMessage(m);
177:             if(m != null && !c.contains(m)) c.add(m);
178:         }
179:     String sql="Select * from outmessage where date_emailed
        is null";
180:         int total = fillArrayUpto(numMsgs,c,sql);
181:         msgs.addAll(c);
185:         return total > 0 ? total - numMsgs : total;
186:     }
```

Listing 18.37 Method doRetrieveMessages( ) in MDataMapper

Method doRetrieveMessages() in MDataMapper

```
191:    private int doRetrieveMessages(String sql,Collection results,
194:    int numMsgs) {
195:        int count = 0, total = 0;
197:        EOutMessage msg = null;
198:        java.sql.ResultSet rs = null;
199:        try {
200:            rs = reader.query(sql);
201:            total = rs.getStatement().getMaxRows();
202:            while (rs.next()) {
203:                count++;
204:                if (count > numMsgs)
205:                    break;
207:                msg = (EOutMessage) createOutMessage();
208:                fillOutMessage(rs, msg);
209:                cache.registerMessage(msg);
210:                results.add(msg);
211:            }
        ...[cut to save space]
216:        return total;
217:    }
```

`MDataMapper` provides some methods to allow the client to query its data. Method `retrieveMessageByOID()` returns an outmessage that corresponds to the given OID (or null if outmessage does not exist) (Listing 18.38). The method simply redirects the query to the cache `EIdentityMap`. Other methods such as `retrieveEmplyeeByOID()` and `retrieveContactByOID()` perform similar actions.

Listing 18.38 Method retrieveMessageByOID( ) in MDataMapper

```
Method retrieveMessageByOID() in MDataMapper

237:    public IAOutMessage retrieveMessageByOID(int oid) {
238:        return cache.findMessage(oid);
239:    }
```

Creating a new outmessage object to be filled and then inserted into the database is done by `retrieveNewMessage()` (Listing 18.39). A new outmessage object is created (Line 221) and its OID is randomly generated (Line 224). The OID needs to be unique for the application and therefore is checked if it does not exist in the cache (by calling `findMessage()` from `EIdentityMap`) (Line 225). A new outmessage ID needs to be retrieved from the database to ensure that the outmessage has a proper primary key (Line 228, `retrieveNewMessageID()`). All newly created outmessages are registered in `newMsgOIDs`. Finally, the outmessage needs to be flagged as dirty and registered in the cache (Lines 231–232).

Listing 18.39 Method retrieveNewMessage( ) in MDataMapper

```
Method retrieveNewMessage() in MDataMapper

220:    public IAOutMessage retrieveNewMessage(){
221:        EOutMessage msg = (EOutMessage) createOutMessage();
222:        int msgOID;
223:        do{ //keep trying when the msgOID has been used
224:            msgOID = rand.nextInt();
225:        }while(cache.findMessage(msgOID) != null);
227:        msg.setOID(msgOID);
228:        msg.setMessageID(retrieveNewMessageID());
229:        newMsgOIDs.add(new Integer(msgOID));
231:        cache.registerMessage(msg);
232:        msg.setDirty(true);
233:        return msg;
234:    }
```

Listing 18.40 Method unloadMessage( ) in MDataMapper

```
Method unloadMessage() in MDataMapper

134:     public void unloadMessage(IAOutMessage msg) throws Exception{
135:         msg.setDirty(true);
136:         cache.unregisterMessage((IEObjectID)msg);
138:         Integer oid = new Integer(((EOutMessage)msg).getOID());
139:         if(newMsgOIDs.contains(oid)){
140:             newMsgOIDs.remove(oid);
141:             return;
142:         }
144:         PreparedStatement st = null;
145:         try{
146:             st = writer.delete("delete from outmessage where
                                    message_id = ?");
147:             st.setInt(1, msg.getMessageID());
148:             st.execute();
             ...[cut to save space]
```

Outmessage saving and unloading

Message unloading requires two steps (Listing 18.40). The first is to unload it from the cache, as done on Line 136. The second is deletion from database as shown on Lines 146–148. If the message is a newly created message, which is not yet saved in the database, then there is no need to remove it from the database (Lines 139–142).

Listing 18.41 shows how an outmessage is stored back in the database. Initially the outmessage needs to be checked to see whether it is newly created and does not exist in the database (Lines 278–282). If it is new, the SQL insert statement is executed (Line 287), otherwise an update on already existing data must be performed (Line 288). Lines 290–306 prepare the PreparedStatement for the insertion into the database, depending on whether it is an insertion or update statement (Lines 302 and 306). If the insertion is successful, then the messageOID is removed from the pool of newMsgOIDs (Line 305).

There is another possibile way to update an outmessage. The outmessage could be marked as sent (Line 308, getSentDate()). If the outmessage is marked as sent, then there is a need to remove it from the cache (Lines 310–323). The EM application is concerned only with unsent outmessages. However, if an outmessage is not marked as sent, then it needs to be re-registered (Lines 325–330) to replace the old reference in the cache.

Listing 18.41 Method storeMessage( ) in MDataMapper

Method storeMessage() in MDataMapper

```
274:    public boolean storeMessage(IAOutMessage msg) {
275:        boolean newMsg = false;
276:        Integer oid = new Integer(((EOutMessage)msg).getOID());
277:        try {
278:            if(newMsgOIDs.contains(oid)){ //store new message
279:                newMsg = true;
282:            }
285:            String sql = null;
287:            if(newMsg) sql = "insert into outmessage(
                    sender_emp_id,creator_emp_id,contact_id,
                    message_subject,message_text,date_scheduled,
                    date_emailed,department_code,message_id,date_
                                                        created)
                    values(?,?,?,?,?,?,?,?,?,?)";
288:            else sql = "Update OutMessage set sender_emp_id = ?,
                        creator_emp_id = ?, contact_id = ?,
                        message_subject = ?, message_text = ?,
                        date_scheduled = ?, date_emailed = ?,
                        department_code = ? where message_id = ?";
290:            PreparedStatement st = writer.prepareStatement(sql);
291:            if(msg.getSenderEmployeeID() == null)
                    st.setNull(1,java.sql.Types.VARCHAR);
292:            else st.setString(1, msg.getSenderEmployeeID());
293:            st.setString(2, msg.getScheduledEmployeeID());
294:            st.setString(3, msg.getCreatorEmployeeID());
295:            st.setString(4,msg.getContactID());
296:            st.setString(5, msg.getSubject());
297:            st.setString(6, msg.getMessageText());
298:            st.setDate(7,msg.getScheduleDate());
299:            st.setDate(8,msg.getSentDate());
300:            st.setString(9, msg.getDepartmentCode());
301:            st.setInt(10, msg.getMessageID());
302:            if(newMsg){
303:                st.setDate(11,msg.getCreationDate());
304:                st.execute();
305:                newMsgOIDs.remove(oid);
306:            }else st.executeUpdate();
308:            if(msg.getSentDate() != null){
310:                msg.getContact().removeOutMessage(msg);
311:                msg.getCreatorEmployee().
                                    removeOutMessageCreator(msg);
311:                msg.getCreatorEmployee().
                                    removeOutMessageCreator(msg);
```

```
312:                    msg.getScheduledEmployee().
                                        removeOutMessageScheduler(msg);
313:                    msg.getSenderEmployee().
                                        removeOutMessageSender(msg);
315:                    msg.setContact(null);
316:                    msg.setCreatorEmployee(null);
317:                    msg.setSenderEmployee(null);
318:                    msg.setScheduledEmployee(null);
319:                    msg.setDirty(true);
321:                    cache.unregisterMessage((IEObjectID) msg);
322:                    return true;
323:                }
325:            cache.registerMessage((IEObjectID)msg);
328:            msg.getContact().addOutMessage(msg);
329:            msg.getCreatorEmployee().addOutMessageCreator(msg);
330:            msg.getSenderEmployee().addOutMessageSender(msg);
331:        } catch (Exception exc) {
332:            System.out.println("ERROR in update/insert");
333:            exc.printStackTrace();
334:            return false;
335:        }
336:        return true;
337:    }
```

18.7 Presentation Layer: Applet Version

As discussed in Section 17.1.3, there are two different types of *applet* – a thin applet and a thick applet. A **thin applet** is a set of classes that make up an application which performs most of its activities on the server. A **thick applet** is a set of classes that is equivalent to an application performing most of its activities on client site rather than on the server.

The applet version implemented in the EM Iteration 2 is a thick applet. It is slower to load, as most of its code is in the client. However, it is easier to develop, as much of the code is already available in the Iteration 2 code for the desktop UI. In fact, the only changes required are to modify PWindow to inherit from Applet rather than from Frame, plus some extra modifications to support the Applet lifecycle.

As shown in Figure 18.17, PWindow is modified to inherit from JApplet. It still has a reference to a Frame since an applet has to be loaded inside a Frame. PWindow has been implemented such that it can run as an application as well as an applet. The main() method serves as the entry point to launch the program as an application. Methods such as getAppletInfo(), getParameter(), and getParameterInfo() are provided to support various services required to be implemented by the applet and available to the environment in which the applet lives (usually a web browser or applet viewer). The init() method is supplied to construct and run the applet in the web browser.

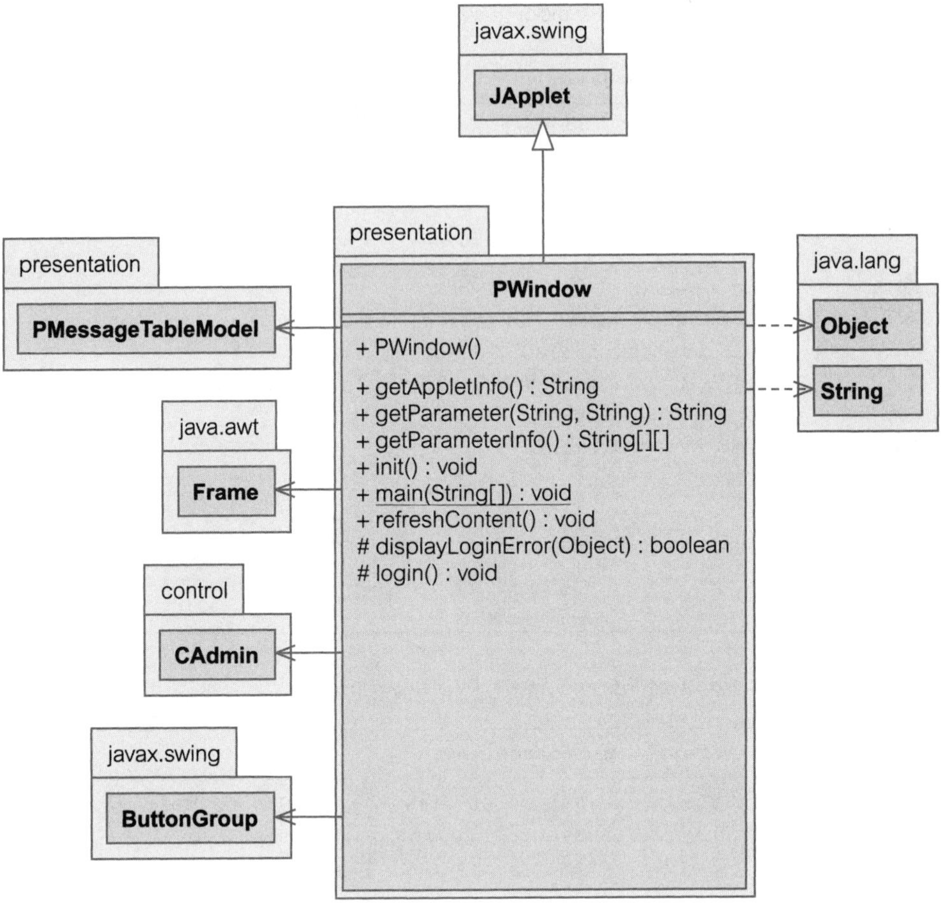

Figure 18.17
Class PWindow in
EM 2 applet

The PWindow construction is almost the same as in Section 18.3.1. The only difference is the removal of Lines 37–45 (Listing 18.42). These lines are moved to the init() method to ensure that the applet UI appears on the screen. The applet lifecycle states that all UI construction should be placed in the init() section rather than other sections. If Lines 37–45 are not moved to init() and left in the constructor, the applet will not show any GUI but rather a simple blank screen.

The getParameter() method allows the applet to query its environment regarding certain parameters or properties (Listing 18.43). The signature of getParameter() specifies that it will find the value corresponding to the given key and if such a key is not found in the system, it will return the default (def) value. If this applet is executed as a standalone application, then the function queries the system properties supported by java.lang.System (Line 51). However, if this applet is executed as an applet, then the queries are redirected through the parent class's getParameter() method (Line 52). Line 52 says that if getParameter() returns a null value, then the default def will be returned instead.

Listing 18.42 Constructor in PWindow.java (applet)

```
Constructor in PWindow.java
31:     public PWindow() throws Exception {
32:         designMode = true;
33:         admin = new CAdmin();
34:
35:         //pop for login
36:         login();
37: /*        model = new PMessageTableModel(retrieveData(1));
38:         initComponents();
39:         model.attachSortHeading(viewTable); //activate the sorting
40:         populateContact();
41:         populateDepartment();
42:         setButtonsEnable(false);
43:
44:         designMode = false;
45: */
46:     }
```

Listing 18.43 Method getParameter( ) in PWindow (applet)

```
Method getParameter() in PWindow.java
50:     public String getParameter(String key, String def) {
51:         return isStandalone ? System.getProperty(key, def) :
52:             (getParameter(key) != null ? getParameter(key) : def);
53:     }
```

The `init()` method of `PWindow` simply constructs a `PWindow` GUI. It does not offer any special code and therefore is not discussed here.

18.8 Presentation Layer: Servlet Version

'Servlet' is short for 'server applet'. It behaves similarly to an applet but is located on the server. It serves user requests using the HTTP standard. Servlet displays the HTML (or other web-enabled) format viewable to the user. The servlet version of the EM Iteration 2 (Section 17.5) requires modifications to the `presentation` layer. All classes in the `presentation` layer are replaced with two classes: `PEMS` and `PEMSEdit`.

Analogous to applet, servlet has some methods that need to be overridden in the implementation. The methods are `getServletInfo()`, `doPost()`, `doGet()`, `init()`, and `destroy()`. The `doPost()` method is said to serve *post* actions in HTML. The `doGet()` method is called to answer *get* actions in HTML. By default, a *get* action is called when a servlet is loaded from web browser unless *post* is specifically requested. The methods init() and destroy() are used to notify the servlet that it is ready to be loaded/unloaded into the environment (server) respectively.

Class PEMS

The PEMS class handles the main interaction between the user and the EM system (Figure 18.18). Apart from standard methods to support the servlet lifecycle, PEMS also supports the actions of sending and viewing outmessages.

There are three fields defined in PEMS (Listing 18.44). The fields are used to identify whether the user is in *View Department Messages* (Line 27), or *View Own Messages* (Line 28), or *View All Messages* (Line 29).

The init() method of PEMS (Listing 18.45) is different from its applet (PWindow) counterpart. In PWindow, there is a need to place all GUI construction code into init(). This is no longer applicable on the servlet as the servlet's GUI is shown only when the user requests it either via doGet() or doPost(). This is why the init() in PEMS calls only its superclass's init() to initialize the servlet.

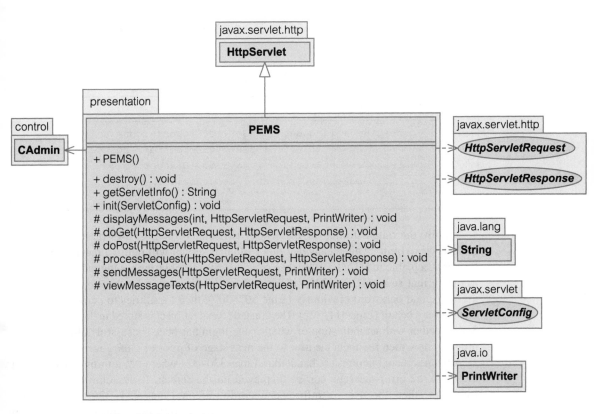

Figure 18.18 PEMS in EM 2 (servlet)

Listing 18.44 Fields in PEMS.java

```
Fields in PEMS.java

25:     public class PEMS extends HttpServlet {
26:         //is it dept, emp, or all messages to be displayed
27:         static final int DEPT_ONLY = 1;
28:         static final int EMP_ONLY = 2;
29:         static final int ALL = 3;
```

Listing 18.45 Method init( ) in PEMS

```
Method init() in PEMS

33:     public void init(ServletConfig config) throws ServletException {
34:         super.init(config);
35:
36:     }
```

Login in servlet

The methods `doGet()` and `doPost()` are the same (Listing 18.46). They forward the requests to `processRequest()`.

Listing 18.46 Method doGet( ) in PEMS

```
Method doGet() in PEMS

349:    protected void doGet(HttpServletRequest request,
                                    HttpServletResponse response)
350:    throws ServletException, java.io.IOException {
351:        processRequest(request, response);
352:    }
```

Initially the output format of the servlet is declared on Line 245 (Listing 18.47) to indicate 'text/html'. This means that this particular servlet will return a result page in the format acceptable to HTML. PEMS then checks if the current user has logged in previously in the current session (Line 248). If the user has not logged in but has supplied his/her username and password previously (Line 307–309), then PEMS tries to perform the login on the user's behalf (Line 311–322). The created CAdmin object is stored in the session (Line 312) together with an indication of whether the login has been successful (Line 315). The program flow then redirects the user to the next stage of `processRequest()` (Line 316).

Any unexpected failures are handled in Lines 320–321 where PEMS throws an error and therefore the error message can be displayed on the screen. If the login does not pass Line 314, then the user is informed accordingly on Lines 324–326 together with Lines 333–343. Lines 327–343 are also used as the starting point for the servlet when the user requests an *http-get* for the first time. This simply displays the login window.

Listing 18.47 Method processRequest( ) in PEMS – login

```
Method processRequest() in PEMS - Login

243:    protected void processRequest(HttpServletRequest request,
                                       HttpServletResponse response)
244:    throws ServletException, java.io.IOException {
245:        response.setContentType("text/html");
246:        java.io.PrintWriter out = response.getWriter();
247:
248:        Object logged = request.getSession().getAttribute("logged");
            ...[cut, discussed on next listing]
306:        }else{ //not logged-in yet, check if username/
            passwd is entered
307:            String username = (String) request.
                                            getParameter("username");
308:            String passwd = (String) request.
                                            getParameter("passwd");
309:            if(username != null && passwd != null){
310:                try{
311:                    CAdmin admin = new CAdmin();
312:                    request.getSession().setAttribute("admin",admin);
313:                    Object o = admin.login(username,passwd);
314:                    if(CAdmin.LOGIN_OK.equals(o)){
315:                        request.getSession().setAttribute("logged",
                                            new Boolean(true));
316:                        processRequest(request,response);
317:                        return;
318:                    }
319:                }catch(Exception exc){
320:                    exc.printStackTrace(out);
321:                    throw new ServletException(exc.getMessage());
322:                }
323:                //display login error message
324:                out.println("<html><head><title>EMS
                                            Login</title></head><body>");
325:                out.println("<h1><center>PSE's Email Management
                            System<br/>Servlet Version</center></h1>");
326:                out.println("<p><H2>Login ERROR...Please try
                                            again</H2>");
327:            }else{
328:                //display standard heading
329:                out.println("<html><head><title>EMS
                                            Login</title></head><body>");
330:                out.println("<h1><center>PSE's Email Management
                            System<br/>Servlet Version</center></h1>");
331:            }
```

```
332:
333:            out.println("<p><center>You need to login before
                                    further processing</center><p>");
334:            out.println("<form method=post>");
335:            out.println("<center><table>");
336:            out.println("<tr><td>Username</td><td><input
                                name=username type=text maxlength=32
                                                    size=16></td></tr>");
337:            out.println("<tr><td>Password</td><td><input
                                type=password name=passwd maxlength=32
                                                    size=16></td></tr>");
338:            out.println("<tr><td align=center><input type=submit
                        value=Submit></td><td align=center>
                        <input type=reset value=Clear></td></tr>");
339:            out.println("</table></center></form>");
340:            out.println("</body></html>");
341:        }
342:        out.close();
343:    }
```

Showing outmessages in servlet

If the user has logged in successfully (Line 249 in Listing 18.48), then PEMS checks whether a *send* outmessage has been requested (Line 264) or perhaps this was a *view*

Listing 18.48 Method processRequest( ) in PEMS – Show Messages

Method processRequest() in PEMS - Show Messages

```
243:    protected void processRequest(HttpServletRequest request,
                                        HttpServletResponse response)
244:    throws ServletException, java.io.IOException {
            ...[cut, refer to Login listing above]
249:        if(logged != null){ //s/he has logged-in successfully
251:            out.println("<html><head><title>EMS Messages</title>");
253:            //define our row colouring for the tables
254:            out.println("<style type=\"text/css\">");
255:            out.println("tr.green { background: #00cc00;
                                            color: #ccffcc }");
256:            out.println("tr.blue { background: #0000ff;
                                            color: #ffff00 }");
257:            out.println("</style>");
259:            out.println("</head><body>");
261:            out.println("<h1><center>PSE's Email Management System
                            <br/>Servlet Version</center></h1><br>");
263:            //try to send those selected messages if user had
                indicated so
264:            if("Send".equals(request.getParameter("actiontype")))
```

```
265:                     sendMessages(request,out);
266:                 else viewMessageTexts(request,out);
268:                 String typeSelected = request.getParameter("type");
269:                 int type = EMP_ONLY;
270:                 if(typeSelected != null){
271:                     try{
272:                         type = Integer.parseInt(typeSelected);
273:                     }catch(Exception exc){
274:                     }
275:                 }
277:                 //display the list of messages
278:                 if(type == EMP_ONLY){
279:                     out.println("<center><font size=\"5\"><a href=EMS
                                                          ?type="+ALL+
280:                         ">View all messages</a> | 
                                                          <a href=EMS?type="+
281:                         DEPT_ONLY+">View department messages
                                                          </a> | "+
282:                         "<a href=\"PEMSEdit\">Create new message</a>
                                                          </font></center><br>");
283:
284:                     out.println("<H3><center>Messages addressed to
                                                          <b>you</b></center></H3>");
285:                 }else if(type == DEPT_ONLY){
286:                     out.println("<center><font size=\"5\"><a href=EMS
                                                          ?type="+ALL+
287:                         ">View all messages</a> | 
                                                          <a href=EMS?type="+
288:                         EMP_ONLY+">View your messages
                                                          </a> | "+
289:                         "<a href=\"PEMSEdit\">Create new message</a>
                                                          </font></center><br>");
291:                     out.println("<H3><center>Messages addressed to
                                                     <b>your department</b></center></H3>");
292:                 }else{
293:                     out.println("<center><font size=\"5\"><a href=EMS
                                                          ?type="+DEPT_ONLY+
294:                         ">View department messages</a> | "+
295:                         "<a href=EMS?type="+EMP_ONLY+">View your
                                                          messages</a>"+
296:                         " | <a href=\"PEMSEdit\">Create
                                                          new message
297:                         </a>"+"</font></center><br>");
299:                     out.println("<H3><center>All types of messages
                                                          </center></H3>");
300:                 }
302:                 displayMessages(type,request,out);
304:                 out.println("</body></html>");
305:                 return;
```

message text request (Line 266). In either case, PEMS sends or shows the content of an outmessage before continuing the process. The `actionType` parameter is discussed in Listing 18.49. Lines 253–257 define two different colors to be used in the table to display outmessages. The colors are needed to differentiate between consecutive rows.

When it is found that the user is in the *View Own Messages* page (Line 278), s/he will be shown a list of hyperlinks labeled 'Display all messages', 'Display department messages', 'Create new message' (Lines 279–282). This gives him/her the flexibility to navigate from one use case to another, as supported by EM Iteration 2. Similar links are offered for the *View department messages* page, except that the links' labels are 'View all messages', 'View your messages', and 'Create new message'. Finally the *View All Messages* page would have hyperlinks labeled 'View department messages', 'View your messages', and 'Create new message'. Following the display of the headings is the display of the outmessage list (Line 302).

Listing 18.49 Method displayMessages( ) in PEMS

Method `displayMessages()` in PEMS

```
45:     protected void displayMessages(int type,
                    HttpServletRequest request,java.io.PrintWriter out){
47:        try{
48:            CAdmin admin=(CAdmin)request.getSession().
                                            getAttribute("admin");
49:            Collection msgs = new LinkedList();
50:            int remainder = 0;
55:            if(type == EMP_ONLY)
56:            remainder=admin.getMsgSeeker().
                        retrieveMessagesForCurrentEmployee(msgs,
58:                        IAConstants.MAX_MESSAGE, null);
60:            else if(type == DEPT_ONLY)
61:                remainder = admin.getMsgSeeker().
                        retrieveMessagesForDepartment(
62:                        admin.getEmployee().getDepartmentCode(),
63:                        msgs,IAConstants.MAX_MESSAGE, null);
66:            else
67:                remainder = admin.getMsgSeeker().
                                            retrieveAllMessages(
68:                    msgs, IAConstants.MAX_MESSAGE, null);
72:            if (msgs.isEmpty()){
73:                out.println("No unsent query messages.");
74:                return;
75:            }
77:            List params = Collections.list(request.
                                            getParameterNames());
78:            StringBuffer buf = new StringBuffer();
79:            buf.append("<form method=post><br>\n");
```

```
80:              buf.append("<center><table border=2
                                        width=\"70%\">");
81:          buf.append("<tr><th>Selected</th>");
82:          buf.append("<th>Contact Name</th>");
83:          buf.append("<th>Company Name</th>");
84:          buf.append("<th>Subject</th>");
85:          buf.append("<th>Created Date</th></tr>\n");
87:          int counter = 0;
88:          for (Iterator it = msgs.iterator(); it.hasNext();) {
89:              IAOutMessage msg = (IAOutMessage) it.next();
90:              counter++;
93:              buf.append("<tr ").append(counter%2==0?
                                  "class=green>":"class=blue>");
96:              buf.append("<td><input type=checkbox name=ck").
                                  append(msg.getMessageID());
99:              if(params.contains("ck"+msg.getMessageID()))
100:                 buf.append(" checked");
101:             buf.append(">");
102:             buf.append("<td>");
104:             IAContact contact = msg.getContact();
105:             buf.append(contact.getFamilyName());
106:             buf.append(", ").append(contact.getFirstName());
108:             buf.append("</td><td>").append(contact.
                                          getOrganization());
109:             buf.append("</td><td>").append(msg.getSubject());
110:             buf.append("</td><td>").append(msg.
                                          getCreationDate());
111:             buf.append("</td></tr>\n");
112:         }
113:         buf.append("</table></center><br>");
114:         buf.append("<center><table><tr>");
115:         buf.append("<td><input type=submit name=actiontype
                                          value=Send></td>");
116:         buf.append("<td><input type=submit name=actiontype
                                          value=View></td>");
117:         buf.append("<td><input type=reset value=Clear></td>");
118:         buf.append("</tr></table></center>\n");
120:         buf.append("</form>");
121:         if(remainder >0)
122:             buf.append("<br>There are ").append(remainder).
                         append(" messages still left in the server");
123:         out.println(buf.toString());
124:     }catch(Exception exc){
126:     }
127: }
```

The three different types of outmessage retrieval are done in Lines 55–67. The retrieved outmessages are displayed in a table with the header defined in Lines 79–85 and the content in Lines 88–112. Line 93 flips the row color from blue to green. Line 99 checks if a particular outmessage was selected on the previous screen and therefore should be shown as selected on the current screen. The actionType attribute is set on Lines 115 and 116, Send and View. The attribute is set depending on the button clicked by the user. ActionType controls the next page to be shown to the user.

18.8.2 Class PEMSEdit

The PEMSEdit class handles outmessage viewing and editing (Figure 18.19). Methods supporting the servlet lifecycle are similar to PEMS. The init(), destroy(), and

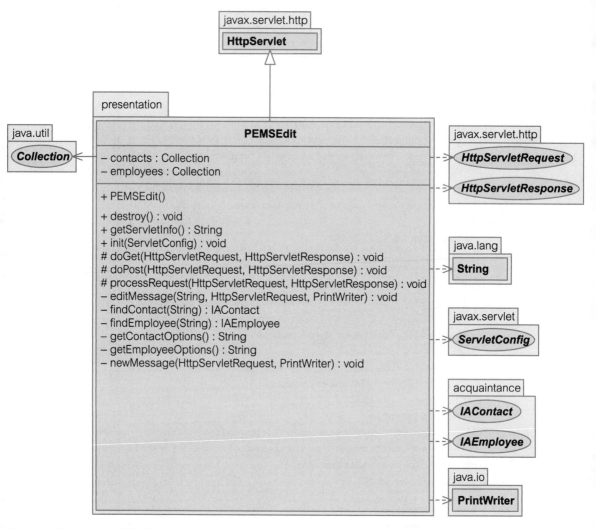

Figure 18.19 Class PEMSEdit in EM 2 (servlet)

`getServletInfo()` methods simply call their superclasses' methods (or provide no implementation for the methods). Both `getContactOptions()` and `getEmployeeOptions()` are used to fill dropdown lists on the form. `doGet()` and `doPost()` act the same way as `PEMS.java`. The `processRequest()` method formats the HTML result and redirects user options (either edit message or create new message) to `editMessage()` and `newMessage()`.

PEMSEdit has two collections to maintain the list of employees and the list of contacts (Listing 18.50). These are the same references as owned by `PMessageDetailWindow` in Section 18.3.1. Those references are required to fill the dropdown list for new outmessage creation.

Listing 18.50 Fields in PEMSEdit.java (servlet)

Fields in PEMSEdit.java
23:       private Collection employees = null;
24:       private Collection contacts = null;

Listing 18.51 Method newMessage( ) in PEMSEdit

Method newMessage() in PEMSEdit

```
166:      private void newMessage(HttpServletRequest request,
                                        java.io.PrintWriter out)
167:      throws ServletException, java.io.IOException {
168:          CAdmin admin=(CAdmin)request.getSession().
                                        getAttribute("admin");
169:          if(contacts == null) contacts = admin.listContacts();
170:          if(employees == null) employees = admin.listEmployees();
172:          DateFormat df = DateFormat.getDateInstance
                                        (DateFormat.SHORT);
173:          StringBuffer buf = new StringBuffer();
174:          buf.append("<form method=post>\n");
175:          buf.append("<table border=0 width=\"70%\">\n");
177:          buf.append("<tr><td width=\"30%\">Subject</td><td>");
178:          buf.append("<input type=text name=subject></td></tr>\n");
180:          buf.append("<tr><td width=\"30%\">Creator</td><td>");
181:          buf.append(admin.getEmployee().getFamilyName()).
                                        append(",");
182:      buf.append(admin.getEmployee().getFirstName()).
                                        append("</td></tr>\n");
184:          buf.append("<tr><td width=\"30%\">Creation
                                        Date</td><td>");
185:      buf.append(df.format(new java.util.Date())).
                                        append("</td></tr>\n");
187:          buf.append("<tr><td width=\"30%\">Addressed
                                        To</td><td>");
188:          buf.append(getContactOptions()).append("</td></tr>\n");
              ...[cut to save space]
```

Creating a new outmessage (Listing 18.51) is achieved as in EM Iteration 2 `PMessage-DetailWindow` (`showNewMessage()`) in Section 18.3.1 and `CAdmin` (`newMessage()`) in Section 18.3.2. The `CAdmin` object created earlier is acquired from the session (Line 168) to retrieve necessary data (Lines 169–170). The data is displayed on Lines 173–188 in the form of dropdown lists populated on Line 188.

Summary

1. The Java code for Iteration 2 conforms strictly to the PCMEF architectural framework.

2. To emphasize the clarity and highlight the simplicity of the PCMEF framework, Iteration 2 restrains the number of classes in each package.

3. Iteration 2 has three different versions: (1) an application, (2) an applet, and (3) a servlet version.

4. Most changes between Iteration 1 and 2 are in the `presentation` layer. Other layers are merely modified to cater for additional functionalities required by the Iteration 2 specifications.

5. Iteration 2 implements a thick applet with a slight modification on `PWindow`.

6. The `acquaintance` package still consists of four interfaces as defined in Iteration 1: `IAConstants`, `IAContact`, `IAEmployee`, and `IAOutMessage`. They are extended with new functionalities to support the idea of *dirty* objects.

7. The `presentation` package contains six classes: `PWindow`, `PMessageDetailWindow`, `PSendPreview`, `PMessageTableModel`, `PDisplayList`, and `PDisplayData`.

8. The `control` package contains three classes: `CAdmin`, `CMsgSeeker`, and `CMsgSender`.

9. Four classes and an interface are in the `entity` package. The classes are `EContact`, `EEmployee`, `EOutMessage`, and `EIdentityMap`. The interface is `IEObjectID`.

10. The `mediator` package consists of two classes: `MDataMapper` and `MModerator`.

11. The `foundation` package consists of three classes: `FConnection`, `FReader`, and `FWriter`. This package is practically unchanged from Iteration 1.

12. The servlet version generates HTML output. It is handled by two classes: `PEMS` and `PEMSEdit`.

Key Terms

cache	609	OIDToObj map	611
dirty	615	PCMEF+ architectural framework	585
dominant class	588	thick applet	620
Javadoc	584	thin applet	620
navigation in entity classes	609	yDoc	584
OID Proxy	609		

Iteration 2 Questions and Exercises

Below is a small set of questions and exercises with regard to the EM Iteration 2 code. More questions and exercises are available from the book's website.

1. What would be the necessary changes required to transform the thick applet version of EM Iteration 2 (Section 18.7) to a thin applet version?

2. Refer to Section 18.8.1 and Listings 18.46 and 18.47. Why do the methods `doPost()` and `doGet()` forward requests to `processRequest()` rather than doing the job themselves?

3. Show and explain the Iteration 2 code fragment that is responsible for the display of Figure 16.21 (Section 16.5). The figure is reproduced below for ease of reference as Figure 18.20.

Figure 18.20
Error 'Unable to Send'

4. Show and explain the Iteration 2 code fragment that is responsible for deleting an outmessage when the `Delete` button is pressed in Figure 16.20 (Section 16.5). The figure is reproduced below for ease of reference as Figure 18.21.

5. Iteration 2 does not allow pre-existing outmessages to be updated before they are emailed. Provide a possible implementation for such updates.

6. Suppose Iteration 2 requires double-clicking on the table of outmessages to view a selected outmessage for update. How could this be implemented?

7. Refer to Section 18.3.3 and the following variant of the `filter()` method (Listing 18.52). Explain the reasons for checking on Lines 68–70.

Figure 18.21
Window to delete
an outmessage

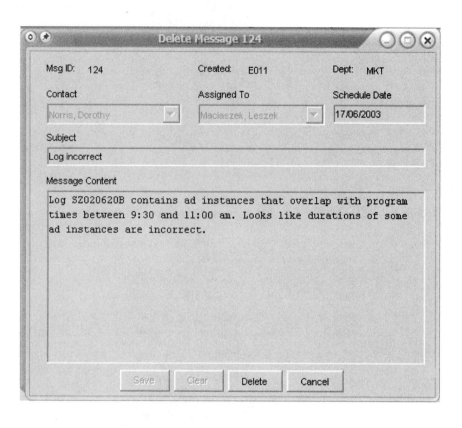

Listing 18.52 Method filter( ) in PMessageTableModel – date only

Method filter() in PMessageTableModel - Date Only

```
67:     public void filter(Object datefilter){
68:         if(datefilter instanceof String){
69:             filter(datefilter.toString());
70:             return;
71:         }
72:         if(ALL_DAYS_FILTER.equals(datefilter)){
73:             data.setFilterDate(3);
74:         }else if(LAST_DAYS_FILTER.equals(datefilter)){
75:             data.setFilterDate(0);
76:         }else if(TODAY_FILTER.equals(datefilter)){
77:             data.setFilterDate(1);
78:         } else if(FUTURE_DAYS_FILTER.equals(datefilter)){
79:             data.setFilterDate(2);
80:         }
81:         fireTableDataChanged();
82:     }
```

8. Explain the purpose of the following code fragment (Listing 18.53).

Listing 18.53 Method getRawData( ) in PMessageTableModel

Method getRawData() in PMessageTableModel
145:     public Object getRawObject(int row){
146:         return data.getOutMessage(row);
147:     }

9. The following is a possible implementation of SortMouseListener in EM Iteration 2 (Listing 18.54). Explain what is going on in this code.

Listing 18.54 Inner Class SortMouseListener in PMessageTableModel

```
Inner Class SortMouseListener in PMessageTableModel

217:      private class SortMouseListener extends
              java.awt.event.MouseAdapter{
218:          JTable tableView;
219:          PMessageTableModel model;
220:          public SortMouseListener(
              JTable table,PMessageTableModel model){
221:            this.tableView = table;
222:            this.model = model;
223:          }
224:          public void mouseClicked(java.awt.event.MouseEvent e) {
225:            TableColumnModel columnModel = tableView.
                                       getColumnModel();
228:            int viewColumn = columnModel.
                                       getColumnIndexAtX(e.getX());
229:            int column=tableView.
                            convertColumnIndexToModel(viewColumn);
230:            model.sort(column);
231:          }
232:      }
```

Data Engineering and Business Components

Chapter 19   Iteration 3 Requirements and Object Model   639

Chapter 20   Security and Integrity   660

Chapter 21   Transactions and Concurrency   700

Chapter 22   Business Components   729

Chapter 23   Iteration 3 Annotated Code   750

T he previous three parts of the book and the previous two iterations of the case-study covered all the typical material expected in a software engineering textbook. However, the promise of this book has been to go beyond simple software engineering projects and address principles and practices for the development of *large enterprise systems*. These principles and practices must extend to the main resource in any enterprise – the *information resource*. An important piece of wisdom, attributed to Bob Epstein of Sybase, says: 'Applications come and go; data stays for ever'. Part 4 of this book places the due emphasis on data sources.

This is not to say that *data sources* were ignored on the foregoing pages of the book. Chapter 10 introduced all basic issues of database design and programming in software engineering. Many sections in other chapters were explicit about the role and place of data sources in software production. Significant aspects of software architectural considerations, discussed in Chapters 9 and 15, related to the organization and manipulation of data sources in programs.

This part of the book continues, reinforces, and builds upon the knowledge about data sources addressed so far. The following discussion embraces the main concepts and issues of data engineering. *Data engineering* is a separate branch of knowledge with its own journals, conferences, technical committees, etc. Data engineering is concerned with the design, storage, management, and utilization of data, information, and knowledge in software systems. Its main emphasis is databases. Modern data engineering embraces many application development issues and reaches to such topics as data warehousing, web mining, multimedia data, metadata and XML.

Business components reside firmly between data sources and the application logic. They are reusable components that come in various shapes and forms, the most popular of which are Enterprise JavaBeans. They can be used to assist in programming and, indeed, to generate application code. They can be deployed into an application or a database server. Business components are given due consideration in this last part of the book.

The main learning objectives of Part 4 and Iteration 3 of the case study are to gain knowledge of:

- security and integrity control principles of database management systems
- programming applications for discretionary authorization-based access to database data and database programs
- programming security and integrity controls into the database
- principles of transaction management in relational and object-oriented databases
- programming concurrency in business transactions performed by the application clients
- transaction services supported by the web, application, and database tiers
- the interplay between user interfaces and business components as well as between business components in the application code and the persistent data in the database
- frameworks of generated Java classes and XML files to manage databases and integrate with applications
- the implementation and deployment of business components into an application server

Chapter

19

Iteration 3 Requirements and Object Model

The focus of Iteration 3 of the Email Management case study is on the improvements to the database and on the refactorings in the lower PCMEF layers of the application code obtained in Iteration 2. As far as possible, the **business logic** of the application is moved from the client to the server. This is expected to bring important portability, maintainability, scalability, security, performance, and related benefits. Whereas previous iterations concentrated on delivering new functionality and (in Iteration 2) on better usability, the emphasis of Iteration 3 is on the remaining features in the FURPS+ acronym – reliability, performance, and supportability (Section 8.4).

As in previous iterations, the Iteration 3 increment is designed to be implementable within two weeks by a small development team. The programming effort combines Java on the client and programs stored in the relational database (stored procedures, stored functions, triggers). The challenge is in removing from the Java application the code that should be centralized in the database for the FURPS+ reasons. This task necessitates further refactoring of Java code, in particular in the `foundation` layer and affecting also the `domain` layer.

19.1 Use Case Model

Figure 19.1 is a use case model for Iteration 3. The boundary of the project, and the actors, which determine this boundary, are unchanged from previous iterations. The actors are, therefore, not shown in the model. The diagram presents use cases and main relationships between them. The Iteration 3 new functionality is embraced by rectangles. There are only four new use cases: `Apply Authorization Rules`, `Maintain Authorization`

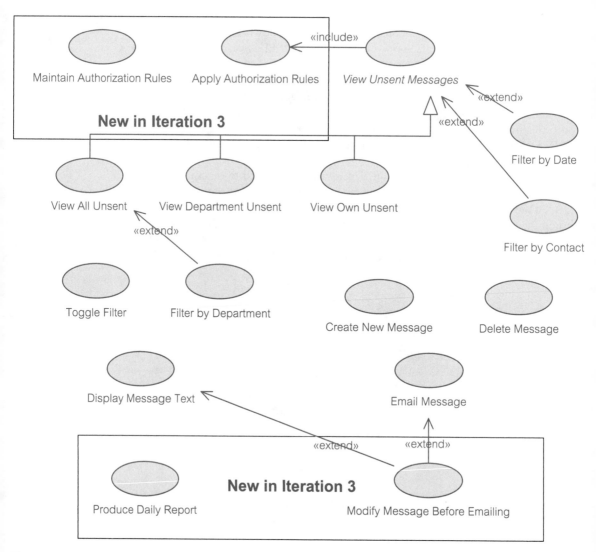

Figure 19.1 Use case diagram for Iteration 3

Rules, Produce Daily Report, and Modify Message Before Emailing. The latter is an extension of Email Message and Display Message Text.

Apply Authorization Rules is included in View Unsent Messages. This means that the display of unsent outmessages is constrained by the authorization rules that may apply to the current user. The rules are recorded in the database. The database ensures that the client application can display only 'authorized' outmessages.

Maintain Authorization Rules is not really part of the EM Iteration 3 application code. A system administrator, not an application user, maintains authorization rules. This use case is really a utility provided to a system administrator. As such it is developed as a separate business component outside of the application code.

Produce Daily Report is introduced to generate daily summary reports about email activities for all contacts. Contacts to whom no emails were sent on a given day are not listed in the report for that day. Reports are displayed to the screen before they can be printed.

Modify Message Before Emailing provides an opportunity to the user to modify the outmessage subject or text before emailing it. The modifications are stored to the database. Only the employee who created the outmessage, or who is a supervisor (manager) of that employee, can modify the outmessage before emailing.

Use Case Document

19.2

The scope of the use case document for Iteration 3 is a union of the requirements of two previous iterations and the new requirements of Iteration 3. That is, the scope corresponds to the use case model in Figure 19.1. The parent use case, which absorbs all iterations, is Manage Email (Figure 8.1).

As demanded by the iterative and incremental development, Iteration 3 delivers an increment on top of Iteration 2. The use case document describes not just functional extensions but also indicates how other FURPS+ features should be implemented.

Brief Description, Preconditions, and Postconditions

19.2.1

Brief description

Iteration 3 of the Manage Email use case allows an employee to create, delete, display, modify, and email outmessages to contacts. It also allows generating basic emailing activity reports. Only one outmessage at a time can be emailed.

The use case can display, modify, and email outmessages previously stored in the database by other processes. It also allows a new outmessage to be created, and displayed, deleted, modified, or emailed, as required. The display of outmessages can be constrained by a number of display conditions (search criteria). A current display can be further filtered on a number of filter conditions. Only authorized users are allowed to view certain outmessages and perform certain operations.

Preconditions

1. A user (actor) is an Employee who works for the Customer Department or is otherwise authorized by the System Administrator to access the EM application.
2. The EM database contains outmessages to be emailed to contacts. Creation of new outmessages is no replacement for outmessages stored in the database by other processes of the AEM system (Chapter 6).
3. An Employee is connected to an email server and is an authorized database user.

Postconditions

1. The program updated the EM database to reflect any successful emailing of outmessages.
2. The EM database is left in an intact state if any exception or error occurred.
3. Upon the Employee quitting the application, all database connections are closed and all application desktop or web-enabled GUI windows are closed.

19.2.2 Basic Flow

Consistent with the approach taken in previous iterations, the description of the flow of events includes prototypes of GUI windows. Iteration 3 retains the GUI presentation of Iteration 2 and extends it to accommodate new Iteration 3 requirements.

Basic Flow

The use case starts when an Employee wishes to create, view and/or email outmessages to contacts.

The system displays an informational message and requests that the Employee provides a username and password (Figure 19.2). The login window is unchanged from Iteration 2.

1. The system attempts to connect the Employee to the EM database.
2. Upon successful connection, the application displays the main application window through which a user can interact with the system (Figure 19.3). The main application window is unchanged from Iteration 2.

Figure 19.2
Prototype of
login window

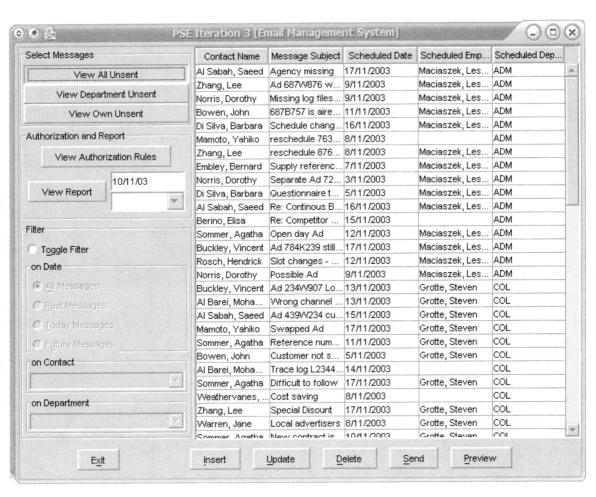

Figure 19.3 Prototype of main application window

3. The application user can perform the following tasks:
   (a) view unsent outmessages to contacts (see 'S1 – View Unsent Messages', below)
   (b) filter the display of outmessages on various criteria (see 'S2 – Filter Messages', below)
   (c) display text of selected outmessage (see 'S3 – Display Message Text', below)
   (d) email selected outmessage (see 'S4 – Email Message', below)
   (e) create new outmessage (see 'S5 – Create New Message', below)
   (f) delete outmessage (see 'S6 – Delete Message', below)
   (g) modify outmessage (see 'S7 – Modify Message Before Emailing', below)
   (h) produce daily activity report (see 'S8 – Produce Daily Report', below)
   (i) quit the application, upon which the use case terminates.

4. A system administrator can additionally perform the task of maintaining authorization rules (see 'S9 – Maintain Authorization Rules', below).

19.2.3 Subflows

S1 – View Unsent Messages

This subflow consists of four options:

- S1.1 – Apply Authorization Rules
- S1.2 – View All Unsent
- S1.3 – View Department Unsent
- S1.4 – View Own Unsent.

S1.1 – Apply Authorization Rules

Each of the three options *specialized from* `View Unsent Messages` is controlled by strict **authorization rules**, shown as the «include» relationship in Figure 19.1. The authorization privileges depend on an employee's department. Currently, the employees are classified into five groups, identified as actors of the AEM system in the use case model in Figure 6.3. The authorization groups are:

- COL – Data Collection Employee (i.e. employee working for Data Collection Department)
- QUA – Quality Control Employee (i.e. employee working for Quality Control Department)
- CUS – Customer Services Employee
- ADM – System Administrator (i.e. employee responsible for the EM system)
- IND – Independent Employee (i.e. employee not assigned to any department or an external consultant, such as Rates Consultant in Figure 6.3).

The following matrix (Table 19.1) controls the authorization **privileges** for viewing outmessages. An employee working for a department in a matrix row can view outmessages of departments listed in columns, if there is 'YES' stated in the appropriate cell.

Note that the introduction of Independent Employee in the Authorization table means that IND will become legitimate code for a department. The IND department does not exist in practice. It is only an informal grouping of Independent Employees. Such a 'virtual' IND department is needed to facilitate managing additional business rules that the database has to enforce with regard to authorization (Section 19.5).

Table 19.1 Authorization matrix for viewing outmessages

	COL	QUA	CUS	ADM	IND
Data Collection (COL)	YES	NO	NO	NO	NO
Quality Control (QUA)	YES	YES	NO	NO	NO
Customer Services (CUS)	YES	NO	YES	NO	YES
System Administration (ADM)	YES	YES	YES	YES	YES
Independent Employee (IND)	NO	NO	NO	NO	YES

S1.2 – View All Unsent

When the user selects the option `View All Unsent`, the application presents a list of unsent outmessages, which the user is authorized to view.

Subject to the authorization matrix in Table 19.1, the system presents the list of all unsent outmessages in the main application window (Figure 19.3). The following are the properties of the list:

- The list shows the columns entitled: `Contact Name`, `Message Subject`, `Scheduled Date`, `Scheduled Employee`, and `Scheduled Department`.
  - `Contact Name` displays the family name of a contact.
  - `Scheduled Employee` displays the family name of an employee or nothing (if scheduled employee is not known). `Scheduled Department` displays department name or nothing (if scheduled department is not known).
- The list is sorted in ascending order by `Contact Name` and `Scheduled Date`.
- The list is scrollable to accommodate situations when the retrieved number of rows exceeds the size of the window.
- Outmessages in the list are selectable with the mouse. The usual functionality of `Ctrl-Click` to select multiple non-adjacent outmessages and `Shift-Click` to select a range of adjacent outmessages should be supported, although this functionality is not used in Iteration 3.

S1.3 – View Department Unsent

When the user selects the option `View Department Unsent`, the application presents a list of outmessages scheduled to be emailed by employees in the department of the current employee (i.e. the current user). This option does not apply to an Independent Employee, who can only view his/her own outmessages (see subflow S1.4).

The GUI presentation uses the same window as in Figure 19.3. There is a clear indication on the window that only outmessages scheduled for a particular department are retrieved from the database and can be viewed.

S1.4 – View Own Unsent

When the user selects the option `View Own Unsent`, the application presents a list of outmessages scheduled to be emailed by the current employee (i.e. the current user). The GUI presentation uses the same window as in Figure 19.3.

There is a clear indication on the window that only outmessages scheduled for a logged-in employee are retrieved from the database and can be viewed.

S2 – Filter Messages

This subflow consists of four options:

- S2.1 – Toggle Filter
- S2.2 – Filter by Date

- S2.3 – Filter by Contact
- S2.4 – Filter by Department.

S2.1 – Toggle Filter

The *filters* panel provides a set of controls to constrain the items selected for display after they have been retrieved from the database by the `View Unsent Messages` subflow. The panel is not active unless a list of outmessages is displayed by `View Unsent Messages` and `Toggle Filter` has been clicked.

By default, the option `Toggle Filter` is turned off. A user can turn this filter on to apply the other filter options: `Filter by Date`, `Filter by Contact`, and/or `Filter by Department`.

The filter is shown as set on when the list of displayed outmessages is restricted by the conditions specified by `Filter by Date`, `Filter by Contact`, and/or `Filter by Department`. When the filter is set on, applying the Toggle Filter action can turn it off. This in effect re-displays the list of outmessages as requested by the `View Unsent Messages` subflow, before any filter was applied.

S2.2 – Filter by Date

The `Filter by Date` panel provides a set of radio buttons to filter on outmessages with a scheduled date (i.e. scheduled for emailing) in the past, future, today, or all (any date). Only one of these buttons can be active at any time. By default, the button `All` is active when the panel is active.

S2.3 – Filter by Contact

The filters panel provides a combo box, which allows the selection of a contact from the dropdown list of contact names or which can be left blank (Figure 14.3). The filter is automatically performed when a contact is selected. This has the effect of modifying the list of outmessages displayed to show only outmessages destined for that contact, excluding any outmessages filtered out by the current scheduled date filter.

S2.4 – Filter by Department

A combo box is provided to allow the user to filter the list of outmessages by a department picked from the dropdown list of department names. Only those outmessages belonging to a particular department (as chosen from the combo box) are listed. A blank entry in the combo box means no filtering on the department has been performed. This filter is automatically performed when a department name is selected. This has the effect of modifying the list of outmessages displayed to show only outmessages assigned to a particular department or, to be precise, outmessages assigned to employees from the selected department. The list excludes any outmessages filtered out by the current scheduled date and contact filters.

Figure 19.4
Dialog box window
showing the
message text
of the currently
selected message

S3 – Display Message Text

The outmessage currently selected (highlighted) in the outmessage list window can be displayed in full in a separate dialog box window (Figure 19.4). The window presents the complete text of the outmessage together with other descriptive information. The text pane is scrollable. The window contains three buttons:

- `Email this Message` – see subflow S4
- `Modify this Message` – see subflow S6
- `Return to List of Messages` – to dismiss this window and return to the main application window.

S4 – Email Message

The dialog box in Figure 19.4, which allows emailing an outmessage, can be produced by the subflow S3 or by this subflow. In subflow S3, double-clicking on a selected outmessage produces the dialog box. In subflow S4, the same effect is achieved by pressing the `Email Selected Message` button from the main application window.

A successful emailing results in updating the database and in an informational message displayed to the user (Figure 19.5).

Figure 19.5
Informational
message after
emailing

S5 – Create New Message

Iteration 2 provided the option to create a new outmessage and save it in the database. Visually this option is unchanged in Iteration 3, but it involves some more work behind the scenes due to the need to enforce the authorization rules presented in Table 19.1. An employee who cannot view outmessages scheduled to other employees or departments, is likewise not allowed to create outmessages for those employees and departments.

Pressing the button `Create New Message` in the main application window, results in a dialog box to type in new outmessages, as shown in Figure 19.6.

Figure 19.6
Dialog box for
creating a new
outmessage

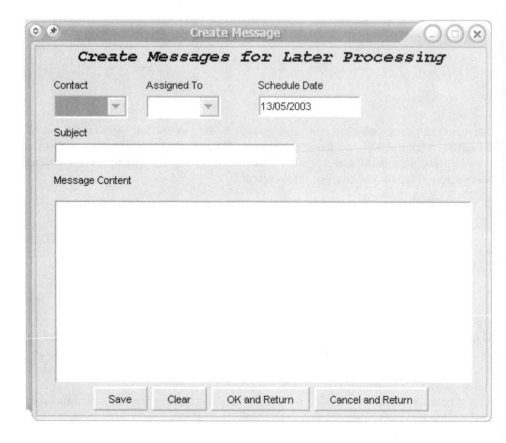

Figure 19.7
Delete message
confirmation

The dialog box allows selecting a contact and assigning a scheduled employee and/or scheduled department. The subject and the outmessage content can be typed in provided fields. The window contains four action buttons:

- `Save` – to save the new outmessage in the database, but keep the dialog box open to allow the creation of the next outmessage.
- `OK and Return` – to save the new outmessage in the database, and then dismiss this window and return to the main application window.
- `Clear` – to clear the current content of the dialog box and permit the user to create a new message from scratch.
- `Cancel and Return` – to cancel the operation, dismiss this window and return to the main application window.

S6 – Delete Message

When outmessages are no longer applicable, perhaps due to corrections made by other employees, then they can be deleted from the database. Pressing the `Delete Message` button when a message is selected in the main window activates this subflow. A simple window to ask the user for confirmation about the deletion is then displayed as shown in Figure 19.7. If the user opts to cancel the deletion, then nothing happens.

S7 – Modify Message Before Emailing

This option extends subflows S3 and S4. These two subflows share the use of the same dialog box (Figure 19.4). The subflow S7 is activated when the user presses the button `Modify this Message`. Pressing this button results in a dialog box (Figure 19.8), which is essentially the same as the dialog box for subflow S5 (Figure 19.6), except that the existing outmessage information is shown.

The dialog box allows selecting a contact and assigning a scheduled employee and/or scheduled department. The subject and the message content can be modified in provided fields. The window contains two action buttons:

- `OK and Return` – to save the modified outmessage in the database, and then dismiss this window and return to the `Display Message Text` window.
- `Cancel and Return` – to cancel the operation, dismiss this window and return to the `Display Message Text` window.

Figure 19.8
Dialog box for
modifying an
outmessage

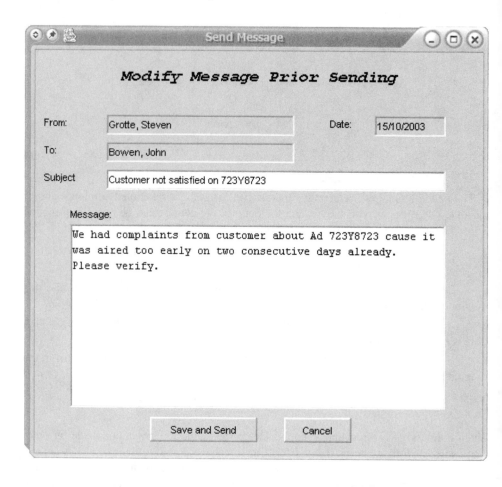

S8 – Produce Daily Report

This option is activated from the main application window (Figure 19.3). It allows construction of a summary report that shows all email activity for a particular day per contact. Upon activating this option, the user is presented with a calendar control that allows selecting the date for which the report is sought. The report displays the following information:

- date of emailing activity
- contact information (first name, family name, organization)
- number of emails created (for this contact on this date)
- number of emails sent (to this contact on this date)
- number of emails outstanding (for this contact and scheduled for this or future dates (and not sent yet))
- number of emails past-outstanding (for this contact and scheduled in the past (and not sent yet)).

Figure 19.9
Format of a daily
activity report

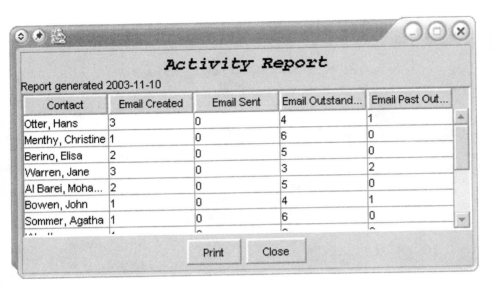

Contact	Email Created	Email Sent	Email Outstand...	Email Past Out...
Otter, Hans	3	0	4	1
Menthy, Christine	1	0	6	0
Berino, Elisa	2	0	5	0
Warren, Jane	3	0	3	2
Al Barei, Moha...	2	0	5	0
Bowen, John	1	0	4	1
Sommer, Agatha	1	0	6	0

Activity Report
Report generated 2003-11-10

[Print] [Close]

Figure 19.9 shows the format of a daily activity report. Once viewed, the report can be printed out.

S9 – Maintain Authorization Rules

This option may or may not be available from the main application window of the EM system (Figure 19.3). It can be implemented as a separate function of a 'system maintenance' application available to system administrators.

The dialog box for S9 (Figure 19.10) is a table similar to Table 19.1. Only a system administrator (the ADM department) is allowed to modify the true/false cells of the table.

Some outmessages in the OutMessage table (Figure 19.15, p. 656) may not be scheduled for any employee or department (i.e. both `sched_emp_id` and `sched_dept_code` may be NULLs). Outmessages in such category are implicitly scheduled to Quality Control (QUA). This means that the EM application should list them for emailing by QUA employees.

Exception Flows

Any exception occurring during runtime should be caught and relayed to the user with an informational message box. The program must not crash on any exception from the database, from the network of email failure, or from the application.

E1 – Incorrect username or password

If, in the *basic flow*, the actor provides an incorrect username or incorrect password, the system displays an error message (Figure 19.11). The message reads: 'Invalid login. Please try again. This will be your second attempt.' The use case continues and allows the user to

Figure 19.10
Maintain
authorization
rules

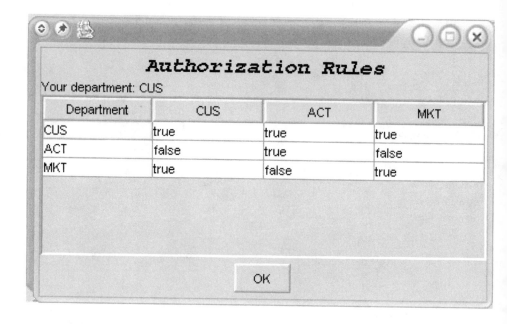

Figure 19.11
Message box for
incorrect login

re-enter the username and password. The second unsuccessful attempt results in the error message: 'Invalid login. Please try again. This will be your last attempt.' The use case continues and allows the user to re-enter the username and password.

The actor is given three chances to provide the correct username and password. If three-times unsuccessful, the system displays the message: 'Exceeded the maximum of three attempts to login. Application will quit' (Figure 19.12). The use case terminates.

E2 – Email could not be sent

If in the S4 subflow the mail server returns an error that the email could not be sent, the system informs the actor that the email was not sent. The message reads: 'Failed in emailing the message. No network connection or invalid email address' (Figure 19.13). The use case continues after the user acknowledges the error message by pressing the OK button.

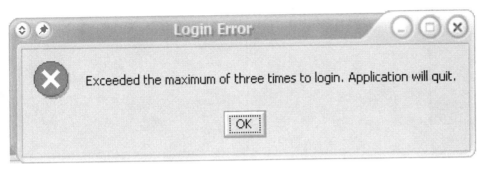

Figure 19.12
Message box after
three unsuccessful
attempts to log in

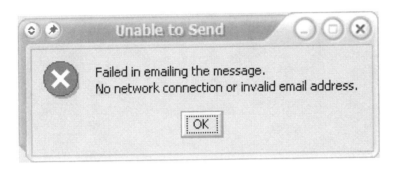

Figure 19.13
Message box
upon email failure

Conceptual Classes and Relational Tables   19.3

The **conceptual class model** for Iteration 3 contains six classes: Employee, Department, Contact, OutMessage, DailyReport, and Authorization (Figure 19.14). Association lines are assigned association names and multiplicities. Association roles are named in most cases. Associations from Authorization to Department are only navigable in one direction (indicated by arrows on the association lines). Primary attributes (identifiers) are typed in bold font.

Employee may be employed_by at most one Department. Department employs many Employees, but it may exist even if it does not employ any Employee. The managerial structure of employees is captured in the employment_hierarchy relationship.

Department may have scheduled OutMessages. There is at most one Department for each OutMessage. There is precisely one Contact for each OutMessage.

Contact may be linked to zero or many OutMessages and to zero or many DailyReports. Each DailyReport object is identified by date_or_report_day and contact_id.

The association named outmsg_creator links OutMessage to Employee who created that OutMessage in the database. The association named outmsg_scheduled identifies the Employee who is scheduled to email the OutMessage. This association links to zero Employees if the OutMessage is not scheduled for any particular Employee.

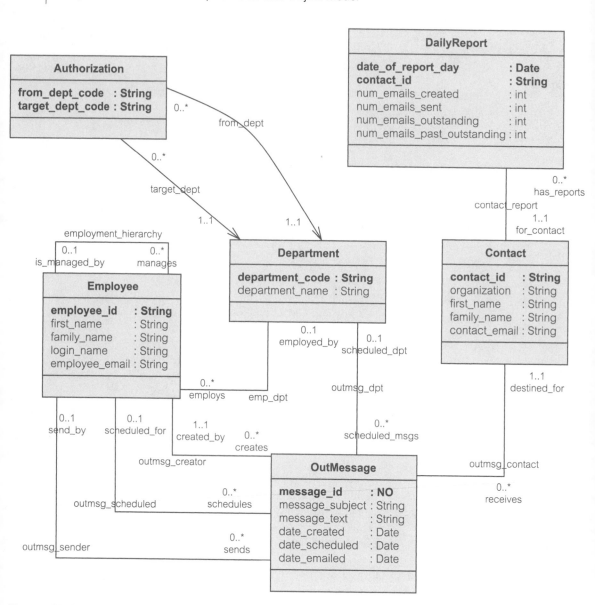

Figure 19.14 Conceptual classes for Iteration 3

The association named `outmsg_sender` identifies the `Employee` who emailed the `OutMessage`. This association links to zero `Employees` prior to `OutMessage` emailing.

Authorization contains only two attributes: `from_dept_code` and `target_dept_code`. This is sufficient to implement the authorization requirements defined in Table 19.1. `from_dept_code` corresponds to the rows and `target_dept_code` to the columns in Table 19.1. The `Authorization` table contains only values for those cells in Table 19.1 that are signified as `true`. The `false` entries are not explicitly stored in `Authorization`.

Associations from `Authorization` to `Department` navigate only in one direction. This signifies the separation between the users of the EM application and system administrators responsible for controlling database authorizations. Of course, the EM application can still query (as it must) the `Authorization` table but there is no navigational dependency from `Department` to `Authorization`. This said, the mapping of the conceptual model to relational schema (Figure 19.15) is not able to capture one-way navigations (because the notion of referential integrity of relational databases is not 'navigational').

Most attributes are typed as `strings`. The type of `message_id` is `number` (signified by NO). The four date attributes are typed as `dates`.

A conceptual class model can be automatically converted to a **relational database model** using the object-relational mapping rules explained in Chapter 10. Figure 19.15 shows the relational model derived from the conceptual model in Figure 19.14. The model defines tables and relationships between them. Each table defines columns, indexes, and user-defined triggers (where applicable). The names of the most important user-defined stored procedures are shown at the bottom of the diagram.

The index compartment identifies the indexes created on primary keys (PK), on foreign keys (FK), and on unique columns (UN). The `Authorization` table does not have an explicit index on its primary key because it is a very small table (but the primary key is of course still enforced by the database).

There are a few changes in the `OutMessage` table compared with Iteration 2. The column `department_code` has been renamed `sched_dpt_code` to hint at this column's purpose. For consistency, the column `scheduled_emp_id` has been renamed `sched_emp_id`. Lastly, the type of `message_text` has been changed to LONG. In Oracle, the LONG data type signifies a variable-length character data up to a maximum of 2 gigabytes.

Supplementary Specification

19.4

Iteration 3 has a significant impact on the FURPS+ features of the EM implementation, and yet this impact is not always directly reflected in supplementary specifications. The **FURPS+** features that are particularly targeted by Iteration 3 are performance and supportability. By moving much of the business logic from the client program to the server database, Iteration 3 makes a movement from 'programming in the small' to 'programming in the large'.

- Functionality
  - EM is a multi-user application.
  - User authorization and privileges to access various features of the application are controlled centrally from a database to which the application program connects.
- Usability
  - There is no training required for a computer-literate user to be able to use the Iteration 3 program. Simple explanation of the aim and basic features of the application will suffice to use the program.

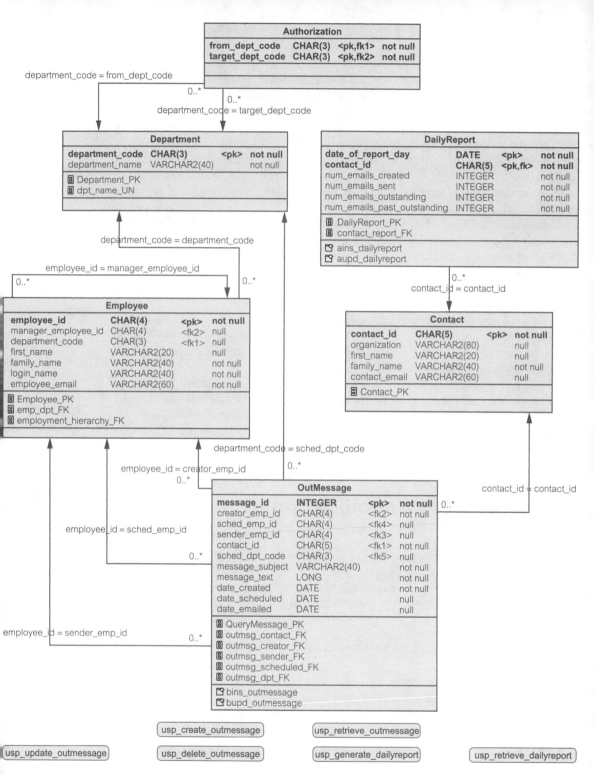

Figure 19.15 Relational schema for Iteration 3

- Iteration 3 is a GUI-based program that provides an intuitive way of using various application options. Only one option at a time may be requested.
- Iteration 3 is executable and can be deployed on a Windows desktop GUI or as a web-based GUI.
- Reliability
  - The application must be available 24 hours a day every day of the week. There must be no database-related downtime. Any scheduled email server downtimes due to maintenance must be notified to EM users by email with at least 24 hours' warning.
  - A failure of the program must not compromise the correctness and integrity of the database. A user must be able to restart the program after failure and find the database information to be consistent and not affected by the failure.
- Performance
  - There is no upper limit on the number of concurrent users.
  - The response time of the system must remain stable for up to 100 concurrent users. A slight degradation in performance is acceptable for a larger number of users.
  - The response time must be less than 5 seconds 90 per cent of the time.
- Supportability
  - The system architectural design must conform to the PCMEF+ framework to allow proper maintainability and scalability.
  - Test-driven development is used for code production. Acceptance testing is used for code validation. Test units obtained from test-driven development and from acceptance tests are used for regression testing when Iteration 3 code is changed.
- Other constraints
  - The project must use Oracle database, but it must be easily portable to other relational databases.
  - Iteration 3 must use Java and JDBC or SQLJ to access the Oracle database from the program.
  - Whenever possible, the business logic must be implemented in the database server as stored procedures or stored functions. Complex business rules must be programmed in triggers.

Database Specification

19.5

Iteration 3 places special demands on the ability of contemporary databases to store programs that applications can call. This ability has tremendous advantages to application clients and to overall characteristics of enterprise information systems. The advantages relate to systems' performance, security, integrity, supportability, etc. The following are the main requirements placed on the database by EM Iteration 3.

- As far as practical, replace all SQL statements in the application to the database by JDBC/SQLJ calls to **stored procedures**. As a minimum, all modification statements (insert, update, delete) must be replaced by calls to stored procedures. Some highly interactive selects on the database, in which the query conditions (in the `where` clause) are dynamically entered by the user, may have to be retained in the client application.

- Once all data required by the client application can be fetched through stored procedures, revoke from the application users the privileges to *insert*, *update*, *delete*, and (possibly also) *select* data from/to the database. Replace these privileges by granting to the users the *execute* privilege on all stored procedures available to the application. This will result in increased database **security** as the users will not be able to damage database objects by connecting to the database with the EM account and by directly accessing data using an interactive SQL tool (i.e. a SQL query tool, such as Oracle's SQL*Plus) (Bonazzi and Stokol, 2001).

- Refactor the application design for **transaction processing**. Identify the transactions, specify where they are started and closed, set transaction isolation levels to maximize concurrency (consider that an isolation level can apply to a table rather than the entire connection or transaction), etc. Whenever possible, control transactional boundaries in stored procedures rather than in the application.

- Required stored procedures and/or functions:
  - Retrieve outmessages and related data from linked tables (`usp_retrieve_outmessage`)
    - viewable by a particular employee
    - assigned to a particular department
    - scheduled to a particular employee
  - Create outmessage (`usp_create_outmessage`)
  - Delete outmessage (`usp_delete_outmessage`)
  - Modify outmessage (`usp_modify_outmessage`)
  - Generate daily report (`usp_generate_dailyreport`)
  - Retrieve daily report (`usp_retrieve_dailyreport`).

- Required **triggers**:
  - When inserting/updating the `OutMessage` table (`bins_outmessage` and `bupd_outmessage` in Figure 19.15):
    - Check that `sched_emp_id` and `sched_dpt_code` satisfy referential integrity between `Employee` and `Department` tables.
    - Ensure that if `sched_emp_id` exists then the corresponding `sched_dpt_code` must exist (in fact, the EM application should request the database to populate `sched_dpt_code` on any insert/update of `sched_emp_id`).
    - Ensure that if both `sched_emp_id` and `sched_dpt_code` do not exist, then `sched_dpt_code` is set to the Quality Control department.
    - Ensure that `manager_employee_id` for each `Employee` record is either NULL or indicates an employee from the same department as the `Employee` record, with the exception of an Independent Employee who can have a manager from any department.
    - `date_scheduled` and `date_emailed` must be greater than or equal to `date_created`.
  - When inserting/updating the `DailyReport` table (`ains_dailyreport` and `aupd_dailyreport` in Figure 19.15):
    - ensure for each record that:

      ```
      num_emails_created = num_emails_sent +
      num_emails_outstanding + num_emails_past_outstanding
      ```

Summary

1. Iteration 3 aims at moving the *business logic* from the application code to the database server. All database processing is done by stored procedures, which are called by the application's Java code as required.

2. Iteration 3 enhances the system's *FURPS+* features of reliability, performance and supportability.

3. There are four new use cases in Iteration 3: Apply Authorization Rules, Maintain Authorization Rules, Produce Daily Report, and Modify Message Before Emailing.

4. Iteration 3 defines and implements strict *authorization rules* for database access by the application users.

5. The *conceptual class model* for Iteration 3 contains six classes: Employee, Department, Contact, OutMessage, DailyReport, and Authorization. The classes map to six tables in the *relational database model*.

6. Iteration 3 defines and implements *transactional boundaries* for accessing data from the application.

7. Iteration 3 uses triggers to control the integrity of the database.

8. Although not raised in this chapter, Iteration 3 variants to take advantage of frameworks for *business components* are available.

Key Terms

authorization rules	644	relational database model	655
business logic	639	security	658
conceptual class model	653	stored procedure	657
FURPS+	655	transaction processing	658
privilege	644	trigger	658

Review Questions

1. In what sense does the use case Maintain Authorization Rules differ from the other use cases in Iteration 3?

2. Explain the intent of the authorization rules in Iteration 3. Can the rules be easily added to or modified?

3. Iteration 3 aims at moving business logic to the database. What does this really mean? How can it be achieved?

4. What functions of Iteration 3 do you think should be embraced by transactional boundaries? What are the implementation consequences of introducing transactions on the current code?

5. What is the role of triggers in Iteration 3? How are they linked to stored procedures?

Chapter

20

Security and Integrity

Software engineering is quite inseparable from *database engineering*. Chapter 10 covered database fundamentals from a software engineering viewpoint. It introduced the relational database model. The topics explained in Chapter 10 included: relational database structures, declarative and procedural referential integrity, stored procedures, indexes, and mapping objects to database records. There are many other issues in software engineering that are intertwined with database engineering. This chapter and the next address database design issues from a software engineering viewpoint.

The concentration of Iteration 3 on database issues brings up the topics of designing *security* and *integrity* (discussed in this chapter) and designing *transactions* and *concurrency* (Chapter 21). These topics span all tiers of multi-tier client/server systems, but the database server tier assumes the bulk of responsibility for actually performing the tasks. From the software engineering perspective, security and integrity are mechanisms to enforce business rules, while transactions and concurrency are means of implementing application logic (and conforming to integrity rules in the process).

Business rules dictate how security and integrity concerns should be implemented. Business rules cut across various applications and various users. A user (or rather job roles that a user is allowed to perform in the enterprise) may be permitted to work with various client applications, but the security authorizations granted to that user/role on data must be the same regardless of which application is used to access data. Similarly, declarative and procedural integrity constraints (Section 10.1.4) must not be violated by any application or user, regardless of the level of authorization granted to them.

From the standpoint of the user community, security has a personal (individual) dimension. Authorization privileges and security clearances are assigned to individual users and roles that they perform. Integrity, on the other hand, has a multi-personal (user community) dimension. Declarative and procedural integrity constraints, as well as other integrity checks, apply uniformly to all users of the database.

Designing Security

Ramakrishnan and Gehrke (2000) list three objectives for designing security in enterprise information systems:

- Secrecy – to disallow revealing of information to unauthorized users and applications.
- Integrity – to disallow modification of data by unauthorized users and applications.
- Availability – to allow access at all times to authorized users and applications.

To achieve these objectives users and applications accessing a database are first authenticated and then granted access rights, called privileges. Authentication is the task of verifying the identity of a user/application trying to connect to a database. In a simple scenario, authentication is done on the basis of user id and password combination.

Granting privileges to access database objects is the technique of so-called discretionary authorization, or discretionary access control (Section 20.1.1). Privileges have several dimensions. Users/applications can be granted privileges on:

- *schema objects* (such as disallowing creation of new tables)
- *data objects* (such as disallowing access to some table columns)
- *SQL operations* (such as disallowing any updates on database)
- *execution of procedures/functions* (such as allowing execution of some stored procedures but not others).

Discretionary authorization is not sufficient in enterprise information systems with various applications and large numbers of users accessing one or more databases. Such systems demand more sophisticated authorization schemes, normally implemented on top of the discretionary control.

One relatively rigid scheme, which works well for many military organizations and security agencies with one-directional flow of information and security clearances, is called the mandatory authorization (Section 20.1.2). In mandatory authorization (Ramakrishnan and Gehrke, 2000), users/applications are assigned clearance levels and database objects are assigned corresponding *security levels*. Then, on a successful connection to database, the system determines how the user/application can access the database. The SQL standard specifies only discretionary authorization, but most database vendors have their own facilities to assist in implementing mandatory authorization.

For business-driven organizations, with high staff turnover and dynamic changes to applications, a more flexible scheme is required. Unfortunately, current database management systems offer little support, even though such complex authorization schemes must be stored and driven from the database itself. For the lack of a better term, these more complex schemes are called here enterprise authorization (Section 20.1.3). Enterprise authorization demands that access rights of all users and applications are stored in an *enterprise authorization database*, which every application must consult to determine what the current user can or cannot do with regard to database objects and with regard to application objects (such as being able to use a menu item).

20.1.1 Discretionary Authorization

The lingo of discretionary authorization is provided by the standard SQL. The lingo is centered on the notion of a **privilege**. All **access rights** to objects must be explicitly granted as privileges. The SQL `grant` and `revoke` commands are used to give or remove a privilege. Some database systems, such as SQL Server, additionally implement the `deny` command, which prevents the user/application from performing certain actions on an object.

Privileges can be granted/revoked to users and/or roles. A **role** is normally related to a job function (e.g. the role of a teacher). Role-based authorization permits specifying access rights in terms of the organizational structure of an enterprise. A *user* can be assigned to one or more roles. Each role represents a set of privileges granted to it. The user's privileges are, therefore, determined by the union of sets of privileges granted to all roles that the user is assigned to. Listing 20.1 is an example of SQL commands to grant privileges to users and roles.

Listing 20.1 Granting of privileges to users and roles

```
Granting of privileges to users and roles

create user anne identified by annepsswd;
create user michael identified by michaelpsswd;
create role student;
create role teacher;
grant create session to anne;
grant create session to michael;
grant select on grades to student;
grant update on grades to teacher;
grant student to anne;
grant student to teacher;
grant teacher to michael;
```

In Listing 20.1, the users `anne` and `michael` and the roles `student` and `teacher` are created. The users are granted `session` privileges. The `session` privileges are necessary to connect to and log in to the database. The roles are then granted additional privileges. The user `anne` is granted the role of `student`. The role `student` is then granted to the role `teacher`. This means that `michael`, in the role of `teacher`, 'inherits' `student` privileges and he can both `select` and `update` the `grades` table.

Once the role privileges are established, changes to them will be rare. The authorization tasks will be dominated by assignments of users to roles. This is consistent with what is happening in organizations – job (role) descriptions are relatively fixed, but users (employees) change jobs frequently. This is also a reason why the role concept has effectively replaced the older SQL notion of user **groups**. Creating 'virtual' group users (i.e. roles) and giving them group accounts replaces a need for a formal notion of a SQL group.

System and object privileges

Privileges are grouped into system privileges and object privileges. **System privilege** is the right to perform a particular action on a database system as a whole or an action with regard to the database schema (logical or physical structure). The `create session` in Listing 20.1 is an example of a system privilege. Other examples of system privileges are the rights to create, alter, and drop tables or to create and drop indexes. In general, system privileges are granted only to database administrators and to software engineers. Application users require only object privileges (and a system privilege to connect to and log in to a database).

Object privileges determine how users/applications can work with the database content (i.e. with the **database extension**, as opposed to the **database intention** defined by the schema). Object privileges determine what SQL operations can be performed on particular database objects. Different privileges are available for different types of objects. Object privileges for tables and views include the rights to `select`, `insert`, `update`, and `delete`. For stored procedures and functions, the only object privilege is `execute` – the right to execute a procedure/function.

Privileges can be passed from a user/role to another user/role. Granting a role to a user is one way of *passing privileges*. The other way, for users only, is with the SQL `with grant option`, e.g.

```
grant delete on grades to diana with grant option;
```

Of course, a user can pass a privilege to another user only if that user has the authority to do so. To start with, a user that creates a table has all applicable privileges on it and can pass these privileges to others. The effects of passing privileges can be depicted in an **authorization graph** (Ramakrishnan and Gehrke, 2000; Silberschatz *et al.*, 2002). The nodes of the graph are users/roles. The arcs (arrows) between nodes denote passed privileges. The passing of privileges begins at the root of the graph, which represents the **database administrator** (DBA). A user/role has a particular privilege only if there exists a path from the root to the node representing the user/role. Figure 20.1 is an example.

The authorization graph in Figure 20.1 distinguishes between user nodes (single circles) and role nodes (double circles). DBA is a root role that represents any user granted that role (in most database systems, the DBA role is a predefined standard role with the most powerful privileges). The graph extends the definitions in Listing 20.1.

The arcs are annotated with information about past privileges. For example, (diana, teacher, delete on grades) informs that the user diana passed a delete on grades privilege to the role teacher. Note that michael, who is in the role of teacher, has select, update, and delete privileges on grades.

Roles can be **authenticated**, if desired. This means that roles can be assigned passwords. This also means that all nodes (users and roles) are *authorization ids*, in SQL technical terms. However, in most database systems, with grant option does not apply to object privileges granted to a role, whether authenticated or not. This prevents users, who were granted certain roles, propagating object privileges of these roles to other users/roles.

Granted privileges can be **revoked**. The SQL revoke statement is used to remove privileges from a user or a role. The syntax of the revoke statement is similar to the grant statement, e.g.:

```
revoke delete on grades from diana;
```

Figure 20.1
Authorization
graph

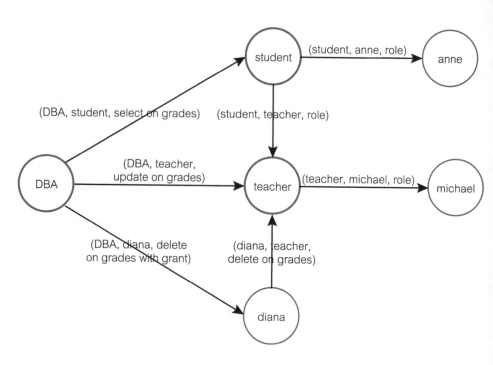

In some systems, such as in SQL Server, privileges can also be **denied** using the non-standard SQL deny statement. A denied privilege at any level (user or any role level) takes precedence over the same privilege granted at another level. The deny privilege overrides other privileges when combining memberships from multiple roles. If the user michael is a member of roles student and teacher, and the role student grants a privilege on an object but the role teacher denies the same privilege, then michael will be denied the access. This is because the denied privilege takes precedence over the granted privilege.

In the presence of revocation and denial of privileges, the **effective privileges** granted to a user on an object are defined by the union of all granted, denied, or revoked privileges defined for the user and for the roles that the user belongs to. Figure 20.2 shows a UML activity diagram for how effective privileges are computed and granted (Maciaszek and Owoc, 2001).

The user Mary attempts to access the object X. The guard condition states that Mary does not have direct privilege on X granted to her user account. To determine if Mary can access X, the system obtains the union of privileges that Mary inherits from her roles. If one of the roles has the required privilege on X *and* if that privilege on X is not explicitly denied in any other Mary's roles, then Mary can access X. Otherwise, Mary is prevented from accessing X until the deny statement is revoked.

Programmatic discretionary authorization

System and object privileges represent SQL **declarative** ways of implementing discretionary authorization. System and object privileges are declared. However, SQL provides

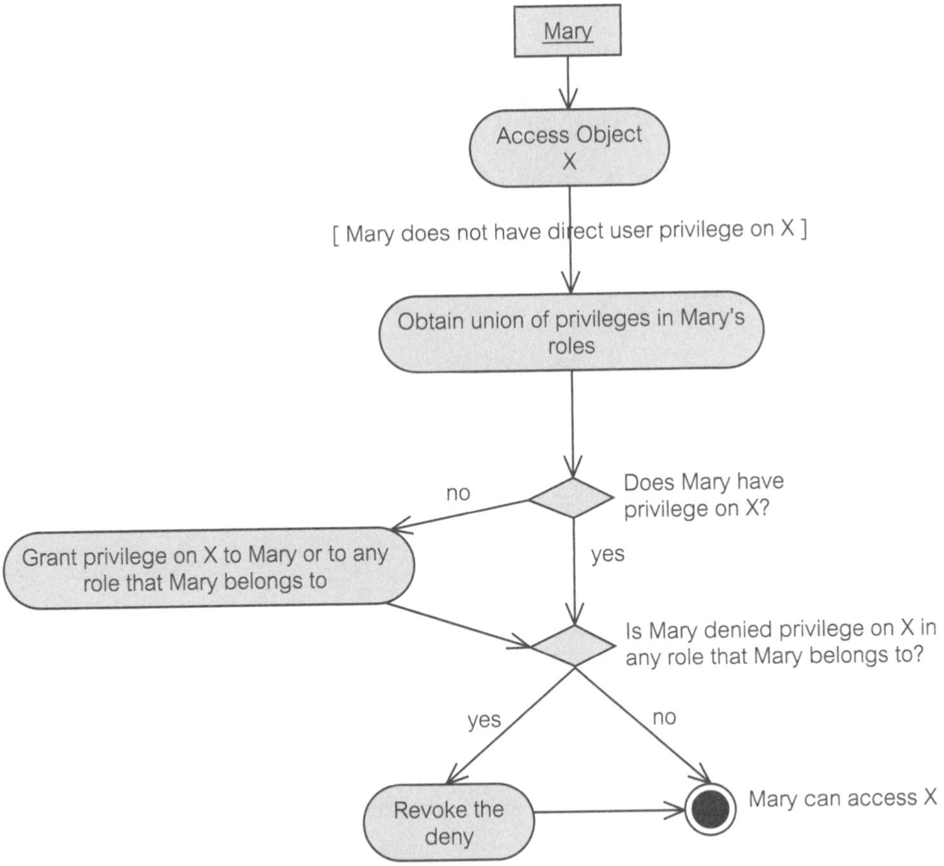

Figure 20.2
Computing and
granting effective
privileges

also **programmatic** (procedural) ways of controlling discretionary authorization. Programmatic authorization requires extra SQL programming with a specific aim to secure access to data. The resulting authorization code, or objects that are results of that code, are successively assigned declarative privileges.

There are three main targets of programmatic discretionary authorization: views, synonyms, and stored procedures. They are discussed next.

Using views

A **view** (or viewed table) is in essence a SQL query (select statement) that is given a name and it can be called by its name. When called, the SQL query executes and produces results in a *virtual table*. A view, therefore, pretends to be a table but in reality it is just a result of executing its query on one or more concrete tables and/or on one or more other views.

Figure 20.3 illustrates three views defined on the MovieActor database, extended here slightly from Chapter 10 (Figure 10.5). The views are presented graphically and the corresponding `create view` statements are also shown (the double quotes around names allow working with case-sensitive names). The views `actor_no_personal_info` and `expensive_actor` are defined on one table, namely on the `actor` table. The former is a

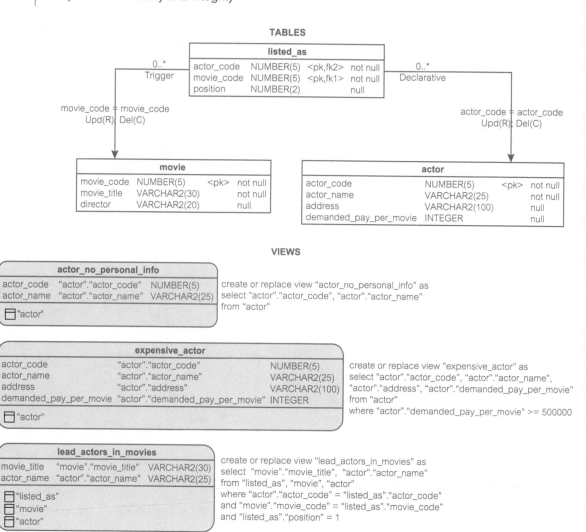

Figure 20.3 Views

projection view that prohibits visibility of two sensitive columns in `actor`. The latter is a *restriction view* that excludes visibility of rows where `demanded_pay_per_movie` is less than 500,000. The view `lead_actors_in_movies` is a *join view* that shows only movie title and names of actors who are listed as lead actors (with `position` equal 1).

Views have many advantages, but also a few significant restrictions. SQL select statements are set-oriented queries acting on entire tables. But some users and roles must not be allowed to see certain rows or certain columns of tables. A solution by splitting data from a table across many tables and granting limited privileges to each table is not an attractive proposition for performance and other reasons. Views provide a desired answer; they provide an additional level of table security by restricting access to a predetermined set of rows and/or columns of a table.

The main restriction is that the most interesting views are not updatable, i.e. they cannot serve as a source of updating (through them) real data in concrete tables. Hence, they are not very useful for controlling privileges for insert, update, and delete operations.

Creating a view does not require a so-called **resource privilege**, which is a system privilege to create database objects. To create a view, a user must only have prior `select` privileges on all tables referred to by the view. After these `select` privileges are granted to the user with `with grant option`, the user can pass the `select` privilege on the view to others.

Using synonyms

Some database management systems, including Oracle prior to Oracle 8.1.6, unite the concepts of user and schema. This one-to-one mapping means that a **schema** is created for each user account. Such an approach favors software engineers and developers, but it is inferior in the context of application users who are only allowed to access a shared database and who never create their own objects in their own schema.

There are a number of solutions to the dilemma. None of them is perfect, short of complete user/schema separation. Some solutions are (Bonazzi and Stokol, 2001):

- Allow all users to share a single schema and, therefore, the same username and password. This solution goes against basic principles of authorization and security.
- Still allow all users to share a single schema but store usernames and passwords in the database (governed by the same schema) to authenticate the users of the system.
- Use multiple **local schemas** (one schema per user), synonyms, and one **global schema**. In this solution, each user has his/her own schema but they do not contain any tables or data; they are only filled with *synonyms*. The synonyms connect each schema to a central (global) schema. All requests performed on the user schemas are redirected to the global schema through the synonyms.

A **synonym** is an alias (alternative name) for a table, view, stored procedure, function, or another synonym. To successfully use the synonym, the user/role must have proper privileges on target database objects. A synonym can be created in one schema to access objects in another schema. This merely allows access to objects in another schema without using the schema qualifier name. The `create synonym` statement is used to create a synonym. The statement below creates the synonym called `actor` in one schema to refer to the table `actor` in schema `MovieActor`:

```
create synonym actor for MovieActor.actor;
```

Synonyms prop up location transparency and data independence. By using synonyms, the user is not aware of the real location of objects. A certain level of data independence is also achieved because some changes to database objects, including name changes, may not impact on applications working with synonyms.

From the authorization perspective, synonyms do not help with the issue of assignment of privileges, but they can provide for improved user authentication in systems that unite schemas and users. Privileges are assigned to objects as needed in the *global schema*, such as MovieActor, which contains all objects for the application. There are no database objects defined in *local schemas* of users, except for synonyms. Users are authenticated on their own local schemas and all local schemas are identical (they contain the same set of synonyms).

An interesting perspective on using synonyms to implement a software development environment is suggested in Bonazzi and Stokol (2001). In their scenario, developers work with global schema objects via synonyms in their local schemas. By revoking from them some privileges, such as `alter` or `drop`, they are not allowed to mess up in the global schema. When an object must be changed, the developer creates the object in his/her local schema to temporarily substitute for the synonym. Once all the programming and testing has been completed, the developer can request that the local object should replace the object in the global schema.

Using stored procedures and functions

Synonyms are just aliases and therefore they do not block certain data from client's visibility (and there will always be some information in the database that is not allowed to be shown to some users/roles). Views can provide assistance in this regard but they have some important drawbacks. A superior solution to access control is offered by stored procedures and functions (Section 10.1.5). Procedures and functions can detect the access level of the connected client and service only permitted activities.

Stored procedures and **stored functions** are precompiled batches of code, which have names and can take parameters. Procedures and functions simplify application programming by shifting the responsibility for performing tasks from the applications to the database itself. Procedures and functions are programmed once and can be invoked from many different applications. This greatly facilitates maintenance of programs. Being precompiled, stored procedures/functions execute much faster than corresponding inter-active SQL statements from the client code. They also reduce network traffic because invoking procedures and functions requires much shorter text strings as compared with interactive SQL commands. The same relates to the possible volume of data returned from the database.

Stored procedures and functions are invaluable from an authorization perspective, as they completely encapsulate actions performed on the database. Some of these may be authorization checks. To the users, stored procedures and functions are black boxes returning data or just performing some actions without returning data. The users do not know what SQL commands are inside a procedure/function and they cannot change the commands prior to execution.

The only authorization privilege assignable to a stored procedure or function is the `execute` privilege. A user can only call a stored procedure or function, pass parameters to it, and receive results back from the database. A desirable implication is that once an application accesses all data by means of stored procedures and functions, then a database administrator can revoke from all application users and roles the privileges to `select`, `insert`, `update`, and `delete` data. An important benefit of such an approach is that the application users cannot circumvent authorization rules by gaining illegitimate access to the database by using an interactive SQL tool.

Listing 20.2 is an example of a stored function called `usp_retrieve_employee_login`. The function accepts two parameter values: `login` is the login name provided by the user and `usern` is the login/username as known to the database. If the two values agree, the stored function retrieves a complete record of information about `Employee` and returns it (in `REF_CURSOR`) to the application.

Listing 20.2 Stored function usp_retrieve_employee_login

```
Stored function usp_retrieve_employee_login

create or replace function usp_retrieve_employee_login(login IN
varchar2, usern in varchar2) return EMS.REF_CURSOR is
    c EMS.REF_CURSOR;
    dummy integer;
begin
    dummy := null;
    select 1 into dummy from dual where upper(login) = upper(usern);

    open c for select * from "Employee" where "login_name" = login;
    return c;
EXCEPTION
      WHEN NO_DATA_FOUND THEN
          raise_application_error(-20023,
'usp_retrieve_employee_login: unmatch username and loginname');
end;
```

Listing 20.3 illustrates how the stored function in Listing 20.2 is called from the application. The method `retrieveEmployeeByName()` builds a call string as a parameter of the `query()` message on a `reader` object (Line 437). This call returns a result set that is stored in the variable `rs`. The comment line (Line 438) shows how a direct SQL `select` statement could replace a call to a stored function.

A careful reader would notice that the call to `usp_retrieve_employee_login()` supplies only one parameter and the procedure in Listing 20.2 expects two parameters. The explanation of this apparent error relates to the one-to-one mapping between a user and a schema in some database management systems.

Instead of using synonyms for stored procedures and functions in local schemas, the developer can create imitations (skeletons) of global stored procedures in local schemas and use these skeletons to redirect execution to the global schema. Listing 20.4 is such a solution. The `call` statement in Listing 20.3 invokes the stored function in Listing 20.4, now with one parameter – the `login` string. The `select` statement on a system table `user_users` supplies the second parameter to the stored function in Listing 20.2.

The table `user_users` stores the username of the connected user. Because of the one-to-one mapping between a user and a schema, there can be only one username connected to the local schema. This username (`usern`) is the second parameter in the call to `usp_retrieve_employee_login` in the global schema (called in Listing 20.4 on the `return` statement). Note that trying just to redirect the call to the global schema and to `select username` on that global schema will fail because the global schema user is different from the current application user (and the application user does not know that user's credentials or privileges).

Listing 20.3 Calling stored function from application method retrieveEmployeeByName()

Calling stored function from application method retrieveEmployeeByName()

```
433:       public IAEmployee retrieveEmployeeByName(String username) {
434:           EEmployee emp = null;
435:           java.sql.ResultSet rs=null;
436:           try {
437:               rs = reader.query("{ ? = call
                       usp_retrieve_employee_login(?)}", new
                                                   Object[]{username});
438:               //reader.query("select * from employee where
                                       login_name = '" + username + "'");
439:
440:               if (rs.next()) {
441:                   emp = (EEmployee) createEmployee();
442:                   fillEmployee(rs,emp);
443:                   cache.registerEmployee(emp);
444:               }
445:           } catch (Exception exc) {
446:               exc.printStackTrace();
447:               return null;
448:           }finally{
449:               if(rs != null) reader.closeResult(rs);
450:           }
451:           return emp;
452:       }
```

Listing 20.4 Stored function usp_retrieve_employee_login in a local schema

Stored function usp_retrieve_employee_login in a local schema

```
create or replace function usp_retrieve_employee_login(login IN
varchar2)
    return PSE3.EMS.ref_cursor is
    usern varchar2(20);
begin
    select username into usern from user_users;
    return PSE3.usp_retrieve_employee_login(login, usern);
end;
/
```

Mandatory Authorization

Mandatory authorization addresses some loopholes of discretionary authorization with respect to user authentication and in terms of user permissions. Firstly, mandatory authorization validates if a user, which passes the username/password test, is really who s/he claims to be. Secondly, mandatory authorization defines top-down **clearance levels** for users and **security classes** for accessed objects in order to eliminate some possible bypasses of security. Mandatory authorization applies in systems where *secrecy* may be a greater concern than information integrity.

The first aspect of mandatory authorization refers more to *authentication* than authorization. Authentication checks the credentials of the user. This can be done in a number of ways. For more secure scenarios, a **challenge–response approach** involving **encryption** can be used (Silberschatz *et al.*, 2002). The process can be as follows:

1. The user/application tries to connect to a database.

2. The database sends a challenge string to the user/application.

3. The user/application uses a predefined password (encryption key) to encrypt the challenge string and sends the encrypted string back to the database.

4. The database decrypts the string with the same password and it allows connection only if it gets the initial challenge string.

Encryption has a benefit that passwords do not travel over the network. A variation of encryption using a **public key** has an added benefit that passwords are not even stored in the database. Public key encryption is also used in **digital signatures**.

The second aspect of mandatory authorization is the authorization aspect per se. The idea is to restrict access to objects based on the sensitivity of contained information (security classes) and based on the clearance levels of users trying to access that information. Security classes and clearance go hand-in-hand; a user has to have the clearance at least as high as the object's classification to gain access to it. The scheme is called mandatory to emphasize the requirement that classifications and clearances are maintained centrally by **security administrators** and cannot be changed by users.

A widely publicized variant of mandatory authorization, called **Bell–LaPadula model**, is centered on four concepts (Ramakrishnan and Gehrke, 2000):

■ objects (e.g. tables, views, columns, rows, stored procedures)

■ subjects (e.g. users, application programs)

■ classifications of objects

■ clearances of subjects.

As stated, classifications and clearances go together. The same set of levels applies to both. One simple possibility is to have four classification/clearance levels:

■ top secret

■ secret

■ confidential

■ unclassified.

Once objects are given classification levels and subjects are assigned clearance levels, a subject with certain clearance can only access objects with the same or lower classification. This rule constitutes additional checking after the subject satisfies discretionary access controls.

20.1.3 Enterprise Authorization

The techniques of discretionary and mandatory authorization are insufficient when faced with enterprise information systems with possibly hundreds of applications, thousands of users, and several corporate databases. In such situations, system-wide authorization policies, that cannot be changed by individual users or even developers, must be adopted. This is the premise of **enterprise authorization**.

Discretionary and mandatory authorizations concentrate on database objects and users and neglect client program objects and applications. In reality, authorization issues span client programs and databases. For example, an application user who is not allowed to see grades of students in the database should not even have a menu option available in the program to attempt viewing the grades. In other words, privileges on database objects and on application objects should be consistent and in sync. Moreover, the same user can be acting in many roles, each with different privileges on the database. The authorization system must be able to determine privileges that apply to a user when that user is using a particular application program.

Since a role is defined as a set of privileges, a role cannot span across different applications accessing the same database. For this reason, an increasing number of database systems implement the notion of an **application role**, as separate from a user role. The availability of application roles introduces a new possibility of integrating authorization on server objects with authorization on client objects.

Like users and user roles, privileges are assigned to application roles. However, there are important differences. Israel and Jones (2001) list the following differences between an application role and a user role in SQL Server databases:

∎ Application roles have no members.

∎ Application roles are inactive by default (they are activated by the application when it starts).

∎ All effective privileges (Section 20.1.1) of the current user are removed and only privileges assigned to the application role are applied.

Database management systems like Oracle, which normally establish a schema for each user, provide *advanced security features* that implement similar concepts, but not always under the same name. Oracle uses the notion of an **enterprise user** (or **schema-independent user**) to support the functionality of an application role. Oracle provides a special directory service to map a user (so called Distinguished Name (DN) of a user) to an enterprise user, when the user accesses the database via an application. The application is associated with a so-called **shared schema**, and a set of privileges for the application on the shared schema is defined.

As opposed to an application role in SQL Server, the set of privileges of an enterprise user in Oracle is the union of the privileges associated with the shared schema and any additional privileges that are associated with the roles granted to the user in the directory service. The mapping of enterprise users via the directory service extends to many databases that a user may need to access and many applications that a user may need to use.

Support given by existing database management systems for enterprise authorization may be sufficient for controlling access of application users to database objects, but they still fall short of providing integrated access control on both database (server) objects and application (client) objects. Also, the authorization machinery of available solutions may be too complex to manage for some organizations. In cases like that, or for extensions of existing solutions, software engineers may decide to create a special **authorization database** in support of enterprise authorization (Maciaszek and Owoc, 2001). Each application, when it is launched by a user, queries the authorization database in order to determine the user's privileges and to customize itself for that user.

Enterprise authorization via the authorization database still requires that the user connects to the database server using a predefined user login (however, the user login alone may only be granted the database connect privilege). Without the user login, the auditing of specific user activities (via the application) on the database may not be possible. Once connected, the login to the application role is transparent to the user and the effective permissions are obtained by the application from the authorization database.

Figure 20.4 is an example of a partial design of an authorization database (Maciaszek, 2001; Maciaszek and Owoc, 2001). The central table in this design is `ApplicationRole`. An application role is activated for a *connection* (user session). The authorization settings that the user obtained from the application role remain in effect until the user logs out of the application program (and, therefore, logs out of the database server).

The model in Figure 20.4 assumes that the authorization database is used by the client program to establish authorization settings with regard to both the client and the server objects. This is consistent with the requirement that an unauthorized user must be refused permission to perform unauthorized activities on the client. If client activity can compromise the integrity of the database then the second level of protection on the server is also enforced.

The authorization database maintains in `ClientObject` a catalogue of all application *client objects* that are subject to authorization settings. The catalogue includes application windows, window fields, and window controls. Any hierarchical relationships between client objects are also maintained (such as panes in a window, fields in a window, or menu hierarchy). The **client privileges** in `ClientPermission` relate to windows and window controls.

Each client object can be granted or denied more than one permission. The *revoked permissions* are not stored in the authorization database – they are not needed to determine the authorization settings for the current user (a revoked permission is simply a permission that has not been granted).

The allowed mappings of permissions to client objects are stored in `ClientObject-ToPermission`. An application role is then assigned its permissions on the application's client objects. The assignment can be either that the permission *is granted* or that it *is denied*. This information is stored in `RoleToClientPermission` (is_granted and is_denied).

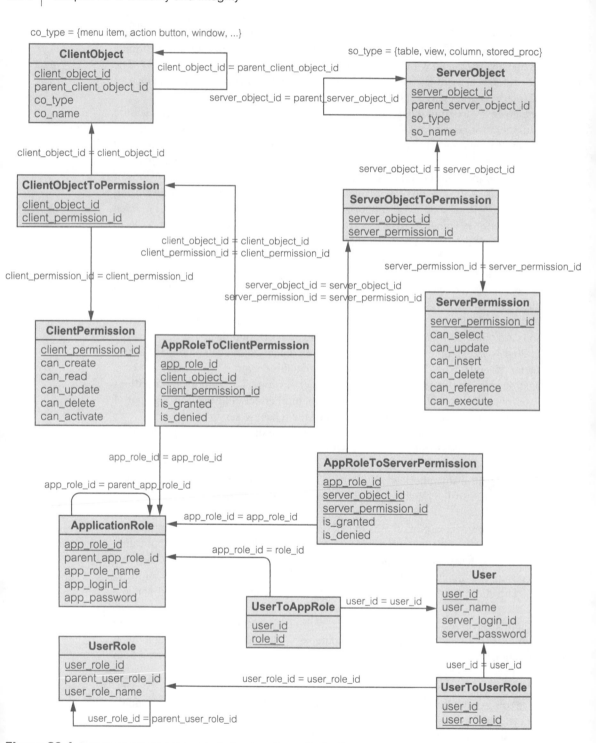

Figure 20.4 Database schema in support of enterprise authorization

Because of possible hierarchical relationships between client objects, complex *integrity rules* are implemented in the authorization database to prevent inconsistencies between granted/denied permissions. For example, it does not make sense to grant permission on a submenu if the permission is denied on a menu that contains it. Similarly, a denied permission for `can_read` precludes a granted permission for `can_update`.

Ultimately the security and integrity of the database is the responsibility of the database itself, not the client applications accessing the database. The client authorizations can only eliminate some security breaches early in the process and can free the database from duplicated and unnecessary checks. Not all potential security breaches can be addressed in the client. For example, most integrity constraints implemented in database triggers can only be enforced once a client-authorized insert, delete, or update operation hits a database table.

The authorization database maintains in `ServerObject` (Figure 20.4) a catalogue of all application *server objects* that are subject to authorization settings. The catalogue includes tables, views, stored procedures and any individual table columns that must be protected from indiscriminate access. Hierarchical relationships between server objects are maintained (such as columns in tables). The **server privileges** in `ServerPermission` relate to database objects – tables, views, columns, stored procedures, etc.

As with client objects, each server object can be granted or denied more than one permission. The *revoked permissions* are not stored in the authorization database.

The allowed mappings of permissions to server objects are stored in `ServerObject-ToPermission`. The application role is either granted or denied permissions to server objects to which the role is linked via a referential relationship. This information is stored in the table called `RoleToServerPermission` (`is_granted` and `is_denied`).

Placing the burden of application authorizations on a database server is a good approach for two-tier client/server systems. The issue gets more complex for *web-based systems* supported by web and application servers. The users of web-based applications are unlikely to have user accounts on the database. In fact, the database may only have a single account for all users of a web server and/or application server. In such systems, authorization tasks shift from the database server to web/application servers or even to client applications. Designing authorizations for such systems is a tricky business with little support from system software.

Designing Integrity

The term integrity in software and data engineering has only weak relevance to its usual meaning of honesty or unity. Integrity is about correctness and consistency of data accessible to the program. Because sometimes the distinction between the data and a process that generates the data cannot be defined, integrity can also apply to processes (operations, programs, etc.).

In the database context, integrity is enforced by **integrity constraints** specified on the database behavior. The constraints enforce the business rules that the database must obey. They are defined in the database rather than in an application. Since databases are active (programmable), the constraints can be declarative or procedural (Section 10.1.4). Typical database management systems support the following *types of integrity constraint* (Silber-schatz *et al.*, 2002):

- null
- default
- domain (data type)
- check (rule, assertion)
- unique (alternate key)
- primary key
- foreign key
- trigger (active rule, assertion).

20.2.1 Null and Default Constraints

The **null constraint** defined on a table column states that the column accepts null values. There are two main meanings of a null value, namely 'value at present unknown' or 'value inapplicable' in the context of the remaining values in the row. The null value is represented by a special database character (i.e. it is not a zero (0) or space).

The **default constraint**, also defined on a table column, provides a value for the column if such a value is not given when a new row is inserted into the table. The default value could be a literal or expression. Expression can include selected database functions, such as the `sysdate` function in Oracle to refer to the current date and time. In the absence of the default specification for a column, its default value is set to `null` (unless, of course, the column is defined as `not null`).

Figure 20.5 shows an example of the definition of table `listed_as`. The column `position` is given the default value of 1. This means that unless a different value is

Figure 20.5
Null and default constraints

listed_as			
actor_code	NUMBER(5)	<pk,fk2>	not null
movie_code	NUMBER(5)	<pk,fk1>	not null
position	NUMBER(2)		null

```
create table "listed_as"   (
    "actor_code"          NUMBER (5)                    not null,
    "movie_code"          NUMBER (5)                    not null,
    "position"            NUMBER (2)                    default 1,
    constraint PK_LISTED_AS primary key ("actor_code", "movie_code")
)
/
```

Figure 20.6
Domain and check
constraints

```
                    ┌─────────────────────────────────────────┐
                    │                 movie                   │
                    ├─────────────────────────────────────────┤
                    │ movie_code   NUMBER(5)      <pk>  not null │
                    │ movie_title  VARCHAR2(30)         not null │
                    │ director     VARCHAR2(20)         null     │
                    │ movie_type   FEATURE_TYPE         null     │
                    └─────────────────────────────────────────┘
```

```
    create domain feature_type varchar2 (20)
    constraint CKC_FEATURE_TYPE
    check (value in ("drama", "comedy", "horror"))
```

```
create table "movie"   (
   "movie_code"          NUMBER (5)                        not null,
   "movie_title"         VARCHAR2 (30)                     not null,
   "director"            VARCHAR2 (20),
   "movie_type"          VARCHAR2 (20)
        constraint CKC_MOVIE_TYPE_MOVIE check ("movie_type" is null or
                    ("movie_type" in ('drama', 'comedy', 'horror'))),
   constraint PK_MOVIE primary key ("movie_code")
)
/
```

provided when performing `insert` to the table, the actor will be considered to be the leading actor for the movie.

Domain and Check Constraints

20.2.2

A **domain** is a user-defined data type. The definition includes the possibility of imposing constraints (additional rules) on the values that the data type allows. The constraints are specified using the **check** keyword. The checks can be of varying nature, such as allowed ranges of values or allowed lists of values. Once defined, the domain can be used as a data type for any column, in place of primitive data types supplied by the database management system.

Figure 20.6 shows an example of the `movie` table extended with column `movie_type`, which type is the domain `feature_type`. The domain is defined with a check constraint, which restricts allowed values for feature types to drama, comedy, and horror. When a `create table` statement is generated based on the `movie` and `feature_type` design, the domain is expanded in the definition of column `movie_type`, to conform to required SQL syntax.

Unique and Primary Keys

20.2.3

Rows (records) in database tables need to be uniquely identified to separate one row from another. Such identification is provided in relational databases by means of unique and primary keys. A **primary key** is one of the unique keys specified on a table, which has

Figure 20.7
Unique and
primary keys

actor			
actor_code	NUMBER(5)	\<pk\>	not null
actor_name	VARCHAR2(25)	\<ak\>	not null
address	VARCHAR2(100)	\<ak\>	null
demanded_pay_per_movie	INTEGER		null

⌖ pk_actor \<pk\>
⌖ ck1_actor \<ak\>

```
create table "actor" (
    "actor_code"                    NUMBER (5)              not null,
    "actor_name"                    VARCHAR2 (25)           not null,
    "address"                       VARCHAR2 (100),
    "demanded_pay_per_movie"        INTEGER                 default 50000,
    constraint PK_ACTOR primary key ("actor_code"),
    constraint CK1_ACTOR unique ("actor_name", "address")
)
/
```

been chosen as more useful for identification than others. This is typically some kind of code or number and it is typically defined on a single column. A **unique key** is also called a **candidate key** or **alternative key**.

Figure 20.7 illustrates the `actor` table with the primary key defined on `actor_code` and the unique key defined on two columns: `actor_name` and `address`.

20.2.4 Foreign Keys

As defined in Section 10.1.2, a **foreign key** is a set of columns (frequently just one column) whose values correspond to the values of the primary key in another (or the same) table. Foreign keys create the basis for **referential integrity** constraints (Section 10.1.4). The constraints can be implemented declaratively or procedurally by triggers.

Figure 20.8 is an example of a declarative integrity constraint, slightly modified from Section 10.1.4. The constraint is defined on the foreign key `actor_code` in `listed_as`. It is a **restrict constraint** for update operations stating that if `actor_code` in `actor` is updated, all associated dependent records in `listed_as` must be correspondingly updated or the update will be refused. The restrict constraint is the default constraint. For delete operations, the constraint is defined as **cascade**. This means that a deletion of a row in the `actor` table will cause an automatic deletion of all associated dependent rows in the `listed_as` table.

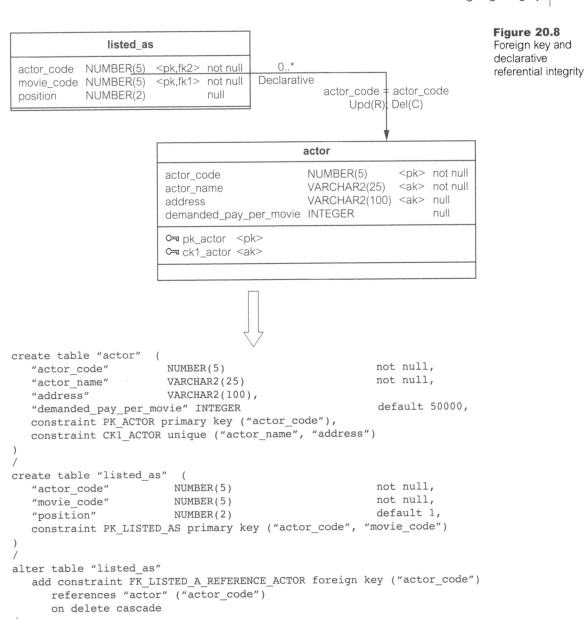

Figure 20.8
Foreign key and
declarative
referential integrity

```
create table "actor"   (
    "actor_code"           NUMBER(5)                              not null,
    "actor_name"           VARCHAR2(25)                           not null,
    "address"              VARCHAR2(100),
    "demanded_pay_per_movie" INTEGER                              default 50000,
    constraint PK_ACTOR primary key ("actor_code"),
    constraint CK1_ACTOR unique ("actor_name", "address")
)
/
create table "listed_as"   (
    "actor_code"           NUMBER(5)                              not null,
    "movie_code"           NUMBER(5)                              not null,
    "position"             NUMBER(2)                              default 1,
    constraint PK_LISTED_AS primary key ("actor_code", "movie_code")
)
/
alter table "listed_as"
    add constraint FK_LISTED_A_REFERENCE_ACTOR foreign key ("actor_code")
        references "actor" ("actor_code")
        on delete cascade
/
```

The SQL standard defines two other declarative constraints: null and default. The **null constraint** states that when referenced data (in the primary table) is updated or deleted, all associated dependent data (in the foreign table) will be set to null. The **default constraint** states that when referenced data (in the primary table) is updated or deleted, all associated dependent data will be set to a default value.

Figure 20.9
Design of triggers
for movie and
listed_as

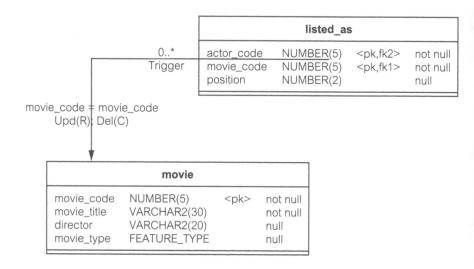

20.2.5 Triggers

Triggers constitute a procedural way of enforcing referential integrity constraints as well as implementing other business rules that the database must satisfy (Section 10.1.4). These other business rules 'asserted' by a trigger can be defined for any column in a table, not just for foreign key columns. Triggers are variants of stored procedures that are automatically fired whenever a predefined insert, delete, and/or update event happens.

Figure 20.9 is an example of a design of triggers for tables `movie` and `listed_as`. Listing 20.5 is an Oracle SQL definition for these triggers.

In the Oracle case (as shown in Listing 20.5), a **trigger action** can be executed `before`, `after`, or `instead of` the insert, update, or delete statement. **Before triggers** execute the trigger action before the triggering event. **After triggers** execute the trigger action after the triggering event is completed.

Instead of triggers are a handy technique for executing the action defined in the trigger instead of the action that the triggering event would normally provide. This technique is particularly useful for telling the system what to do if there is an attempt to insert, update, or delete through a view. Since many views are not updatable, `instead of` triggers provide a custom solution for view modifications, which otherwise would fail. There is no example of an `instead of` trigger in Listing 20.5.

A trigger action can be programmed using `:old` and `:new` values of records that were inserted, deleted, or updated in the event that triggered the action. The action can be performed either once `for each row` modified or only once for the triggering statement for all rows modified. The former is called a **row trigger**, the latter a **statement trigger** (there is no example of a statement trigger in Listing 20.5).

One of the most crucial decisions facing a developer is to decide whether to use *declarative referential integrity* at all or to replace it fully with *triggers*. Triggers corresponding to declarative constraints can be automatically generated by CASE and IDE tools, so there is no manual programming involved. This problem is best answered by studying the pros and cons for the database management system involved.

Listing 20.5 Definition of triggers for movie and listed_as

```
Triggers for movie and listed_as

-- Before insert trigger ""tib_listed_as"" for table ""listed_as""
create trigger "tib_listed_as" before insert
on "listed_as" for each row
declare
   integrity_error  exception;
   errno            integer;
   errmsg           char(200);
   dummy            integer;
   found            boolean;
   -- Declaration of InsertChildParentExist constraint for the parent
   -- ""movie""
   cursor cpk1_"listed_as" (var_"movie_code" number) is
      select 1
      from   "movie"
      where  "movie_code" = var_"movie_code"
      and    var_"movie_code" is not null;

begin
   -- Parent ""movie"" must exist when inserting a child in
                                               ""listed_as""
   if :new."movie_code" is not null then
      open  cpk1_"listed_as"(:new."movie_code");
      fetch cpk1_"listed_as" into dummy;
      found := cpk1_"listed_as"%FOUND;
      close cpk1_"listed_as";
      if not found then
         errno  := -20002;
         errmsg := 'Parent does not exist in ""movie"". Cannot create
                   child in ""listed_as"".';
         raise integrity_error;
      end if;
   end if;

-- Errors handling
exception
   when integrity_error then
      raise_application_error(errno, errmsg);
end;
/

-- Before update trigger ""tub_listed_as"" for table ""listed_as""
create trigger "tub_listed_as" before update
```

```
of "actor_code",
   "movie_code"
on "listed_as" for each row
declare
   integrity_error  exception;
   errno            integer;
   errmsg           char(200);
   dummy            integer;
   found            boolean;
   -- Declaration of UpdateChildParentExist constraint for the parent
   -- ""movie""
   cursor cpk1_"listed_as"(var_"movie_code" number) is
      select 1
      from   "movie"
      where  "movie_code" = var_"movie_code"
      and    var_"movie_code" is not null;

begin
   -- Parent ""movie"" must exist when updating a child in
                                                        ""listed_as""
   if (:new."movie_code" is not null) then
      open  cpk1_"listed_as"(:new."movie_code");
      fetch cpk1_"listed_as" into dummy;
      found := cpk1_"listed_as"%FOUND;
      close cpk1_"listed_as";
      if not found then
         errno  := -20003;
         errmsg := 'Parent does not exist in ""movie"". Cannot update
                   child in ""listed_as"".';
         raise integrity_error;
      end if;
   end if;

   -- Cannot modify parent code of ""movie"" in child ""listed_as""
   if (updating('movie_code') and :old."movie_code" !=
                                               :new."movie_code")
   then
         errno  := -20004;
         errmsg := 'Cannot modify parent code of ""movie"" in child
                   ""listed_as"".';
         raise integrity_error;
   end if;

   -- Cannot modify parent code of ""actor"" in child ""listed_as""
   if (updating('actor_code') and :old."actor_code" !=
                                               :new."actor_code")
```

```
       then
             errno   := -20004;
             errmsg := 'Cannot modify parent code of ""actor"" in child
                         ""listed_as"".';
             raise integrity_error;
      end if;
-- Errors handling
exception
   when integrity_error then
        raise_application_error(errno, errmsg);
end;
/
-- Before update trigger ""tub_movie"" for table ""movie""
create trigger "tub_movie" before update
of "movie_code"
on "movie" for each row
declare
   integrity_error  exception;
   errno            integer;
   errmsg           char(200);
   dummy            integer;
   found            boolean;
   -- Declaration of UpdateParentRestrict constraint for ""listed_as""
   cursor cfk1_"listed_as"(var_"movie_code" number) is
      select 1
      from   "listed_as"
      where  "movie_code" = var_"movie_code"
      and    var_"movie_code" is not null;

begin
   -- Cannot modify parent code in ""movie"" if children still exist in
   -- ""listed_as""
   if (updating('movie_code') and :old."movie_code" !=
                                           :new."movie_code")
   then
      open  cfk1_"listed_as"(:old."movie_code");
      fetch cfk1_"listed_as" into dummy;
      found := cfk1_"listed_as"%FOUND;
      close cfk1_"listed_as";
      if found then
         errno   := -20005;
         errmsg := 'Children still exist in ""listed_as"". Cannot
                     modify parent code in ""movie"".';
         raise integrity_error;
      end if;
   end if;
```

```
-- Errors handling
exception
    when integrity_error then
        raise_application_error(errno, errmsg);
end;
/

-- After delete trigger ""tda_movie"" for table ""movie""
create trigger "tda_movie" after delete
on "movie" for each row
declare
    integrity_error  exception;
    errno            integer;
    errmsg           char(200);
    dummy            integer;
    found            boolean;

begin
    -- Delete all children in ""listed_as""
    delete "listed_as"
    where "movie_code" = :old."movie_code";

-- Errors handling
exception
    when integrity_error then
        begin
        IntegrityPackage.InitNestLevel;
        raise_application_error(errno, errmsg);
        end;
end;
/
```

Firstly, there may be performance differences (usually in favor of declarative constraints). Secondly, mixing declarative constraints and triggers may introduce nasty overlapping and precedence issues. Usually declarative constraints have execution precedence over triggers and can, for example, stop the relevant trigger from firing. However, **instead of** triggers have precedence over declarative constraints.

Thirdly, triggers can be implemented without any direct recognition of the notions of primary and foreign keys. Even if they are recognized, the relationship such as in Figure 20.9 is unlikely to be automatically reverse engineered from the database code if the relationship is implemented by means of a trigger.

Last but not least, once the database is loaded with triggers in place, a later attempt to switch to declarative integrity cannot be done easily (such as by running `alter table` statements on existing tables). This means that the database would have to be dropped, a new schema created, and the whole database reloaded. In many practical situations, re-creating and reloading a database is not a feasible proposition.

Security and Integrity in Email Management

The implementation of EM Iteration 3 gives due consideration to security and integrity controls. The main *authorization* changes are in the area of adding enterprise authorization on top of the discretionary authorization for users, already enforced in previous iterations. The *integrity* changes relate mostly to addition of triggers.

The implementation of enterprise authorization in Iteration 3 includes addition of roles and the introduction of a special table to hold authorization rules. Changes to authorization rules can be made through a new authorization window in the user interface. However, the changes are not as extensive to implement as a separate authorization database for 'computing' a user's privileges on the application's startup and for appropriately customizing the application.

Triggers enforced in Iteration 3 are designed to collaborate with newly introduced stored procedures and stored functions. The triggers are defined on two tables: `OutMessage` and `DailyReport`.

Security in Email Management

The level of granularity of authorization supported by databases is limited to grants on `select`, `update`, and `delete` per table basis. It is not possible to declaratively grant a user a *select* on a *subset* of a table. This is just one of the reasons that forces the implementation of programmatic discretionary authorization in Iteration 3.

Authorization rules in EM Iteration 3 are directed only to the `OutMessage` table. Users can only view and act on a subset of this table depending on a department for which they work. A possible authorization graph for EM Iteration 3 is shown in Figure 20.10. The graph refers to virtual subsets of the `OutMessage` table. For example, `IND-outmessages` represents a virtual subset of the `OutMessage` table available to independent employees (`IND`). A similar approach is applied for other authorization roles.

Figure 20.10 illustrates that the hierarchy of privileges on the `OutMessage` table is from `IND` to `COL` to `QUA` to `CUS` to `ADM`. The smallest subset of the `OutMessage` table is available to independent (`IND`) employees. `Grotte` is an independent employee and is granted the `IND` role. The graph shows that a member of `IND` cannot view other subsets of the `OutMessage` table because `IND` is not granted any additional privileges.

However, employees of the Data Collection department (`COL`) can manipulate all of the `IND` outmessages. This is because the `IND` role is granted to the `COL` role. Moreover, `COL` can view a larger subset of the `OutMessage` table, as reflected in the authorization matrix (Section 19.2.3, Table 19.1). Moving up the hierarchy, it is apparent that the most powerful role, which can access and modify all outmessages, is given to the employees in the System Administration (`ADM`) department. `Dayes` and `Liong`, as the users with granted `ADM` role, can access the entire `OutMessage` table content.

SQL statements corresponding to Figure 20.10 are shown in Listing 20.6. This listing could only apply if there were five different `OutMessage` tables. Dividing the existing

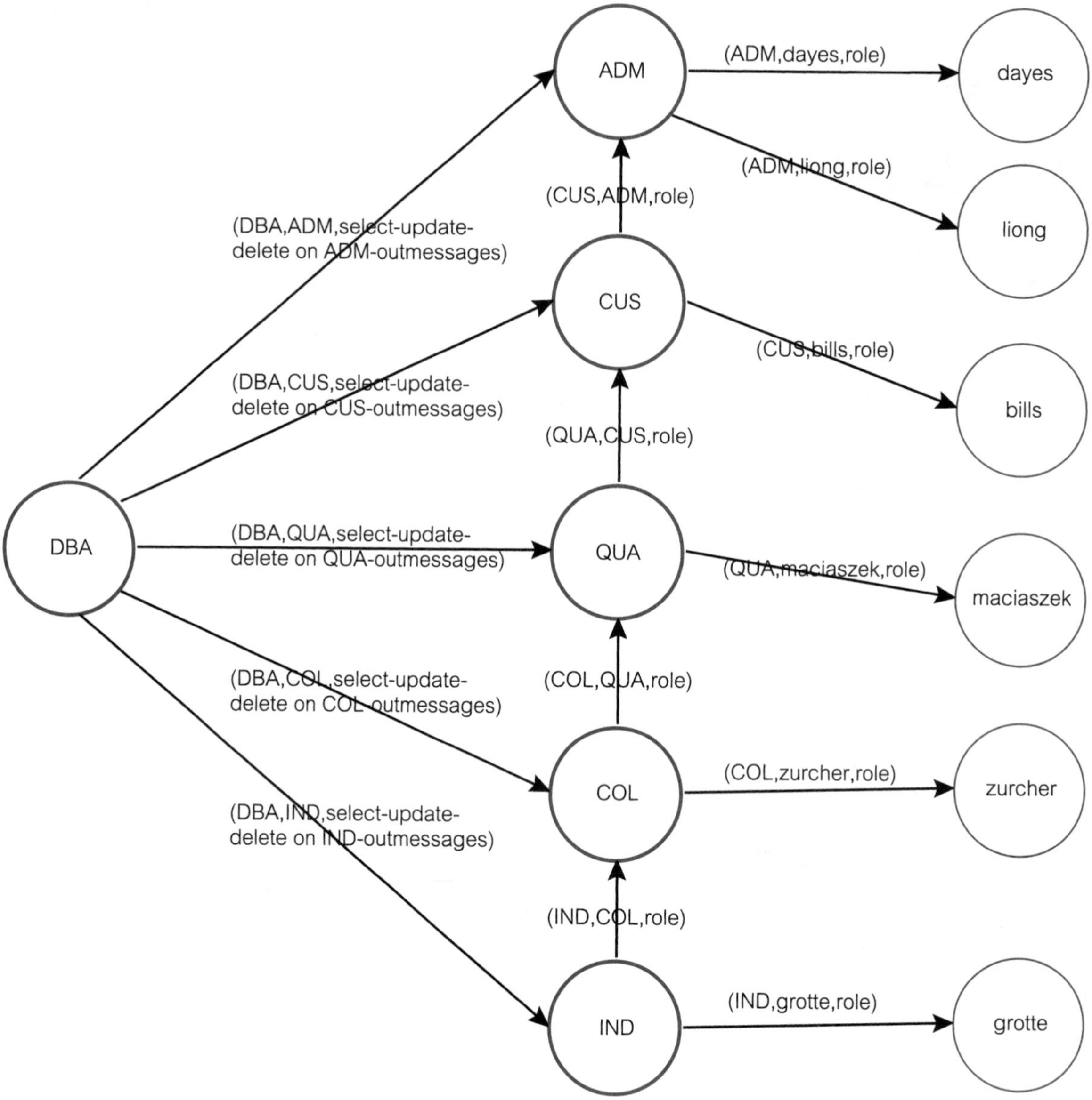

Figure 20.10 Possible EM Iteration 3 authorization graph

OutMessage table into five tables is not practical, especially in that the increase in the number of roles would necessitate even more tables. Moreover, this would not be acceptable from the application code viewpoint. Forcing the application to perform multiple statements on subsets of the OutMessage table in order to access all required outmessages would be a performance and maintenance nightmare.

Listing 20.6 SQL statements to realize authorization rules

```
SQL statements to realize authorization rules
create user Dayes identified by dayespsswd;
create user Liong identified by liongpsswd;
create user Bills identified by billspsswd;
create user Maciaszek identified by maciaszekpsswd;
create user Zurcher identified by zurcherpsswd;
create user Grotte identified by grottepsswd;
create role ADM;
create role CUS;
create role QUA;
create role COL;
create role IND;
grant create session to Dayes;
grant create session to Liong;
grant create session to Bills;
grant create session to Maciaszek;
grant create session to Zurcher;
grant create session to Grotte;
grant select on IND_OutMessage to IND;
grant select on COL_OutMessage to COL; --similar to update/delete
grant select on QUA_OutMessage to QUA; --similar to update/delete
grant select on CUS_OutMessage to CUS; --similar to update/delete
grant select on ADM_OutMessage to ADM; --similar to update/delete
grant IND to COL; --COL can now access IND_OutMessage
grant IND to QUA; --QUA can access IND_OutMessage
grant IND to CUS;
grant IND to ADM;
grant COL to QUA; --QUA can now access COL_OutMessage
grant COL to CUS;
grant COL to ADM;
--etc etc
grant IND to Grotte ;
grant COL to Zurcher;
--etc etc
```

To solve this problem, Iteration 3 uses a programmatic approach to authorization. Privileges granted to roles, as shown in Figure 20.10, are stored in the Authorization table. This table, used together with specially formulated views, synonyms, and stored procedures/functions, can achieve the desired level of enterprise authorization.

Note that in the Oracle case, short of using Oracle's advanced authorization feature, there is an added difficulty of setting each user account on a separate schema. This complicates sharing of global resources (global schema) in situations when various users can only access subsets of these resources. Duplicating global data in local schemas does not make sense. Usage of synonyms would not prevent the users from accessing disallowed subsets of data. Views are set oriented queries and as such require `select` privileges to be granted to the user on the target table. This means that a determined user would be able to discover the whole content of the target table.

In short, proper handling of authorization in EM forces a programmatic solution that combines views, synonyms, stored procedures/functions, and the `Authorization` table. While this approach (presented below) is not the only one possible, other potential solutions are left to exercises.

Explicit Authorization table

The introduction of an explicit `Authorization` table simplifies authentication and authorization processes. Users are authenticated by the database via their local schema. A global schema performs the application-specific authentication via the `Authentication` table. The content of the `Authorization` table reflects the authorization matrix (Section 19.2.3, Table 19.1). Each record in the `Authorization` table registers the role (or employee's department) and one (of possibly many) *accessible* roles (other departments).

In order to control access to outmessages, it is necessary to implement all permissible accesses in stored procedures/functions. A stored procedure/function is able to check whether the current user has the correct privileges. To this aim, the `Authorization` table is accessed by all stored procedures/functions implemented in global schema. As an example, in Listing 20.7, the `Authorization` table is used to produce a subset of the `OutMessage` table that can be viewed by the current employee (as known by his/her `empDept`).

Listing 20.7 Authorization table usage

```
Authorization Table usage (to produce subset of OutMessage)

  Select *
  from "OutMessage"
  where "date_emailed" is null and "sched_dpt_code" in
      (select "target_dept_code"
      from "Authorization"
      where "from_dept_code" = empDept); --empDept is previously known
```

The current employee can only view outmessages addressed to him/her as well as those outmessages that the authorization matrix allows him/her to see (Table 19.1). Using this approach, the authorization rules shown in Figure 20.10 and Listing 20.6 can be implemented with no need for multiple tables to store outmessages.

The `Authorization` table does not provide a mechanism to impose the authorization rules on accesses to the database. It merely records the associations between different roles represented by the departments. The real enforcement of the authorization rules is left to the stored procedures or SQL statements similar to Listing 20.7. This is discussed in more detail in the following two sections.

Using individual schemas, global schema, and stored procedures

A user of the database in Figure 20.10 (single circles) has his/her own **local schema**. A client application accesses the database through this schema and therefore is only aware of his/her own data. S/he logs into the database (or EM application in this case) via his/her own username and password. The user is not aware that the database does in fact perform various checks on his/her privileges.

Global schema is where all the shared data is located. None of this data is copied or duplicated in local schemas. A user is not aware of the existence of this global schema. The global schema provides a set of stored procedures to allow its *clients* (from local schemas) to access its data. These stored procedures/functions check the privileges of the client. Different results and actions are performed depending on the given authorization level of the client.

An example of this approach is already given in Listings 20.2 and 20.3, which show how a call to a local schema is redirected to a stored function in the global schema. The redirection involves a skeleton of the stored function in a local schema. The global schema performs a check of the user's authentication.

Another clear example of such a check is shown in Listing 20.8. The employee id is validated against the login name of the user as recorded in the database. Once the employee id is acquired, its department code is retrieved.

An exception will be thrown to the application if the user supplies a wrong parameter to the stored function and s/he cannot be validated against the appropriate login name and department code. The level of *security* of the above approach is increased by the fact that the client application does not directly access the stored function shown in Figure 20.8. The client accesses the global stored function through his/her own local schema's stored function. The local schema stored function (such as shown in Figure 20.4) ensures that the appropriate parameter is passed to the procedure in Figure 20.8.

In this approach, individual users are not permitted to perform direct `select`, `update`, or `delete` statements on the global schema. The `select`, `update`, and `delete` privileges are revoked for all users except the global schema user. Local schema users are granted only `execute` privileges to be able to invoke stored procedures/functions on the global schema.

Using individual schemas, global schema, views, and stored procedures

A variation to the previous approach is by the addition of **views** in the local schema. Despite the limitations of views (related to the inability to update through views), they remain a convenient approach for authorization management.

Consider the following scenario. A client application connects to the local schema. It executes a statement such as '`select * from uv_outmessages`'. The client application is unaware that the `uv_outmessages` is in fact a view. The `uv_outmessages` view could be constructed by the statement in Listing 20.9. The first part of the `select` statement collects all outmessages that have been assigned to the current employee. The second part of the statement gathers all outmessages addressed to the employee's department.

Listing 20.8 Outmessage retrieval based on employee's authorization

Message retrieval based on employee's authorization

```
create or replace function usp_retrieve_outmessage(usern in varchar2)
return EMS.ref_cursor is
    c EMS.REF_CURSOR;
    inEmpID varchar2(100);
    empDept varchar2(100);
begin
    inEmpID := null;
    select "employee_id" into inEmpID
    from "Employee"
    where upper("login_name") = upper(usern);

    empDept := 'IND'; --default independent employee
    select "department_code" into empDept
    from "Employee"
    where "employee_id" = inEmpID;

    open c for
        Select *
        from "OutMessage"
        where "date_emailed" is null and "sched_dpt_code" in
            (select "target_dept_code"
                from "Authorization"
                where "from_dept_code" = empDept);
        return c;
        EXCEPTION
            WHEN NO_DATA_FOUND THEN
                raise_application_error(-20009, 'usp_retrieve_outmessage:
unmatch username and loginname or you cannot view the message');
end;
```

The authorization mechanism introduced in Section 20.3.1 can take advantage of views. Views can be used to ease the work of stored procedures/functions with respect to selection criteria. Insertions, updates, and deletions are processed through stored procedures/functions, thus counteracting the weaknesses of views.

Consider Listing 20.10 which shows a local schema usage of the `uv_outmessages` view. The view is used to verify whether the message id (`msgID`) identifies an outmessage that can be manipulated by the employee. If the outmessage appears in the view then the user must have access to it and therefore s/he should be able to delete this outmessage. If the user has no privilege to delete the outmessage (i.e. the `select into dummy` fails), then an exception is thrown to the client application to indicate so.

Listing 20.9 View uv_outmessages

```
View uv_outmessages

Create or replace view uv_outmessages as
select *
from PSE3."OutMessage"
where "date_emailed" is null and
("sender_emp_id" =
    (select "employee_id" from PSE3."Employee" emp, user_users u
where upper(u.username) = upper(emp."login_name"))
or
    "sched_dpt_code" in
    (select "target_dept_code"
     from PSE3."Authorization"
     where "from_dept_code" = (select "department_code" from
PSE3."Employee" e, user_users u where upper(e."login_name")
= upper(u.username))
     )
)
```

Listing 20.10 Outmessage deletion after checking authorization via view

```
Outmessage deletion after checking authorization via view

create or replace procedure usp_delete_outmessage(msgID IN varchar2) is
    dummy integer;
begin
    select distinct 1 into dummy
    from uv_outmessages
    where msgID = "message_id";

    delete from PSE3."OutMessage" where "message_id" = msgID;
    --this delete can be replaced with a call to stored procedure
    --PSE3.ups_delete_outmessage(msgID, usern);
    --where usern is acquired earlier as shown in Listing 20-4.
    EXCEPTION
        WHEN NO_DATA_FOUND THEN
            raise_application_error(-20300, 'You are not allowed to
delete the message');
end;
```

The outmessage deletion can simply be performed directly as shown in the `delete` statement in Listing 20.10. A better approach will be to invoke the stored procedure in the global schema. Allowing the direct execution of delete statements exposes the fact that the `OutMessage` table is selectable, updatable, and deletable from the local schema.

In fact, this is the weakness of view. In order to be able to create a view in the local schema, the local schema must have appropriate privileges (minimum the `select` privilege) on the tables involved in the view. This exposes the global schema to individual schema users.

Authorization administration

The `Authorization` table allows dynamic discovery of the authorization rules (Section 19.2.3, Table 19.1) by applications as they execute. Changes to the authorization rules, once recorded in the `Authorization` table, can be automatically picked up by a running application. Similarly, there is no need to update the local schema due to changes to the authorization rules. Views, as shown in Listing 20.9, are also not affected by the modification.

Iteration 3 of EM requires a user interface to allow modification of authorization rules. Furthermore, only employees of the System Administration department (ADM) are allowed to modify the rules. This has been implemented with a set of stored procedures and a GUI shown in Figure 20.11. Figure 20.11 satisfies requirement S9 (Section 19.2.3, Figure 19.10). Instead of using true/false entries, Figure 20.11 uses checkboxes.

Figure 20.11 can only be editable by ADM users. This is achieved by enabling/disabling of checkboxes and enabling/disabling the `Save` button. If the user is not allowed to change the authorization matrix, then the checkboxes are not editable and the `Save` button is not accessible.

The stored procedure to accomplish editing of the authorization matrix is shown in Listing 20.11. The procedure verifies if the user is an employee of the ADM department. If this cannot be asserted then an exception is thrown to indicate that the user is not allowed to modify authorization rules (errors -20040 and -20041).

Figure 20.11
GUI for authorization modification

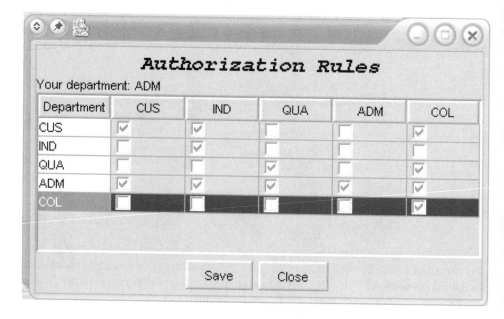

Authorization Rules

Your department: ADM

Department	CUS	IND	QUA	ADM	COL
CUS	✓	✓	☐	☐	✓
IND	☐	✓	☐	☐	☐
QUA	☐	☐	✓	☐	✓
ADM	✓	✓	✓	✓	✓
COL	☐	☐	☐	☐	✓

Save   Close

Listing 20.11 Stored procedure usp_upd_auth_rules

```
Stored procedure usp_upd_auth_rules

create or replace procedure usp_upd_auth_rules(frm in varchar2,
   target in varchar2, usern in varchar2) is
   inEmpID varchar2(100);

begin
   inEmpID := null;
   select "employee_id" into inEmpID
   from "Employee"
   where upper("login_name") = upper(usern) and
      "department_code" = 'ADM';
   if inEmpID is null then
      raise_application_error(-20040, 'usp_upd_auth_rules: '||
         ' You are not allowed to modify authorization rules');
   end if;

   --this will throw exception if the entry exists already therefore
   --make sure usp_clear_auth_rules is called first
   insert into "Authorization"("from_dept_code","target_dept_code")
      values(frm,target);

EXCEPTION
   WHEN NO_DATA_FOUND THEN
      raise_application_error(-20041,'usp_upd_auth_rules: '||
         ' You are not allowed to modify authorization rules');
   WHEN DUP_VAL_ON_INDEX THEN
      --entry already exists which means usp_clear_auth_rules
      --have not been called properly
      raise_application_error(-20042,'usp_upd_auth_rules:'||
         ' Duplicate entries found in authorization table');
end;
```

Once the user is verified, the procedure parameters are passed to the `insert` statement to insert the corresponding authorization rule. The insertion could trigger a `DUP_VAL_ON_INDEX` exception (multiple rows with the same primary key) if the client application did not perform a prior clean-up on the authorization table (if such a clean-up was required).

Integrity in Email Management   20.3.2

The EM database maintains integrity of its data via **declarative integrity** constraints as well as by means of **triggers**. Declarative constraints include specification of nulls, domains, check rules, keys (primary, foreign, and unique), and *referential constraints* from the table's foreign keys to corresponding primary keys in other tables. Business rules, that cannot be represented declaratively, are implemented in triggers.

Listing 20.12 presents declarative integrity constraints with regard to the `DailyReport` table. All columns are declared to be `not null`. This ensures that all data for a record (row) must be provided during inserts into the table. A strict column length is indicated, if necessary, such as for the `'contact_id'` column. Each value in this column must have exactly five characters.

Listing 20.12 DailyReport table definition

```
DailyReport table definition

 1:   create table "DailyReport" (
 2:      "date_of_report_day"              DATE                 not null,
 3:      "contact_id"                      CHAR(5)              not null,
 4:      "num_emails_created"              INTEGER              not null,
 5:      "num_emails_sent"                 INTEGER              not null,
 6:      "num_emails_outstanding"          INTEGER              not null,
 7:      "num_emails_past_outstanding"     INTEGER              not null,
 8:      constraint PK_DAILYREPORT primary key
             ("date_of_report_day", "contact_id")
 9:   )
10:   alter table "DailyReport"
11:      add constraint FK_DAILYREP_CONTACT_R_CONTACT foreign key
12:         ("contact_id") references "Contact" ("contact_id")
```

All tables in EM have a *primary key* to ensure that every single record in the table is unique with respect to other records. Duplicated entries will not be accepted. The `DailyReport` table has the primary key consisting of two columns `'date_of_report_day'` and `'contact_id'` (Line 8).

Listing 20.13 Check rule for num_emails_created check

```
Check rule for num_emails_created check

 1:   create table "DailyReport" (
 2:      "date_of_report_day"              DATE                 not null,
 3:      "contact_id"                      CHAR(5)              not null,
 4:      "num_emails_created"              INTEGER              not null,
 5:      "num_emails_sent"                 INTEGER              not null,
 6:      "num_emails_outstanding"          INTEGER              not null,
 7:      "num_emails_past_outstanding"     INTEGER              not null,
 8:      constraint PK_DAILYREPORT primary key
             ("date_of_report_day", "contact_id"),
 9:      constraint num_created_greater0 CHECK("num_emails_created" >= 0)
10:   )
```

The value of 'contact_id' in each record of DailyReport must be equal to one of the values of 'contact_id' in the 'Contact' table. This specifies a *declarative referential constraint* between 'DailyReport' and 'Contact' tables. Any attempt to enter a daily report record without proper reference to *existing* contact will be rejected by this rule.

Declarative integrity can ensure generic referential constraints. It can also ensure that column values conform to a specific format or fall within a prescribed ranges of values. This can be achieved with a *check rule*. Listing 20.13 shows a check rule in the DailyReport table asserting that the number of emails created cannot be negative (Line 9). This is quite an obvious rule but it may be put to use because the table has no knowledge how the applications are going to try to insert values.

There are referential integrity constraints in EM that cannot be enforced by using declarative integrity. Such constraints are enforced by *triggers*. The constraint in Listing 20.14 is composed of three rules:

1. The manager of an employee (in the manager_employee_id column) may be null to indicate that the particular employee is not managed by anybody.

2. The manager has to belong to the same department as the employee, if the employee has a manager.

3. An employee who is described as independent (IND) is not constrained by the first rule (i.e. s/he may be managed by an employee from any department), provided that s/he has a manager at all.

Listing 20.14 Referential integrity constraint enforced by trigger

```
Referential integrity constraint enforced by trigger

 1:   create or replace trigger bins_upd_employee
 2:   before insert or update
 3:   on "Employee"
 4:   for each row
 5:   declare
 6:       dept_code varchar2(20);
 7:   begin
 8:       if :new."manager_employee_id" is not null then
 9:           if :new."department_code" <> 'IND' then
10:               select "department_code" into dept_code
11:                   from "Employee"
12:                   where "employee_id" = :new."manager_employee_id";
13:
14:               if :new."department_code" <> dept_code then
15:                   raise_application_error(-20102,
                          'The manager cannot be from other department');
16:               end if;
17:           end if;
18:       end if;
19:   end;
```

The trigger, called `bins_upd_employee`, is fired during inserts and updates on the `"Employee"` table (Line 2). Specifically, it is fired for *every* insert or update of a table row (Line 4).

Line 8 checks the first rule. There is no need to check the insert or update entry on the table if the *new* row (indicated by `:new`) has no manager information.

Line 9 specifies that if the employee is discovered to be an independent employee (indicated by belonging to the `IND` department) then there is no need to further check on his/her manager entry. This satisfies the third rule.

The remaining Lines 10–17 satisfy the second rule. The manager's `department_code` is retrieved and stored into a local variable `dept_code` (Lines 10–12). Line 14 checks if this `dept_code` value matches the employee's department code (`:new."department_code"`). If it does not match the employee's department, an application error is thrown to indicate the violation of the second rule.

When an application error is thrown, the trigger is said to be a *failing* integrity event (operation) and therefore the event must be cancelled. This means the insert or update operation will not proceed at all (Line 2). If the trigger is fired *after* an insertion or update instead of *before* it (Line 2 indicates it is fired *before* insert/update), then an exception thrown in the trigger will result in rolling back the effect of such insert/update.

Firing a trigger before or after an operation is quite different, although the difference may be unnoticeable most of the time. If the insertion is allowed to proceed before the trigger fires (an **after trigger**), then there may be other triggers that have been fired before the current trigger fired. Consider if the table has a **before trigger** as well as an *after* trigger. Insertion will fire the *before* trigger, then it proceeds to insert the value, then it fires the *after* trigger. Failure in the *after* trigger will mean rolling back the effect of the insertion as well as the effect of any work done by the *before* trigger. Not all work done on the database is repeatable or recoverable and this has to be given serious attention. It may very well be that the *before* trigger performs an operation that cannot be undone or the undoing of the operation could lead to inconsistency in the database.

Summary

1. *Security* has a personal (individual) dimension. *Integrity* has a multi-personal (user community) dimension.

2. *Authentication* is the task of verifying identity of a user/application trying to connect to a database.

3. *Discretionary authorization* is based on granting *privileges* to access database objects. Privileges can be granted/revoked to users and/or roles. A *role* is normally related to a job function. A *user* can be assigned to one or more roles.

4. A *system privilege* is the right to perform a particular action on a database system as a whole or an action with regard to the database schema. *Object privileges* determine how users/applications can work with the database content.

5. Privileges can be passed from a user/role to another user/role. The effects of passing privileges can be depicted in an *authorization graph*.

6. System and object privileges represent SQL *declarative* ways of implementing discretionary authorization. SQL provides also *programmatic* (procedural) ways of controlling discretionary authorization. Programmatic authorization uses views, synonyms, and stored procedures.

7. In *mandatory authorization*, users/applications are assigned *clearance levels* and database objects are assigned corresponding *security levels*. Clearance levels are used when authenticating the user/application. Authentication checks the credentials of the user. For more secure scenarios, a *challenge–response approach* involving *encryption* can be used.

8. *Enterprise authorization* demands that access rights of all users and applications are stored in an enterprise *authorization database*, which every application must consult to determine what the current user can or cannot do with regard to database objects and with regard to application objects. In enterprise authorization, *application roles* are distinguished from *user roles*.

9. *Integrity* is about correctness and consistency of data accessible to the program. In the database context, integrity is enforced by *integrity constraints* specified on the database behavior.

10. *Triggers* constitute a procedural way of enforcing referential integrity constraints as well as implementing other business rules that the database must satisfy.

11. Iteration 3 implements *enterprise authorization*. It includes addition of roles and the introduction of a special table to hold authorization rules. Changes to authorization rules can be made through a new authorization window in the user interface. All access to the database is peformed via stored procedures/ functions, which are also responsible for enforcing the authorization rules.

12. Iteration 3 enforces database *integrity* by various means, including the use of triggers. *Triggers* are designed to collaborate with newly introduced stored procedures and stored functions.

Key Terms

access right	*See* privilege
after trigger	680, 696
alternative key	*See* unique key
application role	672
authentication	661, 663
authorization	661
authorization database	673
authorization graph	663, 685
availability	661
before trigger	680, 696
Bell–LaPadula model	671
candidate key	*See* unique key
cascade constraint	678
challenge–response approach	671
check constraint	677
clearance level	661, 671
client privilege	673
database administrator	663
database extension	663
database intention	663
DBA	*See* database administrator
declarative authorization	664
declarative integrity	693
default constraint	676, 679
denied privilege	664
digital signature	671
discretionary access control	*See* discretionary authorization
discretionary authorization	661
domain constraint	677
effective privilege	664
encryption	671
enterprise authorization	661, 672, 685
enterprise user	672
foreign key	678
global schema	667, 689

group	662
instead of trigger	680, 684
integrity	661, 675
integrity constraints	675
local schema	667, 689
mandatory authorization	661, 671
null constraint	676, 679
object privilege	663
primary key	677
privilege	661, 662
programmatic authorization	665
public key	671
referential integrity	678
resource privilege	667
restrict constraint	678
revoked privilege	663
role	662
row trigger	680
shared schema	672
schema	667
schema-independent user	*See* enterprise user
secrecy	661
security	661
security administrator	671
security class	671
server privilege	675
shared schema	672
statement trigger	680
stored function	668
stored procedure	668
synonym	667
system privilege	663
trigger	680, 685, 693
trigger action	680
unique key	678
view	665, 689

Review Questions

1. Explain the difference between system security and integrity.

2. Explain the difference between authentication and authorization.

3. Assume an application user who is only allowed to search in the database, but not to make any changes in data. Should/could such a user be granted any system privileges? If yes, what system privileges? Give examples.

4. Can roles be authenticated? What are the consequences?

5. What is the difference between a revoked privilege and a denied privilege? Explain by example.

6. Why do views provide only a limited security mechanism?

7. How does mandatory authorization relate to discretionary authorization? Are they separate or overlapping techniques?

8. Explain the difference between an application role and a user role in enterprise authorization. How are these two concepts related to the notion of an authorization database?

9. What are the declarative and procedural integrity constraints? List and briefly define them.

10. In Figure 20.7, the unique key on `actor` is defined on columns `actor-name` and `address`. However, the `address` column permits null values. Is this allowed? If it is, what will be an outcome of an attempt to insert an `actor_name` with null `address`, if such `actor_name` with null `address` already exists in the table? Explain.

11. Trigger is a kind of stored procedure. Can a stored procedure call a trigger? Explain.

12. How does the Oracle approach of assigning a local schema to each user account influence the design of authorization into an application? Is the Oracle approach helpful or not? Explain.

13. Give an example of a transaction such that the effects of triggers or stored procedures must not be rolled back despite the fact that the transaction has failed.

Problem-Solving Exercises

1. Refer to Section 20.3.1, Listing 20.9. The view produced by this listing will result in duplicate entries. Why? Check this by experimenting on an Oracle database.

2. Refer to Section 20.3.1 and Figure 20.10. Modify the authorization graph shown in Figure 20.10 with this additional requirement: 'QUA employees can read ADM messages but they cannot modify them. QUA employees cannot access CUS messages.'

3. Implement a `before` trigger on the `ListedAs` table of the `MovieActor` database as a replacement for its equivalent declarative referential integrity constraint as follows:

   ```
   ADD Constraint fk_const3 FOREIGN KEY (actor_code)
   REFERENCES actor ON DELETE CASCADE
   ```

Chapter

21

Transactions and Concurrency

Transactions have been referred to informally throughout this book but they have not been addressed yet as a topic in their own right. In practice, designing transactions into enterprise information systems is one of the great challenges for a software engineer. Databases offer extensive support for transaction management but only application developers can define transaction boundaries and decide which transactional mechanisms should be used for each business transaction.

A **transaction** is defined as a logical unit of work that accomplishes a particular business task and guarantees the *integrity* of the database after the task completes (Chapter 20). In this definition the term 'transaction' is an abbreviation for **business transaction**. From the transactional perspective, **integrity** means that the data is left consistent after the transaction completes its execution.

A transaction consists of one or more data manipulation actions. A classic example of a transaction is a money transfer between two accounts, such as paying off a credit card account from a savings account. This involves withdrawing money from a savings account and depositing it to a credit card account. Both actions are demarcated by a single transaction.

Grouping the actions to form a transaction is a business decision, not a technical one. However, a business transaction can consist of a number of shorter **system transactions**. Actions of an executing transaction complete in unison – they either complete successfully and write (**commit**) all the data changes to the database or they fail and undo (**rollback**) all partial changes from the database.

In business applications, transactions executing within applications should be short so that many applications and users working on the same database can have concurrent access to the shared data (i.e. transactions are not blocking each other by holding shareable data resources for prolonged times). **Short transactions** facilitate **concurrency**.

There are applications where short transactions cannot constitute the main transactional boundaries. For example, workgroup computing systems, such as systems facilitating collaboration of office workers, architects, engineers, etc., require long transactions. An office worker writing a document or manipulating spreadsheet data (retrieved from the database) must be allowed to perform these tasks for a longer time and be able to commit changes to the database without blocking other users and without damaging the integrity of the database. Such systems require different concurrency mechanisms, which most traditional (relational) database management systems do not support very well.

The issue of long transactions is an obvious but not the only reason for the need to distinguish between business transactions and system transactions. A system (or database) transaction is defined by the support mechanisms provided to the transaction notion by a database management system or other transaction management system. A system transaction is a technical concept that does not have understanding of the business reasons for the transaction as a unit of work.

A business (or application) transaction is a business concept; it has a business meaning to the user of an application. A customer using a web application to buy books on the Internet defines business transactions. The actions of putting books in an order basket through to specifying payment details and submitting (or canceling) the order constitute a single business transaction. It follows that a business transaction is likely to span multiple system transactions. This constitutes a serious challenge to a software engineer who has to handle some tricky concurrency issues outside of the built-in support mechanisms of a database management system or other transaction monitor.

Apart from concurrency, transaction management is inseparable from database recovery issues. A database management system guarantees that any transaction failures do not leave the database in an inconsistent state. If a transaction fails, the database is recovered to the state in which it was prior to the start of the transaction. The recovery mechanisms extend on non-transactional failures, such as physical damage to a disk containing database or transactional data.

Transaction management for concurrency is a main consideration for a software engineer and developer. Transaction management for recovery is mainly a task of a system/database administrator. Consequently, this chapter addresses concurrency; references to recovery are only marginal.

Concurrency in System Transactions   21.1

Concurrent execution of programs on shared data sources introduces some of the most difficult challenges in software engineering. It is an overwhelming task in which individual transaction requirements of a single user or application must be defined and implemented in the context of all other transactions that can be concurrently executing on the system.

Fortunately, database management systems provide primitive (and not so primitive) mechanisms for relieving the software engineers from responsibility for transactional integrity and from most tricky implementation issues. *System transactions* are defined in terms of these primitive mechanisms.

A transaction is delimited, explicitly or implicitly, by statements that mark its beginning and its end. This act of establishing a transaction boundary is called **demarcation** or **bracketing** of a transaction. Demarcation of a system transaction is known as a **server-side demarcation**, while demarcation of a business transaction is called a **client-side demarcation**.

The beginning of a system transaction is frequently implicit. The transaction starts with the first executable SQL statement in a batch of SQL statements. Some kind of `begin transaction` or `start transaction` statement can be used for explicit starting of a transaction.

The end of a transaction can also be implicit, but it is always better to explicitly demarcate the transaction end. The transaction can end with a `commit` statement or a `rollback` statement. The *commit* means a successful completion of the transaction, which results in writing all transactional changes to the database. The *rollback* usually means that some problem has been encountered and the transaction is aborted and any partial changes made on the database will be undone. In some cases, a rollback can mean an expected ending of the transaction (this happens, for example, when testing database programs and wanting to return the database to its original state after the tests).

21.1.1 ACID Properties

The topic of transactions and concurrency has a close rapport with the notion of data integrity (Section 20.2). Data integrity defines rules for data correctness, accuracy, and consistency. To ensure data integrity in a multi-user system, the database server must implement concurrency mechanisms so that only one user/application can change a particular piece of data at a time and change it in a way that all integrity rules on that data are enforced.

To enforce data integrity in the presence of concurrent access and system failures, system transactions must satisfy four properties known in the literature as the **ACID properties**. The acronym stands for atomicity, consistency, isolation, and durability. Consistency and isolation have mostly a concurrency connotation whereas atomicity and durability have mostly recovery implications.

Atomicity describes a requirement that each transaction represents the smallest possible unit that cannot be further subdivided. An atomic transaction ensures the all-or-nothing requirement; the system must either successfully complete all its transaction-demarcated actions or it must roll back all work. Partial completions of transactions are not allowed. In the example of transaction as a money transfer between two accounts, atomicity ensures that the money will never be withdrawn from a savings account unless it gets deposited to a credit card account. Any such incomplete transaction will be undone (rolled back) and the user/application will be given a chance to repeat the attempt.

There are many reasons why a transaction may not complete. This may be a network or database failure, a conflict (such as a *deadlock*) encountered between concurrently executing transactions, or an unexpected application program failure. There are many software/hardware parties that participate in a transaction, from the client code, via web and application servers, to a database server. Any of these parties can cause a failure. Because no one of these parties knows what happens at other parties, committing (or rolling back) a transaction uses a voting scheme. Each party votes on whether the transaction should be considered successful, and if any vote is negative, the whole transaction must roll back. Two typical voting schemes are called *two-phase commit* and *three-phase commit*.

Durability complements the atomicity property by stating that a successful transaction guarantees that committed changes made to the database are permanent (persistent). That is, the server guarantees that any failures, after the user/application was informed that the changes have been committed, will cause no loss of data. In reality, informing the user that changes are committed and committing the changes are two different events, and a failure may even occur between these two events. In all cases, the server gives the same guarantee to the user.

The server ensures transaction atomicity by **undoing** failed transactions and it ensures transaction durability by **redoing**, if necessary, successful transactions that in reality have not been made persistent at the time when the application was informed about the success. To be able to undo and redo transactions, the database server maintains a transactional log. The *log* remembers (persistently) all changes made by transactions on the database (all writes to the database). The server uses the log to undo or redo transactions, as required by the circumstances.

Consistency is a requirement that each transaction is a transition of data from one consistent state to another, preserving the data semantic and referential integrity. A consistent database state is defined by data integrity rules (Section 20.2). Because the integrity rules are business rules determined by users, ensuring consistency of a transaction is first of all the responsibility of application developers and programmers. The system support for consistency is a guarantee that a transaction will fail if it attempts to violate the specified integrity rules.

Isolation is a requirement that any intermediate changes made to data by a transaction are not visible to other concurrent transactions until the transaction commits. Execution of transactions is isolated so that each transaction produces the results on the database that do not depend in any way on other transactions. This is called **serializable execution**, i.e. a set of transactions produces the same results whether the transactions execute concurrently or serially, one after another in an unspecified order. The database server ensures isolation by placing **locks** on data currently used by a transaction. When one transaction holds a lock on data, other transactions interested in that data must wait until the lock is released.

Isolation Levels   21.1.2

Serializable execution of transactions, in complete isolation from one another, is not always required or practical. For example, a concurrently executing transaction that computes some statistical measures on a large volume of data items is unlikely to care about intermittent changes made by other transactions on one or few of these items. Also, a complete isolation of transactions in serializable execution lowers the potential level of concurrency in the system and leads to lower throughput and performance of the system.

The context for tradeoffs between execution correctness, concurrency and performance is provided by four isolation levels defined in the SQL, Java and other standards. An **isolation level** defines how concurrent transactions are isolated from one another.

The highest isolation level, with the worst concurrency and performance but with strict (isolated) correctness of transactional results, is a **serializable** level. A transaction executing at a serializable level is protected from reading uncommitted changes from other transactions. This level ensures also that reading the same data multiple times within the same transaction will always return the same value even if another transaction has modified that data (*read consistency*). Finally, at serializable level, executing the same query multiple times will always produce the same result even if another transaction inserted new data records that satisfy the query predicate condition (*query consistency*). Serializable execution is achieved by a system placing locks on the transaction's data set, so that other transactions cannot update or insert into the data set until the transaction ends.

The next level down from serializable is called **repeatable read**. This level guarantees read consistency, but does not guarantee query consistency. Not guaranteeing query consistency means that repeatable read permits phantoms. A **phantom** occurs when a transaction executes the same query twice and the second execution shows additional (phantom) data records inserted by other transactions in the meantime. Repeatable read is achieved by a locking mechanism that forbids intermittent updates but allows intermittent inserts.

The third level down from serializable is **read committed**. This level guarantees one of two aspects of read consistency. It guarantees invisibility of any data items modified by another transaction provided that the modification has not been committed yet. However, it allows seeing committed changes, which can lead to **nonrepeatable reads**. Read committed is achieved by placing so-called *shared locks* on data being read by the transaction and honoring so-called *exclusive locks* held on data by other transactions in order to modify that data.

The lowest isolation level is **read uncommitted**. This level does not guarantee any aspect of read consistency. **Dirty reads**, that is reading data modified by another transaction but not actually committed yet, are possible at this level. At this level no shared locks are issued and no exclusive locks are honored.

Table 21.1 summarizes the above discussion by showing what query or read inconsistencies may occur at various isolation levels. A programmer can set different isolation levels for different transactions executing concurrently, but the system would normally disallow changing the level in the middle of a transaction execution. The default isolation level in most systems is read committed.

Table 21.1 Isolation levels behavior

Isolation level:	dirty read	nonrepeatable read	phantom
serializable	not possible	not possible	not possible
repeatable read	not possible	not possible	possible
read committed	not possible	possible	possible
read uncommitted	possible	possible	possible

Lock Modes and Levels

Isolation levels are implemented by locking the data resources. Only the read uncommitted level uses no locks. Locks can be placed on data and process resources. Database systems offer a variety of lock modes and levels and there are significant differences between systems.

The main **lock modes** are (Israel and Jones, 2001; Maciaszek, 2001):

- exclusive (write) locks
- update (write intent) locks
- shared (read) locks.

An **exclusive lock** placed on a resource by a transaction means that only this transaction may access the resource for both writing and reading. This is the most restrictive mode in the sense of restricting access to the resource. Until the transaction holding the lock releases it, no other locks can be acquired on the resource. An exclusive lock is always automatically placed on the resource by the system for the duration of actual updating of the resource.

One problem with concurrently held locks is that a transaction can require locks held by another transaction, and vice versa – the second transaction may require locks held by the first transaction. This situation creates a **deadlock**. A deadlock can be resolved only by rolling back one of the two transactions. Since prevention is better than detection, update locks are used to prevent many deadlocks.

An **update lock** obtained on a resource by a transaction guarantees that the transaction will be able to upgrade the lock to the exclusive mode as soon as it requests such upgrade. Only one transaction can hold an update lock on a resource at a time.

A **shared lock** placed on a resource by a transaction does not restrict other transactions from reading the same resource or from obtaining an update lock on that resource. For the repeatable read or serializable isolation, shared locks are held until the end of transaction. For the read committed isolation level, shared locks are held only for the duration of the server reading the data (that is why nonrepeatable reads may happen at this isolation level).

Locks can be held on resources of various granularity. This is called **lock level**. The three most interesting levels are:

- row
- page
- table.

A **row lock** is the lowest possible lock in relational databases where the smallest accessible object is a row (record) of a table. A **page lock** locks all rows that reside on a single page. A page is a physical part of database disk storage, typically between 8 KB and 128 KB. A **table lock** engages all rows of a database table.

Lock level is a tradeoff between concurrency and performance. Database servers have a capability of **lock escalation**, i.e. automatically increasing the lock level for transactions that access multiple records from the same page or table.

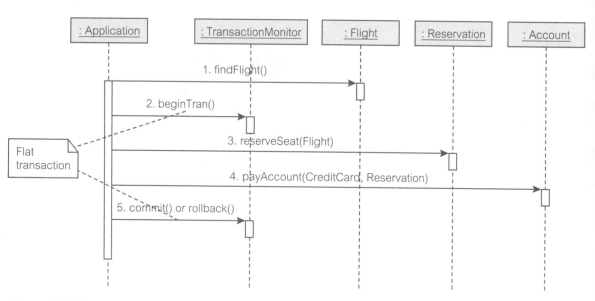

Figure 21.1 Flat transaction

21.1.4 Transactional Models

The discussion so far has related to the simplest transactional model – a flat transaction model. A **flat transaction** is a single unit of work, which ends with a single commit or rollback. A flat transaction model falls short of expectations for some more complex applications, including many web-based applications (Roman *et al.*, 2002).

Figure 21.1 is a sequence diagram that depicts a flat transaction model. The example refers to an application that allows finding suitable plane flight, reserving a seat and paying for the ticket. Seat reservation is not possible unless the payment is made. Therefore, reserveSeat() and payAccount() operations are demarcated by one flat transaction. Searching for the flight, by means of findFlight(), is outside the transaction.

In a flat transaction in Figure 21.1, if the payAccount() operation fails then the entire transaction is rolled back, and the customer loses the seat. Chaining the two operations by means of the transaction savepoint can rectify this. A **savepoint** is a named marker in the program that divides a longer transaction into smaller parts. Savepoints persistently save a portion of work accomplished by the transaction up to a savepoint. This permits partial rollbacks to a savepoint.

In a **chained transaction** in Figure 21.2, a savepoint named Payment is created prior to payAccount(). The savepoint remembers the reservation made by reserveSeat(). If the payAccount() operation fails, the program can roll the transaction back to the savepoint, thus allowing the user to try paying the account again. Eventually, however, the whole chained transaction must either commit or fail in unison. It is not possible to commit partial changes to the savepoint.

Sometimes it is desirable to divide a longer transaction into smaller parts such that the smaller parts are relatively independent and can be committed or rolled back independently,

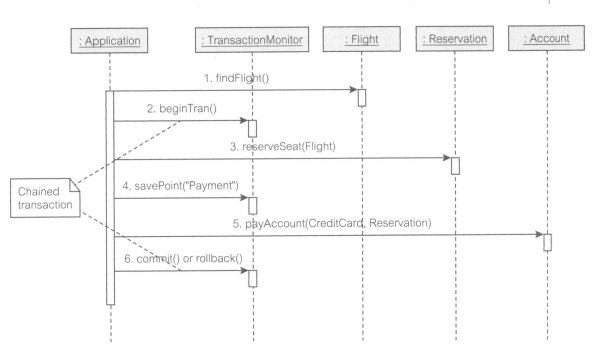

Figure 21.2 Chained transaction

if so desired. Such a model is known as a nested transaction. A **nested transaction** consists of subtransactions (autonomous transactions). The commit or rollback of a subtransaction does not affect the state of the *calling transaction*, which can continue its work regardless. (The term 'nested transaction' is unfortunate as it is really a calling transaction that nests other transactions. Arguably, a more accurate name would be a 'nesting transaction'.)

Figure 21.3 is an example of a nested transaction for reserving various goods and services for a trip. The trip reservation includes reservation of a plane, and then reservation of a car and a hotel. Ideally, the user would like to reserve all elements of the trip in a single transaction. However, reservations of a car and a hotel are made into separate autonomous subtransactions. This allows making individual reservations, if the entire trip cannot be reserved in a single session. So, for example, a flight may be reserved without hiring a car, or vice versa, a car may be booked even if the flight is not reserved.

Concurrency Control Schemes   21.1.5

Concurrency control discussed so far, based on locks, is known as **pessimistic concurrency control**. Pessimistic concurrency control is based on an assumption that conflicts between transactions are likely, i.e. that concurrent transactions are likely to need access to the same data and process resources. Pessimistic concurrency is a conflict prevention scheme whereby the transaction that uses resources locks them from other transactions until it finishes its work. Such a scheme is best suited to conventional enterprise information systems and is the standard scheme in relational databases.

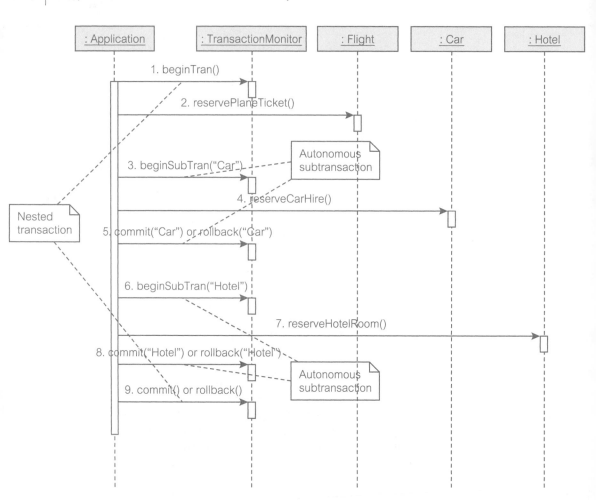

Figure 21.3 Nested transaction

Optimistic concurrency control takes the opposite view that conflicts between transactions are infrequent. This may indeed be the case in some applications, e.g. in a university grading system where grades are allocated to classes of students by a teacher who teaches a class. Optimistic concurrency does not use locks and, therefore, the overhead of managing locks is avoided.

The processing under optimistic concurrency is done in three stages (Ramakrishnan and Gehrke, 2000):

1. The transaction reads data from the database without any restrictions.

2. When the transaction decides to commit changes in the database, the system checks that the changes will not overwrite changes made by another transaction in the meantime (i.e. since the transaction started).

3. If no conflict is detected, the transaction will be allowed to commit; otherwise, the transaction will be rolled back and the user may need to restart it.

Multiversion concurrency control is sometimes treated as a variant of optimistic control. In the multiversion scheme, a transaction never waits to read a data object because it is given the object with a new version number. The reading of an object to the transaction space (of the private workspace of the user/application) is called the **check-out** operation. When the transaction finishes its work, it places the data objects back in the server database in a **check-in** operation. The check-in always succeeds because the object has its own unique version number. However, the system checks for versions in the database that are in conflict and instigates a conflict resolution process, which involves human intervention.

Multiversion schemes have been widely used as a preferred modus operandi in **object databases**, such as Versant or Objectivity/DB. Object databases target applications such as workgroup computing and multimedia systems. Long transactions dominate in such applications. Databases in workgroup computing serve as repositories of such artifacts as architectural and engineering drawings, software engineering models, geographical maps, etc. The users of these applications are architects, designers, etc. who check out data objects to their private workspaces and work on them for a long time, hours or days, before checking the results of their work back to the database.

Object databases offer in one system the most flexible combination of pessimistic, optimistic, and multiversion concurrency control schemes. Such combined use of different schemes results in a scheme termed **collaborative concurrency control**. Object databases are designed to support multi-user access by allowing cooperative access to data in long transactions. The users work on their own workstations with the client portion of the database software running on their machines and using personal databases of data checked out (copied) from a group database. Rather than isolating users, object databases provide an integrative environment in which users are kept aware of the work done by others on shared data items.

Concurrency during a **long transaction** is managed by a **persistent (long) lock**. Such a lock has the normal features of a short lock, but (being persistent) has the ability to span **short transactions** and database **sessions**. To be able to span short transactions in a database (**group workspace**), a long transaction runs in the private workspace of the user. A long transaction can be assigned queuing options (allowing the user to wait for an object) and lock notifications (informing the user of other transactions which use an object). In general, the main objectives of long transactions are to:

- minimize rollbacks and deadlocks
- exchange information (even if inconsistent) between cooperating users
- allow concurrent updates on the same objects (in private databases)
- detect data inconsistencies and mediate their resolutions.

In order to guarantee the ACID properties during check-in or check-out operations, long transactions activate **short locks** (these locks are released immediately after the end of check-in/check-out). Long transactions also activate *persistent locks* placed on objects in the group workspace. Having a long transaction executing in a private workspace and short transactions running in both group and private workspaces, allows the implementation of *nested transactions*. Updates to a workgroup database can be committed or aborted without committing or aborting the surrounding transaction in a private workspace.

Figure 21.4
Collaborative
concurrency
control

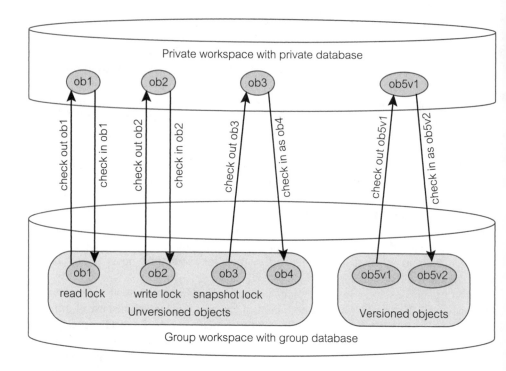

Apart from typical short locks, such as shared or exclusive locks, object databases support **snapshot locks** permitting 'dirty reads'. An object checked out with a snapshot lock is obtained to the private workspace independently of its lock status in the group database. If the object gets modified in the private workspace, it is checked into the database as a new (different) object. This is, in effect, a variant of optimistic concurrency control.

Figure 21.4 illustrates how collaborative concurrency control is used by an object database supporting a workgroup computing system (Hawryszkiewycz *et al.*, 1994). Object resources in the group database can be unversioned or versioned (Section 5.4.2). **Object identifiers** (OIDs) include the identification of a database, and – in the case of a versioned object – the assignment of a version number. Unversioned objects have locks imposed according to the way they are currently used by transactions.

Figure 21.4 demonstrates that the check-out of the object ob1 with a read lock creates a copy of the same object (with unchanged identity) in the private database and it blocks changes to ob1 in the group database for the duration of the persistent read lock (i.e. until ob1 is checked in). The check-out of the object ob2 with a write lock behaves similarly except that it blocks even read access by other transactions in the group database. The check-out of the object ob3 with a snapshot lock creates an identical copy of the object in the private database, but this action does not affect (does not block) other transactions – any subsequent check-in of this object creates a new object in the group database (ob4).

An object in a private database can be accessed in more than one long transaction that the user can attach to. This is achieved by ending the original *session* without ending the long transaction (so called *continue* or *detach* mode) and starting a new session with another transaction. Of course, running multiple long transactions against the same object does not change the association of the object with the original long transaction used to check the object out.

There are myriads of implementation variants of concurrency control schemes. For example, Oracle implements an interesting variant of multiversion concurrency control by replacing read locks with read consistent snapshots of a database. A **read consistent snapshot** (nothing to do with a snapshot lock in Figure 21.4) is a view of the database as it existed at some point in time, which reflects only committed changes at that point. This means that read operations never wait for and never block write operations. Oracle guarantees read consistency by checking (optimistically) if an object has changed prior to the time when the transaction commits. In the case of queries, such as when generating reports from the database, Oracle can use snapshot data and does not worry about changes that the database undergoes. Consequently, Oracle does not need to support lower isolation levels. It supports only read committed and serializable levels.

Concurrency in Business Transactions   21.2

A transaction is a demarcated sequence of work. In a **system transaction**, the demarcation is between the application and the database. A system transaction fulfils a single user request, such as 'modify customer address', 'make a payment', etc. In some well-defined cases of workgroup computing applications, supported by long transactions within collaborative concurrency control, a system transaction can span sessions (Section 21.1.5). In typical scenarios, system transactions are short and do not span sessions or requests.

In a **business transaction**, the demarcation is between the user and the application (Fowler, 2003). A business transaction groups multiple user requests into a demarcated sequence of work. Because each user request corresponds to a single transaction, a business transaction spans a number of system transactions. The steps needed to move from one system transaction to another do not get server-side support similar to concurrency control mechanisms discussed in Section 21.1. The responsibility for the ACID properties of a business transaction is moved up the tiers from a database server towards the application client and the user.

In contrast to **online concurrency** in system transactions, the glue that is required by a business transaction to put together a number of system transactions so that the ACID properties are adhered to is called **offline concurrency** (Fowler, 2003). The J2EE platform provides support for transaction services to assist in the task, but in most cases the resourcefulness and inventiveness of the developer are essential factors in delivering offline concurrency (otherwise, it would not be called 'offline').

Business Transaction Execution Contexts   21.2.1

Program execution occurs in *contexts* (Fowler, 2003). In the case of processing based on system transactions, the contexts are a session and a transaction itself. A **session** is defined by user/computer interactions between the time the user logs into the system and logs out from the system. A session is likely to activate multiple system transactions. A long transaction under a collaborative concurrency control can span multiple sessions (Section 21.1.5).

A system transaction corresponds to a single request, which is another execution context. 'A **request** corresponds to a single call from the outside world which the software works on and for which it optionally sends back a response' (Fowler, 2003, p.65). A business transaction can span multiple requests, such as ordering the goods and then paying for the order. Transactions spanning multiple requests involve offline concurrency.

A session happens between two neighboring software tiers. Hence, there may be many sessions for a single request. For example, a request from a web-based client may engage a HTTP session to the web server, an application session to the application server, and a database session to the database server.

From an operating system perspective, a transaction executes within a process or within a thread. A **process** represents a time slice during which the program executes. A program may be executing in more than one process. Execution of such a program involves interprocess communication. The execution context of a process provides considerable isolation for the data resources that it uses.

Processes are heavyweight in the sense that they tie up a lot of computing resources. A **thread** is a lightweight portion of a process that takes advantage of resources allocated to the process, although it still requires few resources of its own, such as its own execution stack. An attraction of threads for transactions is that multiple threads of a process can run concurrently and perform different tasks. This allows running a transaction on a thread.

21.2.2 Business Transactions and Component Technology

A **component** is a reusable software object. The component technology facilitates construction of multi-tier enterprise applications. The J2EE platform supports a wide range of components, including applets, application clients, JavaBeans, Enterprise JavaBeans (EJB), servlets, and Java Server Pages (JSP) (Singh *et al.*, 2002). Component technology perpetrates business transactions.

Figure 21.5 illustrates how the PCMEF architecture aligns with the system tiers on which components reside. Business transactions cut across all tiers, with most responsibility placed on the database tier and on the middle tier. The middle tier typically consists of an application server and/or web server. The diagram shows that PCMEF presentation and control packages are frequently deployed on a web server, and the remaining three packages on an application server.

System transactions, at least the way they have been treated here, are synonymous with database transactions. Business transactions bring up the topic of transaction services on the tiers above the database server, which is on an application server, a web server, and even in an applet or application client.

21.2.3 Transaction Services across Tiers

The J2EE platform defines components for transaction services within the **Java Transaction API (JTA)** and the **Java Transaction Service (JTS)** (Singh *et al.*, 2002). J2EE-based

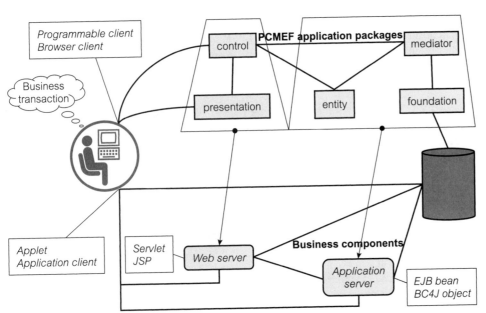

Figure 21.5
PCMEF and
components

servers can employ these services. JTA specifies standard Java interfaces between various application tiers and resources and a transaction manager (JTA, 2003). JTS specifies the implementation of a transaction manager that supports JTA (JTS, 2003). The implementation of such a transaction manager is available within the J2EE platform.

A JTA transaction, governed by the J2EE transaction manager, can be a distributed transaction spanning multiple databases. As these databases can be heterogeneous, the J2EE transaction manager has an advantage over a database-provided transaction manager if an application needs to span databases from different vendors. On the negative side, the J2EE transaction manager supports only flat transactions; it does not support chained and nested transactions (Section 21.1.4).

The J2EE platform offers two kinds of transaction demarcation: declarative and programmatic. Enterprise beans in an application server support the declarative demarcation. **Declarative demarcation** uses the deployment configuration information to select the way of automatically starting and completing transactions. **Programmatic demarcation** requires direct coding of demarcation using JTA. Once demarcation is defined, all other typical functionality of transaction management is given by the J2EE platform.

In most cases, business transactions are initiated in *applets* and *application clients* but the real transactional work is done in the system's lower tiers. The task of demarcating the transactional request received from the user is normally delegated to a web server or application server (possibly via a web server). In the PCMEF architecture, this corresponds to delegating the work from the presentation layer to the control or domain layer.

Web tier

JTA transactions can initiate at a servlet or JSP page in the **web server tier**. So, a JTA transaction may contain a servlet or a JSP page accessing one or more enterprise beans in an application server, which in turn may access one or more databases. Only programmatic demarcation is supported for servlets and JSP pages. A servlet or JSP component can explicitly initiate a JTA transaction using the interface `javax.Transaction.User-Transaction` in the `service` method, as illustrated in Listing 21.1.

Listing 21.1 Business transaction demarcated in a servlet

```
Business transaction demarcated in a servlet

 1:   Context ic = new InitialContext();
 2:   UserTransaction ut =
          (UserTransaction) ic.lookup("java:comp/env/UserTransaction");
 3:   ut.begin();
 4:   try{
 5:       insertMovieToDB(movie);
 6:       Iterator it = actors.iterator();
 7:       while(it.hasNext())
 8:           insertActorToDB((Actor)it.next());
 9:       it = listedas.iterator();
10:       while(it.hasNext())
11:           insertListedAsToDB((ListedAs)it.next());
12:       ut.commit();
13:   }catch(Exception exc){
14:       ut.rollback();
15:   }
```

Invoking `begin` on a `UserTransaction` object assigns the calling *thread* to the transaction. The transaction uses this thread to perform successive transactional actions, such as making a JDBC connection to a database. The transaction must be committed within the service method, which means that a J2EE transaction cannot span multiple *requests* from the web UI.

Application tier

The primary responsibility of the web server tier is handling of UI presentation and interactions, not handling of business logic. *Business transactions* are associated with business logic and, as such, they should be managed by the **application server tier**, whenever possible (unless, of course, they are managed by the database server tier). Transactional enterprise beans are available for this task.

Enterprise beans offer both programmatic (bean-managed) and declarative (container-managed) transaction demarcation. As shown in Listing 21.2, the bean-managed demarcation uses the `UserTransaction` interface in a way similar to the web tier example in Listing 21.1. In bean-managed demarcation the reference to `UserInterface` is obtained by calling `ejbContext.getUserTransaction()`.

Listing 21.2 Business transaction demarcated programmatically in enterprise bean

```
Business transaction demarcated programmatically in enterprise bean

 1:   MovieHome = (MovieHome) PortableRemoteObject.narrow(
                   ctx.lookup("MovieHome"), MovieHome.class);

 2:
 3:   UserTransaction ut = ejbContext.getUserTransaction();
 4:   ut.begin();
 5:   try{
 6:       home.create("Neil Jordan", "Interview with the Vampire",
                     "The vampire bla bla bla");
 7:       ut.commit();
 8:   }catch(Exception exc){
 9:       ut.rollback();
10:   }
```

Listing 21.2 tries to create (insert) a record in the movie table by calling the create() method of the MovieHome interface (described in Chapter 22). Successful creation of a movie record results in commit(), otherwise the transaction's rollback() method is called.

The J2EE platform encourages the use of **container-managed transactional services**. In this approach, methods of a business component (enterprise bean) can be assigned one of six transaction attributes, which determine the transactional behavior of the component. Typically, all methods of an enterprise bean are given the same transaction attribute (except, perhaps, the methods that do not require any transactional support).

Outside of the attribute-determined behavior, the bean has only limited influence on the transaction already started. One thing that it can do is to rollback the transaction with the setRollbackOnly() method. The six attributes are (Singh *et al.*, 2002):

- Required
- RequiresNew
- NotSupported
- Supports
- Mandatory
- Never.

A bean's method with the Required attribute performs always within a JTA transaction context. This context can be obtained from a calling client or, if the client is not associated with a JTA transaction, the container will start a new transaction for the method. Unless the setRollbackOnly() gets involved, the transaction will be committed when the method completes. Methods with Required attributes in various beans can be nicely composed to form a single higher-level multi-method JTA transaction.

A bean's method with the RequiresNew attribute starts only a new JTA transaction. Any transaction context associated with the calling client is suspended and the current thread is used for the new transaction context. The suspended transaction is resumed on the same thread when the new transaction completes.

A bean's method with the `NotSupported` attribute suspends any incoming transactional context and the method executes without transactional demarcation. When the method completes, the container resumes the suspended transaction.

A bean's method with the `Supports` attribute provides a middle-ground solution between the `Required` and `NotSupported` cases. If the method is called with a transaction context, it behaves as for the `Required` case. If it is called without a transaction context, it behaves as for the `NotSupported` case. This is a risky attribute as its 'split-personality' behavior can violate ACID properties.

A bean's method with the `Mandatory` attribute provides a further variation to the `Required` case. If the method is called with a transaction context, it behaves as for the `Required` case. However, when it is called without a transaction context, the container throws an exception.

Finally, a bean's method with the `Never` attribute forbids a transactional context on the method. The method is always invoked without transactional demarcation. If the method is called with a transaction context, the container throws an exception.

Database tier

System transactions are demarcated within the **database tier**. They are small transactions corresponding to an elementary user request involving an atomic insert, update or delete on a database table. A database-demarcated transaction is normally processed within stored procedures/functions invoked as a result of user request. In J2EE specifications, such transactions are called **local transactions** of the resource manager (e.g. a database manager).

Listing 21.3 Business transaction spanning database connections

```
Business transaction spanning database connections

 1:   Collection movies = ...; //a set of movies to be inserted
10:   InitialContext ic = new InitialContext(System.getProperties());
11:   DataSource db1 = (DataSource) ic.lookup("MovieActorDB");//JDBC
12:   ConnectionFactory db2 =
          (ConnectionFactory) ic.lookup("VideoStore"); // Connector CCI
13:   java.sql.Connection con1 = db1.getConnection();
14:   javax.resource.cci.Connection con2 = db2.getConnection();
15:   UserTransaction ut = ejbContext.getUserTransaction();
16:   ut.begin();
17:   try{
18:      // perform updates to MovieDB using connection con1
19:      insertMovies(con1, movies);
20:      // perform updates to VideoStore using connection con2
21:      updateVideoStore(con2, movies);
22:      ut.commit();
23:   }catch(Exception exc){
24:      ut.rollback();
25:   }
```

A recommended practice of the J2EE platform (from the perspective of business transactions) is to demarcate transactions above the database tier. In other words, databases should be accessed within the demarcation of JTA transactions, originating in enterprise beans of the application tier or in the servlets/JSP pages of the web tier. Demarcation above the database tier has multiple advantages, including the possibility of composing short transactions into longer atomic units under the control of application logic. These longer transactions can span more than one database connection.

Listing 21.3 is an example of a business JTA transaction working on two database connections and embracing system transactions on these two connections.

There are cases when a complete business transaction demarcation is not technically possible. This happens when the database server does not support JTA transactions by means of an XATransaction resource adapter or similar device. This happens also when a particular form of database access is not supported by the J2EE platform. At the time of writing, the J2EE platform supports JTA transactions for JDBC and for JMS access. JDBC transactional support is available for servlets, JSP pages, and enterprise beans.

The problem with client-demarcated transactions is that each server transaction ends with explicit commit or rollback. Changes committed to the database cannot be simply uncommitted ('rolled back') by a JTA transaction. To rectify undesirable commits, a separate **compensating transaction** (Maciaszek, 2001; Singh *et al.*, 2002) must be programmed into the application logic. Depending on the business prerogatives, this is a difficult and sometimes impossible task. In some cases, a human intervention on a database, outside of the application scope, may be required to rectify the problem. Listing 21.4 illustrates the principles behind compensating transactions.

Listing 21.4 Compensating transaction

```
Compensating transaction

1:    updateRemoteSystem();
2:    try {
3:        UserTransaction.begin();
4:        updateJDBCDatabase();
5:        UserTransaction.commit();
6:    }catch (RollbackException ex) {
7:        undoUpdateRemoteSystem();
8:    }
```

Offline Concurrency Patterns   21.2.4

Concurrency is best left for the management of the transaction software. However, the transaction concept itself is a business notion. The business rules are full of special cases that sometimes cannot be demarcated by some readily implementable notion of a business transaction. At some other times, the available transaction software is not quite up to the task.

One of the most important challenges facing developers is to address conflicts between concurrent user requests and, therefore, between concurrent business transactions. These issues are addressed by **offline concurrency patterns** (Fowler, 2003). Two of these patterns, Optimistic Offline Lock and Pessimistic Offline Lock, are discussed next. The offline concurrency patterns assume that the application implements some kind of Unit of Work pattern, introduced before in Section 15.3.5.

Unit of Work

The **Unit of Work** pattern 'maintains a list of objects affected by a business transaction and coordinates the writing out of changes and the resolution of concurrency problems' (Fowler, 2003, p.184). 'A Unit of Work keeps track of everything you do during a business transaction that can affect the database. When you're done, it figures out everything that needs to be done to alter the database as a result of your work' (Fowler, 2003, p.184).

The above descriptions of Unit of Work take a somewhat flexible and broader view of what the business transaction is. Earlier in this chapter, and elsewhere in Fowler's book, the notion of business transaction has been restricted to actions taken from an application but affecting persistent data. The Unit of Work pattern prescribes also (if not most of all) what actions should be taken on transient in-memory objects *prior* to opening and demarcating a business transaction aimed at committing changes to the database.

With that in mind, the Unit of Work pattern introduces a class within the `domain` layer. The class can be called `MUnitOfWork` (assuming it is in the `mediator` package). The class keeps track of changes made on in-memory `entity` objects. A possible behavioral structure of the class is as in Figure 21.6 (Fowler, 2003).

`MUnitOfWork` tracks changes on entity objects on behalf of a business transaction. When the application decides that changes should be made persistent in the database,

Figure 21.6
Unit of Work

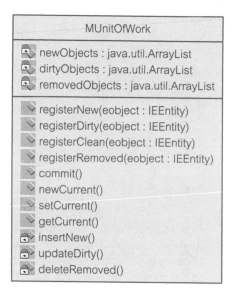

`MUnitOfWork` initiates the business transaction. The changes are kept in three array lists: `newObjects`, `dirtyObjects`, and `removedObjects`. The lists are maintained by the relevant methods: `registerNew()`, `registerDirty()`, and `registerRemoved()`. `registeredClean()` is not relevant for a business transaction as clean objects do not get updated on a database (this method can be used to put registered objects in Identity Map (Section 15.3.1)).

The `commit()` method contains calls to the three private methods: `insertNew()`, `updateDirty()`, and `deleteRemoved()`. The invocation of `commit()` on a current `MUnitOfWork` object results in initiating a business transaction, the purpose of which is to synchronize the state of entity objects in the program's memory with the state of the database. Depending on the frequency with which `commit()` is called, a business transaction is shorter or longer and it may include multiple system transactions on the database.

Figure 21.7 demonstrates a particular simplified scenario with a single change on `EContact` object resulting in `commit()`. To begin, an `MUnitOfWork` object aimed at serving a particular transaction must be instantiated. As discussed in passing, the application transaction can work on a current thread using the `java.lang.ThreadLocal` class (Fowler, 2003). The `newCurrent()` method instantiates the new `MUnitOfWork` object and places it on the current session's thread.

When `EContact` changes its address, it calls `setDirty()`, which in turn registers its dirty status on the current `MUnitOfWork` object. When the decision is taken to propagate changes to the database, `EContact` invokes `commit()` on `MUnitOfWork`. This starts a business transaction, in this case involving only the `updateDirty()` method. The `updateDirty()` method uses `FWriter` to spawn a system transaction, which executes the SQL update on a database.

Optimistic Offline Lock

Unit of Work is a single request, single session, single process, single thread, and single business transaction solution. But in a multi-user system, with many users/applications hitting the database at the same time, the transaction concurrency issues get much more complex. System transaction services resolve many of these concurrency problems automatically (Section 21.1). Some get resolved by business transaction services (Section 21.2.3). However, problems due to conflicting transactions across concurrent sessions by multiple users, require individual programming attention.

The **Optimistic Offline Lock** pattern 'prevents conflicts between concurrent business transactions by detecting a conflict and rolling back the transaction' (Fowler, 2003, p.416). The assumption of the Optimistic Offline Lock is that conflicts are rare. The pattern checks at commit time whether the data objects to be written to persistent store have been changed by another business transaction since they have been read from the store. If they have been changed, the business transaction is rolled back.

In practice, this pattern amounts to application-implemented methods of non-pessimistic concurrency control schemes (Section 21.1.5). In an ideal situation, the application developer gets assistance from a multiversion concurrency scheme supported by the transaction manager. If not, in a typical implementation of Optimistic Offline Lock, a

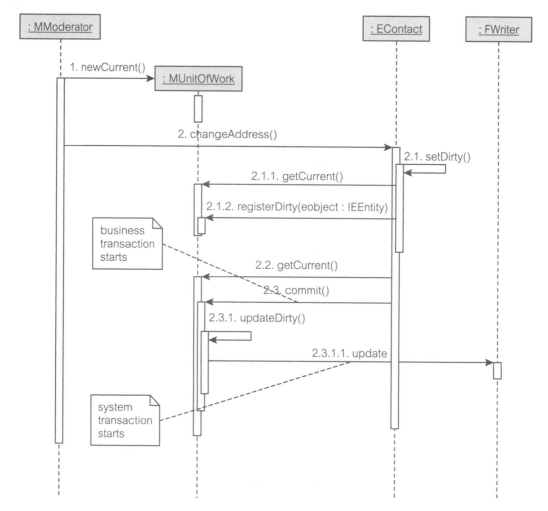

Figure 21.7 Unit of Work activating a business transaction

version number is assigned to each persistent data object in the system (something that multiversion concurrency control can provide 'free of charge').

With version numbers in place, the responsibility of each business transaction is to:

■ acquire an exclusive lock on the persistent object (database record) to be modified by the transaction,

■ use the session's copy of the version number in the `where` clause of a SQL update or delete statement in order to verify if the version of the record has not changed,

■ if the version has changed then the update/delete fails and the business transaction is rolled back.

To resolve conflicts 'offline', Fowler (2003) recommends that apart from a version number, persistent objects are augmented with information about when and who last modified the record. This allows the current user to engage in 'reconciliation discussions' with the users who made recent changes. In fact, this is a standard practice in collaborative concurrency control schemes (Section 21.1.5), which provide automatic notification (e.g. by email) to encourage 'reconciliation discussions'.

Pessimistic Offline Lock

The **Pessimistic Offline Lock** pattern 'prevents conflicts between concurrent business transactions by allowing only one business transaction at a time to access data' (Fowler, 2003, p.426). The pattern amounts to managing multiple business transactions with pessimistic concurrency control schemes. The pessimistic offline lock demands that a business transaction acquires proper locks on data before it can act on this data. This is precisely what pessimistic concurrency schemes do for system transactions. Business transactions need to adopt a pattern like the Pessimistic Offline Lock.

Pessimistic Offline Lock recommends three types of lock on session data used by a business transaction (Fowler, 2003):

- exclusive write lock
- exclusive read lock
- read/write lock.

An **exclusive write lock** ensures that only one transaction at a time can make changes to a set of data processed by a transaction that managed to acquire such a lock. Other transactions can read the same set of data, which of course can mean that they process an inconsistent set, which may change by the time they finish their work.

An **exclusive read lock** removes the loophole of the exclusive write lock. Under the exclusive read lock, a business transaction that acquires a lock on a data set excludes other transactions from even reading the same data set. The other transactions must wait for the release of the lock. Clearly, this lowers the overall system concurrency.

A **read/write lock** allows multiple concurrent read locks under the condition that no write lock is held. This makes read and write locks mutually exclusive. A business transaction cannot acquire a write lock as long as any other business transaction holds a read lock on the same data set.

The implementation of a *lock manager* to support the Pessimistic Offline Lock includes a need for a shareable persistent table in a database that maps locks to business transactions. Such a table is sometimes called a **semaphore table**. The semaphore table stores what is currently locked, which business transaction locks it, and what kind of lock is applied. Business transactions are obliged to query the semaphore table before they can proceed.

The last point raises the issue of the *lock protocol* for Pessimistic Offline Lock that dictates when and what to lock, when the lock should be released, and what to do if the lock cannot be acquired. Not surprisingly, most principles of pessimistic concurrency control employed for system transactions apply also to Pessimistic Offline Lock. Locks should be acquired before the data is loaded. Locks should be placed on identifiers (primary keys) of database records. Locks should be released after the transaction completes. A business transaction should abort if the locks cannot be acquired for some time.

The most troublesome issues in Pessimistic Offline Lock are the definition and granularity of a data set needed by a business transaction (and the identification of business transactions in the first place) and the potential bottleneck created by the semaphore table. A simplistic solution of treating a business transaction on a par with a session can reduce concurrency to an unacceptably low level. The semaphore table is likely to become the main point of lock contention itself and in some cases a business transaction may have difficulty obtaining locks because it is locked out of the semaphore table.

21.3 Transactions and Concurrency in Email Management

The EM application uses Oracle for database storage. This gives EM the advantage of a powerful but complex Oracle transaction manager, which uses a **multiversion concurrency** mechanism with **read consistent snapshots** (Section 21.1.5). Speed of queries is achieved by reading the snapshot without the need to *pause* current updates on the database. However, this approach does not guarantee that up-to-date data is read by queries. However, the data is up to date with respect to the snapshot. Oracle optimistically detects conflicts, which improves concurrency (assuming the conflicts are not frequent).

The use of the Oracle optimistic offline lock requires the client application to supply necessary steps when a commit action could trigger exceptions. The combination of optimistic lock and read consistent snapshot does not give any indication to the client application if committing changes to the database may result in conflict. This is very different from the pessimistic lock in which there is only one transaction at a time that can modify data and therefore other transactions have to wait for the lock. Optimistic locks allow multiple transactions to execute at the same time and only throw the exception when they detect a conflict.

EM Iteration 3 employs a range of transactional models. The flat transactional model is used for simple, straight-to-the-point transactions. Chained transactions are used to ensure that the user is given a second chance to try a failed operation. Chained transactions involve stored procedures/functions as well as triggers. The EM case study does not have a pressing need for nested transactions and autonomous transactions.

21.3.1 Flat Transaction Model

A **flat transaction** is the simplest transaction model to ensure that a single request to modify the database is either committed or rolled back. Figure 21.8 illustrates how the flat transaction model is used to encapsulate the deletion of an outmessage. The client application requests CAdmin to delete the outmessage. The deletion is carried out by MModerator, which creates a new MUnitOfWork and registers on it that the outmessage should be removed. Finally, MModerator asks MUnitOfWork to commit the transaction.

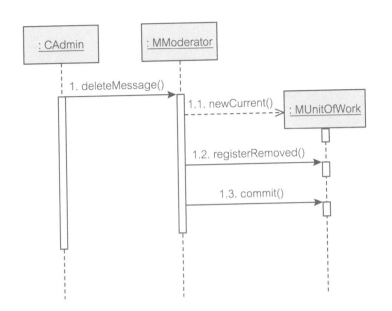

Figure 21.8
Simple flat
transaction in EM

Unit of Work and Transactional Support

21.3.2

The **unit of work** is not only used to encapsulate simple transactions, as shown in
Figure 21.8, but it can be used to encapsulate much more complex transactions. A complex
transaction may be an arbitrary sequence of inserts, updates, and deletes on a database.
Although the EM case study does not currently have complex transactions, MUnitOfWork
implemented in Iteration 3 has the capacity to handle complex transactions.

Figure 21.9 gives an example in which the transaction is a sequence of three operations
on the OutMessage table: insert, update, and delete. MUnitOfWork can be acquired
via its static getCurrent() or newCurrent() method. Using a static method ensures
that a valid instance of MUnitOfWork is returned. Once the unit of work is *initialized*
by its getCurrent() or newCurrent() method, entity objects can register to it by
calling appropriate methods such as registerDirty(), registerRemoved(), or
registerNew() (Messages 2.2 and 3.2).

Once the commit() on MUnitOfWork is executed (Message 4), the whole sequence of
changes is performed in a transactional manner. This involves creating a savepoint on the
current database connection (Message 4.1). Once a savepoint is acquired, the insertions,
updates, and deletions are performed according to the sequence of their registrations
(Message 4.2). At the end, the whole transaction (guarded by the savepoint) is either
committed or rolled back (Messages 4.3 and 4.4).

Figure 21.9 shows that EM forces MModerator to handle the start and finish of a
transaction. If the transaction is started from MModerator then it has to be either rolled
back or committed by MModerator. If the transaction is then encapsulated into MUnitOf-
Work, then the unit of work has to ensure that the sequence of actions is treated as a single
transaction and therefore it has to return either a committed or rolled back state.

Figure 21.9
Unit of Work in
action

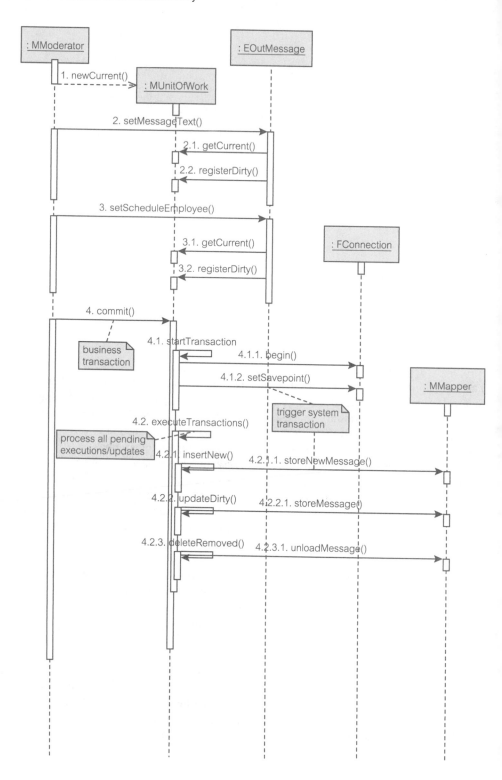

Summary

1. A *business transaction* is a logical unit of work that accomplishes a particular business task and guarantees the *integrity* of the database after the task completes. A business transaction consists of one or more *system transactions*.

2. Transaction management has two main functions: system concurrency and system recovery. This chapter concentrated on *system concurrency* (concurrent execution of programs on shared data sources).

3. A transaction is delimited (demarcated), explicitly or implicitly, by statements that mark its beginning and its end. Demarcation of a system transaction is known as a *server-side demarcation*, while demarcation of a business transaction is called a *client-side demarcation*. The transaction ends with a *commit* or *rollback*.

4. To enforce data integrity in the presence of concurrent access and system failures, system transactions must satisfy the *ACID properties* (atomicity, consistency, isolation, and durability).

5. An *isolation level* defines how concurrent transactions are isolated from one another. SQL standard defines four isolation levels: serializable, repeatable read, read committed, and read uncommitted.

6. Isolation levels are implemented by *locking* the data resources. The main *lock modes* are: exclusive locks, update locks, and shared locks. Locks can be held on resources of various granularity – they can be held on a row, a page, or on the whole table.

7. There are various transactional models. A *flat transaction* is a single unit of work, which ends with a single commit or rollback. Parts of a flat transaction can be chained by using *savepoints*. This leads to the notion of a *chained transaction*. A *nested transaction* consists of subtransactions (autonomous transactions), which can be committed or rolled back independently.

8. *Pessimistic concurrency control* is based on an assumption that conflicts between transactions are likely. *Optimistic concurrency control* takes the opposite view that conflicts between transactions are infrequent. A variant of optimistic control, used routinely in object databases, is known as *multiversion concurrency control*. A combined use of pessimistic, optimistic and multiversion concurrency control schemes results in a scheme termed *collaborative concurrency control*.

9. In a *system transaction*, the demarcation is between the application and the database. In a *business transaction*, the demarcation is between the user and the application. A business transaction can span multiple *requests* and *sessions*.

10. In contrast to *online concurrency* in system transactions, the developer's task of putting together a number of system transactions into a business transaction and satisfying the ACID properties in the process is called *offline concurrency*.

11. A *component* is a reusable software object. The component technology facilitates construction of multi-tier enterprise applications. The J2EE platform defines components for transaction services within the *Java Transaction API* (JTA) and the *Java Transaction Service* (JTS). The J2EE platform offers two kinds of transaction demarcation: *declarative* and *programmatic*.

12. *Business transactions* are associated with business logic, and as such they should be managed by the application server tier. *System transactions* are demarcated within the *database tier*. A database-demarcated transaction would normally be processed within stored procedures/functions invoked as a result of a user request. In J2EE specifications, such transactions are called *local transactions* of the resource manager (e.g. a database manager).

13. *Patterns* for programming *offline concurrency* include Unit of Work, Optimistic Offline Lock and Pessimistic Offline Lock.

14. EM Iteration 3 employs transactional models ranging from simple flat transactions to chained transactions involving stored procedures/functions as well as triggers. The EM case study does not use nested and autonomous transactions or other more complex transactional models.

Key Terms

ACID properties	702
application server tier	714
application transaction	*See* business transaction
atomicity	702
bracketing	*See* demarcation
business transaction	700, 701, 711
chained transaction	706
check-in	709
check-out	709
client-side demarcation	702
collaborative concurrency control	709
commit	700, 702
compensating transaction	717
component	712
concurrency	700
concurrency control	707
consistency	703
container-managed transaction	715
database tier	716
database transaction	*See* system transaction
deadlock	705
declarative demarcation	713
demarcation	702
dirty read	704
durability	703
exclusive lock	705
exclusive read lock	721
exclusive write lock	721
flat transaction	706, 722
group workspace	709
integrity	700
isolation	703
isolation level	704
Java Transaction API	712
Java Transaction Service	712
JTA	*See* Java Transaction API
JTS	*See* Java Transaction Service
local transaction	716
lock	703
lock escalation	705
lock level	705
lock mode	705
long lock	*See* persistent lock
long transaction	701, 709
multiversion concurrency	722
multiversion concurrency control	709

nested transaction	707, 709
nonrepeatable read	704
object database	709
object identifier	710
offline concurrency	711
offline concurrency pattern	718
OID	*See* object identifier
online concurrency	711
optimistic concurrency control	708
Optimistic Offline Lock	719
page lock	705
persistent lock	709
pessimistic concurrency control	707
Pessimistic Offline Lock	721
phantom	704
process	712
programmatic demarcation	713
read committed isolation	704
read consistent snapshot	711, 722
read uncommitted isolation	704
read/write lock	721
recovery	701
redo	703
repeatable read isolation	704
request	712
rollback	700, 702
row lock	705
savepoint	706
semaphore table	721
serializable execution	703
serializable isolation	704
server-side demarcation	702
session	709, 711
shared lock	705
short lock	709
short transaction	700, 709
snapshot lock	710
system transaction	700, 701, 711
table lock	705
thread	712
transaction	700
undo	703
Unit of Work	718, 723
update lock	705
version number	720
web server tier	713

Review Questions

1. Explain the difference between the notions of business transaction and system transaction. How do these two terms relate to the concepts of client-side and server-side demarcation? Does the common use of the term 'transaction' mean business transaction or system transaction?

2. Which of these two pairs of concepts are more intertwined – consistency and durability or consistency and isolation? Explain.

3. What locking strategy is required for ensuring the read committed isolation level? Explain and exemplify.

4. Provide a couple of examples of applications in which the nested transaction model should be used? Explain. Are savepoints necessary for implementation of nested transactions? Explain again.

5. Can long transactions use short locks? Explain.

6. How does a snapshot lock relate to a read consistent snapshot? Explain.

7. Can a request span multiple sessions? Can a session span multiple requests? Explain.

8. Explain the deployment options for PCMEF packages.

9. Explain the pros and cons of declarative and procedural demarcation. Which one is more advocated by J2EE? Why?

10. Is a compensating transaction a system or business transaction? When compensating transactions are used?

11. Is the Unit of Work pattern also the Singleton pattern? Is the Unit of Work pattern a concurrency solution? Explain.

12. How is a semaphore table used in concurrency control?

Problem-Solving Exercises

1. Suppose you are about to develop an application with the following requirements: (1) the application requires reading data from the database, (2) data may be modified in the application, (3) there may be a long time delay between data read and data modification (i.e. users may have been analyzing data before modifying it), and (4) data retrieved has to be the most recent data during which no additional data may be inserted into the database. What isolation level is most suitable for this application? What is the impact of the chosen isolation level on application responsiveness?

2. Suppose you are about to develop an application with the following requirements: (1) the application requires reading data from the database, (2) data may be modified in the application, (3) there may be a long time delay between data read and data modification (i.e. users may have been analyzing data before modifying it), (4) data retrieved has to be the most recent data, and (5) the application polls data frequently from the database to reflect changes in the database via a clever proprietary 'cache and compare' algorithm. What isolation level is most suitable for this application? What is the impact of the chosen isolation level on application responsiveness?

3. The ACID properties do not only apply to database operations. Some or all of these properties apply to any programming operation which stores and shares data. The following statement, if

not guarded by synchronization, could result in non-atomic behavior. Explain why. You may assume the operating system uses time-slicing as its scheduling algorithm. [Hint: multithreading]

```
value = value + newValue;
```

4. The following is the implementation of report retrieval in Iteration 3 (Figure 21.10). There is something not quite right with the sequence of messages. Identify the problem and suggest an approach to fix it.

Figure 21.10
Sequence
diagram for report
retrieval

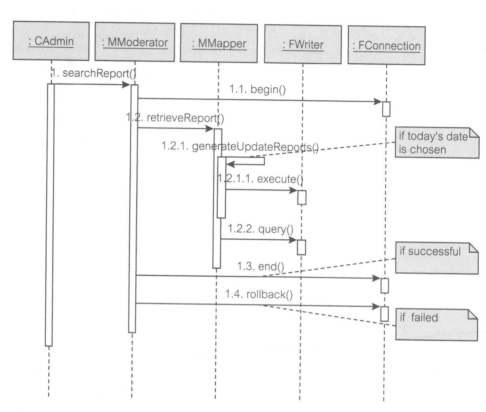

Chapter
22
Business Components

The component technology has been discussed frequently throughout the book. This chapter is meant to put the various 'bits and pieces' together and to explain in more detail the fundamental Java and database technologies which assist in construction of systems from reusable business components. This chapter discusses two representative technologies: (1) the **Enterprise JavaBeans** (EJB), representing the Java world, and (2) **Business Components for Java** (BC4J), representing the database world. Other examples of component technologies include CORBA server objects and ODMG-compliant Object Storage API.

A **business component** is a reusable object that occupies the middle tier between the user interface and the database. Business components represent persistent database objects, implement business logic and business rules, know how to access the database, and can perform business transactions. Physical deployment of business components is usually in an application server, but some components can reside also in a database or web server or even locally within a Java client. There is a close alignment between business components and the `entity`, `mediator`, and `foundation` packages of the PCMEF framework (Section 21.2.2, Figure 21.5).

Business components technologies aim at facilitating rapid development of server-side applications by connecting reusable components via their published interfaces. The components can be freely specialized and customized.

The main philosophical difference between EJB and BC4J is that the latter derives business components from the underlying database design. EJB components do not obtain the business logic from the database; the logic needs to be provided to EJB components by the developer. The components are called **beans** in EJB. EJB offers *entity beans* to contain data and *session beans* to represent transactions, security, and similar functions. This genericity of EJB allows, for example, the deployment of a BC4J application in a EJB session bean.

A good way of understanding differences between EJB and BC4J is by accepting that the two technologies come from two ends of the same spectrum. EJB extends applications towards databases. BC4J extends databases towards applications. The outcome is that EJB provides transaction, security and similar services, already present in databases. On the other hand, BC4J provides GUI components, already present in applications. EJB relies on JavaBeans for GUI components.

22.1 Enterprise JavaBeans

Enterprise JavaBeans (EJB) is the main ingredient of the Java 2 Enterprise Edition (J2EE) framework. The main objectives of the EJB technology are (Johnson, 2002):

■ *Robustness* – the architecture aims at providing reliable host services for the development of J2EE applications.

■ *Scalability* – the application server may be clustered to improve the scalability of hosted applications.

■ *Support OO design principles* – enforcement of OO principles and design patterns is a necessary condition for EJB in order to support large, reusable, and scalable systems.

■ *Portability* – this conforms to the Java ideology to 'build once and use everywhere'.

■ *Server properties* – EJB needs to serve multiple client types, such as applets, stand-alone Swing GUI, web applications (JSP/Servlet), etc.

■ *Single-threaded design with multi-thread features* – although a bean can be running on a single-thread it should demonstrate (simulate) a multi-threaded behavior to clients.

It is necessary to emphasize that EJB is *not* the same as JavaBeans. A JavaBean is more like a standard Java class that has a set of methods for every property that it would like to expose. If the property is called 'hi', then there are `setHi()` and `getHi()` methods. JavaBeans are predominantly used in GUI development to chain a set of components (or beans) together. EJBs have different usage than JavaBeans. EJBs are predominantly used in server-side programming (as compared with GUI for JavaBeans) and support various methods to allow manipulation from a *host server* (a J2EE container).

There are many sources of information which discuss the pros and cons of EJB (and J2EE, in general). This chapter does not get into this debate but rather presents EJB at its best: as a stable and extensible architecture for distributed applications expecting scalable services. Figure 22.1 shows the overall J2EE architecture.

There are two points of view on the J2EE architecture. On the one hand, the architecture can be seen through the Client, J2EE, and Enterprise Information System (EIS) tiers. On the other hand, the tiers are UI (or Presentation), Business Logic (BL), and Information System (IS). The first classification (Client, J2EE, EIS) is concerned more with the technological changes between the tiers. The second (UI, BL, IS) is concerned more with the spread of information and responsibilities.

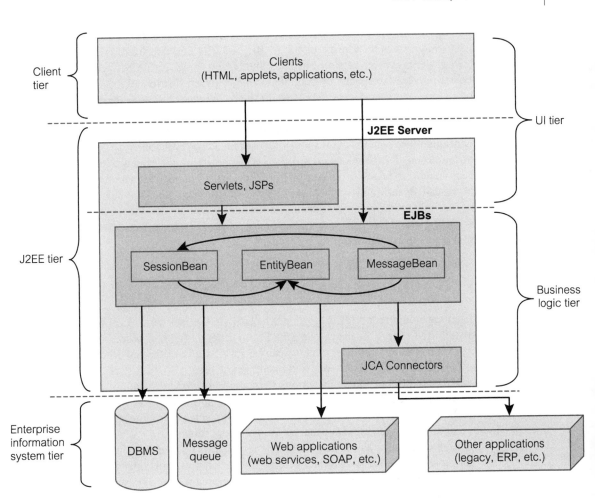

Figure 22.1 J2EE architecture

Applications that interact with users reside on the **Client tier**. This includes applets, console and GUI applications, and HTML web pages. The Client tier communicates with the J2EE tier to obtain necessary information and to process data. The **J2EE tier** consists of servlets, JSP pages, EJB beans and the supporting components (such as Java Connector Architecture (JCA), Java Transaction Service (JTS), JMS, JDBC, etc.). The **EIS tier** consists of databases or other data sources (including legacy systems) to manage persistent storage, Message Queue services to ensure delivery of messages, and related services.

Taking the second perspective on the J2EE architecture, there is no real difference between the EIS tier and the **IS tier**. However, the **UI tier** embraces the Client tier 'gudgets', but it also includes servlets and JSPs as they provide some type of interface between users and the business logic. The exceptions are those servlets/JSPs that do not interact with users directly.

The UI tier relies on the **BL tier** for its business functionality. There are three types of EJB (Sun, 2002a,b). **Entity beans** in BL or J2EE tiers are used as representations of business entities and **session beans** as the driving force for the business logic. **Message beans** provide the means of communication between distributed systems. Both session beans and message beans represent business actions, but message beans are able to interpret and deliver messages to other beans *asynchronously*.

The beans live in a J2EE **application server**, commonly referred to as a J2EE **container**. The container is responsible for the loading, availability, and garbage collection of the beans. The developer has a choice of specifying the container-managed beans or bean-managed beans. The complete names are Container-Managed Persistent (CMP) beans and Bean-Managed Persistent (BMP) beans. With the CMP beans, the container is responsible for providing persistency to the beans. With the BMP beans, this responsibility is on the shoulders (or, rather, the brain) of the developer (this means writing SQL statements to the database).

22.1.1 EJB Fundamentals

The core principle of J2EE (particularly EJB) is the fact that each bean is treated as a **distributed object**. Beans can be called from different types of processes, either remotely located or in the same host. Clients can be Java-based or other-environment-based (such as C++). All clients can invoke and manipulate EJBs.

EJB has strict naming conventions for naming its properties and interfaces that need to be implemented. EJB follows the JavaBeans example for naming the `set()` and `get()` methods. Additionally, EJB requires the implementation of the `find()` and `load()` methods to allow the management of beans by the container.

Figure 22.2 is a simplified version of the overall **EJB architecture**. The figure does not represent the J2EE container despite the fact that the container plays a major role in the maintenance of beans. Figure 22.2 has three interfaces and one class that are user-defined. The three interfaces are `MyEJBHome`, `MyEJBObject`, and `MyEJBInterface`. The user-defined class is `MyEJB`. The remaining classes and interfaces are part of the J2EE API.

The J2EE container generates automatically classes such as `MyEJBHomeImplementation` and `MyEJBObjectImplementation`. Note that the naming of `MyXXX` interfaces and classes are for illustration only. It would be more logical, for example, to have a `BankAccountHome`, a `BankAccountObject`, a `BankAccountInterface`, and a `BankAccountEJB` as the set of classes, if the application relates to the banking domain. Classes automatically generated by the J2EE container are specific to the container. The application has no knowledge of automatically generated classes.

The generated classes in Figure 22.2 form three types of beans. Clients need to refer to them indirectly via interfaces. There exist *Home* and *Remote* interfaces. A client typically obtains a reference to the Home interface (`MyEJBHome`) of the particular bean (`MyEJB`), and then obtains the corresponding Remote representation of the EJB (`MyEJBObject`) from the Home interface. This is the end of the communication path as far as the client is concerned. The client invokes various business activities on the acquired Remote object as if that object represented the real bean. Behind the scenes, the Remote object invokes the

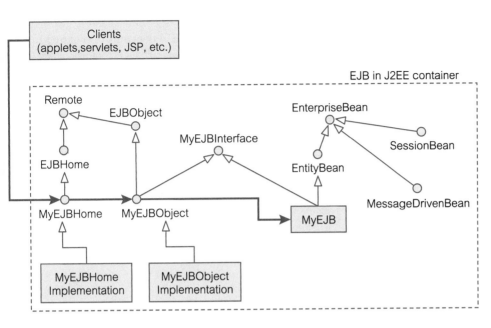

Figure 22.2
EJB architecture from the developer's perspective

bean to perform the job. This path of communication is indicated in Figure 22.2 by the arrow from the Clients box.

A bean is qualified to be called an Enterprise JavaBean if it extends `javax.ejb.EntityBean`, or `javax.ejb.SessionBean`, or `javax.ejb.MessageDrivenBean`. These beans extend `javax.ejb.EnterpriseBean` which is a *serializable* interface (`java.io.Serializable`). User-defined beans will never inherit directly from an `EnterpriseBean` but from one of the three bean types.

The **serialization** feature of an `EnterpriseBean` means that all beans can persist – they are serialized via the appropriate `readObject()` and `writeObject()` methods. This feature allows the beans to be stored or reloaded by the container whenever necessary. For example, if the number of beans in the container exceeds a certain limit then the container may choose to serialize some beans. When these beans are required again, they will be *de-serialized*.

Note also in Figure 22.2 that `EJBHome` and `EJBObject` extend the `java.rmi.Remote` interface. This indicates that both objects are designed to support remote invocation. These objects can be transmitted across the Internet and called from different Java Virtual Machines (JVMs) by using Remote Method Invocation with the Internet Inter-ORB Protocol (RMI-IIOP).

As EJB is designed as a distributed object, its discovery by a Client involves a little work. The client cannot communicate directly with EJB but instead it has to acquire a reference to `EJBHome`. This reference establishes a communication channel to the bean. The `EJBHome` reference is acquired through some Naming Service. Moreover, `EJBHome` cannot acess the bean directly. It can access it by obtaining a reference to an `EJBObject`. The sole responsibility of `EJBHome` is to create, find, and destroy `EJBObjects`. An `EJBObject` is the one with knowledge of how to invoke the bean.

Listing 22.1 shows how a client can acquire references to EJBHome and EJBObject to manipulate the EJB indirectly. Initially the context to an EJB container is acquired from a system property on Line 13. From this context, an alias *MovieHome* is requested. The alias lookup is mapped to a class called MovieHome (Line 15), which is an interface extending EJBHome (MovieHome is shown as MyEJBHome in Figure 22.2). As EJBHome is a remote object (inherits java.rmi.Remote), it needs to be *translated* into a known class. This is achieved by calling the PortableRemoteObject's narrow() method (Line 14).

Listing 22.1 MovieClient uses Movie EJB

```
MovieClient uses Movie EJB

 1:   package presentation;
 2:   import javax.ejb.*;
 3:   import javax.naming.*;
 4:   import java.rmi.*;
 5:   import javax.rmi.PortableRemoteObject;
 6:   import java.util.*;
 7:   import domain.entity.*;
 8:   public class MovieClient{
 9:      public static void main(String args[]){
10:         MovieHome home = null;
11:
12:         try {
13:            Context ctx = new
                           InitialContext(System.getProperties());
14:            home = (MovieHome) PortableRemoteObject.narrow(
15:               ctx.lookup("MovieHome"), MovieHome.class);
16:
17:            home.create("Neil Jordan", "Interview with the Vampire",
18:                     "The vampire bla bla bla");
19:            //...
20:            Iterator i =
                     home.findByDirector("Neil Jordan").iterator();
21:            System.out.println("These movies directed by Neil
                                               Jordan:");
22:            while (i.hasNext()) {
23:               Movie movie = (Movie) PortableRemoteObject.narrow(
24:                  i.next(), Movie.class);
25:               System.out.println(movie.getTitle());
26:            }
27:         }
28:      }
29:   }
```

Once a Home interface is acquired, its create methods can be invoked to create new instances of the beans (Line 17). Lines 20–27 show how `Movie` (a sub-interface of `EJBObject`) is used to represent a `MovieBMPBean` or `MovieCMPBean`. A business method (`getTitle()`) can be invoked from the acquired `EJBObject`.

Entity Beans

Entity beans are the most used beans in J2EE applications. They represent business objects such as the `Movie` class in the `MovieActor` application. The main reason that they are so useful is that they are **persistent**. Because they have persistent storage, they survive server and client machine crashes.

As mentioned before, there are two types of entity beans depending on how their persistence is managed. Persistence of **Bean-Managed Persistent** beans (BMP) is managed manually by the developer. If the persistence management is left to the container, the bean is called **Container-Managed Persistent** bean (CMP). The decision on which persistency management to use depends on various considerations:

- *Maintenance* – CMPs are easier to maintain. There are no SQL statements involved and there is no need for manual preparation of a database connection. There is only a need to provide (mostly) abstract methods all of which will be implemented by the container.

- *Pre-existing database* – If there is a pre-existing operational database, BMPs can be advantageous.

- *Knowledge of SQL* – CMPs do not demand much knowledge, if any, of the SQL language. The EJB-Query Language (EJB-QL) is a simplified SQL variant for CMP if such a need arises.

- *Dependence on container vendor* – Container vendors provide different levels of services in managing persistent storage. This makes CMPs more vulnerable to changes in container capabilities.

Listing 22.2 shows an example of Entity bean implementation for the `Movie` class in the `MovieActor` application. It is a BMP entity bean that implements `MovieInterface`. The bean has methods called `ejbXXX`, such as `ejbFindByDirector()`. These methods are typically implemented to match the *similarly* declared methods in the corresponding `EJBObject`. For example, `ejbFindByDirector()` is provided to serve method calls by the `MovieHome`'s `findByDirector()` method (or `MovieLocalHome`'s `findByDirector()`). The word `ejb` is prefixed to the method name to signify its EJB bean implementation (as compared with its `EJBHome` declaration). The rest of the BMP methods have a similar pattern to `ejbFindByDirector()`. A connection is acquired before a query to the data source can be done. Listing 22.2 shows how the connection is acquired from a connection pool (`ejbPool`). The method also needs to clean up all the acquired resources.

Listing 22.2 MovieBMPBean for MovieActor application

```
MovieBMPBean for MovieActor application

public class MovieBMPBean extends EntityBean, MovieInterface
{
   //declare some fields to be maintained by this bean
   String director, title;
   //...cut to save space
   public void setDirector(String director){
      this.director = director;
   }
   public String getDirector(){
      return director;
   }
   public Collection ejbFindByDirector(String director)
   throws FinderException {
      PreparedStatement pstmt = null;
      Connection conn = null;
      Vector v = new Vector();
      try {
         conn = getConnection();
         pstmt = conn.prepareStatement(
               "select id from movie where director = ?");
         pstmt.setString(1, director);
         ResultSet rs = pstmt.executeQuery();
         while (rs.next()) {
            String id = rs.getString("id");
            v.addElement(new MoviePK(id));
         }
         return v;
      }catch (Exception e) {
         throw new FinderException(e.toString());
      }finally {
         try { if (pstmt != null) pstmt.close(); } catch (Exception e) {}
         try { if (conn != null) conn.close(); } catch (Exception e) {}
      }
   }
   private Connection getConnection() throws Exception {
      try {
         Context ctx = new InitialContext();
         javax.sql.DataSource ds = (javax.sql.DataSource)
            ctx.lookup("java:comp/env/jdbc/ejbPool");
         return ds.getConnection();
      }catch (Exception e) {
         System.err.println("Could not locate data source. Reason:");
         e.printStackTrace();
         throw e;
      }
   }
   //...cut to save space
}
```

Listing 22.3 allows comparison of the CMP implementation with its BMP counterpart in Listing 22.2. The `MovieCMPBean` has a set of `set`/`get` methods with no implementation. The implementations of these methods are left to the container. Also, the bean does not have class fields, unlike BMP.

Listing 22.3 MovieCMPBean for MovieActor application

MovieCMPBean for MovieActor application

```
public class MovieCMPBean extends EntityBean, MovieInterface
{
    //all methods set/get are to be implemented by container
    public abstract void setDirector(String director);
    public abstract String getDirector();

    public String ejbCreate(String director, String title, String desc){
        setDirector(director); //call set() methods rather storing to
                                                                   fields

        setTitle(title);
        setDescription(desc);
        return null; //CMP does not need the return value
    }
    //...cut to save space
}
```

The `ejbCreate()` method is required and reflects the `EJBHome`'s/`EJBLocalHome`'s `create()` method. BMP requires `ejbCreate()` to store the values to persistent fields (class variables), whereas CMP calls the `set()` methods to perform this job. The `set()` methods, implemented by the container, achieve a similar effect (of storing to persistent fields).

Finder methods (`ejbFindXXX()`), although declared, need not be implemented in CMP. The implementation is provided in the deployment descriptor (Listing 22.4) in the form of EJB-QL. By specifying an EJB-QL statement in the deployment descriptor, the container is able to generate its own proprietary classes to implement finder methods.

Listing 22.4 is the deployment descriptor for the `Movie` bean. The declaration specifies that the deployment descriptor follows the EJB 2.0 specification. The name of the EJB is `Movie` with its associated classes (home, remote, local interfaces). Importantly, it also specifies whether it is BMP or CMP. A BMP has its persistence-type set to `Bean`, whereas a CMP would have the `Container` type (the commented lines refer to CMP specific entries).

Since `MovieBMPBean` uses a data source connection, this resource is declared in the deployment descriptor as well. A `reentrant` is a feature that allows the bean to be shared in a *multi-threaded* environment. A reentrant is a condition upon which a bean calls another bean, which in turn calls the initial bean back. Most beans are *single-threaded* but a reentrant indicates to the container that a particular bean supports multi-threaded access. A single-threaded bean still exhibits multi-thread behavior to the client. This is because the container is capable of simulating multiple threads to the client (by using bean pooling).

Listing 22.4 MovieActor's Deployment Descriptor (ejb-jar.xml) – Entity Beans

---

Deployment descriptor, ejb-jar.xml, for MovieApplication - Entity Beans

```xml
<?xml version="1.0"?>
<!DOCTYPE ejb-jar PUBLIC '-//Sun Microsystems, Inc.//DTD Enterprise
JavaBeans 2.0//EN' 'http://java.sun.com/dtd/ejb-jar_2_0.dtd'>
<ejb-jar>
    <enterprise-beans>
        <entity>
            <ejb-name>Movie</ejb-name>
            <home>domain.entity.MovieHome</home>
            <remote>domain.entity.Movie</remote>
            <local-home>domain.entity.MovieLocalHome</local-home>
            <local>domain.entity.MovieLocal</local>
            <!-- <ejb-class>domain.entity.MovieCMPBean</ejb-class> -->
            <ejb-class>domain.entity.MovieBMPBean</ejb-class>
            <!-- <persistence-type>Container</persistence-type> -->
            <persistence-type>Bean</persistence-type>
            <prim-key-class>domain.entity.MoviePK</prim-key-class>
            <reentrant>False</reentrant>
            <!-- below is only required if BMP or explicit resources
                                                    needed-->
            <resource-ref>
                <res-ref-name>jdbc/ejbPool</res-ref-name>
                <res-type>javax.sql.DataSource</res-type>
                <res-auth>Container</res-auth>
            </resource-ref>
            <!--
            the following is only for CMP
            <cmp-version>2.x</cmp-version>
            <abstract-schema-name>MovieBean</abstract-schema-name>
            <cmp-field> <field-name>director</field-name> </cmp-field>
            <cmp-field> <field-name>title</field-name> </cmp-field>
            <!-- put other fields here -->
            <query>
                <query-method>
                    <method-name>findByDirector</method-name>
                    <method-params>
                        <method-param>java.lang.String</method-param>
                    </method-params>
                </query-method>
                <ejb-ql>
                    <![CDATA[
                    SELECT OBJECT(a) FROM MovieBean AS a WHERE
                    director = ?1]]>
                </ejb-ql>
```

```
        </query>
        put other queries here
        -->
    </entity>
  </enterprise-beans>
  <assembly-descriptor>
    <container-transaction>
        <method>
            <ejb-name>Movie</ejb-name>
            <method-intf>Local</method-intf>
            <method-name>*</method-name>
        </method>
        <method>
            <ejb-name>Movie</ejb-name>
            <method-intf>Remote</method-intf>
            <method-name>*</method-name>
        </method>
        <trans-attribute>Required</trans-attribute>
    </container-transaction>
  </assembly-descriptor>
</ejb-jar>
```

The `<res-auth>` specifies the authentication required for the database connection. If the value of this tag is `Container` then the deployer will configure the authorization as part of the deployment descriptor. If the value is `Application` then the EJB has to specify the exact username/password for the connection.

Finally the assembly-descriptor section of the deployment descriptor specifies whether transaction management is required for the beans and, if so, how it is managed and which methods require such a service. `Remote` and `Local` interfaces' methods have been flagged as requiring container-managed transactional support. The wildcard (*) is used to indicate that all methods need transactional support.

Listing 22.4 shows that the descriptor follows CMP version `2.x`. The database schema name is `MovieBean` with a set of field names (columns in the database). The descriptor uses EJB-QL to achieve implementation of the `findByDirector()` method. The EJB-QL query is enclosed in standard XML CDATA keywords to instruct the XML parser to ignore the content of the query. This is necessary because the content of the query may have XML-reserved characters such as less than (<), greater than (>), and other characters.

Session Beans   22.1.3

Session beans represent business logic and business activities. Session beans manipulate entity beans. The main difference between a session bean and an entity bean is the lifespan of the bean. A session bean lives only for the duration of the session whereas an entity bean may live much longer. A session bean is not persistent. It is maintained by the server in memory for the duration of the connection/session.

There are two types of session bean based on their ability to maintain state between invocations. A **stateless session bean** is a bean that serves requests but does not maintain any information state between each request. This is reminiscent of a web server that does not differentiate between the first and subsequent requests. By comparison, a **stateful session bean** has the ability to remember states between requests and therefore is able to enrich the interactions with clients. Second and subsequent client requests to the server can result in different pages being displayed.

Examples of stateless session beans are: (1) a request to download a file from a web server, (2) a web query to a search engine, (3) a web crawler that gathers information based on a specific query, or (4) a translation engine to translate a given text or web page to another language.

Listing 22.5 MovieActor's Deployment Descriptor (ejb-jar.xml) – Session Beans

> Deployment descriptor, ejb-jar.xml, for MovieApplication - Session Beans

```
<!-- this needs to be joined with previous ejb-jar entries -->
<ejb-jar>
   <enterprise-beans>
      <session>
         <ejb-name>MovieSearcher</ejb-name>
         <home>control.MovieSearcherHome</home>
         <remote>control.MovieSearcher</remote>
         <ejb-class>control.MovieSearcherBean</ejb-class>
         <!-- This is for stateless session bean
         <session-type>Stateless</session-type>
         -->
         <session-type>Stateful</session-type>
         <transaction-type>Container</transaction-type>
         <env-entry>
            <description>
               This is an example of passing environment
               variable to bean.
            </description>
            <!--
               The JNDI location identifiable via
               java:comp/env/mycategory/myfield.
            -->
            <env-entry-name>mycategory/myfield</env-entry-name>
            <env-entry-type>java.lang.String</env-entry-type>
            <env-entry-value>Here is the Value</env-entry-value>
         </env-entry>
      </session>
   </enterprise-beans>
</ejb-jar>
```

Examples of stateful session beans are: (1) a shopping cart that maintains a list of items ordered throughout the shopping exercise, (2) a software update manager that remembers selected updates that the client requested before downloading and installing them as a batch, (3) an online doctor that diagnoses an illness by requesting the patient to answer mutiple questions, or (4) an online help system that guides the user through a sequence of questions to determine the problem.

The container determines if its deployment descriptor if a bean is stateless or stateful. This is done in an entry for `session-type` (Listing 22.5). Stateful session beans are seen as normal Java objects in a Java application. The container manages all the necessary background work to handle the availability of the beans.

Business Components for Java   22.2

In the PCMEF framework, business components correspond to the domain (`entity` and `mediator`) and to `foundation` layers. In EJB, business components consist of session and entity beans (and message-driven beans not discussed in Section 22.1). In Oracle's **Business Components for Java** (BC4J), business components are known as **entity objects**. Unlike EJB, BC4J also supports **view objects**. As a result, BC4J enables quick generation of fully functional application modules complete with the presentation layer.

Much of the processing in an enterprise application consists of routine create–read–update–delete (CRUD) operations on the content of business components. Modern integrated development environments (IDEs) are capable of generating code and building applications based on the definitions of business components. The definitions can be obtained from a schema for a database, from an eXtensible Markup Language (XML) schema, or similar sources of metadata information.

IDEs, such as Oracle's JDeveloper, provide design-time wizards, component editors and a programming environment to generate executable Java code and XML code for business components (Bonazzi and Stokol, 2001; Lakshman, 2002). The application code is automatically generated and it can be regenerated at will. Once generated, it can be further customized and integrated into the overall application.

Creating Entity Components   22.2.1

An **entity object** is an in-memory representation of database data – its definition, storage characteristics, and associated business rules. An entity object can be automatically generated based on a database table, view (i.e. relational table view) or based on a union of multiple tables and/or views.

The generation of entity objects using JDeveloper-like IDEs relies on the same object-relational mapping rules as applied in the EM case study and described in Section 10.2.2. However, the EM iterations in this book have not taken advantage of a business components framework, such as EJB or BC4J. For educational reasons, the EM case study elected to implement business components from scratch and in its own way. This allowed an explanation of the PCMEF framework and various crucial patterns, such as *Identity Map*, *Data Mapper*, and *Lazy Load* (Section 15.3). Conceivably, EM could employ an IDE to generate business components and then customize and reprogram them to suit specific EM needs.

A BC4J-generated business components application consists of Java classes and XML files. The application can access data in a relational database, cache entity objects, and render them to a screen as view objects. Creating an entity object entails generation of a Java source and a corresponding XML file. The Java file provides the implementation of the entity component. The Java implementation class uses an XML parser to understand the format of the entity component as well as the applied object-relational mapping and any business rules that the entity object must obey.

XML for entity components

Just as Java is the principal language for Internet-age applications and SQL is the principal language for accessing databases, **XML** is the dominant language for data exchange. XML is a document markup language. As in the typesetting industry, the term 'markup' is anything that instructs how a document is to be printed (rendered) but the printed text itself does not render any markup instructions.

An **XML document** consists, therefore, of textual data (to be rendered) and markup data (not to be rendered). As a **markup language**, XML describes what part of the document is textual data, what part is markup data, and what is the meaning of markup elements and attributes. The meaning of markup data is defined by means of *tag* names. Hence, the content of an XML document is *self-documenting*.

Unlike HTML, XML itself does not define the document formatting rules. A separate XML Stylesheet Language (XSL) is used for this purpose. Also unlike HTML, XML does not define a fixed set of allowed tags. Whereas HTML is mainly a document formatting language, XML is a document representation and exchange language. Because the format of an XML document is not fixed, the document can be modified in the exchange process between senders and recipients of it. New tags can be recognized. Unexpected tags can be ignored.

Listing 22.6 shows selected lines from the `Department.xml` file that defines the `Department` entity object. The XML element called `<Entity>` is the root of the document. It specifies that the `Department` entity object corresponds to the Oracle table called `DEPARTMENT` (Lines 7–9) and that its Java implementation file is called `DepartmentImpl` (Line 12).

The XML file has an `<Attribute>` element for each column in the `DEPARTMENT` table selected by the designer/programmer for object-relational mapping. The `<Attribute>` element in Lines 19–34 defines the properties of the `DepartmentCode` attribute. The properties include Java and SQL data types, whether or not the `null` value is allowed, the precision of the attribute, if the attribute is the primary key, etc.

The `<AccessorAttribute>` element (Lines 48–55) defines the available navigation (association) between the `Department` and `Employee` entity objects. The `<Key>` element (Lines 64–73) captures the fact that `DepartmentCode` is the primary key.

Listing 22.6 Entity object XML file – Department.xml

```
Department.xml (excerpt) for Department entity object

 4:      <Entity
 5:         Name="Department"
 6:         DBObjectType="table"
 7:         DBObjectName="DEPARTMENT"
 8:         AliasName="Department"
 9:         BindingStyle="Oracle"
10:         UseGlueCode="false"
11:         CodeGenFlag="4"
12:         RowClass="PSE2BusinessComponents.DepartmentImpl" >

19:      <Attribute
20:         Name="DepartmentCode"
21:         IsNotNull="true"
22:         Precision="3"
23:         Type="java.lang.String"
24:         ColumnName="DEPARTMENT_CODE"
25:         ColumnType="CHAR"
26:         SQLType="CHAR"
27:         TableName="DEPARTMENT"
28:         PrimaryKey="true"
29:         RetrievedOnUpdate="true"
30:         RetrievedOnInsert="true" >
31:         <DesignTime>
32:            <Attr Name="_DisplaySize" Value="3" />
33:         </DesignTime>
34:      </Attribute>
35:      <Attribute
36:         Name="DepartmentName"
...
47:      </Attribute>
48:      <AccessorAttribute
49:         Name="Employee"
50:         Association="PSE2BusinessComponents.
                                    FkEmploeeRefDepcodeAssoc"
51:         AssociationEnd="PSE2BusinessComponents.
                              FkEmploeeRefDepcodeAssoc.Employee"
52:         AssociationOtherEnd="PSE2BusinessComponents.
                           FkEmploeeRefDepcodeAssoc.Department"
53:         Type="oracle.jbo.RowIterator"
54:         IsUpdateable="false" >
55:      </AccessorAttribute>
...
64:      <Key
```

```
65:                    Name="PkDepartment" >
66:                    <AttrArray Name="Attributes">
67:                        <Item Value="PSE2BusinessComponents.Department.
                                                    DepartmentCode" />
68:                    </AttrArray>
69:                    <DesignTime>
70:                        <Attr Name="_DBObjectName" Value="PK_DEPARTMENT" />
71:                        <Attr Name="_isPrimary" Value="true" />
72:                    </DesignTime>
73:                </Key>
...
96:        </Entity>
```

Java for entity components

The Java implementation file for the entity object described in `Department.xml` is called `DepartmentImpl.java`. The file is automatically generated by IDE. Both the Java class and XML document can be modified to build a customized application. However, the generated default code for entity components is sufficient to build view components (Section 16.4.2) and generate a working application module (Section 16.4.3).

Listing 22.7 contains an excerpt from the code generated by IDE for `Department-Impl.java`. `DepartmentImpl` is a subclass of `oracle.jbo.server.EntityImpl` (Line 11). A significant part of the generated code is the `get()` and `set()` methods for all attributes in `DepartmentImpl`. For example, `getDepartmentName()` (Lines 72–75) calls `getAttributeInternal()`, inherited from `EntityImpl`, to access the value of `DepartmentName` held in the entity object. The Java object type that holds this attribute value is defined in the `<Attribute>` element of `Department.xml` (Listing 22.6). The `DEPARTMENTNAME` constant in Line 14 provides an integer value that serves as an index to a container (array) of attribute values within the `Department` entity object (Bonazzi and Stokol, 2001).

The `getEmployee()` (Lines 126–129) provides access to an entity object (`Employee`) associated with `Department`. This association is defined in the `<AccessorAttribute>` element of the XML document (Lines 48–55 in Listing 16.1).

The `createPrimaryKey()` method maintains the primary key in the `Department` entity object. The primary key is defined in the `<Key>` element of the XML document (Lines 64–73 in Listing 16.1).

22.2.2 Creating View Components

A Java application can benefit by obtaining standard CRUD functionality from business components. Without writing a single line of code, an application is able to display rows of data, to insert new data into a database, to delete data from the database, and update the database content. In the case of BC4J, view objects serve the purpose of providing the presentation layer to the application.

Listing 22.7 Entity object Java file – DepartmentImpl.java

```
DepartmentImpl.java (excerpt) for Department entity object

1:        package PSE2BusinessComponents;
2:        import oracle.jbo.server.EntityImpl;
...
11:       public class DepartmentImpl extends EntityImpl
12:       {
13:          protected static final int DEPARTMENTCODE = 0;
14:          protected static final int DEPARTMENTNAME = 1;
15:          protected static final int EMPLOYEE = 2;
16:          protected static final int OUTMESSAGE = 3;
...
72:          public String getDepartmentName()
73:          {
74:             return (String)getAttributeInternal(DEPARTMENTNAME);
75:          }
...
81:          public void setDepartmentName(String value)
82:          {
83:             setAttributeInternal(DEPARTMENTNAME, value);
84:          }
126:         public RowIterator getEmployee()
127:         {
128:            return (RowIterator)getAttributeInternal(EMPLOYEE);
129:         }
...
145:         public static Key createPrimaryKey(String departmentCode)
146:         {
147:            return new Key(new Object[] {departmentCode});
148:      }
153: }
```

A **view object** represents a visualization of a SQL query on a database. The query can result in a filtered and sorted subset of attributes from one or more entity objects. Obtaining data from multiple entity objects is analogous to performing a join operation on database tables.

A separate concept of **view link** allows visualization of a master–detail relationship, such as between an invoice and invoice lines or between department and employees. The visualization of a master–detail relationship uses a separate view object (called the master view), which provides the master object as a context for all its detail (child) objects. The detail information changes when a different active master object is requested and displayed

XML for view components

Listing 22.8 shows selected lines from the DepartmentView.xml file that defines the DepartmentView view object. The root element called <ViewObject> specifies the

SQL query (Lines 6–8) for `DepartmentView`. The `<EntityUsage>` element informs which entity object is associated with this view object. The `<ViewAttribute>` elements define attributes of the entity object to be 'viewed'. The `<ViewLinkAccessor>` elements specify view links that the view object may use to produce master–detail relationships.

Listing 22.8 View object XML file – DepartmentView.xml

```
DepartmentView.xml (excerpt) for DepartmentView view object
 4:    <ViewObject
 5:       Name="DepartmentView"
 6:       SelectList="Department.DEPARTMENT_CODE,
 7:          Department.DEPARTMENT_NAME"
 8:       FromList="DEPARTMENT Department"
 9:       BindingStyle="Oracle"
10:       CustomQuery="false"
11:       ComponentClass="PSE2BusinessComponents.DepartmentViewImpl"
 . . .
25:       <EntityUsage
26:          Name="Department"
27:          Entity="PSE2BusinessComponents.Department" >
 . . .
32:       </EntityUsage>
33:       <ViewAttribute
34:          Name="DepartmentCode"
35:          IsNotNull="true"
36:          EntityAttrName="DepartmentCode"
37:          EntityUsage="Department"
38:          AliasName="DEPARTMENT_CODE"
39:          ColumnType="VARCHAR2" >
 . . .
48:       <ViewLinkAccessor
49:          Name="EmployeeView"
50:          ViewLink="PSE2BusinessComponents.FkEmploeeRefDepcodeLink"
51:          Type="oracle.jbo.RowIterator"
52:          IsUpdateable="false" >
53:       </ViewLinkAccessor>
 . . .
60:    </ViewObject>
```

Java for view components

Java for view components inherits most of its code from the IDE class library. In the case of BC4J, the parent class is called `ViewObjectImpl` (Listing 22.9). The provided functionality includes the sort order for displayed rows of information, the search criteria to restrict the number of rows displayed, placing the row iterator on a particular row object (first, last, next), etc.

Listing 22.9 View object Java file – DepartmentViewImpl.java

```
DepartmentViewImpl.java for DepartmentView view object

package PSE2BusinessComponents;
import oracle.jbo.server.ViewObjectImpl;

public class DepartmentViewImpl extends ViewObjectImpl
{
    public DepartmentViewImpl()
    {
    }
}
```

Creating the Application Module   22.2.3

An **application module** for business components uses the definitions of entity and view objects in order to provide an application with default functionality. The module is generated by BC4J. The generated code is able to establish a connection with a database and to give a transactional context to operations on the database. The module can be deployed in the middle tier, for example as an EJB.

As in the case of entity and view components, the application module is defined by a pair of XML document and Java file. The module specifies what views are available and integrates the views in a single framework. Figures 22.3 and 22.4 are examples of two views executed from within the generated application module. Figure 22.3 shows a simple view of an OutMessage entity object. Figure 22.4 is a master–detail view that shows the list of Outmessage objects created by the master Entity object.

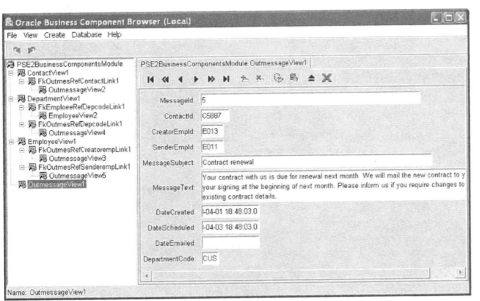

Figure 22.3
Application module showing a simple view
Source: Screenshot of Oracle Business Component Browser from www.otn.oracle.com, reproduced by permission of Oracle Corporation

Figure 22.4
Application
module showing a
master–detail view
Source: Screenshot
of Oracle Business
Component
Browser from
www.otn.oracle.com,
reproduced by
permission of Oracle
Corporation

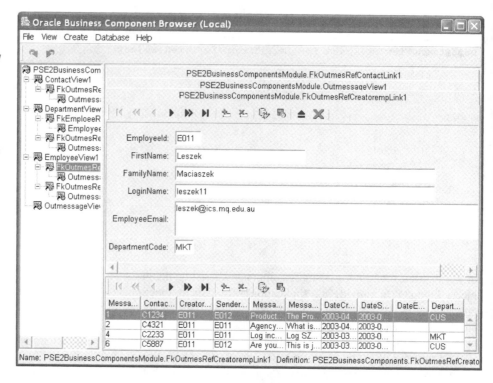

Summary

1. A *business component* is a reusable object that occupies the middle tier between the user interface and the database. Two representative component technologies are: (1) the *Enterprise JavaBeans* (EJB), representing the Java world, and (2) *Business Components for Java* (BC4J), representing the database world.

2. The components are called *beans* in EJB. EJB offers *entity beans* to contain data and *session beans* to represent transactions, security, and similar functions. EJB relies on *JavaBeans* for GUI components.

3. EJB is the main ingredient of the Java 2 Enterprise Edition (J2EE) framework. The beans live in a J2EE *application server*, commonly referred to as a J2EE *container*. Each bean is treated as a *distributed object*.

4. *Entity beans* are the most used beans in J2EE applications. They represent business objects. They are *persistent*.

5. *Session beans* represent business logic and business activities. They manipulate entity beans. A session bean lives only for the duration of the session whereas an entity bean is persistent. Session beans can be *stateless* or *stateful*.

6. In BC4J business components are known as *entity objects*. Unlike EJB, BC4J also supports *view objects*. A BC4J-generated business components application consists of Java classes and XML files.

7. An *entity object* is an in-memory representation of database data – its definition, storage characteristics, and associated business rules. An entity object can be automatically generated based on a database table, view (i.e. relational table view) or based on a union of multiple tables and/or views.

8. A *view object* represents a visualization of a SQL query on a database. The query can result in a filtered and sorted subset of attributes from one or more entity objects.

9. A BC4J *application module* for business components uses the definitions of entity and view objects in order to generate an application with default functionality. The generated code is able to establish a connection with a database and to give a transactional context to operations on the database.

Key Terms

application module	747	entity bean	732, 735
application server	732	entity object	741
BC4J	*See* Business Components for Java	IS tier	731
bean	729	J2EE tier	731
Bean-Managed Persistent bean	735	JavaBeans	730
BL tier	732	markup language	742
BMP	*See* Bean-Managed Persistent bean	message bean	732
business component	729	persistent bean	735
Business Components for Java	729, 741	serialization	733
Client tier	731	session bean	732, 739
CMP	*See* Container-Managed Persistent bean	stateful session bean	740
container	730, 732	stateless session bean	740
Container-Managed Persistent bean	735	UI tier	731
distributed object	732	view link	745
EIS tier	731	view object	741, 745
EJB	*See* Enterprise JavaBeans	XML	742
EJB architecture	732	XML document	742
Enterprise JavaBeans	729, 730		

Review Questions

1. Are business components reusable? Explain.

2. Are business components distributed? Explain.

3. List and discuss the differences between EJB entity beans and BC4J entity objects.

4. EJB uses JavaBeans for GUI components. BC4J view objects are GUI components. What are the differences between JavaBeans and view objects?

5. What is the sequence of steps that the client application needs to perform to run the EJB?

6. What components need to be defined to implement an Enterprise Bean?

7. What are the main steps for developing a BC4J application?

8. Search the Internet for the latest developments and new technologies in business components. Are there any changes of direction? How do EJB and BC4J fit in any new trends?

Chapter

23

Iteration 3 Annotated Code

This chapter presents the code related to the *data engineering* concerns in the Email Management case study. The presentation style employed in this chapter is similar to the approach used in Chapter 18. Snapshots of class diagrams (produced by the yWorks' **yDoc** tool) are presented and accompanied by **Javadoc** documentation. The code that has not changed from the previous iterations is largely omitted from the discussion in this chapter. The complete code for this and the previous iterations can be viewed and downloaded from the book's website.

The chapter begins with the code overview for Iteration 3 followed by detailed visits to individual packages and classes. Particular emphasis is placed on explaining classes and code supporting new functional as well as architectural requirements, such as the daily summary report or the unit of work.

In comparison with Chapters 13 and 18, this chapter includes a separate discussion of the database code (not already covered in the earlier chapters of Part 4). This demonstrates the significant role played by the database code in Iteration 3 in achieving *database security and integrity* and in providing *transactional concurrency control* for the application. Most modifications from Iteration 2 are in the mediator package, where all user transactions are initiated.

Code Overview

The EM Iteration 3 is the final iteration for the case study. This iteration concentrates on the data engineering issues and addresses some unresolved concerns with regard to the PCMEF+ architectural framework. However, the framework remains intact and the number and names of packages are the same as in previous iterations.

Comparing with Iteration 2, major changes introduced in Iteration 3 are:

- the introduction of `MUnitOfWork` to provide *transactional support* for the application
- all SQL code is moved to the database server in the form of *stored procedures/functions*
- all user transactions are initiated in `MModerator`
- the *authorization rules* are applied to all activities to restrict the type of outmessages viewable by employees
- authorization rules can only be modified by the user in the role of the security/database administrator
- the functionality of producing daily *summary reports* is implemented
- outmessages can be modified before emailing.

Figure 23.1 shows the final class model for Iteration 3. Changes from Iteration 2 include additional classes (blue colored). The new classes implement viewing of authorization rules, daily reporting, unit of work, and other minor changes due to refactoring. With the exception of a few associations, the role names for associations have been removed to improve readability of the diagram.

Package Acquaintance

The only additional interface introduced in the `acquaintance` package in Figure 23.2 is `IAReportEntry`. The interface assists in generating daily summary reports of emailing activities. It is also possible to put `IAAuthorizationRule` as an additional interface in this package, although this is not implemented in Iteration 3 and is left for the user as an exercise.

Other interfaces declared in the `acquaintance` package are the same as in Iteration 2.

Interface IAReportEntry

`IAReportEntry` is an interface that signifies a single entry of a report row in the database. A report entry consists of contact information and the statistics regarding this employee's outmessages, such as the number of created outmessages or the number of outstanding outmessages for a specified date. Figure 23.3 shows the definition of the `IAReportEntry` interface.

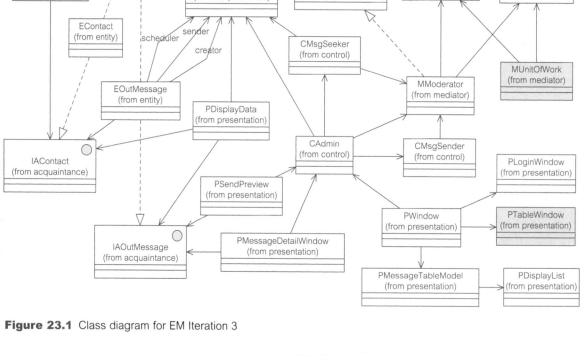

Figure 23.1 Class diagram for EM Iteration 3

Figure 23.2
Package
Acquaintance
and its classes
in EM 3

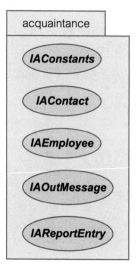

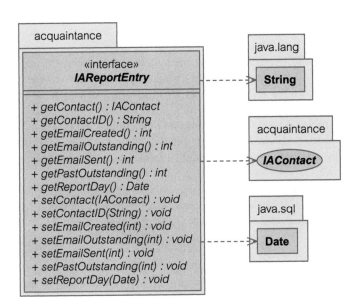

Figure 23.3
Interface
IAReportEntry
in EM 3

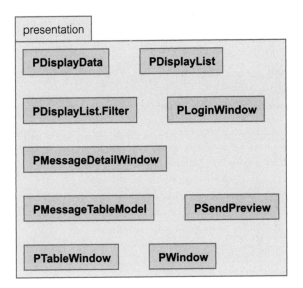

Figure 23.4
Package
Presentation and
its classes in EM 3

Package Presentation

23.3

An extra class is introduced to the presentation package to make a total of eight classes and one inner class as shown in Figure 23.4. The extra class PTableWindow is used to display **authorization rules** as well as daily reports.

23.3.1 Class PWindow

The PWindow's public signature has not been modified from its original version (Figure 18.6). Additional implementation and changes, however, are represented by private methods to PWindow. PWindow becomes a **façade** for various presentation package classes, such as PTableWindow.

Construction of a PWindow follows the same procedure as explained in Section 18.3.1. An association to CAdmin is established, login dialog requests user identification, and data is retrieved to fill appropriate fields. Additional fields such as report contact list are filled in this stage as well.

The following discussion addresses three subflows (Section 19.2.3) of the use case document for Iteration 3. These are subflows S8 (the report generation feature), S1 (the authorization procedure), and S7 (the outmessage modification feature).

Populating report contact list

The use case Produce Daily Report provides an option for the user to generate **daily summary reports** about email activities for specific contacts only. The method populate-ReportContact() in PWindow is used to achieve this (Listing 23.1). The list of contacts is retrieved from admin via its listContacts() method (Line 53). The list-Contacts() method returns a set of IAContact. The names in the contact list are constructed from IAContact's family name and first name (Line 56).

Listing 23.1 Method populateReportContact( ) in Pwindow to populate report contact list

```
Method populateReportContact() in Pwindow to populate report contact
list

49:      private void populateReportContact(){
50:          synchronized(rptContactCmb){
51:              rptContactCmb.removeAllItems();
52:              rptContactCmb.addItem("");
53:              Iterator it = admin.listContacts().iterator();
54:              while(it.hasNext()){
55:                  IAContact ctc = (IAContact) it.next();
56:                  String contactName = ctc.getFamilyName() +", "+
                         ctc.getFirstName();
57:                  rptContactCmb.addItem(contactName);
58:              }
59:          }
60:      }
```

The user may want to generate a report for all contacts rather than for a particular contact. This can be achieved by allowing an empty field in the rptContactCmb combo box (Line 52).

Report window

There are many ways possible to generate a report window. The approach implemented in Iteration 3 takes advantage of a **utility class** created and filled with appropriate data. This is a dynamic and reusable approach. The data needs to be constructed and passed to the utility class beforehand. The utility class does not have any knowledge regarding actions that need to be applied on data.

Listing 23.2 shows how the report is constructed. The data is encapsulated in an `AbstractTableModel` and provided to a utility class called `PTableWindow` (Line 499). At the beginning, there is a need to find out whether the user wants to generate a report for a particular date (i.e. if the `dayTxt` field is filled, Lines 483–488). Report details are retrieved for the date given or, in the case of error, for today's date (Line 487). Similarly, there is a need to know if the report has to be retrieved for all possible contacts or only one particular contact (Lines 489–496).

If the user has indicated that the report is for a particular date without specifying the contact id, then all report details for the date specified are retrieved (Line 492). If the contact id is provided by the user as a report condition, then the program has to retrieve `ContactID`. But `rptContactCmb` returns the contact name, not contact id (Line 489) (see the `populateReportContact()` method in Listing 23.1, Line 56). The contact name has to be converted into a contact id because the method in `CAdmin` requires a contact id (Lines 494–495).

`AbstractTableModel` is constructed from the list of report details by invoking `populateReportTable()` (Line 498). This model is passed to an instance of `PTableWindow` along with appropriate title text and other parameters. The `Print` and `Close` strings (Line 499) are to inform `PTableWindow` to construct two buttons with the given labels. This shows how `PTableWindow` can generate buttons dynamically.

There is no point in generating a button without attaching an appropriate listener to it. Lines 502–516 specify two listeners to be attached to the two buttons created by `PTableWindow`. The first listener (Lines 502–511) monitors the print command. The second listener (Lines 512–516) simply closes the `PTableWindow` instance.

Since the printing action may take a long time, it is advisable to encapsulate such an activity into a *thread* of its own. This will remove from the painting thread the burden of having to wait for the printing command. Note that the printing thread is the same thread as used to call the `actionPerformed()` method upon a mouse-click event.

Listing 23.2 Method reportBtnActionPerformed( ) in PWindow to display report window

```
Method reportBtnActionPerformed() in PWindow to display report window

480: private void reportBtnActionPerformed(java.awt.event.
                                              ActionEvent evt) {
481:        Collection reports = null;
482:        java.sql.Date day = null;
483:        try{
```

```
484:                 java.util.Date d = java.text.DateFormat.
                                                getDateInstance(
                     java.text.DateFormat.SHORT).parse(dayTxt.getText());
485:             day = new java.sql.Date(d.getTime());
486:         }catch(Exception exc){
487:             day = new java.sql.Date(System.currentTimeMillis());
488:         }
489:         String contactID = rptContactCmb.getSelectedItem().
                                                toString();
490:         if(contactID != null && contactID.trim().length() == 0)
                 contactID = null;
491:
492:         if(contactID == null) reports = admin.getReport(day);
493:         else{
494:             contactID = getContactIDFromName(contactID);
495:             reports = admin.getReport(day,contactID);
496:         }
497:
498:         AbstractTableModel md = populateReportTable(reports);
499:         final PTableWindow win = new PTableWindow(this,true,md,
                 "Activity Report",
                 "Report generated "+day+
                     (contactID==null?"":("on "+contactID)),
                 new String[]{"Print","Close"});
500:
502:         win.addActionListener(0, new java.awt.event.
                                                ActionListener(){
503:             public void actionPerformed(java.awt.event.
                                                ActionEvent evt){
504:                 //don't bog the painting thread
505:                 (new Thread(){
506:                     public void run(){
507:                         print(win);
508:                     }
509:                 }).start();
510:             }
511:         });
512:         win.addActionListener(1, new java.awt.event.
                                                ActionListener(){
513:             public void actionPerformed(java.awt.event.
                                                ActionEvent evt){
514:                 win.close();
515:             }
516:         });
517:         win.show();
518: }
```

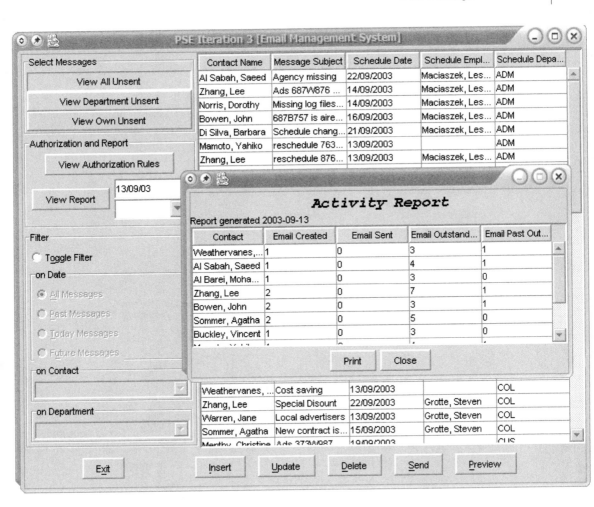

Figure 23.5 Daily report window

Activity report

The **activity report** (called as daily summary report) is shown in Figure 23.5. The report presents the number of outmessages created, updated, and sent by employees on a particular day. The calculations are done by a stored procedure in Listing 23.44 (see p. 803). The implementation leading to the displaying of the report is explained above in Section 23.3.1.

Another new window in Iteration 3, to display authorization rules, has been discussed in Chapter 20 and shown in Figure 20.11.

Printing the report

The logic to print reports is placed in `PTableWindow`. Printing can be performed on data extracted from GUI components or alternatively the printing logic could simply use certain features of GUI components to perform the printing. The second approach is the WYSIWYG (what you see is what you get) principle. This approach relies on the painting logic to perform the job. Iteration 3 implements a mixture of the first and second approach. This is explained in Section 23.3.2.

Listing 23.3 illustrates how the printing logic is placed in PTableWindow and therefore relieves PWindow from any knowledge of printing. PWindow has no influence over the layout or content of the print.

Listing 23.3 Method print( ) in PWindow

Method print() in PWindow
520:    private void print(Printable target){
521:        PrinterJob pj = PrinterJob.getPrinterJob();
522:        pj.setPrintable(target);
523:        if(pj.printDialog()){
524:            try{
525:                pj.print();
526:            }catch(Exception printEx){
527:                printEx.printStackTrace();
528:            }
529:        }
530:    }

PTableWindow, which implements the Printable interface, is fed into the print() method's parameter as the target object (Line 520). The print job is acquired from PrinterJob (Line 512). The printer job is basically a job to be submitted to a print service that contains instructions to the printer hardware. The printable target (PTable-Window) is then registered to the printer job instance (Line 522). This indicates that the printable target is fully responsible for providing all information regarding what to print to the printer job.

Before the printing is performed, the user is given a chance to select the format for the printing (Line 523). This is done by displaying a print dialog box from which the user can specify the printer location, paper format, etc.

Populating the report table

Raw report data, retrieved from CAdmin (Listing 23.2, Line 498), needs to be converted into a format suitable for diplay on screen by PTableWindow. The populateTableModel() method does this (Listing 23.4). The method starts by creating an inner class of DefaultTableModel. This class provides all necessary implementations of Abstract-TableModel. Editing in the DailyReport table needs to be restricted as there is no point in allowing the user to edit the table (Lines 552–554).

The appropriate columns for the DailyReport table are registered on Lines 557–561. Finally, the table model is populated with appropriate entries extracted from the given IAReportEntry list (Lines 562–567).

Listing 23.4 Method populateTableModel( ) in PWindow

```
Method populateTableModel() in PWindow

550:    private AbstractTableModel populateReportTable(Collection
                                                        reports){
551:        DefaultTableModel md = new DefaultTableModel(){
552:            public boolean isCellEditable(int row, int col){
553:                return false;
554:            }
555:        };
556:
557:        md.addColumn("Contact");
558:        md.addColumn("Email Created");
559:        md.addColumn("Email Sent");
560:        md.addColumn("Email Outstanding");
561:        md.addColumn("Email Past Outstanding");
562:        Iterator it = reports.iterator();
563:        while(it.hasNext()){
564:            IAReportEntry re = (IAReportEntry) it.next();
565:            String contactName = re.getContact().getFamilyName() +
                    ", "+re.getContact().getFirstName();
566:            md.addRow(new Object[]{
                    contactName,
                    ""+re.getEmailCreated(),
                    ""+re.getEmailSent(),
                    ""+re.getEmailOutstanding(),
                    ""+re.getPastOutstanding()});
567:        }
568:        return md;
569:    }
```

Showing the authorization window

The **authorization window** uses the same principle as the report window generation. It uses PTableWindow to display the authorization rules. This demonstrates the usefulness of PTableWindow as a utility class. With slight modifications to the ways data is constructed, the same PTableWindow can be used to display the content of various windows.

Listing 23.5 shows how the authorization window is constructed. Only a system administrator (an employee of the ADM department) can modify authorization rules. This modification permission is stored in the database and accessible to canEditAuthoriza-tionRules() from CAdmin (Line 617). The authorization rules are acquired from CAdmin through getAuthorizationRules() (Line 618). They are then returned as a map between 'from_department' and 'target_department' (Section 19.2.3, Table 19.1). The acquired authorization rules are converted into a data structure that can be understood by PTableWindow. This conversion happens in the invocation of the method construct-AuthorizationRules() (Line 619).

Listing 23.5 Method authorizationBtnActionPerformed( ) in PWindow

Method `authorizationBtnActionPerformed()` in PWindow

```
616:    private void authorizationBtnActionPerformed(ActionEvent
                                                      evt) {
617:        boolean canEdit = admin.canEditAuthorizationRules();
618:        Map authorization = admin.getAuthorizationRules();
619:        final DefaultTableModel md =
                constructAuthorizationRules(canEdit,authorization);
620:        String[] buttons = null;
621:        if(canEdit) buttons = new String[]{"Save","Close"};
622:        else buttons = new String[]{"Close"};
623:
624:        final PTableWindow win = new PTableWindow(this,true,md,
                "Authorization Rules",
                "Your department: "+admin.getEmployee().
                getDepartmentCode(), buttons);
625:        int closeIndex = 0;
626:        if(canEdit){
627:            closeIndex = 1;
628:            win.addActionListener(0, new java.awt.event.
                                                  ActionListener(){
629:                public void actionPerformed(ActionEvent evt){
630:                    (new Thread(){
631:                        public void run(){
632:                            saveAuthorizationRules(md);
633:                        }
634:                    }).start();
635:                }
636:            });
637:        }
638:        win.addActionListener(closeIndex, new ActionListener(){
639:            public void actionPerformed(ActionEvent evt){
640:                win.close();
641:            }
642:        });
645:        win.setDefaultRenderer(Object.class,
            new DefaultTableCellRenderer(){
646:            public Component getTableCellRendererComponent(JTable
            table,
647:            Object value,
648:            boolean isSelected,
649:            boolean hasFocus,
650:            int row,
651:            int column){
```

```
652:                    if(value != null){
653:                        javax.swing.JCheckBox ch = null;
654:                        if(value.toString().equals("true"))
                                ch = new javax.swing.JCheckBox("",true);
655:                        else if(value.toString().equals("false"))
                                ch = new javax.swing.JCheckBox("",false);
656:
657:                        if(ch == null)
                                return super.getTableCellRendererComponent(
                                    table,value,isSelected,hasFocus,row,column);
658:
660:                        if(isSelected)
                                    ch.setBackground(java.awt.Color.BLUE);
661:                        return ch;
662:                    }else
                            return super.getTableCellRendererComponent(
                                table,value,isSelected,hasFocus,row,column);
663:                }
664:            });
665:
668:        win.setDefaultEditor(Object.class,
                new DefaultCellEditor(new JCheckBox()));
669:
670:        win.show();
671:    }
```

Lines 620–624 construct PTableWindow for the purpose of the authorization window (this is similar to the approach taken for the report window (Section 23.3.1, Listing 23.2)). Instead of having the Print button, the authorization window has a Save button (Line 621). The Save button is visible only if the user has been identified as a member of the ADM department. If the employee is not allowed to modify the rules then the Save button is not visible and only the Close button is available (Lines 621–622).

Authorization rules are saved through the invocation of saveAuthorizationRules() (Line 632). This method is invoked inside a thread to provide a more responsive user experience.

The customization of PTableWindow to display the authorization matrix goes beyond making the table model exactly as done for the report window implementation. There is a need to display a richer GUI component in the table because the authorization window does not just contain simple text entries. This is achieved by overriding the rendering (painting) method. PTableWindow has such a method called setDefaultRenderer(). The client code needs to specify the class type for which the rendering customization is required and to provide the renderer for the type (Line 645).

Table rendering is performed by JTable by acquiring a component responsible to render the content of JTable from its list of TableCellRenderers (by invoking TableCellRenderer's getTableCellRendererComponent() method, Line 646).

Iteration 3 displays a set of checkboxes as the representation of the authorization matrix and this is achieved by returning an instance of JCheckBox (Lines 653–655). The checkboxes will be created only if the content to be displayed has a true/false value. If the value is other than true/false, then a default renderer registered in JTable is used (Lines 657 and 662). Visual improvement is also provided by coloring the current checkbox with a blue color when the checkbox is marked as selected (Line 660).

Because checkboxes are used as the content of the table window, there is also a need to register an editor in case the user needs to modify values in the checkboxes (Line 668). As mentioned earlier, editing can only be performed by a user from the ADM department.

Conversion from rule matrix to authorization table

Authorization rules retrieved from CAdmin are in the format of a map between 'from_department' and 'target_department'. It is necessary to convert this representation into a representation understandable to PTableWindow, which is an AbstractTableModel. The constructAuthorizationRules() method performs this conversion (Listing 23.6).

The constructed authorization window resembles closely the representation of the authorization matrix (Section 19.2.3, Table 19.1). This means the table is not editable in column 0 (Line 576). The table has the leftmost column and the heading to display the list of departments (Lines 580–589).

Once the construction of table layout is done, the table is ready to be filled with data contained in the map (Lines 592–609). The algorithm constructs an array of rows to represent rows in the table (Line 596). Each row contains the same number of columns, all of which have to have a value of either true or false. The true value represents a direct mapping between the 'from_department' (left side of the table) and 'target_department' (heading of the table). All rows are initially set to false to indicate that there is no such mapping (Line 598). A true value is inserted into the array if the mapping is detected (Lines 599–607, particularly Lines 601 and 606). Finally, the row is inserted as a row in the table via the addRow() method on Line 608.

Saving modified authorization rules

When a modification occurs on the authorization rules and saveAuthorizationRules() is executed (Listing 23.5, Line 632), an attempt to save the rules is performed as shown in Listing 23.7. The user is allowed to try to save multiple times if previous attempts resulted in an error (Line 676 and Lines 683–684).

The authorization rules stored in the modified AbstractTableModel need to be converted back to the representation understandable by CAdmin. Listing 23.6 converts Map (as returned by CAdmin) into AbstractTableModel, and Listing 23.7 reverses the conversion. The conversion is performed by the extractAuthorizationRules() method (Line 679). The converted Map is fed to CAdmin's saveAuthorizationRules() for further processing. This method may throw an exception to indicate that either the saving has failed or the user is in fact not allowed to modify authorization rules. Either way, the user is given an opportunity to keep trying to save the modified values (Lines 683–684).

Listing 23.6 Method constructAuthorizationRules( ) in PWindow

```
Method constructAuthorizationRules() in PWindow
```
```
573:     private DefaultTableModel constructAuthorizationRules(
                 final boolean canEdit, java.util.Map authorization){
574:        DefaultTableModel md = new DefaultTableModel(){
575:           public boolean isCellEditable(int row, int col){
576:               if(col == 0) return false;
577:               return canEdit;
578:           }
579:        };
580:        md.addColumn("Department");
581:
582:        //build the left and heading part of the table
583:        Iterator it = authorization.entrySet().iterator();
584:        List left = new LinkedList();
585:        while(it.hasNext()){
586:           Map.Entry e = (Map.Entry) it.next();
587:           md.addColumn(e.getKey());
588:           left.add(e.getKey());
589:        }
590:        //populate data
591:        it = authorization.entrySet().iterator();
592:        while(it.hasNext()){
593:           Map.Entry e = (Map.Entry) it.next();
594:           List l = (List) e.getValue();
595:           Iterator it2 = l.iterator();
596:           Object row[] = new Object[1+left.size()];
597:           row[0] = e.getKey();
598:           for(int i=left.size();i>0;i--) row[i] = new
                                                Boolean(false);
599:           while(it2.hasNext()){
600:               String match = it2.next().toString();
601:               int index = left.indexOf(match);
602:               if(index == -1){
603:                  System.out.println("WRONG value "+match+
                         " from "+row[0]);
604:                  continue;
605:               }
606:               row[index+1] = new Boolean(true);
607:           }
608:           md.addRow(row);
609:        }
610:        return md;
611:     }
```

Listing 23.7 Method saveAuthorizationRules( ) in PWindow

```
Method saveAuthorizationRules() in PWindow

674:    private void saveAuthorizationRules(AbstractTableModel
                                                            md){
675:       boolean tryAgain = true;
676:       while(tryAgain){
677:          tryAgain = false;
678:          try{
679:             java.util.Map extracted =
                                     extractAuthorizationRules(md);
680:             admin.saveAuthorizationRules(extracted);
681:          }catch(Exception exc){
683:             int ok = JOptionPane.showConfirmDialog(this,
                 "Error in saving modification, would you like to try
                                                            again?",
                 "Error saving Authorization",
                 JOptionPane.OK_CANCEL_OPTION);
684:             if(ok == JOptionPane.OK_OPTION) tryAgain = true;
685:          }
686:       }
687:    }
```

Conversion from authorization table to rule matrix

As just explained, values stored in the authorization table (AbstractTableModel) need to be converted into values understandable by CAdmin (Map). This conversion is performed by extractAuthorizationRules() shown in Listing 23.8.

Each row in the table is traversed and its key–value pair is inserted into a map (Line 695). However, only a mapping with a checked value in the table needs to be inserted into the authorization map. For this purpose, the table needs to be traversed and a value of 'true' will cause the insertion to be made with an appropriate key–value pair (Lines 697–702). The key–value pair is acquired from the column name of the table (left side of the table and its heading) as indicated by Lines 694 and 699, respectively.

Deleting an outmessage

Iteration 3 introduces the possibility that an employee is allowed to delete an outmessage provided s/he has the permission to do so according to the authorization matrix (Section 19.2.3, subflow S6). This is done by using PMessageDetailWindow to display the content of the outmessage and at the same time allowing the user to edit or delete the outmessage (Listing 23.9, Line 718).

Listing 23.8 Method extractAuthorizationRules( ) in PWindow

```
Method extractAuthorizationRules() in PWindow

690:     private java.util.Map extractAuthorizationRules(TableModel
                                                          model){
691:        java.util.Map authorization = new HashMap();
692:        int rows = model.getRowCount();
693:        for(int i=0;i<rows;i++){
694:           Object key = model.getValueAt(i, 0);
695:           authorization.put(key, new LinkedList());
696:           for(int j=1;j<rows+1;j++){
697:              if(model.getValueAt(i, j).toString().equals("true")){
698:                 LinkedList list = (LinkedList) authorization.
                                                              get(key);
699:                 list.add(model.getColumnName(j));
700:                 authorization.put(key, list);
701:                 System.out.println(key+" --> "+model.
                                                  getColumnName(j));
702:              }
703:           }
704:        }
705:        return authorization;
706:     }
```

Listing 23.9 Method deleteBtnActionPerformed( ) in PWindow

```
Method deleteBtnActionPerformed() in PWindow

711:     private void deleteBtnActionPerformed(ActionEvent evt) {
712:        int []rows=viewTable.getSelectedRows();
713:        if(rows.length == 0) return;
714:        boolean needRefreshing = false;
715:
716:        //confirm deletion of messages one at a time
717:        for(int i=0;i<rows.length;i++){
718:           PMessageDetailWindow msgWin =
                    new PMessageDetailWindow(this,true, admin,false);
719:           msgWin.setTarget((IAOutMessage)model.
                                             getRawObject(rows[i]));
720:           msgWin.show();
721:           needRefreshing |= msgWin.hasModified();
722:        }
723:        //refresh when everything finishes, save drawing time
724:        if(needRefreshing) refreshContent();
725:     }
```

When the `Delete` button is clicked, `PMessageDetailWindow` is shown for every selected outmessage in the table (Lines 712 and 718). When the outmessage is modified or deleted, the table is refreshed (Lines 721 and 724).

The method `setTarget()` of `PMessageDetailWindow` is invoked to change the content of the outmessage displayed on it. This window is a modal window and therefore does not allow the user to switch back to the main window while it is still active (Line 718 second parameter is true to indicate modality).

Modifying an outmessage

There is not much difference between outmessage deletion and outmessage modification in the implementation of `updateBtnActionPerformed()` shown in Listing 23.10. Outmessage modification (Section 19.2.3, subflow S7) uses `PMessageDetailWindow` with a slightly different flag (Line 734 fourth parameter has the value true).

Listing 23.10 Method updateBtnActionPerformed( ) in PWindow

```
Method updateBtnActionPerformed() in PWindow
```
```
727:     private void updateBtnActionPerformed(ActionEvent evt) {
728:         int []rows=viewTable.getSelectedRows();
729:         if(rows.length == 0) return;
730:
731:         boolean needRefreshing = false;
732:         //show the content of each selected message
733:         for(int i=0;i<rows.length;i++){
734:             PMessageDetailWindow msgWin =
                     new PMessageDetailWindow(this,true, admin,true);
735:             msgWin.setTarget((IAOutMessage)model.
                     getRawObject(rows[i]));
736:             msgWin.show();
737:             needRefreshing |= msgWin.hasModified();
738:         }
739:         //refresh when everything finishes, save drawing time
740:         if(needRefreshing) refreshContent();
741:     }
```

The fourth parameter specifies whether the outmessage displayed by `PMessage-DetailWindow` is editable. Only modified outmessages will trigger repainting of the outmessage table (Lines 737 and 740).

Creating an outmessage

Creation of a new outmessage relies on `PMessageDetailWindow` as a convenient class that is capable of displaying the content of an outmessage. Listing 23.11 shows how `PMessageDetailWindow` is constructed similar to an edit action in Listing 23.10. An exception, however, is that the constructed `PMessageDetailWindow` does not have a pre-existing outmessage as its content, such as the one shown in Listing 23.10 Line 735 (`setTarget()` method). Instead, an empty outmessage is constructed for this purpose via invocation of `showNewMessage()` (Line 840).

Listing 23.11 Method createNewMsgBtnActionPerformed() in PWindow

```
Method createNewMsgBtnActionPerformed() in PWindow

837:     private void createNewMsgBtnActionPerformed(ActionEvent evt) {
838:         PMessageDetailWindow msgWin =
                 new PMessageDetailWindow(this,true, admin,true);
839:         msgWin.setTitle("Create New Message");
840:         msgWin.showNewMessage();
841:         msgWin.show();
842:         if(msgWin.hasModified()) refreshContent();
843:     }
```

The outmessage table in the main window will be refreshed only if the insertion is successful (Line 842).

Class PTableWindow

23.3.2

`PTableWindow` serves as a **utility class** to display a generic table in a window. This class is capable of generating a number of buttons dynamically. Each button can have multiple listeners.

Listing 23.12 shows the method summary for this class. This class informs the client about the state of the button clicked via its `getReturnStatus()`. Printing capability is provided by the `print()` method. Printing on this class is performed by displaying the content of the table in a simple table format to the print job. Various default editors and renderers for the table can be modified by calling `setDefaultEditor()` and `setDefaultRenderer()`.

As this class is capable of remembering the state of the user's actions, a manual window dispose method is provided to allow the client to control the timing of the window disposal (via the `setDisposeWhenClose()` method).

Dynamic registration of buttons

`PTableWindow` is capable of supporting **dynamic buttons**. This is done in its constructor as shown in Listing 23.13. Lines 22–39 show a standard initialization of properties. When no button is provided for the window, a default `Close` button is created automatically (Lines 41–50). However, if a set of button texts is provided in the parameter, then the dynamic buttons are generated as shown in Lines 55–66.

Listing 23.12 PTableWindow method summary

void	**addActionListener**(int buttonIndex, java.awt.event. ActionListener listener) Allow clients to attach actions to a particular button.
void	**close**() Allow the client to close the window at any time.
int	**getReturnStatus**() Return the status acquired in this window (once it has been closed).
static void	**Main**(java.lang.String[] args) Testing for this window.
int	**print**(java.awt.Graphics graphics, java.awt.print.PageFormat pageFormat, int pageIndex) Print the window as user sees it.
void	**setDefaultEditor**(java.lang.Class c, javax.swing.table.TableCellEditor editor) Change the editor for a component in the table shown in this window.
void	**setDefaultRenderer**(java.lang.Class c, javax.swing.table.TableCellRenderer renderer) Change the renderer for a component in the table shown in this window.
void	**setDisposeWhenClose**(boolean dispose) Allow client to indicate whether the window need to be disposed automatically whenever it is no longer needed.

Listing 23.13 Constructor of PTableWindow

```
Constructor of PTableWindow

33:      public PTableWindow(Frame parent, boolean modal,
            AbstractTableModel model,String title,String subtitle,
            String[] buttons) {
34:          super(parent, modal);
35:          this.model = model;
36:          initComponents();
37:          titleLbl.setText(title);
38:          subtitleLbl.setText(subtitle);
39:
40:          //no buttons given, so provide a default close button
41:          if(buttons == null){
42:              javax.swing.JButton btn = new javax.swing.
                                               JButton("Close");
43:              btn.setToolTipText("Close this window");
44:              btn.addActionListener(new ActionListener() {
```

```
45:                        public void actionPerformed(ActionEvent evt) {
46:                            doClose(0);
47:                        }
48:                    });
49:                    buttonPanel.add(btn);
50:                    return;
51:                }else{ //construct buttons dynamically
52:                    for(int i=0;i<buttons.length;i++){
53:                        javax.swing.JButton btn = new JButton(buttons[i]);
58:                        btn.setActionCommand(""+i);
59:                        btn.addActionListener(new java.awt.event.
                                                   ActionListener() {
60:                            public void actionPerformed(ActionEvent evt) {
61:                                doClose(Integer.parseInt(evt.
                                                   getActionCommand()));
62:                            }
63:                        });
64:                        buttonPanel.add(btn);
65:                    }
66:                }
67:            }
```

Each button created would have the label as indicated by the parameter `buttons` (Line 53). An action command is used to distinguish buttons (Line 58). The action command is used to identify which button is clicked and is also used for listener registration via `addActionListener()` (explained later) and for the value of the return status `getReturnStatus()` (explained later).

Adding listeners to dynamically generated buttons

As buttons are added dynamically to the `PTableWindow`, adding **listeners** after the construction of buttons becomes an interesting challenge. Remember that the buttons are created dynamically and it is difficult to find out which button to refer to for proper listener registration. Also, `PTableWindow` does not return the list of buttons it has created as doing so is not possible in its constructor.

A solution to this problem turns out to be quite simple. All buttons need to be placed into a container that can be referred to based on their order of creation. This way, the first button in the list represents the first index of the `buttons` parameter in the constructor argument. Listing 23.14 shows this idea. The buttons created (Listing 23.13, Line 64) are added to a single container (`buttonPanel`). The method `addActionListener()` requires the index of the button stored in the container (Listing 23.14, Line 76).

Method `getComponent(index)` from `JPanel` (container) is used to retrieve the button at the given index.

Listing 23.14 Method addActionListener( ) in PTableWindow

```
Method addActionListener() in PTableWindow
74:      public void addActionListener(int buttonIndex,
                  java.awt.event.ActionListener listener){
75:          try{
76:              ((javax.swing.JButton)buttonPanel.
                                        getComponent(buttonIndex)).
                  addActionListener(listener);
77:          }catch(Exception exc){}
78:      }
```

Button return status

Clients need to be informed regarding which button has been clicked on PTableWindow. As the buttons are dynamically generated, there are two visible results that can be returned by getReturnStatus(). The index of the button clicked can be returned. Alternatively, the text of the button can be returned. Both approaches allow the client to know which button has been clicked and respond appropriately to the event.

Listing 23.15 shows a surprisingly simple implementation of the first approach. The return status is registered via the parameter given in doClose() (Listing 23.13, Line 61). The doClose() method can either leave PTableWindow on the screen or close it. This depends on the value of disposeWhenClosed, set by the setDisposeWhenClose() method, or on the value of the return status. A value of -1 indicates that the window is to be closed without clicking any of its buttons, but perhaps by clicking the window listener instead (such as represented by the cross symbol in the top right corner of the window).

Listing 23.15 Method doClose( ) in PTableWindow

```
Method doClose() in PTableWindow
142:     private void doClose(int retStatus) {
143:         returnStatus = retStatus;
144:         if(disposeWhenClosed || retStatus == -1) close();
145:     }
```

Printing in PTableWindow

PTableWindow provides a simple printing mechanism. The title of the window along with the table header and content are printed via the print() method presented in Listing 23.16. Initially, the graphics provided in the parameter of the function is translated into a printable area (Line 182). Once this is done, the titles are printed with a little gap between the main title and the subtitle (Lines 183–185). Titles are printed with the help of their paint() method. More space is provided above the table header (Lines 186 and 192). Finally, the content of the table is printed with the help of JTable's paint() method.

Listing 23.16 Method print( ) in PTableWindow

```
Method print() in PTableWindow

179:     public int print(java.awt.Graphics graphics,
             java.awt.print.PageFormat pageFormat,
             int pageIndex) throws java.awt.print.PrinterException {
180:        if(pageIndex == 0){
181:            Graphics2D g2 = (Graphics2D) graphics;
182:            g2.translate(pageFormat.getImageableX(),
                 pageFormat.getImageableY());
183:            titleLbl.paint(g2);
184:            g2.translate(0,40); //move down 40 points
185:            subtitleLbl.paint(g2);
186:            g2.translate(0,30);
187:
188:            //this could be used to print the whole graphics
189:            //paint(g2); //use the paint method to perform the job
190:
192:            table.getTableHeader().paint(g2);
193:            g2.translate(0, table.getRowHeight());
194:            table.paint(g2);
195:            return PAGE_EXISTS;
196:        }else return NO_SUCH_PAGE;
198:     }
```

Package Control

23.4

The control package consists of three classes (Figure 18.9). In comparison with Iteration 2, Iteration 3 only modifies CAdmin to provide features to satisfy additional requirements (see Chapter 19). Other classes in the control package are not modified in Iteration 3.

The new Iteration 3 methods in CAdmin are: canEditAuthorizationRules(), getAuthorizationRules(), saveAuthorization(), deleteMessage(), get-Report(), and updateMessage() (Figure 23.6). These new methods redirect all requests to MModerator and therefore there is no need to cover them in this section.

Package Entity

23.5

The implementation of IAReportEntry has introduced EReportEntry to the entity package. EIdentityMap has been modified slightly to cater for this additional entity class. There is a set of methods to handle report storage and retrieval. Figure 23.7 shows

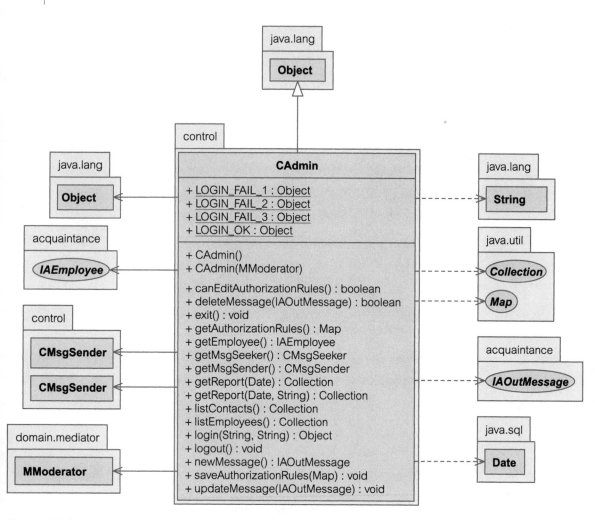

Figure 23.6 Class CAdmin in EM 3

Figure 23.7
Classes in the
Entity package

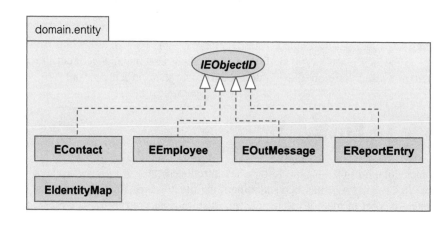

the content of the entity package. There is in fact another inner class called `EIdentity-Map.Epair`, which is used to store a pair of primary keys for `EReportEntry` mapping in `EIdentityMap`. However, this class is a private class in `EIdentityMap` and therefore is not shown in the diagram.

As per other entity objects, `EReportEntry` implements `IEObjectID` and therefore can be referred from `EIdentityMap` and other classes that use `IEObjectID`. References from `EIdentityMap` to `IEObjectID` cannot be generated as the `EIdentityMap` maintains a collection of these `IEObjectID`s.

Class EIdentityMap

Additional methods to support report retrieval and storage have been added to `EIdentityMap`. Figure 23.8 shows the additional methods: `getReports()` and `getReport()`, `registerReport()` and `unregisterReport()`. As `EReportEntry` is a new type of entity, there is also a need to introduce a map called `rptPKToOID` that maps a primary key of a report to its OID. This approach is similar to previous mapping approaches for outmessages, contacts, and employees (Section 18.5.1, Listing 18.29).

Report registration and removal

The `registerReport()` method (Listing 23.17) gets the given `oidObject`'s OID and puts it into the report map (Line 92) and finally into `OIDToObj` (Line 93). Entries of the report map are in the form of an `EPair` object. The `EPair` object contains the date and the contact id, which define the report generation conditions.

Listing 23.17 Method registerReport( ) and unregisterReport( ) in EIdentityMap

```
Method registerReport() and unregisterReport() in EIdentityMap

89:     public void registerReport(IEObjectID oidObject) {
90:         Integer oid = new Integer(oidObject.getOID());
91:         IAReportEntry rpt = (IAReportEntry)oidObject;
92:         rptPKToOID.put(
                new EPair(rpt.getReportDay(),rpt.getContactID()),oid);
93:         OIDToObj.put(oid, oidObject);
94:     }
97:     public void unregisterReport(IEObjectID oidReport) {
98:         IAReportEntry rpt = (IAReportEntry)oidReport;
99:         rptPKToOID.remove(new EPair(rpt.getReportDay(),
                rpt.getContactID()));
100:        OIDToObj.remove(new Integer(oidReport.getOID()));
101:    }
```

Method `unregisterReport()` is done by invoking the `remove()` method from the appropriate maps (Lines 99 and 100). Again, in order to remove a particular report from

Figure 23.8
Class
EIdentityMap
in EM 3

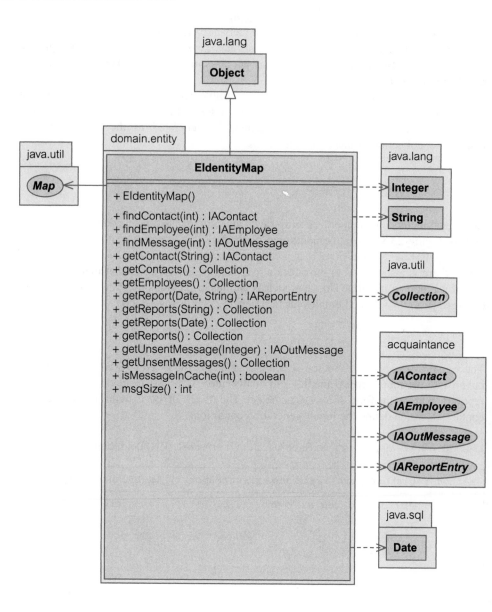

its report map, an `EPair` object has to be formed from the date and contact id of the report and used as the key in the removal process (Line 99).

Report retrieval

There are a number of methods that can be used to retrieve report entries. A list of report entries for a particular day can be retrieved from `EIdentityMap` (cache) via `get-Report()` (Listing 23.18). This method accepts a date and retrieves all report entries for that date. If there are no reports available, then an empty collection will be returned. If the date given is null then it is assumed that the client would like to retrieve all available reports (Line 38).

Listing 23.18 Method getReports( ) in EIdentityMap – retrieval by date

```
Method getReports() in EIdentityMap - retrieval by date

37:        public Collection getReports(java.sql.Date day){
38:            if(day == null) return getReports();
39:
40:            Collection c = new ArrayList();
41:            Iterator it = rptPKToOID.entrySet().iterator();
42:            while (it.hasNext()){
43:                Map.Entry entry = (Map.Entry) it.next();
44:                EPair key = (EPair)entry.getKey();
45:                if(day.equals(key.first)) c.add(entry.getValue());
46:            }
47:            return c;
48:        }
```

Each entry in the report map (rptPKToOID) is traversed and its day value is compared to check if the reports are for the same date (Line 45).

If the user needs to retrieve all available reports, then the getReports() method can be invoked to achieve this (Listing 23.19). The method simply iterates over all recorded reports in the map (Lines 53–57) and finds the report as indicated by its report OID (Line 55). Remember that the mapping maintained in the rptPKToOID is from an EPair to an OID. Therefore, the return value of next() on Line 55 returns the OID value.

Listing 23.19 Method getReports( ) in EIdentityMap

```
Method getReports() in EIdentityMap

51:        public Collection getReports(){
52:            Collection c = new ArrayList();
53:            Iterator it = rptPKToOID.values().iterator();
54:            while (it.hasNext()){
55:                Object o = findReport(((Integer) it.next()).intValue());
56:                if(o != null) c.add(o);
57:            }
58:            return c;
59:        }
```

When an OID of a report is known, it is possible to retrieve the report quickly. This is done by the findReport() method in Listing 23.20. As the OIDToObj map maintains the mapping between all OIDs and their associated objects, a quick search on OIDToObj gives the appropriate report, provided it exists in the cache (Line 77). Data stored in the map has to be objects and therefore the `reportOID` parameter has to be translated into its `Integer` representation.

Listing 23.20 Method findReport( ) in EIdentityMap

Method findReport() in EIdentityMap
76:      private IAReportEntry findReport(int reportOID){ 77:   return (IAReportEntry) OIDToObj.get(new Integer(reportOID)); 78:   }

It is also possible to retrieve report entries for a particular contact id. This is achieved by the method `getReports(contactID)` shown in Listing 23.21. Again, this method is similar to Listing 23.18 with a minor difference in the comparison done to choose a particular report. Listing 23.18 compares the date of the report (Line 45), whereas Listing 23.21 compares the contact id of the report. When the contact id is null, it is assumed that the user would like to retrieve all available reports (Listing 23.19).

Listing 23.21 Report retrieval for a particular contact

Method getReports(contactID) in EIdentityMap

62:      public Collection getReports(String contactID){
63:          if(contactID == null) return getReports();
64:
65:          Collection c = new ArrayList();
66:          Iterator it = rptPKToOID.entrySet().iterator();
67:          while (it.hasNext()){
68:              Map.Entry entry = (Map.Entry) it.next();
69:              EPair key = (EPair)entry.getKey();
70:              if(contactID.equals(key.second)) c.add(entry.
                                                   getValue());
71:          }
72:          return c;
73:      }

23.6 Package Mediator

Many aspects of the `mediator` package have been discussed in previous chapters. For example, Chapter 15 covered the patterns for `mediator`, Chapter 20 used `mediator` (`MDataMapper`) to illustrate stored procedure calls, and Chapter 21 introduced `MUnitOf-Work` in its capacity to manage transactions and concurrency. `MUnitOfWork` is a new class in Iteration 3 (Figure 23.9).

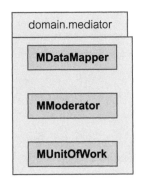

Figure 23.9
Classes in the
Mediator package
of EM 3

Evolution of the `mediator` package from Iteration 2 to Iteration 3 has resulted in the following improvements in Iteration 3:

- All database access through a set of stored procedures/functions.
- Implementation of authorization rules by taking advantage of additional triggers and constraints on the database.
- Transaction and concurrency management by `MUnitOfWork` and `MMediator`.
- Implementation of daily report generation in `MMediator`.

Class MModerator 23.6.1

The `MModerator` class (Figure 23.10) intercepts all entity object retrievals and modifications. It redirects these requests to `EIdentityMap` or to `MDataMapper`, as appropriate. `MModerator` is responsible for ensuring that activities are performed in accordance with their **transactional** nature with the help of `MUnitOfWork`.

Some of the additional methods in `MModerator` are `canEditAuthorization-Rules()`, `getAuthorizationRules()`, `saveAuthorizationRules()`, and `search-Reports()`. Other methods are modified to incorporate the transactional capabilities of Iteration 3.

Authorization rules

Listing 23.22 shows how the modified **authorization rules** are saved into a database. The authorization rules can be modified by the `presentation` package (Section 23.3.1.8). The `saveAuthorizationRules()` method in `MModerator` redirects the execution to `MDataMapper`'s `saveAuthorizationRules()` method. However, it guards the redirection to ensure that the execution of `MDataMapper`'s `saveAuthorizationRules()` is encapsulated into a transaction.

The `saveAuthorizationRules()` method turns on the auto commit to start the transaction (Line 184) and creates a **savepoint** (Line 186). The savepoint has a random number as its label. This is to avoid the chance of conflicting savepoints being created via concurrent access to the database. Note that the usage of savepoints forces the EM application

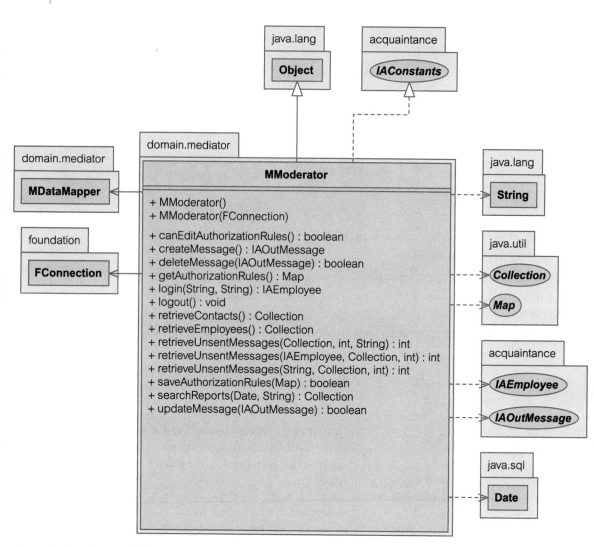

Figure 23.10 Class MModerator in EM 3

to use JDK 1.4 as a minimum. At the time of writing, Oracle has not fully implemented the JDK 1.4 savepoint specifications in the `Connection` interface. However, Oracle provides its own similar savepoint capability. This is shown on Line 186.

Once the savepoint is created, `MModerator` tries to call `MDataMapper`'s `save-AuthorizationRules()` (Line 188). `MModerator` commits the transaction, if it is successful (Line 189). However, if there are exceptions triggered during this execution, the transaction will be rolled back and the savepoint is released (Lines 191 and 192). Irrespective of whether the transaction is successful or not, the connection auto commit is reset to its original state (Line 195).

Listing 23.22 Method saveAuthorizationRules( ) in MModerator

```
Method saveAuthorizationRules() in MModerator

178:    public boolean saveAuthorizationRules(java.util.Map rules)
        throws Exception{
179:        //this could be placed into unit of work, provided the
            following is done:
180:        //* Authorization rule is promoted to a class
            on its own rather than simply Map
181:        //* unit of work is modified to handle any entity objects
182:        //but for now, we'll show the simplified version
183:        boolean origAutoCommit = connection.getAutoCommit();
184:        connection.setAutoCommit(false);
185:        //randomise the savepoint name and therefore
            avoids conflict in DB
186:        oracle.jdbc.OracleSavepoint savepoint =
            connection.setSavepoint("AuthorizationRuleSavepoint"+
            (Math.random()*Integer.MAX_VALUE));
187:        try{
188:            mapper.saveAuthorizationRules(rules);
189:            return connection.commit();
190:        }catch(Exception exc){
191:            connection.rollback(savepoint);
192:            connection.releaseSavepoint(savepoint);
193:            throw exc;
194:        }finally{
195:            connection.setAutoCommit(origAutoCommit);
196:        }
197:    }
```

Report retrieval

MModerator provides a single method to retrieve reports satisfying all allowed report conditions (date only, contact only, or both). Report retrieval is served by the searchReports() method that accepts a date and a contact id as its parameters (Listing 23.23). This listing is the implementation for Figure 21.10 (Section 21.3.3).

The searchReports() method checks if the day parameter is filled. If it is not filled then it is assumed that the user intends to retrieve today's reports (Line 138). The method then starts a transaction explicitly by calling the FConnection's begin() method (Line 144).

Depending on whether or not contactID is provided in the parameter, the method will invoke a different variant of retrieveReports() on MDataMapper. If contactID exists then it is apparent that the user wants to retrieve a report entry for the particular contact on the specified date (Lines 147–152). If the contact information is not provided then the list of reports for all contacts for the particular day is retrieved.

Listing 23.23 Method searchReports( ) in MModerator

Method searchReports() in MModerator

```
136:     public Collection searchReports(java.sql.Date day,
         String contactID){
137:       //if the day is not specified, then it is today's date
138:       if(day == null)
             day = new java.sql.Date(System.currentTimeMillis());
139:
140:       boolean successful = false;
141:       Collection col = null;
142:       try{
143:          //explicitly starts a transaction
144:          connection.begin();
147:          if(contactID != null && contactID.trim().length() != 0){
148:             Object rpt = mapper.retrieveReport(day,contactID);
149:             if(rpt == null) col = new LinkedList();
150:             col = java.util.Collections.singleton(rpt);
151:             successful = true;
152:          }else{
153:             col = mapper.retrieveReport(day);
154:             successful = true;
155:          }
156:       }catch(RuntimeException exc){
157:          throw exc;
158:       }catch(Exception exc2){
159:          exc2.printStackTrace(); //debugging
160:       }finally{
161:          if(successful) connection.end();
162:          else{ //remove all the changes
163:             connection.rollback();
164:             try{
                    connection.setAutoCommit(true);
                 }catch(Exception exc3){exc3.printStackTrace();}
165:          }
166:       }
167:
168:       if(col == null) return new LinkedList();
169:       return col;
170:    }
```

Successful retrieval ensures that the transaction will be committed (Line 161). A failure (exception) causes a rollback of the transaction (Line 163).

Creating an outmessage

MModerator encapsulates outmessage creation in a **transaction**. It uses MUnitOfWork to perform the transaction as shown in Listing 23.24. Before the activity can be performed, a new blank outmessage is retrieved from MDataMapper. This provides a container in which the outmessage data can be stored.

Listing 23.24 Method createMessage( ) in MModerator

Method createMessage() in MModerator
111:     public IAOutMessage createMessage(){ 112:   IAOutMessage msg = mapper.retrieveNewMessage(); 113:   MUnitOfWork work = MUnitOfWork.newCurrent(); 114:   work.registerNew((IEObjectID) msg); 115:   return msg; 116:   }

MUnitOfWork is initialized on Line 113 and changes to entity objects are registered on the new work object (Line 114). Method newCurrent() in MUnitOfWork ensures that a new instance of the **unit of work** is created for the very purpose of this transaction.

The method registerNew() indicates to the unit of work that the outmessage has just been created and therefore an insertion to the database needs to be made when the transaction commits. Notice, however, that the new outmessage is not committed at this time. It is merely marked as new. The commit functionality is incorporated in the updateMessage() method (explained later).

By not committing the newly created outmessages, the program can discard the outmessage if the user decides to cancel its creation. This does not compromise database integrity as there was no insertion or declaration of the new outmessage in the database.

Updating an outmessage

There are two situations in which an outmessage needs to be updated. The update can happen on an *existing* outmessage as well as on a *new* outmessage. Listing 23.25 shows both cases in one method.

During the construction of a new outmessage, a unit of work is explicitly created by the newCurrent() method (Listing 23.24, Line 113). This means that a call to MUnitOf-Work's getCurrent() on Line 101 provides the instance of MUnitOfWork created earlier. However, getCurrent() returns null if there is no instance of MUnitOfWork created earlier. This is possible as there was no invocation of the createMessage() method and in reality the user tries to update a pre-existing outmessage. In this case, a new unit of work needs to be created (Line 105).

Updating an outmessage only registers the outmessage as *dirty* in MUnitOfWork (Line 106). This forces the unit of work to perform an *update* on the dirty entity and save its value to database when the transaction is committed (Line 107).

Listing 23.25 Method searchReports( ) in MModerator

```
Method searchReports() in MModerator

97:       public boolean updateMessage(IAOutMessage msg) {
101:          MUnitOfWork work = MUnitOfWork.getCurrent();
102:
103:          //work could be null in the case there is only
                 //an update (without creation
104:          //of new outmessage)
105:          if(work == null) work = MUnitOfWork.newCurrent();
106:          work.registerDirty((IEObjectID)msg);
107:          return work.commit();
108:      }
```

The deletion of an outmessage is similar to the update procedure explained above except that the unit of work is always created via its newCurrent() method. Accordingly, the call to registerDirty() is replaced by registerRemoved().

23.6.2   Class MDataMapper

Most MDataMapper methods have been modified in Iteration 3 to cater for the fact that all SQL queries are converted into stored procedures or functions. This is discussed in an example in Chapter 20 (Listing 20.3).

Other improvements made on MDataMapper include refactoring of outmessage retrieval. Iteration 2 outmessage retrieval retrieveMessages() can throw an SQL exception to indicate *too many open cursors*. This happens only when there is a large number of outmessages retrieved from the database. The reason for this is due to the requirement that outmessage retrieval must resolve references to other entities. When an outmessage is retrieved, its contact, creator, and sender employees, as well as other references need to be resolved. This issue is resolved in Iteration 3 by delaying the resolution of references till the last stage of outmessage retrieval (i.e. only after all outmessages have been retrieved). The solution (not discussed here) is in the completeReferences() method in MDataMapper.

There are some other methods introduced in MDataMapper. These methods mainly support the storage or retrieval of daily reports and authorization accesses. Figure 23.11 provides a complete list of methods in MDataMapper.

Changes to previous methods

Listing 23.26 shows the Iteration 3 changes in the unloadMessage() method. This change is representative of many similar changes in MDataMapper, which are not discussed here. The interested reader is advised to browse the documentation available on the book's website.

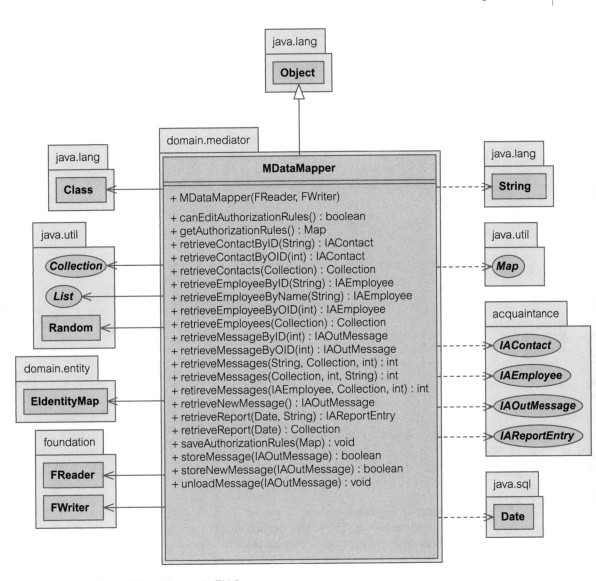

Figure 23.11 Class MDataMapper in EM 3

A simple SQL statement originally used in Iteration 2 (Line 155) has been replaced with a call to a stored procedure (Lines 156–159). FWriter's execute() method is used to achieve the execution of the stored procedure usp_delete_outmessage (Line 156). The method requires a string to specify a call statement on the stored procedure name. The parameters to the stored procedure are marked by the question marks. Each parameter is defined by a Class to indicate the parameter type of the stored procedure and an Object to represent the value of the parameter.

Listing 23.26 Method unloadMessage( ) in MDataMapper

```
Method unloadMessage() in MDataMapper
144:    public void unloadMessage(IAOutMessage msg) throws Exception{
145:        msg.setDirty(true);
146:        cache.unregisterMessage((IEObjectID)msg);
147:        //skip the delete of non-existance msg
148:        Integer oid = new Integer(((EOutMessage)msg).getOID());
149:        if(newMsgOIDs.contains(oid)){
150:            newMsgOIDs.remove(oid);
151:            return;
152:        }
153:
154:        try{
155:    //st = writer.delete("delete from outmessage where
                                              message_id = ?");
156:            writer.execute("{ call usp_delete_outmessage(?)}",
157:                new Class[]{Integer.class},
158:                new Object[]{new Integer(msg.getMessageID())}
159:            );
160:        }catch(Exception exc){
161:            exc.printStackTrace();
162:            throw exc;
163:        }
164:    }
```

Report retrieval in MDataMapper

The burden of retrieving reports is placed on MDataMapper's retrieveReport()
method shown in Listing 23.27. This method simply retrieves data from the database and
stores them in EIdentityMap. Report retrieval from the database assumes that the
database has been filled with reports. This does not necessarily mean that the reports are
generated and stored beforehand. They can be generated by a stored procedure when

Listing 23.27 Method retrieveReport( ) in MDataMapper

```
Method retrieveReport() in MDataMapper
595:    public Collection retrieveReport(java.sql.Date day) {
596:        //compare if the day required is today's date
597:        Date now = new java.sql.Date(System.currentTimeMillis());
598:        Calendar cal = GregorianCalendar.getInstance();
599:        cal.setTime(now);
600:        Calendar dayCal = GregorianCalendar.getInstance();
```

```
601:            dayCal.setTime(day);
602:
603:            boolean isToday = false;
610:            isToday = cal.get(Calendar.DATE) == dayCal.
                                                    get(Calendar.DATE) &&
611:               cal.get(Calendar.MONTH) == dayCal.get(Calendar.MONTH) &&
612:               cal.get(Calendar.YEAR) == dayCal.get(Calendar.YEAR);
613:
614:            if(isToday)
615:                generateUpdateReports();
617:            EReportEntry rpt = null;
618:            java.sql.ResultSet rs=null;
619:            IAContact contact;
620:            Collection results = null;
621:            if(!isToday) results = cache.getReports(day);
622:            if(!results.isEmpty()) return results;
623:            try {
625:                rs = reader.query("{ ? = call
                        usp_retrieve_dailyreport(?)}", new Object[]{day});
626:                while(rs.next()) {
627:                    contact = null;
628:                    contact = cache.getContact
                                        (rs.getString("contact_id"));
629:                    if(contact == null) contact =
                            retrieveContactByID(rs.getString("contact_id"));
630:                    int created = rs.getInt("num_emails_created");
631:                    int sent = rs.getInt("num_emails_sent");
632:                    int outstanding =
                                rs.getInt("num_emails_outstanding");
633:                    int pastout =
                                rs.getInt("num_emails_past_outstanding");
634:
635:                    rpt =
      new EReportEntry(day,contact,created,sent,outstanding,pastout);
636:                    cache.registerContact((IEObjectID)contact);
637:                    cache.registerReport((IEObjectID)rpt);
638:                    results.add(rpt);
639:                }
640:            } catch (Exception exc) {
641:                exc.printStackTrace();
642:                return null;
643:            }finally{
644:                if(rs != null) reader.closeResult(rs);
645:            }
646:            return results;
647:        }
```

needed and temporarily stored in the database for application retrieval. This is the approach taken in Iteration 3.

Listing 23.27 retrieves a list of reports for a particular day. There are some other variations of this method available in MDataMapper, however they are not discussed in this chapter as they differ only in minor details.

Iteration 3 assumes that past reports, for days other than today's date, do not need to be regenerated in the database. However, a request to produce a report for today's date requires generation of a new report every time. This is because today's emails are not in the history yet in the sense that new emails are being handled all the time by various employees using the EM system.

The code in Listing 23.27 detects whether the day of the requested report is today's date (Lines 610–612). If it is today's date, then retrieveReport() generates the report in the database (Lines 614–615). An attempt to retrieve a report from the cache is done if the day parameter is not today's date. This is just to see if the report has been requested recently and is in the cache. If it is, then there is no need for a trip to the database (Lines 621–622). The concrete retrieval from database is performed by Line 625. This utilizes FReader's query() method to query the database. Lines 626–639 show the report construction and registration (to cache).

Authorization rules loading in MDataMapper

Although *authorization rules* are designed in Iteration 3 as a simple map implementation rather than a class on its own, such as EAuthorizationRule, its loading/unloading processes are still managed by a class. This class is MDataMapper. MDataMapper is responsible for all data mapping between raw objects in the database and their entity representation in the application.

Listing 23.28 shows how the authorization rules are retrieved from the database and converted into their entity representation (just a simple Map). The stored procedure usp_retrieve_auth_rules is executed on FReader's query() (Line 794). The result of execution is traversed (Lines 796–813) and a proper map is created with entries similar to those in the authorization matrix (Section 19.2.3, subflow S1.1).

The map contains a mapping from a 'from_deparment' to a list of 'target_department'. Initially the 'from_department' is registered on the map with an empty list (Lines 800–803). Then an entry for the 'target_department' is made to the list belonging to the 'from_department' (Line 804) before the map is updated with the changed list (Line 805). An employee of a department has to be able to access all outmessages from his/her own department and this is realized by the mapping done in Lines 804–812.

Figure 23.12 represents the structure of the map. The figure shows how a list of 'to_department' is mapped to a single entry of 'from_department'. As a minimum, there must be a map from a department to itself, such as shown for from_department3.

Saving authorization rules in MDataMapper

A security administrator can modify the current authorization rules. Saving of modified rules requires a conversion from the map entries into the database entries. This is basically

Listing 23.28 Method getAuthorizationRules( ) in MDataMapper

```
Method getAuthorizationRules() in MDataMapper

789:     public java.util.Map getAuthorizationRules(){
790:        String sql = "{ ? = call usp_retrieve_auth_rules }";
791:        java.sql.ResultSet rs = null;
792:        java.util.Map m = null;
793:        try{
794:           rs = reader.query(sql,null);
795:           m = new java.util.HashMap();
796:           while(rs.next()){
797:              String code1 = rs.getString("from_dept_code");
798:              String code2 = rs.getString("target_dept_code");
799:              java.util.List l = (java.util.List) m.get(code1);
800:              if(l == null){
801:                 l = new java.util.LinkedList();
802:                 if(!code1.equals(code2)) l.add(code1);
803:              }
804:              l.add(code2);
805:              m.put(code1,l);  //replace the old one
806:
807:              //make an entry for code 2 if it does not exists yet
808:              if(m.get(code2) == null){
809:                 java.util.List ll = new java.util.LinkedList();
810:                 ll.add(code2);
811:                 m.put(code2,ll);
812:              }
813:           }
814:        }catch(Exception exc){
815:        }finally{
816:           if(rs != null) reader.closeResult(rs);
817:        }
818:        return m;
819:     }
```

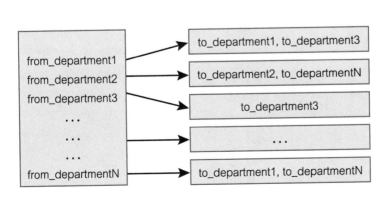

Figure 23.12
Authorization
rules in Map

a reverse of `getAuthorizationRules()`. The method that saves authorization rules is `saveAuthorizationRules()` (Listing 23.29).

Listing 23.29 Method saveAuthorizationRules( ) in MDataMapper

Method `saveAuthorizationRules()` in `MDataMapper`

```
840:    public void saveAuthorizationRules(java.util.Map rules)
        throws Exception{
841:      //clear up the entries in authorization table
842:      String sql = "{ call usp_clear_auth_rules }";
843:      CallableStatement st = null;
844:      try{
845:         st = writer.prepareCall(sql);
846:         st.execute();
847:      }catch(Exception exc){
848:         exc.printStackTrace();
849:         throw exc;
850:      }finally{
851:         if(st != null) writer.closeStatement(st);
852:         st = null;
853:      }
854:
855:      //fill up the entry from the map
856:      sql = "{ call usp_upd_auth_rules(?,?) }";
857:      try{
858:         st = writer.prepareCall(sql);
859:         java.util.Set entries = rules.entrySet();
860:         for(Iterator it = entries.iterator(); it.hasNext();){
861:            java.util.Map.Entry entry = (Map.Entry) it.next();
862:            String key = entry.getKey().toString();
863:            Iterator targets =
                       ((Collection)entry.getValue()).iterator();
864:            while(targets.hasNext()){
865:               st.setString(1, key);
866:               st.setString(2, targets.next().toString());
867:               st.execute();
868:            }
869:         }
870:      }catch(Exception exc){
871:         throw exc;
872:      }finally{
873:         if(st != null) writer.closeStatement(st);
874:         st = null;
875:      }
876:    }
```

Because the authorization rules are received in the format of a table and the map does not remember which of its entries have been modified, the update process becomes slightly difficult. The only way to perform the update is by removing all previous entries in the database and replacing them with the new entries as contained in the Map. This is achieved by executing the usp_clear_auth_rules stored procedure (Lines 842–847). Once the database is cleared, the individual entries of the Map can be inserted into the database one at a time (Lines 856–869, particularly Lines 859–863).

A java.sql.CallableStatement is used to cache the stored procedure strings (Line 858). CallableStatement can be reused with different parameters multiple times after it has been constructed. This is evidenced on Lines 865 and 866 where the parameters of CallableStatement are set dynamically before execution (Line 867). Stored procedure usp_upd_auth_rules was visited previously in Chapter 20, Listing 20.11.

Class MUnitOfWork   23.6.3

This is a new addition to the mediator package to accomplish the **unit of work** in EM (Section 21.2.4). Methods already discussed in Chapter 21 are not to be visited again in this chapter. The current design of MUnitOfWork accepts only IEObjectID as part of its list. Figure 23.13 shows the MUnitOfWork class. Associations to FConnection, MDataMapper, and the Collection framework are not shown to save space.

The MUnitOfWork implementation performs the transaction in the sequence of its entity registrations. Despite the fact that it registers the entities into three distinct

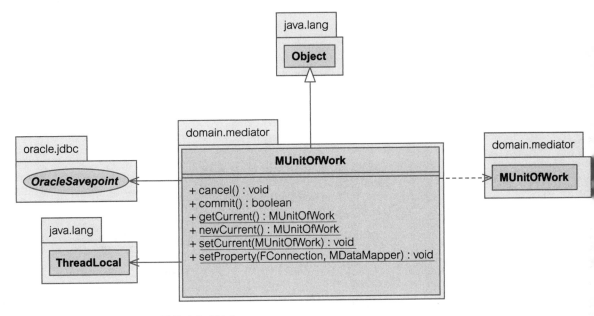

Figure 23.13 Class MUnitOfWork in EM 3

categories (discussed later), it commits changes to the database in the sequence of entity registrations. This ensures that the references from entities registered later to entities registered before are not broken when commiting changes to the database.

Static methods are provided in MUnitOfWork in support of its *singleton* pattern implementation, as discussed fully in Section 21.2.4. Typical activities involving MUnitOfWork are illustrated in Section 21.3.2, Figure 21.9. This chapter explains a few additional details of the MUnitOfWork implementation.

An application designed with concurrency can benefit from the usage of ThreadLocal to keep a unique instance of a variable for the thread (thread based mapping). ThreadLocal is used in MUnitOfWork to provide a unique instance of itself per each transactional request. ThreadLocal can be seen as a mapping from a thread to its own version of the MUnitOfWork.

Once a unit of work is acquired, a series of registrations can be performed for a transaction via the methods registerNew(), registerDirty(), and registerRemoved(). As this is a transaction, a failure in any part of it triggers the rollback.

Acquiring MUnitOfWork

Most methods in MUnitOfWork are static. The method newCurrent() is the only way to get a new instance of MUnitOfWork as shown in Listing 23.30. The default constructor (Line 93) creates a unit of work instance before it is registered as the most current MUnitOfWork, according to the singleton pattern (Line 95).

Listing 23.30 Methods newCurrent( ), setCurrent( ), and getCurrent( ) in MUnitOfWork

```
Methods newCurrent(), setCurrent(), and getCurrent() in MUnitOfWork
92:      public static MUnitOfWork newCurrent() {
93:          MUnitOfWork work = new MUnitOfWork();
95:          setCurrent(work);
96:          return getCurrent();
97:      }
100:     public static void setCurrent(MUnitOfWork unit) {
101:         currentUnit.set(unit);
102:     }
106:     public static MUnitOfWork getCurrent() {
107:         if (connection == null || mapper == null)
                 throw new IllegalStateException(
                     "Please set the connection and mapper first");
108:         return (MUnitOfWork) currentUnit.get();
109:     }
```

The singleton pattern is maintained by a ThreadLocal instance called currentUnit (Line 101). ThreadLocal provides only two methods, a set() to change the value contained in ThreadLocal and a get() to retrieve the stored value. Setting the given unit of work to `currentUnit` forces the latest reference to the subsequent `getCurrent()` method to point to the given unit of work (Line 108).

New entity registration in MUnitOfWork

`MUnitOfWork` can register an entity object as being in one of three states. The entity can be registered (1) as a *new* entry (and, therefore, can be inserted into the database), (2) as a *dirty* entry (which means that the database entry can be updated with the modified version of this entity), or (3) as a *deleted* entry (and therefore the corresponding database entry can be deleted).

Listing 23.31 illustrates the new entity registration to the unit of work. An inner class is used to remember the registration order during the registration. This approach is applied for all registrations (*new, updated*, and *deleted*). The inner class is called `MPair`. This is a simple container of two objects: an integer to represent the registration number, and the entity to be registered. This particular `MPair` is inserted into the `newObjects` container (Lines 115 and 118).

Listing 23.31 Method registerNew( )in MUnitOfWork

```
Method registerNew()in MUnitOfWork

114:    public boolean registerNew(IEObjectID obj) {
115:        MPair p = new MPair(new Integer(index++), obj);
116:
117:        if (dirtyObjects.contains(p) ||
                removedObjects.contains(p) ||
                newObjects.contains(p)) return false;
118:        newObjects.add(p);
119:        return true;
120:    }
```

There is a need to check that the new entity to be registered has not been registered previously. If it has been registered previously, then there is no need to re-register it and therefore the registration will be rejected (Line 117).

Dirty entity registration in MUnitOfWork

Similarly to the `registerNew()` method, `registerDirty()` in Listing 23.32 creates an `MPair` object to be stored in the `dirtyObjects` container (Lines 127 and 132). Again, a careful check is performed to ensure consistency in the unit of work. If the dirty entity to be registered has been registered before for deletion (i.e. it exists in the `removedObjects` container), then the registration is rejected (Line 129). However, if the dirty entity has been registered as new or dirty previously, then the registration is simply ignored.

Figures 21.7 and 21.9 in Chapter 21 show how transactions involving unit of work perform updates of registered dirty entities.

Listing 23.32 Method registerDirty( ) in MUnitOfWork

```
Method registerDirty() in MUnitOfWork

126:    public boolean registerDirty(IEObjectID obj) {
127:        MPair p = new MPair(new Integer(index++), obj);
129:        if (removedObjects.contains(p)) return false;
131:        if (newObjects.contains(p) || dirtyObjects.contains(p))
                return true;
132:        dirtyObjects.add(p);
133:        return true;
134:    }
```

Entity removal in MUnitOfWork

Entity removal follows similar registration principles (Listing 23.33). An MPair object is created to be stored in removedObjects (Lines 142 and 149). Checking is performed to determine if the entity object to be removed exists in the newObjects container. If it exists then it must be removed from the newObjects container (Line 145). This could happen because the user has cancelled the creation of a new entity. Similarly, if the entity to be removed exists in the dirtyObjects container, then it must be removed from this container (Line 149). After all, there is not much point in updating an entity object that is to be removed.

Listing 23.33 Method registerRemoved( ) in MUnitOfWork

```
Method registerRemoved() in MUnitOfWork

141:    public void registerRemoved(IEObjectID obj) {
142:        MPair p = new MPair(new Integer(index++), obj);
145:        if (newObjects.remove(p)) return;
149:        dirtyObjects.remove(p);
150:
151:        if (!removedObjects.contains(p)) removedObjects.add(p);
152:    }
```

The entity object registered to be removed will only be placed in the removedObjects container if it has not been registered in the container previously (Line 151). Duplicate registration may trigger exceptions in the execution of the transaction.

Examples of execution of unit of work for the purpose of removing entity objects are shown in Figures 21.8 and 21.9 in Chapter 21.

Committing MUnitOfWork

MUnitOfWork can have two states once all entities are properly registered: committed or cancelled. A *committed state* will result in writing from the registered entities to database, whereas a *cancelled state* will ignore all registrations.

Figure 21.9 in Chapter 21 shows a complete unit of work in action. Listing 23.34 is the code that conforms to Figure 21.9. The method `startTransaction()` is invoked to get a transaction from the database. If this cannot be acquired then the whole sequence of unit of work execution will not be in a single transaction and therefore it is wise to cancel the operation (Lines 158–159).

Listing 23.34 Method commit( ) in MUnitOfWork

```
Method commit() in MUnitOfWork

155:     public synchronized boolean commit() {
158:         if (!startTransaction())
159:             return false;
161:         //execute the list of transactions
162:         try {
163:             executeTransactions(newObjects.iterator(),
                     dirtyObjects.iterator(), removedObjects.iterator());
164:         }catch (Exception exc) {
165:             rollback();
167:             return false;
169:         }
172:         if(!connection.end()) rollback();
173:         setCurrent(null);
174:         return true;
175:     }
```

Once a transaction has started, a sequence of insertions, updates, and deletions is performed within this transaction by the `executeTransactions()` method (Line 163). This method ensures that the modifications (insert, update, delete) are performed according to their sequence of arrival during their registrations.

When an exception is thrown, the transaction needs to be rolled back (Lines 164–169). Similarly, when an attempt to commit the transaction fails, a rollback has to be done (Line 172).

A successful execution of a unit of work invalidates the current singleton instance held by `MUnitOfWork` (i.e. held in `currentUnit`). This invalidation is done by executing `setCurrent()` with a null unit of work. When the application tries to acquire a null unit of work, it is forced to create a new instance of unit of work via the `newCurrent()` method.

Execution of a transaction

It is necessary to commit changes to entity objects in the database in the order the changes have arrived (have been registered). This is achieved by the `executeTransactions()` method shown in Listing 23.35. A recursive solution in `executeTransactions()` is shown in which the method tries to figure out which of the three entities (from `newIt`, `dirtyIt`, and `removedIt`) must be executed first (Line 197). The method uses a function called `less()` to perform the job. Suffice to say that `less()` will return the earliest registered entity out of the two parameters given to it.

Listing 23.35 Method executeTransactions( ) in MUnitOfWork

```
Method executeTransactions() in MUnitOfWork

188:      private void executeTransactions(
          ListIterator newIt, ListIterator dirtyIt, ListIterator
          removedIt) throws Exception {
189:        MPair newP = null, dirtyP = null, removedP = null;
190:
191:        if (newIt.hasNext()) newP = (MPair) newIt.next();
192:        if (dirtyIt.hasNext()) dirtyP = (MPair) dirtyIt.next();
193:        if (removedIt.hasNext()) removedP = (MPair)
                                              removedIt.next();
194:
195:        if (newP == null && dirtyP == null && removedP == null)
                                              return;
196:
197:        MPair lowestIndex = less(less(newP, dirtyP), removedP);
198:        if(lowestIndex != newP && newP != null) newIt.previous();
199:        if(lowestIndex != dirtyP && dirtyP != null)
                                              dirtyIt.previous();
200:        if(lowestIndex != removedP && removedP != null)
                removedIt.previous();
201:
202:        if(lowestIndex == newP)
                insertNew((IEObjectID) lowestIndex.second);
203:        else if (lowestIndex == dirtyP)
                updateDirty((IEObjectID) lowestIndex.second);
204:        else deleteRemoved((IEObjectID) lowestIndex.second);
207:        executeTransactions(newIt, dirtyIt, removedIt);
208:      }
```

As per all recursive algorithms, there must be a stopping case. The stopping case is when the iterators no longer have any entity in them (Lines 191–195).

The method executes only the earliest entry out of the three possible entries. This means the other two entries, that have been already taken out of the iterators (Lines 191–193), need to be given back to the iterators (Lines 198–200). This allows the two entities to be processed during the next round of the recursive action (Line 207).

Depending on the type of entity, the processing results in invoking of (1) `insert-New()`, if it is a new entity, (2) `updateDirty()`, if the entity has been registered by `registerDirty()`, or (3) `deleteRemoved()`, if the entity is to be deleted (Lines 202–204).

A sequence diagram corresponding to Listing 23.35 is shown in Figure 21.9 in Chapter 21.

Starting a transaction

The method `startTransaction()` ensures that the start (begin) of a transaction is acquired from the database (Listing 23.36). In `MUnitOfWork`, this is accomplished by ensuring that `FConnection` starts the transaction with its `begin()` method (Line 200) followed by the creation of a savepoint to safeguard the executions after the savepoint (Line 220).

Listing 23.36 Method startTransaction( ) in MUnitOfWork

```
Method startTransaction() in MUnitOfWork

218:     private boolean startTransaction() {
219:         try {
220:             connection.begin();
221:             savepoint = connection.setSavepoint("unitofwork" +
                                                    transactionID);

222:         }catch (Exception exc) {
223:             exc.printStackTrace();

224:
225:             //turn back the auto commit
226:             if (!connection.getAutoCommit())
227:                 try{ connection.setAutoCommit(true);
                     }catch(Exception exc2){}
228:             return false;
229:         }
230:         return true;
231:     }
```

In the case of failure, for example due to an inability to acquire a transaction from `FConnection` or to acquire a savepoint, the state of `FConnection` needs to be reset to the original state in which the auto commit is set as true (Lines 226–228).

Package Foundation

Modifications in the `foundation` package in Iteration 3 are quite minor. Most modifications involve the support for **transactions** in `FConnection`. Additional improvements are in `FWriter` and `FReader` to support calls to stored procedures and stored functions.

This section shows only a few code samples to illustrate typical operations within the `foundation` Interested readers can find complete code on the book's website.

23.7.1 Transactions on FConnection

Transactional features of `FConnection` depend on the support provided by the JDBC driver used. Starting from JDK1.4, Java has introduced many new transactional features, which have already been supported by many database vendors. For example, Oracle has been supporting savepoint, rollback with savepoint, and many other features via its own classes. Listing 23.37 shows a method provided by Oracle to perform rollback. Instead of using `java.sql.Savepoint`, the `rollback()` method uses `oracle.jdbc.Oracle-Savepoint()` (Lines 207–208).

Listing 23.37 Method rollback( ) in FConnection

```
Method rollback() in FConnection

207:    //public boolean rollback(java.sql.Savepoint savepoint){
208:    public boolean rollback(oracle.jdbc.OracleSavepoint savepoint){
209:        try{
212:            //connection.rollback(savepoint);
214:            ((OracleConnection)conn).oracleRollback(savepoint);
215:        }catch(Exception exc){
216:            return false;
217:        }
218:        return true;
219:    }
```

Similarly, instead of using `java.sql.Connection`'s `rollback()` method, the `oracle.jdbc.OracleConnection`'s `oracleRollback()` method needs to be invoked (Lines 212–214).

The list of methods in `FConnection` is shown in Figure 23.14. The list contains a set of methods such as `getAutoCommit()`, `setAutoCommit()`, `rollback()`, `setSavepoint()`, `releaseSavepoint()`, `begin()`, `end()` and other transactional features.

23.7.2 Execute Statements in FWriter

A new method introduced in `FWriter` in Iteration 3 is the `execute()` method shown in Listing 23.38. This method allows an arbitrary `CallableStatement` to be executed on a database connection. The `execute()` method assigns parameters to `CallableState-ment`. The method currently supports `null`, `String`, `java.sql.Date`, and `Integer` objects as possible parameters of the execution (Lines 65–69). If the number of parameters declared in `parameters` does not match the `types`, an exception is thrown to the user to indicate so (Line 55).

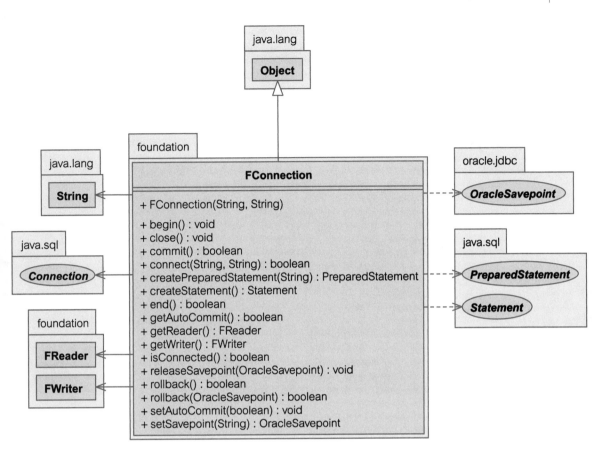

Figure 23.14 Class FConnection in EM 3

Listing 23.38 Method execute( ) in FWriter

```
Method execute() in FWriter
54:     public void execute(String sql, Class[] types, Object[]
        parameters) throws Exception{
55:         if(types != null && parameters.length != types.length)
                throw new IllegalArgumentException(
                "Different sizes of parameters and types given");
56:
57:         CallableStatement st = null;
58:         try{
59:             st = insert(sql);
60:
61:             if(types != null){
62:                 int index;
```

```
63:                    for(int i=0;i< parameters.length;i++){
64:                        index = i+1;
65:                        if(types[i] == null)
                            st.setNull(index,
                                        ((Integer)parameters[i]).intValue());
66:                        else if(types[i] == String.class)
                            st.setString(index, parameters[i].toString());
67:                        else if(types[i] == java.sql.Date.class)
                            st.setDate(index,
                                            (java.sql.Date)parameters[i]);
68:                        else if(types[i] == Integer.class)
                            st.setInt(index,
                                        ((Integer)parameters[i]).intValue());
69:                        else
                            throw new
                                IllegalArgumentException("Unknown type:" +
                            types[i] + " with value:"+ parameters[i]);
70:                    }
71:                }
72:                st.execute();
73:            }catch(Exception exc){
74:                throw exc;
75:            }finally{
76:                if(st != null) closeStatement(st);
77:                st = null;
78:            }
79:        }
```

For every identifiable parameter type, the `execute()` method assigns a corresponding value to the callable statement (Lines 65–58). The statement is created by invocation of the `insert()` method (Line 58). There is no need for separate `delete()` or `update()` methods because Iteration 3 invokes stored procedures and functions by calling `execute()`, as compared to directly issuing SQL `insert()`, `delete()`, or `update()` statements.

23.7.3 Querying the Database in FReader

Stored functions are provided in the database to replace queries from the client. These stored functions are accessible from the `query()` method in FReader, shown in Listing 23.39. The method is similar to `execute()` in the way that it processes the parameters. The `sql` query is assumed to be an invocation of stored functions that return a result list (with type `OracleTypes.CURSOR`, Line 46). Once the `CallableStatement` is created (Line 45), its parameters are assigned one at a time to the statement (Lines 48–51).

Listing 23.39 Method query( ) in FReader

```
Method query() in FReader

41:     public ResultSet query(String sql, Object o[]) throws
                                                    Exception {
42:        CallableStatement st = null;
43:        ResultSet rs = null;
45:        st = connection.prepareCall(sql);
46:        st.registerOutParameter(1,OracleTypes.CURSOR);
48:        for(int i=0;o != null && i < o.length;i++){
49:           if(o[i] instanceof Integer)
                   st.setInt(i+2, ((Integer)o[i]).intValue());
50:           else if(o[i] instanceof java.sql.Date)
                   st.setDate(i+2, (java.sql.Date) o[i]);
51:           else
                   st.setString(i+2,o[i].toString());
53:        }
54:        try{
55:           st.execute();
56:        }catch(Exception exc){
63:           st.close();
64:           throw exc;
65:        }
66:        rs = ((OracleCallableStatement) st).getCursor(1);
68:        return rs;
69:     }
```

Execution of the statement object is carried out on Line 55. This execution could throw an exception which is captured by the catch statement (Lines 56–65) before it is re-thrown to the client. The capture of the exception allows the proper cleanup of the statement via the `close()` method (Line 63). Finally, the output of the execution is returned to the client in the form of `ResultSet`. The result set conforms to the declaration of the first parameter, initially set on Line 46.

Database Code

Some **stored procedures** and **functions** have been discussed in Chapter 21 and therefore are not discussed in this chapter. There are two types of stored procedures/functions created for Iteration 3. The first is a set of functions/procedures to be placed in the **global schema** (Chapter 20, Sections 20.1.1 and 20.3.2). The second is a set of functions/procedures to be deployed in **local schemas** (Section 20.1.1, particularly Listing 20.4).

This section does not discuss procedures/functions for local schemas. They are similar to those presented in Listing 20.4. It concentrates on the global schema's stored functions/procedures. A number of simpler stored procedures and functions are not discussed due to reasons of space (they are available from the book's website).

23.8.1 Ref Cursor for ResultSet

The usage of `ref cursor` in Iteration 3 allows the return of a result set from a stored function. The declaration of `ref cursor` is Oracle-specific. Other database vendors have their own methods of returning result sets. The `ref cursor` declared in Listing 23.40 is placed in a package called EMS.

Listing 23.40 Ref Cursor for ResultSet

Ref cursor for ResultSet

```
create or replace package EMS as
    type REF_CURSOR is ref cursor;
end EMS;
```

Listing 23.41 Stored function usp_retrieve_outmessage_emp( )

Stored function usp_retrieve_outmessage_emp()

```
1:    create or replace function usp_retrieve_outmessage_emp(
2:        empid IN varchar2, usern in varchar2) return EMS.ref_cursor is
3:            c EMS.REF_CURSOR;
4:            inEmpID varchar2(100);
5:    begin
6:            inEmpID := null;
7:            select "employee_id" into inEmpID
8:            from "Employee"
9:            where upper("login_name") = upper(usern);
10:
11:        open c for
12:            Select *
13:            from "OutMessage"
11:            where "date_emailed" is null and
15:                    "sender_emp_id" = empid and
16:                    empid = inEmpID;
17:        return c;
18:        EXCEPTION
19:            WHEN NO_DATA_FOUND THEN
20:                raise_application_error(-20002,
21:                'usp_retrieve_outmessage_emp: unmatch username and
                                                    loginname');
22:    end;
```

Retrieval of Outmessages

There are a number of methods to retrieve outmessages. All outmessages assigned to a particular employee are retrievable via the stored procedure usp_retrieve_outmessage_emp() in Listing 23.41. The given empid is verified with the value indicated by usern (Lines 6–9). If the selection fails then an exception is thrown and caught on Lines 18–21. The exception is further propagated to the client program as an application exception.

A successful verification of the employee as a legitimate application user allows the program to continue selecting outmessages assigned to the employee (Lines 11–17).

Retrieval of Departmental Outmessages

Listing 23.42 demonstrates the function usp_retrieve_outmessage_dept() to retrieve a set of outmessages that have been assigned to all employees from the department of the current employee. Verification of employee id (Lines 47–50) is done the same way as in Listing 23.40. Extra code is added to get the department to which the employee belongs (Lines 52–55). If the employee cannot be verified then an exception is thrown (Lines 67–70).

Listing 23.42 Stored function usp_retrieve_outmessage_dept( )

```
Stored function usp_retrieve_outmessage_dept()

40:   create or replace function usp_retrieve_outmessage_dept(
41:       department IN varchar2, usern in varchar2) return
                                            EMS.ref_cursor is
42:       c EMS.REF_CURSOR;
43:       inEmpID varchar2(100);
45:       empDept varchar2(100);
46:   begin
47:       inEmpID := null;
48:       select "employee_id" into inEmpID
49:       from "Employee"
50:       where upper("login_name") = upper(usern);
51:
52:       empDept := 'IND'; --default independent employee
53:       select "department_code" into empDept
54:       from "Employee"
55:       where "employee_id" = inEmpID;
56:
57:       open c for
58:           Select *
59:           from "OutMessage"
```

```
60:          where "date_emailed" is null and
61:          "sched_dpt_code" = department and
62:          department in
63:              (select "target_dept_code"
64:              from "Authorization"
65:              where "from_dept_code" = empDept);
66:      return c;
67:      EXCEPTION
68:          WHEN NO_DATA_FOUND THEN
69:              raise_application_error(-20004,
70:              'usp_retrieve_outmessage_dept: unmatch username and
                                                    loginname');
71:  end;
```

A verified employee can retrieve all outmessages assigned to his/her department (i.e. outmessages scheduled to all employees in the department) (Lines 57–66). In fact, the employee is able to view all outmessages belonging to other departments as long as this is allowed by the authorization rules (Lines 62–65).

23.8.4 Deleting an Outmessage

Outmessage deletion is preceded by the verification that the employee is allowed to delete the outmessage. An employee can only delete his/her own outmessages (created by him/her) and other outmessages that s/he is allowed to view according to the authorization matrix (Section 19.2.3, subflow S1.1).

The verification is performed by the stored procedure usp_delete_outmessage() (Listing 23.43). Lines 97–108 check whether the employee can delete the outmessage as per the authorization rules (Lines 102–108). Again, if the selection fails then an exception is thrown to the user (Lines 113–116). A successful verification allows the program to proceed with deleting the outmessage (Lines 110–111).

Listing 23.43 Stored procedure usp_delete_outmessage( )

```
Stored procedure usp_delete_outmessage()

80:  create or replace procedure usp_delete_outmessage(
81:      msgID IN varchar2, usern in varchar2) is
82:      dummy integer;
83:      inEmpID varchar2(100);
84:      empDept varchar2(100);
85:      error_msg varchar2(100);
86:  begin
87:      --Cut to save space, the same as Listing 23.41 Line 47-55
96:
```

```
97:     dummy := null;
98:     select 1 into dummy
99:     from "OutMessage"
100:    where "message_id" = msgID and
101:    "creator_emp_id" in
102:        (select "employee_id"
103:        from "Employee"
104:        where "department_code" in
105:            (select "from_dept_code"
106:            from "Authorization"
107:            where "target_dept_code" = empDept)
108:        );
109:
110:    delete from "OutMessage"
111:    where "message_id" = msgID;
112:
113:    EXCEPTION
114:        WHEN NO_DATA_FOUND THEN
115:            raise_application_error(-20007,
116:            'usp_delete_outmessage: unmatch username and loginname
                or you are not allowed to delete the message');
118: end;
```

Creating an Outmessage

23.8.5

Extensive checks need to be performed before a new outmessage can be inserted into the database. The stored procedure `usp_create_outmessage()` performs these checks (Listing 23.44). The standard check to verify that the user is an employee in the `Employee` table is performed on Lines 137–140.

If it is discovered that the creator of the outmessage and the employee who tries to insert the outmessage are different people, an exception is thrown to reject the insertion (Lines 142–145). A further check is performed on Lines 153–169. This check is to ensure that the employee assigns the new outmessage to another employee within his/her authorization reach as dictated by the authorization matrix (Section 19.2.3, subflow S.1.1). Finally, the insertion is done when everything is confirmed (Lines 171–176).

Listing 23.44 Stored procedure usp_create_outmessage( )

```
Stored procedure usp_create_outmessage()
120: create or replace procedure usp_create_outmessage(
121:     senderID IN varchar2,
122:     --The rest of parameters and variables are cut to save space
136: begin
```

```
137:    inEmpID := null;
138:    select "employee_id" into inEmpID
139:    from "Employee"
140:    where upper("login_name") = upper(usern);
141:
142:    if inEmpID <> creatorID then
143:        raise_application_error(-20014, ('You cannot pretend to be
           another person in creator field:' || creatorID));
145:    end if;
146:
147:    --Cut to save space, same as Listing 23.41 Line 52-55
152:    --begin a new transaction in order to handle the exception
                                                              thrown
153:    begin
154:        dummy := null;
155:        if schedulerID is not null then
156:            select 1 into dummy from dual
157:            where schedulerID in
158:                (select "employee_id"
159:                from "Employee"
160:                where "department_code" in
161:                    (select "from_dept_code"
162:                    from "Authorization"
163:                    where "target_dept_code" = empDept)
164:                );
165:        end if;
166:        EXCEPTION
167:            WHEN NO_DATA_FOUND THEN
168:                raise_application_error(-20015,('You are not allowed
                   to schedule this message to ' || schedulerID));
169:    end;
170:
171:    insert into "OutMessage"(
172:        "sender_emp_id","sched_emp_id",
                                    "creator_emp_id","contact_id",
173:        "message_subject","message_text","date_scheduled",
174:        "date_emailed","sched_dpt_code","message_id",
                                                    "date_created")
175:    values(senderID,schedulerID,creatorID,cntID,subject,
176:        text,scheduled,emailed,deptCode,msgID,created);
177:    EXCEPTION
178:        WHEN NO_DATA_FOUND THEN
179:            raise_application_error(-20016, 'usp_create_outmessage:
           unmatch username and loginname');
180: end;
```

A similar idea is applied for updating an outmessage (not shown in this section). The only change for updating is the replacement of the insert statement (Lines 171–176) with an update statement.

Report Generation

The DailyReport table entries are generated with the help of the stored procedure usp_generate_dailyreport(), shown in Listing 23.45. This stored procedure first generates a list of all contacts with created or already emailed outmessages (Lines 5–9 and 15). It then calculates the value of outstanding, past outstanding, created, sent, and total outmessages for each employee (Lines 16–37).

An insertion to the DailyReport table is done if the current contact has no entry yet (for the date of generation) (Lines 51–62), as checked by Lines 45–48. If the Daily-Report table contains an entry for the contact on that particular date, then the data in the DailyReport table will be updated (Lines 64–71).

Listing 23.45 Stored procedure usp_generate)dailyreport( )

```
Stored Procedure usp_generate_dailyreport()

 1:   create or replace procedure usp_generate_dailyreport(usern in
                                                           varchar2)
 2:   is
 3:      cnt_exists integer;
 4:      c EMS.REF_CURSOR;
 5:      cursor contacts_c is
 6:          select distinct "contact_id"
 7:          from "OutMessage"
 8:          where to_date("date_created",'DD/MM/YY') =
                  to_date(SYSDATE,'DD/MM/YY')
 9:          or to_date("date_emailed",'DD/MM/YY') =
                  to_date(SYSDATE,'DD/MM/YY');
10:      outstanding integer;
11:      past_outstanding integer;
12:      sent integer;
13:      created integer;
14:   begin
15:      for selected_contact in contacts_c loop
16:          outstanding := 0;
17:          select count(*) into outstanding
18:          from "OutMessage"
19:          where "contact_id" = selected_contact."contact_id" and
20:          to_date("date_scheduled",'DD/MM/YY') >=
                  to_date(SYSDATE,'DD/MM/YY')
                  and "date_emailed" is null;
```

```
21:
22:          past_outstanding := 0;
23:          select count(*) into past_outstanding
24:          from "OutMessage"
25:          where "contact_id" = selected_contact."contact_id" and
26:          to_date("date_scheduled",'DD/MM/YY') <
                  to_date(SYSDATE,'DD/MM/YY')
                  and "date_emailed" is null;
27:
28:          sent := 0;
29:          select count(*) into sent
30:          from "OutMessage"
31:          where "contact_id" = selected_contact."contact_id" and
                  "date_emailed" is not null;
32:
33:          created := 0;
34:          select count(*) into created
35:          from "OutMessage"
36:          where "contact_id" = selected_contact."contact_id" and
37:          to_date("date_created",'DD/MM/YY') =
                  to_date(SYSDATE,'DD/MM/YY');
38:
39:          cnt_exists := null;
44:          begin
45:              select 1 into cnt_exists
46:                  from "DailyReport"
47:                  where to_date("date_of_report_day",'DD/MM/YY') =
                          to_date(SYSDATE,'DD/MM/YY')
48:                  and "contact_id" = selected_contact."contact_id";
49:
50:              if cnt_exists is null then
51:                  insert into "DailyReport"("date_of_report_day",
52:                  --Cut to save space ...
63:              else
64:                  update "DailyReport"
65:                  --cut to save space
72:              end if;
73:
74:              EXCEPTION
75:                  WHEN NO_DATA_FOUND THEN
76:                      insert into "DailyReport"("date_of_report_day",
77:                      --cut to save space
88:          end;
89:      end loop;
90:  end;
```

A contact may not have an entry in the `DailyReport` table. This will cause an exception when the select statement is executed. For this purpose, an insertion is performed into the `DailyReport` table (Lines 74–77).

Trigger on OutMessage Table

For reasons of space, only one **trigger** is shown in this section. The trigger is for insert and update operations on the OutMessage table (Listing 23.46). The trigger is used to check on the following conditions:

- Check 1: check whether the `dept_code` is filled when `sched_emp` is filled (`dept_code` of employee has to be the same as `sched_dpt_code`).
- Check 2: ensure that when `sched_emp_id` and `sched_dpt_code` are null then the default `sched_dpt_code` is QUA.
- Check 3: `date_scheduled` has to be filled.
- Check 4: `date_scheduled` cannot be smaller than `date_created`.
- Check 5: when the `date_emailed` is filled, it has to be greater than `date_created`.

Listing 23.46 Trigger on OutMessage table

```
Trigger on OutMessage table

create or replace trigger bins_upd_outmessage
before insert or update
on "OutMessage"
for each row
declare
      dept_code varchar2(20);
begin
      if :new."sched_emp_id" is not null then --satisfaction of check 1
      -- dept code cant be null if sched_emp is filled
      if :new."sched_dpt_code" is null then
         raise_application_error(-20100,
         'Schedule Dept Code is empty');
      end if;

      select "department_code" into dept_code
      from "Employee"
      where "employee_id" = :new."sched_emp_id";

      --dept code and sched emp dept code have to be the same
      if dept_code <> :new."sched_dpt_code" then
```

```
                    raise_application_error(-20101,
                    'Schedule Dept Code does not match the employee dept');

           end if;

    end if;

    --both sched_emp_id and sched_dpt_code null,
    --make sure sched_dpt_code is QUA
    --satisfaction of check 2
    if :new."sched_emp_id" is null and :new."sched_dpt_code" is null then
        :new."sched_dpt_code" := 'QUA';
    end if;

    --could happen if created or accessed externally of EMS
    --satisfaction of check 3
    if :new."date_scheduled" is null then
            raise_application_error(-20102,
            'Schedule date of this message is empty');
    end if;

    --schedule date cant be smaller than creation date
    --satisfaction of check 4
    if :new."date_created" > :new."date_scheduled" then
            raise_application_error(-20103,
            'Date scheduled is older than date created');
    end if;

    --emailed date cant be older than creation date
    --satisfaction of check 5
    if :new."date_emailed" is not null and
        :new."date_created" > :new."date_emailed" then
            raise_application_error(-20104,
            'Date emailed is older than date created');
    end if;
end;
```

Summary

1. The iteration 3 implementation addresses the data engineering concerns in the Email Management case study. The PCMEF+ framework is fully retained and adhered to.

2. Iteration 3 introduces MUnitOfWork to provide transactional support for the application.

3. All SQL code is moved to the database server in the form of stored procedures/functions.

4. All user transactions are initiated in MModerator.

5. The authorization rules are applied to all activities to restrict the type of outmessages viewable by employees. Authorization rules can be modified only by the user in the role of the security/database administrator.

6. The functionality of producing daily summary reports is implemented.

7. Outmessages can be modified before emailing.

8. The acquaintance package has an additional interface named IAReportEntry to assist in generation of daily reports with emailing statistics.

9. The presentation package has an extra class PTableWindow that is used to display authorization rules as well as daily reports.

10. The control package consists of three classes, as in Iteration 2. Iteration 3 only modifies CAdmin to provide features to satisfy additional requirements.

11. The implementation of IAReportEntry has introduced EReportEntry to the entity package. EIdentityMap has been modified slightly to cater for this additional entity class.

12. MUnitOfWork is a new class in the mediator package to handle transactions. There are changes in the mediator classes related to the replacement of SQL commands to access the database with calls to database-stored procedures and functions.

13. Modifications in the foundation package are quite minor. Most modifications involve support for transactions. Additional improvements are to support calls to stored procedures.

14. Iteration 3 moved application business logic to the database. This is accomplished with a significant number of stored procedures and functions as well as by implementing triggers to guarantee database integrity.

Key Terms

activity report	757	savepoint	777
authorization rules	753, 777, 786	stored function	799
authorization window	759	stored procedure	799
daily reports	*See* summary reports	summary reports	751, 754
dynamic buttons	767	transaction	777, 781, 795
façade	754	trigger	807
global schema	799	unit of work	781, 789
Javadoc	750	utility class	755, 767
listeners	769	yDoc	750
local schema	799		

Iteration 3 Questions and Exercises

Below is a small set of questions and exercises with regard to the EM Iteration 3 code. More questions and exercises are available from the book's website.

1. Refer to the interface `IAReportEntry` in Figure 23.3. Any reasons, you can think of, why the programmer used `java.sql.Date` to represent report dates instead of `java.util.Date`?

2. Refer to Section 23.3.1 'Populating the report contact list'. State the reason(s) for using the `synchronized` keyword in Listing 23.1, Line 50.

3. Refer to Section 23.3.1 'Report window'. Listing 23.2 illustrates one way of generating the report window. Discuss a few alternative ways.

4. The logic to print reports is placed in `PTableWindow`. Would it not be better to place such logic in `Pwindow` instead? Explain.

5. The printing of reports (Section 23.3.1) is implemented solely in `PTableWindow`. In this implementation any modifications to the printing mechanism or to the choices of components to be printed must go to `PTableWindow`. What would be other, more flexible approaches?

6. Why is the `PWindow` instance in Listing 23.2, Line 499, declared `final`? (Hint: Try to delete the `final` keyword and recompile, and see what happens.)

7. Refer to Section 23.3.1 'Report Window' and Listing 23.2. The anonymous inner class on Lines 502–511 uses its own thread. Why does the next anonymous inner class on Lines 512–516 not use a thread to lift the burden from the painting thread?

8. Refer to Section 23.3.1 and Listing 23.11 (and other listings for `PMessageDetailWindow`). Would it be beneficial to refactor `PMessageDetailWindow`? If so, what would be the refactoring targets? Explain.

9. Refer to Section 23.6.2 'Report retrieval MDataMapper' and Listing 23.27. Speculate why the code in Listing 23.27 uses such complicated checking to see if the day parameter is equal to today's date? Can this be done some other way?

Bibliography

Agile (2003) http://agilealliance.org/home (last accessed July 2003)

Alur, D., Crupi, J. and Malks, D. (2003) *Core J2EE Patterns: Best Practices and Design Strategies*, 2nd edn. Englewood Cliffs, NJ: Prentice Hall

Apache (2003) http://www.apache.org/ (last accessed July 2003)

ArgoUML (2003) http://argouml.tigris.org/ (last accessed August 2003)

Beck, K. (1997) *Smalltalk Best Practice Patterns*. Englewood Cliffs, NJ: Prentice Hall

Beck, K. (1999) *Extreme Programming Explained: Embrace Change*. Reading, MA: Addison-Wesley

Benson, S. and Standing, C. (2002) *Information Systems: A Business Approach*. Brisbane: John Wiley

Boehm, B.W. (1981) *Software Engineering Economics*. Englewood Cliffs, NJ: Prentice Hall

Boehm, B.W. (1984) Software Engineering Economics, *IEEE Tran. Soft. Eng.*, **1**: 4–21

Boehm, B.W. (1988) A spiral model of software development and enhancement, *Computer*, May: 61–72

Boehm, B.W., Abts, C., Brown, A.W., Chulani, S., Clark, B.K., Horowitz, E., Madachy, R., Reifer, D. and Steece, B. (2000) *Software Cost Estimation with COCOMO II*. Englewood Cliffs, NJ: Prentice Hall

Booch, G., Rumbaugh, J. and Jacobson, I. (1999) *The Unified Modeling Language User Guide*. Reading, MA: Addison-Wesley

Bonazzi, E. and Stokol, G. (2001) *Oracle® 8i and Java™. From Client/Server to E-Commerce*. Englewood Cliffs, NJ: Prentice Hall

Borland (2003) http://www.borland.com/together/ (last accessed September 2003)

Brooks, F.P. (1987) No silver bullet: essence and accidents of software engineering, *IEEE Software*, 4: 10–19; reprinted in C.F. Kemerer (ed.) (1997) *Software Project Management: Readings and Cases*. Chicago: Irwin, pp.2–14

Bugzilla (2003) http://gcc.gnu.org/bugs/management.html (last accessed September 2003)

Buschmann, F., Meunier, R., Rohnert, H., Sommerlad, P. and Stal, M. (1996) *Pattern-Oriented Software Architecture: A System of Patterns*. New York: John Wiley & Sons

Cambridge (2003): http://dictionary.cambridge.org/ (last accessed September 2003)

Cattell, R.G.G. (1994) *Object Data Management: Object-Oriented and Extended Relational Database Systems*, rev. edn. Reading, MA: Addison-Wesley

Charette, R.N. (1989) *Software Engineering Risk Analysis and Management*. Reading, MA: McGraw-Hill

Chidamber, S.R. and Kemerer, C.F. (1994) A metrics suite for object oriented design, *IEEE Trans. Soft. Eng.*, **6**: 476–93

CMM (2003) http://www.sei.cmu.edu/cmm/cmm.html (last accessed August 2003)

Codd, E.F. (1982) Relational database: a practical foundation for productivity, *Comm. ACM*, **2**: 109–17

De Millo, R.A., Lipton, R.J. and Perlis, A.J. (1979) Social processes and proofs of theorems and programs, *Comm. ACM*, **5**: 271–80

Eckel, B. (2000) *Thinking in Java*, 2nd edn. Englewood Cliffs, NJ: Prentice Hall. http://www.planetpdf.com/ (last accessed April 2002)

Eclipse (2003) http://www.eclipse.org/ (last accessed September 2003)

Ege, R. (1992) *Programming in an Object-Oriented Environment*. New York: Academic Press

eProject (2003) http://www.eproject.com/ (last accessed July 2003)

eRoom (2003) http://www.eroom.net/eRoomNet/ (last accessed July 2003)

Fowler, M. (1999) *Refactoring: Improving the Design of Existing Code*. Harlow: Addison-Wesley

Fowler, M. (2003) *Patterns of Enterprise Application Architecture*. Harlow: Addison-Wesley

Gamma, E., Helm, R., Johnson, R. and Vlissides, J. (1995) *Design Patterns: Elements of Reusable Object-Oriented Software*. Reading, MA: Addison-Wesley

Gentleware (2003) http://www.gentleware.com/ (last accessed August 2003)

Ghezzi, C., Jazayeri, M. and Mandrioli, D. (2003) *Fundamentals of Software Engineering*. Prentice Hall

Goodwill, J. (2002) *Mastering Jakarta Struts*. New York: John Wiley & Sons

Hawryszkiewycz, I., Karagiannis, D., Maciaszek, L. and Teufel, B. (1994) Response – Requirements specific object model for workgroup computing, *Int. J. Intelligent & Cooperative Information Systems*, **3**: 293–318

Heldman, K. (2002) *PMP®: Project Management Professional. Study Guide*. Berkeley, CA: Sybex Inc.

Henderson-Sellers, B., Constantine, L.L. and Graham, I.M. (1996) Coupling and Cohesion (Towards a Valid Metrics Suite for Object-Oriented Analysis and Design), *Object Oriented Systems*, **3**: 143–58

IBM (2003) http://www-3.ibm.com/software/awdtools/studioappdev/ (last accessed September 2003)

ICE (2003) http://www.iceincusa.com/products_tools.htm (last accessed July 2003)

ISO (2003) http://www.iso-9000–2000.com/ (last accessed August 2003)

Israel, M. and Jones, J.S. (2001) *MCSE: SQL Server™ 2000. Design Study Guide*. Berkeley, CA: Sybex Inc.

Jacobson, I. (1992) *Object-Oriented Software Engineering: A Use Case Driven Approach*. Reading, MA: Addison-Wesley

Johnson, R. (2002) *Expert One-on-One J2EE Design and Development*. Birmingham: Wrox Press

Java (2003) http://java.sun.com/products/ (last accessed August 2003)

JSF (2003) http://java.sun.com/j2ee/javaserverfaces/ (last accessed July 2003)

JTA (2003) http://java.sun.com/products/jta/ (last accessed August 2003)

JTS (2003) http://java.sun.com/products/jts/ (last accessed August 2003)

JUnit (2003) www.junit.org (last accessed March 2003)

Kim, W. (1990) *Introduction to Object-Oriented Databases*. Boston, MA: MIT Press

Kleppe, A., Warmer, J. and Bast, W. (2003) *MDA Explained: The Model Driven Architecture™: Practice and Promise*. Reading, MA: Addison-Wesley

Krasner, G.E. and Pope, S.T. (1988) A cookbook for using the model view controller user interface paradigm in Smalltalk-80, *J. Object-Oriented Prog.*, Aug/Sept: 26–49

Kruchten, P. (1999) *The Rational Unified Process*. Reading, MA: Addison-Wesley

Lakshman, B. (2002) *Oracle and Java Development*. Boston, MA: SAMS

Larman, C. (2002) *Applying UML and Patterns. An Introduction to Object-Oriented Analysis and Design and the Unified Process*, 2nd edn. Englewood Cliffs, NJ: Prentice Hall

Lee, R.C. and Tepfenhart, W.M. (2002) *Practical Object-Oriented Development with UML and Java*. Englewood Cliffs, NJ: Prentice Hall

Lientz, B.P. and Rea, K.P. (2002) *Project Management for the 21st Century*, 3rd edn. New York: Academic Press

Lethbridge, T.C. and Laganiere, R. (2001) *Object-Oriented Software Engineering. Practical Software Development Using UML and Java*. New York: McGraw-Hill

Lieberherr, K.J. and Holland, I.M. (1989) Assuring good style for object-oriented programs, *IEEE Soft.*, **9**: 38–48

Maciaszek, L.A. (1990) *Database Design and Implementation*. London: Prentice Hall

Maciaszek, L.A. (2001) *Requirements Analysis and System Design: Developing Information Systems with UML*. Harlow: Addison-Wesley

Maciaszek, L.A. (2002) Process model for round-trip engineering with relational database, in S. Valenti (ed.) *Software Reengineering*. Hershey, PA: IRM Press, pp.76–91

Maciaszek, L.A., De Troyer, O.M.F., Getta, J.R. and Bosdriesz, J. (1996a) Generalization versus aggregation in object application development – the 'AD HOC' Approach, *Proc. 7th Australasian Conf. on Information Systems ACIS'96*, Vol. 2, Hobart, Tasmania, Australia, pp.431–42

Maciaszek, L.A. and Owoc, M.L. (2001) Designing application authorizations, in E. Boyd, E. Cohen, and A.J. Zaliwski (eds) *Proc. 2001 Informing Science Conference*, Krakow, Poland. Proceedings on CD (ISSN 1535–0703), or http://ecommerce.lebow.drexel. edu/eli/

ManagePro (2003) http://www.managepro.net/ (last accessed July 2003)

Martin, R.C. (2003) *Agile Software Development: Principles, Patterns, and Practices*. Englewood Cliffs, NJ: Prentice Hall

MDA (2003) http://www.omg.org/mda/ (last accessed July 2003)

Microsoft (2003a) http://msdn.microsoft.com/scripting/default.htm (last accessed July 2003)

Microsoft (2003b) http://msdn.microsoft.com/ssafe/default.asp (last accessed September 2003)

Microsoft (2003c) http://www.microsoft.com/office/project/default.asp (last accessed July 2003)

Newkirk, J. and Martin, R. (2001) *Extreme Programming in Practice*. Reading, MA: Addison-Wesley

Netscape (2003) http://wp.netscape.com/eng/javascript/ (last accessed July 2003)

Nomagic (2003) http://www.magicdraw.com/ (last accessed August 2003)

Oracle (2003) http://otn.oracle.com/products/jdev/content.html (last accessed September 2003)

Palisade (2003) http://www.palisade-europe.com/ (last accessed July 2003)

Paulk, M.C., Weber, C.V., Curtis, B. and Chrissis, M.B. (1995) *The Capability Maturity Model: Guidelines for Improving the Software Process.* Reading, MA: Addison-Wesley

Perforce (2003) http://www.perforce.com/ (last accessed September 2003)

Pfleeger, S.L. (1998) *Software Engineering. Theory and Practice.* Englewood Cliffs, NJ: Prentice Hall

PMC (2003) http://www.infogoal.com/pmc/pmcswr.htm (last accessed July 2003)

Porter, M. (1985) *Competitive Advantage: Creating and Sustaining Superior Performance.* New York: Free Press

Pressman, R.S. (2001) *Software Engineering: A Practitioner's Approach*, 5th edn. New York: McGraw-Hill

Primavera (2003) http://www.primavera.com (last accessed July 2003)

Quatrani, T. (2000) *Visual Modeling with Rational Rose2000 and UML.* Reading, MA: Addison-Wesley

Ramakrishnan, R. and Gehrke, J. (2000) *Database Management Systems.* New York: McGraw-Hill

Rational (2002) *Rational Suite Tutorial*, Version 2002.05.00. Rational Software Corporation

Rational (2003) http://www.rational.com (last accessed August 2003)

Responsive (2002) http://www.responsivesoftware.com (last accessed October 2002)

Riel, A.J. (1996) *Object-Oriented Design Heuristics.* Reading, MA: Addison-Wesley

Roman, E., Ambler, S. and Jewell, T. (2002) *Mastering Enterprise Java Beans^{TM}*, 2nd edn. New York: John Wiley & Sons

Rumbaugh, J., Jacobson, I. and Booch, G. (1999) *The Unified Modeling Language Reference Manual.* Reading, MA: Addison-Wesley

RUP (2003) http://www.rational.com/products/rup/ (last accessed July 2003)

Schach, S. (2002) *Object-Oriented and Classical Software Engineering*, 5th edn. New York: McGraw-Hill

Silberschatz, A., Korth, H.F. and Sudershan, S. (2002) *Database System Concepts*, 4th edn. New York: McGraw-Hill

Singh, I., Stearns, B., Johnson, M. and Enterprise Team (2002) *Designing Enterprise Applications with the J2EE^{TM} Platform*, 2nd edn. Reading, MA: Addison-Wesley

SmallWorlds (2003) http://www.thesmallworlds.com/ (last accessed June 2003)

Sommerville, I. (2001) *Software Engineering*, 6th edn. Reading, MA: Addison-Wesley

Sparx (2003) http://www.sparxsystems.com.au/ (last accessed August 2003)

Standish (2003) http://www.standishgroup.com/ (last accessed July 2003)

Sun (2002a) *J2EE BluePrints*, available at http://java.sun.com (last accessed September 2003)

Sun (2002b) *J2EE Platform Specification*, available at http://java.sun.com (last accessed September 2003)

Sun (2003) http://developer.java.sun.com/developer/infodocs/ (last accessed July 2003)

Sun ONE (2003) http://wwws.sun.com/software/sundev/jde/ (last accessed August 2003)

Sybase (2003) http://www.sybase.com/products/enterprisemodeling (last accessed August 2003)

Telelogic (2003) http://www.telelogic.com/ (last accessed August 2003)

Tomcat (2003) http://jakarta.apache.org/tomcat (last accessed December 2003)

UML (2002) *Unified Modeling Language: Superstructure, Version 2 beta R1 (draft)*. U2 Partners

UML (2003a) http://www.rational.com/uml/resources/documentation/index.jsp (last accessed July 2003)

UML (2003b) *OMG Unified Modeling Language Specification, Version 1.5*. Needham, MA: OMG

Unhelkar, B. (2003) *Process Quality Assurance for UML-Based Projects*. Reading, MA: Addison-Wesley

W3C (2003) http://www.w3.org/ (last accessed July 2003)

White, S., Fisher, M., Cattell, R., Hamilton, G. and Hapner, M. (1999) *JDBC^{TM} API Tutorial and Reference*, 2nd edn, *Universal Data Access for the Java^{TM} 2 Platform*. Reading, MA: Addison-Wesley

yWorks (2003) http://www.yworks.de/index.htm (last accessed September 2003)

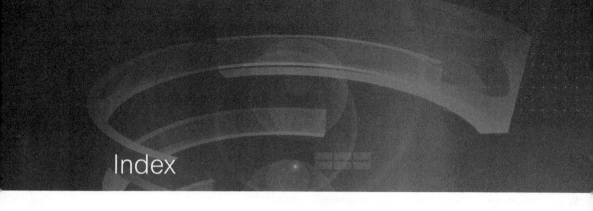

Index

A

Abstract Factory pattern 286–7
abstract use case 465
AbstractButton 522
abstraction 12, 15, 265, 306
acceptance testing 20–1, 31, 365,
    395–6, 463
access rights *see* privileges
Access software 73
accounting systems 138–41, 144–5
accrual of cost 128
achievement theory of motivation 158
ACID properties 702–3
acquaintance 273, 283–5
acquaintance dependency 273–5
acquaintance package 275–7, 283,
    417–21, 586–8, 751–3
action 55
action state 56
activation 50, 347
activity 114
activity diagrams 55–6, 350, 487
activity reports 757
actors 202, 217
actual cost
    from accounting 143–6
    from schedules 142–3
    of work performed (ACWP) 147–8
addition use case 49
Advertising Expenditure Measurement
    (AEM) 196, 200–1
    business use case models 203–5
'after' trigger 684
aggregation 44, 46, 207, 226
Agile Alliance 29
agile software development 29–32, 385,
    462–3, 478
ALAP (As Late As Possible)
    scheduling 119

algorithmic budget estimation 127, 130–8
algorithms 17
alpha-testing 20–1
alternate key *see* unique key
analysis as distinct from design 17–18
anonymous class 524
anonymous inner class 389
«anonymous_type» class 375
applet state transition model 549
applets 516, 541, 620–2
    thin and *thick* 547–51
application class 242, 331
application composition model 135
application module 747
application role 672
application server 510, 732
application tier 714
application transactions *see* business
    transactions
application under development 215
aptitude tests 156
architectural design 18, 20, 69–70, 248
    definition of 248
architectural frameworks *see* frameworks
architectural layers 249
architectural models 12
architectural patterns 285–91
argument type 367
artifacts 169, 199
ASAP (As Soon As Possible)
    scheduling 119
association 44, 46, 202, 207, 226
association attribute 243
association class 45–6, 307
association link 371
asynchronous communication 50, 269
atomicity 702
@ *Risk* 73
attributes 42–4, 225–6

audits 179–80
authentication 661, 663
authorization 661–75
authorization database 673
authorization graph 663, 685
authorization rules 644, 753, 777, 786
authorization window 759
automated verification 396
automatic testing 175
availability 661

B

bar charts 118–23
base user case 49
baselines 127, 138–9, 184
basic flow of events 237–9
BC4J *see* Business Components for Java
Bean-Managed Persistent bean 735
beans 729
'before' trigger 684
Bell–LaPadula model 671
Benson, S. 9–10
best script 176
beta-testing 21
Big-bang testing 20
BL tier 732
black box testing 173–4, 395
BMP *see* Bean-Managed Persistent
    bean
Boehm, B.W. 113
BOM *see* business object model
Booch, G. 248
BorderLayout 518
boundary value techniques 174–5
bracketing *see* demarcation
browser clients 509
budget at completion (BAC) 147–8
budget estimation 126–38
budget tracking 141–8

budgeted cost of work performed (BCWP) 147–8
budgeted cost of work scheduled (BCWS) 147–8
budgets 116
builds 25
build files *see* configuration files
build-and-fix models 32
business actors 201–2
business case models 199, 207–10
business components 95–6, 638, 729
Business Components for Java (BC4J) 377, 729–30, 741–8
business context diagrams 199, 201
business entities 207, 241
business logic 639
business object model (BOM) 199–200, 215–16
business processes 8–10
business rules 307, 660
business transactions 700, 711–22
business use case model 199–207

C

cache 609
callback *see* up-call
callback messages 50, 348
candidate key *see* unique key
Capability Maturity Model 153–4, 168
capture/playback tool 175
cascade constraint 678
cascading group menu 521
CASE *see* computer assisted software engineering
CCAs *see* change control authorities
CCBs *see* change control boards
CEP *see* cycle elimination principle
Chain of Responsibility pattern 287–8, 530–1
chained transactions 706
challenge–response approach 671
change and configuration management 180–90
change control authorities 181–2
change control boards 181–2
change management 97–102, 180, 181
tools for 64, 99
change request forms (CRFs) 181–2
Chaos Report 2
Charette, R.N. 166
check constraint 677

checkbox 523
check-in *see* 'unload' function
checklists 178
check-out 480, 709
Chidamber, S.R. 188–90
circular dependencies 251, 267–9
CK metrics 188–90
Chain of Responsibility pattern 287
class 44, 224
in Java 366–77
class data type 367
class dependencies 254–5
class design 331–2
architectural elaboration of 339–46
class diagrams 43–6
class hierarchies 415
class instantiation 344–6
class interfaces 366
class libraries 514
class members 44
class method 367
class naming principle 283
class protocols *see* class interfaces
class relationships 226–7
class template *see* parameterized type
classifiers 43, 202, 218
clearance level 671
client objects 261
client privileges 673
client tier 731
client/server(s) 509, 543
architecture 285
client-side demarcation 702
clients 543
closure load 483
CM *see* Contact Management
CMM *see* Capability Maturity Model
CMP *see* Container-Managed Persistent bean
CNP *see* class naming principle
COCOMO (COnstructive COst MOdels)
COCOMO 81 133–5
COCOMO II 135–8
code reuse 256
coding of messages 158
collaboration 349
collaboration diagrams 50–3, 332, 349–51
collaboration management 67–8
collaborative concurrency control 709
collections 371

see also containers
collective ownership of code 32
columns 303
combinations counting rule 13
combo box 523
Command pattern 531–2
commit 700, 702
«communicate» relationship 48, 202, 218
communication 158–62
communication diagrams *see* collaboration diagrams
communication forms 158
communication lines 159
'compare-and-merge' capabilities 102
compensating transactions 717
complexity of software systems 13–15
component-based lifecycle 29
component diagrams 56–9
component technology 29
components 56, 170, 285, 712
Composite pattern 387, 563–4
compromise 161
computer assisted software engineering (CASE) 16–19, 29, 38, 64, 74
computer-supported collaborative work (CSCW) 63
conceptual database model 306
conceptual classes 241–3, 317, 331, 474–6, 653–5
concurrency 700–11
in business transactions 711–22
control of 707–11
configuration 11, 183
configuration files 102
configuration management 64, 97, 99, 102, 180, 183
tools for 99, 169
conflict resolution 161–2
confrontation 161
consistency 703
constructor methods 45, 367
Contact Management (CM) 196, 215–19
class models 227–9
domain glossary 222–4
use case model 219–22
Container-Managed Persistent bean 735
container-managed transactions 715
containers 515–20, 730, 732
content management 67–8

context diagrams 40, 199–201
contingency planning 168
continuous integration 20
control flow 56
control layer 281
control package 430–5, 607–8, 771
controller objects 278
controls (in Swing event model) 521–3
correctness 169
cost drivers 134
cost estimation 116, 127–38
cost variance (CV) 147–8
coupling 189, 254
CPM *see* critical path method
CRFs *see* change request forms
critical path method 65, 117
crow's foot notation 42
C/S *see* client/server(s)
CSCW *see* computer-supported
    collaborative work
current cost 142
cursor 316
custom tag library 567
custom tags *see* tags
cycle elimination principle 283

D

daily reports *see* summary reports
data engineering 638
data flow diagrams (DFDs) 39–45,
    199–201
Data Mapper pattern 487–94
data members 44, 366
data store 41
data type 225
database access in Java 377–85
database administrators 663
database code 799–808
database extension and intention 663
database management system 301
database modeling 82–3, 301
database packages 311
database schema 304
database technology 38, 63
database tier 716
database transactions *see* system
    transactions
databases
    business rules for 307–9
    conceptual versus *logical* models 306–7

indexes 311–15
    programming application logic 310–11
    relational 302–15
    see also object databases
DBAs *see* database administrators
DBMS *see* database management system
DDP *see* downward dependency principle
dead code 174
deadlock 705
debugging 19, 90–2
declarative authorization 664
declarative demarcation 713
declarative integrity 693
declarative referential integrity 308
Decorator pattern 530, 565–6
default constraint 676–9
default layer 518
defect script 176
defects in software 101, 185–7, 396
delay dependencies 119
delegation 262, 287
delegator objects 262
deliverables 114, 117, 184
demarcation 702
dematerialization 494
denied privilege 664
dependability of software 170, 664
    see also reliability
dependencies 20, 118–19, 172–3, 189,
    249–50
    see also acquaintance dependencies;
        circular dependencies; class
        dependencies; implementation
        dependencies; inheritance
        dependencies; layer dependencies;
        method dependencies; package
        dependencies; usage dependencies
deployment diagrams 56, 59
deployment of systems 19–21
depth of inheritance tree (DIT) 188–9
derivatives 183
descriptive attributes 216
design classes 250, 331
design patterns 285
desktop GUI 476
detailed design 12, 18
DFDs *see* data flow diagrams
diagrams of models 38–40, 50–9
dialog box 515
digital signature 671

dirty read 704
discretionary authorization 661–70
'Display Message Text' interaction 356–7
distributed objects 732
documentation for users 21
DOM *see* domain object model
domain class 224–9, 241
domain constraint 677
domain glossary 222
domain layer 281
domain object model (DOM) 199, 215–29
domain use case models 217–22
domains 215
dominant class 265, 588
DOORS 77
down-calls 259–60, 263–4
downward dependency principle 282
dropdown list *see* combo box
durability 703
dynamic binding 256, 546, 767

E

EAP *see* explicit association principle
early design mode 136
earned value analysis 141, 146–8
effective privilege 664
effectiveness 8
efficiency 8
effort 131
effort-driven scheduling 122–3
EIS tier 731
EJB *see* Enterprise JavaBeans
elaboration 339
EM *see* Email Management
email 159
'Email Could Not Be Sent' interaction
    361
Email Management case study 196, 215,
    234
    architectural elaboration of class design
        342–3
    class design after architectural
        elaboration 343–4
    classes found from use case
        requirements 333–7
    database design and creation 322–7
    database management system 301
    initial class design 337–9
    integrity 693–6
    interactions 351–61

Email Management case study *(continued)*
  Iteration 1 404–9, 414–15
    extract class and interface 480–4
    refactoring 502–5
  Iteration 2 462–3
    conceptual classes and relational
      tables 474–6
    supplementary specification 476–7
    use case document 465–73
    use case model 464–5
  Iteration 3 639
    conceptual classes and relational
      tables 653–5
    use case documents 641–53
    use case model 640–1
    supplementary specification 655–7
    security 685–93
    servlet implementation 573–80
    test-driven development 389–95
    test input, output and regression
      testing 398–401
    test scripts 396–7, 401–4
    transactions and concurrency 722–4
    user interface 532–7
Email Marketing 235
'Email Message' interaction 357–8
embedded SQL 303, 310
encryption 671
end products 169
engineering change orders 182
enhancements of software 185–7, 396
enterprise application development 93–5
Enterprise Architect 78–9
enterprise authorization 661, 672–5, 685
enterprise information systems 2, 7
Enterprise JavaBeans 377, 558, 638,
    729–41
  architecture of 732
enterprise portfolio management 68–9
enterprise users 672
entities 42
entity beans 732, 735–9
entity components for Java 741–4
entity objects 741
entity package 281, 435–46, 608–12,
    771–6
entity-relationship diagram 42
entity-relationship modeling 42–3, 306
eProject Enterprise 69–70
Epstein, Bob 638

equivalence partitioning 174
ER *see* entity-relationship modeling
ERD *see* entity-relationship diagram
eRoom 68
error correction, cost of 172
estimate at completion (EAC) 147–8
estimation by analogy 127
event handling 523–7
event model 523
event objects 269–70
event processing 268–73, 523
evolutionary maintenance 104
evolvability *see* scalability
Excel software 73
exception flow 241
exclusive lock 705
exclusive read lock 721
exclusive write lock 721
executable specifications 29
execution contexts 711–12
exercising tests 175–6
'Exit' interaction 353–4
expectancy theory of motivation 158
expert judgment 127
explicit association principle 282
«extend» relationship 48–9, 218
extension inheritance 258–9
extension use case 49, 234
external entities 40, 201
extract class refactoring 485
eXtreme Programming (XP) 32, 385
extrinsic motivation 157
extroverts 160

Façade pattern 286, 754
Factory Method pattern 564–5
features 44
feedbacks 22
fields 44
  see class members; data members
fixed costs 143
fixtures 387
flat load 494
flat transactions 706, 722
flow balancing 41
flow of events 237
forcing 161
foreign keys 305, 678–80
formal systems development 29

forming stage of team development 162
foundation layer 282
foundation package 455–8, 795–9
Fowler, M. 479, 484
frameworks 170, 277–85
Front Controller pattern 567
function points (FPs) 131–2
functional decomposition 39
functional paradigm 13
functional requirements 332
functionality 243
FURPS 244
FURPS+ 244, 655

G
Gang of Four patterns 286, 528, 562
Gantt charts 65, 119–20, 123, 140
gates 347
Gehrke, J. 661
generalization 45–6, 202, 207, 226, 321
generic class *see* parameterized type
Ghezzi, C. 10–11, 72, 169
glass box testing *see* white box testing
global schema 667, 689, 799
glossaries 199–200, 206–7, 222–4
GoF *see* Gang of Four patterns
graphical user interface (GUI) 462–3
group communication 161
group workspace 709
guard conditions 54
groups 662

H
heavyweight classes 515
heavyweight Swing components 514
Heldman, K. 155, 157
Herzberg, Frederick 158
hierarchical structures of
    organization 159–60
HTML (HyperText Markup Language)
    27, 541–5
  clients *see* browser clients
  tags 544
hygiene theory of motivation 158

I
IDE *see* integrated development
    environment
Identity Field pattern 438
identity load 494

Identity Map pattern 485–7
impact analysis 262
impedance mismatch 316–17
implementation 18
implementation dependencies 266
implementation diagrams 56–9
implementation inheritance 255, 262–4
implementation of software products 11, 18–19, 22
incidental communication 161
«include» relationship 48–9, 218
'Incorrect Option' interaction 358–9
'Incorrect User Name or Password' interaction 358
incremental versions of software 17, 25
indexes 311–15
inflexible constraints 120
information systems, nature of 7–10
inheritance 312
  dependencies 255–60
  metrics related to 188–9
  without polymorphism 258
  see also implementation inheritance
inner class 38, 286, 524
inspections 17, 19, 178–9
instance method 367
instance variables 366
  see also data members
instances of classes 44
instantiation of classes 344–6
'instead of' trigger 684
integrated development environments (IDEs) 19, 64, 83–6, 93–4
integration
  with business components 95–6
  with change and configuration 97–8
  of modeling and coding 93
  of whole systems 19–20
integration testing 20
integrity 661, 700
  design of 675–84
integrity constraints 675
intentional programming 31, 391
interaction diagrams 50–1
interaction fragments 350
interaction occurrences 350
interaction overview diagrams 350–1
interactions 346–54
  design of 331–2
interactive SQL 303

interfaces 264–75, 331, 510
  adaptability of 513
  consistency, forgiveness and adaptability 512–14
  design of 510
  hierarchies of 415
interim plans 138
internal structure diagrams 349
International Organization for Standardization 168
interoperability of software 171
intrinsic motivation 157
introverts 160–1
IS tier 731
ISO standards 168
isolation levels 703–5
iteration in software development 25
iterative lifecycle 25
iterative processes 196–7

J

J2EE tier 731
Jakarta Straits technology 542
Japplet component 516, 541
JAR *see* Java Archive file
Java 366–85
  business components 741–8
  entity components 741–4
Java Archive file 541
Java Database Connectivity 377
Java Development Kit 377
Java interface 339
Java Server Pages (JSPs) 541–2, 555–9
  reuse of tags in 567–71
Java Stored Procedures 377
Java technologies 85
Java Transaction Service 712
JavaBeans 377, 541, 558, 730
Javadoc 584, 750
JavaMail 435
JavaScript 541, 545
JavaServer Faces 542
JButton 522
JCheckBox 522
JCheckBoxMenuItem 520
JDBC *see* Java Database Connectivity
JDeveloper 95–6
JDK *see* Java Development Kit
JFrame 515
JLayeredPane 518

JList 523
JMenu 520
JMenuBar 520
JMenuItem 520, 522
JOptionPane 515
JPanel 515
JRadioButton 522
JRadioButtonMenuItem 520
JScrollBar 523
JScrollPane 516, 523
JSF *see* JavaServer Faces
JSlider 523
JSP *see* Java Server Page
JSplitPane 517
JTable 517
JTablePane 516
JTextPane 516
JToolBar 521
JTree 523
JTS *see* Java Transaction Service
JUnit framework 386–9
JWindow 515

K

Kemerer, C.F. 188–90
KLOC metrics 131

L

lack of cohesion in methods (LCOM) metric 188–90
Larman, C. 248
late binding *see* dynamic binding
layer dependencies 253–4, 270–1
«layer» package 250, 253
layering 249, 519–20
layout manager 518
layouts 518
Lazy Initialization pattern 494
Lazy Load pattern 493–501
leadership of projects 155–6
legacy systems 5–6, 21, 104–6
Level 0 diagrams 40–1
lifecycle of software development 5–32, 113, 172
  modeling of 21–2
  phases in 5, 15–21
lifelines 346
lightweight classes 515
lightweight Swing components 514
lines of code (LOC) 131–2

list boxes 523
listener objects *see* subscriber objects
listeners 769
load 488
local schema 667, 689, 799
local transactions 716
local variables 367
lock 703
lock modes 705–6
logical database models 305, 317
'Login' interaction 352–3
long lock *see* persistent lock
long transactions 701, 709
look and feel 509

M

MagicDraw 83, 105–6
main method 345
maintainability of software 170
maintenance of software 21
management levels 9
management by objectives 147
ManagePro™ 66–7
mandatory authorization 661, 671–2
manual verification 396
MAPI *see* JavaMail
mapping of objects 315–22
markup language 742
    see also HTML
Maslow's hierarchy of needs 157–8
material resource 121
materialization *see* load
maturity 63, 153–4
MDA *see* model driven architecture
mediator package 281, 446–55, 612–20,
    776–95
Mediator pattern 290–1
member function *see* method
member variables 44
    see also data members
menus 520–1
merging 184
message beans 732
message passing 44
messages 44, 346
metadata 492
Metadata Mapping pattern 492
metamodels 27
method 44, 367
method of coverage *see* operation coverage

method dependencies 260–4
method overloading 256, 367
method overriding 256
method prototypes 367
method reply *see* callback message
method return 50, 348
method signatures 367
metrics 69, 187–90
milestones 114, 117
missing functionality 173
modal layer 519
modal window 476
model driven architecture (MDA) 25, 29
model interfaces 526
model objects 278
Model–View–Controller (MVC) 277–9, 566
modeling 12–13, 38
modules
    architectural 249–51
    specification 41
motivation 155–8
multimedia 216–17
multiplicity 44, 226
multi-tier systems 285, 509
multi-version concurrency 709, 722
MVC *see* Model–View–Controller

N

n-levels load 494
navigation 49, 218, 498–9, 609
navigational links 302, 305
neighbor communication principle 282
nested transactions 706–9
network charts 117
network graphs 65
network organization 155
nodes 59
non-functional requirements 339
non-primitive data types 226
non-repeatable reads 704
non-unique indexes 313
norming stage of team development 162
null constraints 676–9
nulls 304
number of children (NOC) 188–9

O

object behavior 43
object coupling 478
object creation messages 50, 348

Object Data Management Group 316
object databases 316–17, 709
object flow 56
object identifiers 438, 710
object identity 43
Object Management Group (OMG) 29
object-oriented developments 13, 43–6
object points (OPs) 131–3
object privilege 663
object-relational mapping 317–22
object resistance 225
object states 43, 53
Object Storage API 316
observer objects *see* subscriber objects
Observer pattern 288–90, 528–30, 563
ODMG *see* Object Data Management Group
offline concurrency 711, 718
OID *see* object identifiers
OID Proxy pattern 495–501, 609
OLAP (online analytical processing) and
    OLTP (online transaction
    processing) 9
online concurrency 711
online processing *see* OLAP
open systems 171
operation coverage 175
operations 21, 44
optimistic concurrency control 708
optimistic offline lock 719–21
organizational culture 21–2
outer class 386
overallocation of resources 123–6
overlap dependencies 119
overlaps between project phases 23
overloading *see* method overloading
overtime rates 128
overview diagrams 40

P

package dependencies 251–3
package hierarchies 415
packages 250–1
page lock 705
pair programming 31–2
palette layer 519
parameterized type 375
participation 44, 226
partition 253
passivation *see* 'unload' function
path coverage 175

patterns 527–32, 561–73
Patterns of Enterprise Application
    Architecture 562
PCMEF framework 415
PCMEF+ architectural framework 585
PEAA patterns *see* Patterns of Enterprise
    Application Architecture
people management 153–8
percolation 183
Perforce 97–8
performance 170, 243
performance management 66, 147
performed work 148
performing stage of team development 162
persistent bean 735
persistent lock 709
persistent records 315–22
PERT *see* Program Evaluation and Review
    Technique
per-use costs 143
pessimistic concurrency control 707
pessimistic offline lock 721–2
phantoms 704
phases 114
phasing in and phasing out of products
    5, 21
physical database independence 312
physical database model 305
picklist *see* combo box
plan documents 116
platform independent models (PIMs) and
    platform specific models (PISs) 29
pluggability 514
polymorphism 256
pop-up layer 520
portability of software 171
portfolio management 68
Poseidon 79, 81
post-architecture modeling 137
postconditions 237
PowerDesigner 82–4
preconditions 237
predicate load 494
Presentation–Control–Mediator–Entity–
    Foundation (PCMEF) 279–85
presentation layer 281, 620–32
presentation package 422–30, 588–606,
    753–71
Pressman, R.S. 171
pre-use rates 128

primary actors 202
primary keys 677–8
primary windows 515
Primavera Enterprise® 69
primitive data type 225, 303, 366
private workspace 99, 183
privileges 644, 661, 662
proactive dependency management 249
proactive risk strategies 163
procedural referential integrity 308
process 40, 712
process maturities 153
process qualities 169
productivity in software production 171
Program Evaluation and Review Technique
    (PERT) 65
program models 12
programmable clients 509–10
programmatic demarcation 713
programmatic SQL *see* embedded SQL
programme authorization 665
programming 11, 18
programming languages 37, 44
programming tasks 85–93
project calendars 117
project communication 158
project leadership 155
project management 12, 116–17
    tools for 64–73
project managers 155–6
project planning 112–16
Project software 66, 73, 116–32, 139–45
project teams 114–16
project termination 166
prototyping 23–4
provided interfaces 266, 510
psychometric tests 156
public interfaces 510
public keys 671
public workspaces 99, 183
Publish-Subscribe pattern *see* Observer
    pattern
'publisher' object 269, 523
pull technology 559
pure abstract status 265

Q

quality 114
quality assurance 171, 177–80
    see also software quality assurance

quality control 171–7
quality management 168–80

R

radio buttons 523
Ramakrishnan, R. 661
rates 128
Rational ClearQuest 101
Rational Rose 77–80
Rational Unified Process (RUP®) 25–9
RationalRequisitePro 75–6
reactive dependency management 249
reactive risk strategies 163
read committed isolation 704
read consistent snapshots 722
read uncommitted isolation 704
read/write lock 721
records 302–3
recovery 701
recurring tasks 117
recursive association 320
'redo' function 703
reengineering 104–7
refactoring 31, 478–505
reference data type *see* class data type
referential integrity 305–6, 678
reflection 389
registrar objects 269
regression testing 175–6, 245, 396, 399
relational database model 301, 655
relationship multiplicity 208
relationship participation 208
relationships 42, 44, 224, 226
releases of software 20, 183–5
reliability of software 170, 243
remaining costs 142
repairability *see* maintainability
repeatable read isolation 704
report generation 82–3
repositories 38, 224
requests 712
required interfaces 266, 510
requirements 16, 74–6
    analysis of 11–12, 16–17
    changes in 181–2
    documentation of 17, 74–5
resource(s)
    assignment 121–2, 128
    calendars 121–2
    definition 114, 121

resource(s) *(continued)*
  graphs 126
  privileges 667
  usage 123–4
response for a class (RFC) metric 189
responsibility 332
'restrict' constraint 678
restriction inheritance 259
return type 367
reusability of software 170
reverse engineering 19, 64, 79, 82, 95,
    105–6, 249
reviews for quality assurance 178–9
revoked privilege 663
rich clients *see* programmable clients
right-click pop-up menus 521
rigor of software processes 10
risk 72, 115
  analysis of 26, 72
  assessment of 164–7
  avoidance of 168
  components of 165
  exposure to 165
  handling of 167–8
  identification of 115–16, 163–4
  impact of 165
  likelihood of 164
  management of 28, 72–3, 163–8
  minimization of 168
  probability of 164
risk databases 167
Risk Radar™ 72–3
risk reference level 166
robustness of software 170
roles 662
rollback 700, 702
roundtrip engineering 12, 18–19
row lock 705
row trigger 684
RUP® *see* Rational Unified Process®

S

sandbox environment 541, 549
savepoint 706, 777
scalability of software 170
schedule-driven budgeting 127–30
schedule tracking 139
scheduled variance (SV) 147–8
scheduled work 148
scheduling 65, 116–26

schema-independent users *see* enterprise
    users
schemas 667
scripting languages 545–7
scriptlets 542
scroll bars 516
secondary actors 202
secondary windows 515
secrecy 661
security 658
  design of 661–75
security administrators 671
security classes 671
self-directed teams 155
self-referential association *see* recursive
    association
semaphore tables 721
Separated Interface pattern 268
sequence diagrams 30, 50–1, 332, 347–8
serializable execution 703
serializable isolation 704
serialization 733
server privilege 675
server-side demarcation 702
servers 543
servlet active state model 553
servlet containers 552, 554
servlets 541–2, 551–5, 622–32
session beans 732, 739–41
session objects 561
sessions 709, 711
shared lock 705
short lock 709
short transactions 700, 709
signatures 45, 332
    see also method signatures
signed applets 551
single implementation inheritance 265
singleton classes 225
slack time 117
slippage 117
Small Worlds 70–1
smoothing 161
snapshot lock 710
software engineering 2
  definition of 2, 11
  as distinct from programming 11–14
  as distinct from traditional
    engineering 10–11
Software Engineering Institute (SEI) 153

software engineering pentagon 3
software process model 12
software processes in relation to business
    processes 8–10
software product model 12–13
software projects, definition of 2
software prototypes 24
software quality assurance 17, 177
software systems, nature of 7–8
Sommerville, I. 17, 113–14
specifications model 12
spiral model of the lifecycle 25–7
split windows 517
SQA *see* software quality assurance
SQL *see* Structured Query Language
SQL:1999 316
SQL for Java 377
stable frameworks 254
stable layers 254
staff selection 156–7
staffing management plans 155
standard rates 128
standards 114–15, 168–9
Standing, C. 9–10
Standish Group 2
state machines 53
state models 43
state passing 560
state transition 53
statechart diagrams 53–5
stateful session beans 740
stateful systems 560
stateless session beans 740
stateless systems 559–61
statement diagrams 53
statement triggers 684
static binding 546
stereotypes 47–8
stored functions 310, 668, 799
stored procedures 310, 657, 668, 799
storming stage of team development 162
Strategy pattern 565
structured analysis and design 39
Structured English 41
structured information 216
structured modeling 39
structured programming 38
Structured Query Language 301, 316
struts 542, 572–3
subclasses 45, 226

subflows 239–40
subjects 288
subscriber objects 269
subscribers 523
subset classes 44, 226
Subsume Method refactoring 481
summary reports 751, 754
summary tasks 117
Sun ONE Studio 85–97, 103–4
superclasses 45, 226
superset classes 44, 226
supplier objects 261
supportability 11, 70, 170, 243, 478
Swing components 514
Swing event model 521–4
synchronous messages 50, 262, 348
synonyms 667
system building facilities 102–3
system design, definition of 17–18
system development 2
system engineering, definition of 2
system modeling tools 73–4
system transactions 700–1, 711

T

tabbed pages 516
tables 302–3
table lock 705
TableModel 526
tags 542, 567
task dependencies 118
tasks 114, 117
team building *see* team development
team development 156–8, 162–3
team organization 162
teamwork 12, 63, 97
templates 17
test cases 176, 386, 396
test-driven development 31, 365, 385–95, 478
test drives 20
test environments 176
test harness 20
test plans 176
test scripts 176, 395–7, 401–4
test steps 396
test stubs 20
test suites 176, 386, 396
test units 386
testing 17–21, 31, 171–3, 365

execution-based 19
of job applicants 156
manual and automated 175–6
planning of 176–7
'to code' and 'to specs' 19
see also black box testing; white box testing
thick applets 547, 551, 620
thick web clients 285, 542
see also programmable clients
thin applets 547, 620
thin web clients 285, 542
see also browser clients
threads 712
three-tier architecture 285
timeliness 171
Together ControlCenter 93–4
'Too Many Messages' interaction 359–60
toolbars 521
tools
   all-in-one 76
   for software engineering 63
   for system modeling 73–4
top-down approach to programming 39
traceability management 18–19
tracking 112, 116, 121, 138–48
traditional engineering 10
training of users 21
transaction managers 301
transaction processing 658
transaction states 560
transactional models 706–7
transactions 771, 781, 795
   definition of 700
transformation models 29
transient objects 305, 315–22
transition 53
triggers 308, 658, 680–5, 693, 807
trusted applets 550
two-tier architecture 285

U

UI *see* user interface
UI tier 731
UML *see* Unified Modeling Language
underallocation of resources 123–6
understandability of software 170
'undo' function 703
Unhelkar, B. 180

unidirectional relationships 49, 203, 218
Unified Modeling Language (UML) 12, 16–17, 29 37–9, 43–50, 55, 74–6, 79–85, 93
   profile of 37
Unified Process (UP) 199, 339
unique indexes 313
unique key 304, 677–8
Unit of Work pattern 501–2, 718–19, 723, 781, 789
'unload' function 489
UNP *see* upward notification principle
unstable layers 254
unstructured information 216
UP *see* Unified Process
up-calls 260, 263–4
update lock 705
upward notification principle 282
usability of software 170, 243, 510
usage dependencies 266–7
use case diagrams 46–50, 217
use case documents 236–7, 465–73, 641–53
use case models 235–6, 464–5, 640–1
use case relationships 217–18, 332–9
use case specifications 217
user interface 509–14
   components of 514–23
   design of 510
   event handling 523–7
   patterns 527–32
user-in-control 511
user requirements 16
utility classes 755, 767

V

variance 140
variance at completion 147–8
variation control 171
VBScript 545
verification points 176, 396
version control systems 97–9
version derivation graphs 102
version management 11, 182–90, 720
versionable objects 183
view link 745
view objects 278, 741, 745
'View Unsent Messages' interaction 354–6
Virtual Proxy pattern 495–6

visibility of processes 171, 366
visual modeling 73–4, 79–82
  tools for 37–8
Visual SourceSafe 102–3

W

W3C *see* World Wide Web Consortium
walkthroughs 17, 19, 178–9
waterfall model 22–7
web-based applications 476, 541–2
web clients *see* browser clients

web pages 159, 541
web servers 510, 551
web tiers 713
weighted methods per class (WMC)
  metric 188–9
'what if' analysis 70
white box testing 19, 174–5, 385
withdrawal 162
work breakdown structure 114
work products 169
work resources 121

workflow management 100
workgroup computing *see* computer-
  supported collaborative work
World Wide Web Consortium 543

X

XML 568, 742
XP *see* eXtreme Programming

Y

yDoc software 584, 750

The accompanying CD

The CD accompanying this book contains:

1. Software tools and environments relevant to the book content and directly or indirectly discussed in the book.
2. Complete code for case studies:
   - source code
   - compiled code
   - documentation
   - Readme.txt documentation on installation and execution
3. Most figures in the book.

Software tools and environments included in the CD range from IDEs, UML modeling, Refactoring, Metrics, Profiling, Testing, Logging, Documentation and other tools. Each tool is briefly described and, where applicable, a set of web links is given to direct the reader for more resources available in the vendor's website or on the internet.

The tools are included in the hope that the reader would be able to develop and run the case studies, minicases, and other examples discussed in the book. Moreover, the tools can be used for book's exercises and projects as well as for other educational needs related to software engineering. The book's website is frequently updated with exercises that maximize the use of the tools included in this CD.

In some cases readers of the book, who are interested in purchasing the full licence for the tools, will be able to do so for a fraction of the cost, obtaining a student licence.

The breakdown of case studies code is as follow.

1. EMS (Email Management System) case study is included in all of its iterations. This includes Iteration 1, Iteration 1 Refactored, Iteration 2, Iteration 2 Applet Version, Iteration 2 Serviet Version, and Iteration 3.
2. MovieActor case study as discussed in the book. This includes versions of MovieActor for database and MovieActor for serviet.

All figures that are shown in the book are included in the CD. This excludes a small number of figures, which are third party copyrighted images.

Instructions for how to use the CD

Upon being inserted into the CD drive, the disk should auto-execute under any of the common Microsoft PC operating systems. Should this fail to happen, go to readme.txt for instructions on how to install the CD.

IMPORTANT: READ CAREFULLY

WARNING: BY OPENING THE PACKAGE YOU AGREE TO BE BOUND BY THE TERMS OF THE LICENCE AGREEMENT BELOW.

his is a legally binding agreement between You (the user purchaser) and Pearson Education Limited. By retaining this licence, any software media or accompanying ritten materials or carrying out any of the permitted tivities You agree to be bound by the terms of the licence greement below.

If You do not agree to these terms then promptly return the entire publication (this licence and all software, written materials, packaging and any other components received with it) with Your sales receipt to Your supplier for a full refund.

SINGLE USER LICENCE AGREEMENT

] YOU ARE PERMITTED TO:

Use (load into temporary memory or permanent storage) a single copy of the software on only one computer at a time. If this computer is linked to a network then the software may only be installed in a manner such that it is not accessible to other machines on the network

Make one copy of the software solely for backup purposes or copy it to a single hard disk, provided you keep the original solely for back up purposes.

Transfer the software from one computer to another provided that you only use it on one computer at a time.

❑ YOU MAY NOT:

- Rent or lease the software or any part of the publication.
- Copy any part of the documentation, except where specifically indicated otherwise.
- Make copies of the software, other than for backup purposes.
- Reverse engineer, decompile or disassemble the software.
- Use the software on more than one computer at a time.
- Install the software on any networked computer in a way that could allow access to it from more than one machine on the network.
- Use the software in any way not specified above without the prior written consent of Pearson Education Limited.

ONE COPY ONLY

This licence is for a single user copy of the software
PEARSON EDUCATION LIMITED RESERVES THE RIGHT TO TERMINATE THIS LICENCE BY WRITTEN NOTICE AND TO TAKE ACTION TO RECOVER ANY DAMAGES SUFFERED BY PEARSON EDUCATION LIMITED IF YOU BREACH ANY PROVISION OF THIS AGREEMENT.

Pearson Education Limited owns the software You only own the disk on which the software is supplied.

LIMITED WARRANTY

The software is distributed on an 'as is' basis without warranty. Neither the authors, the software developers nor Pearson Education Limited make any representation or warranty, either express or implied, with respect to the software programs, their quality, accuracy, or fitness for a specific purpose. Therefore, neither the authors, software developers, nor Pearson Education Limited shall have any liability to you or any other person or entity with respect to any liability, loss or damage caused or alleged to have been caused directly or indirectly by the programs contained on the media. This includes, but is not limited to, interruption of service, loss of data, loss of classroom time, loss of consulting or anticipatory profits, or consequential

damages from the use of these programs. If the media itself is defective you may return it for a replacement. Use of the software is subject to the individual licence agreements supplied within the media and the single user licence agreement printed in this book. Read the licences carefully, by opening this package you are agreeing to be bound by the terms and conditions of the single user agreement printed here. By installing a specific software program you are agreeing to be bound by the terms and conditions of the licence agreement accompanying that program. If you do not agree, do not open the package.

This licence agreement shall be governed by and interpreted and construed in accordance with English law.